LATIN AMERICA

AN ECONOMIC AND
SOCIAL GEOGRAPHY

J. P. COLE, M.A., Ph.D.

Reader in Geography at
Nottingham University

ROWMAN AND LITTLEFIELD
Totowa, New Jersey

c1975

This edition published in the United States 1975
by ROWMAN AND LITTLEFIELD, Totowa, N.J.
First published 1965
Second impression 1966
Third (revised) impression 1970
Fourth impression 1973
Second edition 1975

© Butterworth & Co (Publishers) Ltd. 1975

ISBN 0–87471–703–5

Filmset on the Photon Pacesetter and
Printed in England at The Pitman Press Bath

PREFACE

In the preparation of the present edition of *Latin America* all but a few sections of the 1965 edition have been completely rewritten. The plan of the book and the emphasis on different regions has also been changed considerably. The first part of the book (Chapters 1–10) treats Latin America systematically, while the second part (Chapters 11–17) deals in turn with the seven largest countries. In the final chapter a brief attempt is made to study prospects for Latin America over the next few decades.

Greater attention is given in the present edition than in the previous one to the provision of numerical data for the seven largest countries on a regional breakdown at major civil division level. Such data can only be obtained from statistical sources published in each country since United Nations and other world bodies usually provide data only for whole countries. Unfortunately the smaller countries of Latin America have been sacrificed in the present book to allow space for an adequate coverage of the larger ones. They do however appear in many of the tables in Chapters 1–9 where they are given in three groups, Central America, the Caribbean islands and the smaller South American countries. Appendix 4 contains a bibliography on the smaller countries. Further reading is also suggested at the end of each chapter on topics relevant to the chapter, but the amount of geographical material on Latin America is now so vast that the references and bibliography are very selective.

An attempt has been made to show on at least one map the location of every place mentioned in the text. The aim of some maps is however to show spatial distributions rather than place names. The source of the numerical data in each table is given at the foot of the table. Where possible data for 1970–71 have been given and use has been made of the census results of six of the seven largest countries for 1970–72. The illustrations are intended to give a visual impression of certain features and situations in Latin America referred to in the text. They are mostly based on photographs taken by the author during travels in Latin America.

Many people have helped in the provision of material for this book and in its preparation. The author is particularly indebted to the following people in Latin America: to Marília Velloso Galvão, Speridião Faissol and Olga Buarque de Lima of the Instituto Brasileiro de Geografia e Estatística in Rio de Janeiro, to María Teresa G. de MacGregor and Silvana Levi López of the Universidad Nacional Autónoma de México, to Maria Teresa de Bravo of the Universidad de Los Andes, Mérida, Venezuela and to José Matos Mar and Denis Chávez of the Instituto de Estudios Peruanos in Lima. Colleagues in England have kindly read and commented on chapters in the book and the help of Cuchlaine King, John Doornkamp, Roy Bradshaw and David Ebdon is greatly appreciated. Paul Mather gave advice on computing and kindly allowed the use of factor analysis and linkage programs written by him for the University of Nottingham computer. Most of the maps were drawn by Mrs. Carol Walter, but the help of Mr. M. Cutler is also appreciated. The illustrations have been drawn by the author's father, Mr. Philip Cole, who also helped with some of the maps and diagrams.

CONTENTS

CONTENTS

CONTENTS

CONTENTS

GENERAL INFORMATION

CONVERSIONS

Distance and altitude

Kilometres to miles
1 km = 0·621 miles

km	miles
5	3·1
10	6·21
50	31
100	62
500	310
1000	621

Metres to feet
1 metre = 3·281 feet

metres	feet
100	328
500	1,641
1,000	3,280
2,000	6,560
3,000	9,840
4,000	13,120

Area

1 sq.km. = 0·3861 square miles
1 sq.km. = 100 hectares = 1 million sq. metres
1 hectare = 10,000 sq. metres = 2·471 acres

Rainfall

Centimetres to inches (1 centimetre = 10 millimetres)

cm	in	cm	in
250	$98\frac{1}{2}$	80	$31\frac{1}{2}$
200	79	60	$23\frac{1}{2}$
150	59	50	$19\frac{1}{2}$
140	55	40	16
130	51	20	8
120	47	15	6
110	$43\frac{1}{2}$	10	4
100	$39\frac{1}{2}$	5	2

Temperature

Degrees Centigrade to nearest whole degree Farenheit

C	F	C	F	C	F	C	F	C	F
0	32	7	45	14	57	21	70	28	82
1	34	8	46	15	59	22	72	29	84
2	36	9	48	16	61	23	73	30	86
3	37	10	50	17	63	24	75	31	87
4	39	11	52	18	64	25	77	32	89
5	41	12	54	19	66	26	79	33	91
6	43	13	55	20	68	27	81	34	93

Quick reference

$0°C = 32°F$
$10°C = 50°F$
$20°C = 68°F$
$30°C = 86°F$

Weight

Unless otherwise stated, all weights are in metric tons (or tonnes) which are slightly less heavy than long tons used in Britain

1000 kilograms = 1 metric ton = 0·98 long tons

EQUIVALENTS

Energy sources are often expressed for comparative purposes in terms of coal equivalent. The *United Nations Statistical Yearbook* uses the following:

1 metric ton of crude petroleum = 1·3 tons of coal
1000 cubic metres of natural gas = 1·332 tons of coal
1000 kWh of electricity = 0·125 tons of coal

Note that in the electricity industry a kilowatt (kW) measures generating capacity, while a kilowatt hour (kWh) measures output.
Electricity is generated both directly from hydro-electric power, a primary source, and from coal, oil, nuclear fuel and other secondary sources.

TERMS

A number of technical or controversial terms used in the book need a brief clarification here:
Country is used to refer not only to sovereign states but to dependent units at sovereign state level (e.g. Surinam in South America, a Netherlands colony).
Developed and *developing* are widely accepted terms used without undue offence to refer to the richer and poorer groups of countries of the world respectively. They do not imply in the present book a clearcut dichotomy.
Iberia (n) means Spain and Portugal.
Major civil division refers to the highest level of administrative subdivisions within a country (e.g. the departments of France, the provinces of Argentina).
Oil is generally used in Britain to refer to the American term petroleum.
Pre-Columbian refers to the period of Latin American history or pre-history before the arrival in the Americas of the European explorer Christopher Columbus in 1492.

PLACE NAMES

Latin America contains place names with a wide variety of origins. Most places mentioned in the present book are of Spanish origin apart from those in Brazil, which are of Portuguese origin. In the text and on maps correct accents and other diacritical marks have been included (e.g. Bogotá, São Paulo) though in words in capital letters they may be omitted. Certain commonly used place names with English equivalents (e.g. Mexico City, Brazil) have been used instead of the Spanish or Portuguese original (Ciudad de México, Brasil).

Some symbols indicate the syllable on which the stress falls in words in which this does not follow recognised rules. Others affect the pronunciation of certain letters. In Spanish (´) as in Mérida and in Portuguese (´) as in Anápolis and (^) as in Rondônia indicate the syllable with the stress. In Spanish (ñ) as in Viña del Mar is pronounced like 'ni' in onion and (¨) which is rare (as in Camagüey) means that the 'u' is pronounced and does not merely harden the 'g' for the following 'e' or 'i' (as in Miguel); in Portugese (˜) is found on certain vowels (as in São Paulo), indicating a nasal sound.

The following terms are used for the groups of countries indicated:

Central America	Guatemala, El Salvador, Honduras, Nicaragua, Costa Rica, Panama
the Islands	All the islands in the Caribbean and Gulf of Mexico between the U.S.A. and South America
Latin America	Everywhere in the Americas south of the U.S.A.
North America	The U.S.A. and Canada
South America	Latin America excluding Mexico, Central America and the Islands

ABBREVIATIONS

To save space certain frequently referred to statistical sources, institutions and technical terms have been expressed in abbreviated form or by initial letters.

AEB	Anuario Estatístico Brasileiro
BOLSA	Bank of London and South America, particularly the monthly review published by Lloyds and Bolsa International Bank Ltd.
ECLA	Economic Commision for Latin America
FAOPY	Food and Agriculture Organization, Production Yearbook
GDP	Gross domestic product
GNP	Gross national product
LAFTA	Latin American Free Trade Association
UNDYB, UNSYB	United Nations Demographic, Statistical Yearbook
UNYITS	United Nations Yearbook of International Trade Statistics

LARGE NUMBERS AND NUMERACY

A large amount of numerical data is presented in this book both in the text and in the tables. The reader should be careful to distinguish between absolute

GENERAL INFORMATION

figures and figures *per caput* (per inhabitant). This material is of little use unless it means something to the reader. In order therefore to provide a very approximate guide to the magnitude of quantities involved, the following may be used for comparison.

1. *Population*

    10,000 a small town
    100,000 a town about the size of York in England
    1 million roughly the population of a British county, and of major civil divisions in larger Latin American countries
    10 million roughly the population of Belgium, of Chile
    100 million somewhat more than ⅓ of the total population of Latin America

2. *Area*

In square kilometres	In hectares	
1	100	a large arable farm
1,000	100,000	a small British county
100,000	10 million	roughly the area of Cuba
1 million		roughly the area of Bolivia
10 million		roughly half the area of Latin America

3. *Cost in United States dollars (U.S. $)*

    10,000 1 small commercial motor vehicle
    100,000 1 cheap oil well
    1 million a few kilometres of unpaved road
    10 million a small factory producing consumer goods
    100 million a small steel mill
    1,000 million a large hydro-electric station
    10,000 million the yearly gross domestic product of Venezuela, early 1970s
    100,000 million the combined yearly gross domestic product of South American countries, early 1970s
    1 million million the yearly gross domestic product of the U.S.A., early 1970s

CHAPTER 1

INTRODUCTION

1.1. UNITY AND DIVERSITY IN LATIN AMERICA

Latin America is defined for the purposes of this book as everywhere in the Americas south of the United States. The Americas are thus divided on a cultural basis rather than on a physical one. Latin America is that part of the Americas conquered, colonised and dominated mainly by Spain and Portugal for some three centuries after the discovery of the American continent by Europeans at the end of the 15th century. The formerly commonly used term Anglo-America may be used to cover the rest of the continent, namely the U.S.A. and Canada.

The division of the Americas into two major cultural regions is convenient but not exact. Latin America contains a number of areas influenced in the past more strongly by Britain, Holland and France than by the two Iberian* powers. Anglo-America contains areas that formed part of the French and Spanish Empires and later of Mexico. In addition the U.S.A. contains many millions of migrants from the Caribbean and Mexico.

In spite of the reservations made about the term 'Latin', over 98 per cent of the population of Latin America lives in countries in which Spanish, Portuguese or French is the official language. In addition the Latin American countries are at least in theory overwhelmingly Roman Catholic. They share, also, many customs and traditions brought originally from Iberia. With the improvement of international transport links, in particular airline services, the more affluent and influential Latin Americans have been able to travel more easily within the region, and since the Second World War there seems to have been a growing awareness among Latin Americans of the common cultural background in their part of the world. In 1970, for example, when their own team was eliminated during the World Cup Football tournament in Mexico City, the Mexicans apparently had no hesitation in switching their support to the more successful Brazilian team. On the other hand, the economic integration of Latin America, officially started in 1962 with the establishment of the Latin American Free Trade Association†, had not made much progress by the early 1970s. The prospect for some kind of political union between pairs or bigger groups of Latin American countries seems distant still in the 1970s.

The political and economic integration of Latin America may be hampered not only by existing fragmentation of political units but also by great distances between units. The distance along a great circle over the Pacific from Tijuana in northwest Mexico to Tierra del Fuego in southern Argentina is 11,000 km. The maximum comparable distances across Anglo-America, Africa and the U.S.S.R. are respectively 7,200 km (Alaska to Florida), 8,800 km (Spanish

* Iberia means Spain and Portugal.
† Abbreviated in Spanish to ALALC and in English to LAFTA.

1

Sahara to Madagascar) and 8,000 km (Armenia to Chukhotka). Even though
Latin America does extend so far round the earth's surface it is remote from
most other land areas of the world, a feature it shares with Australia and New
Zealand. *Figure 1.1* shows the hemisphere that centres on Ecuador. Mexico and
the islands of the Carribbean are situated close to the U.S.A., West Africa is not
all that distant from northeast Brazil, and Antarctica is close to Chile and
Argentina. Other regions of the world are at great distances from Latin
America across the Atlantic or Pacific, which may contribute to the sense of
isolation that occurs sometimes in Latin America and to the lack of concern over
crises in other parts of the world.

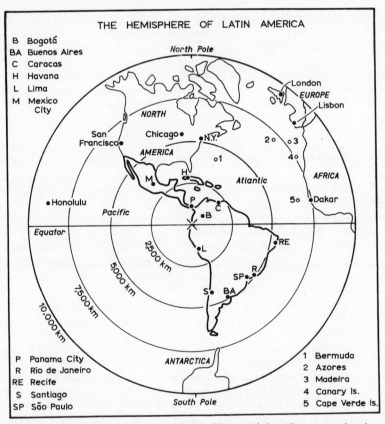

*Figure 1.1. The hemisphere of Latin America. Projection: oblique zenithal equidistant, centred on the coast of
Ecuador at the Equator. Distances are correct only along lines radiating from the centre of the projection*

When one takes a closer look at Latin America, the diversity of the region
becomes apparent. Latin America covers a considerable range of latitude,
stretching from 30° North of the Equator to 55° South. Virtually all imaginable
physical conditions can be found somewhere in Latin America: the driest desert
in the world and some of the areas of heaviest rain, arid lands with no vegetation at all and dense tropical rain forest, vast plains and rugged mountains,
mangrove swamps and glaciers. Politically also Latin America is diversified and

fragmented, with 23 independent countries* in the early 1970s having over ½ a million inhabitants each as well as several smaller independent countries and many small colonies. The countries vary enormously in area and population size and in the composition of their physical conditions and natural resources. Different types of governments, ranging from democratically elected parties of various political shades to military juntas come and usually go with considerable frequency. The establishment of Fidel Castro's communist government in Cuba in the early 1960s brought a new political element into the continent. Culturally, the Spanish and Portuguese influence in Latin America has in many places failed to erase or even modify to any great extent underlying American Indian features, while the arrival at different times of African slaves, Italian, German and East European settlers and even Japanese and Indians of Asia has modified the Iberian tradition.

On a world scale Latin America is popularly thought of as one of the main developing† regions of the world. Average living standards are low in most countries and dependence on agriculture is considerable. Exports consist mainly of food or raw materials, while among imports manufactured goods predominate. This pattern of trade was established in the colonial period. A closer look at the economic structure of the countries of Latin America shows very marked contrasts between different countries and even between regions within countries. At one extreme Argentina and Uruguay are in some respects more like European countries than like Latin American countries. At the other extreme, Haiti resembles the least developed African and Asian countries rather than the other Caribbean countries. Within single Latin American countries there are areas with some of the most simple hunting and gathering communities in the world and places with modern industrial communities in which few of the features of the most developed countries of the world are lacking. One of the main aims of the present book is to identify the regional contrasts in level of development both in Latin America as a whole and within individual countries, and to draw attention to the problems and prospects of various places.

1.2. THE COUNTRIES OF LATIN AMERICA

Latin America has an area of about 20,570,000 sq. km., approximately 14 per cent of the earth's land surface. Its total population was estimated to be 283 million in June 1970, nearly 8 per cent of the world total. During the late 1960s population was increasing at about 2·9 per cent per year and the population of the region had roughly doubled between 1945 and 1970. A United Nations estimate[1] gives 291 million for mid-1971 and a projection of 652 million for the year 2000. By way of comparison it may be noted that Latin America is similar in area to three other large regions of the world, North America, the U.S.S.R. and Africa south of the Sahara, but has rather more inhabitants than they do.

According to the United Nations, there are 45 political units in Latin America, including several very small islands. 13 units are in South America, the rest in Central America, the Caribbean and Atlantic. 25 of the units are

* The term country is used in this book to refer both to sovereign (or independent) and dependent (colonial) political units.

† In accordance with United Nations practice, developing and developed are used in this book to refer to two broad groups of countries, the poorer and the more prosperous.

independent while the remainder have some kind of colonial or dependent status. The 8 largest countries have approximately 80 per cent of the population of Latin America. The location of most of the countries is shown in *Figure 1.2* and in *Figure 1.3* the main countries are drawn according to population size.

Figure 1.2. The countries of Latin America. The inset map shows the eastern part of the Caribbean in greater detail

As pointed out in the previous section, great contrasts exist within individual Latin American countries. These will be described later in the book. At this stage it is convenient to use data for whole countries to provide an introduction to contrasts between different parts of Latin America. Table 1.1 contains data on both the absolute size and the per capita performance of 24 countries. Smaller countries not included in Table 1.1 are listed in Table 1.2; they contain only about one per cent of the total population of Latin America.

The presentation of the data in Table 1.1 allows a quick comparison of the countries of Latin America. Columns 1, 2 and 4 show area size, population size and total national income. Column 1 draws attention to the enormous contrast in real size between Brazil, which is fifth in area among the countries of the world, and the many small countries of Central America and the Caribbean.

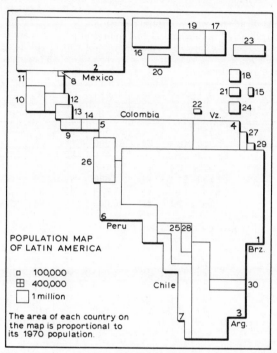

Figure 1.3. Topological map of Latin America in which the area of each country is made proportional to the population size of the country, not its territorial size

1 Brazil	11 Guatemala	21 Martinique
2 Mexico	12 Honduras	22 Netherlands Antilles
3 Argentina	13 Nicaragua	23 Puerto Rico
4 Venezuela	14 Panama	24 Trinidad
5 Colombia	15 Barbados	25 Bolivia
6 Peru	16 Cuba	26 Ecuador
7 Chile	17 Dominican Republic	27 Guyana
8 British Honduras	18 Guadeloupe	28 Paraguay
9 Costa Rica	19 Haiti	29 Surinam
10 El Salvador	20 Jamaica	30 Uruguay

Column 2 shows that contrasts in population size, though still great, are not as marked as contrasts in territorial extent. As a result of the great differences in size and population among countries, density of population varies greatly, as is shown in column 3. The data in column 4 represent the absolute size of the national income of each country, a rough measure of the goods and services produced in a year. The use of U.S. dollars as the measuring unit allows comparison between countries but introduces some bias in conversion from national currencies due to technicalities of exchange rates. While the area data in column 1 are reasonably accurate, in spite of disputes between certain pairs of countries over boundaries, both population and national income figures are only approximate. It is sobering to find that even in the 1970 census of the

Table 1.1

SUMMARY TABLE FOR 24 COUNTRIES OF LATIN AMERICA

1   Area in thousands of sq.km.
2   1970 population in millions
3   Density of population, 1970, persons per sq.km.
4   Total national income in millions of U.S. dollars in 1970 (n.a. not available)
5   Percentage of economically active population engaged in activities other than agriculture, mid-1960s
6   Urban population as a percentage of total population
7   Consumption of energy in kilograms of coal equivalent per inhabitant in 1970
8   Consumption of food in calories per inhabitant, per day, in 1970
9   Literate population over 14 years of age as a percentage of all population over 14 years of age, mostly around 1960

	1	2	3	4	5	6	7	8	9
Seven largest									
Brazil	8,512	94·5	11	32,500	52	46	472	2,540	61
Mexico	1,973	48·4	25	32,000	48	60	1,205	2,620	76
Argentina	2,777	23·2	9	23,000	82	74	1,688	3,170	93
Venezuela	912	10·4	11	8,700	71	76	2,498	2,490	63
Colombia	1,139	21·1	19	7,600	53	53	578	2,190	73
Peru	1,285	13·6	11	4,900	53	52	609	2,200	61
Chile	757	9·8	13	6,000	74	74	1,208	2,520	84
Central America (countries 9-14 on Figure 1.2)									
Costa Rica	51	1·7	34	900	52	35	344	2,230	84
El Salvador	21	3·5	165	1,000	41	38	150	1,880	49
Guatemala	109	5·2	48	1,800	36	34	232	1,950	29
Honduras	112	2·6	23	600	35	32	243	1,930	45
Nicaragua	130	2·0	15	800	41	44	374	2,250	50
Panama	77	1·5	19	900	57	48	1,634	2,450	73
Islands									
Cuba	115	8·4	73	n.a.	61	53	1,039	2,500	78
Dominican Republic	49	4·3	89	1,300	43	40	224	2,080	64
Haiti	28	4·9	175	400	21	12	43	1,930	10
Jamaica	11	1·9	171	1,100	66	37	1,135	2,280	82
Puerto Rico	9	2·7	306	4,500	81	44	3,283	2,530	81
Trinidad	5	1·0	184	700	81	18	4,683	2,360	74
Other South America									
Bolivia	1,099	4·9	4	900	35	34	211	1,760	40
Ecuador	284	6·1	21	1,500	48	38	293	1,850	67
Guyana	215	0·8	4	200	54	30	1,014	2,180	76
Paraguay	407	2·4	6	500	49	36	145	2,730	74
Uruguay	178	2·9	16	2,200	83	81	900	3,020	91
LATIN AMERICA*	20,566	283·0	14	138,000	55	45	1,009	2,318	66

* Totals in Columns 1, 2 and 5 include other units not in this table (see Table 1.2).

Sources:

1–3   *UNSYB 71*, Table 18
4   *UNSYB 71*, Table 185
5   *FAOPY 24*, Table 5
6   *UNDYB 70*, Table 5
7   *UNSYB 71*, Table 137
8   *UNSYB 71*, Table 160
9   *UNDYB 70*, Table 11

Table 1.2

THE SMALLER COUNTRIES OF LATIN AMERICA

Area in thousands of sq.km.
Population in thousands.
Density in persons per sq.km.

	Area	Population	Density
British Honduras	23·0	126	5
Barbados	0·4	256	595
Guadeloupe	1·8	327	184
Martinique	1·1	338	307
Netherland Antilles	1·0	222	231
French Guiana	91·0	51	1
Surinam	163·2	393	2

In addition the following units, some of which gained political independence by the early 1970s, are in Latin America:
Antigua, Bahamas, British Virgin Islands, Cayman Islands, Dominica, Grenada, Leeward Islands, Montserrat, St. Kitts — Nevis — Anguilla, St. Lucia, St. Vincent, Turks and Caicos Islands, United States Virgin Islands, Windward Islands, Falkland Islands.

U.S.A. the census total understated the correct population of the country by about two per cent.[2] The degree of error in some Latin American countries is probably considerably greater.

Columns 5–9 in Table 1.1 contain data expressed in percentage or per capita terms in order to allow the direct comparison of countries of greatly different size. The values for each country may be compared with the Latin American average (mean) value at the foot of the column. To allow a quick appraisal of the extreme values in each column, the five countries ranked highest and the five ranked lowest on each of the five columns are named in Table 1.3.

Table 1.3

HIGHEST AND LOWEST RANKED COUNTRIES ON FIVE VARIABLES

Rank	Non-agricultural	Urban	Energy	Food	Literacy
1	Uruguay	Uruguay	Trinidad	Argentina	Argentina
2	Argentina	Venezuela	Puerto Rico	Uruguay	Uruguay
3	Puerto Rico	Argentina	Venezuela	Paraguay	Chile
4	Trinidad	Chile	Argentina	Mexico	Cost Rica
5	Chile	Mexico	Panama	Brazil	Jamaica
20	El Salvador	Bolivia	Dom. Rep.	Honduras	El Salvador
21	Guatemala	Honduras	Bolivia	Haiti	Honduras
22	Honduras	Guyana	El Salvador	El Salvador	Bolivia
23	Bolivia	Trinidad	Paraguay	Ecuador	Guatemala
24	Haiti	Haiti	Haiti	Bolivia	Haiti

The percentage of economically active population engaged in activities other than agriculture shows concisely the degree to which employment in Latin America has shifted from what a century ago was in most areas the dominant sector of the economy. The Latin American extremes, Argentina and Uruguay with about 80 per cent outside agriculture and Haiti with about 20 per cent have fundamentally different types of economy. Since so much of the population in

Haiti is in agriculture, each farm family does little more than support itself. In Argentina or Uruguay each farm family produces enough to support several other families. Although agriculture is relatively much more important in the economy of Haiti than in that of Argentina or Uruguay, the productivity and absolute output of a farm family is much higher in the latter countries.

The definition of urban in the assessment of urban and rural population is not standard among Latin American countries. Even so, the data in column 6 in Table 1.1 indicate great contrasts in level of urbanisation. Columns 7 and 8 show understandably a much greater range in per capita consumption of energy than of food. Energy consumption is related both to the level of mining, processing and manufacturing and to the standard of living of a country. Literacy (column 9) serves as an approximate guide to general educational levels. The data reveal almost universal literacy in Argentina and Uruguay compared with widespread illiteracy in Haiti.

Some preliminary conclusions, to be reconsidered later in the book, may be drawn from Tables 1.1 and 1.3. It is evident in Table 1.3 that some countries are consistently high on all five variables, while some are consistently low. Argentina and Uruguay are among the top five throughout, Haiti and Bolivia among the bottom five, while Peru and Colombia do not appear at either extreme. As a result of the tendency noted for countries to have similar rankings on the five 'development' variables, there tend to be strong positive correlations between the variables. These can be represented graphically or they can be summarised by a numerical correlation coefficient (see Chapter 9). It can be observed that a country tends to be at roughly the same level on the scale for all the indices that measure 'development' or 'modernisation'. It is unlikely, for example, that a country would be highly urbanised and industrialised and have good health services yet have a very low level of energy consumption and poor educational services. Development may be thought of as a package of closely interrelated material and cultural features. These features can be represented for convenience by precise and concise numerical indices.

Two further points may be introduced here with reference to Table 1.1. Firstly, the level of development of the countries of Latin America apparently has little relationship to their size in terms of *total* area, population or national income. Secondly, great contrasts exist among the countries of Latin America. One might ask: what prospects do the poorer countries have of reaching the level of the more prosperous countries? The question may also be asked with reference to the whole world. In order to put Latin America in the broader world context, Latin American countries are compared with countries in other parts of the world in Chapter 2. In anticipation it may be suggested that Latin America is the most developed of the major developing regions of the world. Whether present trends in Latin America throw any light on future trends in Africa and parts of Asia is a matter that does not seem to have been given much consideration.

1.3. APPROACHES TO THE GEOGRAPHY OF LATIN AMERICA

Since the present book uses a number of relatively new approaches to the study of regional geography it is necessary here to discuss briefly the methodology of regional geography and to justify their use. In the 1960s regional geography came under criticism in some countries from those who considered themselves in the vanguard of innovations in the methodology of geography. Regional geography was criticised both for its descriptive, inventory nature and on account of its superficial approach to complex situations. In a paper published in 1964, W. D. Pattison[3] pointed out that over its long history as a recognised branch of knowledge, geography has consisted of several distinct but not mutually exclusive traditions. He identified four: earth sciences, man-environment relationships, spatial studies and area studies. In the view of the present author the study of distinct areas or regions of the earth's surface can have both academic and practical value. The other approaches or traditions can however be brought into regional studies.

In the methodology of regional geography it is essential to distinguish two basically different aspects, firstly the problem of defining regions and secondly the problem of studying the regions themselves. The division of a country into climatic regions or planning regions is a question of regional definition and delimitation, a matter of classification or taxonomy. The organisation of a backward mountain valley, a growing metropolitan region or indeed a whole country is a matter of appreciating the functioning and interrelationships of the various elements in the region under consideration. D. Harvey[4] refers to the basic distinction between uniform regions and nodal regions.

In the context of Latin America an example may serve to illustrate the distinction between the two kinds of region. The Northern Andes form a fairly distinct physical region with certain accompanying characteristics of human geography. They are distinct from the lowlands both to the west and to the east. The 'uniform' or 'homogeneous' northern Andean region is not however organised as one unit. It is shared among several countries (Venezuela, Colombia, Ecuador, Peru and Bolivia) and for politico-administrative purposes each part is grouped with portions of other uniform regions, notably tropical forest and desert. In the present book the emphasis is on organised regions rather than on homogeneous regions but it must be appreciated that both types can be identified in the real world and that 'functional' and 'formal' regions may be related both conceptually and on the ground.

Regional geography itself has changed in function and approaches in recent decades. One of the main functions of European geography in the period from about 1500 to 1800 was to record the findings of European exploration by collecting information about places, locating the places correctly and describing them. Latin America was one of the parts of the world most involved in this process. During the period of exploration, two characteristics of regional geography emerged, a tendency to detect causal relationships between phenomena found to occur in the same localities and a tendency to base geography as a school subject on a factual knowledge about places. Regional geography has been characterised by many intuitive and often spurious statements about causal relationships. This matter will be discussed again in Chapter 9.

The tendency to equate regional geography with the location and characteristics of places goes back a long way. A child in 18th century Europe privileged enough to be taught geography at all might have been given *The Geography of Children or a Short and Easy Method of Teaching or Learning Geography*,[5] published in London (translation from the French) in 1737. He or she would be confronted by questions such as the following: 'What is Chili? Answer: Chili lies on the coast of the South-sea, beyond the Tropic of Capricorn, and is divided into three provinces, viz. Chili, Imperiale and Chiquito; the chief towns are San Jago of Chili, Imperiale, Angol and Osorno.' It is still convenient in a regional study to know where places are and what they are called, at least the places that recur so frequently that the effort of learning them is less than the effort required to look them up in an index or on a map.

As censuses were carried out with increasing frequency in the 19th century and other information about places became available, books on regional geography tended to place less emphasis on place names and locations, and to become inventories about particular parts of the world. Often the various ingredients of a region were recorded in a particular order, with physical features preceding human ones. European and North American geographers broke away from this approach in the 20th century by using material more selectively, with greater discrimination and with better examples and illustrations. It is evidence of the slow way in which new ideas reach Latin America that many geography books published there in the 1960s still have the traditional form of inventories of facts about places.

It is easy to be critical of regional geography books on regions as vast and diverse as Latin America. Perhaps the fact that virtually no Latin American geographers have attempted a comprehensive survey of their own continent from within is evidence of the difficulty of the task. One must therefore appreciate the work of Preston E. James whose *Latin America,*[6] revised and rewritten on various occasions, is widely held to be one of the best regional geography books written by an English speaking author. It consists mainly of a comprehensive sympathetic appraisal of the physical and human features of the various countries of Latin America. R. Platt's *Latin America: Countrysides and United Regions*[7] uses a different approach, being mainly an account of various case studies of settlements, mines and farms in the region. The difficulty of a geography based on selected case studies is to infer from individual representative known cases to large sets of cases, assumed to be similar. In being more selective in their choice of themes and topics for study, P. R. Odell and D. A. Preston[8] have made a new contribution in *Economies and Societies in Latin America: a geographical interpretation* to the geography of Latin America by presenting in depth some of the current social and economic problems of the region. In regional geography one can in some situations concentrate on particular themes and problems such as oil in Venezuela or the social organisation of the Indians in the Andes. The emphasis in the present book is on areal differentiation within Latin American countries and on the way the countries function through time. Other approaches and traditions of regional geography have been used as well. In the 1970s it would be unrealistic to ignore the help an electronic computer can provide in some types of calculation and study. Appendix 1 contains notes on the various programs used in the present book.

1.4. THE INGREDIENTS OF A REGION

A number of basic features and ingredients of a region can be identified. A region occupies a piece of three dimensional space and exists during a period of time. Four sets of ingredients can be identified within its natural resources, people, routes and organisation. Relationships exist within and between these four sets of ingredients. Within reason, the ingredients can be identified in a region of any size from a village to the ultimate region, the world itself. They can occur anywhere in the world and at any period of time. The larger the region the greater its complexity and the greater the loss of detail in any study of it.

To illustrate the features and ingredients of a region the country of Peru has been chosen. The information on the twelve sketch maps of Peru in *Figure 1.4* is

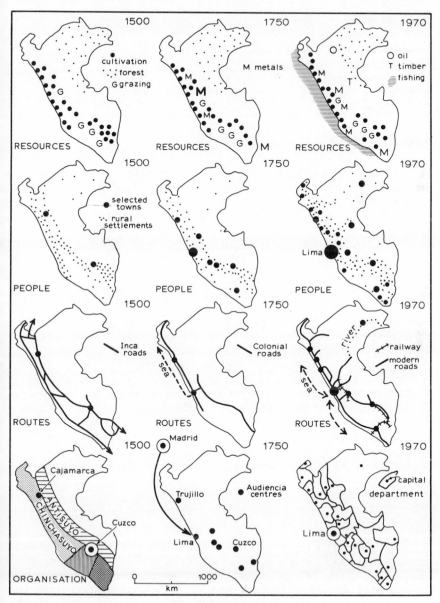

Figure 1.4. Peru used to illustrate the ingredients of regional geography. The information is both selective and approximate

very selective and only approximately accurate. The maps may be compared across the page to show changes in a given ingredient over time and down the page to show the combination of ingredients at any given moment in time.

SPACE

A region occupies a recognised and identifiable space. The land of Peru is limited horizontally by the Pacific coast and by an international boundary touching five other countries and not entirely mutually accepted. It occupies three dimensions and is limited effectively downwards several thousand metres below the surface of the earth and upwards to a boundary somewhere in the atmosphere, as high as its air space is considered to reach.

TIME

A region occupies a span of time. In fact the viceroyalty of Peru and the Inca Empire did not coincide with the limits of modern Peru, which are the limits used in *Figure 1.4*.

NATURAL RESOURCES

Some of these, like agricultural land and forest, occupy large continuous areas while others, like economic minerals, occupy areas that are so small they may be considered as points. The top row of *Figure 1.4* shows how Peru in 1500 was mainly agricultural, with grazing lands and a forest area. After two centuries of Spanish control the country was still predominantly dependent on the land but several mining complexes had been superimposed on the agricultural base. By 1970 new irrigated cultivated land had been added along the coast. Silver, the dominant mineral in 1750, was still mined in 1970 but oil, copper, lead and iron ore were also important. The timber of the interior forests and the fish of the coast were being exploited much more in 1970 than in 1750. Grazing was practised in the Andes in all three years but in 1750 and 1970 Old World livestock increasingly replaced the original llama and guanaco herds. Thus *through time* some natural resources become exhausted or are no longer used while others, often through the introduction of new technology, come into use.

PEOPLE

Regional geography is a highly subjective, biased view of the world seen through the eyes of the species Homo sapiens. A hypothetical ant geographer would no doubt write regional geography from an entirely different angle. People, while referred to often as a resource, are not in the context of regional geography a natural resource. Regions and their natural resources are organised by humans in their own interests.

Between 1500 and 1750 the population of Peru probably did not change much. It did however become more concentrated in certain mining and administrative centres. In 1970 the population was much bigger than in 1750, more highly organised and with about ⅓ of it concentrated in one small spot, the national capital. In spite of changes over time, many of the basic features of distribution of 1500 remained in 1970.

ROUTES

Links between places may be thought of as channels (railway, pipeline, telegraph) which may be used by vehicles for the transference of people, goods or information. Peru in 1500 was served by paths or tracks linking places in the Inca empire. The wheel was not used for transport so movement was only by people moving on foot or by llamas carrying goods. In 1750 the main links were organised to take metals to the coast for shipment to Spain, but many of the Inca routes of 1500 were still kept in use. Between 1750 and 1970 many new kinds of link were introduced: railway, telegraph, pipeline, electricity transmission line, paved motor road. A comparison of routes in 1500, 1750 and 1970 shows some similarities in the three patterns.

ORGANISATION

This heading includes all kinds of miscellaneous and residual features of a region that do not fall into the other three categories. The point must be emphasised here, however, that the ingredients of a region function together, if only loosely, and virtually all parts of the earth's land surface now come under the administration of some country. A region can only be planned and regulated if the way in which it functions is appreciated. In Peru at all three dates in *Figure 1.4* (bottom row), decisions were made in a given place about the broad way in which the empire, colony or country should be run. The 1500 map shows Cuzco, the capital and the place in which the Inca and his Court usually resided and ran their enterprise. The empire was divided into four sectors territorially (shaded). In 1750 Peru was run from Madrid and Seville in Spain through a viceroy in Lima. The country was subdivided for judicial purposes into audiencias (e.g. Trujillo, Cuzco). In 1970, the sovereign country of Peru was subdivided into 23 major civil divisions, the departments. Lima, the national capital, is the place in which most of the big decisions affecting the organisation of the country are taken.

SYSTEM

It may help in the study of the functioning of a region to think of it loosely as a system. The essential concept of a system is the way in which the elements of which it is composed interact. A change in some part of the system may have repercussions elsewhere. The construction of a new motor road between a town and a village serves as a simple example. The creation of a new link in the transport system may make it possible to change the range of crops grown in the village and it may encourage people to migrate to the town thereby changing the demographic structure of both places. The concept of a system and the vocabulary of systems will be referred to again in Chapter 9.

References

1. *UNSYB, 72,* Tables 2 and 3.
2. Hauser, P. M., 'The Census of 1970', *Sci. Am.,* July 1971, Vol. 225, No. 1, pp. 17–25.
3. Pattison, W. D., 'The Four Traditions of Geography', *The Journal of Geography,* LXIII, 1964.
4. Harvey, D., *Explanation in Geography,* 1969, London; Edward Arnold, p. 129.
5. Nicolas Lenglet du Fresnoy, *The Geography of Children,* a 1969 facsimile produced by Johnson Reprint Corporation of the original in London in 1737.
6. James, P. E., *Latin America,* London; Cassell, many editions.
7. Platt, R. S., *Latin America: Countrysides and United Regions,* 1942, New York; McGraw-Hill.
8. Odell, P. R. and Preston, D. A., *Economics and Societies in Latin America: a Geographical Interpretation,* 1973, London; Wiley.

Sources of material in the figures

1.4 More detailed maps of the Inca Empire can be found in V. W. von Hagen, *The Realm of the Incas,* 1961, New York; Mentor Books.

Further reading

Blakemore, H. and Smith, C. T., *Latin America: Geographical Perspectives,* 1071, London; Methuen.
Brookes, J. (Ed.), *The South American Handbook* (yearly), Trade and Travel Publications Ltd., Bath.
Butland, G. J., *Latin America, a Regional Geography,* 1960, London; Longmans.
Dozier, C. L., *Land Development and Colonization in Latin America,* 1969, New York; Praeger (Case studies of Peru, Bolivia and Mexico).
Robinson, H., *Latin America,* 1961, London; Macdonald and Evans.
Schneider, R. M. and Kingsbury, R. C., *An Atlas of Latin American Affairs,* 1966, London; Methuen.
Véliz, C. (Ed.), *Latin America and the Caribbean, A Handbook,* 1968, London; Anthony Blond.
West, R. C. and Augelli, J. P., *Middle America, Its Lands and Peoples,* 1966, Englewood Cliffs; Prentice Hall.

CHAPTER 2

LATIN AMERICA IN A WORLD SETTING

2.1. LATIN AMERICA ON A WORLD DEVELOPMENT SCALE

A study was made by the author of the level of development of the 50 countries in the world with the largest number of inhabitants in 1970. These countries contain about 90 per cent of the total population of the world. They include the 7 largest countries of Latin America, ranked in the world according to population size as follows: 8th Brazil, 14th Mexico, 25th Argentina, 29th Colombia, 42nd Peru, 49th Venezuela, 50th Chile. Lack of space prevents the inclusion of the data used in the study but these have been published elsewhere.[1] Twelve variables were used:

1. Area size of country
2. Population size of country
3. Population increase rate
4. Non-agricultural population
5. Energy consumption per capita
6. Steel consumption per capita
7. Radios in use per capita
8. Doctors per million inhabitants
9. Newspapers sold per capita
10. Food consumption per capita
11. Protein intake per capita
12. Gross domestic product per capita

There is little correlation between variables 1 and 2 and the other ten variables. Variables 3–12 are all expressed in terms that eliminate the direct influence of population size. Strong correlations were found to exist between virtually all pairs of variables 3–12. The application of oblique factor analysis to the matrix of correlation coefficients produced two strongly related factors. These were combined to provide a consensus of the ten variables (3–12) representing different aspects of development. It was then possible to put the 50 countries of the world included in the study on a single scale of development. The numerical position of each country on the scale, given in Table 2.1, shows a relative position, not an absolute one. The exact placing of the countries depends on the particular set of variables used in the study.

The results in Table 2.1 agree fairly well with other such studies including, for example, that made by Berry in *Atlas of Economic Development*.[2] They confirm the statement made in Chapter 1 that Latin America is the least underdeveloped of the major developing regions of the world. The seven Latin American countries rank between 14th (Argentina) and 29th (Peru). The countries below Peru belong exclusively to Asia and Africa.

The level of development of Latin American countries can be expressed in

15

Table 2.1.
COUNTRY SCORES ON TWO COMBINED FACTORS REPRESENTING
10 ASSOCIATED DEVELOPMENT VARIABLES

The standard deviation is ± 20

1	U.S.A.	52	26	N. Korea	− 9
2	Canada	39	27	*Brazil*	− 9
3	W. Germany	32	28	*Colombia*	− 12
4	Australia	29	29	*Peru*	− 12
5	Czechoslovakia	29	30	Iran	− 13
6	France	28	31	China	− 13
7	U.K.	27	32	Malaysia	− 13
8	U.S.S.R.	27	33	Sri Lanka	− 14
9	E. Germany	26	34	Pakistan	− 15
10	Netherlands	26	35	Morocco	− 15
11	Japan	21	36	Algeria	− 16
12	Italy	20	37	Thailand	− 16
13	Poland	18	38	Philippines	− 16
14	*Argentina*	15	39	S. Vietnam	− 16
15	Romania	12	40	Kenya	− 16
16	Spain	9	41	Ethiopia	− 16
17	Yugoslavia	6	42	Nigeria	− 17
18	South Africa	4	43	India	− 17
19	*Venezuela*	1	44	Sudan	− 17
20	*Mexico*	− 5	45	Afghanistan	− 17
21	*Chile*	− 6	46	N. Vietnam	− 18
22	Taiwan	− 6	47	Tanzania	− 18
23	Egypt	− 6	48	Burma	− 18
24	Turkey	− 7	49	Zaire	− 20
25	S. Korea	− 8	50	Indonesia	− 20

terms of per capita availability of various goods and services, and summarised by indices expressing gross domestic product. The relatively low per capita levels are the result of a much smaller absolute production of goods and services than in the developed countries of the world. The Table 2.2 shows the total and per capita gross domestic product of selected areas in 1970.[3]

Table 2.2.
GROSS DOMESTIC PRODUCT OF REGIONS AND COUNTRIES IN 1970 (U.S. DOLLARS)

	Total in millions	Per capita
North America	1,063,000	4,700
Latin America	152,000	550
U.S.A.	973,000	4,750
Brazil	37,300	400
Mexico	33,500	680
Argentina	24,400	1,050
Venezuela	10,400	1,000

Around 1970 North America was producing about 7 times as many goods and services as Latin America for a considerably smaller population. Per capita national income was 8–9 times as high. In the U.S.A. the states of New York and New Jersey produced roughly the same value of goods and services as the whole of Latin America. In the two years from 1968 to 1970 North America *added* to its gross domestic product an amount equal to that possessed by the whole of Latin America in 1968, that is about 120,000 million dollars.

2.2. TRADE, INVESTMENTS AND AID

Since the growth of interest in Latin America by the Europeans after 1500, the continent has been influenced predominantly by two other regions, Europe from the start of colonisation and North America from the start of independence early in the 19th century. On a shorter time scale, the Second World War marked the peak of U.S. influence in Latin America. Since 1945, West European influence has been restored and new links have been established, particularly with Japan and the U.S.S.R. Latin America has little contact at present with the rest of the developing world. The purpose of this section is to illustrate the kinds of link that exist between Latin America and other parts of the world and to show the spatial layout of the networks that provide the links.

Latin America was organised during the 16th to 18th centuries to supply Europe with precious metals, raw materials and tropical food products. In the 19th century the new Latin American states continued to export primary products, supplying both West Europe and North America. In return the region received capital goods and manufactured consumer goods. With some modifications this pattern continues in the 1970s.

The links between Latin American countries and other parts of the world are to a considerable extent related to long established flows of goods and also, though perhaps to a lesser extent, to flows of migrants into the region from Spain and Portugal and more recently from Italy, Germany and Japan. The development of mutual interests and ties between a particular pair of countries depends to a considerable extent on the growth of trade between the two. The establishment of diplomatic relations, of shipping and airline services and of cultural and technical exchanges are often consequences of trade, though the relationship is somewhat circular since they may also pave the way for trade.

It was pointed out in the previous chapter (see *Figure 1.1*) that North America, West Africa and West Europe are the nearest populated regions of the world to Latin America. *Figure 2.1* shows the position of Latin America in relation to Europe (Lisbon) and the U.S.A. (Miami and places along the United States–Mexico boundary). In (a) and (b) distances are correct from Lisbon and Miami respectively. Nowhere in Latin America is less than about 5,600 km (about 3,500 miles) from Europe, whereas more than half of it lies at less than this distance from the U.S.A. In (c), Miami in map (b) is placed on Lisbon in map (a) and Latin America seen from Miami is rotated to show the relative distances from the two places to different parts of the region. In (d), Latin America is divided according to comparative distance from the U.S.A. and Europe. Only the extreme tip of Northeast Brazil is closer to Europe than to the U.S.A., but much of South America is less than twice as far from Europe as from the U.S.A. In contrast, Mexico, Central America and most of the Caribbean are at least four times as far from Europe as from the U.S.A.

Although well organised ocean shipping services allow the low cost movement of certain goods and thus reduce the inconvenience and cost of transport of goods over long distances, proximity tends to generate mutual awareness between a pair of countries. The fact that the U.S.A. shares a long land boundary with Mexico has been the cause of many disputes between the two countries. During the early decades of the 20th century the U.S.A. became deeply involved in the politics of Central America and the Caribbean.

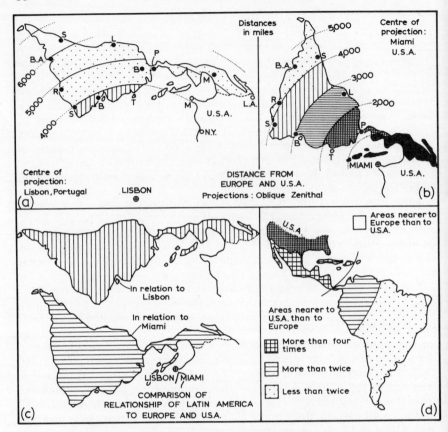

Figure 2.1. The position of Latin America in relation to Europe (Lisbon) and to North America (Miami). Distances are correct from Lisbon in map (a) and from Miami in map (b). In map (c), Lisbon is superimposed upon Miami and maps (a) and (b) are redrawn together

The importance of West Europe and North America in Latin American foreign trade in recent decades is illustrated in a broad way by the following figures: in 1938 West Europe received 47 per cent of the exports of Latin America and North America 31 per cent; in 1953 North America received 47 per cent of the exports of Latin America and West Europe only 27 per cent. When trade between Latin American countries themselves, about 10 per cent of all their trade, is added to the above percentages, it is evident that Latin America had very little trade with any other part of the world before the mid-1950s. Table 2.3 shows more recent trade in greater detail. In the table, the category 'Other' (group 11) includes some Caribbean countries not classed with Latin America in the United Nations source used. The most noticeable trend between 1958 and 1970 has been the relative decline of North America as a market for Latin American exports and the growth of trade with Japan and Comecon.* In the 1960s, however, most of the Latin American trade of Comecon was with Cuba. In 1970 only 3 per cent of the exports of Latin America went to other developing regions (groups 7–10 in Table 2.3) although

* The U.S.S.R. and its East European partners.

together these have almost twice as many inhabitants as the developed regions (groups 2–6).

The provenance of Latin American imports according to the major regions of the world in Table 2.2 is similar to the destination of exports with the notable exception that North America supplied 41 per cent of the imports of Latin America in 1970 while taking only 33 per cent of the exports. Latin America as a whole is therefore not favourably placed in its trade with North America, though the relationship varies greatly from country to country.

Table 2.3.
THE DIRECTION OF LATIN AMERICAN EXPORTS

	Total Value [1] in millions of U.S. dollars		Percentage	
	1958	1970	1958	1970
1 Within region	760	1,700	9·3	11·3
2 U.S.A. and Canada	3,805	4,940	46·5	32·8
3 West Europe	2,420	4,990	29·5	33·2
4 Japan	215	1,020	2·7	6·8
5 Comecon	150	970	1·8	6·4
6 Oceania	10	15	0·1	0·1
7 Middle East	25	60	0·3	0·4
8 China	15	105	0·2	0·7
9 Other Asia	35	155	0·4	1·0
10 Africa	70	115	0·9	0·8
11 Other [2]	680	970	8·3	6·5
TOTAL	8,190	15,040	100·0	100·0

Notes: 1 Note that the U.S. dollar was worth more in 1958 than in 1970
    2 Principally islands of Caribbean and Pacific
Source: *UNSYB 71*, Table 145

Figure 2.2 shows diagrammatically the two largest destinations of the exports (by value) of each of 23 Latin American countries, the eight largest in population in maps (a) and (b), the remainder in maps (c) and (d). As Puerto Rico counts in many respects as a state of the U.S.A. it is not included. *Figure 2.2* is based on 1969 data. Although the U.S.A. had by then become less important relatively as a market for Latin American exports, it was still the biggest export market of 17 out of the 23 countries included in *Figure 2.2* see maps (a) and (c)) and the second market of 3 others (maps (b) and (d)). Only Cuba, trading almost exclusively with Comecon and China, and Argentina and Uruguay, exporting heavily to certain West European countries, do not have the U.S.A. as a first or second export market. The current small value of trade within Latin America is underlined by the fact that in *Figure 2.2,* only three out of 46 possible links are from one Latin American country to another. The export of crude oil from Venezuela to the nearby Netherlands Antilles is only a convenient short step in the export of Venezuelan oil.

It could be argued that the main reason why a country trades is that there are certain goods that it does not or cannot produce at home or that it can obtain more cheaply in a foreign country. It therefore exports to pay for its imports. From the point of view of the imports of Latin American countries, around

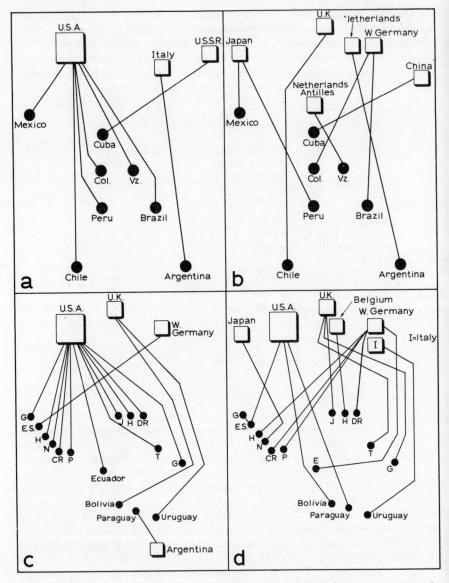

Figure 2.2. The first and second export markets of 23 Latin American countries. Each Latin American country is joined by a line to its first (maps (a) and (c)) and second (maps (b) and (d)) largest export markets. Key to letters in maps (c) and (d):

G	Guatemala	J	Jamaica
E.S.	El Salvador	H	Haiti
H	Honduras	D.R.	Dominican Republic
N	Nicaragua	E	Ecuador
C.R.	Costa Rica	T	Trinidad
P	Panama	G	Guyana

1970 the U.S.A. was the main source for all the larger Latin American countries except Cuba. Table 2.4 shows the three biggest sources of imports of eleven Latin American countries. Dependence on the United States tends to diminish with distance but this is to some extent due to the fact that the products of Argentina and Uruguay are needed more in Europe than in the U.S.A. The complete absence of the U.K. from the list underlines the decline of British influence in Latin America, while France is conspicuous only by being the third trading partner of Cuba. The presence of West Germany is widely felt now in Latin America. As E.E.C. becomes more integrated in the 1970s it will be more realistic to consider the total E.E.C. trade with Latin America rather than the trade of separate member countries.

Table 2.4.

THE PROVENANCE OF IMPORTS OF SELECTED LATIN AMERICAN COUNTRIES:
THREE LARGEST COUNTRIES OF ORIGIN BY VALUE

	Percentage of imports in 1969 obtained from:					
Brazil	U.S.A.	30	W. Germany	13	Argentina	7
Mexico	U.S.A.	62	W. Germany	8	Japan	5
Argentina	U.S.A.	22	Brazil	11	W. Germany	11
Venezuela	U.S.A.	50	W. Germany	9	Japan	7
Colombia	U.S.A.	50	W. Germany	9	Spain	6
Peru	U.S.A.	31	W. Germany	11	Argentina	10
Chile	U.S.A.	39	W. Germany	10	Argentina	10
Guatemala	U.S.A.	34	El Salvador	13	W. Germany	10
Cuba	U.S.S.R.	61	China	6	France	6
Ecuador	U.S.A.	32	W. Germany	13	Japan	9
Uruguay	U.S.A.	14	Brazil	13	W. Germany	11

Source: *UNYITS 69*, various tables

Foreign investments make up only a small percentage of total investments in Latin America. Home investments from the private and public sectors are the main source. Even so, a number of key branches of the economy are dominated or influenced by outside investors. Although data about foreign investments in Latin America are not so straightforward or comparable as trade figures, it is evident that the U.S.A. has by far the largest investments in the region and that there is a broad relationship between value of trade and value of investments. It should be remembered, however, that the U.S.S.R. and its Comecon partners do not have private firms that could invest abroad, since the state owns all means of production. Communist governments are providing loans for projects and accepting interest on the loans.

Table 2.5 shows the value of U.S. direct investments in the larger countries of Latin America and in other major world areas. U.S. investments are relatively large in Venezuela in view of the size of the economy of the country, and they are relatively small in Brazil and Argentina. Latin America in total now has only about $\frac{1}{6}$ of all U.S. foreign investments, compared with Canada and West Europe, each of which has nearly $\frac{1}{3}$. In 1960, Latin America had over $\frac{1}{3}$ of all U.S. foreign investment compared with only $\frac{1}{6}$ now. This trend may be regarded with mixed feelings in Latin America.

The relationship of receipts from U.S. investments to total U.S. investments shown in the third column of Table 2.5 indicates clearly that returns are much higher from the developing regions of Africa and Asia than from the more developed regions of Canada, Europe and Oceania; Latin America occupies an intermediate position. Presumably the developed areas are regarded as being much safer for investments. A commentary on the contrast in receipts from investments in the same industry in different regions is the fact that U.S. investment in petroleum gave the following percentages related to investment: Canada 4 per cent, Venezuela 21 per cent, Middle East 65 per cent.

Table 2.5.
U.S. DIRECT INVESTMENTS ABROAD IN 1968

	millions of U.S. dollars		Receipts as percentage of investments
	Total investments	Total receipts	
TOTAL[1]	64,756	4,985	8
Mexico	1,459	67	5
Other C. America[2]	1,717	123	7
Argentina	1,148	94	8
Brazil	1,484	75	5
Chile	964	144	15
Colombia	629	16	3
Peru	692	99	14
Venezuela	2,620	430	16
Other S. America	298	14	5
LATIN AMERICA[3]	11,010	1,063	10
Canada	19,488	849	4
Europe	19,386	915	5
Oceania	2,821	85	3
Africa	2,673	583	22
Asia	4,693	1,282	27

Notes: 1 Includes some areas and items not listed below
     2 The Caribbean as well as Central America proper
     3 Total of areas listed above

Source: *Statistical Abstract of the United States 1970*, Table 1209, Direct Investments Abroad

Foreign assistance is another aspect of international relations in which the developed regions of the world have become involved with the developing ones. The U.S.A. has been by far the largest source of foreign aid to most Latin American countries since the Second World War. It has, however, been much less generous in Latin America than in certain other parts of the world regarded presumably as being of greater political and strategic concern. Table 2.6 shows the distribution of development *loans,* as distinct from *grants.* The amount authorised during the 1960s was at the rate of one dollar per inhabitant of Latin America per year. Even the limited grants and loans given to Latin America were distributed very unevenly by countries as the per capita values in Table 2.6 show. Ironically the poorest of all, Haiti, received less per inhabitant than any other.

Table 2.6.

U.S. DEVELOPMENT LOANS AUTHORISED TO SELECTED LATIN AMERICAN COUNTRIES DURING 1958–1969 IN MILLIONS OF DOLLARS

	Total	Per capita		Total	Per capita
Brazil	1,029	11	Costa Rica	53	31
Mexico	66	1	El Salvador	43	12
Argentina	98	4	Guatemala	37	7
Venezuela	55	5	Honduras	45	17
Colombia	522	25	Nicaragua	72	36
Peru	96	7	Panama	84	56
Chile	441	45	Dominican Rep.	71	17
Bolivia	109	22	Haiti	6	1
Ecuador	57	9	Jamaica	11	6
Paraguay	37	15	Guyana	38	48
Uruguay	36	12			
			TOTAL	3,117	11

Source: *Statistical Abstract of the United States, 1970*, Table 1219

2.3. INTERNATIONAL LINKS

The overwhelming influence on Latin America of North America and West Europe in terms of foreign trade, investment, aid and cultural exchanges is reflected in the layout of the airline network of each major Latin American country. *Figure 2.3* shows the main features of the international routes served by Varig, the main carrier of foreign air traffic for Brazil, and one of the larger airlines in Latin America. To summarise, Varig has services to eight capitals in

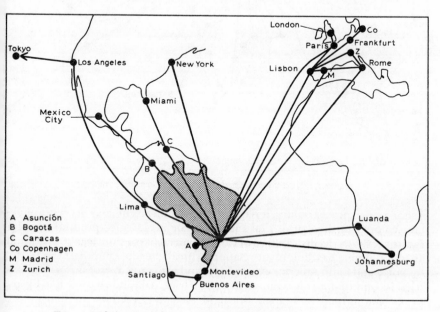

A Asunción
B Bogotá
C Caracas
Co Copenhagen
M Madrid
Z Zurich

Figure 2.3. The international services of the Brazilian airline Varig in the early 1970s

eight other Latin American countries, to eight cities in eight European countries, to three cities in the U.S.A. and less frequent services to Japan and to
southern Africa. *Figure 2.3* does not show several other major Brazilian cities
called at on some of the services. The extent of most of the international systems
of other Latin American countries is more restricted than that of Varig. Most
reach outside Latin America only to North America and West Europe. The
weekly LAN Chile service from Santiago to Easter Island and Tahiti, started in
1970, represents a new direction, as does the proposed route over Antarctica
from Chile to Australia, the first trans-Antarctic commercial air service.

The international airlines of the U.S.A. and of several West European countries are world-wide in extent. From each major West European country, the
Americas tend to be served by several radial lines. *Figure 2.4* uses selected services of the Italian airline Alitalia to exemplify the layout. As many airline
networks spread over large proportions of the earth's surface it is not easy to
appreciate their true layout on the spherical surface. Each tends to be radial in
relation to the country in which it is based. Thus Varig has no direct flights
between Europe and North America or between Europe and South Africa as
these would be circumferential directions in relation to Brazil. Alitalia serves
both these directions, as they are radial to Italy. Varig and Alitalia both reach
Japan, Eastern U.S.A. and South Africa.

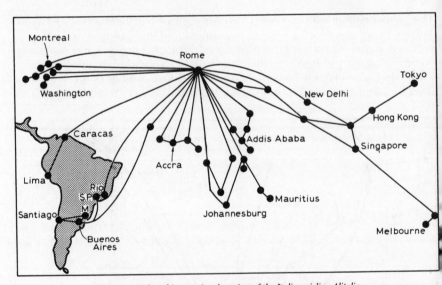

Figure 2.4. Selected international services of the Italian airline Alitalia

For a small, poor country, it is costly to maintain an embassy in every important country in the world. Links may also be avoided for political reasons.
Figure 2.5 shows the distribution of Colombian embassies and legations around
1970. Colombia has diplomatic relations with all the more important countries
of North and Latin America except Cuba and with most West European countries. Its only diplomatic representation in Africa, Asia and Oceania is in Egypt,
the Lebanon, India and Japan. Brazil, Mexico and Argentina are much more
extensively represented outside the Americas and West Europe than Colombia

is: Brazil in 24 countries, Mexico in 22 and Argentina in 28. All three have diplomatic relations with the U.S.S.R. and several of its Comecon partners. Other Latin American countries tend to be more restricted in the extent of their diplomatic relations and more selective. Venezuela, for example, has embassies

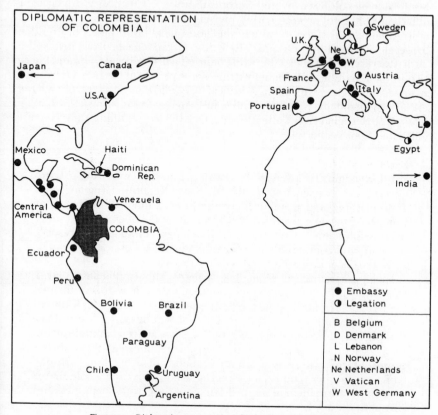

Figure 2.5. Diplomatic representation of Colombia in the early 1970s

in three Middle East oil countries, Iran, Kuwait and Saudi Arabia. Chile has an embassy in another major copper producing country, Zambia. Haiti has embassies in several West African countries.

2.4. VIEWS OF LATIN AMERICA

An addition to the content of geography in the 1960s was the growth of perception studies. Many decisions that determine changes in the human geography of a region are made, it is argued, by decision makers who only have partial information about reality, who are biased in their view and whose judgements are subjective. It has not been easy to transform such loose and broad concepts about perception into rigorous and conclusive statements in which the subjective view of individuals or groups can be related to decisions about the environment and about spatial situations. This section, therefore, only puts forward some tentative ideas about perception in relation to Latin America.

In 1823 President Monroe of the United States, in support of the in-dependence movement in Latin America, declared that in the future the region should not be colonised by any European powers. This policy, which com-mitted the U.S.A. to 'protect' Latin America, has influenced U.S. relations with Latin America ever since, in spite of the 'good neighbour' policy of President Roosevelt, initiated in the 1930s. The U.S.A. became particularly involved in Latin America in 1898 after a war with Spain left it in control of Cuba and Puerto Rico in the Carribbean. Even before this, some people in the U.S.A. envisaged strong economic ties with Latin America. The following extract from a letter[4] sent in 1890 from a U.S. representative in Uruguay to the Minister of Foreign Relations in Uruguay draws attention to a U.S. project to build a railway to link North and South America:

> Excellency,
> I am urgently advised by cablegram this morning of my government's extreme desire that its Sister Republic Uruguay, shall appoint three Representatives, to the International Commission of Engineers, meeting at my country's capital, in October next, 'to study the possible routes, determine their true length, estimate their respec-tive cost, and compare their reciprocal advantages', for a Railroad to unite the systems of South and North America.
>
> In support of my government's earnest wishes in this particular, I trust you will forgive the suggestion, that, vast as may appear the un-dertaking of connecting the three Americas, by a Continuous Railway, for impartial service, to all their different Nations, its successful ac-complishment need not be despaired of, since apart from multiplying many times their material wealth, such a trunk line, with the branches it must attract, will serve to bind with bands of steel, all to harmony with one another, and each to internal tranquility; the whole that is needed to assure them ultimate destinies of the greatest happiness and prosperity.

The above quotation illustrates the U.S. tendency to see Latin America as a whole rather than in terms of individual countries. The Second World War led to an increase in U.S. involvement in Latin America for both economic and strategic reasons. The U.S.A. became the main supplier of manufactured goods for several years while during the war it sought bases in Latin America and per-suaded many Latin American countries to make a token declaration of war on the Axis powers. The Pan-American Highway system, still incomplete in the early 1970s, was proposed at this time.

A further period of concern about Latin America seems to have prevailed in the U.S.A. following the establishment of a pro-Soviet, communist government headed by Fidel Castro in Cuba. Soon after he was elected, President Kennedy established the Alliance for Progress, recognising the continuing economic backwardness of much of Latin America and the desirability that the U.S.A. should help, intending, among other things, to try to weaken or remove Com-munist influence elsewhere. The critical meeting was reported thus in 1961 in the *Fortnightly Review* of The Bank of London and South America:[5]

The conference of the Inter-American Economic and Social Council of the Organization of American States began at Punta del Este, Uruguay, on 5th August. In a message to the conference, President Kennedy stated that the U.S.A. would allocate more than U.S.$1,000 million to Latin America in the first year of the Alliance for Progress programme. The U.S.A. could and should provide sufficient resources to achieve a breakthrough to self-sustaining economic growth. But the U.S.A. would do this only after the Latin American governments had mobilized their internal resources for planned development. The message stressed that social reform was an essential condition for economic growth and political peace, and called for land and tax reform and greater emphasis in government spending on education, health and housing.

Looking back from the early 1970s it can be seen that the Alliance for Progress has so far made little impact on Latin America. For one thing, the financial aid provided by the U.S.A. has been much less than the amount hoped for at the time of its inauguration. In addition several countries have become more openly hostile to the U.S.A., recently, among them Peru since 1968 and Chile during 1970–73.

As has been shown in Section 2.2 of this chapter, the U.S.A. remains a powerful influence in Latin America through its trade, investments and aid. Militarily it is overwhelmingly more powerful than Latin America and economically its productive capacity is about 7 times as great. Since the Second World War the U.S.A. has had political, economic and military worries elsewhere in the world to give it more concern than those in Latin America. In 1973, however, President Nixon[6] apparently planned yet another approach to Latin America aimed at a 'mature relationship' with the region in which countries could 'assume increasing responsibility for ideas, for initiatives and for actions'. To Latin Americans this kind of attitude still leaves the U.S.A. in the position of a condescending neighbour, a powerful self-appointed influence in the region, now pretending to renounce part of its dubious claim to intervene in Latin American affairs. Understandably, Latin American political leaders have themselves attempted to reduce dependence by strengthening links with other parts of the world since the Second World War, in particular with West Europe, Japan and the U.S.S.R. together with its Comecon partners. The Soviet view of Latin America will now be discussed briefly.

Although Russians and Ukrainians have settled in parts of Latin America both before and since the 1917 Revolution in Russia, contacts and transactions have been very restricted until the 1960s when the U.S.S.R. 'adopted' Cuba. Even so, Soviet historians have identified movements in various parts of Latin America sympathetic to the 1917 Revolution in Russia. In an atlas[7] published in Moscow in 1954, for example, revolutionary movements influenced by the Soviet Revolution are noted in seven Latin American countries, Mexico, Haiti, Ecuador, Chile, Argentina, Uruguay and Brazil. More recently, Latin American delegations have been well represented at various Communist Party Congresses in the U.S.S.R. At the 24th Session of the Communist Party of the Soviet Union in April 1971[8] all but a few Latin American countries had representatives who made speeches in Moscow. Cuba and Chile appeared to provide the star delegations, coming first and second in the 'pecking order' among Latin

Americans but preceded by communist countries such as Poland and by other more prominent countries such as France and Italy with big communist movements.

Although the Soviet press has been devoting considerable attention to Latin America since the early 1960s, material links are still very restricted. Foreign trade is relatively unimportant to the Soviet Union. Moreover it is not always easy to establish which part of its trade is essential to the U.S.S.R., and which is carried on for political reasons. Since the Second World War, the U.S.S.R. has been interested in certain Latin American exports such as wool from Uruguay, copper from Chile, and coffee from various countries.

Cuba dominates Soviet trade with Latin America and 1969[9] Soviet trade (imports plus exports) with Cuba was 770 million roubles, about 4 per cent of all Soviet foreign trade. The combined trade with nine other Latin American countries, mainly Brazil and Argentina, was less than 120 million roubles. Since 1969 there has been some increase in Soviet–Latin American trade, as well as in the flow of loans and grants. The Comecon partners of the U.S.S.R. also trade in a limited way with Latin America. In other ways links between the two regions are slight. Since the Second World War the establishment of diplomatic links has been slow. Apart from the Soviet Aeroflot services to Cuba, with proposed extensions to the Andean countries, neither region has airline services to the other.

While Soviet influence in Cuba remains very strong, the overthrow of the Marxist President Allende of Chile in September 1973 appears to be a great setback not only to democracy in Latin America but also, ironically, to the U.S.S.R. No doubt the U.S.S.R. will continue to publish articles in its press deploring the economic and social inequalities in Latin America and the iniquities of foreign investments and political pressure in the region. The two cartoons in *Figure 2.6,* are from *Pravda.*[10] Distance, limited financial resources, linguistic differences and other factors make it difficult for the U.S.S.R. to make much impact on Latin America. Increasingly, Latin American countries are defying the implicit U.S. attitude that they should keep away from Comecon. It is doubtful however if the U.S.S.R. has the military or financial resources to enable it to support another Latin American country, should one follow the path of Castro's Cuba.

One view of Latin America that seems to prevail in many quarters both inside the region and outside is its great potential in terms of natural resources. In 1953, J. A. Comacho[11] introduced a series of eight talks on Latin America by the BBC. The image of Latin America that he conveyed is worth quoting. When asked what their reaction is to Latin America he said:

> 'most people think at once of revolutions. And, of course, there have been and indeed still are from time to time quite a number of revolutions in Latin America .... But it would be a mistake to imagine that revolutions are the only interesting and most important aspects of life in Latin America.'

After describing various aspects of Latin America, Comacho concludes:

> 'But even in those zones that are already peopled and developed, the national wealth is great. Argentina is one of the granaries of the world; Venezuela the world's largest exporter of petroleum; Chile one of the

Figure 2.6. *Two Soviet cartoons from* Pravda *illustrating Soviet propaganda against U.S. investments in and trade with Latin America*

Figure 2.6a. Source: Pravda 4 July 1971
Above the cartoon is the quotation: In a series of Latin American countries the nationalisation of foreign monopolies is taking place, in the first stage, North American, as an effective means of defence of the economy of these countries and the strengthening of their independence (from a newspaper)
In the cartoon: the saw is entitled 'nationalisation', the rake teeth 'robbery' and the sign 'Latin America'
At the foot of the cartoon is its caption: The long rake of Uncle Sam becomes shorter

Figure 2.6b. Source: Pravda 14 May 1972
Above the cartoon is the quotation: In attempting to resolve its economic and exchange-finance difficulties at the expense of other countries, Washington widely uses unfair trade relations with Latin America (from a newspaper)
In the cartoon the sack is entitled: 'Goods of Latin America'. The caption at the foot of the cartoon is: Trade the American way

most important suppliers of copper; Bolivia one of the main suppliers of tin. The wealth of Brazil is so varied and vast that even an inadequate picture would take up the whole of the period of this talk. In fact, in Latin America there is room for expansion and development, for the increased exploitation of a national wealth, whose exhaustion is not even remotely in sight. And there is a rapidly expanding population, with a rising standard of living.

It is not, perhaps, too much to say that Latin America is the land of the future.'

Those who shared Comacho's optimistic view of the future of Latin America in 1953 might query some of his conclusions now.

2.5. PERCEPTION OF PLACES

On a more light-hearted note it may be suggested that the image of Latin America as the land of revolutions is not more than a small part of the mental picture of the region held by the British. The author carried out questionnaire surveys of the views of people in Brazil, Mexico and Britain itself. A study was also made of the frequency of mentions of places in Brazilian, Mexican and Peruvian newspapers, to find which parts of the world readers in those countries read about most. Some of the results will be discussed later in the book under individual countries. To conclude this chapter some general findings are described briefly below.

In a questionnaire circulated in Britain in 1973 and returned by 108 people, one of the parts asked: 'Write down in five single words or short phrases the five features (qualities, places, people) that first come into mind when you think of the following countries'. The list included France, Mexico, China, the U.S.A., Brazil and the U.S.S.R. Table 2.7 lists the most frequently mentioned things

Table 2.7.
A BRITISH VIEW OF BRAZIL AND MEXICO: THE TWENTY MOST FREQUENT REFERENCES

Brazil		Mexico	
Coffee	73	Sombreros	64
Nuts	56	Olympics	39
Amazon	41	Mexico City	25
Brasilia	36	Aztecs	19
Rio de Janeiro	33	Heat	18
Jungles, forests	32	Sun	16
Football (team)	23	Poverty	15
Pele	20	1970 World Cup	15
Large size	12	Cacti	13
Indians	8	Desert, arid	13
Climate	6	Jumping beans	12
Heat, sultry	6	Bandits	11
Political instability	5	Music	9
Revolution	5	Football	8
Coconuts	5	Ponchos	7
Sugar Loaf	5	Moustaches	7
São Paulo	5	Revolution	7
Snakes	4	Horses	7
Carnival	4	High altitudes	6
Portugal, Portuguese	4	Guitars	6

Figure 2.7. Pictorial impressions of the British views of Brazil and Mexico (see Table 2.6)

about Brazil and Mexico. As the question was open, the verbal replies were very diverse and some processing was needed to tabulate the results. It was usually easy to separate specific places and people from classes of objects and from more abstract concepts, but they are listed together in Table 2.6. The items in the table, together with further references, have been combined in *Figure 2.7* to give a pictorial impression of the verbal images.

It must be stressed that what has been discussed is only 'a' British view, not 'the' British view of Brazil and Mexico. The sample is however big enough and representative enough to claim to show reasonably well certain broad features of the British view. Brazilians and Mexicans might be gratified at the few references to political instability or economic backwardness, as well as to the pleasant 'quality' of some aspects of life in their countries. They would certainly be distressed that virtually no-one in Britain made direct reference to industrial developments, power projects or road building, aspects that the two pride themselves on greatly.

The tables are turned on Britain to some extent by the Mexican and Brazilian views of our country. The image of a traditional society with royalty prominent and London dominating the landscape, plus successful pop groups, overshadows a view of a country that prides itself on its strong industrial and technological position in the world. Table 2.8 contains a summary of 'a' Mexican view of four countries, the U.S.A., the U.S.S.R., Britain and France. It should be noted that the Brazilian view of the U.S.A. was rather less critical than the Mexican one, but the Brazilian image of the other three countries was very similar.

A further line of approach to the application of perception in Latin American studies will be mentioned briefly. It is illustrated by a Mexican example. A count of place names mentioned in a sample of daily newspapers in Mexico City shows which parts of the world people are likely to read about most. Table 2.9

Table 2.8.
A MEXICAN VIEW OF FOUR COUNTRIES SHOWING THE 20 MOST FREQUENTLY MENTIONED
TOPICS IN ORDER OF NUMBER OF REFERENCES

U.S.A.	*U.S.S.R.*	*Britain*	*France*
New York	Siberia	Queen (Elizabeth)	Eiffel Tower
Nixon	Lenin	Beatles	Paris
Race	Moscow	Weather	Vines, wine
Hippies	Communism	Royal Guards	De Gaulle
Industries	Red Square	Big Ben	Seine
Drugs	Space race	Industry	Perfume
War	Kremlin	Music	Louvre
Imperialism	Stalin	Empire	Arc de Triomphe
White House	Cold, Snow	Buckingham Palace	Bonaparte
Vietnam	Socialism	Tower of London	Food
Money	Agriculture	Oxford	Museums
San Francisco	Ballet	Royalty	Women
Los Angeles	Imperialism	Liverpool	Sorbonne
Negroes	Taiga	Hippies	Champs Elysées
Technology	Marx	Parliament	Versailles
Dollars	Trans-Siberian	Ireland	Culture
Capitalism	Vodka	Churchill	Paintings
Las Vegas	Workers	Fashions	Industry
Grand Canyon	Industry	Culture	Fashions
Kennedy	Wheat	Castles	Notre Dame

Table 2.9.

AREAL CLASSIFICATION OF PLACES MENTIONED IN THE MEXICAN NEWSPAPER *EXCELSIOR*

		Total	Per cent
	Home		
1	Mexico the country	33	5
2	Mexico State, City and Distrito Federal	48	7
3	Rest of Mexico	99	14
	Sub total	180	26
	Foreign		
4	U.S.A. and Canada	87	13
5	Latin America (except Mexico)	69	10
6	Europe including U.S.S.R.	152	23
7	Africa except Egypt	7	1
8	Middle East	57	8
9	Rest of Asia	85	12
10	Australia and New Zealand	1	0
11	Big areas	49	7
	Sub total	507	74
TOTAL		687	100

Most frequently mentioned individual places

Americas including Mexico		Rest of World	
Mexico (country)	33	U.S.S.R.	15
U.S.A.	25	West Germany	13
Washington	18	Israel	11
Chile	15	France	10
Mexico City	8	Japan	10
University of Mexico	7	China	9
Texas	7	N. Vietnam	9
Santiago (Chile)	7	S. Vietnam	9
Distrito Federal (Mexico)	6	Spain	9
Cuernavaca (Mexico)	6	Lebanon	8
State of Mexico	5	Hanoi	7
Coahuila	5	Tel Aviv	6
New York	5	Peking	6
Brazil	5	Moscow	6
Argentina	5	Paris	5
Nuevo León	4	Italy	5
California	4	Britain	5
		Philippines	5
Latin America	10		
Ibero-america	6	Munich*	13
		Olympic Village*	5
		Europe	6

* The survey period included the 1972 Olympic Games in Munich.

shows the number of occasions on which places in different major regions of the world were mentioned on the front page of *Excelsior* a daily paper published in Mexico City, during September and October 1972. Even when a name was mentioned more than once on the same day it was only counted once. The word Mexico, referring to the country, was mentioned 33 times (every day). Many places only appeared once. The areal distribution of places mentioned in Table 2.9 agrees broadly with that found in Brazilian and Peruvian newspapers. Outside the 'host' country (Mexico), Europe and the U.S.A. receive great prominence. Africa and Australasia are hardly ever mentioned. In the Mexican survey, Israel and Vietnam, and associated places, occupied much of the space devoted to Asia. The pattern of news reported in Latin America resembles the trade, airline and diplomatic links described earlier in this chapter.

References

1. J. P. Cole, *Geography of World Affairs*, 1972 edition and 1974 reprint for a discussion of the data.
2. N. Ginsburg, *Atlas of Economic Development*, 1961, The University of Chicago Press, especially Part VIII, 'A Statistical Analysis' by B. J. L. Berry.
3. *UNSYB, 1972*, Table 188, Estimates of total and per capita gross domestic product in purchasers' values.
4. Part of a letter in *Despatches from U.S. Ministers of Paraguay and Uruguay, 1855–1906*, The National Archives of the United States, 1934.
5. *Fortnightly Review* of the Bank of London & South America Limited, 12th Aug. 1961.
6. *The Times*, May 16, 1973.
7. *Atlas novoy istorii*, 1954, Moscow, chast II, p. 40.
8. *Pravda*, various numbers from 1–10 Apr. 1971.
9. *Vneshnyya torgovlya SSSR za 1969 god*, 1970, Moscow, Table IV.
10. *Pravda*, 4 July 1971 and 14 May 1972.
11. *The Listener*, Oct. 15, 1953, pp. 629–30.

Sources of material in the figures

2.2. The trade data are from *UNYITS 1969*.
2.3. Based on data in *Varig Brazilian Airline International Timetable*, Nov. 1972 (Varig, 235 Regent St., London).
2.4. Alitalia, *Worldwide Timetable*, June 1–July 31, 1973.
2.5. *Statesman's Yearbook*, 1972–73.

CHAPTER 3

HISTORY*

3.1. PEOPLING OF LATIN AMERICA

Speculation as to whether the original inhabitants of Latin America, the American Indians,† had a separate origin in the New World or came from the Old World seems pointless since their obvious membership of the species Homo sapiens points to their common origin with Old World man. Whether American Indians entered the Americas exclusively from northeast Asia across the Bering Strait or arrived from Africa or even across the Pacific seems likely to remain an unsolved problem. A view currently widely held is that small groups of simple hunters and gatherers entered the Americas from Asia, probably on various occasions, in random migrations. Some features of the American Indians such as hair type and shape of face are reminiscent of east Asian features. On the other hand, the indigenous population of the New World has predominantly gene M blood group and locally in northwest North America, mainly gene A, neither of which is common in East Asia. There are no obvious cultural clues as they did not apparently bring with them any cultivated plant species or domesticated animals from the Old World. How long ago early man first settled in the Americas has also been a matter of some interest in the U.S.A. Recent finds of human remains and artefacts suggest that the widely held view that early man reached the Americas about 12,000 years ago will have to be modified. A much earlier date, perhaps between 40,000 and 100,000 years, is now proposed.[1]

If the earliest settlers of the Americas were hunters, gatherers and fishermen with only a modest range of techniques, at least several thousand years ago agriculture was already being practised. Maize, the potato, cotton and other plants were grown, though domesticated livestock were used extensively only in the Andean area. Parts of what are now in Mexico, Central America and northwest South America, supported agricultural civilisations with irrigation in places, urban centres large for the time, and political organisations of some sophistication. By Old World standards of the time American civilisations such as the Maya and Aztec in Mexico and Central America and the Inca centred on Peru in South America lacked certain developments. The wheel was not used for transport, there were no proper written languages and the working of metal was very restricted except for ornamental purposes. These and other shortcomings in no way detract from the impressive achievements of the New World civilisations. On the other hand they may explain to some extent the fragile

---

* See a special note at the end of this chapter for some of the books referred to during the writing of the chapter.

† Amerind for short. When he reached the Caribbean, Columbus thought he had arrived in India and so referred to the area by that name. Unfortunately the area became known as the Indies and the inhabitants as the Indians.

COCAMOS INDIAN, ACRE
TERRITORY, BRAZIL

INDIAN, CENTRAL ANDES, PERU

MESTIZO (INDIAN AND EUROPEAN),
CENTRAL COLOMBIA

MULATO (AFRICAN AND EUROPEAN),
BRAZIL

LATIN AMERICA

CABOCLO (INDIAN AND EUROPEAN),
NORTHEAST BRAZIL

AFRICAN, BAHIA STATE,
NORTHEAST BRAZIL

INSET: EUROPEAN, LIMA SOCIALITE, A MISS UNIVERSE OF LATE 1950's

MESTIZO FAMILY, CIUDAD DE DIOS SHANTY TOWN, LIMA, 1955

nature of American Indian political, economic and social structures when confronted with the early European colonisers and settlers, and they may even contribute to the present difficulties still facing the Indians in many parts of Latin America today.

When the Europeans explored the Americas in the 16th century they found a few very densely populated regions but mainly vast virtually uninhabited areas. There are no records of population numbers in pre-Columbian* America but attempts have been made to assess the number on the basis of the economy of the time and the natural conditions. For the area that became Spanish America, a Spanish source[2] puts the figure at 11¼ million in 1492. With Brazil this makes about 13 million altogether. Such a figure seems low considering that it gives a mean density of about 0·5 persons per sq. km. for all Latin America, including several densely peopled regions. At all events much of the total population was in the highlands of Mexico, the forest lowlands of southern Mexico and northern Central America (4½ m.), in the northern Andes and in coastal Peru (3½ m.), about 8–9 million altogether.

During the three centuries following the early voyages of the Spanish and Portuguese explorers to the Americas two main streams of settlers entered the area and gradually mixed with the indigenous American Indian population: Spaniards and Portuguese from Iberia, conveniently referred to as Iberians, and Africans mainly from the western part of tropical Africa. From Spain immigrants came initially mainly from the southwest and centre, the area of Castilian domination, but later also from other parts. The impact on the Amerind population was devastating in some areas, very slight in others. In the Caribbean islands the Amerinds were reduced after a few decades to about 10 per cent of their original numbers, partly by Old World diseases. The highland Amerinds of Mexico and the Andes resisted more successfully but were eventually reduced by about 20–30 per cent. The Amerinds in Amazonia and Patagonia and in much of North America were not directly affected until the nineteenth century.

During the colonial period, the early 16th to the early 19th century, Iberian colonisers and African slaves reached different parts of Latin America in varying numbers. The total number of Europeans arriving was at most several hundred thousand. The Spaniards tended to settle in existing concentrations of Indians. The Africans on the other hand were deliberately brought to work on plantations in areas from which the Indians had disappeared or in which they had not settled. Smaller numbers of English, French and Dutch settlers also came to Latin America during the colonial period.

Even by 1570 only just over 1 per cent of the population of Spanish America was 'white', and about the same proportion negro, while by 1650 over 80 per cent was still Indian and much of the rest mixed. Rapid mixing of Amerinds and Europeans took place in the early decades due to the lack of European women; this was permitted by the Church, and marriage was encouraged. The result was the emergence of the *mestizo* element. Europeans and Africans also mixed, but marriage with slaves was not usually accepted. The result was the *mulatto* element. When Amerinds and Africans mixed the result was called *zambo,* a type generally considered to be unsatisfactory. By about 1800 all six types were

---

* Pre-Columbian refers to the period before the arrival of Christopher Columbus in the Americas in 1492.

recognised and innumerable local combinations as well. In a total population in Latin America of about 20,500,000 around 1800 the various ingredients represented were divided as shown in Table 3.1.

Table 3.1.

	Spanish areas	Brazil
Whites	3,300,000	800,000
Mestizos	5,300,000	–
Indians	7,500,000	300,000
Negroes	800,000	1,900,000
Mixed (mainly mulatto)	–	600,000

Changes took place in the pattern of migration to Latin America when most of the area became independent of Spain and Portugal around 1820. Africans were still brought in, especially to Brazil, until near the end of the 19th century, but in diminishing numbers. The introduction of steamship services to Latin America in the middle of the 19th century allowed an increase in the flow of Europeans to the region. Spaniards and Portuguese continued to emigrate, while Italians, Germans, east Europeans and others also left Europe, mainly for the southern part of South America. Chinese, Japanese and Asian Indians settled in small numbers in many parts. *Figure 3.1a* indicates the direction of migrations, excluding the Iberian colonisation up to the 19th century. This was so widespread that it covered almost the whole area shaded.

Although European born settlers form only a small minority in Latin America in the 1970s, many people in Argentina are still 'pure' Europeans. Similarly, 'pure' negroes still remain in Northeast Brazil and Haiti and unmixed American Indians are found in many areas, including Amazonia. Most Latin Americans must by now have some mixture of the original ingredients and it is therefore difficult to classify them according to physical characteristics. Some national censuses do however distinguish 'races' though largely on the basis of skin colour and/or cultural characteristics. Often the decision is left to the individual to say what he considers himself to be. Given that 'white' is the most desirable skin colour, people tend to classify themselves as whites when they are brown, and mulatto or mestizo when they are virtually pure African or American Indian. The result presumably is to make the European element seem larger than it is.

In Latin American countries the division of 'races' into such a rigid official twofold division as white and non-white, as in the U.S.A., is not commonly found. Rather there are many rungs on a ladder leading up from darkest to lightest skin or most Indian or negro to most European. Latin America, both past and present, cannot be understood unless it is appreciated that deep underlying prejudices exist over race. They are least of a problem in areas populated mainly by one particular race. To quote Harris:[3] 'In Minas Velhas (a small town in Bahia, Brazil), the superiority of the white man over the Negro is considered to be a scientific fact as well as the incontrovertible lesson of daily experience.' Suitably adapted to local racial conditions, this might be applied in many parts of Latin America, in spite of the professed admiration the Mexicans and Chileans have for their pure Indian minorities and the southern Brazilians for their negro 'brothers.'

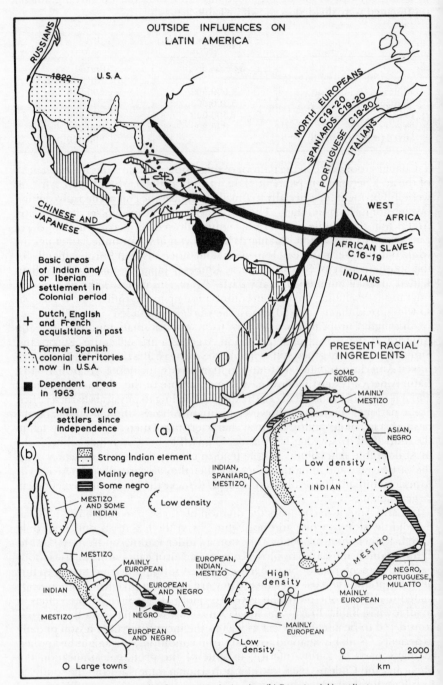

OUTSIDE INFLUENCES ON LATIN AMERICA

RUSSIANS

1822 U.S.A.

NORTH EUROPEANS C19-20
SPANIARDS C19-20
PORTUGUESE C19-20
ITALIANS

WEST AFRICA

CHINESE AND JAPANESE

AFRICAN SLAVES C16-19

INDIANS

Basic areas of Indian and/or Iberian settlement in Colonial period

Dutch, English and French acquisitions in past

Former Spanish colonial territories now in U.S.A.

Dependent areas in 1963

Main flow of settlers since independence

(a)

PRESENT 'RACIAL' INGREDIENTS

SOME NEGRO

MAINLY MESTIZO

ASIAN, NEGRO

Low density

INDIAN

INDIAN, SPANIARD, MESTIZO,

MESTIZO

NEGRO, PORTUGUESE, MULATTO

MAINLY EUROPEAN

(b)

Strong Indian element

Mainly negro

Some negro

Low density

MESTIZO AND SOME INDIAN

MESTIZO

MAINLY EUROPEAN

INDIAN

EUROPEAN AND NEGRO

NEGRO

MESTIZO

EUROPEAN AND NEGRO

EUROPEAN, INDIAN, MESTIZO

High density

E

MAINLY EUROPEAN

Low density

O Large towns

0 2000
km

Figure 3.1. (a) Outside influences on Latin America: (b) Present racial ingredients

Hutchinson[4] points out clearly the differing attitudes to race in Bahia state, Brazil, and in the U.S.A.:

> 'In the United States an absolute "line" is drawn between white and Negro. A person who is not white is a Negro, whatever his percentage of Negro heritage may be. In Vila Reconcavo, this "line" is recognised rather than drawn. A distinction between Negro and white is always kept in mind when classifying an individual. Everyone knows who is "pure" white and who is not. Classification by colour is one of the most important aspects for the outsider to grasp. Reconcavo Bahians feel that one may instantly recognise the difference between a "pure" white and a mixed white-Indian, white-Negro, or Negro-Indian, but they do not let it go at that. They classify or describe minutely each person; they classify according to skin colour, hair form, and facial features. Their classifications of physical types are used in everyday conversation. Just as it would be said in the United States that someone is short and fat, the people of Vila Reconcavo will describe a person's colour and hair form. . . .'

In Mexico, as in Northeast Brazil, complicated mixtures of European and non-European are recognised and terms are given. Galindo Villa[5] in a geography of Mexico, after pointing out that the white is superior intellectually, describes the mestizo: 'He is intelligent, patriotic, just as much as the white and more than the Indian; he disdains his forebear the Indian, however, and also dislikes the Spaniard.' The author then lists some of the variations, which have special terms down to several generations of mixing, and intriguing connotations such as 'salta atrás' (jump back) and 'torna atrás' (turn back) indicating a move, favourable or otherwise, towards a particular 'pure' race, or 'tente en el aire' (stay in the air) for a union of mestizo with mestizo, mulatto with mulatto, when two of the same intermediate colour join to produce offspring not going towards a particular pure race.

In the view of the author a distinction should be drawn between the position of the negro in the U.S.A. and the non-European in Latin America. If the position of the Negroes in the U.S.A. was desperate a few decades ago, moves to secure the vote for them, to give them equal job opportunities and to reduce residential segregation have become a part of deliberate policy in recognition of the problem. In Latin America the problem exists but tends to be ignored.

The present distribution of human groups is summarised below and is very tentatively mapped in *Figure 3.1b*.

1 Indian: (a) Thinly peopled interior of South America (Amazonia)
               (b) Densely peopled rural areas of Southern Mexico and Central America, the Andean countries, parts of Chile, Paraguay.
2 Mestizo: Towns throughout 1(a) and 1(b), many rural areas also.
3 European: (a) Rural in the three southern states of Brazil, in Uruguay, most of Argentina, Cuba, Costa Rica.
               (b) Urban almost throughout Latin America.
4 Mulatto: (a) European strong: parts of Cuba, Puerto Rico, Dominican Republic, Northeast Brazil, Rio-São Paulo area.
               (b) European weak: Jamaica, parts of Northeast Brazil.

5 Negro: Relics in Northeast Brazil, interior Haiti, smaller West In-
                    dian islands.
6 Asian: Considerable element in Trinidad, Guianas, São Paulo state
                    of Brazil.

The official combined percentage of 'whites' and mestizos is shown for the
U.S.A., Canada and each of the main countries of Latin America:

Argentina	99
Canada	98·4
Uruguay	98
Costa Rica	90
U.S.A.	89·5
Cuba	80
Brazil	75
Chile	61
Dominican Republic	58
Venezuela	55
El Salvador	49
Guatemala	46
Mexico	40
Bolivia	31
Peru	27
Ecuador	26
Haiti	2·5

3.2. POLITICAL HISTORY

In most of Pre-Columbian America clearly defined political units did not exist,
though communities operated within recognised territories. Even in Mexico
and Central America, large areas did not fall under one government, though
there were loose associations of quite large groups. For example, Aztec control
from the city of Tenochtitlán at the end of the 15th century diminished sharply
with distance, and was sporadic over peoples on the fringes. Only the Inca Empire was organised as a large political unit with constant communication
between all the parts and the centre. Cohesion was achieved by a remarkable
system of roads, and a system of messengers working in relays. This delicately
balanced system, spreading some 4,500 km along the Pacific side of South
America, like other Indian units of organisation, was quickly disrupted by the
Spaniards.

In 1493–94, a year after Columbus first reached America, the Pope made an
agreement (the Treaty of Tordesillas) with Spain and Portugal, dividing the
world, in effect the tropics, into two spheres of influence. The dividing line on
one side of the world was to be a meridian 370 leagues west of the Cape Verde
Isles. This line passes very close to Belém near the mouth of the Amazon, south
near Goiânia and Curitiba to Araranguá. Subsequently, Portuguese influence
extended west of the Tordesillas line into the interior of South America.

Soon after the arrival of Columbus, the Spaniards began the conquest of
their part of the Americas. From 1493, just a year after the defeat of the last
Moors in Spain, the whole area, initially believed to be part of Asia, and called
the Indies (Las Indias), was considered to be under the crown of Spain. Spain
itself (Las Españas) and America (Reynos de las Indias) became known as the

Monarquía Universal Española. Conquest was largely carried out in the initial decades on a private basis by ambitious and enterprising individuals with small groups of followers, the conquistadores, who with remarkably small numbers of soldiers, overcame populations of millions. From 1493 to about 1520 most of the activity was in the Caribbean, Santo Domingo serving as the first base. When the Aztecs were overcome after a bitter struggle around 1520 and the Inca Empire collapsed in 1533, Mexico (New Spain) and Peru became the main centres for further conquest. *Figure 3.2b* shows the area controlled by Spain in about 1550, and *Figure 3.3b* the situation in about 1800. Two very large areas, Amazonia and southern South America, were not absorbed at all either by Spain or Portugal during the colonial period. During this period there were many mission areas on the fringes of the settled area (see *Figure 3.2d*).

The Portuguese annexation of Brazil was a more gradual and less spectacular process, one reason being that Portugal had interests in other continents in the tropics. The main difficulty was not to establish control of coastal Brazil, the Indians here being relatively few, but later to keep out the Dutch and French. Until the 1540s Portugal left control of Brazil to a number of Captains General (see *Figure 3.2b*), each of whom held a stretch of coast and the land to the west of this; the Captaincies were hereditary. The system was then changed, and the whole of Brazil was subsequently administered from Portugal except during 1580–1640, when Spain and Portugal were united. During the period of union between Spain and Portugal the Tordesillas line established by the Treaty of 1493 was no longer necessary and the Portuguese crossed it both west from São Paulo and along the Amazon. By 1750 they had penetrated in small numbers to within a short distance of the Andes, and in the Treaty of Madrid in 1750, Spain recognised their control of much of Amazonia. In spite of being divided initially, and of being split for a time, when the north, Maranhão, was administered separately, Brazil maintained its cohesion throughout the colonial period and in 1823 remained intact when it became independent. One reason seems to be that all the important centres were in close contact with one another along the coast between São Vicente and Fortaleza. The capital was transferred in 1763 from Salvador to Rio as the southern part gained in economic influence.

While the Portuguese Empire survived as modern Brazil, the Spanish area had broken into 16 independent countries by 1850 and 18 by just after 1900. How the Spanish American countries reached their present form can only be appreciated by following the main administrative developments in the colonial period.

Not long after the arrival of the conquistadores, administrators were sent to the Americas. Those conquerors who had not been killed, either by the Indians or by each other, in many cases lost the grandiose titles and vast lands they had acquired. Administrative centres, Audiencias, were set up by Spain in several places. In 1543, two viceroyalties were created, with their administrative centres in Mexico and Lima. From then until the 18th century almost all of Spanish America fell within one or other of these units though at certain periods Venezuela and various islands came directly under Spain. The viceroy in Mexico controlled Mexico, Central America (except Panama), various Caribbean islands and the Philippines. The viceroy in Lima administered Spanish South America. As the Spaniards settled in other areas, further decentralisation was desirable, and new Audiencias were formed within the two viceroyalties (see dates. *Figure 3.3a*).

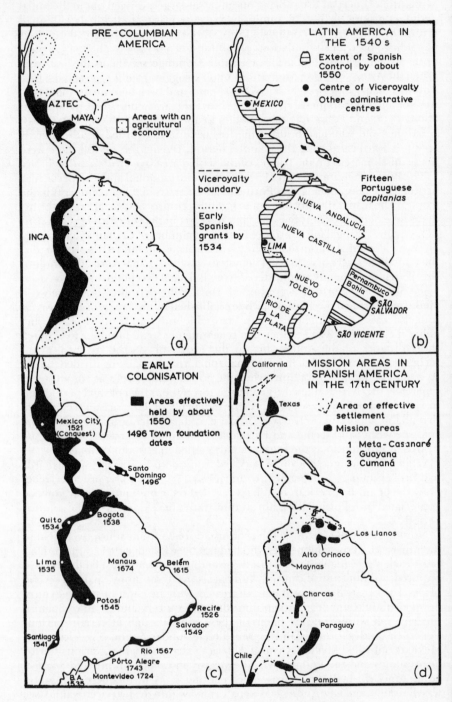

Figure 3.2. Historical maps of Latin America, 15th–17th centuries

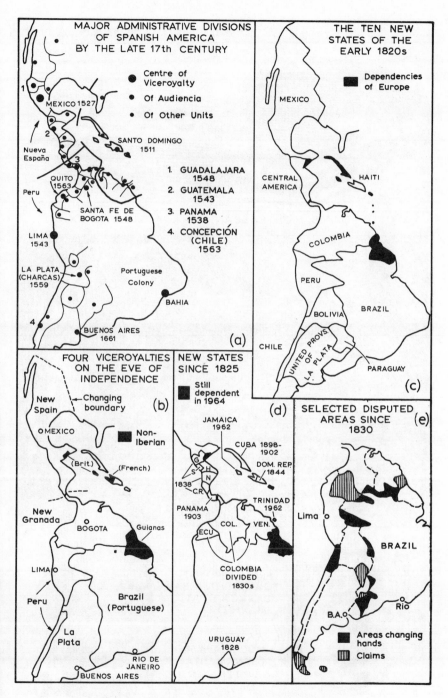

MAJOR ADMINISTRATIVE DIVISIONS OF SPANISH AMERICA BY THE LATE 17th CENTURY

● Centre of Viceroyalty
● Of Audiencia
● Of Other Units

MEXICO 1527

SANTO DOMINGO 1511

1. GUADALAJARA 1548
2. GUATEMALA 1543
3. PANAMA 1538
4. CONCEPCIÓN (CHILE) 1563

Nueva España

QUITO 1563

Peru

SANTA FE DE BOGOTA 1548

LIMA 1543

LA PLATA (CHARCAS) 1559

Portuguese Colony

BAHIA

BUENOS AIRES 1661

(a)

THE TEN NEW STATES OF THE EARLY 1820s

■ Dependencies of Europe

MEXICO

CENTRAL AMERICA

HAITI

COLOMBIA

PERU

BOLIVIA

BRAZIL

CHILE

UNITED PROVS. OF LA PLATA

PARAGUAY

(c)

FOUR VICEROYALTIES ON THE EVE OF INDEPENDENCE

New Spain

– Changing boundary (b)

○ MEXICO

(Brit.) (French)

■ Non-Iberian

New Granada

○ BOGOTA

Guianas

LIMA ○

Peru

Brazil (Portuguese)

La Plata

RIO DE JANEIRO

BUENOS AIRES

NEW STATES SINCE 1825

■ Still dependent in 1964 (d)

JAMAICA 1962

CUBA 1898–1902

G
S H
1838 N
C.R.

DOM. REP. 1844

PANAMA 1903

TRINIDAD 1962

ECU

COL. VEN.

COLOMBIA DIVIDED 1830s

URUGUAY 1828

SELECTED DISPUTED AREAS SINCE 1830 (e)

Lima ○

BRAZIL

B.A. ○

Rio ○

■ Areas changing hands
▓ Claims

Figure 3.3. Historical maps of Latin America, 17–19th centuries

ZAPOTEC TEMPLE, MONTEALBAN, OAXACA STATE, MEXICO

MACHU PICCHU CITY RUINS, SOUTHERN PERU

P. COLE

LEFT:
GOLD MASK
FROM ZAPOTEC
TOMB, MONTEALBAN,
OAXACA STATE,
MEXICO

RIGHT:
MOCHICA *HUACO*
(ORNAMENTAL
WATER JAR),
COASTAL PERU

COLONIAL LATIN AMERICA

ABOVE LEFT:
INCA WALLS WITH COLONIAL
STRUCTURE ABOVE. CUSCO, PERU

ABOVE RIGHT:
THE PROPHET JOËL
BY ALEIJADINHO, LATE
18TH CENTURY, AT
CONGONHAS DO CAMPO,
MINAS GERAIS, BRAZIL

COLONIAL CHURCH, JOÃO PESSÔA, PARAÍBA, NORTHEAST BRAZIL

By 1700 there were some ten Audiencias in Spanish America. Contact between the two viceroyalties was discouraged by Spain for various reasons and apart from limited trade and the movement of administrators there was little contact even between most of the Audiencias. In the 18th century further decentralisation took place, as two new viceroyalties were created: New Granada (1717–24 and from 1740) in Bogota and La Plata (1776) in Buenos Aires. In the 1770s, Cuba, Venezuela and Chile were given more direct links with Spain as captaincies-general. In practice, virtually all major political decisions concerning the Spanish colonies were made in Madrid, and transferred to the Americas through the Casa de Indias in Seville. Local decisions were made in the Americas and local affairs run by the colonies themselves. Between the period of the conquerors of the early 16th century and the liberators of the early 19th there were few outstanding personalities in Latin American colonial history and no constant struggle between political units as in Europe itself during that period.

On the eve of independence, around 1800, Latin America was divided basically into four Spanish Viceroyalties, Mexico (New Spain), Peru, Colombia (New Granada) and Argentina (La Plata), and one Portuguese colony, Brazil. These are the five largest units at the present day, both in population and in area. In addition, several other modern republics could be distinguished as Audiencias or Captaincies: Chile, Venezuela, Bolivia, Ecuador, Cuba, Santo Domingo, Guatemala. England, Holland and France also had colonies in Latin America by 1800. Each had a colony in the Guianas, while France held Haiti and England held Jamaica, Trinidad and smaller islands.

Independence came rapidly to almost all the colonies once the movement started. The main cause was the resentment by the *Criollos,* that is the white settlers in the colonies, against the rigid control by Iberia. The movement was encouraged by the American War of Independence. The weak state of Spain during the Napoleonic wars was the opportunity to declare and fight for independence. The inspiration came from the criollo population, the European element. The Indian and negro masses were possibly pro-criollo in some areas but mainly indifferent or actually hostile both to the criollos and the Spaniards. The complicated and fascinating struggle for independence cannot be outlined here. By the early 1820s the struggle was over. Eight separate independent states emerged from the Spanish colonies (see *Figure 3.3c*), making ten altogether with Haiti and Brazil. Haiti achieved independence from France a little earlier, after a bitter struggle during which those French who did not leave were largely eliminated. Brazil, on the other hand, achieved a less violent compromise, detaching itself from Portugal but retaining as its ruler the son of the King of Portugal. The Court had fled to Brazil during the Napoleonic Wars. Cuba, Puerto Rico and the Philippines remained as Spanish colonies.

In the decades following the main struggle for independence, Central America broke into five separate parts, Colombia into three. Uruguay was recognised by Brazil and Argentina while the Dominican Republic became separated from Haiti. This brought the total number of independent countries to 18 by 1850. In 1898, after a brief war, Spain ceded Puerto Rico, the Philippines and Cuba to the Unites States. Cuba was given independence almost immediately but Puerto Rico remained a U.S. possession, acquiring the status of a commonwealth with some autonomy in 1952. Panama was detached from Colombia at the beginning of the century, becoming another independent

Republic, but the United States was granted the use, occupation and control of the Canal Zone in 1904. The latest colonial areas to become independent in Latin America have been former British colonies, namely Jamaica and Trinidad in 1962 and Guyana (formerly British Guiana) in 1966. Barbados (1966), the Bahamas (1973) and Grenada (1974) are also independent.

After the independence movement in the early 19th century the nature of Latin American political history changed completely. For the first time a large number of new sovereign states came into being outside Europe, many already conscious of their existence as entities in the 18th century. Admittedly they have taken a long time to settle down and in doing so there have been several serious conflicts and many boundary disputes (see *Figure 3.3e*), but the considerable age and experience of Latin American countries should not be overlooked. Most were running their own affairs reasonably successfully several decades before the Europeans even started to colonise Africa in the 1880s.

3.3. ECONOMIC HISTORY

The inhabitants of pre-Columbian America could be divided into hunters and gatherers on the one hand and cultivators on the other. The cultivators were of two main kinds, shifting and sedentary. Shifting cultivation was found mainly in the tropical forest areas, sedentary cultivation in temperate forests, notably in southeastern North America, in drier areas and in mountain areas. Irrigation was practised in parts of Mexico, coastal Peru and Chile, and in the Andes. A fairly high density of population was reached in a few areas of shifting cultivation, notably the Maya areas of southern Mexico and Central America, and also in some areas of sedentary cultivation, especially in mountain basins and valleys (Aztecs, Incas, Chibchas). Towns of considerable size could be supported in all these areas.

As already stressed, the range of crops and livestock used in these basically agricultural economies was limited and the technology was far behind that of contemporary Europe, China or even much of Africa. According to their physical conditions, agricultural communities depended heavily on one particular basic food: maize in Mexico, Central America, the Islands, parts of South America; roots especially manioc, in Amazonia; and potatoes and other tubers in the Andes. Beans, cacao, groundnuts, tomatoes and many tropical fruits were also available, while cotton was used as a fibre, maguey in Mexico as a beverage, tobacco locally for smoking, and the coca leaf in the Andes as a special luxury for the privileged, later to be greatly abused in the colonial period. The only important domesticated animals were the dog, which was widespread, the turkey in Mexico, and the llama, guanaco and alpaca in the Andes. The llama was easily tamed and widely used for carrying goods, for its wool, its dung and on occasions its meat. Animals were not used for draught purposes, either for ploughing or transport, the wheel not being in use. Outside the Andean region all goods were conveyed by humans, and this greatly limited the distance over which most goods could profitably be carried. Even in the civilised areas, the waterways were hardly used for transport and coastal navigation was very limited.

One great weakness of the Amerinds was their failure to develop metal tools, though bronze was made and silver and gold ornaments widely produced.

Without metal tools stone could only be shaped by harder stone, and wood, where available, could only be worked with difficulty. The arms that were in use when the Europeans came were quite inadequate against the crossbow, musket, and armour of the Spaniards, while the horse gave the Spaniards great mobility and the trained hunting dog was also used against the Indians during the decades of the conquest.

Perhaps the main reason why both the Spaniards and the Portuguese acquired an empire was to obtain sources of raw materials, many of them not available in Europe. Other motives should not be overlooked: the prestige of having new lands, the missionary zeal and the desire to convert pagans to Christianity, and an outlet for surplus population from Iberia. Throughout the colonial period the Spaniards were primarily concerned with metals, whereas until the 18th century the Portuguese, like the English, French and Dutch throughout, concentrated on agricultural products, mainly sugar. Although Spain and Portugal were intent on getting everything possible out of the region, they made many changes that in the long run transformed and benefited the economic life of the Americas. Old World crops and livestock were introduced, particularly those used in Europe itself. Horses and asses for transport, the wheel, iron implements, firearms, all spread through the region in the early decades of the 16th century. A further minor contribution was to spread New World crops that had been confined to certain limited parts of Latin America into new areas, as, for example, the potato from the Andes to Mexico. Even to this day, however, Indian populations of remoter areas still tend to depend heavily on their pre-Columbian plants and techniques.

The way of life of the indigenous population of Latin America was soon affected by the impact of the relatively few Europeans. In some areas the Indians were wiped out by fighting and diseases. They moved out of other areas away from the advancing Europeans. The quechua speaking descendants of the Inca Empire held out until after 1570, while the Araucanian Indians in Chile were not tamed until the 19th century. Even now the Amazon Indians take their toll of explorers and missionaries and even interfere with road construction and the exploration for minerals. In Brazil, for example, hostile Indian communities held up the construction of one major road link in the Amazon region in the early 1970s. In most areas, however, the Indian population formed the foundation for the exploitation of the natural resources by the Europeans. Their way of life was undermined and often they were reduced to apathy. Land tenure was changed in favour of European settlers and although the Indians were never considered to be slaves, many virtually belonged to Spanish land-owners under the system of encomiendas in the 16th century, or were organised in large numbers to work in the mines of Mexico and the Andes. At one stage some 80,000 Indians were employed in the Potosi area of Bolivia alone. They provided the labour force for agriculture and the mines and also practised crafts.

Strictly speaking, the organisation of land tenure and agriculture in Spanish America was not feudal, but the result was not unlike that in late Medieval Europe. By 1600, however, the position of the Indian had improved somewhat except in the mining areas, and most Indians were not tied to large estates; many owned land as before. In some areas, especially away from the main area of Spanish penetration, missionaries tried to organise the Indians in ideal communities. In Brazil the Indian population in the areas settled during the colonial period was small. In places it was wiped out, while elsewhere it was absorbed by the European and negro elements. One reason for Portuguese penetration far into the interior of South America was to search for more Indians to bring back as labourers.

For reasons of security and administrative convenience the Europeans first lived mainly in nucleated settlements, and many of the present towns of Latin America were founded in the 16th century. The Spaniards paid great attention to the position, siting and layout of their future urban centres and the foundation was a formal affair. In addition to the administrative and commercial centres there were special settlements in mining areas (*campamentos mineros*), forts (*presidios*) and missionary villages (*reducciones*). Often dispersed Indian rural dwellers were gathered into planned villages.

Where the Indians were few in numbers and commercial agriculture therefore difficult to organise on a large scale, African slaves were brought in. Slavery was authorised in Spanish America shortly after the discovery of the continent. Both Spain and Portugal were already accustomed to slavery in their contacts with North Africa. Ironically, one pretext for bringing in African slaves was to save the American Indians themselves from this form of exploitation. Initially most African slaves were sold in Northeast Brazil. Later they were taken into the Caribbean area and North America in large numbers, especially to the English and French possessions, but also to Spanish Cuba and Puerto Rico. Smaller numbers were taken to or spread to the coastlands of Venezuela, Colombia, Ecuador and Peru, while others spread south from Northeast Brazil to Rio de Janeiro and beyond. The negro element in Mexico, Central America, Argentina, Uruguay and Chile is very small.

Slaves were captured in Africa by European traders or bought from fellow Africans and were transported to the Americas in incredibly bad conditions. The slave trade was a commercial enterprise permitted by European countries, both Catholic and Protestant. Once the survivors who reached the Americas had been sold and were settled, they were in general reasonably well cared for materially, since they were very costly pieces of equipment. They worked either in agriculture, labouring in the sugar and other plantations, or were domestic servants, while some were freed and others escaped. In time mixing with Europeans produced mulattoes.

By about 1600 a new spatial distribution of economic activities had developed in the Americas. It remained with modifications until the early 19th century. The distribution of certain activities can only be fully appreciated by reference to distance from West Europe. *Figure 3.4a* shows the Americas with distances correct from Lisbon. The parts closest to Europe are Northeast Brazil, the coast of Amazonia, the Guianas, the Caribbean islands and eastern North America, all about 6,000 km away. The following types of economy may be distinguished:

1. Almost all the sugar and other tropical crops grown in plantations for export to Europe were produced along the 6,000 km line. The main exception was the coast of Brazil to the south of this. Sugar was grown in smaller quantities elsewhere, but largely for local consumption. In view of the great inconvenience and cost of moving it far by land it had to be produced near the Atlantic coasts. Even moving it across Panama from the Pacific coastlands would have been unthinkable. As it was, given the small size of vessels and the

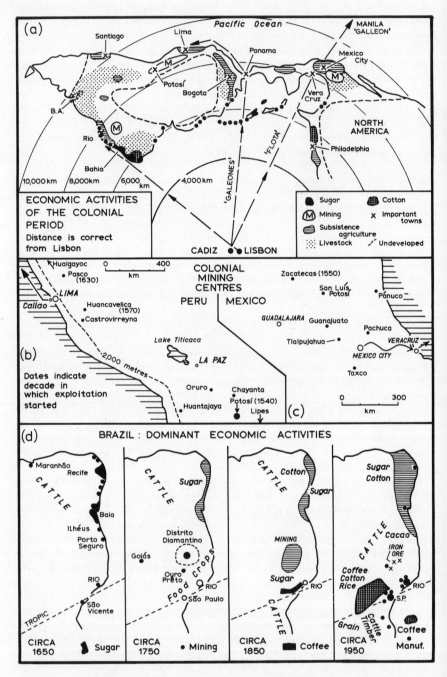

Figure 3.4. Economic History. (a) major economic activities of the colonial period. (b) (c) Colonial mining areas in Peru and Mexico. (d) Dominant economic activities in Brazil at different periods

difficulty of navigation, the transportation of large quantities of sugar in the 17th century, even from the coastal belt of Northeast Brazil, was a remarkable achievement, perhaps the first time in history that such a bulky commodity was taken so far across an ocean. The Portuguese in Brazil were the first Europeans to organise agriculture in the tropics on such a large scale, but in the 18th century, Northeast Brazil was eclipsed by the Caribbean Islands, and Haiti became the world's leading producer of sugar. This area is just as close as Northeast Brazil is to Europe.

2. In contrast to the plantations of tropical crops in the forested coastal lowlands of Atlantic-facing Latin America, the mining areas of Mexico, Peru and Minas Gerais in Brazil were not determined by distance from Europe but by the occurrence of accessible deposits of gold, silver and later precious stones. Once the silver had been refined it could be transported relatively easily, but its great value was obviously an embarrassment and its movement had to be heavily protected in the 16th and 17th centuries when piracy was widely practised and other European powers took a heavy toll of Spanish shipping.

3. Scattered about the Americas were many areas of relatively dense agricultural settlement not producing crops for export to Europe. These included not only such temperate areas as New England in North America and Chile and La Plata in southern South America, but also the interior of Mexico and Central America, and the Andean countries. Here the mining areas were fed by a surplus from the nearer agricultural areas, but there was virtually no export of agricultural products from these remoter areas to Europe.

4. In lands that were neither humid and densely forested nor excessively dry, the raising of livestock, especially cattle, developed in the colonial period. These areas were relatively thinly populated; the cattle were either loosely organised in large estates (estancias) or left to roam wild. Extremely tough types of cattle evolved. Their main contribution to the economy of other parts of Latin America was hides, which were also exported in some quantity to Europe, but were mainly used in the colonies for a large number of purposes such as saddlery, storing water and carrying liquids, and the production of clothing for mining activities. The most extensive areas of cattle raising were in the northern part of Mexico, the northern part of Argentina, the lands behind the coast of Brazil, the llanos of Venezuela, and alone among the islands, Cuba.

5. In the remotest parts of all from Europe either in terms of sheer distance or because of difficulty in penetration, vast areas remained in the hands of hostile Indian tribes until the 19th century: most of North America, Argentina south of Buenos Aires, and the interior of South America. Military expeditions, traders and missionaries did at times penetrate these areas but permanent settlements were few and conditions insecure, particularly in North America where the Indians adapted themselves to European horsemanship and acquired firearms. In the 19th century these Indians were virtually eliminated from the extra tropical parts of North and South America but they remain in Amazonia, little interfered with until the 1970s except along the main rivers.

The impact of the products of the Americas made itself felt in Europe soon after the conquest began. Silver and gold from the Aztec and Inca areas in particular were sent to Europe. Mines were taken over and new techniques introduced from Europe to raise production. Already in the 1540s regular production almost exclusively for export was organised by the Spaniards in

certain areas in Mexico and Peru (see *Figure 3.4b, c*). By the 18th century production here was declining, but in Colombia and in Minas Gerais other mines were
developed. Plantation agriculture was slower to develop, and shipping in the
16th century was not capable of carrying large quantities of goods to Europe.
By the 18th century crop and livestock products had become more important
than minerals and even Spanish America, hitherto organised to produce
metals, was diversifying its exports. During the colonial period, therefore, the
areas in the Americas geared to producing for export were: southern Peru and
Bolivia, central Mexico, Minas Gerais and Colombia, Northeast Brazil and all
the islands except Cuba, and southeastern North America. Other areas only
made a limited contribution, but in some, considerable concentrations of population grew up on regional economies.

Present features and problems of Latin America still reflect the situation in
the colonial period outlined above. It was the policy of European colonial
powers and of Spain in particular to discourage manufacturing in colonial
areas. Manufactured goods made in Spain or elsewhere in Europe and sent
through Seville or Cadiz were sold at very high prices in the colonies. Competition from Asian manufactured goods such as silk was prevented and only one
galleon a year was allowed between Manila in the Philippines and Acapulco
(Mexico). Even so industries did develop in the colonies. Food processing was
often essential before crops could be exported, and large quite highly
capitalised sugar factories were built wherever sugar was grown commercially.
Minerals were also processed, and in the later 16th century a complex process
involving salt and mercury (deposits of which were discovered in Huancavelica,
Peru, in 1563) was used in the Andean mines to refine silver. Mining equipment
had to be maintained and iron, which was often short in the colonies, was
worked in a limited way. Metal working developed particularly in Minas
Gerais, Brazil, where there has been a continuous if modest tradition. All the
ships for use in the Pacific by the Armada del Sur were built on the west side of
the continent (in Guayaquil particularly), while Havana (La Habana) served the
Atlantic side. Cloth was widely manufactured, though the highest quality
textiles came from Europe.

Another feature of colonial Ibero-America was the tendency to work an area
intensively for a particular product and then to abandon it. Brazilian historians
have traced periods in which one product and one area in their country have
been exploited far more than any others (see *Figure 3.4d*).

Throughout the colonial period Latin America was very closely linked to
Spain or Portugal. Trade between colonies was not encouraged, and Mexico
and South America had virtually no contact, due to the rigid organisation of
trade by Spain. Convoys sailing out from Seville (or more often Cadiz in the
18th century) one year and back the next went initially together (1543–64) but
later separately to Veracruz (the Flota) and to Portobello (the Galleons). Here
the products of the colonies were assembled. The convoy system was convenient
in view of the insecurity of the Atlantic crossing but it discriminated against
many places on the periphery of the Empire, especially Buenos Aires, which
could have reached Europe much more easily by other routes. Admittedly the
system was eased in the 18th century and France was allowed to trade in the
Spanish colonies, but the trading pattern changed little. After 1820 Latin
America was still closely tied to Europe, but now to West Europe in general
rather than to Iberia alone.

During the period 1815–25 Latin America was completely transformed politically, but economic changes were more gradual and social changes slower still. In the first place, other European countries were able to trade directly with the new countries. Soon Britain, France, Belgium and later Germany, Italy and other European countries, with manufactured goods to export, needing raw materials and food at home, and having capital to invest, replaced Spain and Portugal as the main trading partners. In the second place, rapid improvements in transportation such as railways, speed and size of vessels, and refrigeration made it possible to bring new areas of Latin America within easy reach of ports and to move more bulky commodities to Europe. Thirdly, it became possible for non-Iberian settlers to emigrate to Latin America, which they did mainly to the extra-tropical southern part.

Though the 18th century pattern of trade continued, the exports of Latin America changed. From about 1800, sugar beet was grown increasingly in Europe and in the 19th century cane sugar declined in relative importance, while coffee, cacao, cotton and later bananas were exported from tropical areas. Cereals and livestock products were exported from Argentina and Uruguay, the organisation of livestock farming having been greatly improved with the introduction of barbed wire fencing. Silver, gold and precious stones were still exported, but other minerals exceeded these in value: guano and nitrates, non-ferrous metals, in the 19th century, oil and iron ore in the 20th.

In the 19th century each Latin American country, like its colonial predecessor, tended to depend heavily on one or a small number of primary products. These had to pay for virtually all capital goods and many consumer manufactured goods as well as services and in some cases food products.

Many of the mines and the rail and shipping services were financed by European countries or by the U.S.A. Before the First World War, manufacturing in Latin America was limited in scale and was confined to certain areas. Monterrey in Mexico had the first modern iron and steel works, Puebla in Mexico, Medellin in Colombia and Juiz de Fora in Brazil had early cotton mills, while the larger capitals had some light industry. The First World War encouraged countries to manufacture goods not easily obtained during this period. Since then most countries have tried to move towards self-sufficiency at least in simpler manufactured goods, often heavily protecting their young industries against outside competition.

Industry is now widespread in Latin America but there are few very large establishments apart from those connected with extractive industries producing minerals for export. That industrialisation was both vital to countries and inevitable was perhaps widely realised already in the 1930s, and these lines published in 1945 show that by then it was clearly the view of one American writer:[6] 'Under the economic and technological circumstances of the modern world, the number of nations which can develop manufacturing industries to advantage has increased considerably. At the same time, it must be recognised that the tempo and character of industrialisation must be adapted to the special circumstances in each country. It is therefore necessary to guard against hasty generalisations about Latin America as a whole, for they tend to obscure the profound differences which exist between the various countries. It is also necessary to avoid conclusions based upon easy analogy with conditions of the U.S.A. and Europe'.

References

1. MacNeish, R. S., 'Early Man in the Andes', *Sci. Am.,* Apr. 1971, Vol. 224, No. 4, pp. 36–46.
2. Vives, J. V., *Historia Social y Económica de España y América,* Vol. III, 1957, Barcelona; Editorial Teide, p. 391.
3. Harris, M., *Race and Class in Rural Brazil,* Ed. C. Wagley, 'Race and Society', 2nd edn, 1963, Paris; UNESCO, p. 51.
4. Hutchinson, H. W. *Village and Plantation Life in Northeastern Brazil,* 1957, Seattle; The American Ethnological Soc., p. 117.
5. Galindo y Villa, J. *Geografía de México* (Colección Labor), 1950, Barcelona; Editorial Labor, pp. 85–90.
6. Wythe, G. *Industry in Latin America,* 1945, New York; Columbia U.P., p. 355.

Sources of material in the figures

3.2. Map (d) is based on a map in Vives (see reference 2 above), p. 391.
3.3. Map (a) as for 3.2 (d), p. 480.

Further sources consulted

The number of books and papers on various aspects of the history and prehistory of Latin America is enormous. This chapter was based particularly on three books:

(1) *Historia Social y Económica de España y América* especially, Vol. III, pp. 387–578, Imperio, Aristocracia, Absolutismo, Ed. by J. V. Vives (Editorial Teide), 1957, Barcelona.
(2) Herring, H. *A History of Latin America,* 1961, New York; McLelland and Stewart.
(3) Bailey, H. M. and Nasatir, A. P., *Latin America,* 1960, London; Constable.

Further reading

Bram, J., *An Analysis of Inca Militarism,* 1966, Seattle; University of Washington Press.
Easby, D. T., 'Early metallurgy in the New World', *Sci. Am.,* Apr. 1966, Vol. 214, No. 4, pp. 72–81.
Lanning, E. P., 'Early Man in Peru', *Sci. Am.,* Oct. 1965, Vol. 213, No. 4, pp. 68–76.
McIntyre, L., 'The Lost Empire of the Incas', *Nat. Geogr.,* Dec. 1973, Vol. 144, No. 6, pp. 729–86.
Million, R., 'Teotihuacan', *Sci. Am.,* June 1967, Vol. 216, No. 6, pp. 38–48.
Moseley, M. E. and Mackey, C. J., 'Chan Chan, Peru's Ancient City of Kings', *Nat. Geogr.,* Vol. 143, No. 3, pp. 318–45.
Pendle, G., *A History of Latin America,* 1963, Harmondsworth; Penguin.
Smith, C. T., Denevan, W. M. and Hamilton, P., 'Ancient Ridged Fields in the Region of Lake Titicaca', *Geog.J.,* Sept. 1968, Vol. 134, Pt. 3.
Stevens, R. L., 'The Soils of Middle America and Their Relation to Indian Peoples and Cultures', *Handbook of Middle American Indians,* Vol. I, 1964, Austin; University of Texas Press.
Von Hagen, V. W., in Mentor Books, New York, New American Library, *Realm of the Incas* (1957), *The Aztec: Man and Tribe* (1958), *World of the Maya* (1960).
Wilgus, A. C. and d'Eça, R., *Latin American History,* 1963, New York; Barnes and Noble.

CHAPTER 4

PHYSICAL CONDITIONS AND HUMAN NEEDS

4.1. INTRODUCTION

The material world of our planet may be subdivided for convenience into natural features and man-made features. In practice, however, it is the constant interaction between man, with his needs, techniques and decisions, and his habitat, the natural environment, that forms one main theme in regional geography. For this reason the physical geography of Latin America is not described in this book in terms of a series of earth sciences, but as the environment in which man obtains resources and encounters obstacles. It should be appreciated, however, that it is possible to distinguish four types of relationship. Some of the relationships are one-way, some, two-way:

1. Physical on physical, as the influence of altitude on atmospheric pressure or of temperature on evaporation and precipitation.
2. Physical on man, as the effect of soil and weather conditions on crop yields or more controversially, the influence of climate on human effort.
3. Man on physical, as the modification, often drastic, of natural vegetation and soil through agricultural practices.
4. Human on human, as the production of smoke and fumes on cleanliness and health.

So numerous and complex are these various influences and relationships as they work in space and time that they cannot easily be taken into consideration all at once. In this chapter, various aspects of the physical environment are for convenience dealt with in turn. Each aspect is related to the way in which it affects and is affected by man's various resource and environmental needs and problems. Table 4.1 indicates in matrix form some of the more obvious ways in which man's needs and activities are related to physical forces and features. *Figure 4.1* shows some of the relationships diagrammatically.

Data about the physical background of Latin America vary in quantity and quality from one country to another and also within countries. Meteorological stations are numerous, for example, in southern Brazil, but few in the Amazon region. Venezuela has been explored intensively for oil but large areas on the interior side of the Andes in Colombia, Ecuador and Peru have only recently been studied. The use of new methods of mapping from aerial surveys and the growing interest in information about physical conditions and human activities transmitted from satellites seem likely to bring about a great increase in the factual knowledge of Latin America during the last decades of the 20th century.

In a single book about an area as large as Latin America one must, when making generalisations about physical conditions and land capabilities, bear in mind the scale or size of a place under consideration. A general statement may

Table 4.1.
THE PRESENCE OF 1 INDICATES A CONNECTION
OBVIOUS PHYSICAL AND HUMAN INTERRELATIONSHIPS

	Structure	Geology	Relief Altitude	Oceans	Atmos-phere	Vegetation Animal Life	Soil
Water				1	1		
Crops			1		1	1	1
Livestock			1		1	1	1
Timber			1		1	1	
Fishing				1		1	
Energy	1	1			1		
Metals	1	1					
Non-metals	1	1					
Transport			1			1	
Housing					1		
Living			1		1		

be made, for example, about the features of the vast Amazon forest. It is characterised over wide areas by undulating relief with a dense vegetation containing very many plant species in any given small area, heavy rainfall, and soils that easily become poor in plant nutrients after cultivation. At a more local level, however, great contrasts may be found in detail between adjoining places in the same general area of forest. Locally, soils may be fertile, vegetation thin, slopes steep, economic minerals available. To the planner assessing the resources of a whole country, general statements about large areas are useful. For a farmer given a piece of forest to clear and cultivate it is of vital interest to know how best to cope with the soil, slope and climatic conditions on his particular plot of land. In *Evaluating the Human Environment,* A. Young describes various methods of assessing the capabilities of land in the chapter 'Rural Land Evaluation'.

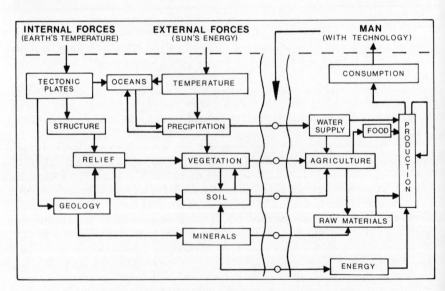

Figure 4.1. Physical and human interrelationships in human geography

4.2. TECTONIC FEATURES AND STRUCTURE

Physical changes, like changes in human activities, take place on enormously varying time scales. The temperature in a place may change markedly in a few hours or even a few minutes. The 'tectonic plates' on which the continents rest have been drifting apart over time spans of tens of millions of years, at the rate of a few centimetres per year. For practical purposes the more immediate, short term changes are of interest in regional geography. Even so, it is of interest to include a brief account of the way in which Latin America fits into the tectonic plates concept of the formation of the earth's crust and mantle, since the occurrence of present day phenomena such as earthquakes, volcanoes and the ocean trenches and continental shelves are related to it. The processes are described clearly by J. F. Dewey.[1]

The supporters of the process of continental drift have for decades noted the similarities of the coasts of Brazil and West Africa, as well as other 'fits' between continents elsewhere in the world. In the 1960s a second theory was introduced, that of sea floor spreading. According to this view, the ocean basins are 'split' along narrow cracks, through which volcanic material in the form of liquid basalt continuously rises from the earth's mantle. Along the cracks the ocean floor is continuously spreading outwards as the rising material adds new oceanic crust.

One of the principal pieces of evidence to support this process is the fact that the periodic reversals in the polarity of the earth's magnetic field affect the magnetisation pattern of the rocks on the ocean floor. Symmetrical patterns of progressively older matching pairs of bands of material, magnetised one way, then the other, are found to occur on each side of the ridge centres.

Thus the ocean floors spread outwards from the cracks, but on a very slow time scale of between 2 cm and 18 cm per year. One implication of this process is that the ocean floors must contain rocks younger than about 200 million years, in contrast to the continents, parts of which are as much as 10 times as old. One requirement of the theory is that if new surface is created, then existing surface must somewhere be destroyed. There are in fact subduction zones along which material descends again into the earth's mantle.

The whole concept of plate tectonics, which encompasses both continental drift and ocean floor spreading, was developed only in the 1960s, yet by the early 1970s was generally accepted. Continents do not drift across the ocean floors, however, but are incorporated in rigid tectonic plates, which may combine both ocean floor and continental crust. Thus plate boundaries are not necessarily the margins of continents.

Latin America thus has a position in the world system of tectonic plates. *Figure 4.2a* shows South America situated on one side of the South American Plate, Mexico as the southern extremity of the North American Plate and the Caribbean area as a smaller Plate, the limits of which are not known exactly. A plate can have three types of boundary. For example, the South American plate is bounded in the east by the Mid-Atlantic ridge, from which it is moving gradually westwards through the addition of new oceanic crust. In the west it is bounded by the Peru–Chile trench, where it is converging with the Nazca Plate. In this subduction zone the Nazca plate is gradually sliding under the 'leading edge' of the South American Plate, as suggested in *Figure 4.2b*. A third type of boundary occurs where plates slide past each other along transform faults.

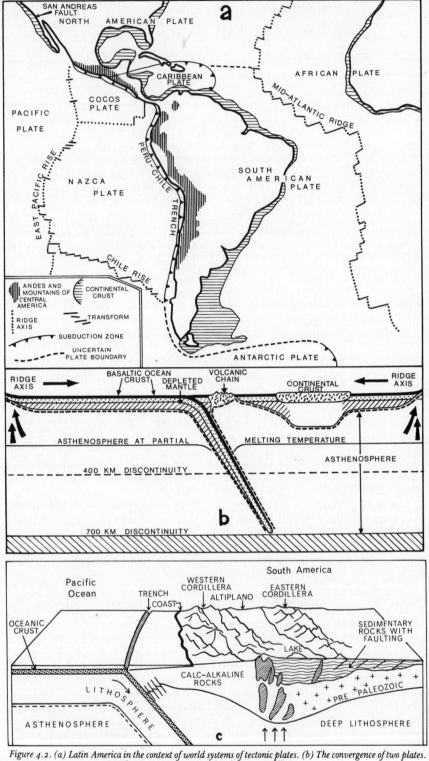

Figure 4.2. (a) Latin America in the context of world systems of tectonic plates. (b) The convergence of two plates. (c) The situation in Peru and Bolivia 1–2 million years ago

Here there is neither creation of new crust nor disappearance of existing crust.

The seismic or earthquake zones of the world, with accompanying volcanoes in places, occur along the boundaries between plates. The plates gradually either slide past each other, separate, or converge. The geometry of their 'motion' is difficult to appreciate as they are situated not on a flat surface but on a spherical one.

In *Figure 4.2b* the lithosphere, about 50–100 km thick, extending to the thick broken line, 'floats' on the asthenosphere, itself several hundred km thick. The ocean floors consist mainly of basaltic crust, while the thicker and higher areas of continental crust comprise both the continental land masses and offshore areas covered by the sea to about the 1,000 fathom depth. Present theories about the geological and structural evolution of such complex areas as the Andes will no doubt have to be modified as new data are collected. One casualty of the plate tectonics concept is the idea that mountain building and the up-lifting of mountain areas is closely associated with the formation of thick layers of sedimentary deposits. *Figure 4.2c* shows the state of the Andes in the last 1–2 million years along a section through southern Peru and Bolivia. The evolution of the Andes is described in a paper by D. E. James[2] from which the diagram is taken.

4.3. GEOLOGY AND ECONOMIC MINERALS

The continent of South America consists of three main elements (see *Figure 4.3a*), the eastern shields, the high western fold mountains (Cordilleras) and an intervening low-lying trough filled largely by Tertiary or Quaternary sediments. In Mexico, Central America and the Caribbean no shield areas occur but the high fold mountains and low-lying Tertiary and Quaternary sediments may again generally be clearly distinguished. Quaternary deposits also occur high in the basins in the mountains of both Mexico and the Central Andes. For a very broad view of the likely occurrence of economic minerals, Latin America may be subdivided into two areas, the fold mountain and shield areas on the one hand and the relatively little contorted sedimentary rocks on the other hand.

Oil and natural gas can be expected to occur almost exclusively in areas underlain by gently folded sedimentary rocks, including offshore areas with such conditions. Non-metallic minerals used for building materials such as limestone, clay and sandstone occur very widely. Coal, metallic ores and non-metallic minerals such as nitrates and phosphates are of limited occurrence, certain metallic ores being almost exclusively found in certain parts of the fold mountains. *Figure 4.3b* shows some of the main areas in which oil and natural gas are at present extracted or are known to exist in commercial quantities. Selected major deposits or areas of metallic minerals are shown in *Figure 4.3c*.

No indication is given in these maps of the actual quantity of mineral reserves in any given locality nor of the intensity of exploration in different areas. Such information is difficult to obtain. Exploration has up to now been slow in many parts of Latin America on account of both physical obstacles such as rugged terrain and dense forest cover, and organisational problems such as lack of communications, reluctance on the part of various countries to let in too much foreign capital and even hostility on the part of Indians. Not infrequently mineral finds have been the result of haphazard exploration and luck rather than systematic planned searches. With the rapidly increasing consumption of many minerals both in the industrial countries and in Latin America itself, and with improvements in exploration techniques and equipment, it may not be long before the inventory of mineral reserves in Latin America is quite well known. For the time being, it is possible only to obtain very approximate estimates. Some data are contained in Table 4.2. Actual production in different countries around 1970 is given in the next chapter and in more detail under individual countries.

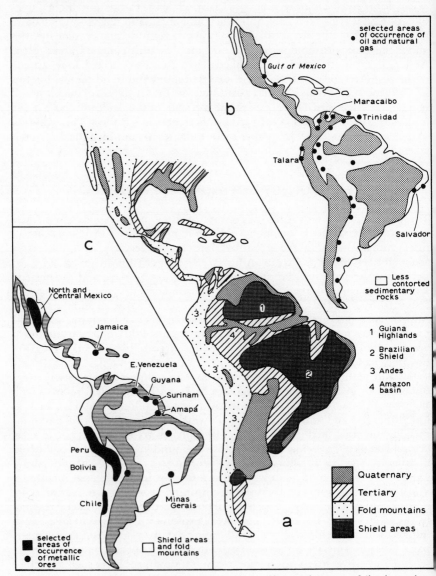

Figure 4.3. (a) Main structural features of Latin America. (b) Possible areas of occurrence of oil and natural gas. (c) Selected areas of occurrence of metallic ores

Table 4.2a.

ESTIMATED RESERVES OF COAL, OIL AND NATURAL GAS IN 1970[†]

1, 2	Coal reserves in millions of metric tons.
	1 measured, 2 measured plus inferred.
3	Oil (crude petroleum) reserves in millions of metric tons.
4, 6	Life in years of 1970 reserves at 1970 production rates of oil and gas respectively.
5	Natural gas reserves in thousand million cubic metres.

	Coal		Oil		Natural gas	
	1	2	3	4	5	6
Brazil	3,175	10,675	114	14	26	21
Mexico	182	3,466	779	35	340	19
Argentina	374	450	220	11	180	30
Venezuela	40	53	2,009	10	719	80
Colombia	n.a.	12,500	224	20	79	53
Peru	211	2,334	68	19	85	*
Chile	96	218	15	10	71	27
Bolivia	38		38	35	85	*
Ecuador			792	*	37	*
Trinidad			86	12	127	79

* over 100 years

† Reserves in Central America, the Islands except Trinidad, Uruguay and Paraguay are non-existent or negligible.

Source: *UNSYB 1971*, Tables 50, 70, 69.

Table 4.2b.

METALLIC MINERALS

P   Some production   R   Reserves considerable

Al — Bauxite, Cu — Copper, Fe — Iron, Pb — Lead, Mn — Manganese, Ni — Nickel, Ag — Silver, Sn — Tin, Zn — Zinc.

	Al	Cu	Fe	Pb	Mn	Ni	Ag	Sn	Zn
Brazil	P		PR	P	PR	P	P	P	
Mexico		P	P	P	P		PR	P	PR
Argentina			P	P	P		P	P	P
Venezuela	PR		PR						
Colombia			P						
Peru		PR	P	P			PR	P	PR
Chile		PR[2]	P		P		P		
Bolivia		P	R	P			P	PR	P
Guyana	PR				P				
Surinam	PR								
Honduras				P			P		P
Nicaragua		P					P		
Cuba					P	PR[3]			
Haiti	P								
Jamaica	PR[1]								

1 Jamaica 10% of bauxite in world.
2 Chile 20% of copper in world.
3 Cuba 25% of nickel in world.

Sources: *UNSYB 71*, various tables
    U.S. Bureau of Mines

It would be premature at this stage to forecast whether there are still great reserves of various minerals in Latin America. It seems certain, however, that coal deposits are both modest in extent and generally difficult to extract. Moreover, the prospect of greatly extending the known oil and gas reserves of Latin America is not apparently thought to be likely in oil circles, and Venezuela is preparing for the phasing out of oil production in the 1980s. On the other hand it has tar sands with several times as much oil content as its remaining oil reserves. Iron ore of high grade seems to be available in abundance in Brazil, Venezuela and Bolivia and bauxite in various areas. New nonferrous metal deposits have also been discovered recently. Economic minerals are unevenly distributed in Latin America. Central America, Paraguay and Uruguay in particular at present have only negligible reserves.

4.4. RELIEF FEATURES

Figure 4.4 shows the main relief features of Latin America. More detailed relief maps are provided for individual countries later in the book. No names have been put on the map as these would have obscured the contours and shading.

The Brazilian Shield has not been covered by the sea since the Palaeozoic, but during periods of deposition much of the original surface has received continental post-Palaeozoic deposits, especially in the later Cretaceous. The landforms of the Brazilian plateau are the result firstly of successive stages of denudation by pediplanation (scarp retreat and pedimentation) followed by deposition from Carboniferous times, and secondly of relatively recent polycyclic stream incision.

Though greatly modified by subsequent stream erosion, several stages of pediplanation remain in the landscape, often terminated by abrupt erosional scarps. For example, many present day flat interfluves are relics of the very widespread early Tertiary Sul-Americana pediplanation; in places these interfluves are extensive, but elsewhere they may be very narrow. Older planations stand above the Sul-Americana, and more recent ones below its level. These surfaces have been warped by later movements.

There is much evidence in the Brazilian plateau, including the presence of Cretaceous continental sands preserved on high watersheds (interfluves), which should have disappeared under a Davisian cycle of erosion, to offer evidence for pediplanation during the earlier evolution of the landscape. Much of Brazil to this day bears traces of these successive cycles of pediplanation and deposition, but subsequent stream erosion has excavated broad valleys in the interior and, where the land is highest, many gorges, especially along the south-eastern coastal margin of the massif.

Most of the present relief was formed as a result of Plio-Pleistocene and recent upwarping. In the Guiana Highlands (see *Figure 4.3a*) older denudational landscapes now stand high, as they do in the Brazilian highlands, but the existing basins of the Amazon and Parana regions were further filled. In the east of Brazil a number of rift valleys associated with upwarping were formed, including the upper and middle São Francisco and the Paraíba trough behind Rio de Janeiro. Nick points of about 100–150 metres on the tributaries of the Amazon are the result of Quaternary rejuvenations. Waterfalls on many other rivers in Brazil mark various substages in relatively recent movements caused by

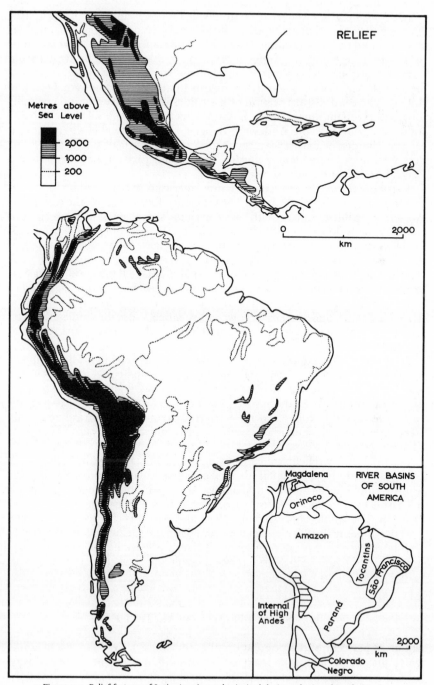

RELIEF

Metres above
Sea Level

2000
1000
200

0   2000
          km

RIVER BASINS
OF SOUTH
AMERICA

Magdalena

Orinoco

Amazon

Tocantins

São Francisco

Internal
of High
Andes

Paraná

0   2000
          km

Colorado
Negro

Figure 4.4. Relief features of Latin America and principal drainage basins of South America

arching. The remarkable scarp formed by the seaward face of the Serra do Mar between Rio and São Paulo (see *Figure 4.5*) is not due to faulting but to erosion.

The Andes may conveniently be subdivided into a number of distinct parts. In Venezuela and Colombia there are several distinct ranges separated by basins caused by block faulting (Magdalena and Cauca valleys). From Ecuador to northern Argentina the Andes widen and are characterised by Western and Eastern Cordillera with intervening plateaux from around 3,000 metres in altitude in Ecuador to 4,000–4,500 metres in altitude in southern Peru and Bolivia. The third distinct section of the Andes is the narrower, and generally lower, single main range, south of Aconcagua (33°S) in central Chile. Finally, south of about 38°S the Andes are rather a series of parallel discontinuous ranges. The detailed relief features of these various parts of the Andes will be described under individual countries. The highest parts of the Northern and Central Andes were glaciated.

A striking feature of drainage in Latin America is the proximity of the continental divide to the Pacific coast. The watershed follows closely the crest of the Western Cordillera much of the way, leaving short rivers with precipitous courses usually flowing directly to the Pacific on the west, but great depressions, in places structural, along the eastern flanks, which are followed for many hundreds of kilometres by the upper courses of rivers flowing to the Atlantic. The central Andes include a large area of internal drainage flanked on the east by canyons over 2,000 metres deep in places draining to the Amazon. In southern Chile and Patagonia (south of about 38°S), the watershed follows a very irregular course, and some rivers rise in Argentina, cross the Andes and enter the Pacific. This region was glaciated, and fiords and limited glaciers remain as evidence today.

To the east of the Andes, the great sub-Andean depression is filled with late Tertiary and Quaternary deposits, including torrential conglomerates, sands and muds. The great extent of Quaternary deposits is shown in *Figure 4.3a*. There are in fact two main basins, joined only by a narrow link between the eastern foot of the Andes and the western extremity of the Brazilian Shield. Deposits are very thick in places, as near the mouth of the Amazon and in the Chaco.

The present day relief of northern Mexico is dominated by the high plateau of the Sierra Madre Occidental; on its flanks, particularly to the west, are relief features similar to those known as basin and range in south-western U.S.A. To the east is the intermont plateau, terminating in the east in the Sierra Madre Oriental. The whole of Mexico and Central America is characterised by high land overlooking the Pacific, a watershed well on the Pacific side of the isthmus, and short rivers on this side; part of north central Mexico has interior drainage, however, and south of the Rio Grande there are no rivers to compare in scale with those of South America.

4.5. SOME EFFECTS OF ALTITUDE

About 20 per cent of the population of Latin America lives above a height at which the effects of altitude make conditions different in one or several ways from those in adjoining lowlands. Much of the population of Mexico and the northern Andean countries lives between 2,000 and 3,000 metres, but only in

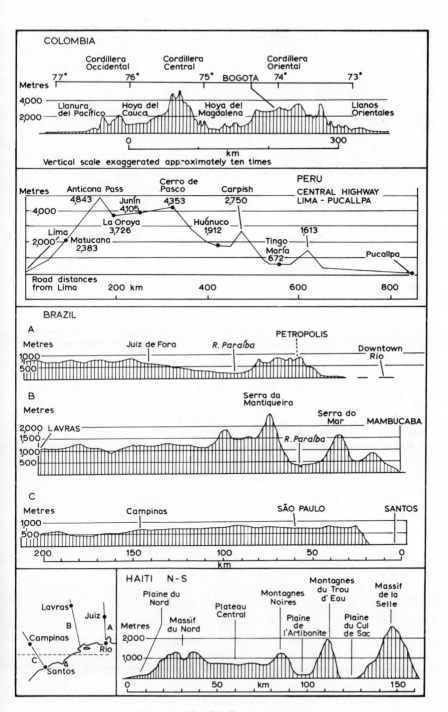

Figure 4.5. Selected profiles in Latin America

Peru and Bolivia do large numbers live between 3,000 and 4,000 metres. There are few settlements anywhere above 4,000 metres, but roads and railways pass above this height in places and many small mining settlements are above 4,000 metres , including one town of considerable size, Cerro de Pasco, Peru, at over 4,200 metres. This section outlines some of the effects of high altitude conditions on human activities.

Pressure decreases with altitude in a predictable way, though small local variations in time and place occur. Table 4.3 illustrates the relationship. At about 5,600 metres the atmospheric pressure is half that at sea-level.

Table 4.3.

Altitude in metres	Expected pressure in millimetres
Sea-level	760
1,000	674
2,000	596
3,000	526
4,000	462
5,000	405

Temperature also diminishes with altitude with reasonable regularity, but since temperatures, unlike pressure, vary enormously from place to place at sea-level and in the same place over time, the temperature at a given altitude can only be predicted, and even then only roughly, if sea-level temperature is known at that place. The following figures show diminution of temperature in Venezuela in an area with a mean annual temperature of 27°C at sea-level. Table 4.4 shows the mean figures at given altitudes.[3] Precipitation and relative humidity are much less precisely related to changes in altitude, but perhaps above 2,500–3,000 metres the rareness of the atmosphere begins to affect its moisture retaining capacity and precipitation appears to diminish, having apparently reached a maximum at least in the northern Andes in a zone around 1,000–2,000 metres.

Table 4.4.

Altitude in metres	Temperature in °C
Sea-level	27°
1,000	21
2,000	15
3,000	9
4,000	2.5

A difference in altitude of about 1,000 metres brings appreciable changes in temperature (e.g. between Santos and São Paulo in Brazil, La Guaira and Caracas in Venezuela). At 2,000 metres, climate vegetation are very different and agricultural patterns distinct. At about 3,000 metres, low pressure, which is roughly $\frac{2}{3}$ sea-level pressure, begins to have profound effects on the physiology of new-comers from lowland areas, though some people are already affected below this altitude and others little affected even at greater heights. Great variations in altitude are often accompanied by widespread steep slopes, and movement is therefore seriously affected. Thus human activities are affected in many ways by appreciable changes in altitude, there being a series of influences originating in: differences in temperature affecting particularly crop farming; differences in pressure affecting animal and human physiology and even the performance of steam and internal combustion engines; and widespread steep slopes affecting cultivation, causing soil erosion, and through steep gradients raising transport costs and requiring detours to avoid physical obstacles.

Agriculture is affected by altitude in various ways, but most profound is the influence of decreasing temperatures. Very broadly the main crops grown in Latin America can occur either below 2,000 metres, above this or throughout. Table 4.5 shows figures for Colombia.[4]

Table 4.5.

Low altitude		High altitude	
Sugar cane	below 1,750	Wheat	1,900 – 3,200
Cotton	750 – 1,750	Potatoes	2,100 – 3,500
Bananas	below 1,900	Beans (haba)	2,150 – 3,500
Coffee (best)	1,100 – 2,000		
	Large range		
Maize		below 3,200	

Lack of oxygen affects animal life above a certain altitude. This problem is serious only in Peru and Bolivia, with their large populations above 3,000 metres. The immediate effect of a visit to a high altitude may be *soroche*—various unpleasant symptoms affecting digestion in particular; these are usually overcome after a short time. A move in the reverse direction may also cause discomfort. More disturbing are the long term effects of infertility on settlers from lowland areas moving into high altitudes and of respiratory troubles for those moving down into lowland areas. When the Spaniards overcame the Inca Empire they soon encountered the problem of infertility, for they could not raise European livestock where they first proposed to put their capital (Jauja at 3,410 metres). But they had eventually to settle in the high Andes to supervise mining activities and themselves long remained either infertile or unable to keep babies alive after birth.

Relief features and altitude also present serious obstacles to the provision and use of transportation networks. Selected profiles are shown in *Figure 4.5*. In an economy in which single communities or small groups of these are largely self-sufficient, transportation is less important than in one in which most products are sold off farms and large quantities of modern manufactured goods are consumed. Road and rail routes between two places are often forced to make detours to avoid excessive gradients, the gradient being more serious for railways than for roads, while even air transport has drawbacks, for take-off is difficult in a rare atmosphere and sites are often dangerous. Detours may be local in nature to negotiate or avoid steep slopes (e.g. hairpin bends), or regional in nature, to avoid major obstacles. But even if gradients are minimised, they cannot be eliminated, and they remain a burden on an upward journey and a hazard on a downhill journey, while curves are also a danger. The implications of these are well illustrated in an extreme case, the railway in Peru from Lima to Cerro de Pasco, which is actually in two parts belonging to separate companies. The direct distance from Lima to Cerro is 185 km. The general course the railway takes to follow the Rimac valley to the summit of the Cordillera is 240 km and the actual rail distance, added by curves and zig zags is 350 km, almost twice the direct distance. In addition, extra fuel is needed to climb, speed is much slower than on a level railway, only one track is possible and time is further lost at passing places. Finally, the load safely pulled by a locomotive is less than normal (e.g. 5–6 passenger coaches). A journey that would take 2–3 hours in a flat area takes about 10 hours, with staff thus engaged longer for the same amount of work. Altogether, transport costs are several times greater.

4.6. THE OCEANS

Interest in the natural resources of the oceans has been growing since the Second World War. In the 1950s, Peru, Ecuador and Chile already established 200 mile fishing limits in the Pacific off their coasts. The search for offshore oil is taking place off Venezuela, Brazil and Peru. Shipping services carry almost all the foreign trade of the countries of Latin America except for Mexico.

The oceans contain over 97 per cent of the water in the world, much of the remainder being in the ice caps. They support a complex system of living organisms, based on plants that obtain inorganic nutrients from the ocean. With the exception of seaweed, used locally in certain parts of the world, the marine plants, called phytoplankton, are not currently directly used by man in significant quantities. They are consumed by small marine animals called zooplankton, themselves eaten by larger ones, which form the basis of the fishing industry. At any given time there exists some kind of balance in the ocean between inorganic materials and living organisms, and between plants and animals. The balance can be upset either by a change in physical conditions or by excessive fishing. The physical change is exemplified by the warm current off Peru that every few years intrudes in the cold waters off the coast, and, by preventing or reducing the normal upwelling which brings nutrients to the surface, reduces the plant and animal life in the fishing area.

There is a fundamental difference between marine and land environments as present and potential future sources of food and organic raw materials. Most marine plants are small, short lived and simple, consisting of many varieties of phytoplankton. They grow only in the lighted surface layers of open water, in which photosynthesis can take place, and are largely concentrated where there is an upwelling of nutrient rich water, as off the coast of Peru and northern Chile. Where the ocean is deep, nutrients tend to descend below the level of light needed for plant growth (photosynthesis). Exceptions occur, as along the Equator, where upwelling occurs in deep waters.

Marine phytoplankton differ from land plants in mobility as well as in size. For the first reason they are difficult to 'cultivate' compared with land plants. For the second reason they occupy a much smaller proportion of the volume of the medium in which they grow than do land plants, such as those in a grassland environment. On average a given area of ocean supports only about $\frac{1}{4}$ the amount of vegetation that an equivalent sized land area supports. In *both* environments, however, plant life is highly concentrated in certain areas, much of the plant life in the oceans being concentrated in about 7 per cent of the total area. In relation to the area of the oceans, marine life is not therefore as abundant as is perhaps popularly thought, and the possibility of actually farming or cultivating marine plants on a large scale as a basis for controlled fishing presents many problems.

The potential of the oceans has been outlined above because around 1970 Peru and Chile together accounted for about $\frac{1}{5}$ of the total tonnage of fish caught in the world (nearly 14 million tons out of nearly 70 million). Their share of the *value* was much less since most of the catch is converted into fishmeal. The whole of the rest of Latin America accounted for only about $1\frac{1}{2}$ million tons. *Figure 4.6* shows the areas of ocean around Latin America where marine life tends to be abundant. The diagram in *Figure 4.6*, with a cut-away of the Pacific off Peru, shows the presence of the occasional warm counter current 'El Niño' which interferes with the normal north-flowing, relatively cold, Peruvian current. Usually there is an upwelling of water along the coast, bringing a rich supply of nutrients to the surface and supporting an abundant plant life. This area has been fished heavily since the late 1950s and it is thought[5] that a combination of the effects of the current from the north and excessive fishing not only caused the disappearance of anchovies in many places in the years 1972–73 but may have done irreparable damage to the fish stocks and breeding pattern. The nature of fishing, which takes adult fish of various ages before they die a natural death, upsets the 'demographic' structure of fish populations and allows a given area to support a stock only somewhere between $\frac{1}{2}$ and $\frac{2}{3}$ the population under natural conditions. Therefore, to ensure the 'maximum sustainable yield', a catch of only a certain size can be taken each year. Such a principle is based on experience and appeals to commonsense. In practice, it is not necessarily applied. Since several Latin American countries see an expansion of their fishing industries as a major part of their programmes for economic development, the limitations of the oceans need to be appreciated. It has been estimated[6] that world fisheries could provide annually somewhere between 110 and 220 million tons of fish a year. 70 million tons in 1970 is not all that far below the minimum potential level, and if the rate of expansion of fishing in the 1960s continued, even the limits of a well managed world fishing industry could be reached by about 1985.

4.7. THE ATMOSPHERE AND WATER SUPPLY

Various attempts have been made by Latin American climatologists to classify weather and climatic conditions on a multivariate basis into climatic regions, the criteria used by Koppen in the 1930s often forming the basis. In the present book it was felt that single feature distributions such as mean annual precipitation would give a more direct appreciation of the potential of different areas for use by man. Again it must be stressed that generalised small scale maps of physical features in a continental area cannot show local details. For this reason *Figures 4.7* and *4.8* also show local temperature and precipitation variations in selected areas.

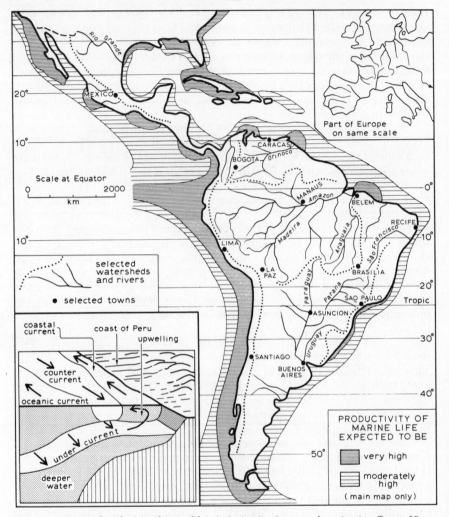

Figure 4.6. Rivers and productivity of marine life in Latin America. Inset map shows situation off coast of Peru

Latin America extends over a great range of latitude, from roughly 30°N to 50°S. Firstly, as mean annual temperature diminishes with increasing latitude, so the seasonal range tends to increase, at least to about 40°S. Secondly, long, relatively narrow but high mountain regions act as barriers, separating the lowest 3,000–6,000 metres of atmosphere on either side over distances of thousands of kilometres. Since about half of the air above any given locality at sea-level is within the first 5,000 metres, the implications of such a barrier as the Andes can be appreciated. Mountain regions also contain their own locally varying climatic conditions. Thirdly, oceanic currents appear to affect profoundly at least the climates of coastal regions, and to be affected by them. The Gulf of Mexico and Caribbean area is virtually sealed off from the penetration of currents from colder latitudes and its surface waters are very warm. In contrast, cold currents converge from north and south along the Pacific coasts of the Americas towards the Panama area and are associated with dry coastal regions. The ocean on the eastern side of South America is warmer than the western side at comparable latitudes, as a result of the warmer south flowing Brazil current.

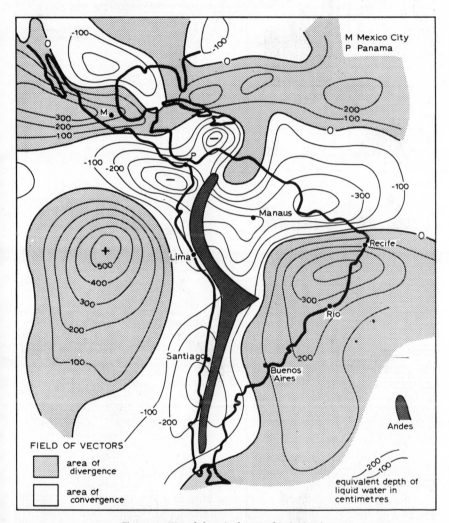

Figure 4.7. Water balance in the area of Latin America

In South America the occurrence of the southern hemisphere summer season in December–February should be borne in mind. Unfortunately, the terms summer (verano) and winter (invierno) are in some areas used to refer to the dry and rainy seasons, which do not necessarily coincide with warm and cool periods respectively.

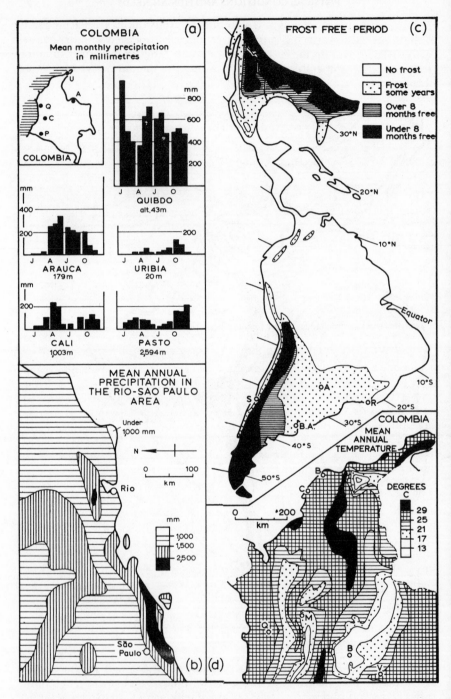

Figure 4.8. Features of precipitation and temperature in Latin America. (a) Precipitation in five selected stations in Colombia. (b) Precipitation in part of Southeast Brazil. (c) Approximate duration of frost free period in Latin America. (d) Mean annual temperature in Colombia

Table 4.6 summarises roughly the temperatures that may be expected at different latitudes in lowland areas of the interior and eastern side of Latin America.

Table 4.6.

Latitude	District	Winter	Summer	Range
30°N	North Mexico	(Jan.) 10°C	(July) 25-30°C	15-20°C
Equator	Amazonia	27°C	27°C	negligible
30°S	Chaco	(July) 10-12°C	(Jan.) 25-30°C	15–20°C
50°S	South Patagonia	(July) 1-2°C	(Jan.) 12-15°C	about 12°C

The mean annual sea-level temperature in South America exceeds about 20°C in lowland areas almost everywhere within 30 degrees of the Equator, but there are considerable regional differences within this generally hot area. In Brazil, for example, the mean annual temperature exceeds 26°C around Manaus and Fortaleza, but is only 16°C at a few hundred metres above sea level in Santa Catarina in the south. The highest summer temperatures occur away from the Equator itself. Hot areas such as the shores of the Gulf of California and parts of the Chaco of Argentina have mean temperatures of over 30°C in the hottest month.

Within about 30 degrees on each side of the Equator, mean annual temperatures are considerably lower along most of the Pacific coastlands of Latin America than on the eastern side at the same latitude. For example, the mean annual temperature of less than 20°C in Lima (12°S) is well below about 25°C at the same latitude in Northeast Brazil. Western Colombia and the southern part of Central America are however as warm as would be expected for their latitude. Great differences also occur as a result of variations in altitude and more, perhaps, than in any other part of the world, it is possible in Latin America to find the extremes of permanent snow and tropical forest close to one another as in the Sierra Nevada de Santa Marta in north Colombia where they are only 50 km apart.

Almost all of Latin America except the limited highest parts and the bleak, windswept extreme south, has high enough temperatures for some kind of agriculture to be practised. Nevertheless, the length of growing season and the cumulative temperatures set limits to different crops at different latitudes and a map summarising the occurrence of frost indicates approximately the limit of tropical agriculture. *Figure 4.8c* shows that except in the very highest parts, almost all of tropical South America is frost free, but whereas in the U.S.A. the period in which frosts may be expected to occur grows in duration rapidly north from the Gulf of Mexico, there is a large area in South America in similar latitudes in which frosts may also be expected to occur, though only in certain years.

At any given time the atmosphere contains only about 1/100,000 of all the water in the hydrosphere. Together with heat from the sun, affecting temperature in the atmosphere, this small quantity of water, as it moves round the hydrological cycle, partly determines the water available for agriculture, livestock, and industrial and domestic uses as well as the hydro-electric potential.

Precipitation and evaporation tend to be thought of from the ground where they occur and are measured. Increasing appreciation of the processes affecting the whole atmosphere together with the availability of electronic computers since the 1950s have made it possible to study the atmospheric part of the hydrosphere in a broader perspective. One study has identified a relationship between evaporation and precipitation in the world. Net flows of water vapour occur in certain directions over a given period of time and areas of divergence and convergence of water vapour can be identified in the lower half of the atmosphere[7] which contains nearly all the moisture in the air. *Figure 4.7* shows areas of divergence (shaded), net sources of water vapour, and areas of convergence (unshaded), net sinks of water vapour. In the former areas, which correspond broadly to the subtropical regions of Latin America, evaporation exceeds precipitation. In the latter areas, which constitute most of the equatorial zone of Latin America as well as the mid-latitudes of southern South America, precipitation exceeds evaporation. The areas of convergence and excess precipitation cover the headwaters of many of the rivers that contribute to the big river systems of South America (see *Figure 4.6*), notably the Amazon itself, the Orinoco and Magdalena in the north and part of the Plate system of the south.

The above brief account of a broad approach to the workings of the atmosphere has been included for two main reasons. Firstly, the existence of a world system, of which Latin America forms part, is an essential view for an appreciation of the atmosphere, as it is for tectonic features (Section 4.2) and for the nature and exploitation of the oceans (Section 4.6). Secondly, if the weather is to be forecast accurately and eventually if the atmosphere is to be controlled by man in any way, the whole atmospheric system must be appreciated. There is little hope of such a development affecting agriculture and water supply in Latin America in the next two or three decades.

A brief description of precipitation as it is at present follows. Since data are lacking for many areas, even this depends on many rough estimates. There are enormous differences in mean annual precipitation between different parts of Latin America. Places in northern Chile with virtually no rainfall at all contrast with part of the Pacific coast of Colombia receiving 600–700 cm per year. With exceptions and reservations it may be said that precipitation rather than temperature determines the broad differences in vegetation type and agricultural possibilities on a regional level, though temperature does this on a continental scale. An appreciation of the quantity, occurrence by seasons and reliability of precipitation in Latin America is therefore essential to an understanding of the human background. *Figure 4.9a* shows the main features of distribution of mean annual precipitation and *Figure 4.9b* gives an idea of the intensity and period of the dry season by showing the mean amount falling in the driest month. Maps with greater detail are given under individual countries.

Although the effectiveness of a given amount of rain varies greatly from region to region in Latin America through differences in evaporation, surface conditions, nature of occurrence and so on, a mean annual rainfall in excess of about 100 cm is usually associated with a forest or savanna vegetation, or where this has been cleared for agriculture, allows cultivation to be practised without the need for irrigation. In contrast, in areas with less than 50 cm per year, xerophytic types of vegetation prevail and irrigation is needed to supplement rainfall for crop farming to succeed.

Marked differences in mean annual precipitation occur over short distances in many parts of Latin America. *Figure 4.9c* shows that in reality in Haiti a

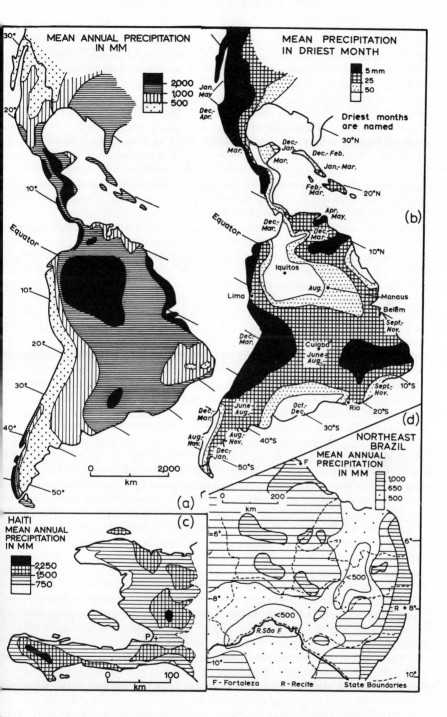

Figure 4.9. Features of precipitation in Latin America. (a) Mean annual precipitation. (b) Precipitation in driest month. (c) Annual precipitation in Haiti. (d) Annual precipitation in Northeast Brazil

number of east-west high areas receive 2–3 times as much rain as the deep intervening lowlands, while the distribution is complicated by the fact that north-
facing sides of the highland areas receive more rain than south-facing sides.
Such marked contrasts as these have been recorded in many parts of Latin
America, including the Islands, Southeast Brazil (see *Figure 4.8b*), and the
Andes. For example, over 200 cm are recorded on one mountain side in the
eastern Andes of Peru, but about 35 cm in a valley floor only 20 km away and
1000 metres below. The transition here from tropical montane forest to cactus scrub
is most impressive. *Figure 4.9d* shows very marked contrasts in precipitation in
Northeast Brazil over short distances even in an area in which relief features are
not pronounced and heights of more than a few hundred metres are rare. *Figure
4.8a* shows precipitation data for five stations (heights indicated in metres) in
Colombia covering tropical rain forest (Quibdo), savanna (Arauca), dry (Uribia)
and mountain (Cali and Pasto), conditions.

Marked seasonal differences in precipitation are found almost throughout
Latin America, even in the areas of heaviest rain (over about 200 cm), which
have no actual dry period. *Figure 4.9b* does not attempt to represent the length
of the dry season but gives an idea of the amount of rain falling in the driest
month in different parts of Latin America, thus representing only the peak of
the dry season. A comparison with the left-hand map suggests a fairly close correlation between total precipitation and the amount of rain in the driest month.
A rainfall regime with rain all the year is characteristic of Southern Brazil and
Argentina, the tropical areas of western Amazonia, and the Caribbean lowlands
of Central America. In contrast, large areas (in black) receive a negligible
amount of rain (under 0·5 cm) in the driest month and may have several dry
months, yet still receive a substantial total for the whole year. This occurs in parts
of northeast Brazil, south Venezuela, and the Pacific coasts of southern Mexico
and Central America.

Within a few degrees either side of the Equator there tend to be two periods
of maximum precipitation around December and June and two periods with
less, around March and October. These differences are more accentuated
towards the eastern end of Amazonia. To the south of the equatorial zone, a
pronounced wet season in the southern hemisphere summer and autumn (from
January on) is characteristic, especially south of about 15°S, but there are many
regional variations of this pattern, and in the west the Andes and the Pacific
coastlands may have quite different regimes. The eastward facing coastlands of
Brazil between Recife and Rio have more rain in winter (May, June) than in the
summer. To the north of the equatorial belt the late summer maximum is in
general more marked than to the south, with a very distinct wet season during
June to August or somewhat later in some places and a relatively dry winter and
spring. Almost throughout Latin America the period of heaviest rain coincides
with the hot season and arrives therefore when most useful for agriculture but
when susceptible to greatest evaporation; central Chile and northwest Mexico
are exceptions.

The above data are based on means for periods of years and in a given year
both the annual total and its occurrence in the year may deviate greatly. The
data in Table 4.7 show the actual amount of rain that fell each month in individual years in Manaus, in the heart of Amazonia, and in Fortaleza in the state
of Ceará, northeast Brazil. It will be seen that values diverge greatly from
monthly averages in both cases.

Table 4.7.

MONTHLY RAINFALL IN MANAUS AND FORTALEZA, BRAZIL, IN SELECTED YEARS IN MILLIMETRES

	Total	Jan.	Feb.	Mar.	Apr.	May	June	July	Aug.	Sept.	Oct.	Nov.	Dec.
Manaus													
1971	2,534	288	368	353	419	316	146	36	9	41	182	282	94
1968	2,841	282	183	635	303	427	128	103	42	243	38	266	195
1967	2,125	305	249	436	496	204	124	34	3	7	11	132	123
1966	2,041	170	248	533	284	269	64	46	3	14	139	77	196
1960	2,580	357	320	229	410	119	174	68	59	80	226	240	299
Fortaleza													
1971	2,094	247	178	329	215	450	259	299	29	8	30	11	39
1968	1,386	260	107	211	342	291	20	60	11	7	27	3	47
1967	1,839	22	403	363	359	338	182	88	32	23	18	2	9
1966	1,629	113	10	219	469	382	314	61	28	14	6	2	10
1960	980	16	10	428	281	95	71	4	6	4	28	2	34

Source: IBGE *Anuario estatistico do Brasil 1972*. p. 24 and various other years.

Precipitation in the interior of Northeast Brazil is notoriously unreliable, but many other areas for which data are limited, and which have attracted less attention because they have fewer people, are as adversely affected by droughts as Northeast Brazil, and also appear to suffer from great year to year variations. For example, desert localities of Peru and northern Chile may receive no appreciable rain for many years and then have all their 'quota' in a few heavy downpours.

Water is not a non-renewable resource like oil or copper ore, since the amount in the world is conserved even when used by man. Nevertheless it is not universally available, in abundance, and increasing consumption of water in some parts of Latin America, including particularly the large cities, has already created water shortages and is likely to produce more in the future.

Although spectacular irrigation works have been built in Latin America and there are a few large hydro-electric power stations in the region, little has been done to assess total water resources. The movement of water over considerable distances to supply large urban consuming areas is very limited. Owing to the complexity of the availability of, and demand for, water, it is difficult to produce a useful map of water resources, but the map showing precipitation (*Figure 4.9a*) gives an idea of where it would be expected to be abundant and where deficient on a regional level.

The principal 'consumer' of water is agriculture. Most is supplied by rain but in recent decades the irrigated area in Latin America has been greatly extended. Hydro-electricity is generated by falling water, the amount that can be expected depending firstly on the volume, secondly on the vertical drop and thirdly on the type of generating capacity actually installed to use this. A reasonably regular flow of water is desirable and a water-course with an irregular regime requires a reservoir constructed above the site of the power station. Other users of water are mining, industrial and domestic consumers. Finally, inland navigation on rivers uses water even if it does not consume it, and inland fisheries should not be overlooked.

To some extent the various users of the water resources compete. If used to generate electricity, falling water may reach too low a level to be available for irrigation where needed. Agricultural and urban consumers may also at times compete. Reservoirs can usefully regulate water supply for power and for other users and even improve navigation, but are liable to silt up in time and if they greatly increase the water surface, evaporation can actually reduce supplies, while in some places loss is caused by seepage of water through the underlying rock. Such hydrological problems have already occurred in western U.S.A. and in the U.S.S.R. in areas in which both the scale of operations and the features of the natural environment resemble those in many parts of Latin America.

Sometimes, on the other hand, several functions may usefully be fulfilled by the construction of a single project. Thus the Tres Marias project in Minas Gerais, Brazil, not only generates hydro-electricity, but helps navigation on the São Francisco River, prevents floods further downstream, regulates the supply of water to the Paulo Afonso station much further downstream, and allows some irrigation.

The work of regulating and using to the full the water resources of Latin America has only just seriously started. In theory, none of the water in rivers flowing across arid areas need ever reach the sea, a situation that may soon exist in western North America. Thus almost all the rivers rising in the mountains of northern Mexico and in the Andes could be exploited to improve water supply in agriculture, even if only to supplement existing precipitation. Northeast Brazil is less fortunate, but the São Francisco can contribute to parts of this dry area. The greatest hydro-electric potential also occurs in the mountain regions, but suitable sites are often remotely placed and the need for great preparatory work such as road building has discouraged efforts so far. Both the Guiana and Brazilian shield areas offer many excellent sites, and the Paraná basin, with a number of rapids, has a very large potential.

In spite of apparently abundant water resources in most of Latin America, water supply is inadequate in most settlements. Large cities such as Mexico, Monterrey, Rio and Lima have already exhausted resources in their immediate vicinity and are having to look further afield. Lima, for example, is now receiving water piped through a long tunnel under the main Andean watershed from the headwaters of rivers flowing to the Amazon. Many mining and smelting centres in dry areas, being large consumers, have also had water problems. Eventually considerable quantities of sea-water may be distilled in coastal areas for human consumption and possibly even for irrigation. This is not an economic proposition at present but is done as a last resort, as in the Netherlands Antilles, which have two large oil refineries requiring far more water than the small islands can provide.

4.8. THE SOIL AND SOIL TYPES

Soil is the basic material in which almost all land plants grow, whether grasses, shrubs or trees. In places the relationship between plants and soil is so close that the soil type may directly determine the natural vegetation or influence the choice of possible crops for cultivation. Some appreciation of the complex needs of plants, whether in natural vegetation or under cultivation, is fundamental to an understanding of the geography of Latin America. In *Figure 4.10* plants and soils are put in a central position in the diagram to show both the ingredients for plant growth (rectangular boxes) and some of the ways (oval boxes) in which growth can be improved either directly, or through the soil. The needs of most if not all land plants are:

1. Light, and a temperature between the threshold levels for that plant.
2. Carbon from carbon dioxide in the air (nitrogen can also be captured from the air by legumes).
3. From water in the soil: hydrogen and oxygen.
4. From soil particles themselves or from dead organic matter in the soil, the macronutrients: nitrogen, phosphorus, potassium, calcium, magnesium, sulphur, and the trace elements: boron, copper, iron, manganese, zinc, molybdenum, chlorine.
5. Soil water to carry the various plant nutrients to be absorbed by the plant.
6. Air in the soil.
7. No extreme acidity or alkalinity of the soil; this property is measured as a pH value.

The eleven oval boxes in *Figure 4.10* show some of the ways in which crop cultivation can be improved by man in appropriate circumstances. Nothing is included in the diagram about harvesting, transporting, storing and processing plants, about social conditions such as land tenure affecting the farmers themselves, or about economic aspects such as finance, mechanisation and marketing. Most of the possible methods of improvement and their aims are self-evident, but problems can arise from their mis-application. Inorganic fertilisers, for example, must be in a form readily available to plants once they are applied. Deep ploughing, which loosens the soil, tends to bring infertile material up to the surface and to bury the more fertile humic top horizon. It may also contribute to soil erosion.

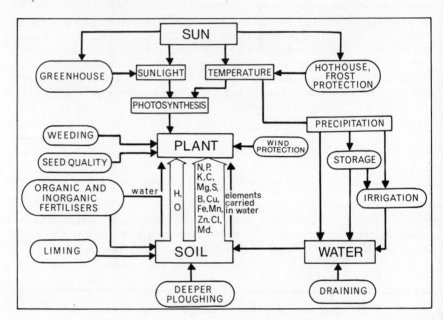

Figure 4.10. Conditions for plant growth in agriculture

The composition and quality of different soils are not easily summarised in concise numerical terms. Even the untrained observer can, however, often see differences in the nature of the soil even in different parts of the same field. On the scale of the map in *Figure 4.11* showing major soil types of Latin America the level of generalisation covers great variations on both regional and local levels. The soil zones on the map in fact show either major types that reflect present, or in some cases past, climatic conditions, or areas of high mountain that cut through the zones. More local soils such as those consisting of volcanic material or of alluvium recently deposited by rivers cannot be shown on this scale.

*Figure 4.11c** shows the general distribution in Latin America of lateritic soils. They are found almost entirely within 30° either side of the Equator and are highly acidic, rich in iron and aluminium, but poor in silica. Lateritic soils are the product of a particular set of climatic conditions, and may form on widely

---

* It is interesting to note the big differences between the lateritic soils in *Figure 4.11c* and the latosols in *Figure 4.11a*. Both maps were made in the early 1960s.

differing kinds of bedrock. Heavy rain, high temperatures and bacteria and insects break down organic material quickly and both this and nutrient elements
such as potassium, calcium and phosphorus are easily leached down through
the well aerated soil out of reach of plant materials. The B and C horizons found .
in many soils are thin or non-existent in lateritic soils. Oxygen from the air
penetrates the soil and forms oxides with the iron and aluminium in it, thereby,
incidentally, capturing oxygen permanently from the atmosphere. Lateritic

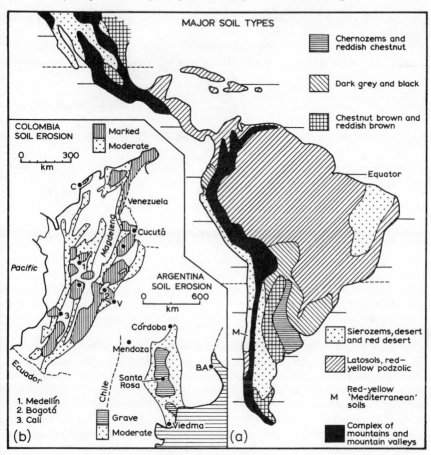

*Figure 4.11. (a) Major soil types in Latin America. (b) Soil erosion in Colombia and in Argentina. (c) Lateritic
soils* (see next page)

soils support dense tropical rain forest in many places but the forest ecosystem
survives only by the continual supply of decaying vegetation from the growing
forest. Experience in many parts of the tropics has shown that when the protec-
tive natural vegetation on the lateritic soils is replaced by crops, particularly
field crops rather than tree crops, the relatively few nutrients in the soil are used
quickly, soil fertility diminishes and oxidisation takes place. This tends to lead
to the formation of a hard lateritic surface. Deep ploughing would further
hasten this process of change. Locally, special conditions such as the presence

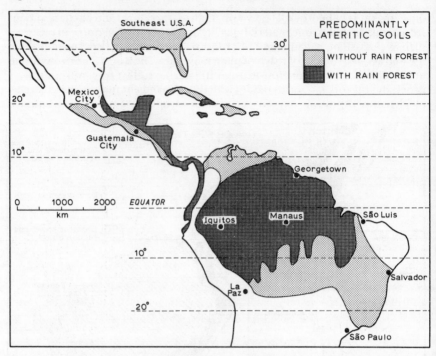

Figure 4.11.(c) Lateritic soils[8]

of alluvial silts may allow cultivation in an area which is surrounded by lateritic soils. Such areas are too small to be shown on either *Figure 4.11a* or *4.11c*. Many experiments have taken place to try to improve cultivation on lateritic soils but most have failed, including that at Iata in the interior of the Amazon region of Brazil.

A particularly distinct set of soils occurs in Argentina and has counterparts in mid-U.S.A. and the blackearth belt of the U.S.S.R., the chernozems (blackearths) and reddish chestnut soils (see *Figure 4.11a*). These are deep, fertile soils formed under grassland conditions. Towards the drier western fringes, however, they become poorer in humus (chestnut brown and reddish brown) and under present climatic conditions, characterised by a low rainfall and strong winds, are easily eroded (see *Figure 4.11b*). Black and chestnut soils have been recorded elsewhere in Latin America at considerable altitudes, as in central Mexico and in Colombia, but they are limited in extent and probably of a different origin.

In the driest parts of Latin America, whether on the dry margin of the chestnut and reddish brown soils as in West and South Argentina, or along the desert coast of Peru and Chile, or in the dry northeast of Brazil, soils are often thin, and poor in organic matter, especially if sandy, but they may be rich in certain mineral nutrients. There is little scope for cultivation without irrigation, but once water is available and suitable fertilisers are added, very high yields may be obtained, as in the irrigated lands of Peru and Mexico.

Other soils tentatively shown on *Figure 4.11a* are a very varied set of dark grey and black soils associated with the sub-tropical fringes of the tropical forest and savannas in South America, the soils of 'Mediterranean' Chile, and the soils of the highland areas. Steep slopes and great differences in climatic conditions over short distances give very varied conditions in the mountain regions, ranging from bare surfaces almost devoid of soil to prairie soils, alluvial soils and in southern Bolivia, saline soils.

Soil erosion is serious in many parts of Latin America. Indeed, almost every existing combination of soil and climate in the region is potentially destructible unless carefully cultivated, but the situation is most serious in the highland areas where excessively steep slopes may be cultivated, and on the semi-arid zone between the pampas and desert areas of Argentina.

4.9. VEGETATION

Of the four aspects of the physical environment most frequently referred to as the background of the activities of man in any large region, relief, climate, soils and vegetation, the last, perhaps, comes closest to summarising the agricultural possibilities of a region. Vegetation regions are no more easy to define with precision than climatic or soil regions, since any given vegetation type is an arbitrarily chosen mass of tree, shrub and herbaceous species. Innumerable combinations are possible and completely different classifications of vegetation types could be devised for any large area by two different authorities. Nevertheless, reasonably distinct types of vegetation are often found over large areas. Those occurring in Latin America have been grouped into four main classes, each of which is mapped separately in *Figure 4.12*. To supplement the relatively simple picture conveyed by these four maps, the vegetation of certain smaller parts of Latin America is shown in more detail in other maps.

The types of vegetation combined are as follows:

1. Humid forest:
   (a) Tropical (i) Rain
                  (ii) Semi-evergreen and deciduous
   (b) Evergreen mixed forest, deciduous beech forest
2. Dry: thorn forest, cactus scrub with or without desert grass, mid-latitude semi-desert scrub (Patagonia), sclerophyllous scrub (Chile and Mexico), desert (Peru, Chile)
3. Mountain: Alpine, tropical montane forest, often with conifers
4. Savanna: grassland including pampa, broadleaved tree savanna (campos in Brazil, llanos in Venezuela), pampas and other temperate grasslands.

In addition to the physical influences that have shaped the various combinations of plant species making up the natural vegetation, the influence of man, in removing the original vegetation by cutting or burning it, in cultivating land and abandoning it, or using it for grazing, is considered to have been very profound over very large areas, even where there is only a low density of population. Before the 16th century, however, the population of Latin America was not large except in certain limited areas. Even so, several thousand years of gradual modification could have had a considerable cumulative influence, and great activity in clearing vegetation in the last few centuries must be added. In

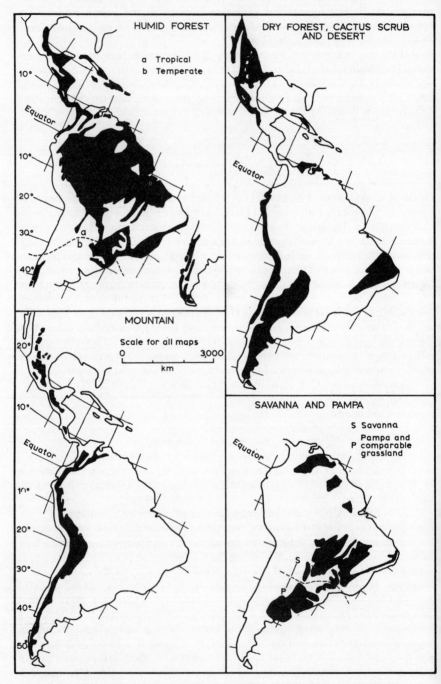

Figure 4.12. Basic vegetation environments in Latin America. See text for further explanation

general, the natural vegetation appears to have been interfered with by man less in Latin America than in Africa. One reason may be the small amount of grazing until the arrival of Old World livestock in the 16th century.

The widespread tropical rain forest is the densest and most continuous mass of vegetation in Latin America. On its drier margins it gives way to semi-evergreen and deciduous forest, or where the transition to dry conditions is abrupt, is replaced by thorn forest with dwarf trees. Where it reaches the margins of highland areas it merges into tropical montane forest, which eventually thins out around an altitude of 2,000–3,000 metres, depending on local conditions. A further reduction in precipitation, or in the length of the rainy season, is frequently associated with savanna in the tropics, and with grassland and scrub further from the Equator. The opposite extreme, desert conditions, is found in Latin America over a large area only in the coastal region of Peru and northern Chile.

Since the tropical rain forest covers such a large part of Latin America its main features deserve attention. This forest has been called equatorial forest, but in certain parts of the tropical world it is found at a great distance from the Equator. Such vegetation is permitted by high temperatures and heavy rainfall interrupted by only very short dry periods. It has at least several thousand different plant species, including in Amazonia some 2,500 species of large tree alone; shrubs are few. The trees are evergreen, since they constantly shed some leaves and at the same time grow new ones. The leaves of the taller trees are leathery and dark green and are able to continue functioning under the strong heat of the sun. Often three distinct levels of forest can be detected. The forest itself generally exceeds 30 metres in height and the uppermost layer is formed by the umbrella-shaped crowns of the tallest species. These alone intercept much of the light, but often two other layers of smaller trees, with their foliage around 20 and 15 metres, grow below. Trees usually have straight trunks with few branches, and the ground beneath the forest is much clearer than is popularly imagined, but on it grow the saplings waiting their opportunity to replace the existing trees as they die. Lianes are frequently found, trailing from tree to tree, and adding to the mass of foliage high above ground level; many species of epiphytes grow on the trees themselves. Well-known species of tall tree are the India-rubber tree (*Hevea braziliensis*) and the Brazil nut (*Bertholletia excelsa*); shorter trees include the cacao (*Theombroma cacao*), and the banana tree (*Musa species*). The tropical montane forest has many of the features of the tropical rain forest but is found mainly between about 1,5000 and 3,000 metres.

The largest area of tropical rain forest in Latin America is in Amazonia and extends several degrees north and south of the Equator with only small interruptions. Smaller areas of this forest are found along the coast of Brazil between 10° and 25°S, in western Colombia, along the Caribbean coast of Central America and in the Islands.

Mainly within the tropics but also in areas with a more limited and more seasonal rainfall (about 75 to 125 cm), the tropical semi-evergreen and deciduous forest displaces the tropical rain forest. The largest area of this forest is in middle Brazil, and long galleries of the forest extend south into the savanna lands. In temperate South America there are two more limited zones of lowland and upland forest. These mainly contain both deciduous and evergreen species and are found in areas with an annual rainfall of more than about 100 cm. The uplands of South Brazil still have large areas of forest with one very

TROPICAL RAIN FOREST IN THE BRAZILIAN AMAZON REGION

TROPICAL RAIN FOREST BEING CLEARED FOR CULTIVATION

DRY FOREST (*CAATINGA*), NORTHEAST BRAZIL

CARNAÚBA PALM,
NORTHEAST BRAZIL

ARAUCÁRIA PINE, SOUTHERN BRAZIL

characteristic species of pine, the *Araucaria angustifolia* (Parana pine), one of the most important commercial trees in Latin America. The other area of forest extends from south central Chile, along the flanks of the Andes to the southern tip of the continent, and also includes valuable coniferous species. The Patagonian side of the Andes has mainly deciduous forest (southern 'beech').

Between the humid forest environments and the decidedly dry environments, large areas of savanna and grassland characterise the central part of South America and much of Argentina. The savanna vegetation has been considered to be associated with a particular climate, but its origin is now in question and in Brazil, at least, it occurs in areas with very different rainfall regimes. It consists of plant communities in which grasses and sedges cover most of the ground but trees also occur, sometimes wide apart, sometimes closer together. It is thought that fires may have had much to do with the development of savanna vegetation, but certain types of soil may also encourage this co-existence of grass and tree species. The savanna belt of Latin America is less continuous than that in West Africa, where the great east-west belt appears to be a transition between the dense humid forest to the south and the desert to the north. Savanna vegetation is rare in Mexico, Central America and the Islands, and in South America occurs mainly in the llanos of the Orinoco valley and in south central Brazil.

In South Brazil, Uruguay and east central Argentina a large area receiving from about 40 to 100 cm of rain per year had a grassland vegetation before most was cleared for cultivation or was intensively grazed in the last 100 years. The grassland was tall prairie with feather-grass and melic growing in closely spaced tussocks. Small areas of tree vegetation were also to be found, and it is thought that possibly these are relics of an earlier forest cover, at least in those parts receiving more than about 75 cm of rain per year. On its northern margins the temperate grassland terminates against the forests of southern Brazil, but in the west, with increasing aridity, the grass is shorter and is replaced by xerophytic shrubs. The grassland area in Argentina is generally referred to as the pampa, but according to usage in the countries concerned, the grasslands of Rio Grande do Sul (Brazil), Uruguay and the Mesopotamian region of Argentina (between the Paraná and Uruguay rivers) are termed provincia Uruguayensis, with vegetación de pradera (meadow).

Most of the dry environment of Latin America consists of varying combinations of scanty grass, dwarf tree species, shrubs and succulent plants adapted to long periods of drought. A large area of dry steppe and semi-desert extends from southern Bolivia, through western Argentina, over almost 40 degrees of latitude, and consists of thorn forest in the north and lower growing scrub in the south. This area is of little use agriculturally except where irrigated. The interior of northeast Brazil also consists mainly of thorn forest, with occasional taller trees (e.g. bottle trees and xerophytic palms). Most of the area receives considerable total precipitation but this occurs with great irregularity, which explains the dominance of drought-resisting species, though underlying rock conditions may also contribute. A smaller area with drier species occurs in parts of northern Venezuela and Colombia, and unexpected dry patches occur also in the Islands and Yucatan. Most of northern and western Mexico consists either of thorn forest where precipitation is sufficient, or towards the north, of semi-desert with cactus scrub; savanna vegetation is not widely found. Central Chile and small areas in the extreme northwest of Mexico have a

'Mediterranean' type of vegetation, with distinct species but many characteristics in common, as a result of dry summer conditions.

In coastal Peru, northern Chile and parts of the central Andes are found the most arid conditions in the whole of Latin America. With a very limited precipitation, large areas are virtually without vegetation and bare rock surfaces and sand dunes are frequent. Desert conditions are only relieved where rivers cross the arid zone from the Andes to the Pacific, where the water table is close to the surface or where ephemeral plants appear in places along the coast exposed to light drizzle (garua) from sea-mists.

The mountain environments are characterised by sharp changes in vegetation with altitude. In general, an increase in altitude above about 3,000 metres is accompanied by diminished precipitation and by a thinning out of forest in areas humid enough for this to occur below this altitude. Four highland environments may be distinguished in Latin America (see *Figure 4.12*; that of southeast Brazil is not shown on the map). Firstly, the Andes north of 30°S are continuous, high and, in places, very wide. In the adjoining lowlands completely different types of vegetation are found, ranging from desert in Peru and Chile on the Pacific side to tropical rain forest on the eastern side. On the western side cactus scrub extends high along the western Cordillera, while on the eastern side tropical montane forest may extend to beyond 2,500 metres. Above about 3,000 metres, however, the characteristic Alpine grassland type of vegetation, with local names (e.g. paramo in the north, puna in the south) according to precipitation and type of grass, occur almost throughout the region, thinning out and disappearing around 4,500 metres into bare rock and small patches of permanent snow. In southern Bolivia and northern Argentina desert-like conditions occur.

The second mountain region consists of the Andes south of about 30°S. The range here is narrower, and for the most part lower, and less continuous. There is a more scanty grassland cover, while the lower flanks are largely covered by temperate forest. The third high mountain region extends discontinuously from northern Mexico far into Central America. The higher ranges in Mexico are distinguished by their relatively dense forest vegetation, containing many conifers, while in southern Mexico and Central America coniferous species appear in the higher parts of the tropical montane forest. The fourth area in which altitude modifies the distribution of vegetation is the high parts of southern Brazil, but here a complicated mixing of lowland vegetation types is the result, rather than the appearance of a particular highland vegetation.

These comments on vegetation give a rough idea of the characteristic types found in various parts of Latin America, but in detail there are many different interpretations of vegetation conditions in different parts of the region. More detailed vegetation maps of selected areas have therefore also been included to give examples of the diversity in some areas and of the Latin American terminology. *Figure 4.13* shows how it is possible in a limited part of Venezuela to pass over a distance of some 200 km in the Maracaibo lowlands from semi-desert, through dry forest and deciduous forest, to tropical rain forest. Over a further 200 km one can pass through mountain forest into the high grassland of the Andes, over permanent snow, and down into savanna (llanos). *Figure 4.14* illustrates the great variety of environments and types of land use encountered in a traverse of the southern Andes of Peru.

It is possible by using as a basis the area of major civil divisions, to calculate the approximate extent of each of the four main vegetation environments in *Figure 4.12*. The forest environment, from which, however, have been subtracted both dry and montane forest, covers almost half of Latin America. Roughly another quarter is accounted for by dry environments, including the dry forest.

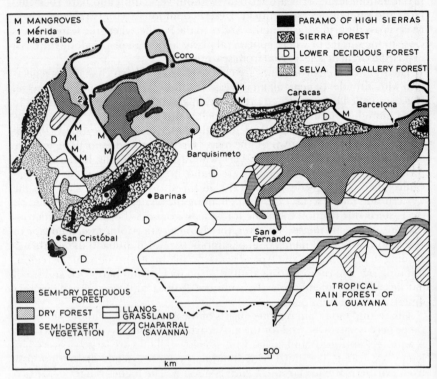

Figure 4.13. Vegetation types in northwestern Venezuela

The remainder is shared by mountain areas above about 1,000 metres (about 8 per cent), savanna (about 12 per cent) and pampa and similar grasslands (about 6 per cent).

4.10. LAND USE AND AGRICULTURAL CONDITIONS

Three main uses of land may be distinguished in Latin America for the purposes of this section: cropland, permanent grazing land and forest land. Land under crops may be further subdivided into land under field crops, fallow and land under permanent (shrub or tree) crops. Some crop land may in fact be used for grazing. The total area of Latin America is distributed in four main categories in percentages as follows:

1. Arable and permanent crops   6
2. Permanent grazing   24
3. Forests   49
4. Other uses (urban, waste, etc.) 21

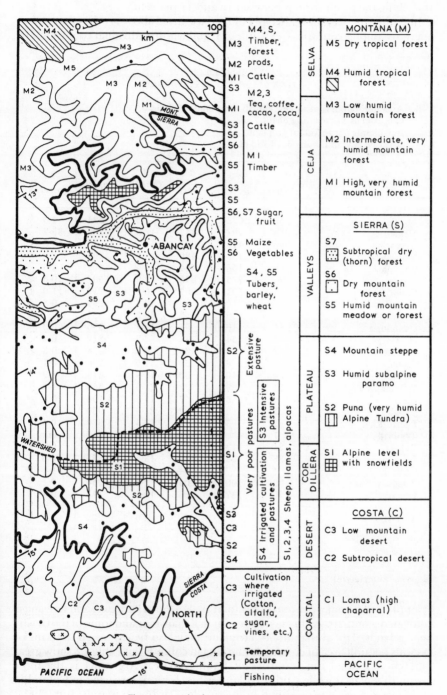

Figure 4.14. A land use transect in southern Peru

By comparison, over 11 per cent of North America is cropland, and in the world as a whole the proportion is between 10 and 11 per cent.

In Latin America, the main types of land use listed above are distributed very unevenly among countries (see Table 4.8) and within individual countries. For

Table 4.8.
TYPES OF LAND USE BY COUNTRIES

1–3 Area in thousands of sq.km., mostly for mid-late 1960s.
4 Cropland as a percentage of total area
5 Inhabitants per sq.km. of cropland
6 Irrigated land in thousands of sq.km.

	1 Crops	2 Grazing	3 Forest	4 Crops/ area	5 People/ Crops	6 Irrigated
Brazil	280	1,073	5,179	3·5	324	4·6
Mexico	238	791	437	12·0	206	35·2
Argentina	330	1,449	627	11·1	73	15·6
Venezuela	52	138	480	5·7	204	2·2
Colombia	50	146	694	4·4	409	2·3
Peru	26	273	870	2·0	507	10·8
Chile	45	101	207	6·0	213	11·0
Costa Rica	6	10	30	12·4	289	0·3
El Salvador	6	6	2	30·2	554	–
Guatemala	15	10	54	13·7	336	0·3
Honduras	8	34	30	7·3	312	0·7
Nicaragua	9	9	65	6·7	218	0·3
Panama	6	8	61	7·5	236	0·1
Cuba	20	40	30	17·9	413	4·9
Dominican Rep.	11	9	22	21·9	380	1·1
Haiti	4	5	7	13·3	1,190	0·4
Jamaica	2	2	2	21·9	980	0·2
Puerto Rico	2	3	1	27·4	1,380	0·4
Trinidad	1	–	2	27·0	750	0·1
Bolivia	31	113	470	2·8	155	0·6
Ecuador	38	22	148	13·4	155	4·6
Guyana	4	27	144	1·9	186	1·1
Paraguay	9	100	205	2·3	256	0·1
Uruguay	20	137	6	10·5	143	0·4
TOTAL*	1,245			6·0	222	

– very small area
* includes other areas, total 3.

Main source: *FAOPY 1970* and *1971.*

example only about 2 per cent of the total area of Peru, Paraguay and Guyana is cultivated, compared with 20–30 per cent in El Salvador and some of the Caribbean islands. The availability of cropland may also be expressed in terms of persons per unit area of cropland. The data in column 5 of Table 4.8 show great differences among the countries of Latin America. Argentina is the most favourably placed while cultivated land is much more restricted in Colombia and Peru and extremely limited in the smaller Caribbean islands. It might be expected that productivity per unit of cropland is higher in the countries in which the land is less abundant but no generalisation seems evident here. Argentina has generally relatively fertile cropland while the quality in the Andes and some of the islands tends to be poor.

The agricultural production of Latin America can be increased in two main ways, firstly by extending cultivation to new areas and secondly by raising yields in existing areas. In both cases a distinction should be made between the inherent or natural quality of a given piece of land as judged, for example, by a land capability survey (soil quality, slope, rainfall and temperature) and the additional productivity that can be achieved by the application of various techniques (fertilisers, irrigation, deeper ploughing). Some of the positive and negative features of the physical background are indicated tentatively in *Figure 4.15.*

Although the exact extent of cropland in Latin America in the past is not known, it would seem that new land has been settled and farmed in three main periods.

1. Pre-Columbian, when some areas already supported very dense agricultural populations by 1500, especially in Mexico and the northern Andean region.
2. Early colonial, when plantations were developed in northeast Brazil, the Caribbean and other areas giving again very high densities.
3. Modern, particularly from about 1870 to 1910, in southern South America, when new European settlers moved into the pampas of Argentina and the coffee lands of southeast Brazil.

Since 1910 the cultivated area in Latin America has been extended only by the addition of small areas in many different localities, except in southeast Brazil (Paraná). The doubtful quality of the widespread lateritic soils in the more humid parts of Latin America has already been noted. In the drier parts of Latin America, irrigation could be extended, but the cost of major works would be very high.

Existing irrigated areas are shown in column 6 of Table 4.8 and *Figure 4.15.* There now seems little future prospect of extending the cultivated area in Latin America much over a short period of time. This situation is comparable with that in North America, Australia and the U.S.S.R., none of which has achieved any major extension of the area under crops in the 1960s.

As will be shown in the next chapter, crop and livestock yields in Latin America tend to be much lower than those for corresponding products in the relatively extensive conditions of North America and Australia and in the more intensive conditions of Japan and West Europe. If Latin American agriculture had the level of productivity found in the 'developed' capitalist countries its agricultural production would be roughly twice as great as it is. Many different factors contribute to the higher productivity per unit of area in the industrial countries, including the widespread use of chemical fertilisers and of high quality seed and livestock. Certain areas of Latin America, such as the wheat and cotton growing areas of northern Mexico and the irrigated oases of coastal Peru do in fact achieve yields comparable with those in the developed countries. This does not imply that such improvements could quickly be made elsewhere in Latin America.

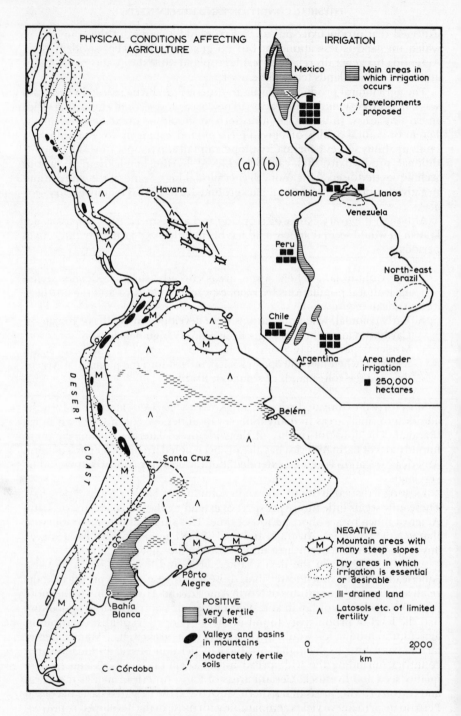

PHYSICAL CONDITIONS AFFECTING
AGRICULTURE

IRRIGATION

Mexico

Main areas in
which irrigation
occurs

Developments
proposed

(a) (b)

Havana

Colombia — Llanos
Venezuela

Peru

North-east
Brazil

Chile

DESERT COAST

Santa Cruz

Argentina

Belém

Area under
irrigation

■ 250,000
hectares

NEGATIVE

M Mountain areas with
many steep slopes

Dry areas in which
irrigation is essential
or desirable

Ill-drained land

Latosols etc. of limited
fertility

Rio

Pôrto
Alegre

POSITIVE

Very fertile
soil belt

Valleys and basins
in mountains

Moderately fertile
soils

0   2000
km

Bahía
Blanca

C - Córdoba

*Figure 4.15. (a) Physical conditions affecting agriculture. Note: This map contains information already presented
in Chapter 4. It is only very general and is to some extent controversial. (b) Irrigation*

References

1. Dewey, J. F., 'Plate Tectonics', *Sci. Am.,* May 1972, Vol. 226, No. 5, pp. 56–68.
2. James, D. E., 'The Evolution of the Andes', *Sci. Am.,* Aug. 1973, Vol. 229, No. 2, pp. 60–69.
3. Santos Rudulfo Cortés, 'Geografía Altitudinal de Venezuela', *Revista Venezolana de Geografía,* June 1961, pp. 45–87.
4. *Atlas de Colombia,* Vol. 1 (Banco de la Republica, 1959), Cartograma No. 6.
5. Idyll, C. P., 'The Anchovy Crisis', *Sci. Am.,* June 1973, Vol. 228, No. 6, pp. 22–29.
6. Holt, S. J., 'The Food Resources of the Ocean', *Sci. Am.,* Sept. 1969, Vol. 221, No. 3, pp. 178–194.
7. Peixoto, J. P., and M. Ali Kettani, 'The Control of the Water Cycle', *Sci. Am.,* Apr. 1973, Vol. 228, No. 4, pp. 46–61.
8. McNeil, M., 'Lateritic Soils', *Sci. Am.,* Nov. 1964, pp. 97–102.

Sources of material in the figures

4.2. Maps (a) and (b) adapted from maps in *Sci. Am.,* May 1972, pp. 57 and 62. Map (c) adapted from map in *Sci. Am.,* Aug. 1973, p. 67.
4.3. Map (a) based on J. H. F. Umbgrove, *The Pulse of the Earth,* 1947, The Hague; Nijhoff, Plate 5.
4.6. Main map, location of productivity of marine life based on map in *Sci. Am.,* Sept. 1969, p. 152. Inset map of Peruvian current based on diagram in *Sci. Am.,* June 1973, p. 25.
4.7. Based on map in *Sci. Am.,* Apr. 1973, p. 52.
4.8. Colombia rainfall graphs and map from *Atlas de Economía Colombiana* (see Chapter 15 for full refernce).
4.9. Map (d) based on map in *Revista Brasileira de Geografía,* Ano XXIV No. 4, p. 511.
4.11. Main map based on map in *The State of Food and Agriculture,* 1963, p. 150 (Food and Agriculture Organisation, Rome 1963). Map of Colombia from *Atlas de Economía Colombiana.*
4.12. Based on maps in S. R. Eyre, *Vegetation and Soils. A World Picture.* 1963, London; Edward Arnold, by courtesy of the publisher.
4.14. From *Plan para el desarrollo del sur del Perú,* 1959.

Further reading

Dawson, J. A., and J. C. Doornkamp, (Ed.), *Evaluating the Human Environment,* 1973, London; Arnold.
Eyre, S. R., referred to in 4.12. above.
Francis, P. W., 'Mysterious Volcanoes of the High Andes' (Chile), *Geogr. Mag.,* Aug. 1970, Vol. XLII, No. 11, pp. 795–803.
Franklin, W. L., 'High, Wild World of the Vicuña', *Nat. Geogr.,* Jan. 1973, Vol. 143, No. 1, pp. 77–91.
Hock, R. J., 'The Physiology of High Altitude', *Sci. Am.,* Feb. 1970, Vol. 222, No. 2, pp. 52–62.
King, Lester C., *The Morphology of the Earth, A Study and Synthesis of World Scenery,* 1962, Edinburgh; Oliver and Boyd.
Thomas, M., 'Down in the Forest', *Geogr. Mag.,* Nov. 1972. Vol. XLV, No. 2, pp. 135–40. .

CHAPTER 5

PRODUCTION

5.1. EMPLOYMENT AND PRODUCTION

In this chapter the production of goods is considered on the basis of countries. In order to make available a large amount of data it has been necessary to base the presentation of the material on tables, with brief comments and some location maps.

In 1970, 88 million people were economically active in Latin America out of a population of 283 million, about 31 per cent of the total. In column 2 of Table 5.1 the absolute numbers employed are given for each country; column 3 shows the proportion of employed to total population. Data for four countries outside Latin America, representative of developed countries, are shown at the foot of the table. Typically the proportion of economically active population to total population is much higher in these countries than in Latin America, with the dubious exception of Haiti and the more reasonable exception of Uruguay and Argentina. The low official level of employment in most Latin American countries is probably due to two sets of influences. Firstly, the number of persons in employment, especially females and children, may have been undercounted. Secondly, such a large proportion of the population consists of young people that members of employable age groups are relatively fewer than in developed countries, though the large proportion of young is to some extent offset by the lack of elderly people. Even when these features have been taken into account, the country figures reflect a lack of jobs in many regions and very high unemployment levels in some localities.

Agriculture, including forestry and fishing, is by far the largest single employer of labour in Latin America, accounting according to one source for over 40 per cent of employment, compared with about 8 per cent in manufacturing. Column 6 in Table 5.1 giving agricultural employment as a percentage of total employment, shows great variations from country to country, with Central America, the poorer islands and the Andean countries being the areas depending most heavily on agriculture. The absolute number engaged in agriculture in the U.S.A. has droped dramatically since the Second World War, from about 7 million to 3½ million between 1960 and 1970 alone. In contrast, the absolute number has risen in Latin America, although relatively agriculture accounts for a smaller proportion of employment than it did in 1950. Out of a total of 162 million inhabitants in 1950, 87 million or 54 per cent were classed as agricultural. In 1970, the figures were 283 million, 118 million and 42 per cent respectively.[1] Most Latin American countries are below the world average of about 50 per cent in agriculture. None approaches either such countries as Nepal, Chad, Mali, Niger and Rwanda, at one extreme, all with at least 90 per cent of their population in agriculture, or at the other extreme the least agricultural countries, the U.K. (3%), U.S.A. (4%), Belgium (5%), Netherlands

(6%) and even certain developed countries with an agricultural surplus such as Australia and Canada, both 8%.

The total number of persons in Latin America employed in manufacturing in 1970 was very roughly 7 million, a mere 8 per cent of the employed population. This small number would be increased considerably by the inclusion of self-employed individuals and persons in very small establishments, not counted in the censuses of many of the countries. The further inclusion of several hundred thousand persons employed in mining and many others in 'services' actually producing 'goods' such as electricity and houses would probably raise the number regularly engaged in industry to 9–10 million. Column 7 in Table 5.1 shows big differences between countries in the proportion of employed population accounted for by industry. No Latin American country approaches the

Table 5.1.
EMPLOYMENT BY COUNTRIES

	1. Total Popn. (millions)	2. Empl. Popn. (thousands)	3. 2/1 %	4. Agric. Empl. (thousands)	5. Indl. Empl. (thousands)	6. 4/2x 100 %	7. 5/2x 100 %	8. Other Act. %
Brazil	93·6	28,860	31	12,610	2,050	44	7	49
Mexico	50·7	14,300	28	6,670	1,300	47	9	44
Argentina	24·4	8,880	36	1,350	1,320	15	15	70.
Venezuela	11·0	3,300	30	870	200	26	23	51
Colombia	21·1	6,090	29	2,750	300	45	5	50
Peru	13·6	4,060	30	1,850	200	46	5	49
Chile	9·8	3,060	31	780	280	25	9	66
Costa Rica	1·8	510	28	230	30	45	6	49
El Salvador	3·4	1,040	31	590	70	57	7	36
Guatemala	5·2	1,590	31	1,000	40	63	3	34
Honduras	2·6	780	30	520	20	67	3	30
Nicaragua	2·0	640	32	360	20	56	3	41
Panama	1·5	450	30	200	20	43	4	53
Cuba	8·4	2,740	33	900	n.a.	33	n.a.	n.a.
Dominican Rep.	4·3	1,190	28	720	100	61	8	31
Haiti	4·9	2,590	52	2,000	n.a.	77	n.a.	n.a.
Jamaica	2·0	650	33	180	50	27	8	65
Puerto Rico	2·8	760	27	110	140	14	18	68
Trinidad	1·1	340	31	60	30	17	9	74
Bolivia	4·9	1,650	34	960	30	58	2	40
Ecuador	6·1	1,850	30	990	50	54	3	43
Guyana	0·8	230	29	80	n.a.	32	n.a.	n.a.
Paraguay	2·4	750	31	400	30	53	4	43
Uruguay	2·9	1,090	38	180	n.a.	17	n.a.	n.a.
LATIN AMERICA*	283·0	87,635	31	36,376		42		
U.S.A.	205·4	81,330	40	3,250	19,170	4	24	72
Australia	12·6	5,160	41	430	1,320	8	26	66
U.K.	55·7	25,180	45	700	8,900	3	35	60
Spain	33·3	12,160	37	4,100	2,000	34	16	50

* Includes countries in Latin America not listed above   n.a. not available
Sources: 1–4 and 6, *FAOPY 1971*, Table 5
    5 *UNSYB 1971*, Table 77

high level of industrialisation found in the developed countries, especially in many in Europe, where over 30 per cent are employed in industry.

Table 5.2 shows that dependence on agriculture can be seen in two different ways. Data for selected countries show that in every case in Latin America agriculture accounts for a much larger share of employment than it does of contribution to gross domestic product.[2] Where the share is roughly the same, as in the U.S.A., Australia and the U.K., it can be said that a person employed in agriculture is roughly as productive as a person in other activities. In Latin America productivity is several times higher in other branches than in agriculture. In Mexico, for example, the 47 per cent of the population in agriculture accounts for 11 per cent of gross domestic product, the 53 per cent in other activities for 89 per cent, a productivity gap of about 7 to 1.

Table 5.2.

RELATIVE IMPORTANCE OF AGRICULTURE AND INDUSTRY IN SELECTED COUNTRIES

1   Persons employed in agriculture as a percentage of total employed population in 1970.
2   a, b, c Contribution (percentage) of a agriculture, b industry, c services to total gross domestic product in 1970.

	1	2a	2b	2c
Brazil	44	14	21	65
Mexico	47	11	29	60
Argentina	15	11	31	56
Venezuela	26	8	40	52
Colombia	45	28	22	50
Chile	25	7	40	53
El Salvador	57	26	21	53
Haiti	77	49	15	36
Puerto Rico	14	3	27	70
Uruguay	17	11	24	65
U.S.A.	4	3	30	67
Australia	8	9	31	60
U.K.	3	3	34	63
Spain	34	14	28	58

Sources: 1, *FAOPY 71*, Table 5
2, *UNSYB 71*, Table 181

The apparently low productivity of agricultural workers in most parts of Latin America is the result of the generally low efficiency and lack of application of mechanised methods and fertilisers. It is also argued that to some extent agricultural products are undervalued. In general, however, mining and industry have become much more highly capitalised, modernised and mechanised than agriculture, a feature characteristic also of the U.S.S.R., where agricultural productivity continues to lag behind industrial productivity. Data for the period 1956–60[3] reveal that even then the productivity of agricultural workers in the United States was more than 10 times as high as that of agricultural workers in Central America or Venezuela and more than 3 times as high as in Argentina. The discrepancy has increased in the 1960s. Similarly it can be calculated that the value of production of a worker in bauxite extraction in Jamaica or the oil industry in Venezuela is 50–100 times as high as the value of production of a farm worker in the same country.

Manufacturing accounts for roughly 20 per cent of the combined gross domestic product of the countries of Latin America but for less than 10 per cent of employment. Mining accounts for about 5 per cent of gross domestic product but less than 1 per cent of employment. Data are not so straightforward for services but here also there are very big contrasts in efficiency in such branches as retailing and transport.

5.2. BASIC FOOD CROPS

Out of over 70 field or tree crops tabulated in the *Production Yearbook* of the Food and Agricultural Organisation of the United Nations (FAO) virtually all are grown in at least one country in Latin America. Whether area under cultivation, weight of crop or its value is considered, however, some crops such as maize, bananas, sugar cane and coffee are far more important than others such as pineapples, sugar beet or tea. In this and the following section certain major Latin American crops are discussed briefly.

The production of crops in Latin America may be viewed from various angles. One may consider, for example, what proportion is exported, whether the crop is a human food, a beverage, or for use as an industrial raw material, whether it is widely grown or is restricted in area, and whether it depends on seasonal labour.

TOTAL PRODUCTION

Table 5.3 shows that in Latin America food production, total agricultural production and population have all increased during the 1960s at roughly the same rate. Indices are in relative values measured against the 1961–65 average. From the table it can be seen that Latin America 'held its own' in terms of per capita production of both food and total production. This is in fact disappointing because it has not allowed a substantial change in the quantity of products available, either for home consumption or for export. The performance of individual countries with regard to food production only is shown in columns 8 and 9 of Table 5.4, the 1961–65 average being 100.

Table 5.3.
AGRICULTURAL PRODUCTION IN LATIN AMERICA IN THE 1960s (1961–65 = 100)

Year	Food Production	Total Production	Food per capita	Total per capita	Population
1961	94	95	99	100	94
1962	96	97	99	100	97
1963	100	100	101	100	100
1964	103	102	101	99	103
1965	106	107	101	101	106
1966	108	106	99	98	109
1967	114	111	102	100	112
1968	116	113	101	98	115
1969	121	117	102	99	119
1970	125	121	103	99	122
1971	124	120	99	95	126

Source: *FAOPY, 1971*, Tables 7, 8

Table 5.4.

THE PRODUCTION OF SEVEN FOOD CROPS IN THOUSANDS OF METRIC TONS

(X SMALL OR NO PRODUCTION, N.A. NOT AVAILABLE)

	1 Maize	2 Wheat	3 Rice	4 Potatoes	5 Cassava	6 Bananas	7 Sugar	8 1961 FOOD (61-65=100)	9 1971 FOOD (61-65=100)
Brazil	13,630	1,300	6,840	1,560	30,070	6,020	5,020	92	136
Mexico	8,830	2,190	370	380	x	1,030	2,400	89	132
Argentina	7,610	5,670	380	2,210	300	140	980	92	105
Venezuela	680	x	240	130	310	950	460	88	157
Colombia	850	80	720	970	920	800	680	94	135
Peru	580	140	450	1,720	500	x	770	95	135
Chile	240	1,250	70	670	x	x	230	98	118
Costa Rica	80	x	90	x	10	970	150	89	182
El Salvador	300	x	80	x	10	x	120	n.a.	n.a.
Guatemala	700	30	20	x	x	80	190	88	130
Honduras	380	x	30	x	20	1,350	50	94	142
Nicaragua	200	x	70	x	10	30	140	n.a.	n.a.
Panama	90	x	170	x	30	900	80	94	138
Cuba	120	x	210	120	220	30	7,560	113	116
Dominican Rep.	40	x	200	x	170	250	1,010	102	127
Haiti	210	x	40	x	110	210	70	n.a.	n.a.
Jamaica	x	x	x	x	10	210	380	n.a.	n.a.
Puerto Rico	x	x	x	x	x	110	410	n.a.	n.a.
Trinidad	x	x	10	x	x	30	220	n.a.	n.a.
Bolivia	290	50	70	630	160	x	120	92	119
Ecuador	200	80	210	380	400	2,700	300	90	118
Paraguay	170	x	30	x	1,550	250	50	95	130
Uruguay	110	420	130	110	x	x	60	89	117
TOTAL LATIN AMERICA	35,300	11,210	10,750	8,870	34,850	16,750	22,250	94	124

Sources: 1–4 Mean annual production 1968–70
UNSYB 71, Tables 33, 42, 38, 37
5, 6 *FAOPY* 70, Table 32 Cassava 1969, Table 71 Bananas 1969

MAIZE

Maize is the principal cereal of New World origin and the most widely grown
cereal in Latin America (see Table 5.4, column 1). In 1970, however, Latin
America only produced ⅓ as much maize as North America. Maize is widely
grown for human consumption, especially in the pre-Columbian Indian areas
of Mexico, Guatemala and the northern Andes. In Argentina it is grown mainly
for animal fodder. Table 5.5 shows that in 20 years between 1948–52 and 1971
maize yields have increased in all the main producing countries of Latin
America but not in a way comparable with the dramatic changes in some
developed countries, exemplified by Italy and the U.S.A. It is some consolation
to think that what has been done in the advanced industrial countries might
eventually be repeated in Latin America in view of the apparently great potential there. Unfortunately, however, maize is grown in many areas in Latin
America where rainfall is inadequate, soils are poor and other conditions are
far less favourable than in Italy or the U.S.A.

Table 5.5.
MAIZE PRODUCTION IN SELECTED COUNTRIES

Area in thousands of hectares
Production in thousands of tons
Yield in hundreds of kg. per hectare

	Average 1948-52			*1971*		
	Area	*Prod.*	*Yield*	*Area*	*Prod.*	*Yield*
Brazil	4,632	5,841	12·6	9,860	14,360	14·6
Mexico	4,101	3,090	7·5	8,000	9,500	11·9
Argentina	1,741	2,839	16·3	4,066	9,930	24·4
Venezuela	310	303	9·8	600	720	12·0
Colombia	731	753	10·3	744	950	12·8
Peru	191	275	14·4	382	650	17·0
Cuba	275	243	8·8	120	115	9·6
Haiti	270	203	7·5	290	235	8·1
Guatemala	538	437	8·1	713	751	10·5
Italy	1,253	2,306	18·4	936	4,469	47·8
U.S.A.	29,856	74,308	24·9	25,826	140,733	54·2
S. Africa	3,228	2,629	8·1	6,000	8,582	14·3
World	88,407	139,852	15·8	112,910	307,796	27·3

Source: *FAOPY 71*, Table 19

WHEAT

While Latin America produces about 14 per cent of the world's maize it only accounts for about 3 per cent of the world's wheat. Wheat is important in the context of Latin America because it is the preferred bread cereal among the settlers
of European origin. As a result it has been the policy to encourage wheat
cultivation in many areas, as in south Brazil, where conditions are not good.
The wheat surplus of Argentina is increasingly sold within Latin America rather

than in Europe as previously. The trend towards higher yields in Mexico started in the 1950s before the 'official' Green Revolution. Table 5.6 shows that increases in yields have been achieved in various Latin American countries but it is in West Europe, exemplified by France, that most progress has been made since the Second World War.

Table 5.6.
WHEAT PRODUCTION IN SELECTED COUNTRIES

Area in thousands of hectares
Production in thousands of tons
Yield in hundreds of kg. per hectare

	Average 1948-52			1971		
	Area	*Prod.*	*Yield*	*Area*	*Prod.*	*Yield*
Brazil	671	498	7·4	2,000	2,056	10·3
Mexico	604	534	8·8	710	1,900	26·8
Argentina	4,487	5,175	11·5	3,750	5,200	13·9
Uruguay	526	469	8·9	350	460	13·1
Colombia	173	124	7·1	52	78	15·0
Peru	158	146	9·2	140	130	9·3
Chile	777	928	11·9	727	1,368	18·8
Australia	4,620	5,161	11·2	7,082	8,380	11·8
France	4,264	7,791	18·3	3,977	15,360	38·6
U.S.S.R.	42,633	35,759	8·4	65,200	92,000	14·1
World	173,285	171,151	9·9	217,220	343,111	15·8

Source: *FAOPY 71*, Table 14

RICE

Rice (or paddy) is grown in Latin America principally in southern Brazil but in some quantities in almost every country; Latin America accounts for about 4 per cent of the world total. The area under cultivation has more than doubled in the last 20 years but again yields are greatly inferior to the highest in the world (Spain, Australia, Japan about 6 tons per hectare) being around 3 tons per hectare in Mexico and only 1½ in Brazil.

POTATOES

Although potatoes originated in the Andes, Latin America now only produces about 3 per cent of the world total and yields are low compared with those achieved in Europe. In the Andean countries potatoes are widely grown at high altitudes in conditions where it is difficult to grow cereals and other food crops. They are principally a crop for local use.

CASSAVA

Cassava (manioc, mandioca) is again a New World crop, widely grown in humid tropical lowland areas for local use. Given its hardy nature and widespread popularity it is likely to continue as a prominent crop but little has been done to improve the quality of the plant. Brazil and Paraguay are the largest producers.

BANANAS

Bananas are cultivated in Latin America both as a local food and for export to industrial countries. Specialist exporters include Central America, many Caribbean islands and Ecuador. On account of their perishability bananas require special handling. Various ways of processing them such as drying and making into flour have been tried.

SUGAR CANE

Sugar cane has been the principal agricultural export of Latin America from the 16th century to the 19th, when coffee, wheat and livestock products gained in relative importance. Cane sugar is grown under very varied conditions in Latin America. Old plantation areas like Haiti and northeast Brazil still have sugar plantations but generally obtain low yields. Some Caribbean islands and the oases of Peru have very high yields. Since the early 19th century Latin American sugar exporters have had to compete increasingly with protected beet sugar producers in many industrial countries. The U.S.A., which itself grows both cane and beet sugar, remains the main importer of Latin American sugar, and a system of quotas under which specified amounts are taken from each country plays a notable part in determining the scale of production. Since 1959, the largest exporter of sugar in Latin America, Cuba, has become linked with the U.S.S.R. and East Europe. Table 5.7 shows the production of raw sugar by the six largest Latin American producers in 1970. Most of the weight of the actual sugar cane is lost by processing into raw sugar, which may then be exported or further refined for home use. In the last 20 years sugar cane yields have only increased gradually both in the world as a whole and in Latin America.

The cultivation of cane sugar has caused many economic and social problems in Latin America. It requires a large labour force per unit of area and was one of

Table 5.7.
SUGAR PRODUCTION IN SELECTED COUNTRIES IN MILLIONS OF TONS

	Cuba	Brazil	Mexico	Dominican Republic	Argentina	Peru
1948	6·1	1·8	0·7	0·4	0·6	0·5
1955	4·7	2·1	1·0	0·6	0·6	0·7
1960	5·9	3·3	1·5	1·1	0·8	0·8
1965	6·1	4·6	2·1	0·6	1·3	0·8
1966	4·9	3·8	2·3	0·7	1·0	0·8
1967	6·2	4·3	2·4	0·8	0·8	0·7
1968	5·3	4·4	2·3	0·7	0·9	0·8
1969	5·5	4·2	2·6	0·9	1·0	0·6
1970	7·6	5·0	2·4	1·0	1·0	0·8

Sources: *UNSYB 63*, Table 81
UNSYB 71, Table 84

the main types of cultivation using slaves. It also requires considerable capital, and can most economically be grown as a monoculture with land under cane as near as possible to the processing factories (centrales), since the cane has to be processed within a very short time of cutting. The crop exhausts the soil quickly. Although only a small part of the cane plant becomes sugar, the rest is not necessarily returned to the soil and may even be used as a raw material for industry. A large application of fertiliser is therefore desirable. Labour is needed in large quantities seasonally and agricultural labour remains idle and in some circumstances unpaid for much of the year. Given the high degree of capitalisation needed to make production efficient and the great interest of the U.S.A. in Latin American sugar it is not surprising that some of the cane is grown in U.S. owned plantations. This is another reason for discontent, especially as the expansion of these has resulted in their encroachment on food producing lands.

OTHER CROPS

Other cereals, including millet and sorghum, barley, oats and rye are all grown in Latin America, Argentina being the principal producer of all those mentioned. Other basic food crops widely grown in Latin America as local sources of carbohydrate and in some cases protein include sweet potatoes and yams, and pulses (dry beans, broad beans and peas, chickpeas and lentils). Apples, pears, citrus fruits and the vine are grown particularly in southern South America but only limited quantities are now exported.

5.3. BEVERAGES, FIBRES AND ANIMAL PRODUCTS

Eight further items of production have been selected for inclusion in Table 5.8 out of many possible ones. All are products of organic nature.

COFFEE

Coffee is one of the principal exports of several Latin American countries though its relative importance in the region has declined since the drop in production in Brazil in the early 1960s. In 1968–70 Latin America accounted for just over 60 per cent of the world's coffee but rival producers in Africa (Ethiopia, Angola, Uganda, Ivory Coast) follow Brazil and Colombia. In the early 1970s there were moves to achieve 'producer power' among the leading producers, to achieve self-imposed quotas and to get higher coffee prices.

Frost damage, tree diseases and government policy contributed to the destruction of about half the coffee trees in Brazil in the early 1960s. There was a reduction in the general area of coffee growing and the virtual disappearance of coffee from the northeast. In the late 1960s coffee and coffee extracts only accounted for about 40 per cent of the value of the exports of Brazil. In spite of policies and frosts (1969 and 1972) Brazil produced a large harvest of coffee again in late 1972. The aim in Brazil is to concentrate on higher quality coffee and on coffee products for export. In the early 1970s, however, Brazil actually

Table 5.8.

SELECTED PLANT AND ANIMAL PRODUCTS

1-3   Annual average production 1968-70 in thousands of tons.
4   Cattle in thousands 1970-71.
5-7   1970 production of meat and wool and 1968-70 average annual production of fish, in thousands of tons.
8   1970 production of sawn wood in thousands of cubic metres.

	1 Coffee	2 Cocoa Beans	3 Cotton Lint	4 Cattle	5 Meat	6 Wool	7 Fish	8 Sawn Wood
Brazil	1,070	196	660	97,300	2,690	29	470	8,040
Mexico	180	22	410	25,120	660		360	1,420
Argentina			100	49,790	3,030	175	210	750
Venezuela	60	19	10	8,500	260		130	330
Colombia	510	20	120	21,080	560		80	1,760
Peru	70	2	100	4,130	160	12	10,800	240
Chile				2,980	250	22	1,200	1,020
Costa Rica	90	6		1,570	60			380
El Salvador	130	1	50	1,490	n.a.			n.a.
Guatemala	130		60	1,450	70			70
Honduras	40		10	1,600	40			n.a.
Nicaragua	30		80	2,550	65			200
Cuba	30	1		7,000	250		80	40
Dominican Rep.	40	30		1,150	30			100
Haiti	30	3		960	20			n.a.
Bolivia	30			2,400	40			90
Ecuador	70	55	10	2,500	80		80	600
Paraguay			10	5,800	150			220
Uruguay				8,500	460	78	10	70
TOTAL LATIN AMERICA*	2,530	366	1,620	248,000	9,000	336	13,500	

* Includes other countries not listed

Sources: *UNSYB 71*, 1 Table 28; 2 Table 27; 3 Table 29; 5 Table 78; 6 Table 43; 7 Table 46; 8 Table 101
FAOPY 71, 4 Table 107.

imported coffee from El Salvador. During the post war period coffee production in the Andean countries has roughly doubled and in Mexico and Central America the increase has been nearly threefold. Colombia, with its high value mild coffee, commands high prices. Table 5.9 shows changes in coffee production in selected Latin American countries.

Table 5.9.

COFFEE PRODUCTION IN THOUSANDS OF TONS IN SELECTED COUNTRIES

	Brazil	Colombia	Mexico	Guatemala	El Salvador	Costa Rica
1948-52	1,080	350	60	60	70	20
1961-65	1,730	470	160	110	110	60
1967	1,510	480	170	110	140	80
1968	1,060	480	170	110	120	70
1969	1,280	480	170	140	140	90
1970	750	570	180	110	130	100
1971	1,800	660	190	130	160	100

Sources: *FAOPY 70*, Table 91
UNSYB 71, Table 28
UNSYB 72, Table 30

COCOA BEANS

Cocoa beans for export are produced in Latin America principally in Northeast Brazil, Ecuador and the Dominican Republic. Latin America provides about 25 per cent of the total world production. Since 1950 production in Africa has risen faster than in Latin America.

COTTON

Cotton is grown both for fibre (lint) and for seed. The distribution of production of seed corresponds approximately to that of cotton lint in column 3 of Table 5.8. Much of the cotton grown in Latin America, 14 per cent of the world total, is consumed in the region, but some areas, particularly those in which irrigated cotton is grown, notably northern Mexico, Nicaragua and coastal Peru, specialise in the export of high quality lint. Cotton cultivation does not require such a complicated organisation as sugar or coffee and it can be successfully cultivated on small farms. Production in Latin America has doubled in the last 20 years but demand for the commodity has not increased greatly in the industrial countries.

CATTLE AND MEAT

Latin America is characterised by the large quantity of livestock rather than by their quality. Large numbers of horses, asses, mules and llamas are used for transport or ploughing. Sheep are numerous in southern South America. Pigs and poultry are also widely kept, but yields of pigmeat are low. Latin America has only 7 per cent of the population of the world but 22 per cent of the cattle. This fact underlines the intermediate position of Latin America in terms of development. Unlike India and China it has large areas of natural grazing land. Unlike West Europe and the U.S.A. it has not generally concentrated on the quality of herds, though in Argentina and locally elsewhere breeding and the improvement of stock has occurred.

A large proportion of the cattle in Latin America graze on poor quality, little improved pastures. Until the introduction of Zebu (Brahman) cattle from Asia in recent decades, cattle in the tropical areas of Latin America were from European breeds. The role of cattle varies from region to region. In some areas they are the main draught animal, in others they are kept for hides. Argentina and Uruguay are the only countries that have a high quality beef industry with a long tradition. Column 5 in Table 5.8 shows meat production, almost all of it beef, but the assessment is on different criteria for different countries. Argentina and Uruguay have a substantial but diminishing surplus for export, but most of the rest is consumed internally. Specialised dairying is practised mainly in the vicinity of the larger towns. There seems then to be great scope for improvement in the livestock sector in Latin America, in the supply of fodder, in the quality of animals and in the organisation of processing and marketing.

WOOL

Wool is a commodity that has had mixed fortunes since the Second World War. It seems likely that the industrial countries will require more in the future, yet in

1970 the whole of Latin America only produced as much wool as New Zealand (each about 12 per cent of the world total) and little over ⅓ the quantity produced in Australia.

FISHING

The limitations of the fishing industry were discussed in the previous chapter. Column 7 in Table 5.8 shows average annual production during 1968–70. The high production of Peru and Chile consists mainly of anchovies, which at present are turned into fishmeal fertiliser for export. Most of the fish caught elsewhere is for internal consumption. There is some scope for processing and preserving fish such as tuna for export outside Latin America.

FORESTRY

Over half the total area of South America is classified as forest and in Mexico, Central America and the Caribbean the proportion is about a third. Much of the forest is of such poor quality that it is of no commercial use. Elsewhere the dense tropical rain forest is difficult to exploit commercially on account of the large number of species occurring in any one locality. Some of the easiest and most successful lumbering operations have been in the pine forests of northern Mexico, Southeast Brazil and Chile. Here, however, little has been done to replant stands. In 1970 Latin America produced about 2 per cent of the world's softwood (coniferous) and 9 per cent of the world's hardwood (deciduous). There is an experiment in Brazil to grow selected tree species on land cleared from the Amazon forest (see Chapter 11). In view of the dangers already noted in using lateritic soils, the idea seems optimistic. The introduction in the last hundred years of eucalypt species from Australia to many of the drier parts of Latin America such as the high Andes of Peru and Minas Gerais in Brazil has been of great benefit regionally.

OTHER ITEMS

Oil seeds are grown in Latin America largely for home consumption except by Argentina. Groundnuts, cottonseed, linseed, rapeseed, sesame, the sunflower and the castor oil seed are all produced. The cultivation of soybeans, almost unknown in Latin America in 1950, has recently expanded greatly in Brazil. Tobacco is grown in virtually every Latin American country but only in Cuba has it been cultivated with high quality export products in view. Fibre plants including sisal (*Agave sisalana*), henequen (*Agave fourcroydes*) and jute are of local importance in northeast Brazil, Mexico, the Caribbean and the Amazon. Very little natural rubber is now produced in Latin America and attempts to cultivate the indigenous *Hevea brasiliensis,* so successful in plantations in Southeast Asia, have so far made little progress. The Brazil nut, gathered from the wild *Bertholletia excelsa* tree in the Amazon is rich in oil and protein but apparently not suitable for cultivation in plantations.

5.4. NON-ENERGY MINERALS

Most of Latin America has not as yet been fully explored for economic minerals and it is a matter of speculation as to how great the reserves are. Only when it has been decided that a mineral deposit is economically worth working are careful calculations made of its extent. Such information may remain confidential.

Mining differs from agriculture above all because it involves the extraction of non-renewable resources, so is rarely more than a temporary activity in a given place. It differs again in the sense that there is little place for the amateur, although alluvial and superficial minerals are still sought in Latin America by small scale prospecting, referred to in Brazil by the term *garimpagem*. Many of the large scale modern mining activities in Latin America have been entirely or partly financed by capital from the leading industrial countries of the world. This has caused friction between foreign companies and the governments of host countries and has led to the nationalisation of some foreign enterprises, such as foreign oil in Mexico in 1938 and in Peru in 1969, and foreign copper in Chile by Allende in the early 1970s.

Latin American countries have been concerned that they should have some control over the exploitation of their own minerals. It is a matter of opinion as to whether the rapid development of minerals for export achieved with foreign capital would be offset by a more gradual rate of extraction which would give host countries a better chance of using some of their own minerals in the future, when they might hope to be more industrialised themselves. Little value is added to minerals that are extracted and shipped abroad in the form of ore or as concentrates. The countries that convert them into manufactured products derive much greater benefits than the source countries.

Modern mining enterprises in Latin America give direct employment to relatively few people. In the early 1970s Brazil, Venezuela and Peru each had only about 50,000 people engaged in all kinds of mining, including oil. The Latin American total was about 500,000. The establishment of mining centres for employees requires the provision of roads, housing and various services for a privileged minority directly employed in the industry. Many more people are often also attracted to the mining areas. There is the constant problem that eventually the minerals will be exhausted.

Table 5.10 shows the main producers of seven metals. Major mining areas will be indicated in later chapters under individual countries. Latin America is well represented in world production of bauxite, but recent expansion of bauxite production in Australia and in Guinea (West Africa) has reduced its share of total world production.

Since Latin America produces less than 2 per cent of the world's pig iron it is evident that most of the iron ore is exported, some after enrichment or pelletelisation. Aluminium smelting has begun in Brazil recently but the capacity of Latin American industry to use non-ferrous metals is very limited and apart from the silver, virtually all the metal mined in the region is exported after refining. Other minerals produced in Latin America included manganese ore in Brazil (about 12 per cent of the world total in Amapá territory), nickel ore in Cuba (about 5 per cent of the world total) and gold, found in many localities. Latin America does not currently produce many non-metallic minerals other than building materials, the Chilean nitrate industry having almost disappeared since its decline began early this century. Mexico, however, is now a leading producer of sulphur and other countries claim to have deposits of fertiliser minerals.

Table 5.10.

PRODUCTION OF METALS (YEARLY AVERAGE 1968–70)

Production in thousands of metric tons except silver (in tons)
Metal content in all minerals except bauxite (ore)

	Iron	Baux-ite	Cop-per	Lead	Zinc	Silver	Tin
Brazil	18,650	330		20		10	4
Mexico	2,210		60	170	250	1,340	1
Argentina	120			30	30	90	
Venezuela	12,140						
Colombia	460						
Peru	5,800		210	160	310	1,070	
Chile	7,180		670			100	
Dominican Rep.		1,040					
Haiti		620					
Jamaica		10,250					
Bolivia			10	20	30	190	30
Guyana		3,840					
Surinam		5,970					
LATIN AMERICA	46,550	21,000	960	410	630	2,790	35
Per cent of world production	12	40	16	13	12	31	18

Source: *UNSYB 71*, Tables 52, 54, 56, 58, 68, 64, 65

5.5. ENERGY

The generalisations made about the mining of metals in Latin America in the last section are broadly true also for the extraction of energy minerals. Increasingly, however, sources of energy have been absorbed internally, and most countries are net importers of energy supplies. Reserves of coal, oil and natural gas, given in Chapter 4, are relatively small in most countries. Even Venezuela, the largest exporter of oil in the world until the 1970s, is concerned increasingly with its own future needs and those of other Latin American countries, and the amount exported to the U.S.A. and West Europe may soon diminish. New finds in Ecuador (see *Figure 5.1*) have however brought that country into prominence as a prospective major exporter of oil. Production exceeded 9 million tons in 1973.

Economic development in Latin America at the level reached in the leading industrial regions of the world requires a much greater per capita consumption of non-animate sources of energy than that achieved at present. With a population growth of around 3 per cent per year this aim is difficult. In spite of population growth, per capita levels of energy consumption increased between 1959 and 1970 from 830 to 1,110 kilograms per inhabitant in the Caribbean area, including Mexico and Central America, and from 475 to 705 in the rest of South America. During the same period, however, the North American figures were 7,610 and 10,940, and the Japanese 970 and 3,210. If the trend of the 1960s were to continue for the next four decades, Latin America would reach roughly the 1970 West European level of energy consumption by 2010. There are various reasons why this prospect seems unlikely.

Figure 5.1. The new oilfields of Ecuador

Latin America has limited and generally poor quality coal reserves with high production costs. Unlike the U.S.A., U.S.S.R. and even the U.K., it cannot turn to or return to coal after oil and gas reserves run down. Its oil and gas reserves, even counting those of Venezuela, are small by world standards. The fact that Brazil is seeking sources of oil in the Middle East reflects thinking in industrial circles there. In other words, Latin American countries cannot base their energy programs far into the future on cheap home produced oil and natural gas. The hydro-electric potential is very considerable in some parts of Latin America, but large sites are mostly distant from existing areas of consumption, and the construction of dams, power stations and transmission lines is costly and slow. It seems unlikely that nuclear power could cater for more than a token fraction of the energy needs of the region for at least two or three decades, though nuclear power stations are in fact under construction near Veracruz in Mexico, near Rio in Brazil, and in Argentina.

So critical is energy to the economic development of Latin America that detailed tables have been included to show present production and consumption, and recent trends. Brief comments on the tables follow.

Table 5.11 shows average annual production of energy in 1968–70. The situation is dominated by oil and gas. Since 1·3 tons of coal are roughly equivalent to 1 ton of crude oil and to 1 thousand cubic metres of natural gas the small contribution of coal to the energy total is clear from the table. Hydro-electric power is the only other major source of energy in Latin America; thermal electricity is generated from other sources already taken into account.

Table 5.11.

COAL, OIL AND NATURAL GAS PRODUCTION

Coal and oil in thousands of metric tons, natural gas in millions of cubic metres

	1968-70 yearly average			1971 production		
	Coal	Oil	Gas	Coal	Oil	Gas
Brazil	2,390	8,150	1,170	2,498	8,395	1,177
Mexico	1,490	21,020	17,130	1,500	21,412	18,220
Argentina	540	18,500	5,560	632	21,578	6,499
Venezuela	30	190,340	8,240	40	185,776	9,365
Colombia	3,140	10,420	1,340	n.a.	11,127	n.a.
Peru	160	3,560	460	n.a.	3,053	n.a.
Chile	1,430	1,710	2,290	1,486	2,102	3,575
Cuba		150			n.a.	n.a.
Trinidad		8,270	1,600		6,671	1,582
Bolivia		1,630	90		1,713	n.a.
Ecuador		210	10		179	n.a.
LATIN AMERICA	9,180	263,960	37,900			

n.a. not available
Source: *UNSYB 71*, Tables 50, 70, 69
          UNSYB 72, Tables 52, 54, 55

About half of the electricity produced in Latin America comes from hydro-electric stations. This 'saves' the equivalent of about 40 million tons of oil in the sense that such a quantity would be needed to generate the electricity. At the official United Nations conversion rate, however, the hydro-electric production of Latin America is equivalent to less than 10 million tons of oil. The share of hydro-electric production in total electricity production varies greatly among the countries, from nearly 80 per cent in Brazil to only 10 per cent in Argentina.

In spite of the apparently small part played by electricity in the energy sector in Latin America, this form of energy is highly flexible in the way it can be distributed, though wasteful both in generation and in transmission. All the leading industrial countries of the world have invested huge amounts of capital in electricity, which has been regarded as a leading link in Soviet planning ever since the 1917 Revolution. Table 5.12 shows the position of the principal countries of Latin America with regard to electricity in 1970. A distinction must be drawn between installed capacity, measured in kilowatts (kW), and production, measured in kilowatt-hours (kWh). 500 kilowatt hours, for example, means that 1 kW of capacity has been producing electricity for 500 hours. It is worth noting that the bar of a conventional 1000 watt domestic electric fire consumes 1 kW hour per hour.

Table 5.12.

INSTALLED CAPACITY AND PRODUCTION OF ELECTRIC ENERGY BY COUNTRIES

1-3   Installed generating capacity in thousands of kilowatts
4   Hydro-electric capacity as a percentage of total capacity in 1970
5   Total output of electricity in millions of kWh and per capita consumption in kWh

	1 1954 Total	2 1970* Total	3 1970 Hydro	4 % Hydro	5 1970 Total	6 1970 Per cap.
Brazil	2,810	11,230	8,830	79	45,460	480
Mexico	1,850	7,410	3,330	45	28,608	600
Argentina	1,970	6,320	610	10	19,879	860
Venezuela	555	3,210	n.a.	n.a.	12,631	1,260
Colombia	480	2,100	1,164	55	8,750	420
Peru	391	1,672	934	56	5,324	380
Chile	878	2,140	1,067	50	7,550	760
Costa Rica	57	244	182	75	1,028	600
El Salvador	55	204	108	52	671	190
Guatemala	41	177	50	28	589	110
Honduras	14	92	35	38	310	120
Nicaragua	38	170	60	35	551	280
Panama	115	420	20	5	859	570
Cuba	530	1,400	953	68	4,266	510
Dominican Rep.	n.a.	273	203	74	855	200
Haiti	25	35	n.a.	n.a.	115	20
Jamaica	64	257	20	8	1,550	820
Puerto Rico	208	1,119	105	9	8,027	2,970
Trinidad	73	334	0	0	1,202	1,200
Bolivia	107	252	171	68	731	150
Ecuador	62	304	106	35	949	160
Guyana	31	114	n.a.	n.a.	323	400
Paraguay	47	110	n.a.	n.a.	220	90
Uruguay	237	470	225	48	2,180	750

* in some cases 1969
n.a. not available
Source: *UNSYB 1963*, Table 131, *UNSYB 1971*, Tables 138, 139

In Table 5.12 no distinction has been made between different types of consumer such as smelting, manufacturing, transport or domestic. The data reveal that the installed capacity of electric power stations in Latin America increased more than three times between 1954 and 1970. This is a reflection more of the lack of electricity before 1954 than of the arrival at a high level of capacity by 1970. In that year France had roughly the same capacity as the whole of Latin America, the U.S.S.R. about 4 times as much and the U.S.A. nearly 10 times as much.

The figures for per capita consumption of electricity in Latin America draw the countries apart even more than a general measure of development such as per capita gross domestic product does. The fact that the consumption of electricity per inhabitant is nearly 150 times as high in Puerto Rico as in nearby Haiti illustrates the development gap in Latin America. It cannot be explained by differences in the physical environment.

Table 5.13 is the most comprehensive and revealing set of data on the energy situation in Latin America. All sources of energy are taken into consideration, but hydro-electricity is undervalued in the conversion used. Some of the salient features of the table may be listed.

Table 5.13.

ENERGY PRODUCTION AND CONSUMPTION BY COUNTRIES

Prod. (production), Cons. (consumption), Bal. (balance)
in millions of metric tons of coal equivalent,
Cap. (per capita) in kilograms

	1960			1970			
	Prod.	Cons.	Bal.	Prod.	Cons.	Bal.	Cap.
Brazil	10·4	24·5	− 14	19·7	45·0	− 25	470
Mexico	32·6	31·9	+ 1	59·2	59·2	B	1,210
Argentina	14·0	22·3	− 8	34·9	39·2	− 4	1,690
Venezuela	201.0	19·3	+182	265·2	26·0	+239	2,500
Colombia	13·6	7·3	+ 6	20·7	12·2	+ 9	580
Peru	3·9	3·8	B	5·4	8·3	− 3	610
Chile	4·0	6·4	− 2	7·7	11·8	− 4	1,210
Costa Rica	0·1	0·3	−	0·1	0·6	− 1	340
El Salvador	0·0	0·3	−	0·1	0·3	−	80
Guatemala	0·0	0·6	−	0·0	1·2	− 1	230
Honduras	0·0	0·3	−	0·0	0·6	− 1	240
Nicaragua	0·0	0·3	−	0·0	0·7	− 1	370
Panama	0·0	0·5	−	0·0	2·4	− 2	1,630
Barbados	0·0	0·1	−	0·0	0·2	−	950
Cuba	0·0	5·8	− 6	0·1	8·7	− 9	1,040
Dominican Republic	0·0	0·5	−	0·0	1·0	− 1	220
Guadeloupe	0·0	0·1	−	0·0	0·2	−	450
Haiti	0·0	0·2	−	0·0	0·2	−	40
Jamaica	0·0	0·8	− 1	0·0	2·3	− 2	1,140
Martinique	0·0	0·1	−	0·0	0·2	−	540
Netherlands Antilles	0·0	3·1	− 3	0·0	4·1	− 4	**
Puerto Rico	0·0	3·4	− 3	0·0	9·3	− 9	3,280
Trinidad	8·8	1·6	+ 7	11·5	5·0	+ 6	4,680
Bolivia	0·7	0·5	−	1·7	1·0	+ 1	210
Ecuador	0·5	0·8	− 1	0·3	1·8	− 2	290
Guyana	0·0	0·3	−	0·0	0·8	− 1	1,010
Paraguay	0·0	0·2	−	0·0	0·4	−	150
Surinam	0·0	0·2	−	0·1	0·9	− 1	2,200
Uruguay	0·1	2·2	− 2	0·2	2·6	− 2	900
TOTAL	290	138	+152	427	249	+178	900*

Source: *UNSYB 1963*, Table 129. *UNSYB 1971*, Table 137
* approximate
** unrealistically large value
+ surplus − deficit B balance

1. Venezuela with a mere 4 per cent of the population of Latin America accounted for nearly 70 per cent of all the energy produced in Latin America in 1960 and for 62 per cent in 1970.
2. Out of the 29 countries listed in Table 5.13 only four had a substantial surplus of energy in 1970. Brazil produced less than half of its total energy needs and Cuba only a tiny fraction. 19 out of 29 countries produce virtually no energy at all.
3. Although Trinidad and Colombia export oil, only Venezuela comes among the top oil exporting countries of the world.
4. The energy gap among Latin American countries, like the electricity gap,

is very marked indeed. A considerable proportion of the total energy used is actually consumed in oil-refining in certain small countries, particularly the Netherlands Antilles, Trinidad and Venezuela itself This fact contributes to their high apparent per capita levels.

5. In all the producing countries the production of energy rose between 1960 and 1970 and even in the non-producing countries, per capita consumption (not shown for 1960), also rose.

Table 5.14 puts energy consumption in a longer time perspective. It shows that per capita energy consumption was higher in 1970 than in 1960 in every country in Latin America.

Table 5.14.
PER CAPITA ENERGY CONSUMPTION 1937–71

	1937	1950	1955	1960	1965	1970	1971
Brazil	130	220	360	370	350	470	500
Mexico	440	600	710	1,010	980	1,210	1,270
Argentina	650	760	890	1,070	1,340	1,690	1,770
Venezuela	300	770	2,030	2,560	2,970	2,500	2,520
Colombia	140	270	470	510	530	580	640
Peru	130	190	300	360	590	610	620
Chile	670	760	990	880	1,090	1,210	1,520
Costa Rica	170	240	330	190	310	340	450
El Salvador	40	90	170	120	170	180	220
Gua.emala	60	160	150	150	180	230	250
Honduras	150	170	170	150	150	240	230
Nicaragua	60	90	120	180	230	370	390
Panama	n.a.	300	360	510	1,120	1,630	2,120
Cuba	340	480	640	860	950	1,040	1,150
Dominican Rep.	40	90	170	160	190	220	260
Haiti	10	20	40	40	30	40	30
Jamaica	80	120	180	530	890	1,140	1,340
Martinique	90	120	250	290	370	540	660
Puerto Rico	190	480	750	1,460	2,130	3,280	3,770
Trinidad	380	1,450	1,870	2,300	3,480	4,680	3,960
Bolivia	40	90	170	140	190	210	220
Ecuador	40	120	140	180	210	290	320
Guyana	90	320	510	510	810	1,010	1,000
Paraguay	10	20	40	90	130	150	140
Surinam	160	420	620	570	1,130	2,200	2,230
Uruguay	400	640	800	750	920	900	960

Sources: *UNSYB* 52, 57, 61, 66, 71, 72
n.a. not available

5.6. INDUSTRY

This section reviews various aspects of industry in Latin America. Several distinctions may be made within this general heading:

1. Small scale, domestic industry is still widely found, especially in rural areas, but for at least a hundred years now factories with modern machinery and equipment have been established in parts of Latin America. Some of the

earliest modern factories made textiles as for example at Puebla and Orizaba in Mexico, Medellín in Colombia, and Juiz de Fora in Brazil. Some of the early mills have now closed down.

2. Processing and manufacturing are also distinct though a clearcut line cannot be drawn between them. The processing of agricultural products, such as sugar processing and wine making, or of minerals, such as copper smelting, often take place in areas of production. Increasingly, however, oil is refined at or near markets rather than on oilfields.

3. A distinction is often made between heavy industry and light industry. At least three features are considered when these two categories are referred to. Firstly 'heavy' implies the actual weight of materials and/or products involved, secondly it may refer to the amount of capital (productive equipment) in relation to wages (labour) and raw materials, and thirdly, it may mean the difference between producer goods and capital goods. In the second sense, light industry has developed in Latin America before heavy industry, and is more widespread. In the third sense, modern industry was first introduced into Latin America for the purpose of 'import substitution', that is to save the need to import consumer goods such as textiles and furniture that could be made nationally. This industrialisation policy needed protection and tended to allow inefficient plants to continue in operation and to cause high prices. More recently the larger countries have become more aware of the desirability of having heavy industry. Iron and steel, cement and some chemicals have been manufactured in Latin America for several decades. Many branches of heavy industry date from the 1940s. The introduction of engineering through the assembly of motor vehicles, the manufacture of rolling stock and small ships, and even of factory equipment, means that several countries in Latin America are beginning to become independent also in this sector. With foreign equipment and often capital and technical help, more sophisticated products such as electrical and electronic manufactures and light aircraft are also being made.

Table 5.15 shows the presence or absence of 19 branches of industry in 23 Latin American countries in 1970. The absence of an industry in the table does not preclude domestic industries and it is possible that some factory industries have been missed. The table gives no indication of capacity or quantity produced. In many cases this is small. The range of branches represented is however much wider in the seven largest countries than in any others. Cuba, eighth in size, with a centrally planned economy, and cut off from the rest of the Americas, might be expected to have more branches than it does. The list of 19 branches is not exhaustive and other selected branches are given below the table. Equivalent tables for 1960, 1950 and earlier dates would show progressively fewer branches of industry. In 1950, for example, the assembly of motor vehicles did not take place in Latin America.

The cement industry has been chosen to illustrate the way in which a particular branch of industry has spread in Latin America. In 1970 cement was manufactured in all 23 countries in Table 5.15. Cement is both heavy in relation to its value and relatively difficult to handle and store. Cement can be made with fairly simple machinery in a small factory, though economies of scale do occur with an increase in size. Limestone is a raw material that is widely available. Cement is essential in modern construction (bridges, dams, multi-storey buildings) and would have to be imported if it was not made nationally. Table 5.16 shows that in 1930 some cement was already being manufactured in at least

CONTRASTS IN PRODUCTIVITY

ABOVE:
WEEDING MAIZE WITH OXEN,
SOUTHERN MEXICO

RIGHT:
SLOW TURNOVER IN A SMALL
MARKET, SOUTHERN MEXICO

PART OF ACESITA, FERRO-ALLOY PLANT AND TOWN,
MINAS GERAIS, BRAZIL

PEUGEOT MOTOR VEHICLE
PLANT, BUENOS AIRES,
ARGENTINA

ABOVE:
SMALL OVERSTAFFED
METAL WORKSHOP,
LA PAZ, BOLIVIA

LEFT:
REMOVAL OF
OVERBURDEN IN
1957, TOCQUEPALA
COPPER DEPOSITS,
SOUTHERN PERU

BELOW:
GIANT MEAT
REFRIGERATION
PLANT, BUENOS
AIRES, ARGENTINA

Table 5.15.

REPRESENTATION OF BRANCHES OF PROCESSING AND MANUFACTURING

	Cement	Tobacco[1]	Beer	Oil Ref.	Cotton Cloth	Nitr. Ferts.	Cotton Yarn	Sulph. Acid	Tyres	Artif. Fibres[2]	Caustic Soda	Synth. Fibres[3]	Paper	Pig Iron	Motor Vehs.[4]	Coke	Radios	Wool Fabrics	Plastics	Total
Brazil	1	1	1	1	1	1	1	1	1	1	1	1	1	1	1	1	1	1	1	19
Mexico	1	1	1	1	1	1	1	1	1	1	1	1	1	1	1	1	1	0	1	18
Argentina	1	1	1	1	1	1	1	1	1	1	1	1	1	1	1	1	1	0	1	18
Venezuela	1	1	1	1	1	1	1	1	1	1	1	1	1	1	1	0	0	1	1	17
Colombia	1	1	1	1	1	1	1	1	1	1	1	1	1	1	1	1	1	1	1	19
Peru	1	1	1	1	1	1	1	1	1	1	1	1	1	1	1	1	1	1	0	18
Chile	1	1	1	1	1	1	1	1	1	1	1	1	1	1	1	1	0	1	0	17
Costa Rica	1	1	1	1	0	1	0	0	0	0	0	0	0	0	0	0	0	0	0	5
El Salvador	1	1	1	1	1	1	1	0	0	0	0	0	0	0	0	0	0	0	0	7
Guatemala	1	1	1	1	0	0	0	0	0	0	0	0	0	0	0	0	0	0	0	4
Honduras	1	1	1	1	1	0	0	0	0	0	0	0	0	0	0	0	0	0	0	5
Nicaragua	1	1	1	1	1	1	0	0	0	0	0	0	0	0	0	0	0	0	0	6
Panama	1	1	1	1	0	0	0	0	0	0	0	0	0	0	0	0	0	0	0	4
Cuba	1	1	1	1	1	1	0	1	1	1	1	0	1	0	0	0	1	0	0	12
Dominican Rep.	1	1	1	0	1	0	0	0	0	0	0	0	0	0	0	0	0	0	0	4
Haiti	1	1	0	0	1	0	0	0	0	0	0	0	0	0	0	0	0	0	0	3
Jamaica	1	1	1	1	1	0	0	1	0	0	0	0	0	0	0	0	0	0	0	6
Puerto Rico	1	0	1	1	0	0	0	0	0	0	0	0	0	0	0	0	0	0	0	3
Trinidad	1	1	1	1	0	1	0	0	0	0	0	0	0	0	0	0	0	0	0	5
Bolivia	1	1	1	1	1	0	1	0	0	0	0	0	0	0	0	0	0	1	0	7
Ecuador	1	1	1	1	1	1	1	0	1	0	0	0	0	0	0	0	0	0	0	8
Paraguay	1	1	1	1	1	0	1	0	0	0	0	0	0	0	0	0	0	0	0	6
Uruguay	1	1	1	1	0	0	0	1	1	1	0	1	0	0	0	0	0	0	0	8
TOTAL	23	22	22	21	17	13	11	10	9	9	8	8	8	7	7	6	6	6	5	

Wood pulp: Brazil, Mexico, Argentina, Chile
Aluminium: Brazil, Mexico, Venezuela
Wool yarn: Colombia, Peru
Motor vehicles: Brazil, Argentina
Merchant vessels: Brazil
Source: *UNSYB 71* various tables from 88 to 122

Notes 1 Tobacco, cigarettes or cigars
      2 Rayon and acetate continuous fibres
      3 Non-cellulosic continuous filaments
      4 Assembly of motor vehicles

nine Latin American countries. Since 1930 the number of countries making cement and the amounts produced have both increased. The number of cement works within countries has also increased. In Brazil, for example, most states now produce some cement. *Figure 5.2* shows graphically the growth of cement production in selected countries.

Like cement manufacturing, oil refining is widely distributed in Latin America. Since oil accounts for over 80 per cent of the energy consumed in the region, it represents the energy base of Latin America. In many of the smaller countries it has been economically feasible and politically desirable to have a national oil refinery to satisfy home needs. Several Caribbean islands refine Venezuelan oil for export elsewhere.

Table 5.16.

THE GROWTH OF CEMENT PRODUCTION IN SELECTED COUNTRIES, 1930–1970, IN HUNDREDS OF THOUSANDS OF TONS PER YEAR

	1930	1935	1940	1945	1950	1955	1960	1965	1970
Brazil	1	4	7	8	14	27	45	55	90
Mexico	2	3	5	7	15	21	31	43	73
Argentina	4	7	11	11	16	18	26	33	47
Venezuela	—	—	1	1	5	13	15	21	22
Colombia	—	1	2	3	6	10	14	21	28
Peru	—	1	1	3	3	5	6	10	11
Chile	2	3	4	4	5	8	8	12	13
El Salvador					—	1	1	1	2
Guatemala					—	1	1	2	3
Cuba			—	2	3	4	8	8	8
Dominican Rep.					1	2	2	2	5
Haiti					—	—	—	—	1
Puerto Rico			1	2	5	7	9	12	16
Bolivia			—	—	—	—	—	1	1
Ecuador	—	—	—	—	1	1	2	3	5
Uruguay	—	1	1	2	3	3	4	4	5

—under 50,000 tons

Source: Various *UNSYB*
1948 Table 100, 1956 Table 107,
1966 Table 125, 1970 Table 119

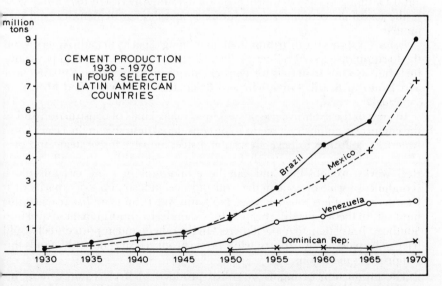

Figure 5.2. Cement production 1930–1970 in Brazil, Mexico, Venezuela and the Dominican Republic

Table 5.17 shows the oil refining capacity of 26 countries in 1971 in hundreds of thousands of tons per year. Venezuela has nearly a quarter of the oil refining capacity of Latin America but only enough to process about one third of its own production of crude oil. The Netherlands Antilles (Aruba and Curacao) has two of the largest oil refineries in Latin America, both receiving Venezuelan oil.

Table 5.17.

OIL REFINING CAPACITY IN HUNDREDS OF THOUSANDS OF TONS PER YEAR

	1950	1960	1970		1950	1960	1970
Brazil	3	101	267	Antigua			8
Mexico	89	168	265	Bahamas			125
Argentina	76	138	316	Barbados			2
Venezuela	142	492	647	Cuba			47
Colombia	12	36	63	Jamaica			13
Peru	18	24	49	Netherlands Antilles	331	368	410
Chile		23	55	Puerto Rico		45	76
Costa Rica			4	Trinidad	51	144	218
El Salvador			7	Virgin Islands			223
Guatemala			12	Bolivia	4	6	12
Honduras			5	Ecuador	3	8	19
Nicaragua			10	Paraguay			5
Panama			35	Uruguay	8	20	20

Source: The Institute of Petroleum, Information Service:
Oil, world statistics, July 1972

Very recently large oil refineries have been opened in the Virgin Islands (U.S.) and the Bahamas, now independent. Oil refining in Brazil has grown from almost nothing in 1950 to fourth position in Latin America in 1971 but in view of the size of the country and the future economic growth plans it is still very limited.

Figure 5.3 shows the distribution of oil refining capacity in Latin America and the location of selected refineries. Several refineries provide not only various fuels but also raw materials for petrochemicals industries, as at Cubatão near São Paulo in Brazil, Minatitlán and Salamanca in Mexico, and Morón in Venezuela.

In view of the extensive use of steel in so many kinds of construction and in the engineering industry it seems to be considered desirable in the larger Latin American countries to have an iron and steel industry for strategic and psychological reasons if not strictly for economic ones. Although small iron and steel works are possible and can be economical in some circumstances, economies of scale operate in the iron and steel industry up to a capacity of at least several million tons per year. No Latin American plant has reached this limit yet. In theory it is still cheaper, for example, to import Japanese steel into Southeast Brazil than to make it there. On the other hand imported steel would have to be paid for by exports, while home produced steel not only avoids this but provides many jobs.

The production of ingots or rolled products of steel requires many ingredients including iron ore, scrap steel, ferro-alloys, coke, electricity, limestone and water. A steel mill can be equipped to make only steel, using pig iron from elsewhere and scrap. A large modern integrated steel mill, such as the one at Volta Redonda in Southeast Brazil, has all the processes.

Mexico was the first country to produce steel in Latin America in its works at Monterrey, established in 1897, though iron had been made in the 18th century in Minas Gerais, Brazil, from local ores and charcoal. In the inter-war period there were several small works in Latin America but even in 1948, only Brazil

1 Salamanca
2 Mexico City
3 Minatitlán

4 Cartagena
5 Barranca-
   bermeja

MEXICO

Matamoros
Ciudad Madero
Poza Rica

HONDURAS
GUATEMALA
EL SALVADOR
NICARAGUA
COSTA RICA
PANAMA

CUBA
JAMAICA
NETHERLANDS
ANTILLES

PUERTO RICO
VIRGIN ISLANDS
ANTIGUA
BARBADOS
TRINIDAD

(see inset map)
VENEZUELA

COLOMBIA

ECUADOR
Talara

PERU

BOLIVIA

PARAGUAY
Campo Durán

CHILE
Concon

ARGENTINA
Luján

BRAZIL

Mataripe

Capuava
Duque de Caxias
Cubatão

Rio Grande
URUGUAY

AVERAGE ANNUAL
OIL REFINING
CAPACITY 1971
IN TONS

64 million

16 million

4 million
under 1·5 million

Selected refineries with
capacity over about
1·5 million tons

6 Campana
7 Avellaneda
8 La Plata

REFINERIES IN VENEZUELA (inset)

Amuay
Aruba
Curacao
Cardón
Bajo Grande
Puerto Cabello
San Lorenzo
CARACAS
Puerto la Cruz
Caripito

0   km   150

Figure 5.3. Average annual oil refining capacity in Latin America in 1971

FISHING BOATS, FORTALEZA, N.E. BRAZIL

PRIMITIVE TRANSPORT, BAHIA, BRAZIL

was producing much pig iron (550,000 tons). In 1970, Latin America produced about 2 per cent of the world's pig iron and steel; the output came exclusively from the seven countries in Table 5.18. All are able to use their own iron ore, though Brazil, Venezuela, Peru and Chile export more ore than they themselves consume, while Argentina produces only part of its needs. None is well provided with coking coal and Venezuela imports all its needs.

Table 5.18.

CEMENT, PIG IRON AND STEEL PRODUCTION (ANNUAL AVERAGE DURING 1968–70)

	Production in thousands of tons			Production in kg per inhabitant		
	Cement	*Pig Iron*	*Steel*	*Cement*	*Pig Iron*	*Steel*
Brazil	8,040	4,200	5,370	84	44	56
Mexico	6,730	2,350	3,850	137	48	78
Argentina	4,430	820	1,820	191	35	78
Venezuela	2,290	520	930	220	50	89
Colombia	2,510	240	240	119	12	12
Peru	1,130	180	90	83	13	7
Chile	1,350	450	550	138	46	56

Source: *UNSYB 71*

In spite of the lack of certain ingredients for the industry and the drawbacks of small scale and of organisational difficulties, Brazil and Mexico have very ambitious plans for the expansion of their industries. It seems unlikely that the smaller countries, as yet unrepresented, will begin to produce steel. The per capita values for Peru and Colombia in Table 5.18 underline the very small scale and precarious position of the industry even in these two larger countries. According to a study of the situation in Latin America, if the plans in various countries all materialise, the production of steel in the region should rise from 13 million tons in 1970 to 28 million in 1975 and 43 million in 1980.[4] Table 5.18 shows the position of the 7 major countries in 1968–70.

References

1. *FAOPY 1971*, Table 6
2. *UNSYB 1971*, Table 181
3. *The State of Food and Agriculture 1963*, Rome 1963.
4. *Peruvian Times*, Nov. 26, 1971, p. 16.

Sources of material in the figures

5.1. *Peruvian Times*, July 30, 1971, p. 10.
5.2. *UNSYB*, various years.
5.3. The Institute of Petroleum, *Oil, Latin America and the Caribbean* (undated) 1969 preliminary figures.

Further reading

Marshall, C. F. 'Coffee, What Future for Cooperation?' *Bolsa Review,* Feb. 1973, Vol. 7, No. 74, pp. 40–46.
Morse, D. A., 'Unemployment, Bitter Burden of Millions in South America', *Focus,* Feb. 1973, Vol. XXIII, No. 6
Shaw, R. d'A., 'A Rural Employment Strategy for South America', *Focus,* Mar. 1973, Vol. XXIII, No. 7.

CHAPTER 6

POPULATION

6.1. INTRODUCTION

The purpose of this chapter is to describe the main features of the population of Latin America around 1970 and to give some views on the reasons for its present distribution and on possible future trends. It has been calculated from sample surveys that even the 1970 census of the United States understated the true population of that country by about 2 per cent.[1] It seems unlikely that any Latin American census is as accurate as the U.S. census. Moreover, it seems likely that the earlier the census the greater the degree of undercounting. The 'official' data used in this chapter, even if census based, could therefore considerably *understate* the present population of Latin America, given that census enumerators are more likely to miss existing people than to invent non-existent ones. A further problem in the study of population in Latin America is that not all countries have censuses at regular intervals and several did not hold one in 1970 (see Table 6.1). Some figures are therefore estimates based on earlier censuses.

The United Nations midyear estimate of the population of Latin America in 1970 was 283 million. Corresponding 1950 and 1960 figures were 162 million and 213 million. The rate of growth during the two decades, 31 per cent and 33 per cent respectively, was similar, but the absolute gain was noticeably greater in the second decade, 70 million during 1960–70 compared with 50 million during 1950–60. Almost all of the increase, in absolute terms, has occurred in the last few decades in the areas of Latin America already having the highest densities of population.

If the population of Latin America were to continue growing at the rate experienced between 1950 and 1970 it could be expected to double in about 27 years and to be some 620 million in the year 2000. This would be about 10 per cent of the total population of the world then; in 1900 Latin America had about 5 per cent.

Table 6.1 shows selected basic data for the main countries of Latin America. There follows a brief note on each column.

Column 1 (the latest census year). Only about half the countries in Latin America had a census in 1970, but several did in 1971 or 1972.

Column 2 (1970 population in thousands). There are great differences in population size among the countries of Latin America. In fact about 20 more units not included in the table are smaller still. Brazil has about 34 per cent of the total population, Mexico about 17 per cent. The seven largest together have nearly 80 per cent. When Latin America is being considered as a whole it is important to keep in mind the weight of the larger countries.

Column 3 The average annual rate of change of population during 1963–70 is measured in per thousands. Thus for example the population of Mexico grew each year by 30 additional inhabitants for every 1000 already there. This amount is calculated from the number of births minus the number of deaths plus the number of people entering the country minus the number leaving.

Table 6.1.
BASIC DEMOGRAPHIC DATA FOR LATIN AMERICA
See text for definition of each column.
See Table 1·1 (page 6) for area and density of population.

	1 Year	2 Popn	3 Change	4 Brate	5 U15	6 Urbn	7 Lurb	8 Infm
Brazil	70	94,510	32	38	43	46	19	80
Mexico	70	48,380	30	41	46	60	23	67
Argentina	70	23,210	15	21	29	74	48	59
Venezuela	71	10,400	36	41	46	76	39	46
Colombia	64	21,120	32	45	47	53	29	70
Peru	72	13,590	31	42	45	52	26	62
Chile	70	9,780	24	27	40	74	37	93
British Honduras	70	130	35	40	n.a.	54	—	52
Costa Rica	63	1,740	32	45	48	35	23	71
El Salvador	71	3,530	38	40	45	38	18	67
Guatemala	64	5,190	31	44	46	34	14	92
Honduras	61	2,580	34	49	51	32	13	34
Nicaragua	63	1,980	37	46	48	44	16	55
Panama	70	1,460	33	41	43	48	29	38
Barbados	70	260	11	21	38	n.a.	—	42
Cuba	70	8,390	21	27	37	53	22	40
Dominican Republic	70	4,330	36	49	47	40	18	62
Guadeloupe	67	330	14	28	42	32	—	45
Haiti	71	4,870	20	44	42	12	7	150
Jamaica	70	1,870	16	33	41	37	24	32
Martinique	67	340	20	27	42	42	—	35
Netherlands Antilles	60	220	14	23	n.a.	n.a.	—	20
Puerto Rico	70	2,720	10	26	39	44	23	28
Trinidad	70	950	3	20	43	18	15	37
Bolivia	50	4,930	26	44	44	34	17	77
Ecuador	62	6,090	34	45	48	38	21	86
Guyana	70	760	30	36	46	30	27	38
Paraguay	62	2,390	32	45	45	36	18	36
Surinam	64	390	31	42	46	34	69	30
Uruguay	63	2,890	12	21	28	81	45	54
OTHER		950						
TOTAL				38	43	45		61

n.a. not available
—has no town with over 100,000 inhabitants
Main sources: UNSYB 71 and UNDYB 71

During the period 1963–70, permanent international migration into or out of the larger countries of Latin America was relatively very small. The values in column 3 therefore largely reflect differences between birthrate and deathrate within countries. The relatively slow rate of increase in Argentina, Uruguay and several of the islands contrasts with some of the highest rates in the world to be found particularly in Central America and certain South American countries. The intermediate positions of Chile and Cuba may be noted.

Column 4 (birthrates in per thousands). Birthrates differ widely among Latin American countries. They reflect the present widespread tendency to have large families.

Column 5 shows the high proportion of children under 15 years of age to total population, which contrasts with European figures of between 20 and 30 per cent. This figure is not only an indication of a high birthrate but also the result of an increasing population over a previous period of some decades. If most children in Latin America now under 15 live until the age of 70, a hope that they may be expected to have, then we already know approximately the number of people between 55 and 70 *as far ahead* as the year 2025, as well as the number of school and hospital places, jobs and retirement benefits, if any, to be provided for that age group until then.

Columns 6, 7 (percentage of total population defined as urban and percentage of total population living in towns with over 100,000 inhabitants). The definition of urban varies considerably from country to country. Usually it is based on a minimum settlement size, on status, or function, or on a combination of these criteria. In spite of the inconsistencies in definition the urbanisation indices in column 6 are sufficient to indicate the enormous differences that can be observed in Latin America between the extremes of about 10 per cent in Haiti and about 75 per cent in southern South America and Venezuela. Column 7 is more selective in definition, showing the proportion of total population living in towns with over 100,000 inhabitants. Urbanisation reflects changing employment structure, itself a result to a large extent of the application of modern technology. Existing urban centres themselves attract more people and more jobs in services and industries.

Column 8 (deaths of children under 1 year of age per thousand births). The level of infant mortality varies greatly among the countries of Latin America. It reflects fairly closely the availability of medical services. Should these be improved in the less well served areas, infant mortality in particular and mortality in general should diminish, thus widening the gap between birthrate and deathrate and producing a faster rate of growth of population in poor areas such as Haiti, Northeast Brazil and South Mexico.

6.2. PRESENT DISTRIBUTION AND DENSITY OF POPULATION

Figure 6.1 shows the broad features of the spatial distribution of population in Latin America. The seven largest countries in population and three others (Ecuador, Bolivia and Paraguay) are broken down into major civil divisions but the remaining countries are treated as single units. 1970 census data or estimates are used. Four density classes have been mapped. The unshaded and dotted areas have densities below the mean for Latin America of approximately 13·5 inhabitants per square kilometre. It must be appreciated that even within the units used, great differences in density occur. For example in São Paulo state, Brazil, about half of the population is in Greater São Paulo.

Amazonia stands out as being only very sparsely populated, while Patagonia and northern Mexico are also large areas below average. Equally striking is the occurrence of distinct clusters of population, several of which form the main concentration of individual countries. In this respect Latin America is similar to Africa but contrasts with North America, characterised by its one outstanding cluster of population in Northeast U.S.A.

It is possible to supplement the visual and verbal descriptions of the distribution of population in Latin America by numerical indices. It turns out, for example, that the 25 per cent of the population in the most densely populated units live on only about 2·5 per cent of the total area. In contrast, the least densely populated 50 per cent of the area of Latin America contains only about 5 per cent of the population. A study of past data in Latin America suggests that while the absolute number of people has grown greatly since censuses began to be held frequently, the degree of concentration has not changed appreciably. The principal reason seems to be that the continuing dispersal of some people into new areas of settlement has been offset by the attraction of urban concentrations.

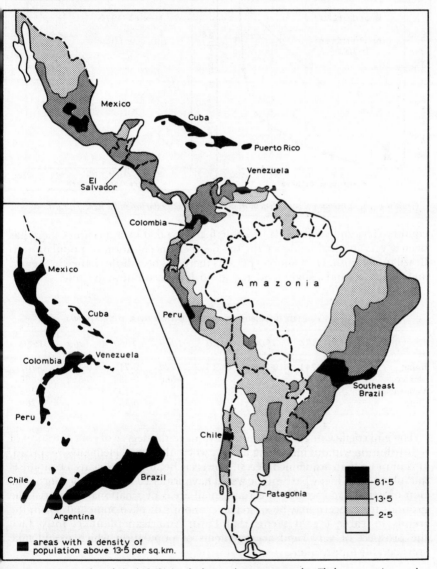

Figure 6.1. Density of population in Latin America in 1970 in persons per sq. km. The larger countries are sub-divided on the basis of their major civil divisions

In a brief study of the distribution of population in four Latin American countries the use of the Lorenz curve and the gini coefficient showed remarkably stable distributions. If a set of elements has a distribution with a gini coefficient of o it is evenly spread.* If all elements are concentrated in one locality the coefficient is near 1. *Figure 6.2* shows the 1970 Lorenz curve distribution for Brazil and for Mexico based on data for the major civil divisions of each

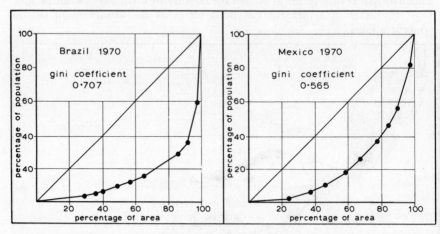

Figure 6.2. The distribution of population in Brazil and in Mexico expressed in the form of a Lorenz curve

country. The gini coefficients in Table 6.2 show that over a century there has been a very gradual tendency for the degree concentration of population in Brazil to diminish. Over shorter periods there has been little change in Mexico and Venezuela and a slight tendency towards concentration in Chile.

Table 6.2.

GINI COEFFICIENTS FOR THE DISTRIBUTION OF POPULATION OVER THE NATIONAL AREA

	1872	1900	1920	1940	1950	1960	1970
Brazil	0·741	0·725	0·715	0·722	0·719	0·711	0·707
Mexico				0·560	0·554	0·552	0·565
Venezuela					0·757		0·758
Chile					0·755		0·769

The gini coefficient gives a numerical value to the degree of concentration of a distribution without indicating how or where the actual elements are spread. It is of more than academic interest, however, because politicians, economists and planners in many parts of the world have criticised the growing concentration of people and wealth in certain small areas of a national territory. The grounds for concern may be strategic, economic or environmental. From the trends in Table 6.2, it seems that Latin American planners must face the prospect of very rigid arrangements of population which would take considerable time to alter.

* See Appendix 1 for a simple example.

The Lorenz curve reflects the relative density of different areas. It stays unchanged over time if growth rates are uniform in all areas. If densities vary greatly, then absolute increases also vary greatly among different areas. The following example illustrates this point. Two sets of major civil divisions in Latin America were considered, those having the highest density of population in 1960 and containing in that year some 25 per cent of the total population of Latin America on 2·5 per cent of the total area, and those having the lowest density of population in 1960 and containing in that year about 5 per cent of the population on 50 per cent of the area. During 1935–60 the total population of Latin America increased from 118 million to 210 million, or by 78 per cent. During the same period population in the first group of major civil divisions rose from 30 million to 54 million or by about 80 per cent, while that in the second group rose from 6.8 million to 10.2 million or by 50 per cent. Thus 24 million more people appeared on a mere 2·5 per cent of the total area while only about 3½ million more appeared on half of the total area.

6.3. URBANISATION

Even in pre-Columbian times parts of Latin America supported big urban populations. For reasons of organisation, Spain and to a lesser extent Portugal both encouraged the establishment and growth of urban centres in their colonies. Parts of Latin America were already very highly urbanised by 1900. Even so, the absolute number of people living in towns in Latin America is many times greater now than it was in 1900. Urban growth is therefore a major feature of the demographic situation in Latin America, since urban populations not only reproduce themselves but are continually supplemented by arrivals from rural areas.

Figure 6.3 (main map) shows the location of the 168 towns in Latin America with over about 100,000 inhabitants in 1970. Where two towns occur close together they have been joined. Large agglomerations are taken where possible as single units even when, as in Mexico City and Rio, their official administrative populations are more restricted. Table 6.3 contains the names and populations of the 50 largest towns in Latin America in 1970; the remainder are listed in Appendix 2. The towns are mapped and discussed in greater detail under individual countries in later chapters.

Table 6.3 shows that all but 14 of the 50 towns had rates of increase of population faster than the Latin American average (33 per cent or 133 when 1960 population = 100). Most of the ones with a slower rate of growth than this grew more quickly than the total population of their own country.

The towns of Latin America are characterised by the presence of a few very large agglomerations dominated by capital cities. The ten largest together contain about 42 million inhabitants, ⅐ of the total population of Latin America, but have a considerably bigger share of manufacturing, services, purchasing power and wealth in general. They include the capitals of seven of the eight largest countries (Rio de Janeiro was replaced as capital by Brasilia in 1960). The 50 largest towns contain nearly 67 million inhabitants, nearly ¼ of the population of Latin America.

There is nothing special about a size of 100,000 inhabitants but it serves as a convenient point in the list at which to cut off population living in 'larger'

Figure 6.3. The largest towns of Latin America in 1970

urban centres. The proportion of total population (not just total urban population) living in such centres is given by countries where relevant in Table 6.1, column 7. Apart from Surinam, Argentina and Uruguay show the greatest degree of concentration of population in such large centres.

6.4. DISTANCES IN LATIN AMERICA

The creation of the Latin American Free Trade Association in 1961 established in principle the need for greater contact and trade between the countries of Latin America. Although changes in this direction had been small by the 1970s

Table 6.3.

THE POPULATION IN THOUSANDS OF THE FIFTY LARGEST TOWNS IN LATIN AMERICA IN 1970

			1970	1960	Change (1960 = 100)				1970	1960	Change (1960 = 100)
1	MEX	Mexico City	8,363	4,871	172	26	BRZ	Belém	573	381	150
2	ARG	Buenos Aires	8,352	6,763	124	27	BRZ	Fortaleza	530	471	113
3	BRZ	São Paulo	6,738	3,872	174	28	SAM	La Paz	525	340	154
4	BRZ	Rio de Janeiro	5,622	4,370	129	29	ISL	Kingston	500	380	132
5	PER	Lima	2,738	1,978	138	30	ARG	Mendoza	500	380	132
6	CHI	Santiago	2,587	1,989	130	31	BRZ	Curitiba	498	351	142
7	COL	Bogotá	2,294	1,329	172	32	SAM	Quito	496	362	113
8	VEN	Caracas	2,184	1,265	172	33	BRZ	Santos	462	359	128
9	ISL	Havana	1,566	1,220	128	34	ISL	San Juan	455	280	163
10	MEX	Guadalajara	1,456	737	197	35	SAM	Asunción	440	310	142
11	BRZ	Recife	1,360	974	139	36	CHI	Valparaíso	436	368	118
12	SAM	Montevideo	1,260	1,173	108	37	CAM	Panama City	418	273	153
13	MEX	Monterrey	1,213	597	203	38	MEX	Puebla	413	289	143
14	COL	Medellín	1,196	691	173	39	MEX	Ciudad Juárez	407	262	155
15	BRZ	Belo Horizonte	1,126	684	166	40	ARG	La Plata	406	330	123
16	BRZ	Pôrto Alegre	1,037	722	144	41	BRZ	Goiânia	371	133	279
17	BRZ	Salvador	1,018	639	159	42	VEN	Valencia	366	161	227
18	ARG	Córdoba	846	590	143	43	MEX	León	365	210	174
19	COL	Cali	821	693	118	44	CAM	San Salvador	349	253	138
20	COL	Barranquilla	817	474	172	45	CHI	Concepción	340	232	147
21	ARG	Rosario	751	670	112	46	ISL	Port-au-Prince	340	250	136
22	SAM	Guayaquil	739	515	143	47	VEN	Barquisimeto	334	197	170
23	CAM	Guatemala City	731	407	180	48	BRZ	Campinas	334	185	181
24	ISL	Santo Domingo	655	370	177	49	MEX	Tijuana	327	152	215
25	VEN	Maracaibo	650	433	150	50	COL	Cartagena	299	185	162

ARG—Argentina
BRZ—Brazil
CAM—Central America
CHI—Chile
COL—Colombia
ISL—Islands
MEX—Mexico
PER—Peru
SAM—Smaller South America
VEN—Venezuela

it is relevant to look at the distribution of population in Latin America in terms of future integration. To this end a brief exercise has been carried out to illustrate how the problem of comparing distances between centres of population in Latin America with distances in other large regions may be approached. From among the larger urban centres of Latin America, North America and West Europe, ten randomly chosen pairs were taken. The great circle distance between each pair was measured to the nearest 100 km. The average great circle distance on the West European journeys was about 1,100 km., that for North America about 2,000 km. and that for Latin America about 4,200 km. To give more accurate values, more pairs of places should be taken and places weighted according to population. Even so, the big size of Latin America, with its various clusters of population, is clearly reflected in the results.

While air journeys in all three regions are more or less direct, surface journeys in Latin America are in many cases characterised by big detours caused by the arrangement of land and sea, and by the absence or poor quality of land routes in many areas. Possible land and sea journeys between Valparaiso in Chile and Sao Luis in Brazil are shown in *Figure 6.4*. Table 6.4 contains the actual distances in Latin America. From the situation described it may be inferred that in Latin America *either* much greater effort will be needed to achieve the degree of integration achieved in North America and West Europe, or for the same degree of effort much less interregional movement will be possible.

6.5. REASONS BEHIND THE PRESENT DISTRIBUTION OF POPULATION IN LATIN AMERICA

This and the following sections contain some ideas that help to account for the present distribution of population in Latin America. More detailed accounts of countries and case studies later in the book will provide examples. Two broad sets of factors influencing the distribution of population in any area are related to natural resources and to relative position. As technology changes, the importance of different aspects of both natural resources and relative position changes. Productive or potentially productive land is counted here as a natural resource. The factors mentioned may be illustrated with Latin American examples.

The attraction of resources may be illustrated by the fact that in the Spanish colonial period population was attracted or was moved to silver mines. Deposits of copper ore were largely ignored during the colonial period but in the 19th century themselves started to attract population. Bauxite was little used until the 20th century. The influence of location may be illustrated by the desirability of having commercial sugar cultivation near the coast during the colonial period. Improved communications have made it possible to grow coffee, cereals and other export crops far from the coast in the 20th century. Proximity to large urban areas tends to be a major influence, however, in locating industries.

Two basic types of population may be distinguished, firstly population spread over a large area in order to use resources of the land and secondly population concentrated in urban centres (central places), carrying out other kinds of employment. The two types in fact merge and overlap. *Figure 6.5* illustrates with a diagram and a simplification of the situation in Venezuela the way in

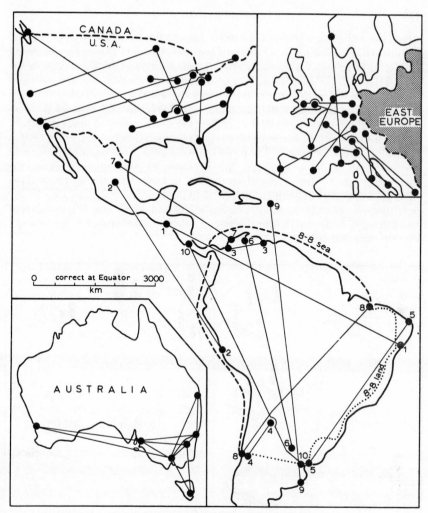

Figure 6.4. *A comparison of distances in the Americas, West Europe and Australia*

Table 6.4.
DISTANCES BETWEEN SELECTED PAIRS OF TOWNS

From		To		Great Circle km
Town	Country	Town	Country	
1 Aracajú	Brazil	1 El Salvador	Central America	6,500
2 Lima	Peru	2 San Luis Potosí	Mexico	4,800
3 Valencia	Venezuela	3 Montería	Colombia	900
4 Santiago	Chile	4 Tucumán	Argentina	900
5 Montevideo	Uruguay	5 Natal	Brazil	3,800
6 Paraná	Argentina	6 Maracaibo	Venezuela	5,000
7 Barranquilla	Colombia	7 Monterrey	Mexico	3,200
8 Valparaíso	Chile	8 Sao Luís	Brazil	4,400
9 San Juan	Puerto Rico	9 Mar del Plata	Argentina	6,500
10 Buenos Aires	Argentina	10 San José	Costa Rica	5,800

which the population of an area can be separated into the two types. The distribution of population depending on resources of the land may be concerned with crop farming, grazing or forestry. The number and density of people involved depends on the productivity of the land, or whether the area has been used to the full yet, and on the degree of application of labour saving machinery. In Venezuela the mountains of the north still support a dense agricultural population, while the plains to the south support a lower density of cattle ranchers and the forest south of the Orinoco a very low density of Indian cultivators and lumber men. The present distribution of rural population could be modified in many ways, as, for example, in the longer term by the mechanisation of farming, reducing the labour force, by a change in the types of crop grown, by the introduction of irrigation and crop-farming in the grazing area or by the exhaustion or erosion of soil. More immediate causes of local, smaller scale population change include natural disasters such as floods, earthquakes and erupting volcanoes.

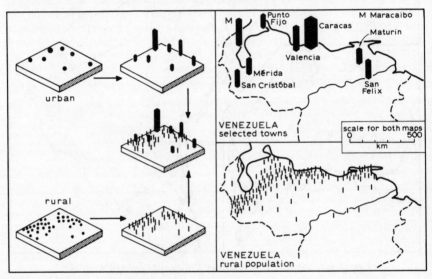

Figure 6.5. Aspects of the distribution of population illustrated by the situation in Venezuela

The distribution of urban centres is influenced by a different set of factors. Many urban centres in Latin America owe their existence and growth directly to the presence of rural populations, for which they provide various services and some manufactures. In Venezuela examples are San Cristóbal and Mérida which serve the western part of the Andes. Other urban centres have grown up by mineral deposits. In Venezuela, Maturín and Maracaibo have grown from very small places early in the century to major oilfield centres, the oil industry now either directly or indirectly supporting a large part of their labour forces. Centres of communications, administration and industry are other types of urban centre. Examples in Venezuela are Punto Fijo, the site of a major oil refinery and outlet for Venezuelan oil, Caracas the national capital, which also has many industries, San Felix, a new industrial centre associated with raw materials, and Valencia, both a regional centre for an agricultural area and a centre for new light industries.

The above account greatly oversimplifies the situation in Venezuela but it is well to remember that population is broadly distributed according to jobs (or to where people expect jobs to be) and that the resource base, used with given technology, is the direct or indirect reason for most jobs. Unfortunately Latin America data for the employment structure of major civil divisions and towns are incomplete and are widely scattered among various census and other publications.

It is more difficult to categorise location in terms of its influence on the distribution of population than to show the effects of natural resources. Relative location in Latin America seems to have played a part during the post-Columbian period in determining which resources were discovered first and which were exploited first. Although the Spanish colonists spread out widely over Latin America they were most active along certain 'corridors'. Proximity to Europe and proximity to the coast to some extent explained the intensity of their influences. In Brazil, also, most of the population remained close to the east facing coast until the 18th century. The influence of proximity to the coast on development and settlement must be treated with reservations because any generalisation must not overlook the fact that long stretches of the coastlands of Latin America are virtually uninhabited (see *Figure 6.1*). A 'remote' location is not necessarily remote in relation to the coast. It may be remote in relation to the major cluster of population in a country or remote from the national capital. The first major oil producing fields of Latin America were in coastal areas in Mexico and later in Venezuela. Only in the 1960s have the 'remote' fields lying behind the Andes of Colombia, Ecuador and Peru been properly explored and large scale production is only starting in the 1970s.

6.6. MIGRATION

In a given region of the world, as opposed to the whole world, population change over time is the result of two influences, the difference between the number of births and deaths within the region and the difference between the number of migrants entering and leaving. For the purposes of this section, three basic types of population movement may be distinguished, tourist, temporary migration and permanent migration. While tourists may learn a great deal about the places they visit, they generally return home and are not a permanent influence on population change. Similarly temporary migrants, such as Mexican farm workers in the U.S.A. or Latin American students who visit educational establishments outside the region, eventually return home, or, by definition become permanent migrants by not doing so.

In a spatial sense, three types of permanent migrant may be distinguished in the context of Latin America: 1. migrants between Latin America and some other part of the world, 2. migrants between Latin American countries and 3. migrants within Latin American countries.

1. Ever since the 15th century Latin America has received permanent migrants from other continents, in particular Europe. The greatest influx into the region was roughly between 1870 and 1910 and the receiving area mainly southern South America. In the inter-war period and again after the Second

World War there was some migration from Europe but the rapidly diminishing share of foreign born citizens even in Argentina underlines the decline of outside sources. Indeed with the movement of people out of Puerto Rico, Cuba and the British West Indies to the U.S.A. and Britain it is possible that at times in the 1950s and 1960s more people have left Latin America than have arrived. The trend may change in the future but for convenience it has been assumed in the projections that follow there will be no net movement either way.

2. With a few exceptions there has never been much migration between pairs of Latin American countries. The exceptions include in recent decades a net flow from Chile to Argentina, Colombia to Venezuela and El Salvador to Honduras. Again, the present situation could change, but for convenience it has been assumed in the projections that follow that there will be no net movement either way.

3. Recent censuses of Latin American countries show increasing mobility in many countries. Two causes are changing employment structure leading to the creation of new (often better paid) jobs in urban areas and the rapid development of road transport. The following net flows of migration have been widely noted in Latin America: from rural areas to urban areas in general, from smaller towns to larger towns and from older densely settled rural areas to new settlements where land is becoming available. The first two flows accentuate the concentration of population but the third leads to dispersal.

One main cause of migration is the search for better employment. People who are poorly paid, or even unemployed, if offered a better job elsewhere, may or may not move. They may decide to move even without the certainty of a specific job, in which case, at least in Latin America, they will tend to move to a big town where there are many jobs altogether and a big turnover of jobs. People may also migrate for health, educational or retirement reasons. Various data suggest, however, that an above average proportion of migrants are somewhere in the age groups 20–40, people likely to be able to change jobs and people also likely to produce children. The movement of population within Latin American countries will be discussed later in the book under individual countries.

6.7. THE REGULATION OF POPULATION SIZE

The demographic structure of a region can be one of three types: 1. Birthrate and deathrate can both be high (as among Amazonian Indians and to some extent in Haiti), 2. Birthrate can be high and deathrate low (as in Venezuela and Mexico) or 3. Birthrate and deathrate can both be low (as to some extent in Uruguay and Argentina). The first and the third type give a slow rate of increase but the second type gives a fast rate of increase. The greater the gap between birthrate and deathrate, the more unstable the population and the greater the increase or decrease.

Since natural change depends mainly on the difference between birthrate and deathrate, and much less on migration, then the number entering a region by being born and the number leaving by dying must be balanced if a stable population is required. Birthrate and deathrate depend on fertility and mortality respectively. These will be considered in turn, mortality first.

In Latin America the widespread introduction of medical facilities and hygiene has helped to eliminate many diseases in recent decades. In some areas, improvements in diet may also have contributed to reduce mortality. In particular the infant mortality rates have been greatly reduced, though by the standards of West Europe and North America they are still high in many countries. Thus more children have become adults and more adults are living to greater ages. In strictly biological terms it is the life expectancy of women up to the age when they cease to be potentially child-bearing that most affects population trends. In theory, and occasionally in practice, as in Paraguay after a war in the 19th century, a greatly reduced number of males could 'service' a larger female population to repopulate a region.

Fertility is largely independent of mortality once most women reach the age of about 45. To state the obvious, births are provided almost exclusively by women between about 15 and 45. Whether they are married or not when they give birth is a social, not a biological question and hardly relevant in some parts of Latin America (Jamaica, southern Mexico, the Andes) where around half the births may be illegitimate.

In theory a woman might be expected to produce a child about every 15 to 18 months, allowing some time after the previous birth before she becomes fertile again, and a further short time for conception.[2] This biological fact may be unpalatable to some readers but it must be accepted. Therefore the biological extremes of population change can be established between a theoretical 20 births per woman during her productive life and 0 births. As some women do not produce children, an increase of population somewhat below ten times in a generation can be achieved (males *and* females are born). In 1969 the author watched a television programme in Rio de Janeiro in which the two rival cities, Rio and São Paulo located their most prolific mothers. São Paulo found a woman with 23 children but Rio capped this with one with 24. The *average* number of children per mother in many regions of Latin America is five or six. In some areas it is higher, while in towns, where children can be regarded as a liability, and among some classes of people, it tends to be lower.

In rural areas it has been customary for most women to have a very large number of children both because this happens naturally and because the high rate of infant and child mortality requires prolific child bearing to maintain population. Moreover middle class and wealthy families have tended also to have large numbers of children for the same basic reason.[5] Although infant and child mortality have dropped, their relative affluence has still allowed them to support large numbers of children.

The degree to which the Catholic Church has influenced family size and planning is difficult to estimate but it must be pointed out firstly that Spain, Italy and other *Catholic* countries of Europe now have very low birthrates while many *non-Catholic* countries elsewhere, as in North Africa and Southeast Asia, have very high birthrates.

What are the prospects, then of actually beginning to control fertility and the birthrate in Latin America? There are four stages at which 'unwanted' potential children can be disposed of to keep women from their maximum theoretical potential of some 20 children.

1. No intercourse: abstinence, asceticism, late marriage, domestic service, common in 19th century Europe.[3]
2. Copulation with prevention of conception. Many different devices from

'safe' periods and pills to pessaries and condoms are available even in parts of Latin America. They require some level of organisation (in fact family planning!) in production and application to be effective and are costly for people with very low incomes.

3. Conception followed by abortion during pregnancy, a practice widely used in certain countries (Japan, East Europe) but not legal anywhere in Latin America,[4] somewhat dangerous unless properly carried out, and costly in developing countries with limited hospital facilities.

4. Infanticide after birth, a practice now almost universally condemned in the world though quite common in both Europe and Latin America in the 19th century.

The situation in Latin America must be seen in a world context. Until about 1700 rapid population changes were confined to limited parts of the world at certain periods of time. Before 1700 the average rate of increase for the world has been estimated to be 0·002 per cent per year.[5] Since 1700 one region after another has begun to experience rapid growth. In some, such as West Europe and Japan (where the birthrate dropped from 35 per thousand in 1948 to 18 per thousand in 1958) the rate of growth has tended to diminish in recent decades. This fact has led to the assumption that as a country develops above a certain level of production of goods and services, families get smaller. Nevertheless the world as a whole is increasing at 2 per cent per year and Latin America at nearly 3 per cent per year. The highest rates of growth attained at any period since rapid change began never exceeded 2 per cent per year in Japan or Russia, two major developed countries that were little affected by large in or out migrations. One reason is that the mortality rate has dropped much more quickly during the 20th century in developing countries than it did in the 19th century in now more highly developed ones. In *Figure 6.6,* recent population change rates* are plotted against GDP per capita (on a logarithmic scale), for

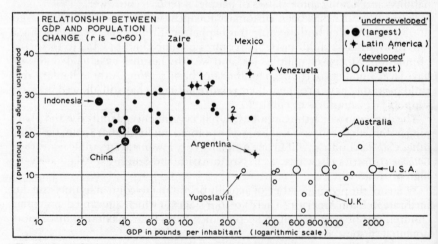

Figure 6.6. Graphical representation of the relationship between per capita gross domestic product and rate of population change 1963–70 for the fifty largest countries of the world (see Section 2.1). Numbers on the graph: 1 Peru, Brazil and Colombia, 2 Chile

* Migration affects Australia and Canada.

the 50 largest countries of the world. The 7 Latin American countries are fairly central on the income scale but vary considerably among themselves. The position of Mexico and Venezuela, so far above the poorer European countries in natural increase rate, but with similar income levels, should be noted.

In conclusion, it seems that there is no one easy way to introduce birth control in Latin America even where enough policy makers and individual citizens

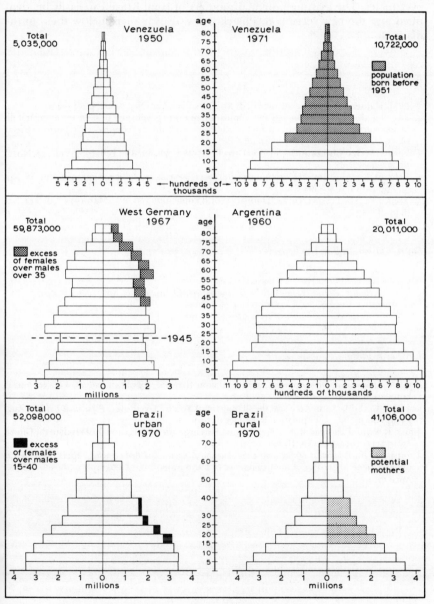

Figure 6.7. Age pyramids for six selected demographic situations. Note that the scale for Venezuela and Argentina differs from that for West Germany and Brazil. Attention is drawn to selected features of the pyramids

want it. It is said by some that the future of an individual is written on the palm
of his hand. Whether this is so or not, the future of a population is to some extent written on its age pyramid. The six examples in *Figure 6.7* illustrate this
thought. For example almost all the people in Venezuela in 1950 apart from
those over 50–55 are now the shaded portion of the 1971 population. The West
German pyramid still carries the scars of two world wars in the excess of females
over males. The existing potential mothers of rural Brazil can easily be identified and the new recruits to this class are already there below them in the
diagram.

References

1. P. M. Hauser, 'The Census of 1970', *Sci. Am.*, July 1971, Vol. 225, No. 1, pp. 17–25.
2. Since on average approximately one copulation in thirty produces a positive result, then if no
   birth control is used it is only a matter of a few weeks before conception occurs, once the effects
   of a previous pregnancy have worn off.
3. Langer, W. L., 'Checks on Population Growth: 1750–1850', *Sci. Am.*, Feb. 1972, Vol. 226, No. 2,
   pp. 92–99.
4. Behrens, K., 'Abortion: the continuing controversy', *Population Bulletin*, Aug. 1972, Vol. 28, No.
   4, Population Reference Bureau.
5. Frejka, T., 'The Prospects for a Stationary World Population', *Sci. Am.*, Mar. 1973, Vol. 228, No.
   3, pp. 15–23.

Sources of material in the figures

6.7. Venezuela: XI *Censo general de población*, Caracas 1972.
     W. Germany: *Statistiches Jahrbuch für der Bundesrepublik Deutschland*, 1969, p. 34.
     Argentina: *Censo Nacional de Población*, p. 4, Table 2.
     Brazil: *Tabulações avançadas do censo demográfico*, 1970, p. 3.

Further reading

Berg, A., 'Nutrition, Development, and Population Growth', *Population Bulletin*, Vol. 29, No. 1,
    Population Reference Bureau.
Cook, R. C. (Ed.), 'Latin America, the "Fountain of Youth" Overflows', *Population Bulletin*, Aug.
    1958, Vol. 14, No. 5, Population Reference Bureau.
Smith, R. V., and Thomas, R. N., 'Population Crisis in South America and the March to the Cities',
    Focus, Sept. 1972, Vol. XXIII, No. 1.
Thomas, R. N., *Population Dynamics of Latin America, A Review and Bibliography*, Papers presented at
    the 2nd General Session of the Conference of Latin Americanist Geographers, Boston, Mass.,
    April 17, 1971.

CHAPTER 7

TRANSPORT AND COMMUNICATIONS

7.1. GENERAL FEATURES

Some features of transport and communications in Latin America are introduced in this chapter. The following features may be noted: a movement, journey, or flow of things (goods, passengers or information) takes place with or without a vehicle between a pair of terminals or nodes, along a path, route, link, arc or edge (railway, pipeline, telegraph line). A given link between two places may be used for various transactions (e.g. a road to carry agricultural produce, people, mail). It may form part of a larger network or system. When a journey between origin and destination uses more than one medium, a change of conveyance may be necessary and transhipment takes place (as at a port between sea and land transport). The increasing use of containers reduces this inconvenience. Journeys may be assessed in terms of distance (length in km), time taken, or cost.

In the study of transportation, various media are distinguished and often studied separately. In fact, they tend to be interdependent, especially in underdeveloped parts of the world like Latin America, where there may be only one means of transport available between two places. Table 7.1 lists some of the principal forms of transport used in Latin America. The particular advantages and disadvantages of each form will be noted in the sections that follow. The common features shared by all media will now be considered.

Figure 7.1 shows three fictitious situations. Ten places are (a) only partly connected, (b) connected in such a way that each place can be reached from every other though in many cases with a big detour, and (c) more completely, with more direct links between many places (e.g. P and Q) than in situation (b). Network (b) is known as a 'tree' network because it has no enclosed 'regions'. In network (c) there are many different possible paths or routes between any pair of places.

In *Figure 7.2*, Venezuela is used to illustrate the concept of completeness of a system. Map (a) shows the sea and the main inland waterway, the Orinoco. The sea is a continuous surface over which direct (or great circle) journeys may be made between pairs of ports as long as there is no land or shallow sea in the way. The Orinoco can be used by sea-going vessels for several hundred kilometres inland but by the nature of a river system it is a tree network.

In Venezuela, few railways now operate (see map (b)). They connect certain pairs of towns and, like (a) in *Figure 7.1*, do not form a single integrated system. The same is true of the oil pipelines shown on the same map.

Only selected main roads in Venezuela are shown on map (c). Enough are included to reveal a network with alternative routes between the main towns. The network is elaborate and integrated in the northern half of the country but hardly penetrates the area south of the Orinoco. The selected air services in

Table 7.1.

TRANSPORT MEDIA USED IN LATIN AMERICA

Internal	I	short distances
	II	long distances
International	III	between Latin American countries
	IV	Latin America and rest of world

	I	II	III	IV	
1 Human transport	X				Rugged areas, especially Haiti, the Andes
2 Pack animal	X				Mountain areas
3 Canoe, raft	X				Amazonia, other remote lowland areas with suitable rivers
4 Wheeled cart	X				Plantations, agricultural areas in general
5 Internal powered navigation	X	X	X		Large South American rivers, some lakes
6 Railway	X	X	(X)	(X)*	Most areas with above mean density of population for Latin America
7 Coastal navigation		X	X		South American countries, especially Chile, Brazil, Argentina, Peru; also Mexico
8 Trans-Oceanic navigation		(X)	X	X	Latin America to North America, Europe, Japan
9 Motor Vehicles	X	X	(X)	(X)*	Most settled areas are being reached
10 Pipelines	X	X			Venezuela, Mexico, Argentina, other oil and gas producers
11 Electricity transmission	X	(X)			Long distance limited. Brazil, Mexico
12 Air: passengers	X	X	X	X	Widespread except in very rugged and/ or high areas
13 Air: freight		X	(X)	(X)	Limited except for inaccessible localities. Often subsidised

(X) Not much used.
* Mexico – U.S.A.

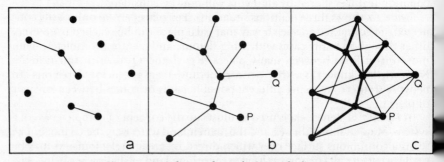

Figure 7.1. Basic features of networks. See text for discussion

7.2(d) show direct links between the capital, Caracas, and various regional centres. Direct links between pairs of regional centres are not numerous. In more detail, several regional centres, as for example Maracaibo and Maturín, have links radiating from themselves to smaller centres. When the radial arrangement of links predominates it often gives a great advantage in terms of centrality and accessibility to a particular centre or a few centres. Air transport is very flexible, however, as aircraft are not confined to specially built channels and air services can be changed quickly and easily.

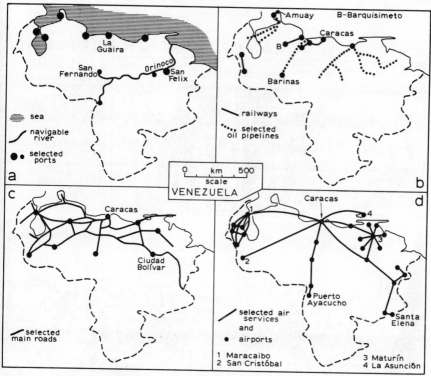

Figure 7.2. Aspects of a national transportation system, exemplified by Venezuela

Transportation systems can be classified by their scale as well as by their layout. It was shown in Chapter 2 (*Figure 2.4*) how Latin America can be seen in the context of a world-wide network, exemplified by the Italian Airline Alitalia, which forms a radial system on the spherical surface of the world, with Rome at the centre. In a similar way, European shipping companies serve all parts of the world and their routes reach out to various Latin American ports. The Panama Canal (*Figure 7.3a*) must also be seen in a world context since its presence shortens routes between many pairs of ports in the world.

On a continental scale, land links between Latin American countries are weak and little used compared with sea and air links, though integrated systems have been proposed. In the 19th Century (see Chapter 2) it was hoped to build a rail system to integrate Latin America. This project never materialised, and physical obstacles, national policies, different gauges and great distances make its completion unlikely. During the Second World War, enthusiasm for integration was renewed, this time with the proposal of the Pan American Highway. It is now possible to cross the boundary between most adjoining pairs of Latin American countries somewhere by road. The continuity of the Pan American road system is however still broken by gaps between Costa Rica and Panama, Panama and Colombia, and Ecuador and Peru. Since the Second World War the concept of the Pan American Highway has acted as an incentive to many coun-

TRANSPORTATION PROBLEMS

LEFT:
PORTERS CARRY-
ING HEAVY
EQUIPMENT,
ANDES OF PERU

BELOW:
IMPRESSION
OF DIFFICULT
CONDITIONS
IN THE ANDES
OF PERU

TRANSPORT
WITH OXEN
IN SAN
SALVADOR,
EL SALVADOR

TOTORA REED
FISHING BOATS,
LAKE TITICACA,
BOLIVIA

IN LATIN AMERICA

RIGHT:
'ASSEMBLING A LORRY
FLOWN IN BY AIR,
TARAPOTO, PERU'

MIDDLE:
DIFFICULT MOUNTAIN
ROAD NEAR SAN MATEO,
CENTRAL ANDES OF PERU

BELOW:
SHIPS TOWED BY 'MULES'
PASSING IN MIRAFLORES
LOCKS, PANAMA CANAL

VIADUCT ON CHIHUAHUA-PACIFIC RAILWAY, MEXICO

SANTOS-SAO PAULO HIGHWAY, BRAZIL

tries to improve their road systems, but distances are so great that the movement of goods or passengers commercially from one end to another is unthinkable.

Latin America lacks the degree of integration of road and rail networks found in North America. Each country tends to develop its transportation system in the context of its own territory. The movement of both goods and passengers between pairs of Latin American countries is often catered for by North American or European shipping and air services in spite of attempts by various Latin American governments to encourage the use of Latin American services.

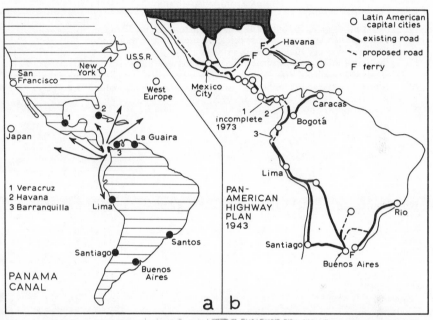

Figure 7.3. (a) The position of the Panama Canal. (b) The Pan-American highway system as envisaged in 1943

On a national scale it is difficult to generalise about transportation systems within Latin American countries though they share certain common features. As in Venezuela the national capital and in some cases other major centres tend to dominate the system, while routes between ports and interior sources of exports are also numerous. The trend has been for both road and air transport to gain in relative importance at the expense of railways since about 1930 and particularly since about 1950.

7.2. THE RELATIVE IMPORTANCE OF DIFFERENT MEDIA

Table 7.2 shows the availability and use of four main types of transport in Latin America in 1970. Unfortunately data are not readily available to allow direct comparisons between the media used.

Column 1 The large merchant shipping fleet registered in Panama uses that country to provide a 'flag of convenience'. The remaining merchant fleets of

Latin America are small, given the size of the countries that own them. If Panama is excluded, Latin America had only about 2 per cent of the world's merchant shipping in 1971, a smaller share than it had around 1950. Vessels are mostly small and are used to provide coastal services, some of which cover very large distances. The development of shipbuilding may make it easier for countries to expand their fleets and the expected growth of trade between member countries of the Latin American Free Trade Association is a further incentive.

Table 7.2.

TRANSPORT BY COUNTRIES

1   Merchant shipping in thousands of gross registered tons, 1971
2,3   Passenger cars and commercial vehicles in use, 1970, in thousands
4   Passenger cars per 10 commercial vehicles
5,6   Railways: millions of passenger/kilometres (5) and millions of ton/kilometres of goods (6) handled, 1970.
7,8   Internal air transport: millions of passenger/kilometres (7) and millions of ton/kilometres of goods (8) handled, 1970.
9   Cars in use per 1000 inhabitants

| | 1 | 2 | 3 | 4 | 5 | 6 | 7 | 8 | 9 |
| | | Road | | | Rail | | Air | | Cars |
	Ships	Cars	Com.	2:3	Pass.	Goods	Pass.	Goods	Cap
Brazil	1,730	2,003	656	31	13,340	25,210	2,107	36	21
Mexico	400	1,234	558	17	4,530	22,860	1,493	20	25
Argentina	1,310	1,304	715	18	12,830	13,360	975	13	56
Venezuela	410	522	230	23	36	13	378	5	50
Colombia	210	151	135	11	235	1,170	1,181	45	7
Peru	420	230	118	19	250	590	107	7	17
Chile	390	177	150	12	2,340	2,530	413	24	18
Costa Rica	–	39	27	14	55	18	23	2	23
El Salvador	–	35	19	18	–	–	–	–	10
Guatemala	–	43	24	18	–	106	19	1	8
Honduras	70	19	17	11	–	–	31	1	7
Nicaragua	–	34	19	18	35	13	6	–	17
Panama	6,260	68	15	45	–	–	–	–	47
Barbados	–	19	4	48	–	–	–	–	73
Cuba	390	71	31	23	–	–	317	4	8
Dominican Republic	–	39	22	18	–	–	–	–	9
Guadeloupe	–	23	13	18	–	–	–	–	70
Haiti	–	11	2	55	–	–	–	–	2
Jamaica	–	64	23	28	58	132	10	–	34
Martinique	–	25	11	23	–	–	–	–	74
Netherlands Antilles	–	33	4	83	–	–	–	–	150
Puerto Rico	–	500	103	49	–	–	–	–	184
Trinidad	–	75	20	38	–	–	8	–	79
Bolivia	–	19	29	7	249	316	64	1	4
Ecuador	–	40	51	8	85	56	78	7	7
Guyana	–	19	5	38	45	1	–	–	6
Paraguay	–	15	13	12	28	22	–	–	6
Surinam	–	11	5	22	–	–	–	–	28
Uruguay	160	121	88	14	–	–	–	–	42

Sources: *UNSYB 1971* 1, Table 149; 2–4, Table 148; 5–6, Table 146; 7–8, Table 152
— negligible value or none

Column 2 shows the number of passenger cars in Latin America. Some passenger cars are used as taxis but nearly all are the private vehicles of the small sector of the community in Latin America wealthy enough to afford them.

Column 9 shows the number of passenger cars in circulation per thousand total population. In West Europe the figure is over 200 in many countries and in some states of the U.S.A. it exceeds 400. In Latin America most passenger cars are used in and around the larger towns where the condition of roads is generally at its best and where repair and maintenance facilities are widely available.

Column 3 shows commercial vehicles. While private cars are a luxury in Latin America, reflecting the very uneven spread of income, commercial vehicles have become one of the main necessities for the development of the region. The U.S.A., with a smaller population, has more than six times as many commercial vehicles as Latin America. The ratio of passenger cars to commercial vehicles has been calculated in *column 4* and is expressed as passenger cars per 10 commercial vehicles. The ratio seems to reflect several influences including heavy import restrictions on the importation of passenger cars in some countries.

Columns 5 and *6* show the performance of the railway systems of the major countries in Latin America. The data for passenger/km and ton/km represent the sum of the number of units carried, multiplied by the distance. For example 5 tons carried 20 km is 100 ton/km. The amount of ton/km carried on railways of the U.S.A. is about 50 times as great as that carried on the railways of Mexico or Brazil. The role of rail transport is negligible in many of the smaller Latin American countries.

Columns 7 and *8* may be compared with 5 and 6 respectively. The relative importance of air and rail transport is clearly revealed by the data. In Mexico, for example, the railways handle 1,000 times the ton/km of goods handled by air transport, whereas they only account for 3 times as many passenger/km as the air lines. In Colombia in particular air transport caters for a large part of passenger movement. Air transport is responsible for moving goods of high value and/or perishability and 'expensive' passengers between major centres. It also reaches many small, remote places in thinly peopled areas.

As Latin America is so varied physically and economically and so divided politically it is not possible to make a general statement about the relative cost of different forms of transport. This has been done in the U.S.S.R.[1] where in 1970 the cost of moving 10 ton/km of goods was 1·5 kopeks by sea, 2·3 by rail, 2·5 by inland waterway, but 57·1 on the roads. By contrast, the figures for passenger/km were rail 5·5, road 9·9, inland waterway 15·5 and sea 47·2. Estimates of the cost of moving oil in the U.S.A. in the 1960s showed that sea and pipeline were much cheaper per ton/km than rail or road.

The figures referred to above are very general. Since all the forms of transport are used in Latin America, each has a particular place in the overall system. The global figures quoted vary greatly according to local conditions. For example the cost of sea transport depends on the size of ship, the cost of pipeline transport on the diameter of the pipeline, the cost of road transport on the quality of the road and the size of vehicles using it.

The following generalisation may be made about the more favourable means of transport in Latin America according to distance covered.

1. Intercontinental journeys of several thousand km depend almost

exclusively on sea transport for goods and increasingly on air transport for passengers.

2. Long journeys within Latin America are mostly provided by road services, both lorry and coach. Some such as Montevideo – São Paulo or Lima – La Paz cross international boundaries. Others within countries as Tijuana – Mexico City, Rio – Fortaleza, Belém – Brasília, are long internal journeys of 2000–3000 km. Air, coastal shipping services and railways in some cases compete with road services.

3. Journeys of 100 to several hundred km are catered for mainly by roads and railways, but by air in special circumstances and waterways where available.

4. Short, local journeys are made almost entirely on roads either by motor vehicles or animal transport. Suburban train services in big towns are very limited in Latin America, Rio and Buenos Aires being exceptions. Underground railway systems have been started in some cities, notably Mexico City, Rio and São Paulo; the system in Buenos Aires dates from early in the 20th century.

The choice of a means of transport depends not only on cost but also on comfort and on the duration of the journey. Between a pair of towns in Latin America a few hundred km apart the prospective traveller might have choices like those below showing relative cost in money units and estimated time required for the journey.

(i)	Air	100 units	1 hour
(ii)	Collective taxi	40 units	5 hours
(iii)	1st class coach	20 units	10 hours
(iv)	2nd class coach	10 units	15 hours

Rail travel tends to be cheaper than good quality road travel, but slower except on certain routes such as the lines between Buenos Aires and the main regional centres of Argentina.

7.3. CHARACTERISTICS OF DIFFERENT MEDIA

SEA TRANSPORT

Table 7.3 shows that in 1970 about 400 million tons of goods were shipped from the seaports of Latin America and over 100 million tons are unloaded. Only two countries, Bolivia and Paraguay, are land-locked, but each has access to ports in neighbouring countries. The provision of adequate port facilities to cope with the changing growth and nature of foreign trade has been a constant preoccupation in Latin America, since most countries have high import coefficients (the value of their imports expressed as a percentage of their total income in a given period).

Two main types of port exist in Latin America, ports such as Santos, Buenos Aires, Veracruz and Valparaiso, equipped to handle various kinds of cargo and also passengers, and ports equipped with special facilities such as Amuay Bay in Venezuela and Vitoria in Brazil for the export of oil or metallic ores. In fact, roughly half of all the cargo leaving Latin American ports is Venezuelan oil.

Table 7.3.

GOODS HANDLED AT LATIN AMERICAN PORTS IN 1970 IN MILLIONS OF METRIC TONS

	Loaded	Un-loaded		Loaded	Un-loaded
Brazil	40·0	28·0	Ecuador	1·8	1·5
Mexico	9·7	3·7	Central America	5·5	9·3
Argentina	15·2	10·9	Dominican Republic	2·7	1·4
Venezuela	204·5	4·3	Haiti	0·8	0·2
Colombia	6·7	2·2	Jamaica	10·2	2·9
Peru	14·3	2·1	Netherlands Antilles	39·3	44·9
Chile	12·3	5·4	Trinidad	21·4	15·5
Uruguay	1·6	2·4	Guyana	3·8	0·8

Source: *UNSYB 71*, Table 151.

some of this is double-counted by being received in the Netherlands Antilles, refined there and again exported. Mineral exports figure prominently also among the exports of Brazil, Peru, Chile and Trinidad.

INLAND WATERWAYS

There are five main inland waterway systems in Latin America, the first two international: the Amazon, the Parana-Paraguay, the Orinoco, the Magdalena and the São Francisco. All suffer from various physical obstacles along their courses, including the occurrence of rapids and shallows, of floods and dry periods. In some cases these have to be by-passed by a special railway or road. Since they follow fixed courses, waterways do not necessarily go in the 'best' directions. They also have to be supplemented by rail or road feeders to serve areas at some distance away. The speed of movement on the waterways is slow and often possible only during the day due to navigational hazards at night.

RAILWAYS

Rail transport is relatively important in Latin America in four main areas, the northern two thirds of Mexico, the populated parts of Argentina, southeast Brazil and central Chile. Even in these areas the networks are restricted in layout, with radial lines from major centres such as Mexico City, Buenos Aires and São Paulo tending to dominate the pattern. Differences in gauge in some countries make the provision of an integrated system difficult.

Few railways have been built in Latin America since about 1930. One new railway was completed in Mexico in 1961. It is shown in *Figure 7.4a*. The line crosses the very rugged terrain of the Sierra Madre Occidental. It is single track. At first sight a road might have seemed more appropriate, but a single track railway can in fact be carried on a much narrower bed than a motor road with one lane each way. The construction of tunnels, embankments, cuttings and bridges for the railway was also much cheaper. A major rail link in the Magdalena valley of Colombia was completed in the early 1960s and new lines have been proposed in Brazil and Venezuela. Several lines have been electrified

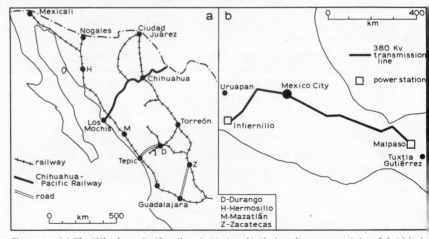

Figure 7.4. (a) The Chihuahua – Pacific railway in Mexico. (b) The long distance transmission of electricity in Mexico

and diesel traction has now replaced steam widely. Many lines carry very little traffic, some have been deliberately abandoned and some have just become impossible to run through neglect.

ROADS

The development and present state of road transport will be dealt with in each country in later chapters. Here the rapid expansion of road transport in Latin America must be stressed. *Figure 7.5* shows that in the case of Mexico between the early 1950s and 1970 the number of passenger cars in use increased about 6 times and the number of commercial vehicles about 3 times. Throughout the 1950s and 1960s only about 10 per cent of the vehicles were actually assembled in Mexico and the manufacture of entirely Mexican vehicles was only beginning

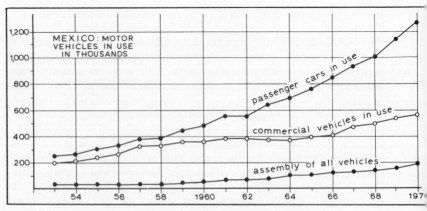

Figure 7.5. The growth of motor transport in Mexico, 1953–1970

around 1970. The growth of vehicles in use was paralleled by the development of a system of paved and unpaved roads both in areas already served by rail transport and in areas hitherto untouched by modern transport. The Mexican example is typical of all the larger Latin American countries.

In many situations, roads offer a quick way of improving the transportation system and allowing the movement of a few vehicles to and from small villages, which can be reached at least by single lane dirt roads at the periphery of the main systems. In fact, most of the main roads in Latin America are of a poor standard with regard to surface quality, width, signs and services compared with those in West Europe, North America or Australia. Unpaved roads are easily worn away by traffic and rain. After less than a decade, the original course of the hastily built road between Belém and Brasília, as well as having several unfinished bridges, was in 1969 already unsuitable for traffic on many stretches.

OTHER MEDIA

Many other more specialised forms of transport and communications are used in Latin America. Oil and gas pipelines are increasingly playing a part in the movement of these products in all the larger Latin American countries. The construction of large hydro-electric power stations in areas remote from centres of population with little prospect of using the current locally has necessitated the building of long distance high voltage transmission lines. Two projects in Mexico are shown in *Figure 7.4*. In Brazil electricity will have to be transmitted a great distance from new stations on the Parana system to the São Paulo area. In the field of communications there are plans to establish links between South American capitals via satellite.

In conclusion one may ask what the relationship is between transportation systems, the other two material ingredients of a region, resources and people, and the less tangible aspect of organisation. The relationship seems to be circular. Goods and people have to be moved in any system that has areal specialisation. Three basically different relationships can be seen.

1. New transport media may be established in existing areas of settlement. Many of the railways built in Latin America in the 19th century linked existing towns and villages previously linked only by animal transport.
2. Transport links and settlements may be established simultaneously. As the new capital of Brazil, Brasília, was built, road, rail and air links were established to supply it with materials and to enable it to communicate with the rest of the country. Subsequently the airline and road networks of Brazil have been considerably modified with the introduction of the new node.
3. Lines of transport can precede settlement and development. The Amazon waterway system, of no more than local importance to the indigenous Indian population of the region, determined the lines of exploration of the region by Europeans and the establishment of commercial centres. In Argentina in the 1880s the settlement of farmers in the pampas south of Buenos Aires followed the building of railways into the area after it had been cleared of Indians. In the 1970s, the construction of new roads through the Amazon forest, built from specially established temporary

encampments, is preceding the establishment of planned agricultural and commercial centres along them.

Reference

1 *Narodnoye khozyaystvo SSSR v 1970 godu*, Moscow, 1971, p. 429.

Sources of material in the figures

7.3(b) *Peruvian Times*, Jan. 8, 1943.
7.5   *UNSYB 1963*, Table 146, *UNSYB 1971*, Table 148.

CHAPTER 8

ORGANISATIONAL ASPECTS

8.1. POLITICO–ADMINISTRATIVE UNITS

When almost all of Latin America broke away from the colonial rule of Spain and Portugal early in the 19th century (see Chapter 3), the concept of the national sovereign state was already strong in Europe. As the new sovereign states of Latin America emerged and gained their identity and recognition in the world they tended to borrow political features from both Europe and the newly created U.S.A. Most Latin American countries follow the U.S. pattern of combining head of state with political leadership. On the other hand, most are strongly unitary, and even in the self-defined federal countries, state powers are very limited compared with federal powers.

The result of over 150 years of independence has been the establishment by 1970 of 25 sovereign countries of greatly different size. During the process there were bitter conflicts in the 19th century as between Chile, Peru and Bolivia in the Pacific War (1879–81) and between Paraguay and its neighbours. Disputes continue over frontier areas between several pairs of countries but there has been very little armed conflict in recent decades. Venezuela claims part of Guyana (formerly British Guiana), while Peru and Ecuador dispute a large area. Several countries claim fishing rights over greatly extended territorial waters, notably Ecuador, Peru and Chile to 200 miles.

In general the countries of Latin America have strong national consciousness and their educational systems tend to encourage this, instilling pride in the flag and awareness of independence day. Although the countries tend to be highly centralised, with much power concentrated in the national capital, regional movements have at times been strong in Brazil, Argentina and Mexico.

The human geography of Latin America, with its underlying distributions of resources and units of production, population, and links, described in the preceding chapters, is greatly influenced in an organisational sense by the network of politico–administrative units into which each country is divided. Each national government strongly influences not only the flow of goods, people and information into and out of the country it controls but also, with varying degrees of intensity, flows within the national territory. Home industries are often protected by tariffs, strategic roads are built to frontier areas and industries of national importance developed on an uneconomic base.

Each sovereign country of Latin America is divided into a number of major civil divisions, referred to as states (in federal countries), departments (French style), provinces or by some other name. The major civil divisions in nearly all Latin American countries are further subdivided at least once more into smaller units (minor civil divisions) such as municipios or comunidades. One of the main functions of the local government units at major and minor civil division level is to allow a spatial breakdown of the business of political administration and judicial matters. Central government funds to provide schools, roads and other services are allocated regionally.

Local government units in Latin America are heavily dependent on central government funds, and the raising of local money through rates as in Britain is very limited. In the federal countries, particularly Brazil, the state governors are individuals of some influence. Local mayors and deputies may also have some influence on national affairs. Each local politician and government official is concerned with promoting the interests of his own particular community and in attracting industry, services and any other innovations and improvements available. The mosaic of major and minor civil divisions with their respective capitals or centres, together with the sovereign countries that contain them, thus form the framework in which many decisions are made that affect the economic conditions of a private enterprise, competitive, market economy. For example, in most Latin American countries the public sector owns the means of production of many goods (oil, tobacco, salt) and services (education, roads, airlines).

The distribution of the major civil divisions of each of the main countries of Latin America are shown in maps in later chapters. Ideally, each political unit on the same level in the hierarchy should have approximately the same number of inhabitants and approximately the same area. In practice, this is impossible on account of the great variations in density of population within a country. The result is that the units that are largest in area tend to have the smallest number of inhabitants. At the other extreme, some towns, including the capitals of federal countries, have territorially very small areas with large populations.

In some countries, major civil divisions with very few inhabitants are not given full status but are defined as *territories,* administered directly from the central government. *Figure 8.1a* shows the main units of this kind, there being three in Brazil,* two each in Mexico and Venezuela, and two different kinds, Comisarias and Intendencias in Colombia. In addition Argentina has a territory in Tierra del Fuego and Nicaragua one in its eastern part. At the other extreme there is a number of areally very small units, also shown in *Figure 8.1a* (black dots). Major civil divisions may be changed at times, as in Colombia in the 1960s. In fact, local government reform often lags behind economic and demographic changes, and existing systems tend to reflect earlier situations, as do the cantons of Switzerland and the counties of England in Europe. On the other hand, when new units are created, the comparability of sets of data before and after the change is affected and the continuity of statistical data interrupted.

For purposes of more strictly local government, each major civil division is broken down into minor civil divisions. The shape and size of these again both reflects underlying economic and demographic distributions and influences them. So large are some of the minor civil divisions of Brazil, the municipios, that in the thinly populated Amazon region, several, exemplified in *Figure 8.1b* by the municipio of Altamira (in Pará state) are larger not only than whole states of Brazil (see Sergipe superimposed on Altamira) but exceed in area whole countries such as those of Central America, or even England. In 1970, Altamira had an estimated 15,000 inhabitants on 150,000 sq. km. (England and Wales nearly 49 million on 151,000 sq. km.).

---

* The former territory of Acre became a state in the late 1960s.

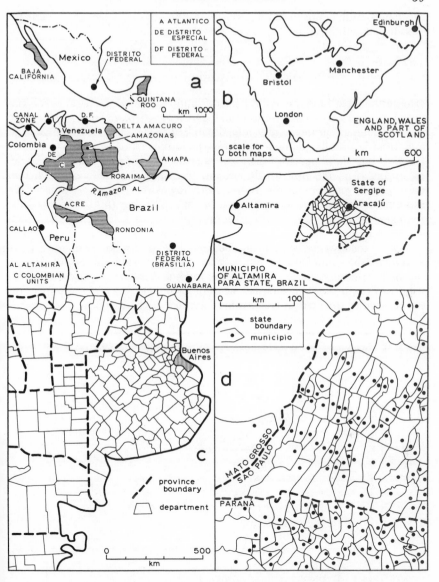

Figure 8.1. Aspects of major and minor civil divisions in Latin America. (a) Territories and other similar low density units, (b) Comparative size of the minor civil division of Altamira, Brazil, Sergipe state, Brazil and England and Wales, (c) Departments in the pampa of Argentina, (d) Municipios in the coffee growing area of Southeast Brazil

The layout of the networks of minor civil division throws light on many features of a region. In *Figure 8.1c*, the provinces of part of Argentina are subdivided into departments. The 'geometrical' appearance of many of these reflects the way the land of the pampas was surveyed and subdivided before settlement took place. In *Figure 8.1d*, parts of three states of Brazil are shown. In

São Paulo, municipios have formed around the original ridge-top settlements established with the spread of coffee growing into the area.

8.2. OWNERSHIP OF THE MEANS OF PRODUCTION

One of the most fundamental differences between (to use the United Nations terms) countries with market economies and centrally planned economies is in the ownership of the means of production of goods and services. In the U.S.S.R. and other centrally planned countries including Cuba since 1959 private property (e.g. clothing, cars, furniture) can exist, but the state owns virtually all the means of production. In the remaining countries of the world, whether developed or developing, the public sector owns varying proportions of the economy and the private sector the rest. In the U.S.A. the proportion belonging to the public sector is small while, for example, in Italy and the U.K., it is considerably larger.

Figure 8.2 shows the relationship between level of development and type of economy. The countries selected for inclusion are located only approximately on the horizontal scale. Level of development as measured by gross domestic product does not correlate clearly with the proportion of the economy in the public sector. After 1959, Cuba moved far across the diagram. The gradual

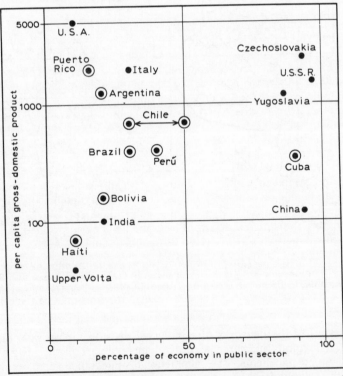

Figure 8.2. *The relationship between percentage of the economy of a country in the public sector and per capita gross domestic product for selected countries around 1970*

nationalisation of the economy in most Latin American countries is also moving them across. Unless a country is almost entirely controlled by the public sector it cannot be completely centrally planned with legal sanctions tied to plan fulfilment. In market economy countries, plans tend to be a series of recommendations. Since 1969, apart from Cuba, Peru has come nearest to becoming centrally planned while still retaining a large private sector. During 1970–73 Chile under Allende was moving in the same direction.

In a given Latin American country capital can be obtained from four main sources, and means of production can be owned in four main ways: internal public sector, internal private sector, foreign public and foreign private. In practice the third category provides both grants (gifts) and loans and credits, but does not have much of a share in the ownership of means of production. It has been estimated[1] that in the early 1960s, about 30 per cent of economic activity in Latin America was government controlled and 70 per cent private. Of the private sector about 90 per cent was domestically owned. These proportions are still approximately correct.

INTERNAL PUBLIC SECTOR

Certain parts of the economy of virtually all Latin American countries are in the hands of the State. These include defence, education and some aspects of health and of communications such as the postal system and the building of roads. These sectors of the economy together take up a large proportion of budget expenditure. Internal public sector enterprises in Latin America tend, under-standably, to be prominent among the largest companies and corporations. In Brazil in 1969,[2] for example, of the 23 largest in terms of capital, the public sector had the majority share in 18. National or individual state concerns dominate or hold a strong position in the production or running of steel, elec-tricity, railways, telephones and water undertakings. Most of the capital in agriculture, in most kinds of light industry and in commerce comes from private sources. The situation is broadly similar in most countries. In addition the State has a monopoly of the handling of certain goods such as tobacco, salt and in the Andes coca leaves.

In addition to the activities mentioned above, the public sector has control of the oil and gas industry in several Latin American countries. Mexico took over its foreign owned oil industry in 1938, Peru in 1969. Venezuela is increasing-ly participating with foreign companies, while Brazil and Argentina have kept control from the start. The oil and gas industry is the major source of energy in most Latin American countries and foreign investment in it has not been per-mitted by certain countries. The internal private sector has generally lacked the large amounts of capital needed to expand such an industry. Electricity supply and the railways also need heavy investment and central coordination and their progress has tended to be increasingly related to government and public sector policy and funds.

INTERNAL PRIVATE SECTOR

It is understandable that no private Latin American companies figure among the largest private companies in the world.[3] Even in Brazil, Mexico and

Argentina, foreign private companies are larger than internal ones. In Brazil, for example, the five largest motor vehicle concerns are all subsidiaries of U.S. or West German firms. In such industries as textiles, chemicals, wood products and food, private internal capital is the main source. There is a growing amount of private capital available in certain parts of Latin America, including São Paulo, Buenos Aires, Mexico City and Caracas. Agriculture belongs almost entirely to the internal private sector in Latin America although certain parts of it are foreign dominated. The ownership of land itself will be discussed under land tenure problems in the next section.

FOREIGN INVESTMENT

A distinction must be made here between actual investment in activities such as oil extraction, fruit growing or vehicle assembly by private foreign companies, and foreign loans whether private or public to help in the construction of projects, themselves to belong eventually to Latin American countries. A question certain to arouse emotions in any group of Latin Americans is that of the profits made by foreign companies 'at their expense'. One such industry, the oil industry of Venezuela, will be dealt with in some detail in Chapter 14.

In view of the limited amount of capital available in Latin American countries many of the larger projects would not have been possible without foreign private capital. The construction of railways, the opening of copper mines, the necessary exploration to locate major oilfields and the establishment of large motor vehicle plants are examples of enterprises that would have been beyond the financial reach and organisational ability of Latin American entrepreneurs of the time.

By far the largest single source of foreign investment in Latin America in recent decades has been the U.S.A., which had about 30 per cent of all its foreign investment in Latin America in 1930, though little more than 15 per cent in 1970. The relative importance of Britain and France has declined in recent decades but since the Second World War, West Germany and Japan have become major sources of capital for several Latin American countries. In Brazil, Japan has some support from Japanese settlers. Private foreign capital in Latin America has increasingly become tied to enterprises in which it is used in participation with internal capital, often on a basis that keeps more than half of the capital and therefore of decision making in internal hands.

8.3. OWNERSHIP OF AGRICULTURAL LAND

The ownership of agricultural land in Latin America has both economic and social implications. Economically land tenure is related to the productivity of both workers and units of land. Socially it is related to the evenness of distribution of wealth among the rural population and to satisfaction and status. The economic and social aspects at times conflict, since efficiency and equality are not necessarily equivalent.

Units of land tenure in agriculture, referred to hereafter as farms, can be classified according to many criteria, including size, ownership, degree of specialisation, and type of crop or livestock. Farm size and type of ownership are closely connected in some respects.

Farms in Latin America vary enormously in size. In 1960, for example, many farms were less than 1 hectare in area while some exceeded 2,500 hectares. The average size of holding in Colombia is about 25 hectares, but the average amount of crop land per holding only about 4 hectares. Such variations about mean values must be borne in mind in a consideration of the values in column 5 of Table 8.1. There has been a tendency for land to become increasingly concentrated in a relatively few large units. Such a process occurred in Mexico between 1850 and 1910 and has been noted in Brazil in the last two decades.

Table 8.1.

COMPARATIVE FIGURES FOR FARM SIZES

1   Agricultural holdings in thousands
2   Area of holdings in thousands of hectares
3   Area under arable and permanent crops in thousands of hectares
4   Farm families in thousands, estimated from figures for total agricultural population
5   Average area of farm holding including land not under crops
6   Cropland (column 3) per farm family
7   Holdings per 100 farm families

	1 Holdings	2 Area of holdings	3 Crop land	4 Farm families	5 Average holding size	6 Arable per farm family	7 Holding 100 families
Brazil	3,350	265,450	29,800	8,970	79	3·3	37
Mexico	1,370	169,080	23,800	4,930	123	4·8	28
Argentina	470	175,140	32,000	1,130	372	28·3	42
Venezuela	320	26,010	5,200	620	81	8·4	52
Colombia	1,210	27,340	5,100	2,000	23	2·6	61
Peru	870	17,720	2,600	1,290	20	2·0	68
Chile	260	30,640	4,500	610	118	7·4	43
Uruguay	90	16,990	2,000	120	189	16·7	75
Guatemala	420	3,410	1,500	640	8	2·3	66
Dominican Rep.	450	2,260	1,070	480	6	2·2	94
Puerto Rico	50	660	240	170	13	1·4	29
U.S.A.	3,710	454,660	176,400	3,890	123	45·1	95
Australia	252	464,580	44,500	330	1,840	135·8	76
Spain	3,010	44,650	20,300	3,390	15	6·0	88
India*	48,880	123,050	163,800	75,700	3	2·2	65

* Inconsistency whereby cropland exceeds land in agricultural holdings occurs in source.
Source: *FAOPY No. 24, 1970* Tables 1, 3, 5

Great variations in the average size of holding can be seen in Latin America, with Argentina and Uruguay at one extreme, Guatemala and the Caribbean islands at the other. In the world as a whole, however, Australia and India stand near the extremes of average size, well outside the range found among the Latin American countries shown.

The type of ownership of land also varies greatly among the countries of Latin America. Column 7 in Table 8.1 shows the relationship of holdings to farm families. The figures give a very rough idea of the proportion of farm population that is landless. As expected, and in spite of the recent growth of big companies in agriculture in the U.S.A., the number of farm families corresponds closely to the number of farm holdings, suggesting that the family farm is well represented. Similarly the correspondence is fairly close in Spain (and many other parts of West Europe). In Mexico and Chile there is a big discrepancy in spite of land reform and in Brazil and Argentina the proportion of farm families without land is over half. In fact, land is owned both collectively and privately on the *ejidos* of Mexico, each unit containing a large number of families. The result of land reform in the Dominican Republic since the 1930s is evident in the figure of 94.

Virtually all Latin American countries have carried out land reform programmes of some kind in the 20th century but each country has tackled its problem separately and in its own way. Very broadly there are two main aims of land reform in Latin America, the first to distribute land more evenly, the second to make farm units commercially viable and efficient in accordance with modern needs and techniques. The redistribution of existing land means that larger owners lose land, for which they may or may not be compensated, and landless farm families are given land or owners of very small farms are given extra land. The modernisation of farms often requires an increase in size as well as the introduction of new methods. This in turn may mean that some farm families have to move or be moved out of their home areas entirely, either to new areas of agricultural resettlement, if new land is conveniently available, or to jobs in other activities outside the agricultural sector. In either case, the provision of new farms or of new non-agricultural jobs represents a big investment.

If land reform is to be carried out seriously, a programme has to be worked out and legislation provided to see that it is enforced. When as many as several hundred thousand farms and families may be involved in a given regional project it is hardly surprising that the organisation needed to carry out the reform is often inadequate.

Figure 8.3 shows basic features of land reform in Latin America. Three types of unit may be suggested:

1. The relatively large unit (latifundio, hacienda, estancia, plantation) with a single owner, owned usually by an individual family but in some cases by the Church, the State or a foreign company, with a large number of workers themselves landless or owning only very small pieces of land. In the past the farm workers would have been slaves or Indians tied closely to the farm unit. Today they are employed as labourers hired for given periods of time by the owner (diagram *b*), exist as tenants paying the owner a rent for a portion of land or share croppers paying part of their produce for use of the land. It has been noted that in some cases share croppers, knowing that they have to give half (or some other agreed proportion) of their produce to the land owner, deliberately produce less than they could in order to spite the owner!

2. The state farm (diagram *f*), accounting for about half the agricultural land in the U.S.S.R., and found in Cuba. Workers own no land other than token allotments for their own use. The collective farm (diagram *d*) of the U.S.S.R. is a variation in which farm workers have small private plots and also have some direct interest in the unit as a whole. The *ejidos* of Mexico are of this kind but the proportion of private land to collective land is greater than in the U.S.S.R.

3. The family farm. Ideally farms would be roughly equal in size at least in an area with similar physical conditions, and there would be a one-one correspondence between farm family and farm unit. The peasant family farm is

Europe and the larger family farm in the U.S.A. have been the basis of land tenure in these two developed regions of the world. Both are satisfactory since the intensity of production in Europe and the large size of farm in North America ensures a reasonable standard of living. In Latin America many family farms are very small (they are often referred to as *minifundio*) and whether the social satisfaction they provide outweighs the disadvantages of their small size is debateable.

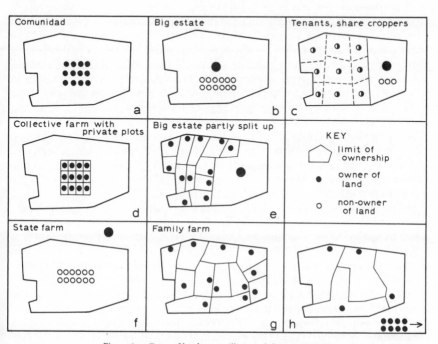

Figure 8.3. Types of land tenure illustrated diagrammatically

Land reform in Latin America has tended to be directed towards the creation of family farm units rather than collective or state farms but with a minimum size according to conditions in different areas. It has been assumed that under a system of family farms not only would social satisfaction be achieved but farmers would be more concerned about the running of their own farms, and about long term improvements in them. In *Figure 8.3*, then, the reform has tended to transform situation *b* into *e*, the large landowner retaining part of his big holding; *b* into *g*, the large landowner losing his holding entirely (or taking a family farm unit out of it); or *c* into *g*, with tenants and share croppers being given the land they already work. The ancient comunidad type of farm system, characteristic of the Andean area in pre-colonial times, but much reduced in colonial times, still exists, though now often with privately held land as well as communal land.

If the more egalitarian distribution of farm land among farmers brings social satisfaction, there are at least two sets of reasons why it has not always brought economic improvements. Firstly, many owners of farms newly allocated after land reform have had no experience of running their own affairs, more often than not are illiterate, and usually lack capital to buy equipment, good quality seeds, fertilisers and other means of improving their land. Secondly, many farm areas in Latin America have between about 10 and 50 times as many farm families per unit of crop land as are found in North America or Australia. It might therefore be assumed that the quality of the land is much higher in Latin America than in North America or Australia. In fact this is not so. One is forced to conclude, therefore, that either there are too few farmers in North America and Australia or too many in Latin America. Since the farm population in North America is now only about half as large as it was in the 1950s, it is difficult to argue that there are too few farmers in North America. The fact is that in many parts of Latin America if land were distributed to farmers in the form of family farms of a minimum desirable size for the farm to have a surplus and not just become self-supporting, there would be enough land only for one family in five or even no more than one family in ten. C. T. Smith[4] refers to part of the Sierra of Peru with 600,000 families eligible to benefit from land reform but only enough land for about 60,000 to have suitably large farms. Even where a country has suitable unused land available for resettlement of farmers the cost of resettlement is very large. The number resettled under such schemes in various parts of Latin America has been very small. For example only 30,000 farmers have been resettled in the eastern lowlands of Bolivia between the Agrarian Reform Act of 1953, and 1970.

If land reform in Latin America follows the pattern of previous sporadic efforts, decisions in the agricultural sector in Latin America will eventually be taken by tens of millions of small farmers. This trend towards fragmentation of ownership of means of production contrasts with the trend in mining, manufacturing and many 'non-goods' activities towards increasing concentration of ownership in relatively few companies, corporations or families.

In conclusion, it must be stressed that land reform in agriculture cannot be separated from other aspects and problems of the economy of Latin America. The view that land reform is one of the keys to development in Latin America, a view widely held both outside the region and inside, does not seem to take into account the possibility that there are already far too many people on the cultivated land to create viable, modern, efficient farms for every family. The gloomy view expressed in the following lines shows that at least one of the principal authorities on the subject of agriculture in developing regions, the Food and Agricultural Organisation[5] had arrived by the early 1970s at a much more pessimistic view of Latin America than that previously held:

'The degree of under-utilisation of the economically active population of the region, including both unemployment and under-employment, is estimated at a full employment equivalent of 28 per cent of the labour force. Much of this unemployment is in agriculture, on which about 145 million inhabitants of the region (*60 per cent of the total population*) depend for a living. Land resources in many areas, particularly zones of small cultivators, are so scanty in relation to population, and so deteriorated from overuse that even the most effective program of rural development cannot be expected to improve significantly rural living standards until many people are shifted out of agriculture. Land tenure reform and opening up new land, therefore, cannot afford a complete solution to rural unemployment. At the same time, already widespread urban poverty and unemployment mean that little or no relief of rural unemployment can be expected from the movement of population to the cities.'

8.4. DECISION MAKERS AND THE SPREAD OF IDEAS

When it appeared in 1965, A. Samson's *The Anatomy of Britain*[6] caused considerable interest. One of the main themes of the book was the question of who runs Britain. Since there appears to be nothing strictly comparable on Latin America, a very provisional attempt has been made to answer the question who runs Latin America, with particular reference to Mexico and Peru. In a small, simple isolated community, such as that of the cave-dwelling Tasadays[7] in the Philippines, the Tsembaga group in New Guinea[8] or many a village of Indians in Amazonia, each member of the community, or at least each family in the community, does roughly the same amount of work as every other, and receives roughly the same amount of what is produced.

In a modern Latin American country the 'cake' is shared out very unevenly, as will be shown in Chapter 10. The influence of an individual in the community and the relative weight his or her decisions make in the functioning of the community and on its future changes may be measured in two related ways. Influence in a community is determined firstly by ownership of the means of production and secondly by purchasing power or 'right' to consume a certain proportion of goods and services produced. The difference is illustrated in the following example. In a system of large agricultural holdings with private owners and landless workers, decisions about production, marketing, modernisation and other aspects of the farm economy are largely in the hands of a few per cent of the population. In a hypothetical large farm it could be that a landowner had 50 workers and that the value of production was 100 units. The owner might take half of the production. He would probably spend some of his income on a range of manufactured goods which would not be bought by the workers whether they received 1 unit per head as now, or 2 units per head in the event of the landowner being dispossessed and the land being shared among them.

In other sections of the community it is by no means so easy to put numerical values to the distribution of ownership and purchasing power among groups and individuals. A tentative attempt is made to indicate where the power lies in Latin American countries, as the power structure differs considerably from that in Britain and the U.S.A.

1. The *Head of State* in Latin American countries is usually also the leader of the political party or military group in power. Latin American countries are Republics so there is no hereditary monarch and there are no titles as in Britain. The president of a Latin American country holds great power but he may be prevented from using it by a majority of opposition party deputies in the house of representatives.

2. *Political Parties* are less well organised than in Europe or the U.S.A., and at times tend to depend on a particular personality or to have supporters concentrated only in one part of the country. In some cases, as in Mexico, one Party dominates the political scene. The central government, whoever controls it,

tends to be strong, local government weak. The national capital is often a key place in the affairs of the country since not only is political power there but often also financial and industrial power.

3. The *Civil Service* and particularly central government Ministries tend to be large and influential. They have been criticised[9] for excessive size. The collection of income taxes is particularly difficult in Latin America and duties on imports and exports tend to be a major source of revenue.

4. The *Armed Forces* in Latin America are usually in a position to take over a country if they wish to and agree between themselves to do so. The key to their strength lies in the communications system at their disposal over the national area and the cohesion among the officers as well as their actual arms. The large following of uneducated conscript other ranks are easily controlled. The police are not usually so well organised or powerful as the armed forces.

5. Some *Professions* are strong in Latin America, especially the legal and medical professions. Engineering and architecture tend to be well developed but pure science and scientific research have little finance and as yet very few achievements to its credit. University education lacks permanent teachers and tends to be poor in buildings and equipment. In the early 1960s the U.S.A. spent about 50 times as much on its Universities as Latin America did. Secondary and primary school teachers tend to be very poorly paid and most schools have poor quality buildings and very little in the way of materials such as books and visual aids.

6. *The Church* appears to be more influential in some countries (Colombia, Brazil) than others (Mexico, Argentina, Cuba). Altogether however its influence has been declining for many decades. In many cases difficulty is encountered in recruiting priests for service in rural areas.

7. The *Press* and broadcasting are relatively influential at least in cities and in areas where the population is educated. Relatively cheap transistor radios have extended communications to more remote areas even without electricity supply. Control of the broadcasting network is essential for the group in power.

8. *Finance and business* have been strongly influenced in the private sector by the presence of foreign capital and companies. Big companies run entirely, or in the majority, by Latin Americans are still few. Large landowners are perhaps the nearest to a European type of aristocracy, and ownership of land in Latin America has often been valued as much for the social status it brings as the economic potential.

9. *Trade Unions* in most activities are weak compared with unions in West Europe or North America. It seems difficult for them to run at national level. They tend to be fragmented.

The organisation of Latin American countries tends to be based on a restricted network with links between various parts of a country passing through the capital, a radial system with few secondary links. The person or group at the hub of the spokes in the wheel is powerful through position. A. Sampson[6] wrote of Britain: 'In the 18th century, it was not difficult to answer the question: "Who rules Britain?" It was ruled by the ruling classes. More specifically, it was governed by the monarch and by two principal families. . . .' Such simplicity may be true today only of a few small Latin American countries (Haiti, Nicaragua, Paraguay) but power does seem to become concentrated easily in a few hands in Latin America.

The question may then be asked, which individuals and groups favour

hange, which are indifferent to it and which are against it? For change can be
isted: 1. Left wing political parties, trade unions and land-less agricultural
vorkers, the change they want being a more equable share of national income,
. Scientists, technologists, financiers, businessmen, private industry, who want
nodernisation and economic growth. Their aims are generally supported by
he press, advertising and planners. Against change are generally the landed
lasses, certainly the large landowners, possibly also smaller landowners, the
Church, the Civil Service and usually until the 1960s the Armed Forces. The
Church has however produced very active members who have advocated land
eform and other measures to share the economic wealth more evenly. The
Armed Forces have turned up at times with Revolutionary ideas, as in Peru
ince 1969 and in a sense in Brazil where they have supported vast economic
hanges and developments since they took control of the country in 1964.

There are many reasons why major decisions often come from relatively few
people or groups in Latin American countries, while the masses participate
ardly at all. Some reasons for the lack of participation may be suggested.

1. Political elections at both national and local level are often not held
egularly or when they should be. Chile has had a long record of stable politics,
ompared with Bolivia, constantly upset by changes of government. Peru,
Argentina and Brazil have had alternating periods of representative govern-
nent and military or civilian dictators. Mexico has tended to be dominated by
one party. Even when elections are held, a large part of the electorate has
ended to be excluded from the franchise through inadequate qualifications,
uch as inadequate level of literacy or failure to own property. In the Peruvian
lection of 1963, many people eligible to vote did not in fact do so.

2. Educational levels are so low in many rural areas that knowledge of the
ffairs of the country does not penetrate to the mass of rural population. In
igure 8.4, maps *a* and *b* show the level of literacy in the States of Venezuela in
941 and 1971. The proportion of literate population grew by 30–40 per cent in
nost states, but the 1971 population of Venezuela was more than twice as big as
he 1941 population so the absolute number of illiterates has changed little.
.evels of literacy in Latin American countries around 1970 are shown in the
ext chapter, Table 9.2.

3. In many parts of Mexico, Central America, the Andes and Amazonia the
peaking of Spanish or Portuguese is an attribute of only part of the popula-
ion. *Figure 8.4c* shows that according to the census in 1961 there were still four
lepartments in Peru in which less than $\frac{1}{3}$ of the population could speak
panish. Most people there are quechua or aymara speaking.

4. The mobility of people at both a local level and a national level is
estricted by lack of transport facilities and the cost of travel in relation to in-
ome. Rightly or wrongly the private car has made people in North America
nd West Europe much more mobile than they were a few decades ago. *Figure*
.4d shows the level of private car ownership in Brazil in the late 1960s. The
umber of private cars per thousand people (and therefore approximately per
oo families) diminishes away from São Paulo. In Northeast Brazil, private car
wnership is restricted almost entirely to the towns. Many rural settlements still
ave no cars at all.

5. The spatial perception of places encourages people in Latin America to
ravitate towards or remain in certain places. The national capital or a major
egional centre is attractive for the large number and wide range of jobs

available, for proximity to people in power, and for services and amenities such as good educational facilities and electricity. On the other hand, some areas are unpopular for their undesirably hot and humid climate, as, for example, the port of Buenaventura in Colombia, or for their excessive altitude, as the mining town of Cerro de Pasco in Peru, 4,300 metres above sea level.

Some towns that at one time flourished in a system of slow communications have not been reached by railways or roads. One such place is Ayacucho in the Peruvian Andes. D. W. Gade[10] studied the views of people in this formerly

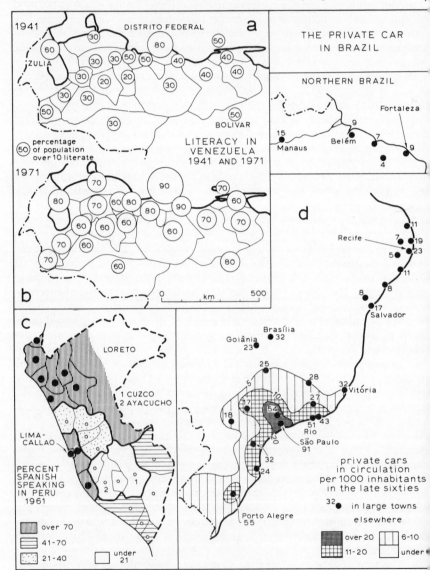

Figure 8.4. Aspects of the diffusion of cultural and technological features illustrated by (a)–(b) Literacy in Venezuela 1941 to 1971, (c) Spanish speaking population in Peru, 1961 and (d) private cars in circulation in Brazil, late 1960s

prosperous and influential town. The illiterate Indians and working class mestizos were less conscious of a feeling of isolation than the literate mestizos and the 'whites'. Virtually all the last group went to Lima at least once a year. They blamed isolation on the lack of a good road to Ayacucho, government neglect and lack of industry. Initially Brasília was regarded as unattractive by many of the people who were compelled to move there with the transference of the national capital. They returned to Rio de Janeiro as frequently as possible. A study in 1968[11] showed however that among children, including those actually born in Brasília, there was a preference for the new environment.

The author made brief studies of the residential preference of samples of middle class people in Rio de Janeiro (1969) and Mexico City (1972). When asked to which states of the country they would choose to move if they had to leave their present home (Rio or Mexico City) they showed preference for states in certain regions and especially states with large towns.

References

1. 'Foreign Investment in Latin America', *BOLSA (QR)*, July 1963, p. 132.
2. *Banas*, 15 de junho, 1970, pp. 13–36.
3. *The Times 1000 1972/73*, 1972, London; Times Newspapers Ltd.
4. In the seminar paper given in Centre for Latin American Studies, University of Liverpool, Mar. 3, 1973.
5. *The State of Food and Agriculture 1971*, 1971, Rome; FAO, p. 71.
6. Sampson, A., *The Anatomy of Britain Today*, 1965, London; Hodder and Stoughton.
7. MacLeish, K., 'The Tasadays, Stone Age Cavemen of Mindanao', *Nat. Geogr.*, Aug. 1972, Vol. 142, No. 2, pp. 219–48.
8. Rappaport, R. A., 'The Flow of Energy in an Agricultural Society', *Sci. Am.*, Sept. 1971, Vol. 224, No. 3, pp. 116–32.
9. Lambert, F. J. D., 'Planning for Administrative Reform in Latin America: the Argentine and Brazilian Cases', *Occasional Papers*, No. 3, 1971, Institute of Latin American Studies, University of Glasgow.
10. Gade, D. W., 'Ayacucho, Peru: un caso notable de aislamiento regional en Latinoamérica', *Unión Geográfica Internacional*, Conferencia Regional Latinoamericana, *Tomo I*, 1966, Mexico, pp. 89–95.
11. Bardawil, J. C. and H. Ribeiro, 'Aqui se pode pisar na grama', *Realidade*, Julho 1969, pp. 17–26.

Sources of material in figures

8.4 For Venezuela see Chapter 14. Peru: *Censo Nacional de Población* 1961, Vol. III Brazil: IBGE, *Veículos licenciados em 1967* (Deicom 1969)

Further reading

Les problèmes agraires des Amériques Latines, Paris 11–16 Oct. 1965, Colloques Internationaux du Centre National de la Recherche Scientifique, 1967, Paris.
Crossley, J. C., 'Continuing Obstacles to Agricultural Development in Latin America', *Journal of Latin American Studies*, 4, 2, 293–305.

CHAPTER 9

RELATIONSHIPS AT COUNTRY LEVEL

9.1. THE DATA USED

Table 9.1 contains 18 sets of data about 24 countries of Latin America in or near 1970. Each variable is defined in full in Table 9.2 and the source is given. In order to reduce the direct influence of the population size of countries on the data in Table 9.1 and on the conclusions that follow, all values are expressed in per capita terms or in some other appropriate way. Values may therefore be compared down the columns, though not across the rows. For convenience the columns will be referred to as variables (V). Columns 1 to 11 contain data about employment structure, the production of goods and the availability of services. Columns 12 to 17 contain demographic information. The final column shows per capita income.

Each column is of interest in its own right. A study of any of the first eleven columns reveals great contrasts among the countries of Latin America. A preliminary study of the data in Chapter 1 showed that Argentina, Venezuela and Puerto Rico usually have high scores, which reflect their relatively high levels of development. Haiti is almost always at or near the bottom while Bolivia and Paraguay also tend to have low scores. Among the demographic variables marked contrasts also occur.

The data for four of the variables, V1, V2, V12 and V17 are mapped in *Figure 9.1*. Shading and dots indicate the countries at the extremes on each of the four scales while those near the average are unshaded. A visual comparison of the distributions for variables V1, V2 and V12 shows that there is a considerable degree of correlation between each pair of variables. Thus where employment in activities other than agriculture is high, so also are per capita energy consumption and percentage urban population. On the other hand natural increase of population does not appear to correlate closely with the other three.

The visual comparison can be extended from the four shaded maps to the eighteen variables in Table 9.1. As it is difficult and time consuming to compare by eye every column with every other column, the degree of correlation between each pair of variables can be calculated numerically. The method will be discussed in the next section.

9.2. THE CORRELATION MATRIX

The correlation between a pair of variables can be shown graphically, as in *Figures 9.2a* and *9.2b*. Each of the 24 countries is located on the graph according to its value (see Table 9.1) on each of two variables, the horizontal scale representing one variable, the vertical scale the other. Three kinds of correlation can occur:

1. A significant positive correlation, in which case the 24 countries tend to spread from the lower left to the upper right of the graph. In *9.2a*, the correlation is fairly high.
2. A significant negative correlation. The 24 countries tend to be spread from the upper left to the lower right of the graph, as in *Figure 9.2b*, in which, however, the negative correlation is quite weak.
3. No correlation or a correlation that is positive or negative but not significant.

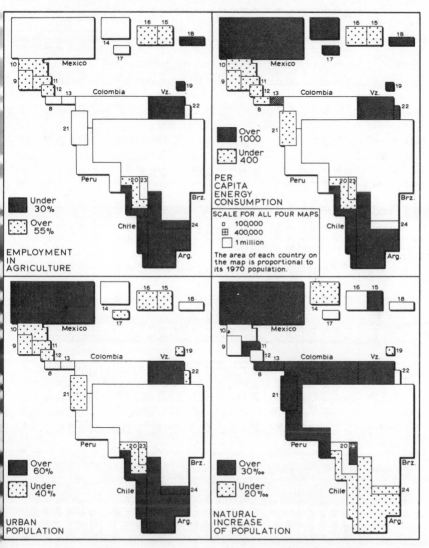

Figure 9.1. Levels of employment in agriculture, energy consumption, urban population and population increase in 24 Latin American countries. The area of each country is proportional to its population (see Figure 1.3). For the numbering of countries, see Table 9.1. Energy consumption is in kgs of coal equivalent in 1970. Natural increase is in per thousands per year

Table 9.1.

DATA FOR 24 COUNTRIES OF LATIN AMERICA MEASURING DEVELOPMENT AND SOPHISTICATION

	1 Not Agr.	2 Eng.	3 Stl	4 Cemt.	5 News.	6 Com. Vehs.	7 Food	8 Lit.	9 Rad.	10 Hosp.	11 Phys.	12 Urb.	13 Brate.	14 Drate.	15 Lt.15	16 Inf. Mort.	17 Incr.	18 Nat. Inco.
1 Brazil	52	472	64	85	29	7	2,540	61	60	31	5	46	38	10	43	80*	28	341
2 Mexico	48	1,205	82	139	31	12	2,620	76	276	18	5	60	41	9	46	67	32	632
3 Argentina	82	1,688	135	191	108	31	3,170	93	370	61	20	74	21	9	29	59	12	914
4 Venezuela	71	2,498	155	220	72	22	2,490	63	164	31	9	76	41	8	46	46	33	837
5 Colombia	53	578	32	119	24	7	2,190	73	105	22	4	53	45	11	47	70	34	358
6 Peru	53	609	34	83	35	9	2,200	61	134	22	5	52	42	11	45	62	31	363
7 Chile	74	1,208	81	138	51	15	2,520	84	143	34	4	74	27	9	40	93	18	613
8 Costa Rica	52	344	53	91	50	16	2,230	84	71	40	5	35	45	8	48	71	38	501
9 El Salvador	41	150	12	44	32	5	1,880	49	115	20	3	38	40	10	45	67	30	271
10 Guatemala	36	232	17	43	15	5	1,950	29	115	29	2	34	44	16	46	92	27	338
11 Honduras	35	243	15	51	5	7	1,930	45	57	16	2	32	49	17	51	34	32	249
12 Nicaragua	41	374	22	60	19	10	2,250	50	55	22	6	44	46	17	48	55	30	387
13 Panama	57	1,634	49	80*	40	10	2,450	73	157	32	5	48	41	9	43	38	32	629
14 Cuba	61	1,039	46	93	27	4	2,500	78	159	49	8	53	27	8	37	40	19	290*
15 Dominican Rep.	43	224	22	93	7	5	2,080	64	38	26	6	40	49	15	47	62	34	270
16 Haiti	21	43	5	11	1	0†	1,930	10	17	7	1	12	44	20	42	150*	24	70
17 Jamaica	66	1,135	62	228	36	13	2,280	82	230	41	4	37	33	7	41	32	26	545
18 Puerto Rico	81	3,283	150*	567	100*	38	2,530	81	250*	45	11	44	26	7	39	28	20	1,650
19 Trinidad	81	4,683	105	254	59	21	2,360	74	281	51	5	18	20	7	43	37	14	700
20 Bolivia	35	211	14	15	9	5	1,760	40	288	19	4	34	44	19	44	77	25	180
21 Ecuador	48	293	29	74	27	8	1,850	67	279	20	3	38	45	11	48	86	34	247
22 Guyana	54	1,014	60*	100*	9	6	2,180	76	105	44	3	30	36	8	46	38	29	300
23 Paraguay	49	145	2	17	17	5	2,730	74	71	20	6	36	45	11	45	36	34	230
24 Uruguay	83	900	13	167	72	30	3,020	91	374	61	9	81	21	9	28	54	12	773
MEAN	55	1,009	52	124	36	12	2,318	66	163	32	6	45	38	11	43	61	27	487

Table 9.2.

DEFINITION OF VARIABLES USED IN TABLE 9·1

Sources

S1 *FAOPY* Vol. 24, Rome 1971
S2 *UNSYB, 1971,* N.Y. 1972
S3 *UNDYB, 1970*
S4 *Population Reference Bureau,* 1971

Variable

1	Percentage of economically active population *not* engaged *in agriculture,* 1965 (S1, Table 5)
2	Consumption of *energy* in kilograms of coal equivalent per inhabitant, 1970 (S2, p. 337)
3	Consumption of *steel* in kilograms per inhabitant, 1970 (S2, p. 578)
4	Production of *cement* in kilograms per inhabitant, annual mean 1968–70 (S2, p. 285); (dummy consumption figures added for non-producers)
5	Consumption of *newsprint* in kilograms per inhabitant, 1970 (S2, p. 527)
6	*Commercial vehicles* in circulation per 1000 inhabitants, 1970 (S2, pp. 412–13)
7	Consumption of *food* in calories per inhabitant, per day, 1970 or nearest (S2, p. 504)
8	*Literate population* over 14 years of age as a percentage of all population over 14 years of age, mostly around 1960 (S3, Table 11)
9	*Radio receivers* in use per 1,000 inhabitants 1970 (S2, p. 807)
10	*Hospital beds* per 10,000 inhabitants, 1970 (S2, p. 712)
11	*Physicians* per 10,000 inhabitants, 1970 (S2, p. 712)
12	*Urban population* as a percentage of total population (S3, Table 5)
13, 14	Crude *birthrates* and *deathrates* per 1,000 inhabitants (S3, Table 3)
15	Persons under 15 years of *age* as a percentage of total population (S4)
16	*Infant mortality,* deaths under age of 1, per thousand live births (S3, Table 16)
17	*Natural increase* of population, per 1000 inhabitants (S3, Table 3)
18	*National income* in U.S. dollars per inhabitant, 1970 (S2, p. 594)

Just as the distribution of the countries on the graph shows visually the correlation between a pair of variables, so the Pearson product moment correlation coefficient can be used to calculate a numerical correlation coefficient. The coefficient lies at or between −1·0 and +1·0, the former being a perfect negative correlation, the latter a perfect positive correlation. Coefficients around zero occur when the relationship between the two variables is random. It is possible, with the help of a computer, to calculate quickly the correlation coefficients between each pair of variables in a data matrix such as that in Table 9.1. These are shown in Table 9.3. To save space, each calculated coefficient has been rounded to one decimal place and then multiplied by 10. The 10s along the principal diagonal (upper left to lower right of the matrix) are the perfect positive correlations of +1·0 between each variable and itself. Other correlation matrices will be used in later chapters and the reader who is not sure of the significance of the data in the matrix should refer to Appendix 1 where the method of calculation is shown and further reading is suggested. Even from a glance at Table 9.3 it can be seen that variables 1–12, representing features associated with development and modernisation all correlate positively with each other and also with variable 18, national income. In contrast variables 1–12 and 18 all correlate negatively with the demographic variables 13–17. The latter, however, correlate positively among themselves. When 24 cases (the countries) are correlated, the level of significance of *r,* with 95 per cent confidence, is 0·39 and with 99 per cent confidence, 0·49. In other words, when *r* is further from 0 (zero) than about ±0·50, the relatively high positive or negative correlation obtained could be reached only very rarely by chance. The two sets

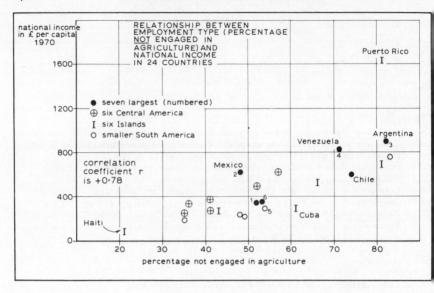

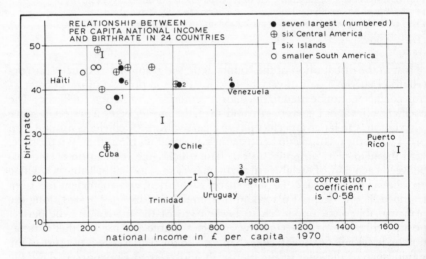

Figure 9.2. Graphical representation of relationship between two pairs of variables in Table 9.1. The seven largest countries in the graph are numbered 1–7, as in Table 9.1

of data are presumably therefore related in some way. Reference to column 18 of the matrix shows that several correlation coefficients are as high as +0·9. Thus the levels of consumption of cement and newsprint and the availability of commercial vehicles all correlate closely with per capita national income, to which of course each makes some contribution. Similarly, as might be expected, population increase (V17) correlates highly with birthrate (V13). The application of factor analysis to the data in the matrix makes it possible to

Table 9.3.
MATRIX OF CORRELATION COEFFICIENTS

The matrix shows the Pearson product moment (r) correlation coefficient between each pair of variables. For quick reference and to save space coefficients have been rounded to one decimal place and then multiplied by 10. e.g. 0·7405 becomes 7.

		1	2	3	4	5	6	7	8	9	10	11	12	13	14	15	16	17	18
Non-agricultural	1	10	7	7	7	9	8	7	8	6	8	7	6	-8	-8	-7	-5	-6	8
Energy	2	7	10	8	8	7	7	4	4	5	6	4	1	-6	-6	-3	-5	-5	7
Steel	3	7	8	10	8	8	7	5	5	4	5	6	4	-5	-6	-3	-3	-3	8
Cement	4	7	8	8	10	8	8	4	5	5	5	5	2	-6	-6	-4	-4	-4	9
Newsprint	5	9	7	8	8	10	9	7	6	6	7	8	6	-7	-6	-6	-3	-5	9
Commercial vehicles	6	8	7	7	8	9	10	7	6	7	7	7	5	-7	-5	-6	-4	-5	9
Food	7	7	4	5	4	7	7	10	7	4	7	8	7	-6	-6	-7	-3	-5	6
Literacy	8	8	4	5	5	6	6	7	10	5	7	6	6	-6	-8	-5	-6	-3	5
Radios	9	6	5	4	5	6	7	4	5	10	6	5	4	-7	-4	-6	-2	-6	5
Hospitals	10	8	6	5	5	7	7	7	7	6	10	7	4	-8	-7	-7	-5	-7	6
Physicians	11	7	4	6	5	8	7	8	6	5	7	10	6	-5	-4	-7	-3	-5	6
Urban	12	6	1	4	2	6	5	7	6	4	4	6	10	-3	-4	-5	-2	-3	4
Birthrate	13	-8	-6	-5	-6	-7	-7	-6	-6	-7	-8	-5	-3	10	6	8	3	9	-6
Deathrate	14	-8	-6	-6	-6	-6	-5	-6	-8	-4	-7	-4	-4	6	10	3	5	2	-6
Under 15	15	-7	-3	-3	-4	-6	-6	-7	-5	-6	-7	-7	-5	8	3	10	1	8	-5
Infant mortality	16	-5	-5	-3	-4	-3	-4	-3	-6	-2	-5	-3	-2	3	5	1	10	0	-4
Population increase	17	-6	-5	-3	-4	-5	-5	-5	-3	-6	-7	-5	-3	9	2	8	0	10	-4
National income	18	8	7	8	9	9	9	6	5	5	6	6	4	-6	-6	-5	-4	-4	10

group closely correlated variables into 'families'. The initial large number can often be reduced considerably to a number of 'collective' new 'super-variables' or factors.

9.3. FACTORS

Factor analysis is a relatively complex, sophisticated and time consuming procedure. It can be applied only with the help of a computer when the data matrix has more than a few variables or cases. In the present book the author has used throughout a program for oblique factor analysis written by Dr. P. M. Mather.[1] In order to introduce the procedure, a simpler method of grouping variables has first been applied to the correlation matrix in Table 9.3. The result is shown in *Figure 9.3*. Each variable is linked by an arrow to the variable with which it has the highest index of correlation. Reference was made to the original correlation matrix, which has several decimal places. Newsprint (V5) and commercial vehicles (V6) are the most highly correlated pair. Several other variables link with these to form Group I. Four separate groups emerge. Intergroup linkages would begin to occur if each variable was also joined to its second highest partner.

Factor analysis takes into account not only the highest correlation of each variable, but all its other associations as well. Table 9.4a shows the relationship of each of the 18 variables to the four strongest factors. The further from zero the coefficient towards +1 or −1, the higher is the degree of correlation of the variable with the factor. Thus the variables correlating most highly with Factor F1 variables 13 (birthrate), 15 (age) and 17 (natural increase), are precisely the ones that form Group 3 in *Figure 9.3*. There is a close similarity between the other three groups and the other three factors.

When oblique factor analysis is used, it is also possible for factors to be inter-correlated (this is not possible with orthogonal components or factors). Table 9.4b, a 4 × 4 correlation matrix, shows the degree of intercorrelation between the factors.

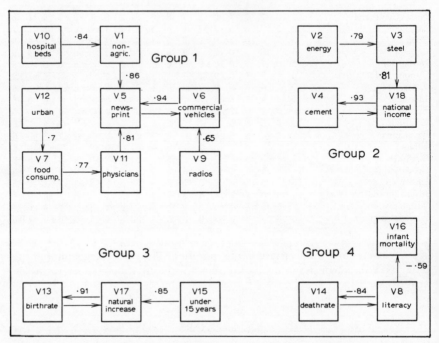

Figure 9.3. Grouping of variables according to associations in the matrix of correlation coefficients, Table 9.3. Note that the grouping in the diagram has been made on the basis of a correlation matrix with values to several decimal places

From the study of the relationships between the variables at least two further studies can be made. Firstly it is possible to use the factors to form the basis for a multi-variate classification of the cases (the 24 countries). This is done in Section 9.4. Secondly, it is possible to use the information about the relationships between variables to help in a study of causal relationships between variables. The structure of development may be worked out with a combination of empirical data such as that processed from the original data matrix in Table 9.1 and deduction, plus some common sense and imagination.

9.4. LINKAGE ANALYSIS

Each of the 24 countries in Table 9.1 can be given a score on each of the four factors. The relative position of each country is shown in Table 9.5. The first fac-tor, expressing demographic features, gives high scores to countries with a high rate of population increase. On the other three factors, the composition of each

of which can be seen in Table 9.4a, the higher the score of a country the higher
its level of development.

Table 9.4a.
FACTOR STRUCTURE MATRIX

The 18 variables are fully defined in Table 9.2.

	Variable	F1	F2	F3	F4
1	Non agricultural	−0·6767	0·9111	−0·8888	0·7181
2	Energy	−0·5348	0·6647	−0·6314	0·8192
3	Steel	−0·3783	0·6366	−0·7636	0·8123
4	Cement	−0·4642	0·6431	−0·7460	0·9608
5	Newsprint	−0·5940	0·7310	−0·9774	0·8006
6	Commercial vehicles	−0·5916	0·6650	−0·9469	0·8612
7	Food	−0·5486	0·6785	−0·7856	0·3743
8	Literacy	−0·3567	0·8688	−0·6950	0·4314
9	Radio receivers	−0·6300	0·5455	−0·6526	0·4701
10	Hospital beds	−0·7421	0·8163	−0·7544	0·5065
11	Physicians	−0·5219	0·5104	−0·8650	0·4744
12	Urban	−0·2907	0·4443	−0·6539	0·2339
13	Birthrates	0·9500	−0·8028	0·7002	−0·5341
14	Deathrates	0·3138	−0·9433	0·6275	−0·5456
15	Young population	0·8594	−0·5620	0·6991	−0·3058
16	Infant mortality	0·0946	−0·5237	0·3833	−0·3961
17	Natural increase	0·9909	−0·4890	0·5624	−0·3865
18	National income	−0·4825	0·6513	−0·8810	0·9456

Table 9.4b.
FACTOR INTERCORRELATION MATRIX

	F1	F2	F3	F4
F1	1·0000	−0·5887	0·6134	−0·4364
F2	−0·5887	1·0000	−0·7407	0·6084
F3	0·6314	−0·7407	1·0000	−0·7616
F4	−0·4364	0·6084	−0·7616	1·0000

It is possible to use the data in Table 9.5 to cluster the countries into
homogeneous groups. Colombia and Ecuador turn out to be the most similar
pair on the verdict of the data used. A comparison of rows 5 and 21 in Table 9.1
shows that in the original data matrix (the values of which are standardised in
the procedures that follow) Colombia and Ecuador have identical or very
similar values on most variables. They are the first pair of countries to be joined
in the linkage tree in *Figure 9.4*. Mexico and Panama turn out to be the next
most similar pair and they are the second pair to join. It should be remembered
that size of country is not taken into account. Each country is represented by per
capita values. On the whole the less developed countries are the least differen-
tiated and tend to join one another first. The top six join to form a more
'sophisticated' group characterised by special demographic and social features.
Puerto Rico and Venezuela are among the last to associate. While the linkage
analysis ensures a more objective grouping of countries than that to be
expected by a visual or intuitive clustering, the countries themselves are not very

Table 9.5.
SCORES OF INDIVIDUAL COUNTRIES ON EACH OF THE FOUR FACTORS

		F1	F2	F3 †	F4
1	Brazil	51	51	47	45
2	Mexico	56	52	50	52
3	Argentina	30	61	77	56
4	Venezuela	59	52	62	62
5	Colombia	59	48	46	47
6	Peru	55	48	48	47
7	Chile	38	59	55	52
8	Costa Rica	63	53	52	51
9	El Salvador	54	49	44	45
10	Guatemala	52	37	41	46
11	Honduras	59	35	39	45
12	Nicaragua	55	37	46	45
13	Panama	56	53	51	50
14	Cuba	39	60	49	42
15	Dominican Rep.	60	40	43	43
16	Haiti	49	29	35	40
17	Jamaica	47	60	50	55
18	Puerto Rico	39	63	72	87
19	Trinidad	31	65	55	65
20	Bolivia	50	33	41	41
21	Ecuador	59	47	45	46
22	Guyana	51	57	42	46
23	Paraguay	59	48	45	39
24	Uruguay	30	62	66	53

* The mean score on each factor is 50 and the standard deviation 10.
† For technical reasons the countries have been rearranged in reverse order about the mean on factor 3.

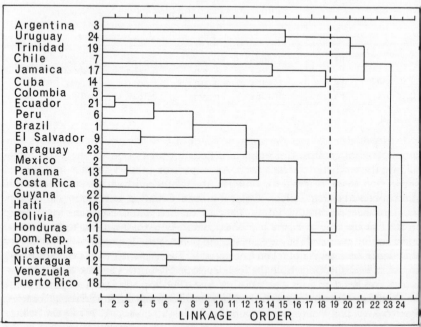

Figure 9.4. Linkage diagram showing the joining sequence of the countries of Latin America according to their similarity resulting from the multi-variate processing of the data in Table 9.1. See text for explanation

good units of study. If comparable data were available for enough major civil divisions within Latin American countries a study on that level could be much more rewarding.

9.5. THE INGREDIENTS OF DEVELOPMENT

The development or modernisation of a country is the result of many simultaneous changes in the economic and social structure of the country and in the relationship between various regions of the country. Some kind of impulse comes to the country, either from inside, or from outside, to change a state of equilibrium into one of instability and change. As changes take place, causal relationships between different ingredients of the country become very complex and sometimes circular. For example areas that have become urbanised tend to attract industry, but at the same time industrial establishments tend to contribute to the formation of urban settlements. The following associated changes have occurred in many Latin American countries in recent decades.

1. For some reason (the use of fertilisers, of mechanisation) the productivity of agricultural workers increases and population is released from the land because a farm family can support other people as well as itself. Employment structure changes and the proportion of population in agriculture diminishes.
2. Part of the population tends to concentrate in towns (central places) because industries and services can often be carried out more effectively in small areas.
3. Local and regional self-sufficiency tend to diminish, subsistence agriculture changes to commercial agriculture and regional exchanges of goods and services take place.
4. Transportation links improve and more goods and passengers can be moved or move more quickly over greater distances than previously. Flows of passengers include permanent migrants moving in particular from rural to urban areas.
5. Material living standards tend to rise. Conditions tend to improve more quickly in urban areas than in rural areas and regional differences in income grow. Housing, health and educational standards tend to improve.
6. Improvements in health tend to reduce the deathrate more quickly than the birthrate. The rate of natural increase of population grows and population begins to increase fast. This leads easily to pressure of population on existing farm land and contributes to migration flows.
7. Improvements in educational standards both increase the readiness of the population to accept innovations and can lead to the expectation of better jobs and improved material standards. If these cannot be satisfied, disillusionment seems likely to cause social and political unrest.

Many other associated changes take place. These and the above kinds of change will be found to occur in the individual Latin American countries described in Chapters 11–18. Each country has its own particular features and problems but most seem to be experiencing precisely the kinds of change outlined. Some, such as Argentina and Puerto Rico, have become much more modernised than others, such as Paraguay and Haiti. It must be remembered, however, that all are 'second generation' developers. Unlike the early industrial countries, the Latin American countries are receiving from outside, over a very short period, many of the technological advances that took decades and even centuries to become established in such countries as England, France and Holland.

It is extremely difficult to tie together all the variables involved in development. This has been tried in various ways recently. One method is to attempt to construct a flowchart or systems diagram to show diagrammatically the links between various elements and forces in the overall system of a country. The application of systems concepts and vocabulary to regional geography has not made much progress and it would not be appropriate to do more than suggest the possibility in the present book. The reader may find the next section both confusing and controversial but at least it may prove thought-provoking.

9.6. THE IDEA OF A SYSTEM

A great deal has been written about systems since the Second World War though relatively little use has been made of systems terms or concepts by geographers. A system in technical terms is basically similar to the popular use of the term. A system may be thought of as a set of interacting or interrelated elements. A change in the state of one element causes a change in the state of other elements. Existing elements may also disappear from the system or new ones appear in it. Most systems likely to be of interest to geographers are open systems in the sense that a system under consideration and defined for a particular purpose will be influenced by changes outside itself, that is in the environment in which it exists. For the purposes of this section, the concept of a system will be illustrated by three simple examples. They may not match up to the rigorous requirements of systems analysis and can perhaps better be described as flowcharts.

A DOMESTIC GAS CENTRAL HEATING SYSTEM

Figure 9.5 shows diagrammatically the main elements of a central heating system. The temperature of the inside of a house tends to be equal to the temperature outside. When the temperature outside drops, heat is lost from the building. To maintain the temperature at a desired level above that outside, heating is provided. In order to maintain a reasonably steady temperature inside the house a thermostat is used to regulate or control the stove producing heat. It monitors the inside temperature. Gas is burned then cut off again as required. A real central heating system may be represented diagrammatically as a flow diagram. The system and its immediate environment are the house. Outside influences are the temperature out of doors and the gas supply. A change in the value of any element in the system has an immediate effect on the values of the element or elements to which the arrow points. The ability of a system to control itself is called homeostasis. An example of this is the way in which the body temperature of mammals maintains itself close to a particular temperature. The information needed to control a system is called feedback. In

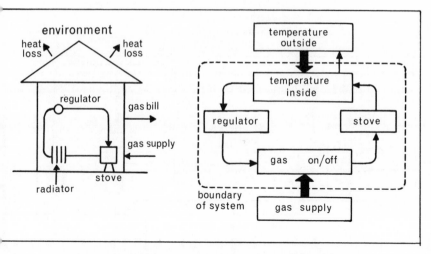

Figure 9.5. The idea of a system, exemplified by the central heating system of a house

the central heating system this is the change of temperature recorded by the thermostat. The central heating system described above is an open system because it interacts with its environment.

A SYSTEM ILLUSTRATING THE ORGANISATION OF A VILLAGE

Figure 9.6 shows some of the main elements and some of the links between elements in a hypothetical village in the Andes. The scheme is actually based on a village in the Central Andes of Peru visited briefly by the author in 1970. The village has a few hundred inhabitants. The land or soil is its only natural resource. Influences outside the system, particularly precipitation, temperature and frosts affect the harvests and yields of crops and livestock. Most of the food, clothing, housing and fuel used are produced locally. A small surplus of livestock products and crops are sold outside the village. The prices received depend on outside influences. Services, consumer goods and capital goods are purchased outside the village. Government policy and spending pay for certain benefits to the village, a school building, teachers, a road.

The diagram in *Figure 9.6* is only one of many possible ways of representing the way in which the village works. Other boxes and arrows could be added and the network could be rearranged. On the whole, however, it is not difficult to separate the village system on its own particular territory from the outside environment, the rest of the country in which it is located. To construct the relatively complex diagram, however, a mass of detail has been abandoned or simplified. For example several hundred people of different ages and both sexes are put indiscriminately into one box. It is opportune here to stress that the larger the system studied the greater the loss of detail, and the more drastic the level of simplification, generalisation and degree of abstraction required to obtain a viable model. The next system shows a concise eight box representation of certain major world elements and relationships.

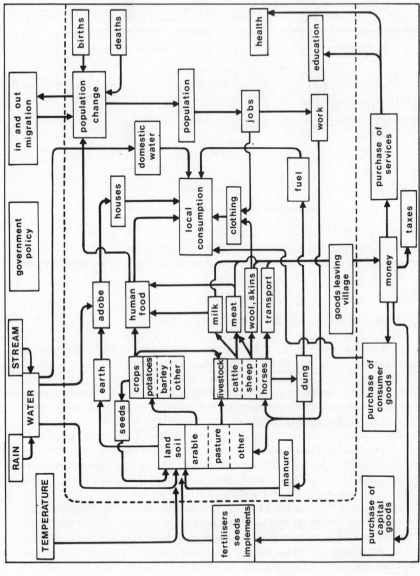

Figure 0.6 Some of the relationships in an Andean village. See text for explanation and Section 16.1 on page 208.

A WORLD MODEL

Figure 9.7 shows an adaptation of various simplified models used in *The Limits to Growth*.[2] They are based on a full model with about 100 elements used to make various futures. Central in the model is 'industrial output' representing agriculture and services as well as manufacturing. The scale of output depends on productive capacity (industrial capital) and on the use of non-renewable (as well as renewable) resources. Food, services and pollution, as well as other items are produced by industrial output. They in turn influence the structure of population through fertility and mortality. Such a model could be applied to a single country rather than to the whole world, but it would then be necessary to establish interconnections with the rest of the world beyond the country itself to allow for the flows in and out of the country of capital, goods, services and people.

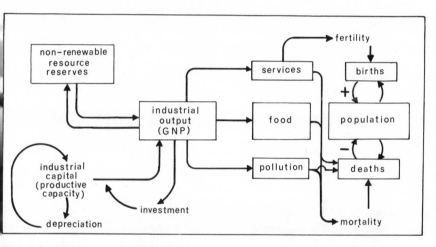

Figure 9.7. Basic aspects of relationships in a world system, based on diagrams and ideas in The Limits of Growth

In conclusion it should be noted that the world system, at least from the point of view of outside human influences, is a closed system, whereas any regional part of the world is an open system. Moreover the world system has no obvious control or homeostasis and it seems unlikely that it will have until human beings work out some way to regulate their activities more consciously. From the point of view of regional geography, the village system and the world system illustrated above have one serious defect: they are not broken down on a spatial or regional basis.

References

1. The factor analysis program was adapted by Dr. P. M. Mather from material in Kaiser, H. F. A second-generation 'Little Jiffy'. *Psychometrika,* 1970, Vol. 35, pp. 401–415.
2. Meadows, D. H. and others, *The Limits to Growth,* 1972, London; Earth Island Limited.

Further reading

Robinson, R. J., 'Latin America's Economic Situation, The Use of the Rank Correlation Coefficient', *Teaching Geography,* No. 13, 1970 (The Geographical Association).

United Nations *Economic Survey of Latin America* 1971, U.N., New York, 1973 (yearly, by the Economic Commission for Latin America).

United Nations *Boletín Estadístico de América Latina,* Vol. VIII, No. 2, Oct. 1971 (monthly).

CHAPTER 10

POVERTY AND UNDERDEVELOPMENT

10.1. THE IDEA OF GROWTH

As a result of colonial influence and then the influence of industrialised countries in the 19th century, growth and 'modernisation' have taken place in Latin America ever since the 16th century. As pointed out in Chapter 3, even after a few decades sophisticated silver mines, sugar plantations and sailing vessels were providing Spain and Portugal with a large revenue from their colonies. Since the Second World War however an unprecedented absolute growth of population and productive forces has taken place in Latin America. On the same area, population more than doubled and the capacity to produce goods and services grew about three times during 1940–70.

Two features of modernisation in Latin America stand out. Firstly, the process has been less even in both a spatial and a temporal sense than in West Europe itself, where the process originated. As a result some areas are much more modernised than others. Secondly, many innovations and decisions affecting change in Latin America have come from outside the region. Inventions, techniques, experts, capital and sophisticated manufactured goods still have a net flow into Latin America even if political independence is carefully guarded by each country. Even in the 1970s the development of Amazonia is as much influenced by pressures from financiers outside Brazil as by politicians and business-men in Brazil itself. There even seems to be a growing voice in circles outside Brazil, notably in West Europe and the U.S.A., to try to stop the process of integration of the last large almost untouched portion of tropical forest in the world on grounds of conservation. While one would not expect conservation conscious Brazilians to offer opinions on the building of a pipeline across Alaska or of nuclear power stations in the Highlands of Scotland, outsiders still feel qualified to advise Latin Americans on their decisions.

The rapid growth of population and means of production during recent decades is not confined to Latin America. Economic 'miracles' in many industrial countries and in some developing countries gave rise after the Second World War to a feeling of optimism about the possibilities of increasing production and improving living standards throughout the world. In the late 1950s Soviet politicians and planners projected their economic growth against that of the Americans and predicted that by the early 1970s they would overtake the U.S.A. The American W. W. Rostow[1] argued that economic growth had nothing to do with capitalism or communism. Given the right conditions and organisation any country, once it broke out of a traditional society, could pass in a few decades through certain stages of growth and emerge industrialised, modernised and affluent.

The views of the Swedish economist. G. Myradl,[2] in the 1950s were less optimistic and simplistic than those of the Soviet leaders or Rostow. He stressed the already wide gap between developed and developing countries and argued that conditions in the developing countries would have to get worse before they could improve beçause big savings and sacrifices would have to be made to get enough capital to invest in rapid economic growth.

In the 1950s, economists identified various stages of growth. The stages overlap to some extent and are not so clear cut as they appear below:

1. *Subsistence economy,* based on agriculture but with other needs such as houses and clothing also produced locally. Little specialisation in jobs. Very low standard of living, common in Haiti, southern Mexico, parts of the Andes, the interior of Northeast Brazil, Amazonia.

2. The production of agricultural items or minerals for *export.* Early examples were the colonial sugar plantations of Northeast Brazil and the Caribbean, and the silver mines of the Andes and Mexico. More recent export orientated activities include the oil of Venezuela, the copper of Chile and the coffee of Colombia and Central America. Specialisation in jobs and the use of modern methods of production and processing.

3. *Industrialisation,* based on local resources and capital, and concentrated in relatively few towns, not necessarily, but often, in national capitals. More specialised industrial towns than the national capitals include for example Medellín in Colombia, Monterrey in Mexico, Blumenau and Juiz de Fora in Brazil.

4. *Tertiary and quaternary activities,* services or non-goods branches of the economy, such as administration, health services, publishing, education and research.

The level of development of a country or of a region in a country is related to a considerable extent to the proportion of each of the above four stages or sectors in its total economy.

Experience shows, and it seems generally to be accepted,[3] implicitly if not explicitly even in Communist countries, that as modernisation takes place, a given country or large region goes through three stages.

1. Every area is on average poor to start with in a traditional society.

2. As modernisation takes place, for various reasons ᴄertain areas develop sooner than others and as a result marked regional differences occur in the country as a whole.

3. The economic and other forces that favoured certain areas are checked by political forces for social reasons to help the poorer, more backward areas. Such a process forms for example a major part of regional policy in the European Economic Community in the early 1970s.

In the 1970s, most Latin American countries find themselves at the second stage, with very big internal regional differences in development levels. It would be safe to say that most, if not all governments in Latin America are anxious to remove poverty, to reduce disparities between regions and to achieve continuing high rates of growth of the capacity to produce goods and services. Some advocate bigger populations as well. Are all these aims and aspirations possible or are some mutually exclusive?

The total wealth of the country (goods and services) produced in a given period (say a year) in a Latin American country is distributed very unevenly among the population, with a few very rich and many poor, as will be shown in the next section. If the same sized total were shared exactly evenly among the population (which is organisationally virtually impossible), everyone would be poor. What is more, if income did not grow, but population continued to grow (as it is bound to do for some decades), in whatever way income was shared out, everyone would gradually get poorer. Therefore the economy has to grow at least as fast as population to maintain existing levels. It has to grow at a faster rate than population, as in fact it has tended to do in Latin America in recent decades, if improvements are to be made. Either economic growth at a rate hoped for by governments can be sustained in Latin America into the forseeable future or it cannot. In the rest of this chapter it is assumed that it can, and various views on economic growth and the solution of regional problems are discussed with reference to the situation in Latin America. In the chapters that follow, the prospects of each Latin American country will be critically examined. The final chapter in the book will attempt to outline the prospects of the whole of Latin America in the light of the recent less confident view about future development in the world that now challenges the optimism of the 1950s. Non-renewable resources, the limits of food supply, pollution, conservation and the population explosion are all involved.

The author is struck by the depressing thought that a time lag of at least a decade or two occurs before influential people in Latin America receive and begin to consider ideas originating in the so-called developed countries. Latin Americans in the 1970s still have the optimism that pervaded views in the 1950s about the possibilities of unlimited economic growth, provided organisational problems can be overcome. In a world in which changes occur with ever increasing frequency and major decisions and events are telescoped in time, such information delays may prove unfortunate.

According to the former President of Chile, Salvador Allende,[4] writing early in the 1970s, serious development was only about to begin in his country. Typically the shareout of the national 'cake' is a greater preoccupation than the problem of making the 'cake' bigger.

> 'From the economic point of view our country, like many others in this and other continents, was a dependent one; its basic resources were controlled by foreign capital. For many years the country lived through a stage of deformed capitalism, producing solely to satisfy the needs of a minority. Our development process was never oriented towards satisfying the needs of the people—a fact proved by statistics on food consumption, education, housing and health. The economy was a dependent one. Some progress was made, but it was based on techniques brought from abroad and often irrationally applied in the local situation. . . .
>
> We must produce to satisfy the needs of the Chilean masses. To achieve this, the Government planned the creation of a socially owned property sector, a mixed sector and a private sector. We began to create the socially-owned sector by nationalising essential resources under foreign control, by taking over a number of monopolistic industries—textiles and tyres, for example—and by bringing the private banks into state ownership.'

10.2. THE DISTRIBUTION OF WEALTH

The wealth of Latin American countries is distributed very unevenly among the population. Put slightly more fully, both the ownership of means of production and the power to purchase goods and services are unevenly distributed among social classes or individuals and also among regions. In this section the shareout among population will be discussed briefly. In the following sections regional disparities will be studied in more detail. It is not within the scope of the present book to argue for or against a more even shareout of wealth. The problem is one of equity versus efficiency and welfare versus incentive, a social rather than a geographical question.

The distribution of wealth in a country can be described in various ways. *Figure 10.1* shows three ways of looking at the shareout diagrammatically. These will be discussed. *Figure 10.2* shows the shareout by income groups according to the Lorenz curve. The eight kinds of house in the accompanying illustration on housing show regional housing conditions.

The upper drawing in *Figure 10.1* shows a 'typical' poor rural family and rich urban family in Latin America. Both have several children but in the poor family it is probable that some of the children will die before they mature. The poor family grows most of its own food, makes some of its clothing, builds its house. The diet tends to lack protein and vitamins. In a poor year food is short. There is no gas, electricity, piped water or sewage. Possessions inside the house include one or two beds and chairs, a few cooking utensils and a fire or stove using dung, firewood, charcoal or sometimes kerosene as fuel. The members of the family rarely wash themselves or their clothes. The nearest doctor may be a journey of several hours on foot. His fees would be so high that his services would be used only in a serious emergency. Most of the children could expect to complete five years of primary education but prospects for secondary education are limited.

The rich family has many of the standards of its counterpart in a developed country. Consumer durables such as a car (or two), a refrigerator, washing machine, vacuum cleaner, may be imported or, increasingly, nationally produced. Two or three servants can be afforded. They help with cooking, cleaning and child-minding. A very affluent family might have a servant simply to look after the dog. Medical services, though expensive, are available. The children will receive secondary education and in some cases higher education. Ironically, while the servants of the rich family are relatively poorly paid, their food, material comforts and probably even health and educational prospects are better than those of the poor rural family.

How many people are in fact rich and how many poor in Latin America? Both terms are relative. Moreover there are big differences between the Latin American countries. One study of the distribution of purchasing power in Latin America estimates that the richest 2 per cent of the population have about 30 per cent of the income and the poorest 60 per cent also have about 30 per cent of the income. This is shown diagrammatically in *Figure 10.1d*. Thus the *average* in the top 2 per cent is about 30 times as high as the average in the bottom 60 per cent. The two families illustrated in *Figure 10.1a* and *b* might represent the average for these two groups.

The distribution of purchasing power is in fact only broadly related to the distribution of ownership of means of production. This may be illustrated by

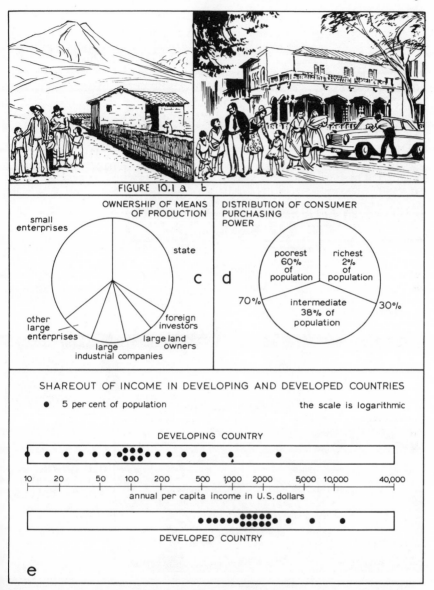

Figure 10.1. Three views of the uneven distribution of wealth in Latin America. (a) and (b) compare two families, (c) and (d) compare distribution of ownership of means of production and purchasing power and (e) compares income levels in a developing country and a developed country

the examples of a hypothetical large farm with one owner and 20 landless labourers. All the land and farming equipment are owned by the one family and the labourers are paid a wage for working the land. The shareout of means of production is 100 per cent to the owner, 0 per cent to the 20 labourers. The returns on the sale of produce, however, would be shared out for example with 50 per cent to the owner and 50 per cent shared among the 20 labourers.

RURAL HOUSING TYPES

TYPICAL HOUSE
OF THE TROPICAL
RAIN FOREST,
IQUITOS, PERU

ADOBE AND
THATCH HOUSE,
COMMON IN
SUB-HUMID
AREAS

OLD AND NEW
HOUSES WITH
ADOBE WALLS,
NEAR LAKE
TITICACA,
BOLIVIA

HOUSING IN
A COTTON
PLANTATION,
ARID ZONE
OF PERU

P. COLE

IN LATIN AMERICA

OLD AND NEW
RURAL
DWELLINGS,
VENEZUELA

TIMBER HOUSE,
PINE FOREST
AREA, SOUTH-
ERN BRAZIL

COFFEE
PLANTATION
OWNER'S
HOUSE,
SAŌ PAULO
STATE, BRAZIL

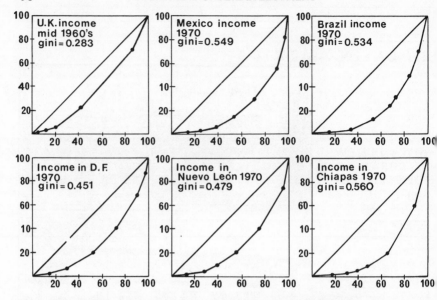

Figure 10.2. The distribution of income by income groups in six selected areas, by the Lorenz curve. The three lower graphs represent the situation in three major civil divisions of Mexico

In *Figure 10.1,* the shareout of purchasing power described above is shown in diagram *d.* In comparison, means of production (other than labour itself) are shared out very differently, as in the hypothetical situation in diagram *c.*

1. The state 'owns' a certain proportion (in a communist country, virtually all) and in theory everyone therefore has an equal stake in this sector.
2. Foreign companies or individuals own a few per cent of the means of production in most Latin American countries. Profits are shared between the host country and the foreign investor.
3. Relatively few families own much of the land and own or have shares in the larger industrial, commercial, transport and other enterprises.·
4. There are many small landowners, retailers and manufacturers with land, buildings and/or equipment.
5. Many people have no share of the means of production other than their stake in the state sector. They may be poorly paid agricultural workers or relatively well paid manual workers in mining and industry, or professional people such as teachers and lawyers, with nothing to 'sell' but their own labour and skills.

Figure 10.1e compares the distribution of purchasing power plus entitlements to state services and benefits in a hypothetical developing country with that in a hypothetical developed country. The use of a logarithmic scale for purchasing power should be noted. The mean income is about $400 per capita in the developing country, about $2,400 in the developed. The logarithmic scale obscures the fact that both distributions are skewed with the median income below the mean. The distribution is more skewed in the developing country than in the developed one. At the lower end it is virtually impossible for a person to exist in a developed country below a certain level. With certain services provided to everyone by the state, plus unemployment benefits and other allowances, no one falls below the level of several hundred dollars. In a developing country, on the other hand, there are families with only a nominal income, living in a subsistence economy. The food and other goods they produce and consume are not however formally recorded in the national income, though they may be calculated.

At the upper end of the scale in *Figure 10.1e,* the effective incomes of people with the highest incomes in developed countries, whether earned or unearned, tend to be much less than their apparent incomes due to severe progressive income tax. In Latin America only a very small proportion of the population has very high incomes and the mean for even the highest 5 per cent (right-hand dot in diagram *e*) is quite low. Income tax tends however to be less drastic than in developed countries.

Table 10.1 shows the distribution of income in Britain, in Mexico and in selected states of Mexico. The application of the Lorenz curve (see Appendix 1) to the data gives the gini coefficients shown in Table 10.2. They show that income is much more evenly spread by income groups in Britain than in Mexico or Brazil. Within Mexico itself the greatest disparity is in Chiapas, the poorest state. A paper[5] on incomes in Brazil showed that the shareout of wealth among income groups became *less* even during the 1960s. The comment was that this reflected progress in the country, that even if the poor were worse off relatively they were better off absolutely, and that education and enterprise had been justly rewarded by the improvements among the already better off classes.

It was suggested that in a developed country it is virtually impossible to have completely poor people. In the same way, in a large urban centre in a developing country, though for environmental rather than social reasons, it is not 'convenient' to have completely poor people living, sleeping and even dying on the streets. A minimum standard of living is desirable. Even Calcutta,[6] reputedly the poorest very big town in the world, cannot absorb too many beggars and other unemployed. On the other hand, in a Latin American country, although the rural community can theoretically have no money income at all, there will be means for people to make their own living until bad conditions bring diseases and famine.

Income level very broadly depends on type of employment. In Latin America labour in agriculture is generally very poorly rewarded. Workers in modern mining and industrial activities are relatively well paid on the whole. White collar or office workers are not all well off and some professional jobs such as teaching seem relatively depressed. On the other hand lawyers, doctors, architects and high-up people in the military establishment are among those who are well paid. Owners of land, factories, shops and other such enterprises can also do very well materially.

The final point leads directly to the next section. The prosperity of a given region in a country in Latin America, measured for convenience in terms of per capita income or some similar index, *depends to a considerable extent on the proportion of the different sectors of the economy and of the jobs that it has.*

10.3. THE REGIONAL DISTRIBUTION OF INCOME

Not many geographers took an interest in the distribution of wealth and poverty within countries before the 1960s. In Italy, the economist G. Tagliacarne[7] has

Table 10.1a

DISTRIBUTION OF INCOME IN BRITAIN[*]

A   people receiving income, in thousands
B   income in millions of pounds

	I	II	III	IV	V	VI	VII	VIII	IX
					Categories				
A	4,3	18,6	84,0	193,0	370,0	725,0	3,400,0	10,900,0	6,300,0
B	129	242	588	695	888	1,233	4,250	8,720	2,520

[*] Note that the wealthiest class comes first for Britain, the poorest first for Mexico in Table 10.1b.   Source: Sampson, A., *The Anatomy of Britain Today*, London 1965, p. 15

Table 10.1b

DISTRIBUTION OF INCOME IN MEXICO AND IN SELECTED STATES OF MEXICO, 1970

A   people receiving income, in thousands
B   income in millions of pesos

Areas		I	II	III	IV	V	VI	VII	VIII
						Categories			
All Mexico	A	2,144	3,083	3,137	1,474	952	556	200	108
	B	300	925	2,353	1,843	1,714	1,668	1,200	1,512
Baja California	A	9	19	42	54	43	28	9	4
	B	1,2	5,6	31,4	67,3	77,8	84,6	55,2	56,0
Distrito Federal	A	78	267	675	494	329	206	81	36
	B	10,9	80,1	506,3	617,5	592,2	618,0	486,0	504,0
Nuevo Leon	A	35	80	158	92	55	28	12	5
	B	4,9	24,0	118,5	115,0	99,0	84,0	72,0	70,0
Tlaxcala	A	23	39	18	7	3	1	0,3	0,3
	B	3,2	11,6	13,6	8,3	5,2	3,0	1,8	4,2
Chiapas	A	135	140	39	13	9	5	1,6	2,1
	B	18,9	42,1	29,6	15,6	15,5	14,1	9,6	29,4

Source: *X Censo 1970*, pp. XII, 19, 117, 257, 397, 89

Table 10.2.

Whole country		Unit within Mexico	
U.K.	0·283	Distrito Federal	0·451
Mexico 1970	0·549	Baja California	0·471
Brazil 1960	0·469	Nuero Leon	0·479
Brazil 1970	0·534	Tlaxcala	0·490
		Chiapas	0·560

published data about purchasing power in Italian provinces since the end of the Second World War. In a lively exchange of views in the mid-1950s, North and Tiebout[8] argued as to the importance of export orientated production as a means of generating regional development. E. Ullman[9] was one of the first geographers to make specific statements about the distribution of wealth in a country. He sees a stark contrast in India:

'In some cases, as in India, one has an impression of two worlds—(1) the great cities with education, libraries, utilities, etc. connected with each other by strategic transport, but floating like islands in (2) a vast sea of rural villages without schools and facilities of any kind'.

On the other hand he draws attention to the social and political forces that may help to even out regional contrasts:

'Some characteristics of political units also favour the equal spread of opportunity; this is one reason why national states have considerable validity as units of measurement. Common schools, roads, armies, markets, services of all kinds, relative freedom to migrate, and subsidy to the poorer regions, are all features of political area and work powerfully to even out the differences, although many remain and are even accentuated, as Myrdal notes, in spite of this political uniformity.'

One possible reason why geographers paid little attention to the distribution of wealth in countries was that unlike mountains, plants, buildings and transport links, it does not have an obvious physical or material representation in the landscape. The distribution of wealth is in fact related to aspects of the physical and human geography of a region and in a sense measures concisely the material achievements and successes of this or that region in a given part of the world.

In the U.S.A., per capita income is measured on a state and county basis[10] in order to identify and eventually assist backward areas. Poverty is represented by a certain minimum income and areas with over a given percentage of their population below this level may be defined as poor. In West Europe, the European Economic Community is attempting to identify regions that are eligible for community aid. Here again some standard measure of poverty is needed. Unfortunately no standard measure exists in Latin America and wealth and poverty can only be identified within each country. In many Latin American countries, meaningful income figures are not readily available but other more specialised measures, such as private cars in circulation or medical facilities can act as approximate surrogates.

Figure 10.3 identifies in Latin America the wealthiest and poorest areas within each main country according to a suitable available measure. Dots are located in the wealthiest major civil divisions, the poorest are shaded, and the intermediate ones remain blank. Each major country will be discussed in detail in the following chapters. What does emerge from the map in *Figure 10.3* is that in spite of the lack of detail there is no obvious spatial pattern of distribution of wealth and poverty. Each country has to be taken on its own merit. On the other

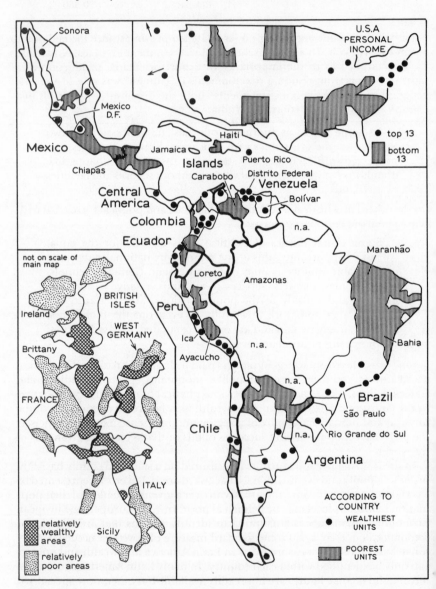

Figure 10.3. The most developed and least developed parts of Latin America. Note that as no standard set of criteria is available, a different measure has been used within each of the larger countries

hand, countries have one feature in common, namely that the units with the national capitals or other large towns tend to be in the wealthiest group. The inset maps show a simpler spatial pattern in both the U.S.A. and the European Economic Community. In the U.S.A. the wealthiest areas are in the industrial Northeast and in the West (extended to include Alaska and Hawaii). The poorest areas are mainly in the deep south but include lagging relatively rural states such as the Dakotas. In the E.E.C. there seems to be a more wealthy centre and a poorer periphery, but a relatively poor area occurs in the heart of E.E.C. in eastern France, southern Belgium and the adjoining part of West Germany.

In a study of the problem of the E.E.C.,[10] the following types of problem area were identified:

1. Those still depending heavily on employment in agriculture, over 20 per cent being considered 'heavy' (southern Italy, parts of south-west France).
2. Old industrial areas, especially those associated with old, declining coalfields (South Wales, parts of Ruhr).
3. Congested areas, notably the London and Paris areas.

Figure 10.3 is interpreted in some detail here to avoid repetition of certain features of the distribution of wealth common to various countries. In the view of the author the following influences are considered to be relevant to an appreciation of the distribution of wealth and development in Latin America:

1. RESOURCES

1a. The more heavily an area depends on agriculture the poorer it tends to be. Heavy here might be over about 50 per cent employed in farming.

1b. The quality of the same resource varies from one place to another. A mineral may be less costly to mine in one place than another and soil fertility also varies from place to place. The higher the production costs the poorer the area.

1c. If an area specialises in an export product that can compete in the world market, by definition production costs will tend to be low. The area will also be favoured on account of its national importance and will tend to be more wealthy than an area producing for the local or home national market.

2. CULTURE AND TECHNOLOGY

The earlier an area has become modernised, the more advanced its stage of development should be. Modernisation has tended to be carried out in areas with European settlers rather than in predominantly Indian or negro areas. Cultural and linguistic differences affect educational standards, which in turn are related to the degree to which modern innovations can be absorbed and applied. It could however also be argued that the new European settlers arriving in the 19th and 20th centuries have found their way to the areas with good resources, such as the good agricultural lands of the pampas of Argentina and the interior of São Paulo state.

3. POSITION

It has often been said that the coastal regions of Latin America are the most developed. There are too many exceptions for this to be more than just a tendency. There may be however an advantage in being on or near a coast for a centre of production of export commodities. Given two places with the same resource and equal production costs, the one nearer to the coast, if the product is to be exported, will be the preferable one to use first. There may for example be large bauxite deposits in the interior of Brazil but those near the coast in Guyana, Surinam and Jamaica have been exploited and used first.

4. PRESSURE OF POPULATION ON RESOURCES

Some of the poorest areas in Latin America are deeply rural areas such as Haiti, Southern Mexico, Northeast Brazil and the Andes of Southern Peru. In all these areas the actual density of farm population to cultivated area seems very high indeed. Paradoxically, however, urban areas may be even more densely populated, have few local natural resources, and depend on materials assembled from elsewhere and on the provision of services to areas around, and yet be relatively prosperous. As the larger urban areas grow however they seem to accumulate many unemployed and underemployed. Perhaps the term job congestion rather than overpopulation might be applied to those parts of Latin America in which there are too many people for the resources or jobs.

Table 10.3 shows how selected regions have different combinations of the various features mentioned above. The areas exemplified are named on the main map in *Figure 10.3*. The table is intended to be thought provoking rather than an exact representation of the overall quality of each region. It seems reasonable however to suggest that whatever precise criteria were used and whatever weight they were given the regions would be ranked roughly in the same order as they are ranked in the final column. São Paulo could never be at the bottom and Chiapas never at the top.

From the table it is possible to suggest three broad types of area in Latin America:

1. A large relatively prosperous urban centre with the area around, offering jobs in industry and services. The danger for such places is that they may become swamped out as their attraction outgrows their ability to provide more jobs. They face problems also of physical congestion, pollution, and supply of water, food and other needs.
2. A thinly populated area with many potential resources, such as Amazonsas in Brazil, Loreto in Peru and Bolívar in Venezuela, with their forest and mineral reserves. Again, the attraction of such areas to settlers may be too great for their resources, and initial prosperity may decline.
3. A densely populated predominantly agricultural area with few resources other than land of limited quality, a remote position, and low educational standards, unlikely to attract new jobs in industry or services.

Regional disparities in the distribution of income in countries can be represented on Lorenz curves. For example, gini coefficients of 0·314 in 1958 and 0·283 in 1968 for the distribution of income by states in Brazil show that regionally income has tended to become more evenly spread in a spatial sense in the 1960s even if not in a social sense. This matter will be taken up again in Chapter 11 on Brazil.

Table 10.3.

RATINGS OF DEVELOPMENT PROSPECTS IN SELECTED LATIN AMERICAN MAJOR DIVISIONS

2   very good   1   satisfactory   0   poor

	1a Non agricultural employ-m-t	1b Good quality resource	1c Export orient.	2 Educ-ation high	3 Position good	4 Little con-gestion	Final Score
Mexico							
Distrito Federal	2	0	1	2	2	1	8
Sonora	1	1	2	2	1	2	9
Chiapas	0	0	0	0	0	0	0
Islands							
Puerto Rico	2	0	2	2	1	0	7
Jamaica	1	1	1	1	1	0	5
Haiti	0	0	0	0	1	0	1
Venezuela							
Distrito Federal	2	0	1	2	2	1	8
Bolívar	1	2	2	1	1	2	9
Carabobo	0	0	0	0	1	0	1
Peru							
Ica	1	1	1	2	2	1	8
Loreto	1	1	1	1	0	2	6
Ayacucho	0	0	0	0	0	0	0
Brazil							
São Paulo	2	2	2	2	2	2	12
Rio Grande do Sul	1	2	1	2	1	2	9
Amazonas	1	1	1	1	0	2	6
Bahia	0	1	0	1	2	1	5
Maranhão	0	0	0	0	1	0	1

In conclusion, the following points may be made:

1. In the context of Latin America, an area with a combination of good natural resources (including agricultural land), proximity to a port and/or a large urban centre, high educational levels and not too many people, financial capital and an appreciation of technology, and favourable political and administrative circumstances, is likely to be relatively wealthy.

2. In view of the lack of data it is difficult to show convincingly where in Latin America regional differences in level of development are increasing, where they are not changing and where they are diminishing. With

evidence from several countries Williamson[3] supports his argument that regional disparities in development are greatest in countries at an intermediate stage of development. Many Latin American countries would fall in this category. This view agrees with the evidence of early stages of development when certain areas begin to modernise rapidly and draw ahead of others. Williamson's data and other data show that in Sweden, West Germany and the U.S.A., regional disparities are relatively less marked than they were a few decades ago. In very poor countries such as Haiti, Ethiopia or Nepal, there has been so little development that again regional disparities are not very marked. The reader interested in following up this particular matter further is referred to the paper by Williamson.

10.4. FEATURES OF UNDERDEVELOPMENT

What characteristics distinguish a developing country from a developed one? It is easy to compare numerical indices expressing per capita production and consumption of goods and services and to see big differences in average per capita values between different countries of the world. This section is a brief verbal account of impressions gained by the author during various visits to Latin America. Five arbitrary headings have been chosen.

1. HUMAN BEHAVIOUR AND ATTITUDES

There is generally a more happy-go-lucky attitude to life in Latin America than in West Europe. People more often fail to carry out promises and tend to be less punctual and in general less reliable than West Europeans. Failure to reply to letters is very common. As a result there is less mutual confidence among people. There is less regard for courtesy in public places. Traffic, for example, is usually chaotic in towns and consideration for other drivers and pedestrians minimal. It is said that at traffic lights an English driver never sounds his horn, a Frenchman does so to tell the driver in front of him when the lights turn to green, but a Brazilian hoots at the lights when they are red. Incidentally it is said that in Rio cars have special gadgets fixed to their exhausts to increase noise, not to muffle it.

In Latin America there seems to be little consideration for animals, whether livestock, draught animals or simply pets. Pets tend to be left to fend for themselves and draught animals may be beaten even when they are making every effort to satisfy their masters. On the matter of blood sports, some people may find it hard to distinguish between bullfighting and hunting.

Old ideas are difficult to change. It is said in some parts of Latin America, for example, that people who eat sugar get intestinal worms. This idea seems to come from earlier times when plantation owners, who themselves often died of diabetes through eating too much sugar, tried to keep their slaves from acquiring a taste for it. In the Andes, it is still widely believed that winds are the cause of earthquakes. After crops have been harvested, the plants remaining in the fields are often burned, a procedure that destroys many potential nutrients. All over Latin America the negroes and Indians are regarded as generally inferior intellectually, a quality attributed to inherent physiological characteristics rather than environmental difficulties. When such people do 'make good' they receive excessive credit and praise. In Mexico and to a lesser extent other Latin American countries *machismo,* the cult of masculinity, is widespread. Men should be tough, have a lot of children, carry a gun if possible and drink heavily. Machismo does not contribute towards quiet or stable family homes and it no doubt helps in the population explosion.

2. EDUCATION

In West Europe and the U.S.A., there has been a gradual change towards methods of teaching that at times at least encourage children to think for themselves. In Latin America, memory learning still appears to prevail in many schools. It is common to hear children repeating what they have been taught in 'parrot fashion'. Teachers tend to shout and bully. On the other hand, education is regarded widely, though uncritically, as a 'good thing'. The general enthusiasm for education is not usually matched either by the quality of teachers or by equipment and buildings. Classes may be very large indeed. Many children receive no education at all.

The advantage of being literate, an attribute regarded as a necessity and very much taken for granted in developed countries, is based on a number of considerations. They are worth listing because they are easily overlooked.

(i) A person who cannot read can easily be cheated in a legal or commercial transaction, such as the signing of a contract. There are many stories of the selling of trams, statues, buildings and even whole towns by the confidence man in the town to the newcomer from the country.[11]

(ii) Instructions on such diverse pieces of technology as tractors, bags of fertiliser, contraceptive devices and medicines cannot be read. There is the story of one ill Latin American who mistakenly tried to cure himself with a dose of hair tonic twice a day.

(iii) For an illiterate it is difficult to exist in an urban environment. Street and shop signs are not usually provided in pictorial form though the Metro maps in the underground trains in Mexico City have a distinct picture for each station as well as a written caption.

(iv) The news cannot be read in newspapers. Small transistor radios are rapidly growing in use.

(v) Inability to read has usually meant exclusion from the franchise in political elections. In the early 1960s, for example, about $\frac{3}{4}$ of the otherwise eligible population in some Departments of Peru were excluded from voting in national elections on the grounds of illiteracy.

(vi) An illiterate person may also be unable to tell the time, not a serious drawback in the countryside, but inconvenient in a town.

(vii) Without a basic knowledge of reading it is difficult to start study or self-instruction in any other subject.

(viii) Reading as an occupation of leisure time is not possible.

Altogether, full participation in a modern 'developed' community is unthinkable without an ability to read. Other considerations like wealth and appearance may also contribute to success and even survival.

3. INEFFICIENCY

Most sophisticated machines still come from abroad to Latin America. Often their capabilities are not fully appreciated. Bicycles, for example, are made to carry excessively heavy loads. Ageing machines are constantly patched up and repaired even after they should have been thrown away altogether. In 1955 the author made a journey of about 150 km into the Andes by lorry. The lorry had four punctures on the journey because the tyres were in such bad condition. On the return journey, the back axle in one of a group of several lorries broke. Not surprisingly, perhaps, another lorry was carrying a spare one, which was fitted after a delay of several hours. Systems of electricity, telephones and water supply are often suspect in Latin America and breakdowns are frequent. Wrong voltages may cause domestic light bulbs to become two or three times as bright as they should. Domestic plumbing is often inadequate, and smells from the sewer often find their way up pipes into bathrooms.

The postal service in Latin America is usually very poor. People often prefer to send mail in the personal charge of bus or long distance taxi drivers rather than by the official post office. Post Office employees have been known to steam stamps off letters and parcels handed to them, to return the stamps to the counter and take their value in money. Not only does such mail fail to reach its destination, it never leaves the place where it was posted.

4. TRAVEL

Unless one has private means of transport it is almost always necessary in Latin America to book a place on a train or bus well before it leaves. Vehicles tend to travel at full capacity or with an excessively large load. To run profitably, vehicles often wait until they are full before setting out on a journey. In poorer classes of bus service, enormous amounts of luggage and even livestock are carried in or on the roof of vehicles. In fact fares tend to be very cheap considering distances covered. On the other hand, poorly paid people, the under-employed or marginally employed, and those migrating in search of a job, do not rate their *time* as valuable and can afford to undertake slow journeys even when they are over big distances.[12] This gives them considerable mobility.

5. THE URBAN SCENE

Theoretically, urban areas are among the more affluent parts of Latin America. In most of the larger towns pleasant, tidy, quiet areas of upper class and better off middle class housing can be identified. The rest of the town is fraught with numerous physical hazards and spoilt by wretched disregard for appearance and design. Even in central business areas, public clocks are often not working, lifts in tall buildings inadequate, and fire escapes not provided. Drivers are noisy and inconsiderate and petrol fumes acrid. Driving is immature, lanes are often changed, and traffic lights sometimes deliberately ignored. A pedestrian walking along the pavement has to keep an eye constantly on the ground in front for irregular or broken paving stones, sometimes for unprotected and un-signed street works in the ground. Even an ordinary downpour of rain can leave streets impassable for some time.

If underdevelopment has to be summarised in a few phrases it can be said that virtually everything found in a developed country can also be found in a Latin American country. The difference is that there is much less of it to go round and it is much more widely misused.

10.5. REMEDIES FOR UNDERDEVELOPMENT

Probably most people in Latin America are just as satisfied or dissatisfied with what they have (or do not have) as people in West Europe or North America. Nevertheless, there seems to be growing awareness of the development gap between Latin America and the western industrial countries and a feeling there that more of the benefits of the affluent society should be found in Latin America. Whether they will or not remains to be seen. There is no harm, however, in identifying a number of possible futures for Latin America. In the simple scheme that follows, three kinds of change are considered possible within any given country:

A Population may increase, stay roughly stable or decrease.
B The capacity to produce goods and services may increase, stay roughly the same or decrease.
C The distribution of wealth (by class and/or region) may become more even, stay the same or become less even.

In Table 10.4 that follows, 1 means increase, 0 little change, −1 decrease

Table 10.4

Situation	A population	B production	C distribution
(i)	1	1	0
(ii)	1	1	1
(iii)	0	1	1
(iv)	−1	1	1
(v)	1	−1	−1

When there are three situations (A, B, C) and three possibilities for each, there are 27 possible futures, only five of which are shown in the table.

(i) represents the situation in Latin America in the 1960s; population and production were growing but the shareout was not changing much (e.g. less even in Brazil by classes but more even by regions).
(ii) is the situation in which 1960 population and production trends continue but are accompanied by an attempt to share wealth out more evenly. This was the aim in Chile during 1970–73 and is probably what occurred in Cuba in the 1960s, though production seemed to falter for a time.
(iii) and (iv) are likely to achieve greater average per capita production than

(i) and (ii) because in these situations population changes only slightly or actually diminishes.

(v) is the worst possible situation for Latin America because population continues to grow but production drops (perhaps through lack of resources or organisational failure) and wealth becomes more concentrated.

Although there is talk in some Latin American countries of the need for more people, the most reasonable and desirable future seems to be situation (iii), stable population, growing production and a more equable shareout of wealth. At the moment only production is doing what it should according to (iii), namely growing, but growth is sporadic in time and uneven in space both in Latin America as a whole and within countries.

The following assumptions are necessary for situation (iii):

1. Population growth needs to be slowed down and stopped. At the moment it is beyond the control of any government to make much impact on population trends, which, as explained in Chapter 6, are characterised in most countries by rapid growth.

2. Economic growth is necessary. This is controlled partly by the quantity and quality of natural resources. It depends also on the investment rate. Fairly steady and fast economic growth has been achieved in the U.S.S.R. for long periods through control by central planning of the level of consumption of the population of the country. Myrdal pointed out in the 1950s that things would have to get worse in underdeveloped countries before they got better. Consumption has to be forgone now to allow investment in the expansion of the means of production for the future. Few Latin American governments have either the necessary control or the desire to curb consumption at present. Sustained growth is for this reason difficult to achieve in Latin America. *Figure 10.4* shows diagrammatically the kind of situation found in a developing country.[13]

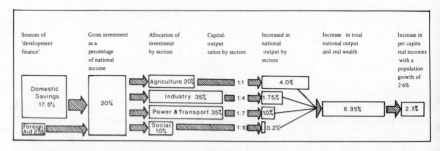

Figure 10.4. The prospects of investment in different sectors of the economy in a developing country

3. A more even shareout of wealth among classes is generally though not universally accepted as desirable. This can be achieved by sharing out consumption more evenly but such a process implies either that increased production of consumer goods and services is directed to lower income groups or that wealthier groups lose part of their wealth, or both. It is thought likely, however, that if a given amount of wealth were more

evenly shared among the population there would be less saving and less capital for future expansion.

4. A more even shareout of wealth among regions has been a major preoccupation of politicians and economists in many countries at least since the First World War. One of the principal aims of Lenin was to eliminate the backwardness of the former colonial areas of the new U.S.S.R. The economic depression afflicting the capitalist countries in the early 1930s drew attention to the problems of areas dependent heavily on one or a few declining industries, such as cotton manufacturing in Britain. Since the Second World War much has been written about regional development problems.

It was suggested earlier in this chapter that Latin America is at a stage in which some regions were much more highly industrialised and modernised than others. How can the poorer lagging regions be helped? They may be suitable for expansion but neglected through regional prejudices or through lack of information about their advantages. In this case their prospects could be improved with a change of image. On the other hand they may be inherently unfavourable, having poor quality agricultural conditions, no sources of energy or minerals, a low level of education, or a remote position. In this case help can only come through political force or persuasion. Two questions then arise. Firstly, is it in the national interest to direct capital to a backward region where returns might be low when it could more advantageously be used in an existing well endowed and advanced region? The corrective political forces may be uneconomic. Secondly, if aid is to be directed to a poor, backward region, should it be spread roughly evenly over the region according to population through investment in an infrastructure of roads, schools, electricity and water supply, or should it be concentrated in a few localities, 'growth poles'?

It is of relevance to the development of Latin America to note that in the 1950s the Cassa per il Mezzogiorno in Italy used a considerable part of its funds to help the South and Islands by providing a very dispersed infrastructure. In the 1960s, on the other hand, development in South Italy tended to be concentrated in a few places (e.g. Taranto and Brindisi in Apulia, Gela in Sicily). In Latin America many of the early improvements in Northeast Brazil were spread thinly over large areas. In the 1960s, the largest towns obtained many of the new industries. In Venezuela, the heavy industrial complex of Ciudad Guyana and the huge petrochemicals complex in Morón represent big investments in small areas. Brasília, capital of Brazil, may also be regarded as a special kind of growth pole.

It is ironical that at a time when 'disenchantment' with indiscriminate economic growth is spreading in the already relatively affluent developed capitalist industrial countries, economic growth is the main aim in life in both the more developed communist countries and in many developing countries. Since the value of the total production of goods and services in Latin America is only about $\frac{1}{4}$ the value of that of the United States, rapid sustained growth is needed for several decades before anything like present West European standards can be expected. At present very little of the development in Latin America is financed by outside gifts. Unless the attitude of developed countries changes radically, Latin America will be financing this future expansion largely on its own.

10.6. GROWTH POLES

A number of terms such as growth pole (French *pole de croissance*), development pole, and growth centre have been used to refer to places of special significance to surrounding areas. The pole is a centre from which innovations and new economic activities are expected to spread or 'filter' down. In fact the term *pole de croissance* was first used by the French economist Perroux[14] not in a spatial sense but with reference to a firm or branch of industry economically strong enough to influence and attract others. In Soviet planning, leading links have been recognised in the economy and growth complexes with various associated activities have been consciously established in certain areas. In the mid 1960s, engineering and chemicals were regarded as growth industries in the U.S.S.R. In Western Europe the motor vehicles industry, with its varied components, has been a rapidly expanding branch of the economy.

The Cerro de Pasco Corporation of Peru (see *Figure 10.5*) serves as an example of a complex of activities resulting from one main 'pole', the non-ferrous

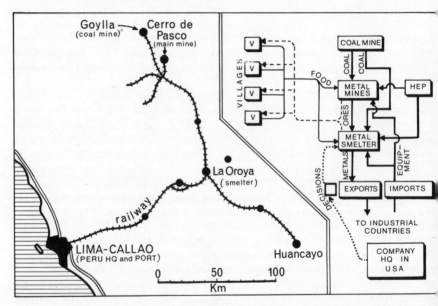

Figure 10.5. Selected spatial and organisational aspects of the operations of a large U.S. mining company, the Cerro de Pasco Corporation, in Peru. The company was taken over by the Peruvian Government in 1974

metal mines at Cerro de Pasco and smaller mines in the area. To refine the ores before export a smelter was built at La Oroya. It became advantageous to exploit coal deposits for the smelter at Goylla and power needs of the mines were catered for by the building of a hydro-electric station at Paucartambo. The mines and smelter have become markets for food produced in the adjoining region and have drawn on the area around for labour. Both remittances and ideas have been fed back to the countryside around.

Many examples of such growth centres exist in Latin America. For the most part they have arisen spontaneously, rather than as part of plans to raise the level of backward areas. Since the 1950s, however, the conscious planting of growth centres has been widely advocated in Latin America.

It seems to be widely assumed that a spread effect or filtering down of material benefits from a growth centre takes place in the area around the centre. Friedman[15] stresses the influence of large urban centres as places of innovation. The influence of São Paulo and Buenos Aires extends hundreds of kilometres in their respective countries. In Peru it is said: 'Lima is Peru'. The concept of centre and periphery suggests that some places are superior to others either in a spatial sense or in an organisational sense. With a little imagination a centre and periphery can be identified in most countries and in regions within countries.

Hirschman[16] is more concerned with the nature of development projects than with their spatial effects. He stresses the difficulty of knowing beforehand with any accuracy or certainty what problems will be met during the construction of big projects and what the subsequent effects will be. Mankind always takes up only such problems as it thinks it can solve. He stresses the role of perception in deciding on places for development and the esteem in which certain places within a country are held. In Brazil, São Paulo is regarded as a particularly go-ahead and favourable place. Similarly, in Colombia, Medellín is regarded as a special place.

The effects of a growth centre on its surrounding area may bring both benefits and disadvantages. The centre may have the effect of stirring things up in the area around and stimulating changes in employment structure and the economy by, for example, stimulating efficiency in agriculture in the region around and setting up new factories in secondary centres within reach of the main centre. The growth centre can also absorb surplus labour from the area around. On the other hand as its industries are more efficient it may affect local activities adversely. Moreover, the people it attracts from the area around may be the more enterprising and/or educated individuals.

At all events, it would be expected that some impact of a growth centre would be felt in the area around. The results of studies conflict, however. In a study of the Department Antioquía in Colombia, A. Gilbert[17] found that level of development of municipios partly diminished with distance from Medellín, the capital, and partly correlated positively with the proportion of urban population in the municipio. In a study of minor civil divisions round many urban centres in Mexico, Colombia and Peru, on the other hand, D. Olden[18] found little difference between smaller settlements very close to the urban centres and smaller centres much further away. This was the impression of the author after brief visits to four metropolises in Northeast and North Brazil, Salvador, Recife, Fortaleza and Belém. Ten or twenty kilometres outside the big towns one can be in deeply rural surroundings.

One reason why spread effects may fail to reach out from urban centres as far or as intensively as might be hoped or expected in Latin America may be the extremely rural and backward nature of places even in their immediate vicinity and the lack of mobility of people in the absence of private cars and other modern means of communications. In Northeast Brazil, private cars are owned by one family out of several hundred in much of the rural area. The way of life of the rural dwellers is such that they do not need contact with the big towns.

Another reason for the difficulty of establishing effective growth poles in Latin America has been suggested by P. R. Odell,[19] the large scale of most countries in Latin America. He showed how in Puerto Rico it was quite feasible to decentralise industry and services by encouraging growth in towns away from the capital San Juan, while maintaining contact between places in the island. Puerto Rico is roughly equal in area to the Federal District of Venezuela. *Figure 10.6* shows the comparative sizes of Puerto Rico, northern and central Venezuela and Spain. In the period 1964–67 there were seven growth poles in Spain. There is some indication[20] that these have had spread effects on municipios in their provinces up to 20–30 km away. Venezuela is more typical of the scale of things in most Latin American countries. Everything is much more thinly spread in Venezuela, which has only about $\frac{1}{3}$ as many inhabitants as Spain. A distance of 20–30 km or even 50 km around Maracaibo or Ciudad Guyana includes only a minute part of the area of Venezuela.

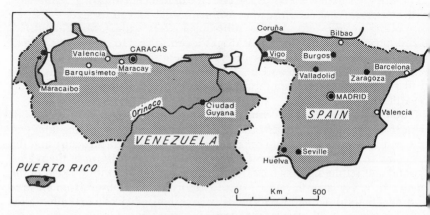

Figure 10.6. A comparison of the sizes of Puerto Rico, Venezuela and Spain. Seven official growth centres of Spain in the 1960s are shown (black dots)

A. Gilbert[21] suggests another reason why spread effects are difficult in Latin America. There are relatively few large firms with branch factories, subsidiaries and complex networks and also less contact between different firms than in a highly industrialised country.

There seem therefore to be several reasons why the spread of innovations is slow in Latin America. The increase in literacy all over Venezuela between 1940 and 1970 shown in *Figure 8.4a* suggests a spread from the capital and the oilfield centres. It depends, however, on the policy of the ministry of education as to where new schools and other educational facilities should be placed. Rural areas tend to receive less attention than urban ones. In Chapter 11 the spread of banks in the State of Bahia, Brazil, is studied briefly. It shows that for decades Salvador was the only place with a bank. Even now, many rural areas in Bahia state are still too far from a place with a bank to use banking facilities regularly. Pedersen[22] shows how various new ideas spread in Chile and notes that the ease with which diffusion takes place is greater now than previously.

Growth poles have appeared, flourished and declined in Latin America ever since the 16th century. In general they have two potential defects. Firstly, the creation of jobs in a new growth pole tends to attract far more job seekers (and their families) than there are new jobs. This tendency has been experienced in such different situations as the heavy industrial centre of Ciudad Guyana in

Venezuela, the construction of Brasilia and the creation of new farms in irrigation projects in Peru. Secondly, when the number of jobs in a centre is reduced
through the exhaustion of resources or for some other reason, the opposite of
spread effects, whatever they may be called, can be seen in many places in Latin
America. The abandonment of irrigation works in Haiti after the French left
around 1800 is an outstanding example. The lavish buildings of Manaus and
Iquitos in the Amazon recall the rubber boom before the First World War. Both
towns suffered a serious decline after the success of rubber plantations in
Southeast Asia. The exhaustion of mineral reserves has also left numerous
ghost towns in Mexico and the Andes which have seen better days and which, in
their time, presumably had spread effects on areas around.

Even when a special development pole has been established in a backward
area there is always the possibility that it will be dragged down by the conditions
in the area around. In Peru, for example, the village of Vicos in the Department
of Huaraz was given special treatment as a 'model' village. Many innovations
were introduced. Such a minipole, intended to serve as an example to villages
around, seems to some extent to have been reverting to its former state once
outside support was removed.

The conclusion seems to be that there are too few rich areas in Latin America,
too few funds, and too few real growth centres. Communications are not
sufficiently good at the moment for large areas to become transformed permanently by regional improvement schemes. This conclusion is drawn from
evidence in many countries, some of it contained in data in the next chapters.
The essence of the argument is this: in West European countries a relatively
prosperous 70–80 per cent of the country is expected to help the remaining
20–30 per cent, though the ratio is less favourable in Spain and Italy. In Latin
America, a relatively prosperous 10–20 per cent is expected to help the
remaining 80–90 per cent; there may be a small amount of outside aid as well.

Chapter 10 has described some of the features and problems of development
in Latin America. These will be illustrated in the chapters that follow with
studies of individual countries. What has been said is to a considerable extent
summarised in the following view expressed by the Food and Agricultural
Organisation:[23]

> 'There is a powerful incentive in the region (Latin America)
> therefore, to think afresh about development strategies and
> policies. The main general problems are seen to be, first the inabili-
> ty to achieve a balanced economic growth of rural and urban areas,
> in which increases in manufacturing activity are matched by im-
> proved agricultural output and productivity; second, the inability
> to provide productive employment for the whole annual increase in
> the labour force and the already existing unemployed; and third the
> extreme inequality of income distribution coupled with con-
> spicuous consumption at the expense of saving in the small high in-
> come group, which limits investment capacity and restricts growth
> of demand by the greater part of the population.'

The present edition of this book, completed in 1973, was written at a time
when attitudes towards development in the *developed* countries were rapidly
changing. In addition to a growing awareness that there is no obvious, easy

path to affluence for the poorer countries of the world, the view was spreading that it would be difficult to maintain recent rates of economic growth in the developed countries themselves and even that the high levels of consumption achieved in North America, West Europe and Japan might themselves be difficult to maintain. The quality of life could deteriorate temporarily or permanently in the industrial countries. The implications of these new lines of thinking on the future of Latin America were difficult to assess at the time of writing.

References

1. Rostow, W. W., *The Stages of Economic Growth*, 1960, Cambridge; The University Press.
2. Myrdal, G., *Economic Theory and Under-developed Regions*, 1957, London; Duckworth.
3. Williamson, J. G., 'Regional Inequality and the Process of National Development: a Description of the Patterns', *Regional Analysis*, L. Needleman (Ed.), 1968, Harmondsworth; Penguin.
4. Zammit, J. A. (Ed.), *The Chilean Road to Socialism*, 1973, University of Sussex; Institute of Development Studies.
5. 'A renda dos brasileiros', *Veja e Leia*, No. 196, 7 de Junho de 1972, pp. 67–74.
6. White, P. T., 'Calcutta, India's Maligned Metropolis', *Nat. Geog.*, Apr. 1973, Vol. 143, No. 4, pp. 534–63.
7. Tagliacarne, G., 'I conti provinciali e regionali', *Moneta e Credito, Dic.* 1970–N. 92.
8. North, D. C., (Location Theory and Regional Economic Growth',*J. Pol. Econ.*, 1955, 63, No. 3, pp. 243–58, and
   Tiebout, C. M., 'Exports and Regional Economic Growth', *J. Pol. Econ.*, 1956, 64, No. 2, pp. 160–64.
9. Ullman, E. L., 'Geographic Theory and Underdeveloped Areas', *Essays on Geography and Economic Development*, 1960, Chicago, University of Chicago Research Papers, No. 62, ch. II, pp. 26–32.
10. Ezra, D., 'Regional Policy in the European Community', *National Westminster Bank Quarterly Review*, Aug. 1973, pp. 8–21.
11. A remarkable true case of fraud was reported in *O Globo* (Rio de Janeiro, 5. 7. 1969). In 1966 some 60 young men and women from the State of Rio Grande do Norte in Northeast Brazil were offered, and accepted, transport to a place with good jobs in the South. They were instead taken to a remote fazenda (farm) in Goiás in the interior of Brazil and held captive there by armed guards to work on the farm. To discourage the men from escaping they were forced to live without trousers. Eventually one man did escape and managed to write to his family. The farm was finally identified and the matter sorted out only in 1969.
12. Hay, A. M. at Institute of British Geographers, Leicester, and Brindley, J. and Hay, A. M. 'Passenger Transport Demand in West Africa: Submarkets and their Spatial Structure', *Econ. Geogr.*, July 1972, Vol. 48, No. 3, pp. 258–69.
13. Patman, C. R., 'Probing Potential in Developing Nations', *Geogr. Mag.*, June 1973, pp. 641–7.
14. Pérroux, F., *L'économie du XXeme siécle*, 1961, Paris, Presses Universitaires de France, Deuxième Partie, Les poles de croissance.
15. Friedman, J., 'A General Theory of Polarised Development', *Growth Centres in Regional Economic Development* (N. M. Hansen Ed,), 1972, New York; Free Press.
16. Hirschman, A. O., *Development Projects Observed*, 1967, Washington D.C. The Brookings Institution.
17. Gilbert, A., 'The Spatial Distribution of Social Variables in Antioqufa, Colombia,' *Discussion Paper No. 38,* Graduate School of Geography, London School of Economics.
18. Olden, D., *The Spatial Distribution of Population in Relation to Wealth in Colombia, Mexico and Peru,* M.A. thesis, London School of Economics, 1971.
19. Odell, P. R., 'The Problem of Geographical Scale in Approaching Regional Development Issues and Policies', *IGU Commission on Regional Aspects of Economic Development*, Rio de Janeiro, 1971.
20. Bradshaw, R. P., unpublished paper on growth poles in Spain (Geography Department, Nottingham University).

1. Gilbert, A., 'Growth Poles—the Instant Solution to Regional Problems?', *IGU Commission on Regional Aspects of Economic Development,* Rio de Janeiro, 1971.
2. Pedersen, P. O., *Innovation Diffusion within and between National Urban Systems,* mimeographed, The Technical University of Denmark, undated.
3. *The State of Food and Agriculture 1971,* 1971, Rome; FAO, p. 71.

Further reading

Back, K. W. and Sullivan, D., 'The Decline of the Ideology of Growth', *Population Reference Bureau,* Selection No. 41, Sept. 1972.
Keeble, D. E., 'Models of Economic Development' in *Socio-Economic Models in Geography* (R. J. Chorley and P. Haggett, Eds.), 1968, London, Methuen.
Lewis, O., 'The Possessions of the Poor', *Sci. Am.,* Oct. 1969, Vol. 221, No. 4, pp. 14–24.
Todd, D., 'The Development Pole Concept . . .', *Discussion Paper,* No. 47, Graduate School of Geography, London School of Economics.

CHAPTER 11

BRAZIL

11.1. INTRODUCTION

The choice of material for inclusion in this chapter has been difficult in view of the large number of geographical and statistical sources produced by the Institute Brasileiro de Geografia e Estatística. It is hoped, however, that the contents will help the reader to gain a fuller appreciation of the demographic resource and spatial situation and problems of Brazil.

Views about the present situation in Brazil and about future prospects vary greatly both within the country and outside it. Brazil has been referred to as an example of success in the tropics and as the great power of the 21st century. On the other hand, it has been criticised for its widespread poverty, hollow frontiers and empty interior. The recent 'economic miracle' of São Paulo state has led to speculation about the possibilities of a brilliant new 'Japan' set in a vast 'India'. Brazilians are very proud of their country and of their achievements and, like everyone else, do not like to be criticised. They seem to have a blind faith in the future of the country, for which perhaps they gain support from the saying that 'God is a Brazilian'.

Economically modern Brazil has tried to be as self-sufficient as possible and generally independent from foreign influence in key sectors such as the oil industry. The fact that it is the only Portuguese speaking country in Latin America further strengthens its isolation in a cultural sense. The many people of African origin, brought in originally as slaves, emphasise its similarity to the Caribbean area and offer scope for the establishment of relations with the new African countries. The 'new' European settlers who came to Brazil in the 19th and 20th centuries, Germans, East Europeans, Italians and Spaniards, are an element found also in neighbouring Argentina.

Brazil is the fifth largest country in area in the world, following the U.S.S.R. Canada, China and the U.S.A. in size. It is somewhat larger than Australia, but about three times as large as the next country in Latin America, Argentina. As a result of the splitting of Pakistan, Brazil has become the 7th largest country in the world in population and by the mid-1970s should overtake Japan and become the 6th. In spite of its large area and population the total gross domestic product of the country is comparatively small, as Table 11.1 shows. In an area nearly the size of Europe, Brazil produces only slightly more goods and services than the Netherlands or Sweden.

Hydro-electric power is one of the two main sources of energy in Brazil yet in 1970 Norway, with about 1/20 as many inhabitants, produced 40 per cent more hydro-electric power than the whole of Brazil. Venezuela produces as much oil in two or three weeks as Brazil does in a year. Its coal output is equal to that of two or three average sized coal mines in Britain. In 1970 the sales of the U.S firm General Motors (about $24,000 million) were two thirds as large as the

value of the whole gross domestic product of Brazil in the same year. It is true
that the rate of economic growth in Brazil has been faster than that of most
countries since the late 1960s but population is also growing fast. The weakness
of the present boom in Brazil goes back a long way.

Table 11.1.

1   thousands of sq.km
2   millions
3   thousands of millions of dollars
4   dollars

	1 Area	2 Population	3 GDP	4 Per capita GDP
Brazil	8,512	93	37	400
Australia	7,687	13	37	2,900
Netherlands	41	13	32	2,400

The coastlands of what is now Brazil were occupied and settled by the Portuguese in the 16th and 17th centuries. It has been estimated that Brazil then
had about 3 million Indians. Slaves were brought into the country from Africa
for over three centuries. The Portuguese established settlements at various
points along the coast. Their administration was initially based on a number of
captaincies, each with an arbitrary territory extending inland from the coastal
settlement as far as the line of the Treaty of Tordesillas (see Chapter 3). During
1580–1640 Spain and Portugal were united and Portuguese settlers from Brazil
were able to penetrate much further west than the Tordesillas line. On the coast
some settlements were more successful than others in both an economic sense
and in acquiring territory in their hinterlands. The capital of Brazil was
Salvador in Bahia until 1763, when it was transferred to Rio de Janeiro. In the
south, however, São Paulo was a powerful influence with connections reaching
far into the interior of South America.

Throughout the colonial period, Brazil was thinly populated and in the 19th
and early 20th centuries people from various European countries and from
Japan were encouraged to settle there. These new settlers are almost all in the
southern part of Brazil. The north and west of Brazil are only very thinly populated. In *Figure 11.1,* map *a* shows an advertisement appearing in Brazilian
publications in the early 1970s. Its caption reads: 'now the turn of the other half
has come'. The other half refers to the empty 'interior', so clearly revealed in
map *c* and by the marked sag in the Lorenz curve in *Figure 11.1d.* It is therefore
not surprising that many people in Brazil feel their country is still underpopulated. They should remember however that Brazil already has about seven
times as many inhabitants as Australia.

Brazilian economic historians have drawn attention to a feature of development not peculiar to Brazil but particularly marked there and considered one of
the weaknesses of the country. Since the 16th century there has been a tendency
to use a particular resource in some part of the country so intensively that the
resource becomes exhausted and the region in which it was exploited tends to

be left stranded. A number of such economic 'cycles' have been identified. They
are listed and discussed briefly below. Places referred to in the text are located
in *Figure 11.1b*.

1. The first product to attract the attention of the Portuguese was the Brazil
wood (*Caesalpinia echinata* or *pau-brasil*), a tree from which a dye was extracted
and sent to Europe. This tree grew in the northern coastlands.

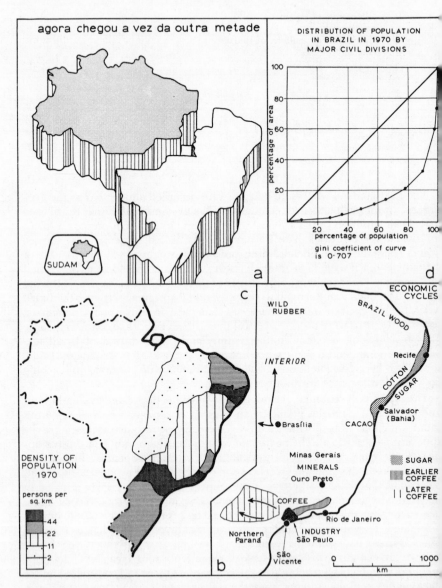

*Figure 11.1. Brazil: (a) The two Brazils according to an advertisement; (b) Areas and towns referred to in Sec-
tion 11.1; (c) Density of population by major civil divisions; (d) Lorenz curve representation of the areal distribution of population in Brazil*

2. In the decades following the settlement of Northeast Brazil, the cultivation of sugar cane, an Old World plant, was introduced at many places along the east facing coast of Brazil from north of Recife to São Vicente (near Santos). This area was one of the main European sources of sugar during about 1550–1700. Thereafter sugar continued to be cultivated in Brazil for export but the competition of the Caribbean sugar plantations in the 18th century, European beet sugar in the 19th and Southeast Brazil in the 20th caused the gradual relative decline and stagnation of the Northeast. Sugar cane is still grown there but natural conditions are not the best in Brazil and technology tends to be backward.

3. After about 1700 the area of economic growth and attraction to settlers in Brazil moved from the Northeast to the area that is now Minas Gerais. Here gold and precious stones were mined during the 18th century. In their turn, the easily accessible mineral resources of Minas Gerais were largely used up and only in the middle of the 20th century has Minas Gerais regained its prominence as a mining area with the growth of the extraction of iron ore and bauxite.

4. Coffee was grown in Brazil in the 18th century but the large scale cultivation of the coffee tree dates from the 19th century. Coffee was first grown in the Paraíba valley behind Rio de Janeiro, then in São Paulo state and finally in northern Paraná. Coffee cultivation left a 'hollow' frontier, as after a few decades land that had been used for its cultivation tended to decline in productivity. Many areas that were originally forest and then coffee plantations are now used as poor pasture or are virtually useless.

The end of the dominance of coffee in the Brazilian economy came around 1960 when no large new frontier areas remained for coffee cultivation to move into, severe frosts in the south affected existing plantations, competition was growing from other coffee-growing countries and, a little later, a disease affected the trees. It must be appreciated that during the coffee 'cycle' other commodities, such as cotton, cacao and wild rubber were also being produced in Brazil. Moreover, Brazil is still the largest producer of coffee in the world.

5. Some Brazilians have identified in the great expansion of industry in Southeast Brazil their next economic 'cycle'. Industrial growth, supported to a considerable extent from capital accumulated in the coffee estates of São Paulo, has been rapid since the Second World War. It is too soon to say if and when the industrial boom will encounter difficulties, but problems may not be all that far off. Three types may be mentioned. Firstly, Brazilian industrial growth rests on a weak energy base provided mainly by hydro-electricity and by oil, increasing amounts of which are being imported. Secondly, current good job prospects in the São Paulo area are attracting very large numbers of migrants from other parts of Brazil; saturation could easily be reached. Thirdly, the great concentration of industry in São Paulo has given the area a much higher standard of living than that found in most other parts of the country. Other states want a share of industrial capacity and employment. For various reasons, then, São Paulo could suffer the fate of other areas left stranded by economic cycles.

6. The next economic cycle in Brazil can be predicted with some confidence. The capital of Brazil was moved from the coast at Rio de Janeiro to a new Federal District, Brasília, about 1000 km to the northwest. This move could be regarded as the symbolic opening of a new phase in Brazilian economic life, a serious attempt to penetrate, exploit and integrate the empty interior. Since the

Second World War many mineral deposits have been discovered there. The mass of tropical rain forest seems to promise vast forest products even if the soil of the area is mostly lateritic and generally unsuitable as a basis for the continued cultivation of field crops. In the advertisement in *Figure 11.1a,* SUDAM stands for the Superintendencia do Desenvolvimento da Amazonia (desenvolvimento means development), an agency set up to encourage development of the Amazon region. The whole process is likely to be rapid, to lack careful planning and to result in a matter of decades in the elimination of the Indian population and the permanent destruction of the large areas of forest.[1]

11.2. PHYSICAL BACKGROUND

Physical contrasts in Brazil tend to be less extreme than those in the Andean countries or in Mexico. There is no great mountain range like the Andes. No part of Brazil is desert, though the interior of Northeast Brazil is afflicted by serious droughts at times. There are few sudden transitions from one type of physical environment to another.

Brazil occupies the crystalline shield of eastern South America but this is buried along the valley of the Amazon by thick Tertiary and Quaternary sedimentary rocks, leaving to the north the Guiana highlands and to the south the Brazilian massif, with its covering in many places of older sedimentaries, not, however, of marine origin. *Figure 11.2a* shows the main geological features of Brazil. The highlands and uplands of the Brazilian shield are referred to very broadly as the Planalto Brasileiro, which is mainly between 300 and 1,000 metres and rarely exceeds 1,000 metres. Relief is to some extent related to solid geology, as where in places the basalt plateau of the south ends abruptly, or where some particularly resistant part of the shield remains as a scarp or isolated mountain. In spite of the widespread use of the term serra (= range), the 'ranges' of Brazil are not usually the result of folding, uplift and subsequent

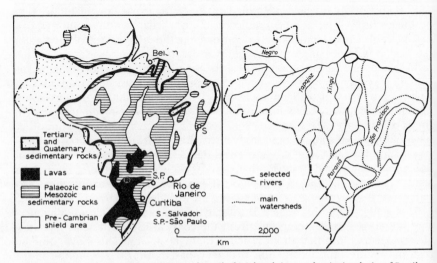

Figure 11.2. (a) Main geological features of Brazil. (b) Selected rivers and main river basins of Brazil

rosion, but are the relics of pediplanation and are often markedly
asymmetrical. Such are many of the chapadas of the Northeast and the serras of
the Southeast. One of the most striking features of the relief of Brazil is the so-
called escarpment, which lies close behind the coast over great distances in
southern Brazil. It is irregular both in altitude and in distance from the coast
but is responsible for bringing the watershed between the rivers of the Paraná
basin and those draining direct to the Atlantic very near indeed to the sea (see
figure 11.2b).

The main features of relief are shown in *Figure 11.3a*. Very rugged conditions
are of limited extent in Brazil and much of the countryside consists rather of
plateaux at various levels, separated by abrupt slopes. In some areas, isolated

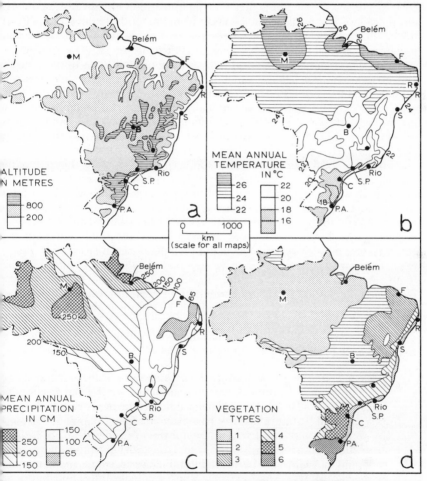

Figure 11.3. Brazil: (a) altitude, (b) temperature, (c) precipitation, (d) vegetation types (see text for
explanation). Key to place names on map, from north to south:

M	Manaus	S	Salvador	C	Curitiba
F	Fortaleza	B	Brasília	P.A.	Porto Alegre
R	Recife	S.P.	São Paulo		

mountain massifs stand above extensive low plateaux. Only about 10 per cent of the country could be considered lowland, but even the largest area of this, in Amazonia, is mostly a very low plateau, in which the present flood plain of the Amazon is cut. Penetration from the coast towards the interior of Brazil is nowhere so difficult as it is along the Pacific side of South America. The Amazon offers easy access to the interior in the north and there are reasonably straight-forward ways in from the Northeast. The most difficult conditions are behind Rio, while at São Paulo a climb of nearly 1,000 metres has to be negotiated before the plateau is reached.

The principal drainage basins of Brazil are shown in *Figure 11.2b*. By far the largest basin in Brazil is that of the Amazon (Amazonas) which occupies 56 per cent of the total area of Brazil or 4,750,00 sq. km and extends outside Brazil to cover 6,500,000 sq. km altogether. The main stream is already only 80 metres above sea level when still about 3,000 km from its mouth. In the south of Brazil the Paraná basin occupies about 10 per cent of the total area of the country and in the east, the São Francisco only 7 per cent or 670,000 sq. km. The Amazon has a complicated regime since it drains areas lying on both sides of the Equator and also derives much of its water from the Andes. South of the Amazon, January to March is the season in which most of the rivers are at their full flow.

Figures 11.3b and *c* show mean annual temperature and precipitation. The northwest of Brazil is defined as super-humid, having a very heavy annual rain-fall, with over 190 cm, and rain at all seasons. The eastern part of the Amazon basin is similarly wet but has a marked dry season. An annual rainfall of over 190 cm occurs locally also in places in southern Brazil, as along the coast of the Paraná and Santa Catarina, and behind Rio. A large part of Brazil receives between about 190 cm and 130 cm of rain per year and is classed as humid rather than super-humid. Almost throughout there is a marked dry season. The general area of the Northeast is considered to be semi-humid and receives un-der 130 cm. Within this area, the *sertão nordestino* and the middle São Francisco valley receive only 25–60 cm. The map of temperatures in *Figure 11.3c* is self-explanatory, but it should be appreciated that in spite of high mean annual temperatures throughout the country, cold conditions occur in the southern part. Snow sometimes falls in the mountains of the south, while frosts and oc-casional snow reach Paraná and São Paulo states and the highest parts of Minas Gerais.

Figure 11.3d is simplified from a much more detailed map of vegetation types in Brazil. Each of the six types is described briefly.

1. *Equatorial forest* occurs in two areas, in Amazonia in the northwest and along an almost continuous narrow coastal belt south from Recife. The so-called *floresta equatorial* or *Hileia* occupies about 40 per cent of the total area of Brazil. Its main features have been noted in Chapter 4. Trees are 40–50 metres high and lianas and epiphytes are widespread. In Brazil a distinction is drawn between forest on land above the flood plains (*terra firme*) and that subject to periodical flooding (*varzea*) or permanently sub-merged (*igapó*). The Amazon forests at present make little contribution to the economic life of the country, and the whole area is sometimes referred to as the *inferno verde,* the green inferno.

2. Second in extent is the *cerrado,* the savanna vegetation. In Brazil the trees are generally no more than 3–6 metres high while the herbaceous plants

reach about 50 cm. There are considerable variations in the closeness of the tree cover and the nature of the grassland, and local conditions of soil and slope appear to have considerable influence. Along the main river valleys the tongues of forest stretch south from the Amazon forest lands. At present the cerrado lands of Brazil are devoted largely to extensive cattle raising.

3. The *caatingas* (also catingas) consist of small trees and shrubs in a very hot environment with a moderate but very irregular rainfall. Many species are equipped to store water, while leaves are small and wax covered. Once rain has fallen, many plants are able to come to life quickly after long dry periods. Much of the caatingas is poor grazing land and only limited areas have been brought into cultivation.

4. The *floresta tropical* consists of a fairly humid belt behind the coast with mainly evergreen species, like those in the Amazon forest, and behind this, mixed evergreen and deciduous forest, more open than along the coast. Most of the cultivated land in tropical Brazil has been cleared from this forest.

5. South of the tropic is the so-called *floresta subtropical* of the uplands of the southern states. The widespread occurrence of the pine *Araucaria angustifolia* has given this area the name of *pinheirais* (pine forests). In the 1950s and 1960s it was the main source of timber in Brazil.

6. The *campos limpos* (limpo = clear, clean) of the extreme south of Brazil consisted of a grassland vegetation in an area of undulating relief. Most of the original vegetation has now been cleared for cultivation or grazing. The campos limpos resemble closely the grasslands of Uruguay and Argentina.

A number of wild or semi-wild plant species are of local commercial importance in Brazil. Their presence and growth is sometimes helped by the deliberate clearance of other vegetation but they are not usually found in plantations. They include the rubber tree (*Hevea brasiliensis*) and Brazil nut (*Bertholletia excelsa*) in the Amazon, the babaçu oil palm (*Orbigny speciosa*) and carnaúba wax palm (*Copernicia cerífera*) in the Northeast and the *erva-mate* plant, source of 'green tea', in the southern forests.

11.3. ADMINISTRATIVE AREAS AND POPULATION

It is convenient at this stage to introduce the main features of the system of major civil divisions of Brazil as they are used in later sections as a means of studying the regional breakdown of various distributions. The distribution of population itself will also be discussed here.

Table 11.2a contains the 22 states of Brazil, three of the four territories and the Distrito Federal. The former territory of Acre became a state in the late 1960s but is treated as a territory in this chapter. The small Atlantic island territory of Fernando de Noronha is not included. The present Distrito Federal contains the national capital Brasília and is in the state of Goiás. The former Distrito Federal and national capital, Rio de Janeiro, is now the state of Guanabara. The parts of the *state* of Rio de Janeiro adjoining Guanabara contain much of the built-up area of Greater Rio, including Niteroi. The number

Table 11.2a.
ALPHABETICAL LIST OF MAJOR CIVIL DIVISIONS OF BRAZIL WITH AREA AND POPULATION

1 Area in thousands of sq.km.
2 Population in 1970 in thousands
3 Density of population, persons per sq.km.

		1	2	3
1	Alagoas	28	1,606	58
2	Amazonas	1,564	961	1
3	Bahia	561	7,583	14
4	Ceará	148	4,492	31
5	Distrito Federal	6	546	95
6	Espírito Santo	46	1,618	35
7	Goiás	642	2,998	5
8	Guanabara	1	4,316	3,686
9	Maranhão	329	3,037	9
10	Mato Grosso	1,232	1,624	1
11	Minas Gerais	587	11,645	20
12	Pará	1,248	2,197	2
13	Paraíba	56	2,445	43
14	Paraná	200	6,798	35
15	Pernambuco	98	5,253	53
16	Piaui	251	1,735	7
17	Rio de Janeiro	43	4,795	114
18	Rio Grande do Norte	53	1,612	30
19	Rio Grande do Sul	282	6,755	25
20	Santa Catarina	96	2,930	31
21	São Paulo	248	17,959	73
22	Sergipe	22	911	41
T1	Acre*	153	218	1
T2	Amapá	140	116	1
T3	Rondônia	243	117	0
T4	Roraima	230	42	0
	BRAZIL TOTAL	8,512†	94,509	11

* Acre is now a State, not a Territory
† Includes land plus inland waters.
Source: *Annario estatístico do Brasil 1972*, pp. 20, 40, 42

Table 11.2b.
POPULATION BY MAJOR REGIONS 1872–1970

	1872	1890	1900	1920	1940	1950	1960	1970
Total population	9,930	14,334	17,438	30,636	41,236	51,944	70,992	94,509
Percentage	100·0	100·0	100·0	100·0	100·0	100·0	100·0	100·0
Norte	3·4	3·3	3·4	4·7	3·6	3·6	3·7	3·9
Nordeste	46·7	41·9	38·7	36·7	35·0	34·6	31·2	30·3
Sudeste	40·5	42·6	44·9	44·6	44·5	43·4	43·8	42·7
Sul	7·3	10·0	10·3	11·5	13·9	15·1	16·8	17·7
Centro-Oeste	2·2	2·2	2·1	2·5	3·1	3·4	4·2	5·5

Source: *AEB 1972*, p. 42.

of the units in Table 11.2a is used to identify the units in *Figure 11.4*, maps *a* and *b*.

Column 1 in Table 11.2a shows the area of each major civil division. The three largest units Amazonas, Pará and Mato Grosso are in the interior and north. Amazonas is nearly three times as large as France. The arrangement of

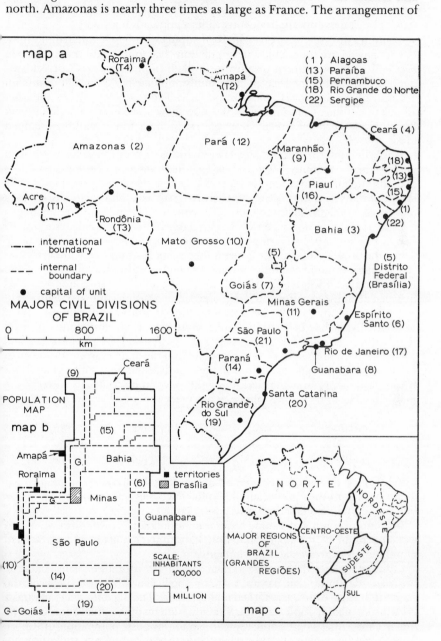

map a

Roraima (T4)
Amapá (T2)

(1) Alagoas
(13) Paraíba
(15) Pernambuco
(18) Rio Grande do Norte
(22) Sergipe

Ceará (4)

Amazonas (2)   Pará (12)   Maranhão (9)

(18)
(13)

Acre (T1)

Rondônia (T3)

Piauí (16)

(15)
(1)
(22)

----- international boundary

Mato Grosso (10)   Bahia (3)

--- internal boundary

(5)

(5) Distrito Federal (Brasília)

● capital of unit

MAJOR CIVIL DIVISIONS OF BRAZIL

Goiás (7)

Minas Gerais (11)

Espírito Santo (6)

0   800   1600
km

São Paulo (21)   Paraná (14)

Rio de Janeiro (17)
Guanabara (8)

POPULATION MAP

map b

Ceará
(9)

Santa Catarina (20)

(15)

Rio Grande do Sul (19)

Amapá
Roraima

G   Bahia

(6)

■ territories
▨ Brasília

NORTE

Minas

Guanabara

São Paulo

SCALE: INHABITANTS
□ 100,000

NORDESTE

CENTRO-OESTE

(10)
(14)
(20)
(19)

G-Goiás

☐ 1 MILLION

MAJOR REGIONS OF BRAZIL (GRANDES REGIÕES)

SUDESTE

SUL

map c

Figure 11.4. (a) Major civil divisions of Brazil (Acre is now a state). Numbering corresponds to that in Table 11.2a. In map (b) the units are drawn proportional in size to their 1970 populations. Map (c) shows the major regions into which states are grouped for planning and other purposes

states in the Northeast still reflects the original form of the captaincies of the 16th century, in which penetration from different coastal settlements took place. There are still small areas of disputed territory between some pairs of states. Each state is subdivided into a number of minor civil divisions, the *municipios*. These units are frequently split as population grows.

Column 2 in Table 11.2a gives the 1970 population of each unit in thousands. The territories are the smallest in population. The topological map, map *b* in *Figure 11.4,* shows units in proportion to their population size. Correct contiguity of units is retained except in the thinly populated interior. The dominant position of the Southeast comes out clearly. The interior of Brazil collapses almost to nothing. Column 3 in Table 11.2a shows the density of population in Brazil. These data have already been referred to in Section 11.1 and are mapped in *Figure 11.1c.*

Since the mid-1960s the major civil divisions of Brazil have been grouped into five major regions. These are mapped in *Figure 11.4c.* Table 11.2b shows that although the major regions have changed in relative importance over the last hundred years, the Norte and Centro-Oeste have never had more than a few per cent of the total population of the country. The most marked change in relative population size since 1872 has been the decline of the Nordeste and the rise of the Sul, especially Paraná state, and recently of the Centro-Oeste, in which the presence of Brasília is beginning to make a noticeable impact.

The effect of modern immigration was felt most strongly in the states of São Paulo, Paraná and Santa Catarina. Only about 5 million immigrants remained in Brazil during the main period of modern immigration, compared with about 35 million in the U.S.A. Nevertheless, the economic and cultural life of southern Brazil has been transformed by the modern immigrants. A small number of Swiss settled in Brazil as early as 1818 (Nova Friburgo near Rio) and some Germans in 1824 (Rio Grande do Sul) but the main reasons for the great influx were the demand for labour in the rapidly expanding coffee plantations from about 1870, and the decline of the slave trade (officially after 1850). Between 1884 and 1941 the following numbers were involved (in thousands):

Italians	1,413	Japanese	189
Portuguese	1,222	Various Slavs	180
Spaniards	582	Germans	172

Table 11.3 shows selected demographic data for Brazil. The major civil divisions are grouped in this and the following tables under major regions, as indicated, not in alphabetical order, as in Table 11.2a.

In columns 1 and 2 of Table 11.3, recent population growth is shown in two ways. In column 1, the 1950 population of the unit is equal to 100 and the 1970 population is expressed as a percentage of it.

Column 2 shows the average annual rate of growth in the 1960s. Data for birthrate, deathrate and natural increase show that differences between the states of Brazil are not very marked in this respect. The big differences in rate of growth revealed in Table 11.3 are therefore due mainly to migration between units. Thus Minas Gerais and Espírito Santo have lost population to Rio de Janeiro (with Guanabara) and to São Paulo, while Paraná was still attracting large numbers of new agricultural settlers from various states until the 1960s. Certain places in the interior and the Amazon region have also attracted migrants. On the other hand, during the 1960s the Nordeste began to lose large numbers of people to the Sudeste. It is possible, however, that in some parts of the Nordeste the birthrate is now actually dropping in response to pressure of population on jobs and resources and to the loss through out-migration of many of the women of child bearing age.

Ever since early colonial days key towns have played an important role in the life of Brazil. A few decades ago, however, Brazil was still basically a rural country and even in 1940 only just over 30 per cent of the population, or under 13

Table 11.3.
BRAZIL: SELECTED DEMOGRAPHIC DATA

1 Population growth 1950-70, 1950 = 100
2 Annual rate of population growth, 1960-70, as a percentage of total population
3 Urban population as a percentage of total population
4 Percentage of total population of unit living in unit capital
5,6 Females as a percentage of males in urban and in rural areas of unit

	1 50-70	2 60-70	3 Urban	4 Cap.	5 Urban sex	6 Rural sex
SUDESTE						
Minas Gerais	150	1·6	53	11	108	94
Espírito Santo	169	1·3	45	8	106	93
Rio de Janeiro	209	3·5	77	7	102	91
Guanabara	182	2·7	100	100	109	—
São Paulo	196	3·3	80	33	102	89
SUL						
Paraná	331	5·0	36	9	103	91
Santa Catarina	188	3·2	43	5	104	94
Rio Grande do Sul	162	2·2	54	13	108	90
NORDESTE						
Maranhão	192	2·0	25	9	111	97
Piauí	166	3·2	32	13	112	99
Ceará	167	3·0	40	19	113	99
Rio Grande do Norte	166	3·4	47	17	113	99
Paraíba	143	1·9	42	9	116	103
Pernambuco	155	2·4	54	21	113	101
Alagoas	147	2·4	40	17	113	99
Sergipe	141	1·8	46	21	113	102
Bahia	157	2·4	41	14	112	100
CENTRO-OESTE AND NORTE						
Mato Grosso	311	6·0	43	6	102	85
Goias and Distrito Federal	292	4·4*	50	13*	103	89
Pará	196	3·5	47	29	110	91
Amazonas	187	2·9	42	33	108	92
Rondônia	316	5·1	52	76	99	74
Acre	190	3·1	28	39	105	87
Roraima	230	3·5	43	89	102	89
Amapá	310	5·4	55	75	106	48
BRAZIL	182	2·9	56		106	90

* Excluding Brasília
Source: *AEB 1972*, pp. 42, 45, 46, 55

million, was classified as urban. In 1970, 53 million were classified as urban, 56 per cent of the total population. Even when some allowance is made for differences in the definition of urban population, a four-fold increase in the number of town dwellers in a generation, a mere three decades, is an enormous demographic change. The time lag in providing jobs and food, let alone housing, amenities and services, means that increasing numbers of Brazilian town dwellers live in slums and shanty towns not integrated in the already weak urban structure of most Brazilian towns.

The proportion of urban population to total population (Table 11.3 column 3) varies greatly among the units of Brazil, Maranhão and Piauí for example being little urbanised compared with São Paulo and Rio de Janeiro. For such a poor region, however, the Nordeste of Brazil from Ceará to Bahia is more highly urbanised than might be expected.

Column 4 in Table 11.3 shows that a large proportion of the population of the states and territories in the Norte is in the capital of each unit.

Columns 5 and 6 show considerable differences in the sex ratio between urban and rural areas. Urban areas tend to have more females than males, a feature very marked in the Nordeste. Rural areas tend to have a greater proportion of males than females. The main reason must be that far more women than men migrate from rural areas to urban areas, not a tendency that would seem obvious at first sight.

Figure 11.5 shows the towns of Brazil with over 70,000 inhabitants in 1970. They are listed in Table 11.4. The nine largest towns include the population of adjoining municipios in the urban 'micro-region'. The growing inconvenience of administering and planning urban agglomerations consisting of many municipios led to an investigation of Metropolitan areas by the Instituto Brasileiro de Geografia e Estatística. At least 9 large urban areas have been given Metropolitan status. On the basis of established criteria such status is sought by various other towns for reasons of prestige and in view of the prospect of receiving special federal funds. Further research in Brazil has made it possible to show approximately the spheres of influence of the 9 metropolitan areas, together with that of Goiânia (see Figure 11.6).

As national capital, Brasilia has a special role, while also at a national level São Paulo is increasingly replacing the former cultural and financial dominance of Rio de Janeiro. Figure 11.6 shows that the regional sphere of influence of Rio de Janeiro is restricted by the presence of Belo Horizonte to the north. São Paulo on the other hand serves northern Paraná and southwest Minas Gerais as well as its own state and much of Mato Grosso. The São Paulo area on the map contains about 25 million people, compared with about 10 million in the Rio area. The 9 largest urban concentrations of Brazil themselves contain nearly $\frac{1}{4}$ of the total population of Brazil and nearly $\frac{1}{2}$ of the urban population. This apparently large share is still far below the concentration of population found in the largest towns in Australia and Argentina.

11.4. THE MAIN BRANCHES OF THE ECONOMY

For the purposes of simplicity the economy of Brazil has been divided in this section into three main sectors, agriculture, industry and services. Agriculture includes pastoral activities, forestry and fishing as well as crop farming.

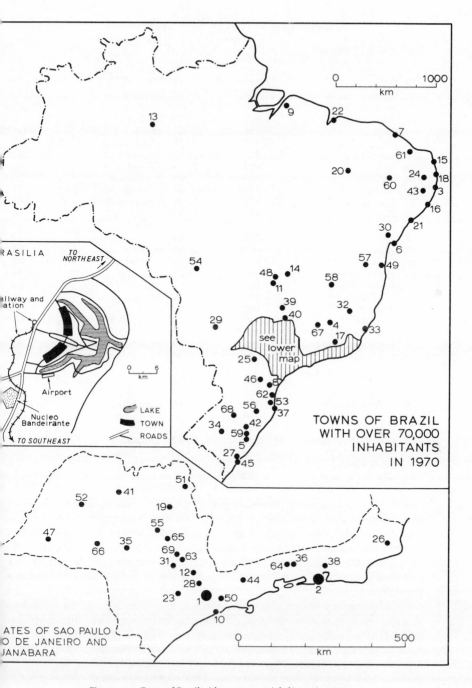

Figure 11.5. Towns of Brazil with over 70,000 inhabitants in 1970

Table 11.4.
TOWNS OF BRAZIL WITH OVER 70,000 INHABITANTS IN 1970

Population in thousands

1	São Paulo	8,137		36	Volta Redonda	122
2	Rio de Janeiro	6,893		37	Florianópolis	120
3	Recife	1,730		38	Petrópolis	119
4	Belo Horizonte	1,646		39	Uberlândia	112
5	Pôrto Alegre	1,548		40	Uberaba	110
6	Salvador	1,196		41	São José do Rio Preto	110
7	Fortaleza	1,038		42	Caxias do Sul	109
8	Curitiba	821		43	Caruarú	102
9	Belém	670		44	Taubaté	101
10	Santos	462		45	Rio Grande	100
11	Goiânia	371		46	Ponta Grossa	94
12	Campinas	334		47	Presidente Prudente	93
13	Manaus	286		48	Anápolis	92
14	Brasília	277		49	Itabuna	91
15	Natal	256		50	Moji das Cruzes	91
16	Moceió	249		51	França	88
17	Juiz de Fora	224		52	Araçatuba	87
18	João Pessoa	204		53	Blumenau	87
19	Riberão Preto	197		54	Cuiabá	86
20	Teresina	190		55	Ararquara	84
21	Aracajú	182		56	Lages	84
22	São Luis	171		57	Vitória da Conquista	84
23	Sorocaba	168		58	Montes Claros	83
24	Campina Grande	165		59	Novo Hamburgo	82
25	Londrina	160		60	Juazeiro do Norte	81
26	Campos	155		61	Mossoró	79
27	Pelotas	155		62	Joinvile	78
28	Jundiaí	147		63	Limeira	78
29	Campo Grande	134		64	Barra Mansa	76
30	Feira de Santana	129		65	São Carlos	76
31	Piracicaba	128		66	Marília	75
32	Governador Valadares	127		67	Divinópolis	71
33	Vitória	125		68	Passo Fundo	71
34	Santa Maria	125		69	Rio Claro	70
35	Bauru	123				

Industry includes mining, processing and the supply of items such as electricity and gas as well as manufacturing. Services include commerce, transport, administration and a wide range of other non-goods activities. The 1968 value of production of each sector for each state is given in millions of cruzeiros in Table 11.5. The territories have been included with Pará or Amazonas. In 1968 the free market selling rate for the exchange of cruzeiros to U.S. dollars was 3·83 cruzeiros per dollar.

From the values of total production in column 1 of Table 11.5 the contribution of each state to total national production can be seen. The large contribution of São Paulo is the outstanding feature. The relative importance of agriculture and industry to the total of each state are shown in columns 5 and 6. It can be seen that dependence on agriculture varies greatly among the states. In column 7 the total value of production of goods and services in a year (column 1) is divided by the total population of the state (see Table 11.2). The result is the per capita production in cruzeiros for each state. This has been converted at the free market rate of 3·8 cruzeiros per U.S. dollar in 1968 to give per capita

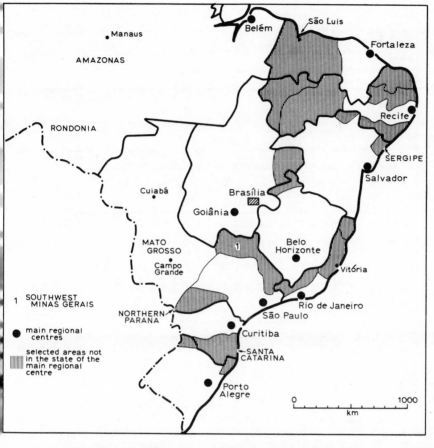

Figure 11.6. Spheres of influence of main regional centres in Brazil around 1970

production in dollars in column 8 and further converted to pounds sterling in column 9. Even during 1968 itself exchange rates changed considerably, and care should be taken when cruzeiro values in different years are compared. It should also be noted that the official rate was more in favour of the cruzeiro than the market rate used above. Even so, the result gives a value of total production not very different from that arrived at by other measures.

Columns 1–4 show clearly the dominant position of the SUDESTE and SUL in total production not only in the industrial sector but also in the agricultural sector. The heavy dependence of the NORDESTE on agriculture might be expected, but the equally high dependence of the SUL and of Espírito Santo is more of a surprise. In effect, São Paulo and Rio de Janeiro with Guanabara are the only units in Brazil in which industry accounts for a greater share of the value of production than agriculture. Minas Gerais, Espírito Santo and the SUL are characterised by greater *productivity* in their agricultural sector than the NORDESTE rather than by greater *dependence* on agriculture.

In view of the fact that services are built upon those sectors of the economy

Table 11.5.

BRAZIL: AGRICULTURE, INDUSTRY AND SERVICES BY STATES

1-4   Internal product* in millions of cruzeiros in 1968 by states, 1 General total, 2 Agriculture, 3 Industry, 4 Services.
5,6   Percentage of total internal product accounted for by 5 Agriculture, 6 Industry
7   Internal product in cruzeiros per inhabitant in 1968. Free market rate was 3·8 cruzeiros
8,9   Column 7 values converted to U.S. dollars and to pounds sterling.

	1	2	3	4	5	6	7	8	9
					Per cent in				
	Total	Agr.	Ind.	Serv.	Agr.	Ind.	Cap. inc. cruz.	Cap. inc. doll.	Cap. inc. £
SUDESTE									
Minas Gerais	7,870	2,131	1,446	4,292	27	18	675	178	74
Espírito Santo	1,011	374	68	568	37	7	625	165	69
Rio de Janeiro	3,808	601	1,231	1,976	16	32	794	209	87
Guanabara	9,026	110	1,877	7,039	1	21	2,091	550	229
São Paulo	27,657	3,407	10,927	13,324	12	39	1,540	405	169
SUL									
Parana	4,815	2,101	480	2,235	44	10	688	181	75
Santa Catarina	2,076	705	453	918	34	22	709	187	78
Rio Grande do Sul	6,721	2,201	1,134	3,386	33	17	995	262	109
NORDESTE									
Maranhão	831	416	60	355	50	7	274	72	30
Piauí	390	169	21	201	43	5	225	59	25
Ceará	1,691	680	141	869	40	8	376	99	41
Rio Grande do Norte	673	294	61	319	44	9	417	110	46
Paraíba	811	402	75	333	50	9	332	87	36
Pernambuco	2,658	692	446	1,521	26	17	505	133	55
Alagoas	570	270	82	218	47	14	355	93	39
Sergipe	390	161	28	201	41	7	428	113	47
Bahia	3,312	1,209	291	1,812	37	9	437	115	48
CENTRO-OESTE AND NORTE									
Mato Grosso	758	316	44	399	42	6	467	123	51
Goias + D.F.	1,806	858	82	767	48	5	510	134	56
Pará†	1,101	198	185	718	18	17	477	125	52
Amazonas‡	530	164	91	275	31	17	395	104	43
BRAZIL	78,587	17,458	19,222	41,827	22	24	828	218	91

that produce goods, the fact that well over half of the value of production in such a poor country as Brazil comes from services is thought provoking. It will be seen in the chapters that follow that a similar situation occurs in other Latin American countries.

Column 7 in Table 11.5 is of particular interest because it measures the extent of the regional disparities in Brazil at state level. The average annual per capita value for the state of São Paulo is nearly 7 times as high as that for the poorest state, Piauí. In the U.S.A. the *ratio* of the median income in the poorest state to that in the most prosperous state is only about 1:2, though the *absolute* difference is greater. It is possible that to a small degree some compensation takes place by the flow of 'aid' and investment from the richest to the poorest parts of Brazil but this is not enough to alter the numerical values much or to remove the image of 'two nations'.

11.5. AGRICULTURE, FORESTRY AND FISHING

In 1970 about six times as many people were employed in agriculture in Brazil as in the U.S.A. The value of Brazilian production was about 4,000 million dollars compared with over 30,000 million dollars in the U.S.A. The productivity per agricultural worker in the U.S.A. is therefore on average nearly 50 times as high as that of one in Brazil. The labour force in agriculture in Brazil increased from over 11 million in 1940 to over 18 million in 1970. Table 11.6 reveals some basic features about the structure of agriculture in Brazil. The location of the states listed in Table 11.6 can be found in *Figure 11.4*. The territories are of limited importance agriculturally and are omitted.

Columns 1–2 show the number of persons employed in agriculture in each state in 1940 and in 1970.

Column 3 shows that only Rio de Janeiro (with Guanabara) and São Paulo had fewer persons in agriculture in 1970 than in 1940. The rate of increase varies greatly among the other states. The settlement of new land accounts for the big increase in Paraná in the south and also in Maranhão, Mato Grosso and some other areas in the interior.

Columns 4–5 show that the number of tractors in use in Brazil was still small in 1970 and that over $\frac{2}{3}$ were in São Paulo and Rio Grande do Sul. The almost complete lack of mechanisation in the NORDESTE is evident in the very small number of tractors per 10,000 persons engaged in agriculture.

Columns 6–7 show that the value of agricultural production per person engaged in agriculture varies enormously in Brazil. There are at least three main causes of the regional discrepancies. Firstly, some areas are naturally more fertile than others. São Paulo and Rio Grande do Sul have extensive areas of good quality soil. Secondly, some uses of land are of higher value than others. Intensive cultivation occurs around the larger towns both on account of the need for market garden products and because the towns draw on labour from the land around and tend to make labour more scarce. Thirdly, the productivity of an agricultural worker is related to the degree of mechanisation, although even the 434 tractors per 10,000 agricultural workers in São Paulo state is not a high level of mechanisation compared with that in Australia, where there are nearly as many tractors as persons engaged in agriculture.

The above remarks about Table 11.6 are only offered tentatively as reasons

Table 11.6.

EMPLOYMENT AND MECHANISATION IN BRAZILIAN AGRICULTURE

1,2   Persons employed in agriculture in 1940 and 1970 in thousands
3   Change in employment in agriculture (1940 = 100)
4   Tractors in use in 1970
5   Tractors in use per 10,000 persons employed in agriculture in 1970
6   Value of agricultural production in millions of cruzeiros in 1968 (data as in column 2 of Table 11.5)
7   Value of agricultural production in cruzeiros per person employed in agriculture (1968 value divided by 1970 agricultural workers)

	1	2	3	4	5	6	7
	Persons occupied		*1940-*	*Tractors*		*Value*	*Value Per*
	1940	*1970*	*70*	*1970*	*Per 10,000*	*1968*	*capita*
SUDESTE							
Minas Gerais	1,974	2,127	108	9,245	43	2,131	1,000
Espírito Santo	231	309	134	984	32	374	1,210
Rio de Janeiro	454	254	56	3,479	137	601	2,366
Guanabara	21	14	67	125	89	110	7,860
São Paulo	1,840	1,513	82	65,731	434	3,407	2,250
SUL							
Paraná	261	2,015	772	17,190	85	2,010	1,042
Santa Catarina	314	774	246	5,026	65	705	910
Rio Grande do Sul	917	1,467	160	38,317	261	2,201	1,500
NORDESTE							
Maranhão	446	1,205	270	122	1	416	345
Piauí	263	521	198	167	3	169	324
Ceará	714	1,085	152	577	5	680	626
Rio Grande do Norte	255	313	123	488	16	294	939
Paraíba	490	614	125	687	11	402	655
Pernambuco	748	1,155	154	1,328	11	692	599
Alagoas	248	460	185	924	20	270	587
Sergipe	152	274	180	374	14	161	588
Bahia	1,256	2,209	176	1,366	6	1,209	547
CENTRO-OESTE AND NORTE							
Mato Grosso	86	380	442	3,926	103	316	832
Goiás + D.F.	290	569	196	5,633	99	858	1,507
Pará	260	591	227	866	15	198	335
Amazonas	97	287	296	57	2	164	571
BRAZIL	11,343	18,249	161	156,592	86	17,458	760

Source: *AEB 1972*, pp. 146–7

for such marked regional differences in the productivity of agricultural workers in Brazil. The truth, easily overlooked or conveniently forgotten by politicians and planners of growth in Brazil, is that several times as many people are engaged in agriculture in Brazil as need be. Even if a large area of good quality land were readily available in Brazil, which is not so, the cost and inconvenience of resettling even a small part of the 18 million farm workers would be enormous. In practice, many people are moving to the towns in the hope of finding jobs in sectors outside agriculture.

In 1960 about 30 million hectares (roughly the *total* area of Italy) were cultivated in Brazil out of a total area of 850 million, that is about 3·5 per cent. This total included some fallow and other unsown land. Several million more hectares have been brought under cultivation in Brazil since 1960.

Agricultural production and productivity can be assessed in various ways. The total value of production and the value per worker have already been discussed. The value and weight per unit of area can also be calculated from Brazilian data. Space does not allow a detailed study on the basis of these criteria. To summarise the production of organic commodities from agriculture, forestry and fishing in Brazil, the value of each of the main categories is given on a state basis in Table 11.7a. The main producing state of less important categories is given in Table 11.7b.

Table 11.7a shows the value of production of timber and fish, of the two main livestock products, beef and milk, and of the ten most valuable field and tree crops. Among the crops, two broad types can be recognised. Some crops are grown and consumed regionally or locally mainly for their carbohydrate content: maize, rice, manioc, beans, wheat and to some extent bananas. Other crops are grown largely or partly for the export market: coffee, sugar cane, cotton and cacao. A brief comment follows on the data in Table 11.7a.

Column 1 shows that at present Amazonia (roughly Pará, Amazonas and the 4 territories) provides a negligible proportion of Brazil's timber. There are at present two main areas of timber production, Minas Gerais, with extensive areas of eucalyptus species, which also produces charcoal, and the SUL, where the forests of Paraná pine (*Araucaria angustifolia*) have been drastically depleted in recent decades.

Column 2. Sea fishing is carried on from all the coastal states of Brazil and is supplemented by fresh water sources. The total catch is however small and the industry is characterised by primitive methods and low labour productivity.

Column 3 shows that the cultivation of coffee, still Brazil's most valuable crop, is concentrated in two states, Paraná and São Paulo. In the early 1960s about $\frac{1}{10}$ of the area under coffee was changed to other uses under a government scheme. In the winter of 1963 frost damaged or destroyed many more coffee trees. In 1964 Brazilian coffee production dropped to its lowest for many decades, about 600,000 tons, compared with an average of 2,200,000 tons during 1959–62. The latest figures available at the time of writing were 755,000 for 1970 but 1,795,000 for 1971, about $\frac{1}{3}$ of the 1971 world total. In the early 1970s coffee still accounted for about $\frac{1}{3}$ of the value of Brazilian exports. Coffee growing still employs a large labour force in western São Paulo and northern Paraná.

Columns 4, 5 and *8* show that maize, rice and beans are widely grown in Brazil. Yields per unit of area of both maize and rice are generally lowest in the NORDESTE.

Column 6. Between the late 1950s and early 1970s the annual production of sugar in Brazil, all from cane, roughly doubled. The original sugar growing area, the NORDESTE, accounts for less than $\frac{1}{2}$ of the national total, a disappointing performance compared with that of São Paulo state, alone accounting for about another third.

Column 7. Manioc is a New World root crop grown mainly for local consumption. It is widely cultivated in the NORTE and CENTRO-OESTE in areas newly cleared from the forest.

Column 9. Cotton is grown both for seed and lint. Climatically only the drier areas of the NORDESTE and SUDESTE are suitable.

Table 11.7a.

PRINCIPAL PRODUCTS OF AGRICULTURE, FORESTRY AND FISHING IN BRAZIL, 1969

Values in millions of cruzeiros

	1 Timber	2 Fish	3 Coffee	4 Maize	5 Rice	6 Sugar cane	7 Manioc	8 Beans	9 Cotton	10 Wheat	11 Bananas	12 Cacao	13 Beef	14 Milk
SUDESTE														
Minas Gerais	129	4	119	264	302	107	82	145	30		71		408	600
Espírito Santo	9	11	37	26	15	9	20	21			22	11	57	42
Rio de Janeiro*	4	91	3	10	32	98	25	3			63		179	107
São Paulo	51	72	663	304	275	429	67	89	300	3	99		895	410
SUL														
Paraná	58	5	1,173	301	151	37	82	193	239	92	7		152	148
Santa Catarina	63	35	1	131	53	17	74	29		36	9		87	88
Rio Grande do Sul	109	33		328	321	16	187	74		469	42		404	193
NORDESTE														
Maranhão	16	36		33	104	10	50	20	8		14		30	14
Piauí	6	2		11	19	4	21	17	15		5		17	11
Ceará	22	19	5	59	25	34	66	59	173		80		83	50
Rio Grande do Norte	7	12		13	1	16	16	26	56		16		34	29
Paraíba	13	12		30	8	40	28	36	77		23		47	28
Pernambuco	16	21	7	47	3	203	84	87	54		36		127	40
Alagoas	4	4		13	5	114	25	47	11		19		20	18
Sergipe	5	3		8	5	10	36	9	4		4		32	12
Bahia	47	23	18	41	17	72	127	118	35		25	425	268	87
CENTRO-OUESTE AND NORTE														
Mato Grosso	13	2	7	24	87	6	43	21	20		9		92	26
Goias + D.F.	56		5	76	243	15	55	59	24		13		164	88
Pará	3	21		9	13	1	25	3			3	1	48	6
Amazonas	2	14			1	1	7	1			1	1	14	7
4 Territories	1	2		2	9		11	3			1		13	6
BRAZIL	509	421	2,039	1,730	1,691	1,242	1,136	1,060	1,049	600	565	438	3,171	2,012

Column 10. Wheat is the main bread flour in the urban areas of Brazil. Climatic conditions are not good for wheat cultivation even in the states of Rio Grande do Sul and Paraná, where most is grown. Most of the needs of Brazil are imported from Argentina.

Column 11. Cacao is a very localised crop in Brazil. The only important area of cultivation is that behind the port of Ilhéus, in the southern part of Bahia state.

Columns 13, 14. Cattle are the main type of livestock kept in Brazil. They are raised throughout the country, both in combination with crop farming and in the vast grazing areas of the interior. The distribution of pigs and poultry corresponds roughly with the distribution of cattle, and the production of pigmeat for local consumption is a valuable item of livestock farming. Sheep raising on the other hand is very limited. In addition, horses, asses and mules are kept throughout Brazil to perform with oxen most of the ploughing and transport work in rural areas. Increased mechanisation would release fodder required to keep draught animals, but great improvements in livestock quality could also be achieved in Brazil by improvements in breeding and the feeding of cattle.

Table 11.7b shows 22 other products of the land in Brazil not included in Table 11.7a. Their combined value is not much greater than that of coffee alone. Many of them are concentrated in one or a few states and are of regional rather than national significance.

São Paulo, Paraná, Rio Grande do Sul and Minas Gerais were the four largest states in Brazil in agricultural production. About 3 million agricultural

Table 11.7b.
BRAZIL: SELECTED AGRICULTURAL AND FOREST PRODUCTS IN 1969 NOT INCLUDED IN TABLE 11.7a

Product	millions of cruzeiros	Leading producer	millions of cruzeiros
Oranges	345	São Paulo	140
Potatoes	318	São Paulo	102
Groundnuts	267	São Paulo	199
Soybeans	265	São Paulo	181
Tomatoes	255	São Paulo	107
Tobacco	250	Rio Grande do Sul	97
Sweet potatoes	142	Rio Grande do Sul	31
Vines	128	Rio Grande do Sul	53
Hides and skins	117	São Paulo	41
Castor oil plant	114	Bahia	50
Coconuts	113	Bahia	33
Charcoal	109	Minas Gerais	70
Onions	106	Rio Grande do Sul	43
Wool	97	Rio Grande do Sul	94
Babaçu palm	80	Maranhão	66
Sisal or agave	78	Rio Grande do Norte	24
Pineapple	69	São Paulo	14
Wild rubber	67	Territories	32
Carnaúba palm	29	Ceará	11
Erva mate	27	Rio Grande do Sul	14
Jute	25	Pará	15
Brazil nuts	21	Pará	10

Source: *Anuario estatístico do Brasil 1972*, pp. 131–165 and p. 247

workers in São Paulo and Rio Grande do Sul produced considerably more in value than nearly 8 million in the NORDESTE. There seems to be scope for increasing agricultural production in Brazil in several ways. The already relatively successful Southeast is technologically sufficiently advanced for the expansion of more sophisticated farming methods. A large increase in production could also be achieved if the Northeast could even be brought to the present level of the Southeast. In the vast interior there must be some areas in which new agricultural land can be found, but the remoteness of potential areas here makes commercial farming difficult due to the great road distances over which products have to be moved to the existing concentrations of population.

11.6. MINERALS AND ENERGY

Brazil is widely spoken of as a country with vast mineral resources. The present production of minerals and the proved reserves of most minerals actually found in Brazil do not fit this very flattering image. The extraction of minerals accounts approximately for 1 per cent of the gross national product of Brazil and employs about 1 per cent of the labour force of the country. As in other Latin American countries there is a great contrast in productivity between relatively well paid personnel in highly mechanised enterprises such as the oil industry and manganese ore extraction, and the amateurs practising what is called *garimpagem,* a term that implies 'scratching the surface' for various minerals such as alluvial gold and precious stones. The main mineral products of Brazil are listed and discussed briefly. Places mentioned in this section will be found on maps in Sections 11.10 to 11.12.

1. IRON ORE

The annual extraction of iron ore has increased about three times during the 1960s. In 1969, 27,160,000 tons were extracted with an iron content of 18,470,000 tons, giving the very high average of 68 per cent. In 1970 about 30 million tons of ore were produced. The price of a ton of iron ore is only a few dollars, and the 1969 production amounted to a value of only about $ U.S. 130 million.

Virtually all the iron ore of Brazil is produced in the state of Minas Gerais. Some is smelted locally, some sent by rail to other states in Brazil, particularly to Volta Redonda in the state of Rio de Janeiro, and the rest is exported. To handle the increasing exports the railway to the port of Vitória has been improved and a special terminal completed in Vitória itself.

Iron ore has been found in other parts of Brazil. A deposit in the state of Pará at Serra dos Carajas (near Marabá) is estimated to have at least 1,500 million tons of ore with 68 per cent iron content. Work started on the preparation of the site for exploitation in the early 1970s but some $ U.S. 600 million, shared by Brazil and U.S. Steel, will have to be invested in the project. A railway of between 400 and 600 km will have to be built to carry the ore to a suitable port for export.

Expansion of iron ore extraction continues in Minas Gerais where an investment of some $ U.S. 150 million at Aguas Claras allows the production of 10 million tons of iron ore a year. This ore is to be exported from a new port at Sepetiba Bay near Rio de Janeiro.

2. MANGANESE ORE

Manganese ore is produced in two areas in Brazil, in Amapá territory in the extreme north, and in Minas Gerais. The 1,150,000 tons of manganese content produced in 1971 by Brazil represented about 14 per cent of the world total.

3. OTHER METALS

Other metals are produced in very limited quantities in Brazil but tin reserves in the form of large cassiterite deposits have been found in the interior near Porto Velho in Rondônia territory. The 10 million tons of cassiterite claimed to exist would be $1\frac{1}{2}$ times all the tin reserves known at present in the world. Brazil probably also has large reserves of bauxite. Its own aluminium industry is supplied from deposits in Minas Gerais. A deposit near the Trombetas River in Amazonia is to start production in 1975 after the investment by Alcan of $ U.S. 90 million.

4. SALT

Salt is the most valuable non-metallic mineral extracted in Brazil. Of about $1\frac{1}{2}$ million tons produced in 1971, over $\frac{2}{3}$ came from the state of Rio Grande do Norte.

5. COAL

About $2\frac{1}{2}$ million tons of coal a year were produced in Brazil around 1970. At the present rate of production the measured reserves of over 3,000 million tons would last indefinitely. Nearly 80 per cent of the coal is extracted in the state of Santa Catarina and the rest in adjoining states. The present coal production provides only about 5 per cent of the energy needs of Brazil. It contributes in particular to the coal needed for coking in the iron and steel industry.

6. OIL AND NATURAL GAS

The exploration and extraction of oil and natural gas have largely been controlled by the State in Brazil. Around 1970 Brazil was producing about $1\frac{1}{4}$ thousand million cubic metres of natural gas, equivalent to less than 2 million tons of coal per year. Almost all the natural gas in Brazil comes from the state of Bahia. Around 1970 Brazil was producing about $8-8\frac{1}{2}$ million tons of oil per year, less than $\frac{1}{4}$ of its total energy needs. Almost all the oil extract in Brazil in the early 1970s came from the Salvador area of Bahia state and the adjoining part of Sergipe state, both in the Nordeste. The estimated oil reserves of Brazil in 1971 were only 113 million tons, giving little more than a decade of production even at present limited rates.

7. HYDRO-ELECTRICITY

Hydro-electricity is an attractive source of energy as it uses a renewable 'resource', falling water, rather than non-renewable combustible fuels. The construction of hydro-electric power stations is often costly, however, and transmission from remote sites to consuming areas a problem. Silting of reservoirs and evaporation of water from their surfaces are other problems. Hydro-electric power is now of declining relative importance as a source of energy in the U.S.A., U.S.S.R., Italy, Japan and other developed countries. In Brazil, on the other hand, the expansion of home produced energy depends heavily in the next two or three decades on the construction of hydro-electric stations. In 1970 the capacity of the hydro-electric stations of Brazil was about 8 million kW. This represents about 10 per cent of the ultimate theoretical hydro-electric potential on Brazilian rivers. The output of about 40×10^9 kWh from this source in 1970 when 'officially' converted to coal equivalent at $0 \cdot 125$ tons of coal per 100 kWh gives a mere 5 million tons of coal equivalent. To generate the same amount of electricity in thermal power stations using coal, however, some 25 million tons of coal would be needed. The importance of hydro-electricity in the Brazilian economy is evident from the second conversion. In 1970 roughly another 8 million kW of capacity were under construction.

Of the total theoretical hydro-electric capacity of Brazil (about 80 million kW), about 60 per cent is in the Paraná and Uruguai basins in southern Brazil, nearly 20 per cent in the São Francisco basin and less than 10 per cent in the Amazon basin. The distribution of capacity by states is shown in Table 11.8. The five states with the largest capacity are São Paulo, Minas Gerais, Mato Grosso, Bahia and Rio de Janeiro. The much publicised Paulo Afonso power station on the São Francisco river in the Nordeste (Bahia) produces as much as only one large modern West European power station but the electricity it generates is distributed over an area with about 20 million people. New stations on the Paraná and its tributaries are further increasing the concentration of hydro-electricity production in southern Brazil.

In conclusion, it is apparent that although Brazil is well provided with a few metallic minerals it lacks many altogether. Its energy base is weak and is concentrated in a few places (see Table 11.8), though the prospect seems good of finding oil in the extreme northwest of the country by the adjoining new oilfields of Colombia, Ecuador and Peru, and the hydro-electric potential is considerable. Very large amounts of capital are however needed to explore for oil, to provide access to known new mineral reserves and to build large hydro-electric power stations and high voltage transmission lines. Foreign participation, not regarded desirable in excess in many quarters in Brazil, seems necessary if the expectations of Brazil are to be realised in the next few decades.

11.7. INDUSTRY

Although Brazil is thought of as a developing country, the growth of industrial capacity in recent decades has brought it to a level of industrialisation where the value of industrial production is estimated to exceed considerably the value of agricultural production. Even so, agriculture still employs more than eight times as many people as industry. Thanks to the size of Brazil and to its recent industrial growth the country now has a large absolute industrial capacity and a labour force of over 2 million. The states of Rio de Janeiro, Guananbara and São Paulo together have about ⅔ of the total value of industrial production and if they were a separate country they would be similar in many respects to less highly industrialised 'developed' countries such as Spain or Poland. Increasingly Brazil is exporting manufactured goods and in the early 1970s the value of these was roughly equal to the value of coffee exports.

The apparent success of industrial development in Brazil must be attributed to some extent firstly to the large size (by Latin American standards) of the national market, secondly to the enterprise and enthusiasm of the citizens of São Paulo, the *paulistas,* and thirdly to a general policy of import substitution and protection of industries. Local capital, raw materials and hydro-electric power favoured the São Paulo area initially and it has been difficult to reduce the monopoly the Southeast has acquired in many branches of industry.

The production of energy in Brazil was discussed in the last section. About ⅓ of Brazil's energy requirements are imported, mostly in the form of oil, and like many other developing countries it is competing increasingly with the industrial countries for the world's oil. In 1971 Brazil imported over 21 million tons of crude oil and refined products, costing it about $ U.S. 500 million. It also imported about 2 million tons of coal. Columns 1–4 in Table 11.8 show where in Brazil the electricity is generated and the oil refined (an incomplete total is shown in column 4). About ⅓ of the oil refined in Brazil is from refineries in São Paulo state and another ⅓ from Rio de Janeiro where it is also refined for sale in Minas Gerais. The Bahia refinery at Mataripe near Salvador uses local oil, while a refinery in Rio Grande do Sul caters for the extreme south of Brazil.

The data in column 5 of Table 11.8 show that about ⅔ of all industrial employment in Brazil is in Rio de Janeiro and São Paulo. The Nordeste has only about ⅒ of the total. The value of industrial production per person in industry is much higher in São Paulo and Guanabara than in most other parts of Brazil and is very low in the states of the Nordeste. The high productivity in São Paulo and Rio de Janeiro (see column 6) is due both to the greater efficiency of industrial plant and to the nature of the branches of industry present. In 1965 São Paulo state alone accounted for about 60 per cent of the total value of Brazilian industrial production, although it had only about 20 per cent of the total population of Brazil. In contrast the Nordeste had only about 10 per cent of the value of production. Since 1965, industrial capacity in Brazil has grown considerably, as has the labour force. New developments outside São Paulo state had probably slightly reduced its dominant position by the early 1970s.

Table 11.9 contains data for industrial production in selected states of Brazil, giving the number (in thousands) of persons employed in manufacturing industry in 1970. The seven largest branches in terms of employment are listed in order of size. Separate data are given for 5 of the largest industrial states. The last column shows that certain industries are more concentrated in São Paulo than others. Very broadly, metallurgical, chemical, engineering and electrical branches of industry are more advantageous in terms of growth prospects and general sophistication than food, textiles and clothing. Column 2 shows that

Pernambuco (like most of the other states in the Northeast) depends more heavily on the food industry than São Paulo or Guanabara.

Columns 7 and 8 in Table 11.8 illustrate the wide difference in degree of regional concentration that occurs among industrial sectors in Brazil. Pig iron, the principal ingredients in the production of which include iron ore, coke (or charcoal), ferro-alloys, limestone and water, is made most cheaply in relatively large mills with several million tons per year capacity. In fact even the largest single mill in Brazil, at Volta Redonda, produces little more than 1 million tons

Table 11.8.

ENERGY AND INDUSTRY IN BRAZIL BY STATES

1,2 Hydro-electric and thermal electric generating capacity in thousands of kilowatts
3   Production of electricity in millions of kWh
4   Oil refining capacity in thousands of tons
5   Persons employed in industry in 1965
6   Value of industrial production per person employed in industry to the nearest thousand cruzeiro
7   Steel production in thousands of tons
8   Cement production in thousands of tons
9   Percentage of cement producing capacity idle

	1 Hydro	2 Therm.	3 Prod.	4 Oil ref.	5 Emplt.	6 Value per cap.	7 Steel	8 Cement	9
SUDESTE									
Minas Gerais	2,791	44	10,577		175	8	2,296	2,293	2
Espírito Santo	59	25	293		16	6	19	335	7
Rio de Janeiro	1,036	209	6,814	8,784	140	11	1,808	1,566	6
Guanabara		241	1,006	502	206	10		239	0
São Paulo	3,054	758	15,342	8,155	1,083	12	1,593	2,753	1
SUL									
Paraná	436	88	1,802		89	11	20	491	20
Santa Catarina	100	158	1,167		88	5		159	12
Rio Grande do Sul	241	400	2,292	3,659	193	8	197	331	10
NORDESTE									
Maranhão	1	12	9		21	3			
Piauí	108	11	122		6	4			
Ceara	5	35	19	70	29	7		84	7
Rio Grande do Norte		4	1		25	3			
Paraíba	4	11	5		45	3		188	37
Pernambuco	6	27	51		95	6	67	577	34
Alagoas	2	9	24		41	3			
Sergipe	1	2	3		16	3		77	36
Bahia	1,081	55	4,387	2,856	57	7		235	19
CENTRO-OESTE AND NORTE									
Mato Grosso	1,134	46			11	5		216	2
Goias + D.F.	177	27			15	9		157	2
Pará		116	313		15	5		101	33
Amazonas		61	182	383	6	10			
BRAZIL	10,244	2,426	50,988	24,409	1,973		5,997	9,532	9

Sources: Columns 1–4 and 7–9, *AEB 1972*, pp. 205–6, 231; Columns 5 and 6 *Registro Industrial*

Table 11.9.
PRINCIPAL BRANCHES OF INDUSTRY IN BRAZIL

	Brazil	Pernam-buco	Minas	GB	RGS	S.P	% S.P
TOTAL	2,099	70	139	203	176	1,054	50
Textiles	298	13	31	18	8	158	53
Food	273	25	17	20	30	84	31
Metallurgical	249	3	42	15	23	66	27
Non-metallic minerals	156	7	14	14	8	127	81
Transport material	154	1	1	9	6	122	79
Clothing and footwear	122	3	5	21	33	48	39
Engineering	108	1	3	9	10	77	71
Per cent food	13	36	12	10	17	8	

Source: *AEB 1972*, pp. 178–186

a year. As might be expected the production of pig iron (4,686,000 tons in 1971) is confined only to three states (Minas Gerais 2,690,000 tons, Rio de Janeiro, 1,240,000 tons and São Paulo 750,000 tons). Column 7 in Table 11.8 shows that nearly 6 million tons of steel were made in Brazil in 1971 the discrepancy between pig iron and steel being accounted for mainly by the addition of scrap steel. Four other states produced small quantities of steel but the three pig iron producers accounted for nearly all of the total.

Column 8 in Table 11.8 shows that the cement industry in Brazil is much less concentrated than the iron and steel industry. Only 5 out of the 21 states in the table produced no cement at all. Column 9 illustrates a feature of Brazilian industry, the failure of areas away from the main industrial concentration to use their capacity to the full. This is one of several reasons why there are some reservations in Brazil about dispersing industry indiscriminately about the country.

Like cement, other branches of industry, including food processing and to a lesser extent textiles, are fairly widely distributed over the national area according to population. Others, including most branches of engineering, are highly concentrated in São Paulo. In view of the inter-dependence of different sectors of engineering and electrical industries, the large size of Brazil and the inadequate interregional transport links it is highly desirable for many industries to be as near as possible to São Paulo. Moreover, many industrial establishments that hope to sell their products throughout the national market of Brazil can expect an appreciable proportion of it in São Paulo itself. About ⅔ of the purchasing power in Brazil is within a few hundred kilometres of São Paulo, compared with a mere 10 per cent in the whole of the Northeast, about 10 per cent in Rio Grande do Sul, and virtually none in the Amazon area or even within a radius of several hundred kilometres around Brasília.

In 1965, about 60 municipios in Brazil had more than 4,500 persons employed in industry. These municipios are listed in Table 11.17 on page 257 and most are located in regional maps in Sections 11.10 and 11.12. There were 5 in the Northeast, 2 in the North and none in the Centro-Oeste. All the municipios from 16 to 24 belong to Greater Rio de Janeiro, which had about 250,000 persons in industry. The municipios attributed to Greater São Paulo

are indicated. This region had about ¾ million in manufacturing, a concentration rivalled in Latin America only by those in Buenos Aires and Mexico City.

Table 11.17 shows for each municipio the branch of industry that employed
the largest number of persons in 1965. The more desirable branches of industry
appear almost exclusively in the municipios of the state of São Paulo.

11.8. TRANSPORT AND LINKS

Brazilian statistical sources do not make it easy to work out the relative importance of different transport media in the movement of passengers and goods.
Table 11.10 simply states whether or not a particular means of transport is
relatively important for a given function and length of journey.

Table 11.10.
MEANS OF TRANSPORT IN BRAZIL

1   implies important

	International		Regional		Local		Urban	
	Pass.	Goods	Pass.	Goods	Pass.	Goods	Pass.	Goods
Sea		1		1				
Inland water	1	1	1	1	1	1		
Rail			1	1	1	1	1	
Road			1	1	1	1	1	1
Air	1		1		1			
Electricity				1		1		1

The movement of goods by sea was increasing during the 1960s but
passenger traffic was tending to decline in the face of competition from air
transport. The inland waterways of both the Paraná and Amazon systems carried
some international traffic. Passenger traffic on the railways of Brazil declined
sharply during the 1960s while goods traffic stayed roughly the same. The rail
network itself was reduced in total route length from about 38,000 km in 1960
to 31,000 km in 1970. Internal air services carried an increasing number of
passengers but even in the early 1970s only took about 1/1000 of all goods
traffic handled in Brazil.

The most spectacular change in Brazilian transportation has been the growth
in the extent of the road system and in the number of vehicles in use. During the
1960s the number of passenger cars registered in Brazil increased about four
times and the number of commercial vehicles roughly doubled. Before 1960
there were few good road links between states and much of the road traffic was
within or around the larger towns. As a result of a vigorous road building campaign, the length of paved federal and state road was increased from 13,000 km
in 1960 to 55,000 km in 1971. The length of such roads was however less than $\frac{1}{20}$
of the 1,220,000 km of motor road of all kinds in Brazil, $\frac{4}{5}$ of it actually defined
as municipal, implying local roads, generally of poor quality and in some areas
seasonal.

Private car ownership in Brazil is very unevenly spread regionally as was shown
in Chapter 8 (see *Figure 8.4d*). The higher standard of living in the Southeast partly
accounts for the relatively high level of car ownership there.

In many parts of the Northeast and Interior, roads are unsuitable for any but the most sturdy vehicles, and garages and service facilities are still very limited.

The more important federal and state roads are shown in *Figure 11.7*. The map shows that by 1970 it was possible to travel from Rio Grande do Sul (capital Porto Alegre) to Recife in Northeast Brazil almost all the way by paved road. Direct links between Brasília and the Northeast and Amazonia and the Northeast had not been provided by 1970.

Figure 11.7. Main roads of Brazil in 1970

One of the most remarkable pieces of road construction in Brazil was the Belém – Brasília, about 2,200 km, built in 1960–61 in little over a year but unfinished in several respects. Many concrete bridges over smaller streams were incomplete in 1969 when the author travelled along the road by bus from Belém to Brasília, a journey that took over 60 hours. The road was unpaved except for short stretches at either end and in 1969 many stretches of the original road had already been abandoned, traffic being diverted to new provisional carriageways. During the rainy season the pink lateritic material becomes sticky and impassable and in places the road surface has become

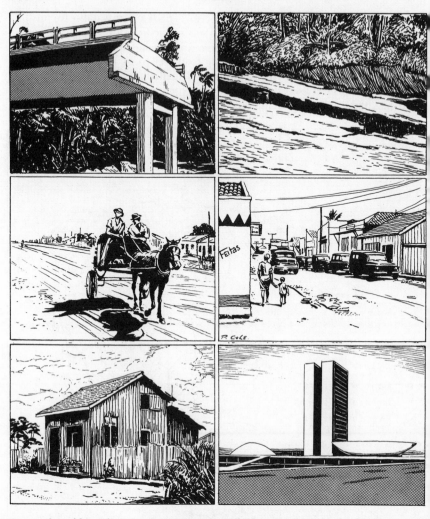

Scenes on the road from Belém to Brasília in 1969. Unfinished bridge and eroded road surface. Local transport uses the road near the town of Araguaia. Typical housing contrasts with the dazzling view of the Parliament building at Brasília, start or end of the journey

eroded by miniature gullies. During the dry season the surface is dusty and travel unpleasant. There are no towns of importance on the road and little sign of forestry, cultivation or grazing along much of the route. Conditions in settlements along it contrast markedly in quality and appearance with Belém and Brasília at the two ends. Some of the features of the Belém–Brasília road are illustrated in the accompanying drawings based on photographs.

In Sections 11.10–12, regional rail networks are shown and the new roads of Amazonia are discussed. Table 11.11 included for reference lists the main ports of Brazil according to the value of international cargoes handled. The large contribution of Southeast Brazil to the foreign trade of the country comes out clearly from the table. Vitória, exporting about 24 million tons of iron ore in

1970, accounts for a large share of the total weight of exports, while Rio de Janeiro (11 million tons in 1970) and Santos (6 million tons) receive most of the oil imports of Brazil, by far the heaviest commodity coming into the country. Salt, coal, oil and oil products are the heaviest goods carried by coastal shipping services, Northeast Brazil providing most of the salt and oil, Santa Catarina the coal.

Table 11.11.

FOREIGN TRADE OF PRINCIPAL PORTS OF BRAZIL IN 1971, LISTED FROM NORTH TO SOUTH

	Exports	Imports
	millions of cruzeiros	
Manaus*	70	350
Belém	200	150
Macapá	210	30
Fortaleza	280	100
Recife	520	380
Maceió	280	20
Ilhéus	310	0
Salvador	500	450
Vitória	1,440	600
Rio de Janeiro	1,050	4,710
Angra dos Reis	110	100
Santos	5,100	7,760
Paranaguá	2,350	150
Itajaí	130	50
Pôrto Alegre	340	490
Rio Grande	820	310
Uruguaiana*	240	230
BRAZIL	15,370	19,220

* River ports
Source: AEB 1972, pp. 275–8

Internal flows of goods between states in Brazil are recorded and published in the *Anuario estatístico do Brasil, 1972*. Shipping, road and rail services handle nearly all the goods traffic, though pipelines, air services and electricity transmission lines are of local importance. The main interstate flow of goods, according to value, are shown in *Figure 11.8*. The data have been extracted from very detailed tables of interstate movements. The dominant position of São Paulo emerges once again in this view of the economic life of Brazil.

11.9. REGIONAL CONTRASTS IN BRAZIL

One of the main aims of the present book is to provide evidence of regional differences in development both in Latin America as a whole and within individual countries. Such differences can be described visually, with the help of pictures, verbally, in the form of text, or numerically. This section is devoted to a numerical assessment of regional differences in Brazil at state level. Readers who are not accustomed to handling and interpreting numerical data and who have not used or become acquainted with multi-variate methods may find difficulty in appreciating the message that emerges from the various data in this

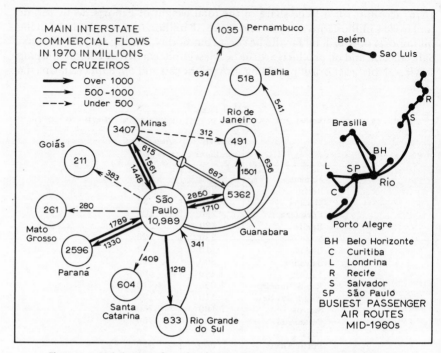

MAIN INTERSTATE
COMMERCIAL FLOWS
IN 1970 IN MILLIONS
OF CRUZEIROS

→ Over 1000
→ 500 -1000
- - -> Under 500

Figure 11.8. Main interstate flows of goods in Brazil in 1970 and main passenger air routes

section and in later chapters. To help in the appreciation of the methods, the second data matrix (Table 11.13) and its corresponding correlation matrix (Table 11.14) use data in ranked form. Such data are easy to interpret and when two variables are correlated, one of the easiest correlation procedures can be used, Spearman rank correlation.

The 21 states of Brazil are listed in 4 regional groups in Table 11.12. Each state has an index on each of 9 variables according to the availability in the state of 9 aspects of material and cultural development. On all 9 variables the values are expressed in per capita terms in order to eliminate the influence of the different population sizes of the states on the original absolute data. In Table 11.13, the 21 states have been ranked 1–21 according to their order on the variables in Table 11.12. Thus, for example, in column 1, Guanabara, with a consumption of 270 kg of cement a year per inhabitant has the highest score and is ranked first. Amazonas and Maranhão have scores of 10 kg, the lowest in the column and have been ranked 20th and 21st respectively. States such as the two referred to above that have the same score in Table 11.12 have been ranked according to the more detailed data from which the Table 11.12 values have been rounded.

In Table 11.12, the data can only be compared down the columns as different units are used to measure each variable. In Table 11.13, the data can be compared not only down the columns but also across the rows. Even at a glance it is easy to see that Guanabara and São Paulo occupy the first and second positions on most variables while Maranhão and Piauí occupy the 20th and 21st positions

1 Consumption of cement in kilograms per inhabitant in 1970
2 Consumption of electricity in kWh per inhabitant in 1970
3 Passenger cars (automóveis) in circulation per 1000 inhabitants in 1970
4 Telephones in use per 1000 inhabitants in 1970
5 Hospital beds in use per 1000 inhabitants in 1970
6 Doctors per million inhabitants in 1970
7 Students in higher education per 10,000 inhabitants in 1970
8 Percentage of municipios with water supply in municipio centre (sede)
9 Internal product, 1968, in cruzeiros per inhabitant

	1 Cem.	2 Elec.	3 Cars	4 Tels.	5 Hosp.	6 Doct.	7 Educ.	8 Water.	9 Cap. Inc.
Minas Gerais	81	440	12	13	35	402	53	87	675
Espírito Santo	108	260	8	8	23	184	44	88	625
Rio de Janeiro	153	540	16	11	43	541	53	99	794
Guanabara	270	920	59	70	76	1,881	146	100	2,091
São Paulo	180	970	45	56	42	673	114	85	1,540
Paraná	53	210	13	6	24	303	41	45	688
Santa Catarina	53	250	15	5	43	253	29	27	709
Rio Grande do Sul	53	260	24	9	42	495	81	64	995
Maranhão	10	20	1	1	3	46	16	20	274
Piauí	14	20	1	2	12	98	6	48	225
Ceará	30	70	3	7	18	179	23	62	376
Rio Grande do Norte	30	70	3	3	16	186	25	14	417
Paraíba	46	90	4	4	20	243	30	42	332
Pernambuco	76	230	8	6	26	348	44	50	505
Alagoas	36	100	3	4	22	284	21	39	355
Sergipe	54	130	5	2	22	222	16	35	428
Bahia	58	140	5	5	12	184	23	48	437
Mato Grosso	110	150	6	6	22	258	26	61	467
Goias + D.F.	81	110	13	12	26	532	56	30	510
Pará	43	100	6	4	23	207	31	70	477
Amazonas	10	120	7	3	27	97	35	50	395
BRAZIL	95	400	19	15	32	453	59	59	828

Source: AEB 1972, pp. 496, 506, 402, 433, 566, 567, 824, 521, 515–17

Table 11.13.

STATES RANKED ACCORDING TO VALUES IN TABLE 11.12

	1 Cem.	2 Elec.	3 Cars	4 Tels.	5 Hosp.	6 Doct.	7 Educ.	8 Water	9 Inc.	10 Total 1-9	11 Rank 1-9
Minas Gerais	6	4	8	3	6	6	6	4	7	50	5
Espírito Santo	5	5	10	7	11	17	7	3	8	73	6
Rio de Janeiro	3	3	4	5	2	3	5	2	4	31	3
Guanabara	1	2	1	1	1	1	1	1	1	10	1
São Paulo	2	1	2	2	5	2	2	5	2	23	2
Paraná	11	9	6	11	10	9	9	14	6	85	10
Santa Catarina	13	7	5	12	3	7	13	19	5	84	9
Rio Grande do Sul	12	6	3	6	4	5	3	7	3	49	4
Maranhão	21	21	21	21	21	21	19	20	20	185	21
Piauí	19	20	20	20	19	19	21	12	21	171	20
Ceará	18	19	19	8	17	18	17	8	17	141	18
Rio Grande do Norte	17	18	18	18	18	15	15	21	15	155	19
Paraíba	14	17	16	16	16	12	12	15	19	137	17
Pernambuco	8	8	9	10	9	8	8	10	10	80	8
Alagoas	16	15	17	15	15	10	18	16	18	140	16
Sergipe	10	11	14	19	13	13	20	17	14	131	15
Bahia	9	10	15	13	20	16	16	13	13	125	13
Mato Grosso	4	12	12	9	14	11	14	9	12	97	11
Goias + D.F.	7	13	7	4	8	4	4	18	9	73	7
Pará	15	16	13	14	12	14	11	6	11	112	12
Amazonas	20	14	11	17	7	20	10	11	16	126	14
MEDIAN	11	11	11	11	11	11	11	11	11	99	11

on most variables. From what has been said about Brazil in the previous sections it is not surprising that the units with the two largest and most industrialised cities in Brazil should head the list in the 'pecking order' of material and cultural quality of life. The states of the Northeast have low rankings on most variables but there is sufficient evidence to show that Pernambuco, with Recife, is higher than the rest of the Northeast, while Maranhão and Piauí represent the most backward part of the whole country, if primitive Indian tribes in the Amazon are not considered.

One may think of the 9 variables as different judges of conditions in Brazil. Each judge has ranked the states of the country on his particular rating. In column 10 of Table 11.13 the 'consensus' of the nine variables or judges has been calculated by adding the rankings for each state along each row. The states have then been reranked in column 11 according to their scores in column 10. On the consensus, the five states of Southeast Brazil, together with Rio Grande do Sul in the South, and Goiás (which includes Brasília) in the Interior, occupy the highest 7 places. All the lowest 7 places (15–21) are occupied by states of the Northeast.

The data in Table 11.13 can be processed further to measure how closely each pair of variables agrees. A comparison of the values for each state in columns 5 and 6 shows that in most states the rankings are similar. For example, Minas Gerais is 6th on both variables, Guanabara 1st on both. The rankings of some states vary considerably, however, suggesting discrepancies in Brazil with regard to the distribution of doctors and of medical facilities.

The point has already been made in this book that it is difficult for an area to be highly developed in one respect and very backward in another. One would not expect São Paulo to be 1st in terms of energy consumption per inhabitant but only 15th or 20th in availability of medical or educational facilities. In fact, as noted above, apparent discrepancies or anomalies can be found in the table. Ceará in the Northeast is generally ranked low but scores relatively high on the telephone and water supply variables. The situation may be due to the presence of Fortaleza, a large urban area, and to the emphasis on improving water supply in Ceará, the worst affected part of Northeast Brazil when dry years occur.

The closeness of similarity, association or correlation of a pair of ranked variables can be calculated from the Spearman rank correlation coefficient. The formula and procedure are explained in Appendix 1. With the help of a computer the correlation coefficient of each variable with every other variable can quickly be calculated. The coefficient lies between +1 (perfect positive correlation) and −1 (perfect negative correlation). A coefficient around 0 (zero) implies no correlation. Table 11.14 contains the coefficient between each pair of

Table 11.14.

MATRIX OF COEFFICIENTS OF CORRELATION BETWEEN VARIABLES IN TABLE 11.13

Variables	1 Cem.	2 Elec.	3 Cars	4 Tels.	5 Hosp.	6 Doct.	7 Educ.	8 Water	9 Inc.	Cons.
1 Cement	1·00									
2 Electricity	0·85	1·00								
3 Cars	0·73	0·90	1·00							
4 Telephones	0·80	0·78	0·79	1·00						
5 Hospitals	0·59	0·82	0·94	0·71	1·00					
6 Doctors	0·74	0·76	0·84	0·77	0·79	1·00				
7 Education	0·68	0·77	0·88	0·84	0·82	0·75	1·00			
8 Water	0·59	0·62	0·52	0·69	0·52	0·36	0·61	1·00		
9 Income	0·77	0·91	0·96	0·82	0·86	0·82	0·84	0·55	1·00	
Consensus	0·85	0·94	0·95	0·89	0·88	0·83	0·91	0·68	0·95	1·00

variables and every other one. The matrix has the same number of rows as columns, and the upper right hand half is omitted because its values 'mirror' those in the lower left hand half of the matrix. The 1·00 on the principal diagonal of the matrix is the perfect correlation between each variable and itself. As would be expected, all the coefficients are positive. The consensus ranking, the tenth variable considered (column 11 in Table 11.13), agrees most closely with variables 3 (cars) and 9 (income); the latter itself is a kind of consensus of the elements affecting standard of living. It must be stressed that the aim of the study described above has been simply to assess the similarity of different variables and of different states, not to look for causal relationships between variables. The general conclusion is that different aspects of development vary regionally in Brazil in broadly similar ways, but that considerable anomalies exist.

The second part of this section contains a study of the 21 states of Brazil on similar lines to the foregoing study but using a different set of variables and a different method of calculating the correlation coefficient. The study is also taken further to produce factors and to work out a clustering of the states into homogeneous groups.

Table 11.15 contains 12 variables for the 21 states of Brazil. Some of the variables are the same as those used in Table 11.12, but they are for two or three years earlier. The matrix of correlation coefficients in Table 11.16a shows considerable intercorrelation among the variables. The reason for the negative correlation between natural increase and the other variables is that it tends to be high where other variables are low and vice versa.

When factor analysis is applied to the correlation matrix it shows that 69 per cent of all the variation among the 12 variables can be represented on the first (and strongest) factor. Another 11 per cent falls on the second factor. Table 11.16b shows that the colour of population is the variable least associated with the other variables but even this associates to some extent with levels of development. The states are arranged in Table 11.16c according to their scores on factor I. The values are only relative. The mean score is 0, and one standard deviation from the mean is ± 100. The distribution is very skewed owing to the artificial influence of Guanabara, containing the city of Rio de Janeiro on a very small area. Factor I represents a development consensus similar to column 10 in Table 11.13, derived from the summing of the rankings given by the 'judges' of development in that table. In fact when the ranking of the states in Table 11.16c is correlated with that in column 11 of Table 11.13, there is a remarkably high Spearman coefficient of + 0.93. The development scale in Brazil is resilient enough to show a very similar picture on the basis of two different sets of variables.

The 21 states of Brazil have been grouped according to their scores on the first three factors derived from the above study. The linkage tree is shown in *Figure 11.9a* and the six groups obtained from it when cut where indicated are mapped in *Figure 11.9b*. The 7 highest and 7 lowest scoring states on factor I are mapped in *Figure 11.9c*.

For the purposes of the next three sections Brazil is divided into three major regions, the Southeast and South, the Northeast, and the 'Interior' (Centro-Oeste and Norte). The evidence in the above studies from the position of the states of Brazil on a development scale and from the clustering suggests that the threefold division used corresponds fairly closely to the actual situation. On the development scale of factor I, Minas Gerais would have come above Goiás until the 1960s when the influence of Brasília began to be felt. Espírito Santo and Pernambuco, for different reasons, occupy intermediate positions between the Southeast and Northeast.

11.10. SOUTHEAST AND SOUTH BRAZIL

Southeast and South Brazil together cover about 17·6 per cent of the area of Brazil but have over 60 per cent of the population, about 57 million people in

1 Density of population, persons per sq.km. in 1970
2 Average annual natural increase of population in persons per thousand during 1950-60
3 Persons born in other states as percentage of total population of state in 1950
4 Whites (brancos) as a percentage of total population
5 Urban population as a percentage of total population
6 Persons employed in manufacturing per thousand total population
7 Electricity consumed in kWh per inhabitant
8 Telephones per thousand inhabitants
9 Cars per thousand inhabitants
10 State budgets in cruzeiros per inhabitant per year
11 Literate population as a percentage of total population
12 Hospital beds available per 10,000 inhabitants

States	1	2	3	4	5	6	7	8	9	10	11	12
1 Amazonas	1	34	10	37	32	7	70	6	7	75	43	29
2 Para	2	29	6	29	41	8	60	4	7	53	49	23
3 Maranhão	11	30	10	34	18	7	10	1	3	11	25	4
4 Piauí	6	35	8	28	24	5	10	2	3	15	26	14
5 Ceará	26	37	4	44	34	8	40	7	7	30	31	17
6 Rio Grande do Norte	24	33	8	29	37	20	50	4	7	31	32	19
7 Paraíba	40	33	6	67	35	21	90	4	3	30	29	18
8 Pernambuco	48	30	6	50	45	21	170	5	9	63	32	25
9 Alogoas	51	34	6	41	34	30	70	3	5	30	24	20
10 Sergipe	39	34	6	50	39	20	90	2	6	30	34	20
11 Bahia	12	28	3	30	35	9	90	4	7	40	32	13
12 Minas Gerais	20	30	3	58	40	15	290	12	12	63	44	35
13 Espírito Santo	42	34	11	59	32	11	90	9	10	46	47	22
14 Rio de Janeiro	107	24	16	60	61	33	430	15	16	89	56	39
15 Guanabara	3,593	17	43	70	98	53	750	99	43	395	85	89
16 São Paulo	67	26	13	86	63	70	790	36	42	322	65	51
17 Paraná	36	29	32	86	31	14	160	6	17	70	53	22
18 Santa Catarina	28	37	10	95	32	35	180	5	19	72	64	46
19 Rio Grande do Sul	25	25	1	89	45	31	190	12	20	127	66	45
20 Mato Grosso	1	32	18	53	40	9	60	6	13	37	51	24
21 Goiás + D.F.	5	28	23	58	40	5	110	12	18	535	33	24

Sources: Anuario estatístico do Brasil (especially 1968 edition): IBGE
Subsídios a regionalização, IBGE
Contribuições para o estudo da demografia do Brasil, IBGE 1961

Table 11.16a.

MATRIX OF PEARSON PRODUCT MOMENT CORRELATION COEFFICIENTS FROM TABLE 11.15

	1	2	3	4	5	6	7	8	9	10	11	12
1 Density of population	1·00											
2 Natural increase	−0·65	1·00										
3 In migration	0·70	−0·57	1·00									
4 Colour (white)	0·18	−0·29	0·35	1·00								
5 Urban percentage	0·80	−0·80	0·58	0·36	1·00							
6 Employment in industry	0·46	−0·51	0·29	0·61	0·73	1·00						
7 Electricity consumption	0·61	−0·73	0·50	0·54	0·87	0·88	1·00					
8 Telephones	0·94	−0·74	0·70	0·33	0·91	0·65	0·82	1·00				
9 Cars	0·62	−0·70	0·63	0·66	0·82	0·81	0·92	0·83	1·00			
10 State budgets	0·48	−0·60	0·60	0·37	0·61	0·42	0·60	0·64	0·74	1·00		
11 Literacy	0·58	−0·60	0·54	0·70	0·73	0·66	0·74	0·71	0·85	0·44	1·00	
12 Hospital beds	0·77	−0·66	0·55	0·59	0·88	0·77	0·85	0·88	0·88	0·59	0·89	1·00

Table 11.16b.

LOADINGS OF VARIABLES ON FIRST TWO FACTORS

		Index		Percentage	
		I	II	I	II
1	Density	0·80	−0·47	63	22
2	Natural increase	−0·80	0·25	64	6
3	In migration	0·70	−0·38	49	14
4	Colour (white)	0·59	0·67	34	44
5	Urban	0·93	−0·15	86	2
6	Industry	0·79	0·41	62	17
7	Electricity	0·92	0·16	85	3
8	Telephones	0·93	−0·29	87	8
9	Cars	0·95	0·18	91	3
10	State budgets	0·71	−0·17	50	3
11	Literacy	0·85	0·27	73	7
12	Hospital beds	0·95	0·10	89	1

Table 11.16c

AREA SCORES ON FACTOR I, THE 'DEVELOPMENT CONSENSUS'

1	Guanabara	351	12	Pará	−41
2	São Paulo	180	13	Amazonas	−48
3	Rio de Janeiro	70	14	Sergipe	−51
4	Rio Grande do Sul	55	15	Paraíba	−52
5	Santa Catarina	23	16	Rio Grande do Norte	−58
6	Goias and D.F.	22	17	Alagoas	−60
7	Paraná	17	18	Bahia	−61
8	Minas Gerais	− 5	19	Ceará	−74
9	Mato Grosso	−20	20	Maranhao	−92
10	Pernambuco	−25	21	Piauí	−96
11	Espírito Santo	−35			

1970. The two regions together contain about ⅕ of the whole population of Latin America and have more inhabitants than France or Italy. Data for the 8 states of the Southeast and South can be found in various tables in earlier sections of this chapter. For convenience the two regions will be referred to in the rest of this section as Southern Brazil.

Figure 11.10 shows the main relief features of Southern Brazil, distinguished by the 800 metre contour. Two mountain areas of a rugged nature may be distinguished, one between Belo Horizonte, Rio and São Paulo, and one shared by the states of Paraná, Santa Catarina and Rio Grande do Sul. The land rises steeply behind the coast itself or from a narrow coastal plain almost everywhere between Porto Alegre and Vitória. Land is flat or gently undulating in the southern part of Rio Grande do Sul and the west of São Paulo. Almost the whole region is sufficiently broken or rugged for relief to have made the construction of railways and modern roads difficult and costly. Contact by land between São Paulo and Rio Grande has been restricted until the 1960s and movement inland from both Rio de Janeiro and Santos, the two principal ports of Brazil, is hindered by steep gradients and winding routes. The presence of large areas over 500 metres above sea level makes most of Southern Brazil subtropical rather than tropical.

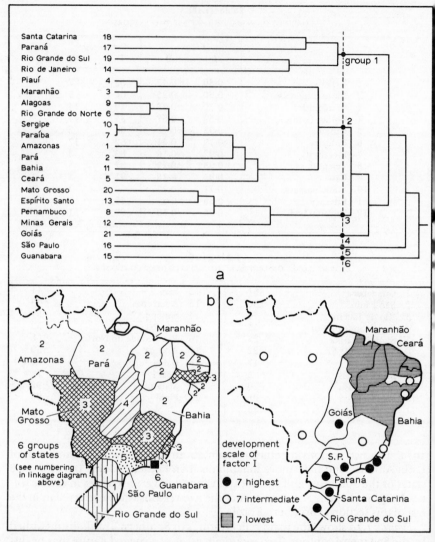

Figure 11.9. The results of the application of factor analysis to data in Table 11.15. (a) Linkage diagram and (b) map of groups from (a); (c) Positions of states on factor I (see Table 11.16c)

Before the colonisation of southern Brazil, most of the area was forest covered, a result of the heavy rainfall, which exceeds 120 cm per year almost everywhere. Dense tropical forest covered the coastal lowlands, thinner deciduous forest extended over much of the interior and coniferous forest occupied the higher parts of the three southern states. Only in the extreme southwest was the region characterised by grassland (campo limpo).

The first agricultural settlements of the colonial period were along the coast, but in the 18th century farming spread into Minas Gerais and Rio Grande do Sul. The settlements of São Paulo, Paraná and Santa Catarina are associated mainly with the new inflow of immigrants from 19th century Europe as well as the movement of more local migrants from Rio Grande do Sul. Coffee plantations, roads and railways spread across São Paulo along east-west ridges to the Paraná in the west. The intervening valleys were settled later. The interior of São Paulo is relatively fertile and includes areas of *terra roxa* derived from lava flows. The clearance of the forest and the introduction of agriculture continued into northern Paraná and finally around the fringes of the southern mountain area. The state of Paraná had only 330,000 inhabitants in 1900, 1¼ million in 1940 but nearly 7 million in 1970. Municipio population changes show a rapid

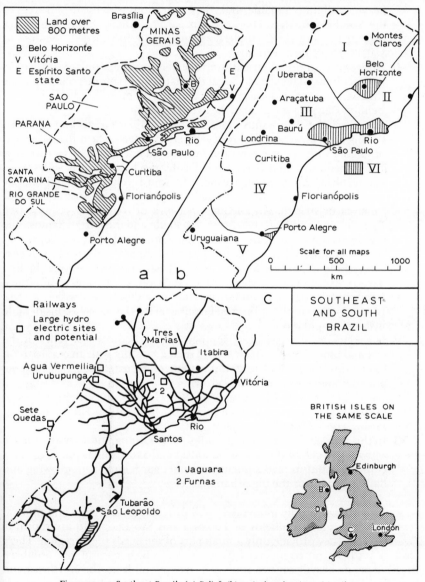

Figure 11.10. Southeast Brazil: (a) Relief, (b) agricultural regions, (c) railways

growth of rural population in the 1940s and 1950s. The frontier or pioneer period of southern Brazil ended with the settlement of Paraná state but continues beyond the Paraná river in Mato Grosso and Goiás.

Table 11.7a in Section 11.5 shows the distribution by states of the main crops cultivated in Brazil. The *Atlas do Brasil* distinguishes six types of regional economy in southern Brazil. These are shown in *Figure 11.10b:*

   I Northern Minas Gerais is part of the tropical grazing area of Brazil. Like the interior of Northeast Brazil it is a thinly populated area but rainfall is heavier and more reliable, and communications with the urban areas of the Southeast better. The northern part of Minas Gerais is however regarded as sufficiently underdeveloped to be included in the area of SUDENE (see next section).

  II An area of traditional agriculture, relatively densely populated, with relics of the colonial slave society. Sugar cane is the main commercial crop along the coast and coffee is still grown in places in the more mountainous areas behind. Dairying is typical in the livestock sector.

 III The interior of São Paulo state, southwest Minas Gerais and northern Paraná form an area of highly developed commercial farming associated originally with coffee cultivation but now characterised by its diversity. The agricultural land is relatively fertile, mechanisation is widespread and fertilisers are used increasingly. Output is relatively high both per unit of area and per worker, though still below that in Australia, North America or Britain. An adequate network of roads and railways (see *Figure 11.10c*) connects the area to São Paulo and the port of Santos. The region accounts for nearly all the coffee produced in Brazil. Sugar and cotton, traditional crops of Northeast Brazil, are now also grown very successfully in São Paulo state. Area III has also been among the first parts of Brazil to introduce new crops such as soybeans and groundnuts. In addition maize, sorghum, rice, potatoes and beans are widely grown. In spite of the emphasis on crop farming, area III also has a considerable livestock population.

 IV The Planalto Meridional or southern plateau consists of relics of the original pine forest set in an area of mixed farming with an emphasis on food crops for regional needs rather than for export. Maize, rice, manioc, potatoes and wheat are widely grown.

  V The southern part of the state of Rio Grande do Sul specialises in livestock farming with the emphasis on beef cattle. The main sheep raising area of Brazil is also here.

 VI In this area agriculture is overshadowed by mining, industry and service activities. Much of the land around Rio and São Paulo is too rugged for cultivation but in places intensive market gardening, fruit growing and dairying cater for the big urban markets.

Southern Brazil is only moderately well provided with energy and mineral resources. The small coalfields of Tubarão and São Leopoldo are shown in *Figure 11.10c.* They provide only a small part of the needs of the region. There have as yet been no commercial discoveries of oil or natural gas. Southern Brazil depends heavily on two sources of energy, oil from the Northeast and from foreign sources, and hydro-electric power. The earliest hydro-electric stations in Brazil were built in the mountains behind Rio de Janeiro and Santos. The headwaters of tributaries of the Paraná river were diverted over the scarp to give big vertical falls of water to generators at the foot. One such station is at Cubatão near Santos. Local hydro-electric capacity was limited and in the 1950s it became necessary to look for sites further away from the main industrial centres. Two examples are Furnas and Tres Marias. Transmission distances are considerable. Since the early 1960s the Paraná itself has come under consideration. There is a very large hydro-electric potential here but the cost of building suitable dams and long distance transmission lines is high. For example Jupia, which is one of the sites, is about 600 km in a straight line from São Paulo.

Table 11.17 shows the main industrial municipios of Brazil, those with over 4,500 persons employed in industry in 1965. 24 of the total of 59 listed are in the

Table 11.17.
MANUFACTURING CENTRES OF BRAZIL

All states except São Paulo			São Paulo state		
Manaus	Amaz.	5 wood	São Paulo	1	552 textiles
Belém	Pará	9 food	Americana	2	8 textiles
Fortaleza	Ceará	13 textiles	Araraquara	3	5 food
Recife	Pern.	32 food	Campinas	4	21 electrical
Arapiraca	Ala.	5 tobacco	Cubatão †	5	15 metals
Maceió	Ala.	5 textiles	França	6	5 clothing
Salvador	Bahia	13 textiles	Guarulhos *	7	20 electrical
Belo Horizonte	M.G.	23 food	Jundiaí †	8	17 textiles
Contagem	M.G.	13 metal	Limeira	9	7 clothing
João Monlevade	M.G.	5 metal	Mauá *	10	6 non-metal
Juiz de Fora	M.G.	9 textiles			
Nova Lima	M.G.	6 minerals	Mogi das Cruzes *	11	8 engineering
Timoteo	M.G.	5 –			
Barra Mansa	Rio	5 metals	Mogi Guaçu	12	5 non-metal
Campos	Rio	10 food			
Duque de Caxias	Rio	15 chemicals	Osasco *	13	16 transport
Mage	Rio	7 textiles	Piracicaba	14	11 engineering
Niteroi	Rio	14 transport			
Nova Friburgo	Rio	6 textiles	Riberão Preto	15	8 textiles
Nova Iguaçu	Rio	8 metals	Santo André *	16	50 chemicals
Petrópolis	Rio	14 textiles			
São Gonçalo	Rio	6 food	Santos †	17	7 food
Volta Redonda	Rio	16 metals	Sao Bernardo do Campo *	18	55 transport
GUANABARA		206 textiles	São Caetano do Sul *	19	25 transport
Curitiba	Par.	21 furniture	São Carlos	20	5 electrical
Blumenau	S.C.	13 textiles	São José dos Campos	21	9 chemicals
Criciuma	S.C.	5 minerals			
Joinvile	S.C.	12 metals	Sorocaba	22	11 textiles
Canoas	R.G.S.	5 food	Taubaté	23	5 textiles
Caxias do Sul	R.G.S.	12 metals	Votorantim	24	7 textiles
Novo Hamburgo	R.G.S.	15 clothing			
Pelotas	R.G.S.	8 food	The numbering of the municipios Sao Paulo state corresponds to numbering in *Figure 11.11a*		
Porto Alegre	R.G.S.	50 metals			
Rio Grande	R.G.S.	5 food			
São Leopoldo	R.G.S.	6 metals			

* Greater São Paulo (inner)
† Greater São Paulo (outer)
Source: *Registro Industrial 1965*, Fundação IBGE, Rio de Janeiro, 1968.

state of São Paulo. Those in the state of São Paulo near the state capital are located in *Figure 11.11* map *a,* and are numbered according to the list in Table 11.17. The extended Greater São Paulo is shown in *Figure 11.11b* with the 11 municipios having more than 4,500 workers in industry. There are many other industrialised municipios in the area with fewer than this number of workers. The following industrial concentrations may be noted in southern Brazil. The approximate number of workers is also given

1. São Paulo itself   550,000
2. The rest of Greater São Paulo   260,000
3. Other towns of São Paulo state   270,000
4. Greater Rio de Janeiro   250,000
5. Volta Redonda area   25,000
6. Belo Horizonte area   50,000
7. Porto Alegre area   80,000

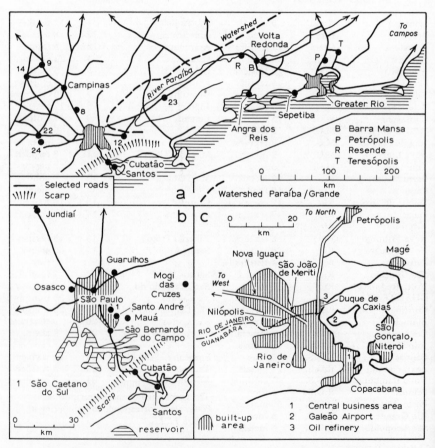

Figure 11.11. (a) The area between São Paulo and Rio de Janeiro and selected places around, the numbering as in Table 11.17, (b) São Paulo and (c) Rio de Janeiro

Contrary to what might have been hoped, the concentration of the value of total Brazilian industrial production in São Paulo state increased between 1950 and the mid-1960s. In 1950 São Paulo was estimated to have 47·5 per cent of the value but in 1964, about 62 per cent. In the late 1960s it dropped to around 57 per cent; Greater São Paulo itself then had about 38 per cent of the national total. Guanabara has about 10 per cent of Brazilian industrial capacity. São Paulo state has over 70 per cent of the value of production of rubber goods, transport and electrical materials and engineering items in general. In Guanabara, pharmaceutical, plastic and publishing branches and the production of beverages are strongly represented.

Outside the two main industrial concentrations, Volta Redonda has the largest iron and steel works in Brazil and the area around has metal working industries. Belo Horizonte itself is more a commercial and administrative centre than an industrial one but it is in a general area of iron and steel making and metal working. Porto Alegre and associated municipios form a bigger and more varied industrial complex than that of Belo Horizonte. In the part of São Paulo state nearest to São Paulo itself, centres like Sorocaba and Campinas are growing industrially as good roads place them within easy reach of São Paulo itself. Away from the areas noted there are many isolated industrial centres such as the old textile centre of Juiz de Fora between Rio and Belo Horizonte, and Blumenau and Joinvile in Santa Catarina. Curitiba, the state capital of Paraná, and one of the Metropolitan Areas of Brazil, also seems likely to grow industrially.

11.11. NORTHEAST BRAZIL

In 1970 the 9 states of the Northeast contained 30 per cent of the total population of Brazil; the population roughly doubled during 1940–1970 (14½ million to 28½ million). An older, 'inner' Northeast, excluding the states of Maranhão, Piauí and Bahia was previously recognised in Brazilian statistical publications, but the latter group, together with the northern part of Minas Gerais, are now within the area of SUDENE (the Superintêndencia do Desenvolvimento do Nordeste).

The Northeast is considered to be one of the main problem areas of Brazil. It declined in relation to Brazil as a whole after the 17th century. Since then it has had little to export and since Brazil became independent has not attracted much foreign investment. It has stagnated on the remains of an economy based along the coast on large sugar plantations, in the dry drought-afflicted interior on cattle raising, and in the northwest on forest products of limited potential. There are however six times as many people in Northeast Brazil as there were even in 1870 and the pressure on limited natural resources has left the region with one of the lowest per capita incomes in Latin America.

Northeast Brazil might have attracted more attention if it had been an independent country. It would be 23rd in population in the world, comparable in size with Iran or Burma. It has been suggested that by being within Brazil instead of independent the Northeast has suffered from competition from the more modernised and industrialised Southeast, which (like North Italy in relation to South Italy) has drawn on the raw materials of the Northeast and has sold manufactured goods there in return. It is agreed that industrial development was held up in the Northeast through lack of protection from the Southeast. Virtually all recent foreign investment and aid to Brazil has gone to the Southeast, which has also felt the benefit of the modern influx of immigrants from Europe.

Since the key politicians and capitalists of modern Brazil are mainly from the Southeast, the argument is that they have arranged trade policy and exchange rates to favour their own region. By keeping low export prices on primary products they have helped the more efficient agriculture in the Southeast. At the same time, low tariffs on the importation of capital equipment and high tariffs on the importation of consumer manufactures have helped to build up and protect the industries of the Southeast.

Whatever the truth of this complex situation, Northeast Brazil in total had an overall per capita income of only about $ U.S. 70 in 1950, about half the Brazilian average and only about $\frac{1}{5}$ the figure for São Paulo state ($ 353). In 1968 the per capita figure was $ 140 for the Northeast and $ 465 for São Paulo state. It was shown in Section 11.9 that according to various criteria measuring development, apart from Pernambuco, raised by the presence of the most sophisticated town in the Northeast, Recife, the states of the region consistently came low in the rankings of the 21 states of Brazil.

The backwardness of Northeast Brazil may be attributed to a number of influences. On the resource side, good quality agricultural land is limited in extent, though there are possibilities of increasing irrigation. There is no coal, only a limited hydro-electric potential, and only one relatively small oilfield, which, being the principal one in Brazil, in fact sends much of its crude oil to Southeast Brazil. Educational levels are very low and land tenure conditions are generally considered to be socially unsatisfactory. In spite of the favourable position of Northeast Brazil in relation to Europe and North America, even at international level the region is now by-passed by almost all inter-continental air services and many shipping lines. In short, there seems little prospect for any rapid improvements in conditions in the Northeast. Agriculture accounts for about 40 per cent of the income of the region, industry only about 10 per cent. Unemployment and underemployment appear to be high everywhere. One study made in 1969 put the level of unemployment at 30 per cent implying that about 5 million more persons could be employed. Since the paving of the main road to Southeast Brazil, emigration from the region seems to have increased considerably. Nevertheless the problem in the Northeast is still to create many new jobs within the region as quickly as possible.

In 1877 a serious drought affected Ceará and it was estimated that about half the population of the State died through starvation, thirst or diseases. Some people died from food poisoning through eating unsuitable vegetation or even soil. Many left the dry interior of the Northeast, moving to the east coast or into Amazonia. The first measures on a national scale to assist Northeast Brazil date from this period. The main achievement was the construction of a large number of reservoirs (açudes) to store water for domestic purposes and livestock use in periods of drought. In spite of attempts to improve water supply in Northeast Brazil the region has been badly affected by droughts as recently as 1958 and 1970.

The second major scheme to assist the Northeast dates from the 1940s with interest centering on the São Francisco river and the construction of a large hydro-electric power station at Paulo Afonso. The capacity of the station is now about 1 million kW, $\frac{1}{10}$ of the total Brazilian hydro-electric capacity. The benefit of Paulo Afonso has perhaps been more psychological than economic. An electricity supply has been made available in about 1000 towns and villages in the region, but there is not enough to provide a basis for heavy industry. A second but smaller hydro-electric station, Boa Esperança, in Piauí, fulfils a similar function in the northern area.

A third step towards encouraging development in the Northeast was the establishment of the Banco do Nordeste do Brasil in 1952. The droughts of 1958 were followed by the establishment in 1959 of SUDENE, mentioned above, with funds specifically provided, mainly by Southeast Brazil, for development projects in the Northeast. Before the present developments and problems of the Northeast are considered it should be noted that some modernisation did take place in the region before the 1950s. A number of railway lines were built in the area, leading mostly from interior areas with livestock products, cotton and other agricultural surpluses, to the main ports. Some modern factories were built as long ago as 1900, but industry was restricted mainly to food processing and textile manufacturing.

According to the agricultural census of Brazil, agriculture employed over 8 million people in Northeast Brazil in 1970. What happens to agriculture is therefore of fundamental importance to the region. In area the Nordeste is nearly three times the size of France, so the convenient division shown in *Figure 11.12c* into four land use areas is greatly oversimplified. Maps *a* and *b* in *Figure 11.12* show the relief features and annual rainfall of the region. Few areas are over 800 metres in altitude and the region consists generally of low plateaux (*tabuleiros*) with occasional isolated mountains, rolling hills and twisting, abrupt scarps. In view of the high temperatures throughout the year evaporation is high and the rainfall, which is markedly seasonal and also highly unreliable over most of the region, is not very effective for agricultural purposes. The numbering that follows refers to areas in *Figure 11.12c*.

1. There is a narrow, discontinuous belt of former tropical forest along the eastern coast (the *terras úmidas*). This area is intensively cultivated and sugar cane is still the principal crop except behind the port of Ilhéus where cacao is cultivated. Coconut palms are widely planted in the area. Commercial agriculture is characteristic but food crops such as manioc, maize, beans and rice are also grown for local use. There is a general lack of protein in the diet, partly supplemented by fishing.
2. This area is sometimes referred to as the *agreste*. In places soil is fertile and commercial crops of cotton and tobacco are grown. Much of the area is used for grazing.
3. This is an area of cattle raising where much of the original vegetation remains in the thorn forest of the drier areas and in the *cerrados* further south. Little has been done to improve pastures or the quality of stock. Locally there are possibilities for irrigation and throughout the area there are patches of cultivation, some of commercial importance; manioc, cotton, sisal and the castor oil plant are grown.
4. The northwest is the fringe of the Amazon forest. Here agriculture, mainly subsistence farming, is supplemented by forest products.

Reference to Table 11.7a shows that every state in the Northeast has a wide range of agricultural products but the value of production of most items is small. The production of certain commercial crops including cocoa beans, cotton seed, cotton lint and carnaúba wax has remained static during the 1950s and 1960s. The cultivation of sugar cane, sisal, tobacco and the castor oil plant has tended to increase. There seems to be scope for introducing certain new crops more widely; the vine is a possibility.

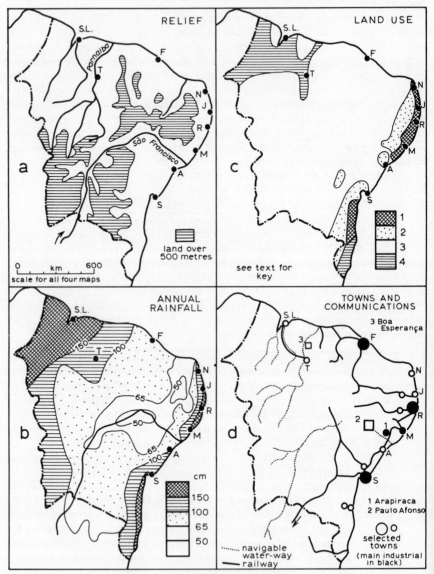

Figure 11.12. Northeast Brazil: (a) Relief, (b) Rainfall, (c) Agricultural regions, (d) Towns, railways and navigable waterways. Towns on map from north to south:

S.L.	São Luis	N	Natal	M	Maceió
F	Fortlaleza	J	João Pessoa	A	Aracajú
T	Terezina	R	Recife	S	Salvador

Many problems face the agricultural sector in the Nordeste in the 1970s. There is far too big a farm population for the limited area of good quality land available. Climatic conditions are unreliable and soil over most of the area is of poor quality. Land tenure is unsatisfactory because units tend to be too large or too small. Not much of the land is owned by the people who work it and land reform has not made much impact on the area. There is not sufficient land to grow enough food crops or to produce adequate protein for the population of the Northeast. Wheat and other food products are imported. The success of commercial cultivation is hampered by lack of good transportation, storage and marketing facilities. Commercial farmers lack support prices and their position is weak. Livestock farming is of a low standard.

In the face of all the drawbacks mentioned it is understandable that there is a big movement of population into the towns of the Northeast and to other parts of Brazil as far away as Rio de Janeiro and Brasília. One reason for establishing new settlements in Amazonia is to take people from the Northeast, but the number that can actually be moved and resettled in reasonable sized farms with adequate capital to start life in a new and difficult environment is very limited. Meanwhile rural areas of Northeast Brazil have a high rate of natural increase and any out migration is quickly replenished from within.

One of the main aims of SUDENE has been to promote industrial development in Northeast Brazil. Table 11.18 shows the projects recorded in 1971 and their value by sectors and states. Most are industrial, though electricity supply, the road network and water supply have also been extensively improved.

Table 11.18.
PROJECTS IN NORTHEAST BRAZIL

Value in millions of cruzeiros
Per capita value in cruzeiros

Branches	Projects	Value	Areas	Projects	Value	Per capita
Agricultural	106	602	Bahia	20	874	115
Chemicals	4	575	Pernambuco	24	393	74
Non metallic minerals	3	237	Ceará	33	348	77
Textiles	1	199	Paraíba	35	301	123
Metallurgical	6	158	Piauí	11	229	132
Food	12	132	Minas Gerais *	19	215	140
Raw materials	2	102	Maranhão **	13	145	47
Rubber	2	91	Rio Grande do Norte	11	61	38
Engineering	3	56	Alagoas	n.a.	42	26
Paper	3	48	Sergipe	3	19	21
Others	27	428				
			Brazil	169		

* Only the extreme northern part
** part is included in Amazonia
n.a. not available
Source: *AEB 1972*, p. 445

The question of what kinds of new industry are most suitable for the Northeast has not been solved. Some branches need a great amount of capital yet create relatively few jobs. Such industries include the manufacture of iron and steel and of chemicals, and oil refining. Textiles, clothing, light engineering and the manufacture of wood, on the other hand tend to employ larger numbers of workers.

A second question to be decided is where to put new industries. SUDENE has been criticised for concentrating industrialisation in a few main centres and neglecting most of the region. The three largest concentrations of existing industry in the Northeast, Recife, Salvador and Fortaleza, all have big new industrial estates. Salvador, for example, has two main types of industry, that associated with the oil refinery at Mataripe, and that established in the Aratu industrial estate. By 1970 about $ U.S. 320 million had been invested in Aratu and there were about a hundred firms. The investment of 320 million dollars was expected eventually to provide about 20,000 jobs, at over $ 15,000 per job. It was estimated that similar jobs could be created in Southeast Brazil for about half the cost.

During 1969–73 it was hoped to achieve an annual rate of growth of industry of 9 per cent in the Nordeste. Even if this rate of growth were sustained for a decade, however, little impact would be made on the employment situation. It was proposed, therefore, to make a very large number of new jobs in semi-domestic industries such as embroidery, lace making and the manufacture of hats. This is virtually an admission, however, that the region can expect to have modern factory industry only in a few places and only on a limited scale.

As new roads link the main centres in the Nordeste, a new spatial arrangement of life in the region is taking shape. The three biggest towns have much of the modern industry as well as the best services. They are privileged growth poles but they do not seem to have made much impact on places beyond their immediate limits. There are also places with special resources such as the oilfields, the hydro-electric stations, the saltpans of Rio Grande do Norte and the areas of commercial agriculture. Some smaller towns also form centres of modernisation as a result of the growth of commercial activities, rather than industry; such places are Feira de Santana, Caruarú and Campina Grande. Virtually all the rest of the Nordeste is little affected as yet by change. There are blind spots even in the more sophisticated areas such as the Recôncavo of Bahia and eastern Pernambuco. The whole of the states of Piauí and Maranhão seem completely stagnant.

If the population of the Northeast continues to grow in the 1970s at about 2·2 per cent per year, as it did in the 1960s, then by 1980 there will be another 7–8 million people. During the 1960s, about 200,000 people a year left for southern Brazil. One needs to be an optimist to predict even a slight increase in the standard of living of the Northeast in the next 2–3 decades. It may be irresponsible and even heretical to make such a suggestion, but it seems that the region could only hope to have a reasonable standard of living for everyone in it if it could suddenly cut its population down to $\frac{1}{4}$ or $\frac{1}{3}$ of the present size.

11.12. THE INTERIOR OF BRAZIL

The North and Centre-West regions of Brazil, referred to in this section for convenience as the interior, contain 64 per cent of the total area of Brazil (the North alone has 42 per cent) but have less than 10 per cent of the total population of the country. Over 1$\frac{1}{2}$ million people live in the four largest towns, Belém, Goiânia, Manaus and Brasília, but the rest of the population is widely scattered in many small towns and villlages. Much of the area is virtually uninhabited or only occasionally used by Indians practising shifting agriculture. Although the region has very few people for its size it is not necessarily underpopulated. Attention in Brazil is now being directed towards the interior, however, as though it was just through a historical accident that it has remained so empty for so long. The region will be considered for convenience under a number of headings.

THE FOREST

The interior of Brazil was explored by many Spaniards and Portuguese during the colonial period and the Indians there were regarded by the Portuguese as a source of labour for their settlements along the coast. Only during about 1870–1910 did Amazonia become an area of world interest when the wild rubber tree, *Heavea brasiliensis,* was exploited in the region and the Amazon and its tributaries became a major transportation network. Rubber is still extracted from wild trees and attempts have been made to grow the rubber tree in plantations as at Fordlandia and Belterra. Brazil nuts and a number of other forest products are extracted from the forests of the interior but their value is very small. The amount of timber produced in the region for sale outside is also at present very small.

CATTLE

Cattle raising is practised in the cerrado or savanna lands to the southeast of Amazonia in the states of Goiás and Mato Grosso as well as in more open country in the coastlands of Amazonia and in the territory of Roraima. The cattle lands are mostly very remote from the main centres of population in Brazil and it is difficult to move products out of the region. Improvements in transportation have come in the southern parts of Goiás and Mato Grosso.

CROP FARMING

Crop farming is very restricted in the interior of Brazil. The potentially fertile alluvial flood plains of the big rivers are at present hardly used and the scale of work needed to control the rivers is so great that no serious projects have yet been considered. Elsewhere in the region, lateritic soils lose their fertility easily when the forest is cleared and field crops are grown. Locally there are areas suitable for tree or field crops, as around Goiás and to the east of Belém. Many tropical plants are cultivated in the interior, including industrial plants such as jute and the oil palm, and food crops such as manioc and maize. Bananas are easily grown and provide a major item of diet in Amazonia, supplemented along the rivers by fishing. Erva mate and quebracho are gathered in the extreme south of Mato Grosso.

MINERALS

Since the Second World War interest in the mineral potential of the Amazon region has increased greatly. Several large mineral deposits have been discovered by accident rather than through methodical exploration, but since the mid-1960s new sensing methods have helped to overcome the difficulty of exploring the geology and structure of the earth's surface through dense vegetation. The minerals of Amazonia were discussed in Section 11.6 of this chapter. The positions of the localities concerned are in *Figure 11.13*.

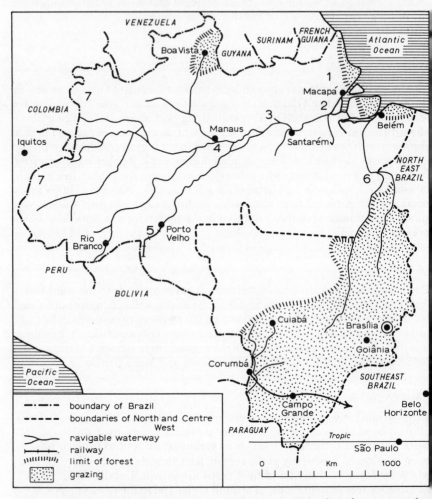

Figure 11.13. The interior of Brazil. The numbered places are referred to in the text on page 269.

INDUSTRY

Industry in the interior of Brazil is restricted mainly to the processing of the forest, agricultural and mineral products of the region. In 1965 only Belém and Manaus had more than 5,000 persons employed in industry. Manaus has a small oil refinery, providing the main source of energy in Amazonia. At Belém there are a number of modern factories including a jute mill employing over 1,000 persons and using locally grown jute, and a new brewery.

MANGANESE

The ICOMI manganese mine in Amapá territory illustrates the impact of a big modern enterprise on a simple Indian society. In 1956 the extraction of manganese ore started at Serra do Navio at the end of a specially built 200 km railway from Santana near Macapá on the Amazon. Serra do Navio is in a rugged, forest covered mountain area. A large cover of overburden had to be removed before the ore, with a 45–52 per cent manganese content, could be reached. The ore is extracted by large excavators, crushed, graded and sent by rail in two or three trains daily, moving out several thousand tons per day.

Although roughly $ U.S. 50 million were initially invested in the project, little more than 1,000 people are directly employed in the two settlements. The cost of creating each job was therefore about $ 50,000. Most of the labour in the enterprise was recruited locally. With dependents of the workers and other people not directly employed by the company, the two settlements each have several thousand inhabitants. Houses, schools and medical facilities are provided by the company.

In the first decade of operation the way of life and attitudes of the workers changed markedly. Data collected by the company show that there was a dramatic drop in the birthrate and a sudden interest in family planning. Greatly improved medical facilities kept far more babies and children alive than under previous primitive conditions, while at the same time parents realised that a large family made it more difficult for them to acquire the high quality consumer goods available. The presence of the interior settlement of Serra do Navio has had a miniature spread effect on the people of the forest around, who produce food for the settlement, and who are not refused medical assistance when they need it badly even though they do not belong to the company.

Manganese ore reserves seem adequate for some decades as production is restricted to about 1 million tons per year and reserves in 1970 were about 30 million tons. Even so there is concern about jobs in the area if and when the mining activity runs down. Some of the profits of the enterprise are kept in Amapá territory and have been invested in an experimental farm at Campo Verde, on which citrus fruits, coconuts and sugar cane are grown and cattle, pigs and poultry raised.

BRASÍLIA

Brasília became the capital of Brazil in 1960 though it was some time before most of the national government functions were transferred there from Rio de Janeiro. *Figure 11.13* shows that Brasília is only just inside the Centro-Oeste. In fact it is about 1000 km northwest of Rio de Janeiro but 3000 km from the other side of the country near Colombia.

The site, layout and buildings of Brasília have attracted considerable interest in many countries but will not be discussed at length here. The town is about 1000 metres above sea level and this altitude and the very dry atmosphere reduce the unpleasant effect of heat in the humid tropics. The area around is poor grassland with stunted trees. The town itself was unfinished when the author visited it in 1969 and almost treeless. Like Canberra, Brasília is a very open town designed primarily for a community of car owners. Many of the

FOREIGN MINISTRY BRASILIA

RIO DE JANEIRO

people whose jobs were moved from Rio de Janeiro to Brasília preferred the former capital and there have been many stories of actual cases of people commuting weekly by air between the two towns. One survey[2] made in the late 1960s showed, however, that children brought up in Brasília tended to prefer the new capital to the old.

One of the main purposes of the transference of the capital of Brazil to the new position was to draw the attention of people to the empty interior of the country and to form a place around which the transport system of Brazil could be reshaped. Good road links were provided with São Paulo, Belo Horizonte and Rio de Janeiro to the south and the Belém–Brasília road, already referred to in Section 11.8, was built though not entirely completed in detail, around 1960. Even by 1970, however, there was no good direct paved road from Brasília to the Northeast.

The internal airline network of Brazil was greatly changed with the growth of Brasília but by the early 1970s the new capital had still failed to attract more than a few international services per week. Rio de Janeiro remains the busiest international airport in the country.

Brasília is essentially a uni-functional city. Its services are for its own use as the area within 50 km is virtually uninhabited. It has no large scale industries. With a few other towns, including Goiânia and Anápolis, and a sparse rural population in southern Goiás and the adjoining parts of Minas Gerais, there are little more than 1 million people within a radius of 200 km of Brasilia. One per cent of the national market is not even enough to attract factories producing on a regional scale, while those expecting to sell their products over the whole of Brazil would find the position very unfavourable.

It is difficult to say whether Brasília is a success or a failure. The author has hardly met any Brazilians who seem certain either way, but the general view seems to be that it will achieve something in the end. A book has been written on Brasília entitled 'How much did Brasília cost?'[3] Nowhere in the book is it stated plainly exactly how much each stage in the creation of Brasília *has* cost, and probably no one knows. What is certain is that its progress has been sporadic because from time to time funds have been cut.[4]

NEW PROJECTS IN AMAZONIA[5]

The following numbers refer to localities in *Figure 11.13*.

1. The ICOMI manganese mine in Amapá has already been referred to.
2. The multi-million tree growing project of the U.S. millionaire, Daniel K. Ludwig, experimenting with the possibility of growing just a few commercial species for timber in place of the hundreds of species typical in any part of the natural forest. There is a Netherlands forestry project in the same area.
3. Bauxite to be exploited on the Rio Trombetas.
4. Finds of minerals, including oil, in the 1950s.
5. Cassiterite deposits of Rondônia.
6. Iron ore deposits of Marabá.
7. Oil in commercial quantities is already extracted in structurally similar parts of Peru, Colombia and Ecuador.

One big drawback still faces the developers of Amazonia. Distances are so great and hauls of agricultural or mineral produce 2000–3000 km by road from the interior to the Southeast are ridiculously costly. The Amazon itself takes only relatively small ocean going vessels. The exploitation of oil or gas in the interior would need very long pipelines to move it out. Ironically they might have to be built to the Pacific (see map) rather than the Atlantic, even with the Andean barrier in the way.

11.13. THE NEW ROADS OF AMAZONIA

Until the early 1970s the Norte and Centro-Oeste regions of Brazil were almost completely lacking in roads or railways and depended on the limited facilities of the waterways and air services. *Figure 11.7* (p. 243) shows the road system of Brazil in the late 1960s. In 1970 a plan was launched to open up Amazonia by the construction in a decade of 10,000 km of roads. Considering there were already over 1 million km of road of varying quality in Brazil, 10,000 km does not in fact appear all that impressive. Moreover it must be appreciated that a road only opens a narrow band of country 20–30 km wide unless appropriate secondary feeder roads are built out from it. What follows is a summary of a Brazilian article published in 1971[6] plus some comments. *Figure 11.14* should be referred to for the location of the roads under consideration.

Serious droughts in Northeast Brazil in 1970 turned a long term idea of moving people from this area into the Amazon region into an actual plan of action. Nearly all the land in Amazonia belongs to the State and little is in the

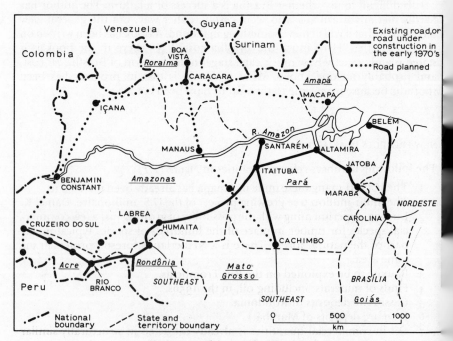

Figure 11.14. The new roads of Amazonia

ands of farmers, mining companies or other private concerns. The original
ndians might dispute the ownership of the land. In 1970 a crash plan called the
lano de Integração Nacional was formulated to develop a road–river
ransport system to open up Amazonia. It had two main aims:

1. The resettlement of an unspecified number of families from Northeast
   Brazil after 1970 droughts, where 400,000 families had been affected by
   the 'emergency'. The families from the Northeast are to be transferred to
   Amazonia and resettled in 20 nuclei, each 100 km apart, along the new
   roads. Saw mills, oilseed processing plants, seeds, tractors, schools,
   medical facilities and banks would have to be provided.[7]
2. To link Amazonia better with Southeast Brazil. Resettlement would be less
   urgent from here, but the raw materials of Amazonia should reach the
   Southeast and the industrial goods of the Southeast be transported more
   easily into Amazonia.

The first stage of the project was to build 2,775 km of new road in 520 days. It
ould be necessary to cut down millions of trees and to move 42 million cubic
netres of earth. The project was advertised, and bids offered for the work.
idders had to be *bona fide,* for example to have enough capital to participate
nd also to have experience. The Belém–Brasília road had still not been *properly*
ompleted 10 years after it had been started. One criterion was that a firm
hould already have moved more than 2 million cubic metres of earth in less
han 361 days (sometimes the Brazilian mind works in strange ways). The total
ost of the 2,775 km road project was estimated to be 320 million Brazilian
ruzeiros or about 30 million U.S. dollars, or about £12 million. This works out
) be about £40,000 per km, compared with several million pounds for an ur-
an motorway in Europe or North America.
The deal was clinched on June 18, 1970 and, in the event, four private com-
anies in particular and three Brazilian army batallions formed a consortium
or the project. 15,000 men were to be employed, 200 tractors used, and various
ther equipment required.
The project included the following items:

1. The construction of small river ports at navigation heads on some south
   Amazon tributaries.
2. The construction of 2,775 km of road between mid-1970 and the end of
   1971 (520 days).
3. The construction of 895 km in 1972.
4. The 'opening' to development of a 20 km wide band of country along the
   roads; this would be an *area* of approximately 60,000 sq. km, but with a
   greatly elongated shape.
5. The 'conquest' should be scientific and humanitarian. Indians along the
   route should be pacified and moved back from the road.

Basically, two roads should be built:

TRANSAMAZONICA (1,290 km), roughly east-west, from Tocantinópolis
n the Tocantins River south of Imperatriz to Humaita on the Madeira River,
ending north to touch the heads of navigation of the Xingu, Tapajos and other

rivers. To link this to the road system of Northeast Brazil a major link road would be needed *east* of Tocantinópolis or Carolina.

CUIABA-SANTAREM (1,485 km), roughly south-north, from Cuiabá in Mato Grosso to Santarém on the Amazon.

The second phase of the campaign to open up Amazonia is apparently based on the construction of two other roads also with a combined length of nearly 3,000 km, the northern peripheral road from Macapá to Cruzeiro do Sul, running close to the boundary between Brazil and its northern neighbours, and a road from Cachimbo on the Cuiabá–Santarém road to Boa Vista via Manaus.

Road builders in Amazonia can expect to run into many construction problems. Some are listed below:

1. The tropical rain forest is costly to clear (though new equipment does this more easily than previously). The soil and underlying rock are mainly lateritic and after rain very slippery, but during the dry season very dusty.
2. Heavy rain most of the year washes exposed soil away quickly and easily floods low lying areas. Though climatic conditions are far from uniform over Amazonia, typically there are several dry or 'drier' months, roughly December to May. During this period, only about 30 cm of rain (12 in) fall, out of a yearly total of 200–250 cm (80–100 in).
3. Long stretches of river flood plain have to be crossed in places. The causeways and viaducts required to avoid floods are expensive.
4. Big rivers need costly bridges or otherwise are crossed by inefficient ferries.
5. There are many steep slopes locally, though mountain areas are few on the south side of the Amazon.
6. Insects and other wild life are hazards.
7. Indians are potentially hostile and dangerous. They held up the completion of a road from Manaus to Boa Vista.

It seems appropriate to conclude this section with an epilogue to the Indians of Amazonia, about 100,000 altogether, many of them in areas as yet hardly ever reached by outsiders. There has been growing concern outside Brazil about their fate.[8] Several not entirely mutually exclusive alternative futures seem to lie ahead for them:

1. They may be wiped out, either deliberately in the way that North American and Argentinian Indians were in the 19th century, or simply a a result of the impact of new diseases from outside.
2. They may survive but then gradually become assimilated in the genera Brazilian population as other peoples have before.
3. Certain areas could be reserved exclusively for them and these area somehow protected from the outside world.

What does seem inevitable is that if the serious onslaught on Amazonia tha started in the late 1960s continues for two or three decades it will rightly o wrongly modify the physical environment and the economic and social life o the present population to such a degree that it will upset the precarious balanc still maintained there at the moment.

11.14. THE BANKS OF BAHIA STATE

It was shown in the previous section how a large area in Brazil is faced with the prospect of the rapid penetration of modern technology. In this section, by way of contrast, the very slow spread of an innovation over a smaller area, the state of Bahia in Brazil, is illustrated with historical data. The availability of the facilities of a bank are useful if not essential in promoting the transformation of areas of subsistence agriculture into areas of commercial agriculture and in allowing internal trade. In the interior of Brazil the actual replacement of worn out paper money in a country characterised by inflation and the almost complete absence of coins is more than a trivial matter. More importantly, the presence of a bank helps to encourage both saving and the use of loans. Long distance transactions can also be carried out. The state of Bahia is larger in area than France and had $3\frac{1}{2}$ million people in 1930 yet in that year there were only 13 actual bank offices in the whole state.

The publication *Movimento Bancario*[9] contains a complete list of the 360 banks in the state of Bahia in 1968. The date of opening of each head office and branch is given for all but a few of the banks. With this information it is possible to trace the spread of availability of banking facilities during time over area in a relatively underdeveloped part of Brazil.

Figure 11.15b shows the distribution of banks in Bahia by municipio. Owing to slight discrepancies in the basic data source, it was not possible to identify and consider exactly 360 banks. For this study the state of Bahia was divided into five areas. The number of banks in each is as follows:

Salvador municipio	111
Other Recôncavo municipios	36
Coast (east of road BR116/110)	109
Interior (BR116/110 to River São Francisco)	91
Far West (River São Francisco and beyond)	10
	357

The data below show the earliest banks in Bahia according to the date of opening of a head office (Matriz), regional office (Filial) or local branch (Agencia). The earliest banks in Bahia were the following:

1	1834	Matriz	Banco Económico da Bahia S.A.	Salvador
2	1858	Matriz	Banco da Bahia S.A.	Salvador
3	1864	Filial	Bank of London and S. America Ltd.	Salvador
4	1910	Agencia	Banco do Brasil S.A.	Salvador
5	1913	Matriz	Banco Bahiano da Produção S.A.	Salvador
6	1917	Agencia	Banco do Brasil S.a.	Ilhéus
7	1919	Agencia	Banco da Brasil S.A.	São Félix
8	1922	Agencia	Banco do Brasil S.A.	Santo Amaro
9	1923	Agencia	Banco do Brasil S.A.	Jequié
10	1924	Agencia	Banco do Brasil S.A.	Juazeiro
11	1927	Agencia	Banco do Brasil S.A.	Itabuna
12	1930	Agencia	Banco Económico da Bahia S.A.	São Félix

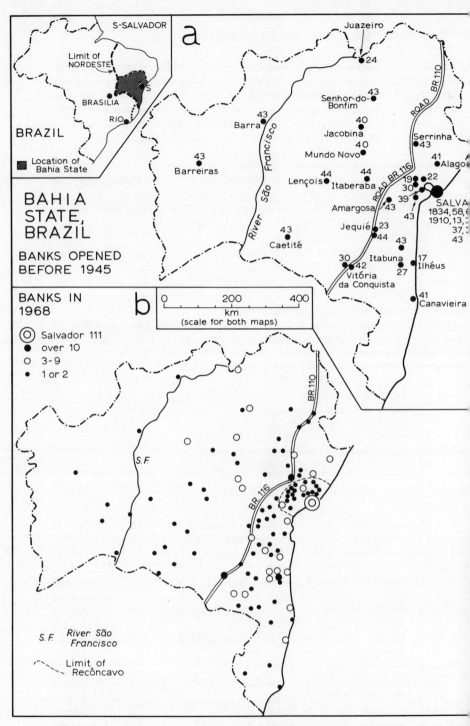

Figure 11.15. Banks in the state of Bahia: (a) Opening dates of banks opened before 1945, (b) Municípios in the state with one or more banks

The first bank in the state of Bahia was opened in 1834 in Salvador. Almost a hundred years passed before any other town in the state had a bank, one being opened in 1917 in Ilhéus, the second port. By the end of the Second World War Bahia still had only 37 banks for a population of some 4 million people. 12 were in Salvador. In contrast, over 320 banks were opened in the period 1946 to 1968.

Figure 11.15a shows the location and date of opening of all Bahia banks opened before 1945. If the presence of a bank in a municipio or a group of municipios marks the entry into or at least strengthening of the position of a place in the commercial, money economy of a country, then only Salvador was integrated before the First World War. During the interwar period, banks were opened elsewhere in the Recôncavo, on the coast and at a few places in the interior. During the Second World War, the western part of the state was reached for the first time. The 'colonisation' by banks was achieved both by those based in Salvador, and by the Banco do Brasil, S.A., from outside the state. The process in total was in fact the result of combined efforts by various banks presumably working out their own systems. The lack of banks as recently as 1945 is indicated by the fact that Feira de Santana, supposedly a commercial centre of wide influence, had no bank until 1947.

The spread of banks in Bahia since 1945 compared with that before 1945 is dramatic. In 1963 alone, 32 new banks were opened in Bahia, almost as many as during the whole of the state's history before 1945. The period of maximum expansion was in the early 1960s. An examination of the distribution of new banks since 1945 suggests that the coastal part of the state has been affected as much as the interior. Banks have proliferated in Salvador and the Recôncavo as much as in the interior and west. Even so, in 1968, 224 municipios out of 336 in the state altogether still had no bank at all.

11.15. THE CARIOCA'S* VIEW OF BRAZIL AND OF THE WORLD

Relatively little is available in English about the way in which ordinary people in Latin America see their own country or the rest of the world. This chapter on Brazil ends, therefore, with an account of a study made by the author in Rio de Janeiro to try to find out the Carioca's view of his own country and the rest of the world. A questionnaire asking for views of Brazil and the world was answered by 65 people in Rio de Janeiro in September 1969. The sample was biased, because circumstances only allowed the questionnaire to be given to certain office workers and their friends. It is representative only of a well informed and well travelled sector of the middle class population of Rio de Janeiro. It is of some interest simply because it shows a view of the world obviously very different from that held by Europeans. The results are tabulated and discussed below. Questions 1–7 are about Brazil, questions 8–10 about the rest of the world. Question 4 was badly expressed and misunderstood and has not been included. Age, sex and place of birth and residence were asked, but the sample was too small to justify the application correlations between these variables and any of the answers.

* Citizen of Rio de Janeiro

Figure 11.16. Britain seen from Rio de Janeiro. The results of a questionnaire answered by Cariocas in 1969

Question 1: Brazil now has about 90 million inhabitants. How many inhabitants do you suppose it will have in 50 years, in 100 years?

60 out of 65 answered the question.

Table 11.19 shows the estimates for the years 2020 and 2070, given by each of 60 people answering question 1. Estimates for 2020 range from 96 million to 400 million and for 2070 from 120 million to 600 million.

Question 2: Most of the population of Brazil lives near the coast (litoral). In your opinion, will this concentration, (a) become greater, (b) stay the same, (c) diminish?

Results (total 64)

(a) 33   (b) 17   (c) 14

Question 3: In 1960 the capital of Brazil was transferred to Brasília. Indicate the decision that in your opinion would have been the best decision for the location of the capital:

(a) remain in Rio de Janeiro, (b) move to the interior, but not so far inland as Brasília, (c) in Brasília, (d) further towards the interior, in the territorial centre of Brazil, (e) in the Northeast (Nordeste), (f) some other suggestion.

Table 11.19.
POPULATION ESTIMATES FROM 60 ANSWERS TO QUESTION 1

Initial population: 90 million in 1970. Numbers in millions

2 020	2 070	2 020	2 070	2 020	2 070	2 020	2 070	2 020	2 070
202	300	200	270	220	400	100	120	270	420
260	320	200	300	180	300	150	190	180	350
150	200	130	190	150	350	100	110	360	450
190	290	240	360	130	180	120	170	150	200
180	220	250	400	230	500	180	260	145	225
200	280	140	180	96	100	180	270	135	270
140	170	220	400	98	120	150	230	150	220
200	220	200	250	98	150	180	290	150	230
120	160	200	300	100	120	240	340	400	600
180	420	120	200	100	120	230	300	250	400
190	350	200	450	180	250	250	470	200	400
200	300	180	250	100	120	250	300	200	350

Results (total 65)

(a) Rio   8   (d) Centre of territory 1

(b) To the interior   4   (e) Nordeste   2

(c) Brasília   46   (f) Other suggestions 4

Question 5: Assuming you live in one of the larger towns of Brazil, if you were offered permanent employment of a kind acceptable to you in Amapá, Rondônia, Roraima or Acre (remote territories of Brazil), what would be the minimum salary you would want in order to move?
(a) what you get now,   (b) 50% more than this,   (c) 100% more, (d) 200% more,   (e) you would not accept under any circumstances.

Results (total 65)
(a) 1   (b) 5   (c) 11   (d) 15   (e) 33

Question 6: If you could no longer live in the state in which you currently reside (Guanabara in the case of almost all the people questioned), write in descending order of preference the five states which in this case you would choose.
(Five points were awarded to the first state name, four to the second, and so on.)

São Paulo	217	Espírito Santo	17
Rio Grande do Sul	138	Brasília	13
Minas Gerais	136	Amazonas	9
Paraná	107	Maranhão	6
Bahia	100	Goiás	6
Estado do Rio*	95	Mato Grosso	6
Pernambuco	52	Acre	3
Santa Catarina	27	Pará	1
Ceará	20		

* State of Rio de Janeiro

Not mentioned at all: Piauí, Rio Grande do Norte, Paraíba, Alagoas, Sergipe, Rondônia, Roraima, Amapá.

Question 7: Have you been abroad?
Results   Yes 31   No 34
If so, which countries have you visited?

Results (number of mentions, maximum 31)

Americas		*Europe*		*Asia and Africa*	
U.S.A.	21	France	18	Israel	5
Argentina	15	Italy	18	Japan	2
Uruguay	10	Portugal	14	Lebanon	2
Canada	8	Germany	13	Turkey	1
Mexico	6	England	13	Jordan	1
Paraguay	5	Switzerland	12	Thailand	1
Chile	4	Spain	10	Morocco	1
Peru	4	Holland	7	Mozambique	1
Cuba	2	Greece	5	Senegal	1
Colombia	1	Belgium	5		
Trinidad	1	Austria	4		
Bahamas	1	Denmark	3		
		Sweden	3		
		Luxembourg	1		
		Czechoslovakia	1		

Question 8: If you had to leave Brazil, write in order of preference the five countries that you would choose to live in:

Results (Five points were awarded to first choice, four to second, and so on):

France	162	Chile	32	Austria	10
U.S.A.	155	Argentina	31	Holland	10
England	96	Mexico	31	Greece	9
Italy	92	Sweden	28	Australia	8
Portugal	75	Canada	27	Cuba	6
Germany	59	Spain	23		
Switzerland	59	Uruguay	20		

5 or less: Norway, Finland, Belgium, New Zealand, Venezuela, Denmark, Israel, Senegal, Mozambique, Japan, U.S.S.R.

Question 10: Write down in a word or short phrase the five features that first occur to you when you think of the following countries:
France, U.S.A., U.S.S.R., England.

Only the features referred to five times or more are included in Table 11.20. Some very similar features (e.g. *tecnologia* and *técnica*) have been joined under one heading for simplicity. The illustrations on page 276 gives an artist's impression of the Brazilian view of England expressed in the questionnaire.

There follow brief comments by the author on the answers to the questions.

Question 1: Even the most conservative estimates of future population trends in Brazil would suggest a population of over 200 million in 50 years' time and of over 350 million in 100 years time. In each case, however, about ¾ of the estimates timates were below these figures. In thinking of the future population of Brazil, Brazilians seem to be affected by two considerations, firstly an awareness of the need to populate the empty interior and secondly an awareness that too great a population explosion would put excessive pressure on existing resources, material and financial.

Table 11.19.

FEATURES MENTIONED ABOUT THE FOUR COUNTRIES IN QUESTION 10

France		U.S.A.		U.S.S.R.		England	
Eiffel Tower	26	Race	24	Cold	20	Queen	26
De Gaulle	18	Technology	21	Communsim	15	Traditions	18
Wines	16	Industry	11	Socialism	12	Beatles	17
Culture	14	Progress	10	Oppression	10	Fog	10
Paris	13	New York	8	Iron Curtain	10	Big Ben	10
Perfumes	12	Cars	7	Siberia	8	Hippies	9
Fashion	12	Economic		Kremlin	7	London	7
Art	9	imperialism	7	Steppes	7	Buckingham	
Arc de		Comforts	6	Technology	7	Palace	6
Triomphe	8	Hippies	6	Vodka	7	Royal Guard	6
Seine	8	Moon	6	Ballet	7	Industries	6
Louvre	7	Space Race	6	Red Square	6	Parliament	5
Notre Dame	5	Niagara Falls	5				
Cheeses	5	Dollar	5				
Tourism	5	Capitalism	5				
History	5	Cinema	5				
		Apollo	5				
		Democracy	5				

Question 2: Less than a quarter of the people asked thought that there would be a relative shift of population towards the interior in the future. Over half anticipated a still greater concentration in the coastal belt.

Question 3: In spite of the general view expressed in Question 2, over three quarters felt that Brasília was the best location for a new national capital.

Question 5: However over half would not move under any circumstances to live in one of the four territories on the opposite side of Brazil, and most of the remainder would go only with substantial financial incentives.

Question 6: Asked where they would prefer to live if they had to leave Guanabara, most preferred São Paulo, Rio Grande do Sul or Minas Gerais, but in the Northeast, Bahia and Pernambuco, with the large towns of Salvador and Recife, were fairly popular.

Question 7: Nearly half the people asked had been abroad. In almost every case, those who had been abroad had visited several countries. The list of countries mentioned shows a clear preference on the part of Cariocas, living in the most developed part of a developing country, for other countries with a relatively high standard of living.

Question 8: The list of countries people would like to live in is fairly similar to the list of countries visited by those of the total who had been abroad.

Question 10: It was not feasible to list all the words or phrases used with reference to each country. What was remarkable, however, was the very distinct range of concepts produced for each of the four countries. While industry, progress and technology (*tecnologia* or *técnica*) were mentioned frequently for the U.S.A. they were mentioned much less in relation to England and hardly at all to France. The main impression of England seemed to be a mixture of tradition, quaintness and London scenes, not forgetting the occasional Scottish castle in 'England'. Perhaps the posters of Britain, displayed prominently in various tourist offices and offices representing British interests, are responsible.

References

1. Richards, P. W., 'The Tropical Rain Forest', *Sci. Am.,* Dec. 1973, Vol. 229, No. 6, pp. 58–67.
2. Bardawil, J. C. and H. Ribeiro, 'Aqui se pode pisar na grama', *Realidade,* Julho 1969, pp. 17–26.
3. Vaitsman, M., *Quanto custou Brasília?,* 1968, Rio de Janeiro, Editora PS.
4. Crease, D., 'Brasilia becomes a capital city', *Geogr. Mag.,* Mar. 1969, pp. 419–28.
5. Maynahan, B., 'Brazil: the Big Carve Up', *Sunday Times Magazine,* Oct. 7, 1973.
6. 'Rodovias na Amazônia', *Transporte moderno* (Edição especial), No. 86, Setembro 1970.
7. According to a BBC television programme in Dec. 1973, only 5,000 out of a proposed 80,000 families had actually been settled in Amazonia from the Northeast by then.
8. Brookes, E., 'Twilight of Brazilian tribes', *Geogr. Mag.,* Jan. 1973, pp. 304–10.
9. Estado da Bahia, Departamento Estadual de Estatística, Sept. 1968, *Movimento Bancario.*

Sources of material in the figures

11.1   Map (a) based on map in *Manchete,* 30 Oct., 1971, pp. 94–5.
11.3   Based on maps in IBGE, *Atlas Nacional do Brasil,* 1966.
11.6   IBGE, Divisão do Brasil em regiões funcionais urbanas, 1971.
11.9   Data for flows from IBGE, *Anuario estatístico do Brasil,* 1972, p. 349.
11.14   Location of new roads from *Peruvian Times,* Feb. 16, 1973.
11.15   See reference 9 above.

Further sources consulted

Fundação IBGE (Ministerio do Planejamento e Coordenação Geral), Rio de Janeiro.
  a) *Anuario estatístico do Brasil,* 1972 and earlier years
  b) *Boletim geográfico* (periodical)
  c) *Revista Brasileira de Geografia* (periodical)
  d) *Sinopse preliminar do censo demográfico,* VIII Recenseamento geral – 1970
  e) *Paisagens do Brasil* (Serie D, No. 2), 1968
  f) Valverde, O. and C. V. Dias, *A Rodovia Belém-Brasília* (serie A, No. 22), 1967
  g) Faissol, S., *Problemas Geográficos Brasileiros, Análises Quantitativas,* Ano 34, Ns. 1/4
  h) *Atlas Nacional do Brasil,* 1966

Marcio, D., *Geografia do Brasil,* 1969, Belo Horizonte; Editoria Bernardo Alvares.
IV Plano Director de desenvolvimento econômico e social do Nordeste (SUDENE), Recife, 1968.
Programa estratégico de desenvolvimento 1968–1970, Zonamento agrícola e pecuario do Brasil, Feb. 1969, Rio de Janeiro.
Simonsen, M. H., *Brasil 2001,* 1969, Rio de Janeiro; Apec Editoras A.
Petroleum Press Service, Apr. 1971 and June 1972 on oil production and imports.
de Araujo, O. E., 'Produção industrial no Grande São Paulo', *Industria e Desenvolvimento,* São Paulo, 2 (10), 22–26, Outubro 1969.

Further reading

Crease, D., 'Dynamic City that Nobody Loves' (São Paulo), *Geogr. Mag.,* May 1969, Vol. XLI, No. 8, pp. 615–23.
'Development in Brazil', *The Times,* Oct. 8 1973 (A Special Report to mark the Brasil Export 73 fair in Brussels from Nov. 7–15).
Kendall, S., 'The Development of Transport in Brazil', *Bolsa Review,* Oct. 1972, Vol. 6, No. 70, pp. 540–50.
Leahy, E. P., 'Trans-Amazonica the rainforest route', *Geogr. Mag.,* Jan. 1973, pp. 298–310.
McIntyre, L., 'Amazon, The River Sea', *Natl. Geogr.,* Oct. 1972, Vol. 142, No. 4, pp. 456–95.
'The Medici Administration – Performance and Prospects', *Bolsa Review,* Apr. 1973, Vol. 7, No. 76, pp. 152–63.

Morris, F. B. and G. F. Pyle, 'The Social Environment of Rio de Janeiro in 1960' *Econ. Geogr.*, June 1971, Vol. 47, No. 2 (Supplement), pp. 286–302.
'The State of São Paulo', *Bolsa Review,* Oct. 1973, Vol. 7, No. 82, pp. 473–8.
Taylor, J. A., 'New Brazilians set the pace in Parana' (progress in coffee technology), *Geogr. Mag.,* Mar. 1972, Vol. XLIV, No. 6, pp. 420–3.
Wilson, J., 'Drought Bedevils Brazil's Sertão', *Nat. Geogr.,* Nov. 1972, Vol. 142, No. 5, pp. 704–23.

CHAPTER 12

MEXICO

12.1. INTRODUCTION

During the period 1960–70 the gross domestic product of Mexico grew at an average annual rate of 7·3 per cent *at constant prices*. This was higher than the comparable rate for any of the other large Latin American countries (Brazil, 5·5, Argentina 4·2, Colombia 5·1, Venezuela 5·4, Peru 5·5, Chile 4·4). The fastest growing major sector was manufacturing (9·7 per cent), the slowest, agriculture (3·8). In spite of the overall annual growth of 7·3 per cent, real gross domestic product per inhabitant rose only by 3·6 per cent annually on account of population growth. 1970 data show that income is very unevenly distributed both by class and by region.

The per capita national income of 630 dollars in Mexico in 1970 is comparable with that in Japan around 1960. It is three times as high as the average for all developing 'market economy' countries (210 dollars per inhabitant), though less than $\frac{1}{4}$ the average for all developed 'market economy' countries (2,670). There is a feeling in Mexico that if economic growth can be held long enough at about 7 per cent per year, Mexico will move into the group of developed countries. In fact, as in Brazil, regional differences are so great that part of Mexico already has a much higher level than the average of 630 dollars.

The purpose of this chapter is firstly to provide a brief factual survey of the main features of the geography of Mexico, secondly to examine critically the regional differences in development, and thirdly to assess future prospects. Two books recently published in Mexico reflect the new interest in growth and also an awareness of the difficulties ahead. *Mexico: desarrollo con pobreza*[1] (Mexico: development with poverty) draws attention to the irregularity of economic growth and to the uneven shareout of wealth. The author seems to settle for a kind of mini-affluence within a still low income country. *El perfil de México en 1980*[2] (The profile of Mexico in 1980) reviews many trends in Mexico over the last few decades and carries them to 1980. Two drawbacks of the book may be noted. In the first place, it covers a very short time span. Secondly, it relies on a continuation of recent trends and does not consider alternative futures to any great extent.

Much of the area of present day Mexico has been the home of relatively advanced civilisations before the Spaniards arrived early in the 16th century, at which time the south central area was dominated by the Aztecs. The Spaniards quickly took over the densely peopled high basins of this area, organised mining, especially to the north, and spread their influence over most of the country during the following decades. Later in the colonial period the viceroyalty of Mexico also had loose control over much of what is now southwestern U.S.A.

Independence from Spain came around 1810, but in the mid-19th century the expanding U.S.A. acquired from Mexico by various means the large but thinly peopled lands north of the Rio Bravo (Rio Grande). For over a century now Mexico has had approximately its present form, with a fairly centralised government after the breakdown of several experiments in federation. Modern industry and railways penetrated the country slowly until the last part of the 19th century. Since the Revolution around 1910 and especially since the late 1930s, the government has taken an increasing share in the economic organisation of the country. Land reform has been widely introduced, the oil industry was taken over by the State in 1938, and new irrigation, hydro-electric and manufacturing projects are encouraged if not actually financed by the government.

Mexico in the 1970s is a land of great contrasts, both physical and human. The dry northern part of the country includes the most productive, irrigated, agricultural areas, as well as many industries. It resembles adjoining parts of the U.S.A. in certain respects. Greater Mexico City, with nearly 10 million inhabitants in 1970, has many of the problems of a typical U.S. city. On the other hand, many parts of Mexico, in particular the poorest states of Guerrero, Oaxaca, and Chiapas in the south, have conditions as poor as those in many parts of the underdeveloped world. Several hundred thousand pure Indians remain in the remotest and most isolated parts of the country, the areas of no interest to the Spaniards during the colonial period and not touched by roads and railways in recent decades. Mexico is however more homogeneous than many Latin American countries in the sense that the population is essentially mestizo. There has been very little migration of Europeans since the colonial period and few negroes were brought in as slaves.

Mexico is less than ¼ the size of Brazil but it has about ½ as many inhabitants. It is about 3,000 km in great circle distance from Tijuana in the northwest to Chetumal in the southeast, and the official road distance from Tijuana to Mérida is over 4,400 km. About half the population of Mexico lives in settlements of more than 5,000 inhabitants. The employment structure of Mexico has changed greatly since 1910 when about 85 per cent of the population was in agriculture; the percentage in 1970 was only about 45 per cent.

The present position and future prospects of Mexico are closely connected with the fortunes of the neighbouring U.S.A. which shares with Mexico one of the longest international boundaries in the world. As the population of the U.S.A. is more than 4 times as large as that of Mexico and the total economy nearly 30 times as large, there is no doubt as to which is the dominant partner in this relationship. Some Mexicans regard with satisfaction the fact that their population is growing faster than that of the U.S.A., but this is actually so only in a relative sense. The foreign contacts of Mexico may be summarised under the following headings.

1. MEXICANS IN THE U.S.A.

In a study of people with Spanish surnames in the U.S.A. it was found that in 1969,[3] there were 4½ million in 5 states alone. The *Chicanos* are the Mexicans who have entered the U.S.A. legally or illegally to work there for varying lengths of time. Some 400,000 agricultural workers in California alone are of Mexican origin. In 1971, however, nearly 350,000 Mexicans were expelled from the

U.S.A. The Chicanos send or take back money to Mexico as well as ideas, both favourable and unfavourable, about the technically more advanced conditions in the U.S.A.

2. TOURISM

In 1971, Mexico was visited by 2,530,000 million tourists (cf. 1,664,000 in 1968). Receipts were estimated to be $ U.S. 1,580 million, an amount considerably in excess of the value of $ U.S. 1,470 million for Mexican exports in the same period. Over 90 per cent of the visitors were from the U.S.A. or Canada. Mexican 'tourists' from the northern fringe of the country also move across the border to use the shopping and other facilities in U.S. border areas, thereby losing some of the advantages of the flow of tourists into Mexico.

3. FOREIGN TRADE

The exports of Mexico are more varied than those of most other large Latin American countries. About 40 per cent consist of food items, including fresh vegetables, sugar and coffee. Cotton is another major item of export. Mexico is using its minerals increasingly for its own industries and zinc ore and sulphur only account for a few per cent of total exports. The increasing amount of manufactured goods exported by Mexico includes various processed metals. Although trade with the U.S.A. has declined relatively since the Second World War (it was about 80 per cent around 1950), the U.S.A. still supplies about 62 per cent of the imports of Mexico and takes about 56 per cent of Mexican exports. West Germany and Japan are the second and third suppliers of Mexican imports. Any study of the future of the Mexican economy has to take into account the likely needs of the U.S.A. In spite of spectacular increases in agricultural production in Mexico in the 1950s and 1960s, the country is likely to find surpluses increasingly hard to produce as its own population grows.

12.2. PHYSICAL FEATURES OF MEXICO

Figure 12.1a shows the main relief features of Mexico. The outstanding feature of the northern part of Mexico is the presence of two ranges, a higher western Sierra Madre Occidental and a lower, less continuous eastern Sierra Madre Oriental. The Sierra Madre Occidental, which extends from the U.S. border as far south as the Lerma valley (1, which marks Guadalajara in *Figure 12.1a*), is mainly between 2,000 and 3,000 metres above sea-level but is broken by deep valleys and gorges. Between the two ranges is the northern plateau, the Altiplanicie Mexicana (2 on map), which is mainly 1,000–2,000 metres above sea-level. To the south again are the higher tablelands of the Meseta Central and Meseta de Anáhuac. The two Sierra Madres drop to coastal plains along the Gulf of California in the west and Gulf of Mexico in the east.

At the latitude of Mexico City the Eje Volcánico (volcanic axis) runs in an east to west direction for several hundred kilometres; to the south the land drops to

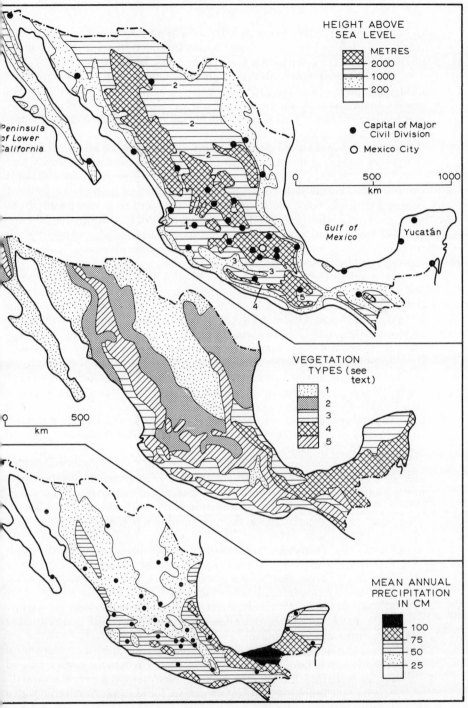

Figure 12.1. Physical conditions in Mexico. (a) Relief, (b) Vegetation types, (c) Precipitation. For the key to map (b), see text. Numbering in map (a) refers to the following

1 Guadalayara and the Lerma valley
2 Northern plateau
3 Balsas valley
4 Sierra Madre del Sur

the Depresión del Balsas (3 on map). The area of the Eje Volcánico consists of a number of high valleys and enclosed basins separated by some of the highest mountains of Mexico, including three peaks over 5,000 metres.

Southern Mexico consists of two distinct areas, the coastal plains of the Gulf of Mexico and the low limestone plateau of Yucatan, and a number of ranges and mountain masses from the Sierra Madre del Sur (4 on map) and mountains and basins of Oaxaca (5 on map) to the coastal range and Meseta of Chiapas, adjoining Guatemala.

The complex and varied geology, structure and relief of Mexico influence both other aspects of the physical geography, and the human geography very profoundly. Features of climate and vegetation reflect regional and local variations of altitude rather than broader influences of latitude. Minerals of commercial importance are found in every state and soils vary greatly from place to place. Both tropical and temperate crops can be cultivated in Mexico. Much of the population lives above about 2000 metres. Roads and railways are in places forced to make detours to avoid physical obstacles and are characterised by steep gradients.

Mexico is situated between about 15° and 32°N. Its climate is complicated by the great variety of relief features and the presence of two seas with somewhat different temperature conditions at the same latitudes. *Figure 12.1c* shows mean annual precipitation. This varies from less than 20 cm in large areas of the north and northwest to over 200 cm along the southern shores of the Gulf of Mexico. Most of Mexico is distinguished by a very marked dry season in the first part of the year and heavy rain in the summer and autumn, but much of the south has no true dry season. Precipitation is generally very unreliable. One assessment of the usefulness of precipitation in Mexico classifies 52 per cent as arid, 41 per cent as semi-arid and only 7 per cent as humid. Unfortunately, even the limited parts that receive a heavy and reasonably reliable rainfall include the more rugged parts of the country such as the Sierra Madre Occidental and the southern mountain masses.

Temperatures are related to altitude and bring temperate climatic conditions into the high central basins, as well as frosts much of the year. The southern part of the country is completely frost free, however, as are the Pacific coast north to the middle of the Gulf of California and most of the Gulf of Mexico coastlands.

In *Figure 12.1b,* vegetation[4] has been grouped into five types.

1. The *matorral desértico* and *matorral espinoso* is the driest part of Mexico, with mostly under about 30 cm of rain per year, very hot summers and a desert or semi-desert vegetation of xerophytic plants, shrubs and small trees. Cultivation is possible only with irrigation.
2. The *matorral espinoso con plantas carnosas y pastizal* and the *chaparral,* a semi-arid zone on the fringes of the desert and semi-desert with plants suitable for pasture as well as shrubs.
3. Low and medium selva and savanna, a sub-humid area in which tropical forest is widely found but the trees lose their leaves in the dry season and do not reach their full size on account of inadequate and irregular rainfall. Much of the limestone plateau of Yucatán, for example, is covered with a low but very dense forest.
4. Tropical rain forest or selva alta with a dense vegetation and trees that keep their foliage all or nearly all the year.

5. Mountain forests consisting mainly of pines but also containing deciduous species. Much of this area is still forested, soils are usually poor and slopes too steep for cultivation. In small areas above about 4,000 metres the forest gives way to high grassland and to permanent snow on the highest peaks.

12.3. ADMINISTRATIVE AREAS, POPULATION AND COMMUNICATIONS

For purposes of internal political and administrative organisation, Mexico is subdivided into 32 major civil divisions. It is a federal country and Mexico City, the national capital, is situated in the special Distrito Federal, the built-up area of which now spreads a long way into the adjoining state of Mexico. Two of the 32 units are defined as territories (3 and 23 in *Figure 12.2*). Each of the remaining 29 states has its own governor, a person of some influence in local politics.

The 32 major civil divisions are used as the basis for the regional breakdown of data in tables in this and the following sections. Their location can be seen in *Figure 12.2a*. In *Figure 12.2b*, the units are redrawn according to their population size instead of their area size. The extreme northwest and southeast of the country diminish greatly in size and the two units of the Distrito Federal and the state of Mexico are greatly enlarged. Table 12.1 shows the area, 1970 population and density of population of the 32 units. Column 3 in the table, density of population, is mapped in *Figure 12.3b*.

As in Brazil, urban population has grown rapidly in Mexico and many towns have doubled in size in the last 10–15 years. A comparison of *Figure 12.3a* with *Figure 11.5* (p. 227) shows that the larger towns of Mexico are much more evenly distributed over the national area than the larger towns of Brazil. Table 12.2 is a list of all towns with more than 50,000 inhabitants in 1970. In some cases adjoining urbanised areas have been added to the official municipio population of the main town. The figure for Mexico City includes about $2\frac{1}{2}$ million people from the adjoining state of Mexico. Seven of the 32 state capitals of Mexico are above 2,000 metres (Mexico City itself is at 2,240) and nine others are between 1,500 and 2,000 metres above sea level.

During 1930–1970 the total population of Mexico increased approximately three times. Table 12.3 shows the population of the 32 major civil divisions of Mexico according to the five most recent census (1930–70). The last four columns show intercensal increases, each value representing the percentage increase over a decade. For example for Aguascalientes, in column 30–40 the 22 means the 1940 population is an increase of 22 per cent over the 1930 population or 1940 is 122 if 1930 is 100. The four values for Mexico at the foot of the table show that the *rate of increase* has itself *increased* in each of the four periods, *in addition to* an increase in the absolute amounts involved. In detail this is reflected in a comparison of the following periods for the 32 units:

1. In 27 of the states, the increase rate was greater during 1940–50 than during 1930–40.
2. In 20 of the states, the increase rate was greater during 1950–60 than during 1940–50.

3. In 18 of the states, the increase rate was greater during 1960–70 than during 1950–60.

If the population of Mexico were to increase by 40 per cent during each of the three decades between 1970 and 2000 it would reach the following totals: 1980: 67,700,000; 1990: 94,800,000; 2000: 133,000,000. The question of projecting the population of Mexico is discussed more fully in Appendix 3.

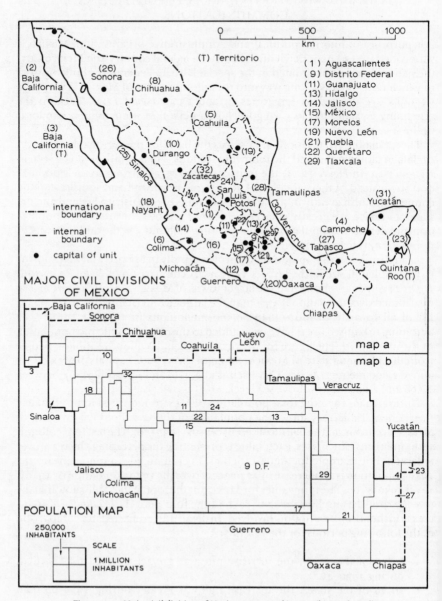

Figure 12.2. Major civil divisions of Mexico, represented in map (b) Topologically

Table 12.1.

AREA AND POPULATION OF THE MAJOR CIVIL DIVISIONS OF MEXICO IN 1970

1   Area of unit in thousands of sq.km.
2   Population in 1970 in thousands
3   Density of population in persons per sq.km.

		1	2	3			1	2	3
1	Aguascalientes	6	338	61	17	Morelos	5	616	125
2	Baja California	70	870	12	18	Nayarit	28	544	20
3	Baja California(T)	74	120	2	19	Nuevo León	65	1,695	26
4	Campeche	52	252	5	20	Oaxaca	95	2,172	23
5	Coahuila	152	1,115	7	21	Puebla	34	2,508	74
6	Colima	5	241	44	22	Querétaro	12	486	41
7	Chiapas	74	1,569	21	23	Quintana Roo(T)	50	88	2
8	Chihuahua	247	1,613	7	24	San Luis Potosí	63	1,282	20
9	Distrito Federal	1	6,874	4,586	25	Sinaloa	58	1,267	22
10	Durango	120	939	8	26	Sonora	185	1,099	6
11	Guanajuato	31	2,270	74	27	Tabasco	25	768	31
12	Guerrero	64	1,597	25	28	Tamaulipas	80	1,457	18
13	Hidalgo	21	1,194	57	29	Tlaxcala	4	421	108
14	Jalisco	80	3,297	41	30	Veracruz	73	3,815	52
15	Mexico	21	3,833	179	31	Yucatán	39	758	19
16	Michoacán	60	2,324	39	32	Zacatecas	75	952	13
						MEXICO TOTAL	1,967	48,382	25

(T) territory

Source: *Anuario estadístico compendiado 1970.*

Space does not allow a discussion in any detail of transport and communications in Mexico. *Figure 12.4* shows the main railways and roads of the country around 1970. A summary of the basic layout of the Mexican transportation system is given in the lower inset map in *Figure 12.4*. The dominant role of Mexico City as a source and destination of traffic flows has made it desirable to provide good links and services between the capital and other parts of the country not only in the rail and road systems but also in the internal air system and in radio communications. The result is basically a radial system centring on Mexico City and elongated in a northwest-southeast direction. The presence of the Sierra Madre Occidental and of other more local physical obstacles has made it difficult to provide links between some parts of the country. Until recently, for example, it was impossible to travel by rail and extremely difficult to travel by road from the Pacific coast to the Mexican plateau anywhere north of Guadalajara (place 1 on the maps in *Figure 12.4*). The completion of the Chihuahua-Pacific railway (place 4 to place T on map *12.4a*) provided this interregional link only in 1961.

Passenger and goods traffic have both increased greatly in Mexico in the 1950s and 1960s. Goods traffic on the railways (in ton km) has more than doubled since the early 1950s. During the same period, however, the number of commercial vehicles in use increased 3 times and the number of passenger cars nearly 5 times. The relative importance of road transport has therefore been growing and the main interregional road links in Mexico are nearly all of a good standard. Coastal shipping and pipelines (see *Figure 12.5b*) handle most of both the crude oil and refined products distributed in Mexico from the oilfields, while shipping handles bulky goods between places along each of the

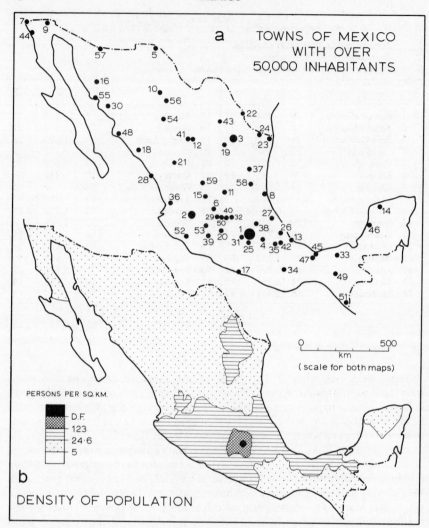

Figure 12.3. Towns with over 50,000 inhabitants, and density of population in Mexico, 1970. For key to towns in map (a), see Table 12.2

two coasts, though the detour through the Panama Canal from one coast to the other makes journeys by sea between the Gulf of Mexico and the Pacific very long indeed.

12.4. AGRICULTURE

At the time of writing it was difficult to obtain data for some aspects of Mexican agriculture around 1970 so it has been necessary to make use of 1960 data. In 1960 about 12 per cent of the total area of Mexico was under field or tree crops, an area of about 24 million hectares. About 40 per cent of the country was

Table 12.2
TOWNS WITH OVER 50,000 INHABITANTS IN 1970

1	Mexico City	8,363	31	Toluca	114
2	Guadalajara	1,456	32	Querétaro	113
3	Monterrey	1,213	33	Villahormosa	100
4	Puebla	413	34	Oaxaca	100
5	Juárez	407	35	Orizaba	93
6	León	365	36	Topic	88
7	Tijuana	327	37	Ciudad Victoria	84
8	Tamico-C. Madero	271	38	Pachuea	84
9	Mexicali	267	39	Uruapan	83
10	Chihuahua	257	40	Celaya	80
11	San Luis Potosí	230	41	Gómez Palacio	80
12	Torreón	223	42	Heroica Córdoba	78
13	Heroica Veracruz	214	43	Monclova	78
14	Mérida	212	44	Ensenada	78
15	Aguascalientos	181	45	Coatzacoalcos	70
16	Hermosillo	177	46	Campeche	70
17	Acapulco	174	47	Minatitlán	68
18	Culiacán	168	48	Los Mochis	68
19	Saltillo	161	49	Tuxtla Gutiérrez	67
20	Morelia	161	50	Salamanca	61
21	Durango de Victoria	151	51	Tapachula	61
22	Neuvo Laredo	149	52	Colima	58
23	Heroica Matamoros	138	53	Zamora de Hidalgo	58
24	Reynosa	137	54	Hidalgo del Parral	58
25	Cuernavaca	134	55	Heroica Guaymas	57
26	Jalapa	122	56	Delicias	52
27	Poza Rica	120	57	Heroica Nogales	52
28	Mazatlán	120	58	Ciudad Mante	51
29	Irapuato	117	59	Zacatecas	50

classified as pasture and 22 per cent as forest. The cultivated area has been slightly extended during the 1960s with new irrigation and reclamation schemes but most of the increase in agricultural production in Mexico has come from higher yields in existing areas of cultivation. During 1961–71, total agricultural production increased by 40 per cent and food production by nearly 50 per cent. The growth in agricultural production is reflected in both increased exports and higher average per capita consumption of calories (2370 per day in 1954–56, 2620 in 1964–66).

According to the 1970 census, 40 per cent of the employed population of Mexico or 5,130,000 people, were employed in agriculture. They only accounted for 11 per cent of total gross domestic product, a fact underlining the low productivity of labour in agriculture compared with that in other types of employment. The regional distribution of employment in agriculture is shown in Table 12.6 in the next section. In 1970, Mexico had about 90,000 tractors in use, compared with about 5 million in the U.S.A. Mechanisation is concentrated mainly in a few states of the north and centre.

It is perhaps more important in a country like Mexico to achieve higher yields per unit of area than to aim for a big reduction in the labour force in farming. Large increases in the yields of certain crops have been achieved since the early 1950s. Some will be noted below. Again, the improvements have largely been in the north and parts of the centre of Mexico. It is also hoped that new areas can be brought under cultivation in the next two or three decades.

Table 12.3.
POPULATION CHANGES IN THE MAJOR CIVIL DIVISIONS OF MEXICO 1930–70

		Population in millions					Percentage increase during the decade		
		1930	1940	1950	1960	1970	30-40	40-50	50-60	60-70
1	Aguascalientes	133	162	188	243	338	22	16	29	39
2	Baja California	48	79	227	520	870	65	187	129	67
3	Baja Calif. (T)	47	51	61	82	128	9	20	34	56
4	Campeche	85	90	122	168	252	6	36	38	50
5	Coahuila	436	551	721	908	1,115	26	31	26	23
6	Colima	62	79	112	164	241	27	42	46	47
7	Chiapas	530	680	907	1,211	1,569	28	33	34	30
8	Chihuahua	492	624	846	1,227	1,613	27	36	45	31
9	Distrito Federal	1,230	1,758	3,050	4,871	6,874	29	73	60	41
10	Durango	404	484	630	761	939	20	30	21	23
11	Guanajuato	988	1,046	1,329	1,736	2,270	6	27	31	31
12	Guerrero	642	733	919	1,187	1,597	14	25	29	35
13	Hidalgo	678	772	850	995	1,194	14	10	17	20
14	Jalisco	1,255	1,418	1,747	2,443	3,297	13	23	39	35
15	México	990	1,146	1,393	1,898	3,833	16	22	36	102
16	Michoacán	1,048	1,182	1,423	1,852	2,324	13	20	30	25
17	Morelos	132	183	273	386	616	39	49	41	60
18	Nayarit	168	217	290	390	544	29	34	34	39
19	Nuevo León	417	541	740	1,079	1,695	30	37	46	57
20	Oaxaca	1,085	1,193	1,421	1,727	2,172	10	19	22	26
21	Puebla	1,150	1,295	1,626	1,974	2,508	13	26	21	27
22	Querétaro	234	245	286	355	486	5	17	24	37
23	Quintana Roo (T)	11	19	27	50	88	73	42	85	76
24	San Luis Potosí	580	679	856	1,048	1,282	17	26	22	22
25	Sinaloa	396	493	636	838	1,267	24	29	32	51
26	Sonora	316	364	511	783	1,099	15	40	53	40
27	Tabasco	224	286	363	496	768	28	27	37	55
28	Tamaulipas	344	459	718	1,024	1,457	33	56	43	42
29	Tlaxcala	205	224	285	347	421	9	27	22	21
30	Veracruz	1,377	1,619	2,040	2,728	3,815	18	26	34	40
31	Yucatán	386	418	517	614	758	8	24	19	23
32	Zacatecas	459	565	666	818	952	23	18	23	16

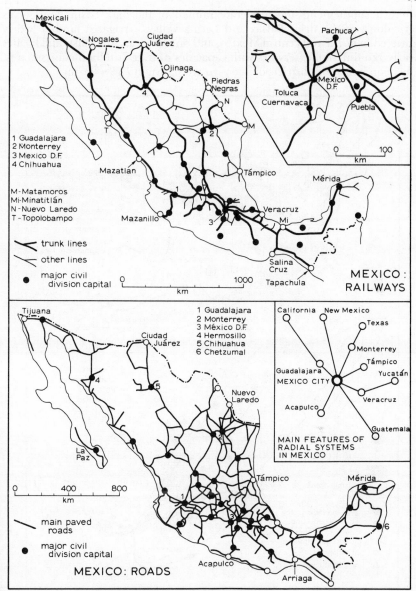

Figure 12.4. Railways and roads in Mexico

In 1950, 2,430,000 hectares were irrigated, and in 1960, 3,520,000 hectares, about 15 per cent of the area under crops. The irrigated area was 4,200,000 by 1970. About ⅔ of the irrigated land in Mexico is in the drier northern part either in the basins of the Rio Grande and Colorado by the U.S. boundary or along the rivers flowing from the Sierra Madre Occidental to the Pacific coast and interior desert. Much of the remainder of the irrigated land is in central Mexico,

where it supplements the moderate rainfall of the high basins and serves
agriculture in the drier Balsas and Lerma valleys. Irrigated land is widely
scattered in north and central Mexico, and one Mexican Atlas[5] lists and locates
nearly 140 different reservoirs with capacities of over 5 million cubic metres.
The main irrigation districts of 1969–70 are shown in *Figure 12.5a*.

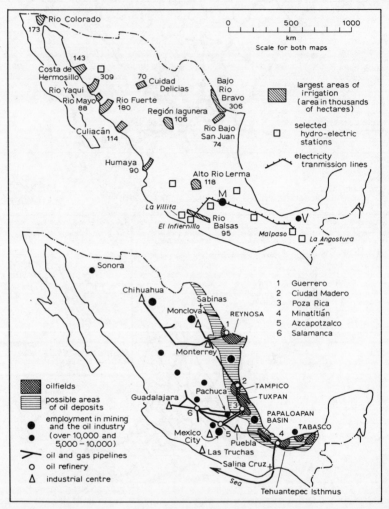

Figure 12.5. Irrigation, electricity, oil and natural gas and mining in Mexico. In upper map M is Mexico City, V Villahermosa

About $\frac{3}{4}$ of all the run off of Mexican rivers occurs in about 15 per cent of the
total area in the south of the country, the area of heaviest rainfall. The
Usumacinta basin, with its headwaters in Guatemala, alone carries over $\frac{1}{3}$ of the
water in Mexico (51×10^9 cubic metres out of about 140×10^9). The extension
of irrigation in the rest of the country is likely to be on a restricted scale as many
of the more easily controlled rivers have already been used. The problem along

the Southern Gulf coast is one of flood prevention in the potentially fertile lowlands, not one of introducing irrigation works.

Table 12.4 shows the principal crops grown in Mexico according to the value of their production in 1970; yields per hectare are shown where relevant. Comparable livestock figures are not readily available, but the total value of production from cattle alone was probably about three times that of the total value of maize production.

Table 12.4.

PRINCIPAL CROPS IN MEXICO IN 1970 ACCORDING TO VALUE OF PRODUCTION IN MILLIONS OF PESOS
AND YIELDS IN 100 KGS PER HECTARE

		Value	Mexico			World	
			1948-52	1961-65	1970	1948-52	1970
1	Maize	8,460	7·5	10·5	12·0	15·9	24·1
2	Cotton	2,493	3·3	6·4	7·2	2·4	3·5
3	Sugar cane*	2,441	513·0	594·0	625·0	423·0	512·0
4	Coffee	2,115					
5	Wheat	2,088	8·8	20·2	28·4	11·3	11·7
6	Beans	1,750	2·8	4·2	5·9	6·4	8·0
7	Sorghum	1,603	n.a.	22	25	6	12
8	Alfalfa	1,218					
9	Oranges	1,020					
10	Bananas	992					
11	Tomatoes	979					

* Yields include weight of whole plant, not only the sugar content.
Sources: *AEC 1971* and *FAOPY 1971*.

1. *Maize* is by far the most widely grown crop in Mexico, which is understandable in view of the fact that it was the principal food in the region before the 16th century. It can be cultivated virtually anywhere in Mexico but tends to be particularly widely grown in high central Mexico. It gives very high yields in the irrigated lands of the north but elsewhere is grown in such varied conditions, including land of very poor quality, that overall yields are very low. In comparison to the performance of Mexico in increasing maize yields from 750 kg per hectare around 1950 to 1,200 around 1970, the U.S.A. has achieved an increase from 2,500 kg per hectare to around 5,000 during the same period. Maize is widely used as the main source of carbohydrate in Mexico especially among poorer people. It is perhaps surprising that the potato, suitable for the temperate conditions of central Mexico, but an Andean crop originally, is little grown in Mexico (value 1970, 424 million pesos).

2. *Cotton* is grown in Mexico only to the north of about 25° N almost exclusively in the irrigated lands, and both for lint and for seed. The crop is of good quality and high yields are obtained per unit of area. The crop is one of the main exports of Mexico. Henequen, cultivated almost entirely in Yucatán, where little else can be cultivated commercially, is the second textile fibre crop of Mexico.

3. *Sugar cane* is widely grown in Mexico but areas that specialise in its cultivation include some of the irrigated lands of the Pacific side and the Gulf lowlands. The prospects of the crop for export depend on quotas and policies in the U.S.A. and E.E.C.

4. *Coffee* production has risen in Mexico in the last two decades. Its cultivation is restricted to the lower slopes of the mountains along the Gulf of Mexico and south Pacific coasts. Production could easily be increased but export quotas have to be considered.

5. *Wheat* is the crop in which the greatest increases in yields have been achieved in Mexico recently. Wheat is considered worth growing on the irrigated lands of the north as well as in the cooler basins and valleys of central Mexico. It is the main bread cereal and has generally been preferred by the Spaniards to other cereals.

6. *Beans (frijoles)* are widely grown in Mexico and form a source of protein especially among poorer rural families.

7, 8. *Sorghum* and *alfalfa* are fairly new crops in Mexico, both grown particularly in the north and centre.

9, 10, 11. *Oranges, bananas* and *tomatoes* are a few of the large variety of fruits and vegetables grown in Mexico. Other fruits of some value include avocado pears, lemons, apples, mangoes and pineapples.

Rice, soybeans, tobacco, chickpeas, Chile peppers and rapeseed still do not complete the list of significant crops that can be cultivated in Mexico thanks to the varied possibilities of tropical, subtropical and temperate climatic conditions.

The number of cattle in Mexico has nearly doubled between 1950 and 1970 and was about 25 million in 1970 according to the Food and Agriculture Organisation. The Gulf coast area of Veracruz is one of the main cattle raising areas of Mexico and the extensive pastures of the northern plateau and associated irrigated areas are also used. Fishing and forestry products were valued at 1216 and 2203 million pesos respectively in 1970, only about $\frac{1}{2}$ and $\frac{1}{4}$ the value of maize production alone. Most of the fish catch is accounted for by ports along the Gulf of California in Sonora and Sinaloa, and in Veracruz and Campeche. The distribution of the forests of Mexico is shown in *Figure 12.1b*.

Improvements in Mexican agriculture of both a social and an economic nature have given rise to satisfaction and even complacency in Mexico. Nevertheless, pressure on land suitable for cultivation is already very considerable and some areas are too poor to be considered satisfactory. There is no one obvious way in which extensive improvement could be made and Mexico lacks a large fertile area comparable to the pampa of Argentina or the good soils of São Paulo in Brazil. The consumption of nitrogenous and phosphate fertilisers, very low in 1950, is now considerable, but that of potash fertilisers is still limited.

12.5. MINING AND INDUSTRY

Although Mexico was predominantly an agricultural country until the Second World War, it has had industries based both on local crafts and on the processing of mining products since the 16th century. Several districts rose to prominence at different periods on account of their mines, among them San Luis Potosí, Zacatecas, Guanajuato and Pachuca to the north of Mexico City and Taxco to the south. Textiles, leather, wood, and in a limited way, iron, were manufactured. In the 19th century the production of non-ferrous metals led to the introduction of new techniques for extracting and processing ores and the growth of the oil industry early in the 20th century to the establishment of oil refining. As early as 1830–40 textile machinery was imported by capitalists in certain centres such as Puebla and Orizaba. The first steel to be made in Latin America was produced before 1900 in Monterrey, but engineering dates only from the 1950s, with, for example, the beginning of the manufacture of railway wagons in 1954, textile machinery in 1955 and sewing machines in 1958. During the same period a motor vehicles industry was formed, based initially on assembly. The modern chemicals industry dates from the 1940s.

The ingredients of modern industry in Mexico are based on home produced oil, gas and hydro-electricity, on other minerals, both metallic and non-metallic, including non-ferrous metals, iron ore and sulphur, and on agricultural products such as cotton and henequen, imported machinery and both home and foreign capital. Some idea of the great expansion of industry in Mexico is given by the fact that industrial activity increased on average 9 per cent per year during the 1960s; the comparable rate for Brazil was only 6·4 per cent. Electricity production increased nearly 3 times during the 1960s.

The energy base of Mexican economic life and industry is provided mainly by home produced oil and natural gas. Hydro-electricity and coal make a much smaller contribution. A disturbing trend since 1968, when Mexican energy production almost exactly balanced energy consumption, is the recent increase in dependence on imported sources. The gap was about 5½ million tons of coal equivalent in 1971, nearly 10 per cent of the 65 million tons consumed. In terms of coal equivalent, home produced oil accounted around 1970 for about 28 million tons a year and natural gas about 25 million tons. The hydro-electric contribution was under 2 million tons of coal equivalent at the official conversion, but about 10 million tons of coal if the same amount of electricity were generated from coal. About half the electricity produced in Mexico is generated in thermal stations with oil or gas, and hydro-electricity accounts for only about half.

Figure 12.5b shows the location of the oilfields of Mexico and Table 12.5 shows the quantity of oil and natural gas produced in each of the main areas. Most of the 1,500,000 tons of coal produced in Mexico came from mines near Monclova. Some of the main hydro-electric stations of Mexico are shown in *Figure 12.5a*. The two largest are at El Infiernillo in Michoacán on the Rio Balsas and at Malpaso in Chiapas. Two other large projects, La Villita and La Angostura, are also shown.

The oil and natural gas fields are fairly conveniently located for the distribution of their products over the national area. Pipelines carrying crude oil, refined products or natural gas are shown in *Figure 12.5b*. The principal directions of flow from the Gulf coast are to northern mining and industrial areas such as Monterrey and Chiahuahua, to the central area of Mexico with its large population and big industrial concentration in Mexico City, and to Pacific coast ports from Salina Cruz, which is served by pipelines across the Isthmus of Tehuantepec. Two of the six main oil refineries, Azcapotzalco in Mexico City and Salamanca to the west have market locations.

The greatest hydro-electric potential in Mexico is in the mountains of the south, where at present there is little local use for electricity. Transmission lines of 380 kV link El Infiernillo and Malpaso to Mexico City, which takes a large part of the energy produced. Lower voltage transmission lines form more local systems for the movement of both hydro- and thermal electricity.

Mexico is not only unable to satisfy its growing energy needs; equally serious is the fact that the production of several of the main raw materials of the country was less around 1970 than around 1960. This is true of cotton, lead, zinc and sulphur. As national industries take increasing quantities of raw materials, so the proportion that can be exported declines. The seven most valuable mineral products of Mexico apart from oil and natural gas are shown in Table 12.5b.

Table 12.5a.
OIL AND GAS BY AREAS 1970

	OIL thousands of cubic metres	NATURAL GAS millions of cubic metres
Northwest — Reynosa	990	6,210
North — Támpico	1,380	520
South — Támpico	2,560	410
Papaloápan Basin	30	390
Tehuantepec Isthmus	2,170	490
Tabasco	10,820	7,600
Poza Rica	9,030	3,030
Nueva Faja de Oro	1,270	180
MEXICO	28,240	18,840

Table 12.5b.
OTHER MINERALS

	Value*	Main producing area
Zinc	1,166	Chihuahua
Copper	1,105	Sonora
Silver	949	Hidalgo
Lead	771	Chihuahua
Iron	666	Chihuahua, Durango
Sulphur	590	Veracruz (Jultipan)
Fluorite	408	San Luis Potosí

* Millions of pesos 1970
Source: AEC 1970. pp. 209, 211.

Altogether mining and the oil industry together employed about 180,000 people in 1970. Their distribution by states is shown in Table 12.6. The oil industry employs large numbers in Tamaulipas and Veracruz along the Gulf coast and in Mexico City. The main oil producing and mining states are shown in Figure 12.5b (black circles).

Mining and industry now employ about half as many people in Mexico as agriculture but their contribution to gross domestic product is more than 2½ times as great. Column 4 in Table 12.6 shows that agriculture accounts for greatly different proportions of total employment in different units of Mexico. In the Distrito Federal there are about 14 persons in industry per person in agriculture, and in Nuevo León, containing the industrial centre of Monterrey, the ratio is nearly 2 : 1. In contrast, in the most heavily agricultural states,

Chiapas and Oaxaca, there are about 10 workers in agriculture for every worker in industry. The gap is even wider than these figures suggest because most of the larger mines and factories, with the highest productivity per worker, are in the more heavily industrialised states and the industries in many of the predominantly agricultural states include many workers in small establishments and in crafts.

Table 12.6.
EMPLOYMENT IN AGRICULTURE, MINING AND MANUFACTURING IN 1970 BY STATES

1,2,3 persons employed in agriculture, mining and oil, and manufacturing, in 1970, in thousands to nearest thousand.

4 Percentage of total employed population (including services not shown in the table) in agriculture.

		1	2	3	4
1	Aguascalientes	32	1	14	37
2	Baja California	49	1	40	22
3	Baja California (T)	12	1	3	35
4	Campeche	33	—	10	46
5	Coahuila	86	12	52	30
6	Colima	30	1	6	44
7	Chiapas	293	1	21	73
8	Chihuahua	151	12	52	36
9	Distrito Federal	49	18	665	2
10	Durango	124	5	21	55
11	Guanajuato	276	8	97	49
12	Guerrero	238	2	31	62
13	Hidalgo	185	6	31	61
14	Jalisco	306	4	188	34
15	Mexico	300	6	246	30
16	Michoacán	320	2	57	59
17	Morelos	74	1	22	43
18	Nayarit	87	—	12	59
19	Nuevo León	85	3	146	17
20	Oaxaca	402	3	50	72
21	Puebla	380	4	92	56
22	Querétaro	62	3	16	48
23	Quintana Roo (T)	13	—	2	53
24	San Luis Potosí	175	9	36	53
25	Sinaloa	178	2	31	51
26	Sonora	109	5	28	38
27	Tabasco	116	6	12	59
28	Tamaulipas	126	18	44	33
29	Tlaxcala	58	—	18	55
30	Veracruz	531	37	95	53
31	Yucatán	111	1	21	55
32	Zacatecas	139	8	14	64
	MEXICO TOTAL	5,132	180	2,173	40

— under 500
Source: *XI Censo General de Población, 1970.*

The following are the main concentrations of industry in Mexico, in order of number of persons employed.

1. Greater Mexico City has about 850,000 persons employed in industry. Within this area the main industrial concentration is on the northern side of

the built-up area. Like São Paulo in Brazil, Mexico City has a big share of sophisticated and growth industries such as engineering and electrical manufactures.

2. Guadalajara, second city of Mexico, has about 100,000 persons in industry. Consumer goods industries predominate.

3. Monterrey itself has about 100,000 persons in industry. The iron and steel industry and engineering here are associated with heavy industry in other centres of the northeast such as Monclova.

4. The Gulf coast ports of Támpico, Veracruz and the area of Minatitlán and Coatzacoalcos have the principal oil refineries and petro-chemicals plants of Mexico.

5. Policy has been to divert new factories to other suitable towns away from the three biggest concentrations. Thus Puebla, with a new Volkswagen plant alongside the older textile industry, is a secondary centre near the capital. Similarly, for example, Querétaro and Salamanca to the north of Mexico City and Toluca to the west have new industries. The towns in the extreme north of Mexico, along the Pacific coast, and in the south of the country, have not taken much part in recent industrial growth. The difficulty of reaching the main concentrations of the national market makes such places as Mexicali in the extreme northwest and Mérida in Yucatán unattractive. One new development that may make some impact on the backward state of Michoacán is the new integrated steelworks at Las Truchas (see *Figure 12.5*). This is to use local iron ore and imported coal.

Industrialisation is without doubt one of the reasons why the three largest towns of Mexico have been growing in population so quickly recently. The size of Mexico City in particular is beginning to cause problems. Energy supplies and food have to be brought in over increasing distances, local water supply is restricted, and many areas of the valley in which the town is situated, part of it a former lake, make the provision of foundations for large modern buildings difficult. As the area of the city is enclosed by surrounding mountains and the air often calm, atmospheric pollution has become a problem, there being probably nearly 1 million motor vehicles in use in Greater Mexico City as well as an oil refinery and large thermal electric stations to contribute. People arriving from other parts of Mexico tend to settle in shanty towns especially on the northeast and east sides of the city and as older shanty towns are improved and become absorbed into the city, new ones appear. In 1970 2¼ million people in the Distrito Federal, ⅓ of the population, were born in other parts of Mexico while the adjoining state of Mexico had about 1 million people born elsewhere.

12.6. A MULTI-VARIATE STUDY OF DEVELOPMENT IN MEXICO

This section includes the original data used for a multi-variate study of Mexico based on states from the 1970 census together with a brief account of the results and findings. Table 12.7 contains data for 18 variables representing aspects of the economic, demographic and cultural life of Mexico. Table 12.8 contains a definition of the variables in Table 12.7.

Each variable in Table 12.7 is of interest in its own right and may be examined in detail by the reader. Four of the variables are mapped separately in *Figure 12.6* on the topological base map of Mexican population. It is possible

		1 Agr.	2 Mf.	3 Ser.	4 Prof.	5 Setl.	6 U.10	7 Fert.	8 Mig.	9 Ch.	10 Mat.	11 Sex	12 Edn.	13 Lit.	14 Rms.	15 Wat.	16 El.	17 Meat	18 Inc.
1	Aguascalientes	37	16	15	6	80	34	65	17	180	24	98	80	85	74	79	65	63	55
2	Baja California	22	18	24	11	96	33	55	41	384	6	100	79	88	77	67	79	80	88
3	Baja Calif. (T)	35	8	19	9	68	34	57	17	210	7	105	80	88	67	64	50	85	81
4	Campeche	46	14	13	7	84	32	51	17	207	6	101	73	77	50	48	56	88	50
5	Coahuila	30	18	19	9	87	32	57	13	155	12	102	81	88	71	74	73	78	64
6	Colima	44	9	17	7	86	33	60	27	215	7	101	75	80	46	78	58	84	70
7	Chiapas	73	5	7	4	63	34	52	2	172	2	102	57	57	39	38	31	82	32
8	Chihuahua	36	13	19	8	79	33	57	11	191	7	102	80	87	70	66	62	70	68
9	Distrito Federal	2	31	32	16	100	29	47	34	225	10	93	86	91	71	96	95	95	85
10	Durango	55	9	11	6	72	35	62	7	149	7	104	78	86	69	53	47	59	50
11	Guanajuato	49	17	10	5	76	34	63	6	171	26	101	61	65	64	56	52	62	50
12	Guerrero	52	8	11	5	73	34	53	3	174	5	100	55	55	39	38	37	72	45
13	Hidalgo	61	10	8	4	70	33	56	4	140	3	101	62	62	54	48	38	71	36
14	Jalisco	34	21	17	8	83	33	61	11	189	16	98	74	81	72	66	64	78	64
15	México	30	25	15	7	91	35	56	27	275	9	102	69	75	62	63	62	86	65
16	Michoacán	59	10	9	5	76	34	62	4	163	13	101	62	66	55	53	49	70	48
17	Morelos	43	13	17	7	94	33	52	27	226	3	99	71	75	55	68	64	87	55
18	Nayarit	59	8	11	5	83	34	60	15	187	3	103	74	79	48	47	58	81	69
19	Nuevo León	17	30	22	11	87	32	55	24	229	14	101	85	89	64	81	78	87	77
20	Oaxaca	72	9	6	4	78	33	51	3	153	3	98	59	58	41	35	28	75	32
21	Puebla	56	14	11	5	86	33	55	6	154	19	99	66	67	53	48	48	78	41
22	Querétaro	48	13	12	5	69	35	61	8	181	15	100	62	62	54	52	38	56	49
23	Quintana Roo	53	6	13	7	68	36	53	45	326	5	108	74	76	41	42	44	84	54
24	San Luis Potosí	53	11	11	5	69	34	59	7	150	7	102	68	71	57	46	41	55	42
25	Sinaloa	51	9	14	7	75	34	58	12	199	2	104	75	79	53	51	53	81	77
26	Sonora	38	10	19	10	81	32	57	16	215	5	101	79	86	74	68	65	77	83
27	Tabasco	59	6	10	5	76	36	56	23	212	2	103	72	76	46	34	32	90	46
28	Tamaulipas	33	12	20	9	80	33	54	23	203	5	99	79	86	60	67	64	77	66
29	Tlaxcala	55	17	9	4	90	34	60	6	148	8	103	75	77	56	49	64	76	42
30	Veracruz	53	9	12	6	79	33	52	9	188	2	101	67	71	53	51	49	80	48
31	Yucatán	55	11	13	6	87	30	50	2	147	8	100	70	74	50	42	53	83	35
32	Zacatecas	64	7	8	5	66	37	67	5	143	17	100	75	81	68	43	33	48	41

Table 12.8.
DESCRIPTION OF VARIABLES USED IN TABLE 12.7

1	Persons employed in *agriculture*, forestry and fishing as a percentage of total employed population
2	Persons employed in *manufacturing* (industrias de transformación) as a percentage of total employed population
3	Persons employed in *services* as a percentage of total employed population
4	*Professional, technical* and *managerial* employees as a percentage of all occupied population
5	Percentage of total population living in *settlements of 500 inhabitants* or over
6	Population *under the age of 10* years as a percentage of total population
7	Average *number of children* per 10 women
8	Population *born outside* unit in which now residing as percentage of total
9	Population *change 1950-1970*, 1950 = 100
10	Couples officially *married* per couple living together *unmarried* (en unión libre)
11	*Males per 100 females*
12	Children with some *education* as a percentage of all children
13	Percentage of population over the age of 9 able to *read and write*
14	Percentage of population living in a dwelling with *more than 1 room*
15	Percentage of dwellings with *piped water* (agua entubada)
16	Percentage of dwellings with *electricity*
17	Percentage of families eating *meat* at least one day a week
18	Percentage of wage earning population earning *500 pesos* per month or more.

Source: All the variables used in this study come from *IX Censo General de Población, 1970,* Resumen de las Principales Características por Entidad Federativa, Mexico, D.F. Nov. de 1970.

even by comparing the four maps by eye to see close correlations between any pair. In fact the correlation coefficients between all possible pairs of variables have been calculated. With the help of factor analysis they were used to identify associated variables in an attempt to reduce the large number of variables to a more limited number of development or modernisation factors. These were then used to produce a multi-variate classification of the states of Mexico into homogeneous groups.

Space does not allow the inclusion of the 18 × 18 matrix of correlation coefficients. Table 12.9a shows the four main factors on which the common variance between the 18 variables load. Their respective percentage shares of total variation are I 47, II 36, III 9, and IV 8, which means that the first two factors carry much more weight than the last two. The association of a variable with a factor is measured by the indices in Table 12.9a. The nearer to + 1 or − 1 the index, the higher the degree of association. Since oblique factor analysis was used, intercorrelation of factors was to be expected. The degree of intercorrelation between the factors is shown in Table 12.9b. The first two factors are closely associated. The following verbal descriptions of the factors are suggested.

    I Economic development and material conditions
   II Cultural development, associated highly with economic development
  III Demographic change, places receiving migrants and growing fast recently
  IV is more obscure but might be clearer if more variables were included. I seems to associate high fertility (variable 7) with the predominantly non meat consuming areas (variable 17), that is the 'old' maize growing heartland of Mexico. It is not suggested, however, that there is a direct causal relationship between these two variables.

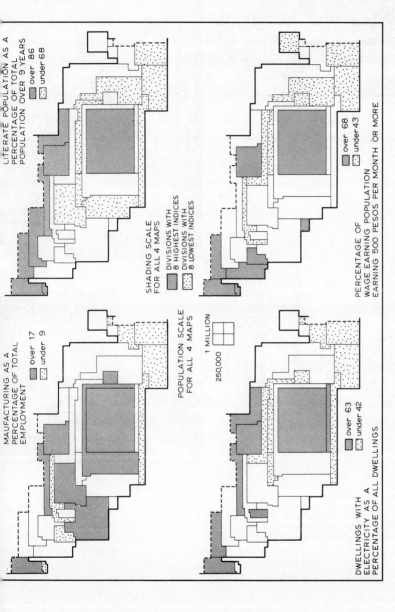

LITERATE POPULATION AS A
PERCENTAGE OF TOTAL
POPULATION OVER 9 YEARS

■ over 86
▦ under 68

MAUFACTURING AS A
PERCENTAGE OF TOTAL
EMPLOYMENT

■ over 17
▦ under 9

SHADING SCALE
FOR ALL 4 MAPS

■ DIVISIONS WITH
8 HIGHEST INDICES
▦ DIVISIONS WITH
8 LOWEST INDICES

POPULATION SCALE
FOR ALL 4 MAPS

1 MILLION

250,000

PERCENTAGE OF
WAGE EARNING POPULATION
EARNING 500 PESOS PER MONTH OR MORE

■ over 68
▦ under 43

DWELLINGS WITH
ELECTRICITY AS A
PERCENTAGE OF ALL DWELLINGS

■ over 63
▦ under 42

Figure 12.6. Four aspects of development in Mexico. The data used are in Table 12.7. The states are proportional
in area to their population size

Pictures illustrating development.
Upper left, rural house in Yucatan
Upper right, urban slum, Puebla
Lower left, urban slum, Mexico City
Lower right, high class housing Pedregal, Mexico City

Industry: upper, modern textile mill, Puebla
lower, oil refinery, Salamanca, Central Mexico
Hotel Mexico, Mexico City, unfinished 1972
Central business district of Mexico City

Table 12.9a.
FACTOR STRUCTURE MATRIX

Short definition of variable	I	II	III	IV
1 Agriculture	−·98	−·72	−·55	−·26
2 Manufacturing	·77	·41	·21	·14
3 Services	·97	·77	·60	·41
4 High salary employment	·94	·76	·59	·45
5 Settlements over 499	·69	·43	·30	·43
6 Under age of 10	−·58	−·26	·04	−·64
7 Number of children	−·22	·08	−·25	−·95
8 Migration	·64	·57	·93	·36
9 Change 50-70	·49	·37	·94	·33
10 Marital status	·20	·09	−·18	−·63
11 Males per 100 females	−·41	−·00	·20	−·21
12 Education	·74	·99	·47	·07
13 Literacy	·74	·99	·47	·02
14 Dwellings over 1 room	·66	·70	·16	−·31
15 Piped water	·90	·71	·38	·10
16 Electricity supply	·92	·74	·44	·27
17 Meat	·41	·25	·48	·78
18 Incomes over 499	·82	·77	·68	·18

Table 12.9b.
FACTOR INTERCORRELATION MATRIX

	I	II	III	IV
I	1·00	·75	·54	·32
II	·75	1·00	·49	·05
III	·54	·49	1·00	·33
IV	·32	·05	·33	1·00

Table 12.9c.
HIGHEST AND LOWEST QUARTILE AREA SCORES ON FIRST THREE FACTORS

Rank	I Economic change		II Cultural change		III Demographic change	
1	Distrito Federal	3·1	Distrito Federal	1·6	Baja California	2·8
2	Nuevo León	1·7	Nuevo León	1·3	Quintana Roo (T)	2·7
3	Baja California	1·7	Baja Calif. (T)	1·2	Mexico	1·2
4	Coahuila	1·0	Coahuila	1·1	Distrito Federal	0·9
5	Tamaulipas	0·8	Baja California	1·1	Colima	0·8
6	Sonora	0·8	Chihuahua	1·0	Baja Calif. (T)	0·8
7	Jalisco	0·7	Sonora	1·0	Morelos	0·7
8	Chihuahua	0·6	Tamaulipas	0·9	Neuvo León	0·7
25	San Luis Potosí	−0·6	Puebla	−0·8	Guanajuato	−0·8
26	Michoacán	−0·7	Michoacán	−1·1	Michoacán	−0·8
27	Guerrero	−0·7	Guanajuato	−1·2	Zacatecas	−0·9
28	Tabasco	−1·0	Querétaro	−1·3	Puebla	−0·9
29	Hidalgo	−1·0	Hidalgo	−1·3	Tlaxcala	−1·1
30	Zacatecas	−1·1	Oaxaca	−1·7	Hidalgo	−1·1
31	Oaxaca	−1·4	Chiapas	−1·8	Oaxaca	−1·1
32	Chiapas	−1·5	Guerrero	−2·0	Yucatán	−1·3

Each of the 32 states has a position or score on the new scales representing each of the factors. In Table 12.9c the positions of the eight highest and eight lowest states are shown on each of the first three factors. Since the first two factors are fairly similar they have been considered together in identifying the most developed and least developed states of Mexico. They are mapped in *Figure 12.7a*. The more developed northern part of Mexico shows clearly. The urban areas of Mexico City and Guadalajara (Jalisco) pull their respective units into

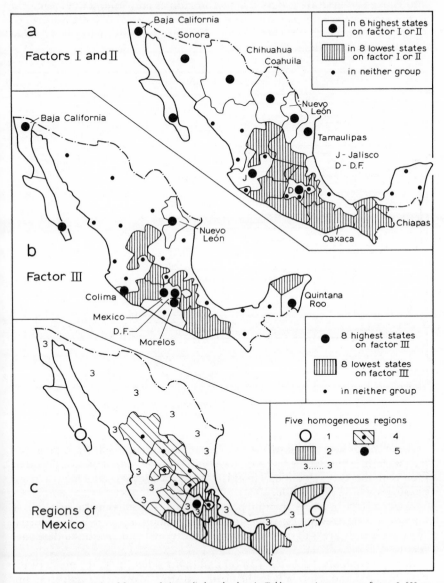

Figure 12.7. The results of factor analysis applied to the data in Table 12.7. Area scores on factors I–III are shown in Table 12.9c and the regions mapped in (c) are from the linkage tree in Figure 12.8

the highest group. Greater Mexico City itself is surrounded, however, by some of the least developed states of Mexico. Chiapas and Oaxaca in the extreme south have the lowest scores of all on many variables. The position of the states on factor III is shown in *Figure 12.7b*. The eight highest, this time, are those in which population growth has been fastest. These are not necessarily the most developed.

Figure 12.8 shows the linkage diagram resulting from the application of cluster analysis to the data used in this study. The most similar pair are Oaxaca and Chiapas. These are grouped first. Tamaulipas and Sonora then join. The last to associate are the two thinly populated territories of Baja California and Quintana Roo, and the Distrito Federal. The linkage tree is cut to give 5 regions and these are mapped in *Figure 12.7c*.

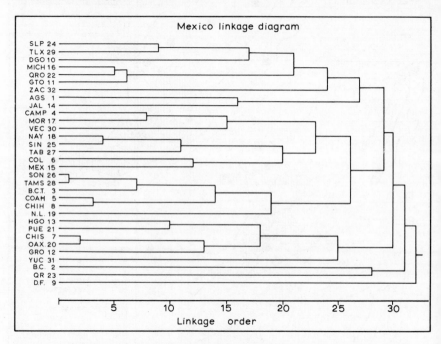

Figure 12.8. The linkage of the states of Mexico into homogeneous groups according to the data in Table 12.7, after the application of factor analysis. The numbering of the states corresponds to that in Table 12.7

Region 1 consists of the two territories already mentioned. Both areas are backward in some senses but are attracting 'pioneer' population still as they represent the two remaining 'frontier' areas of Mexico, and have a comparatively young population.

Region 2 is the most deeply rural part of Mexico. The states in this group have limited mineral resources, poor agricultural conditions and little industry. They are mostly areas of out-migration. Educational and health standards are very low.

Region 3 contains the states with oil and many other minerals, much of the irrigated land and, especially in the north, tourism. Most of the industries not actually in the Distrito Federal are in region 3. Roads and railways between the

S.A. and the rest of Mexico cross this area, which also includes the main
ⱥports.

Region 4 has some of the features of region 3 but contains many areas that are
ⱴy poor locally as well as towns in which industry is growing. It is more rugged
ⱥ the whole than region 3.

Region 5 is the Distrito Federal, the industrial and service functions of which
ⱥce it in a completely different class from all the other states.

The regions described above are only one of many possible outcomes that
ⱥight be obtained from a multi-variate classification of administrative units in
ⱥxico. The result depends on the variables included. It should also be ap-
ⱥeciated that within each state, great variations occur in both physical and
ⱥman conditions. More detailed studies have been made at the level of the
ⱥnicipios, of which there are several thousand in the country. In several states
ⱥt have been studied at this level poorer and more prosperous areas emerge.
ⱥe state capital and a few other urban centres tend to have high scores on
ⱴelopment factors, while deeply rural areas can also be identified, their
ⱥckwardness often associated either with heavy dependence on agriculture in
ⱥficult physical conditions or a strong indigenous element in the population.
The kind of study made in this section draws attention to regional contrasts
ⱥ Mexico and helps to identify in a reasonably objective way the prosperous
ⱥd backward parts of the country. It does not answer the question as to how
ⱥe existing situation might be changed. In Mexico, as in Brazil, it is hoped to
ⱥise the level of the poorest areas but it would hardly be realistic to spend too
ⱥuch on projects in areas in which the cost of making new jobs is very high or in
ⱥmote places without particularly favourable natural resources.

12.7. A MEXICAN VIEW OF MEXICO AND THE WORLD

ⱥe last section of the chapter on Brazil contained the results of a questionnaire
ⱥ perception given to a set of people in Rio de Janeiro. This section contains
ⱥe results of a comparable questionnaire given to a set of people in Mexico
ⱥty. During September 1972 a questionnaire with 8 questions was answered
ⱥ 104 Mexicans. The replies have been analysed and are tabulated and briefly
ⱥscussed, question by question, below. Not all questions were answered
ⱥ everyone, which explains apparent discrepancies in reply totals.

The sample of Mexicans who answered the questionnaire is highly biased and
ⱥt large. Under the circumstances in which the questionnaire was given out it
ⱥs not possible to do better. The results do show a few broad trends. The sam-
ⱥe is biased because it represents the view of middle class Mexicans living in or
ⱥar Mexico City, many of them either geographers, friends of geographers, or
ⱥher social scientists. It is doubtful if most members of the agricultural sector
ⱥ Mexico could have given any meaningful answers at all to the questionnaire
ⱥough one suspects a growing awareness even in remoter parts of Mexico both
ⱥout Mexico itself and about the rest of the world. The questions were actually
ⱥven in Spanish but have been translated here:

ⱥestion 1: At present (1972) **Mexico** has about 50 million inhabitants. How
ⱥany inhabitants do you think it will have:
(a) in the year 2020? (in 50 years' time)
(b) in the year 2070? (in 100 years' time).

Virtually all answers were rounded to the nearest 5 million. The following e timates were given for the year 2020 (A population in millions, B number persons estimating that population).

A	B	A	B	A	B
70	6	100	29	140	2
75	1	105	1	150	15
80	14	110	3	180	1
85	1	120	12	200	2
90	5	125	2	250	2
95	1	130	3	400	1
		135	1		

and the following for the year 2070

A	B	A	B	A	B	A	B
85	1	150	8	230	1	450	6
90	2	160	3	250	9	500	3
100	6	170	4	260	1	520	1
110	4	180	8	280	4	550	1
120	6	190	2	300	6	1,000	2
130	7	200	11	350	1		
140	1	210	2	400	1		

In general, people giving a relatively low estimate for 2020 tended to give comparably low estimate for 2070 and people giving a high estimate for 20 also gave a high one for 2070. Certain numbers are particularly popul because they are very 'prominent' or 'round', especially 100 m., 200 m. and 2 m.

The consensus obtained from the mean of all estimates for each of the tw years was as follows:

2020 : 115 million
2070 : 235 million

Such a consensus might be called a collective 'informed' estimate of the futu population of Mexico. It is interesting to compare the above estimates wi projections reached on the basis of different assumptions about the decline fertility. The following are the five projections in millions discussed in Appe dix 3.

2020	2070
195	463
186	317
171	305
160	253
132	110

Question 2: A large proportion of the population of Mexico is concentrated the central part of the country. In your opinion in the future will th concentration

(a) become more marked?

(b) keep the same proportion as it has now?

(c) diminish?

Replies: (a) 59, (b) 23, (c) 21.

uestion 3: In certain countries of the world the national capital has been
*u*nsferred to a new position. Would it in your opinion be an advantage to
*u*nsfer the capital of Mexico from the present Distrito Federal to another
*u*ace?
If you replied in the affirmative, which place would you choose for the posi-
*u*n of the new capital?

78 did not favour transferring the capital while 25 did. Of the 25 who
*u*commended another place, some replies mentioned a specific town (e.g.
*u*ernavaca, Guadalajara) others a state (e.g. Jalisco) and some were very vague.
u states, the following were noted:

Querétaro	4	Guanajuato	1
Jalisco or Guadalajara	3	Chiapas	1
State of Mexico	2	Puebla	1
Cuernavaca	2	Monterrey	1
San Luis Potosí	2	Aguascalientes	1

	also	South in general	3
		North in general	1

The sample of positive replies, 25, is too small for inferences to be made but
*u*e tendency was to move the capital to the north or west rather than the south.

uestion 4: Assuming that you live in the national capital or in another large
*u*wn of Mexico, if you were offered an acceptable job in a relatively backward
*u*gion of Mexico (for example Chiapas, Oaxaca), what salary would you want
*u*fore migrating:
(a) what you earn now?
(b) 50 per cent more?
(c) more than double what you receive now?
(d) you would not accept under any circumstances?

*u*eplies: (a) 20,   (b) 32,   (c) 33,   (d) 14
(several did not answer this question).

uestion 5: If it was no longer possible for you to live in the state (district) in
*u*hich you live at present, where in Mexico would you prefer to move to? Please
*u*rite the names of 5 Mexican states or territories in order of preference.

*u*otes. 1) Virtually all the people answering the questionnaire live in the Distrito
*u*ederal of Mexico or the adjoining State of Mexico.
   2) Points were given to the 5 preferred states listed by each person as
*u*llows: 5, 4, 3, 2, 1, for the 1st, 2nd, 3rd, 4th, 5th respectively.
   All 31 units were mentioned (but not, of course, the Distrito Federal). They
*u*e listed in order of popularity on points.

1	Jalisco	278	12	Puebla	66	22	Durango	12
2	Guanajuato	154	13	Chiapas	44	23	Tabasco	10
3	Nuevo León	112	14	Sinaloa	43	23	Campeche	8
4	Morelos	95	15	Sonora	41	25	Hidalgo	7
5	Michoacán	90	16	Mexico	30	26	Tlaxcala	6
6	Guerrero	75	17	Querétaro	27	27	Nayarit	5
7	Veracruz	74	18	Quintana Roo	27	28	Aguascalientes	5
8	Chihuahua	69	19	Tamaulipas	23	29	Zacatecas	4
9	Baja California	69	20	Coahuila	21	30	San Luis Potosí	3
10	Yucatán	69	21	Baja Calif.(T)	13	31	Colima	2
11	Oaxaca	67						

Comments

1 Jalisco and Nuevo León contain the second and third cities of Mexico, Guadalajara and Monterrey.

2 The State of Mexico probably received fewer points than it should have because people would associate it with Greater Mexico City (mainly in the Distrito Federal) and might feel it could not be included.

3 There is a great range in popularity and preference among various parts of Mexico.

4 It would be interesting to calculate the degree of correlation between popularity and

a) distance from Mexico City   c) income level of units
b) degree of urbanisation of units   d) some quality of the environment

Several of the poorest states (Michoacán, Guerrero, Oaxaca, Chiapas) are quite popular. It could be that such states, though poor, are attractive on account of their forest cover and other environmental features, including coastal regions. The higher, more arid, poor states come low in the list.

Question 6: Have you visited a foreign country?
Replies: Yes: 59   No: 45
If you replied in the affirmative, please write the names of the countries you have visited.

Americas		*Europe*		*Other*	
U.S.A.	48	France	13	Japan	4
Canada	12	Italy	11	Thailand	4
British Honduras	6	Britain	9	Hong Kong	3
Guatemala	5	Germany	9	India	2
Argentina	4	Holland	9	Malaysia	2
El Salvador	3	Spain	9	Indonesia	2
Colombia	3	Switzerland	9	Korea	1
Peru	3	Belgium	8	China	1
Brazil	3	Portugal	3	Philippines	1
Nicaragua	2	Austria	2	Singapore	1
Costa Rica	2	Denmark	2	Morocco	1
Panama	2	Turkey	2	Ethiopia	1
Venezuela	2	Greece	2	Kenya	1
Bolivia	2	U.S.S.R.	1	Uganda	1
Chile	2	Czechoslovakia	1	Congo	1
Central America	2	Yugoslavia	1	Nigeria	1
Cuba	2	Sweden	1	Ghana	1
Paraguay	1	Norway	1	Guinea	1
Ecuador	1	Finland	1	Senegal	1
Haiti	1	Luxembourg	1		
Trinidad & Tobago	1				

Question 7: If you had to leave Mexico and to live in another country, which would you prefer? Please write five countries in order of preference.
Note. Points were given to the five preferred countries listed by each person as follows: 5, 4, 3, 2, 1 for the 1st, 2nd, 3rd, 4th, 5th respectively,

Americas/Australia		Europe		Africa/Asia	
U.S.A.	120	France/Monaco	185	Japan	62
Brazil	94	Spain	135	Israel	11
Canada	69	Switzerland	111	China	9
Chile	49	Great Britain	104	Algeria	7
Cuba	41	Italy	104	Korea	3
Argentina	34	Germany	68	S. Africa	3
Australia	33	U.S.S.R.	43	Uganda	3
Peru	26	Sweden	23	Guinea	2
Puerto Rico	14	Holland	22	India	2
El Salvador	10	Norway	18	Libya	2
Venezuela	8	Denmark	14	Kenya	1
Ecuador	6	Belgium	11		
Guatemala	6	Austria	10		
Uruguay	5	Finland	9		
Costa Rica	4	Iceland	9		
Nicaragua	4	Greece	9		
Bolivia	3	Czechoslovakia	8		
		Yugoslavia	6		
		Portugal	4		
		Hungary	1		

The data in the table are mapped topologically in *Figure 12.9*. The popularity of Europe stands out in the results. The U.S.A. is not so popular as one might have expected considering (see Question 6) that it is the country most visited

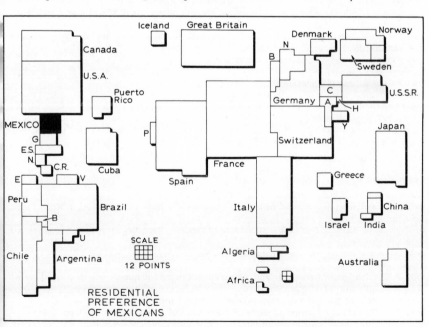

Figure 12.9. *The residential preference of Mexicans. See Section 12.7*

and best known. Certain Latin American countries are quite well represented among the preferences of the Mexicans who answered the questionnaire, but Colombia is not mentioned at all. Cuba and the U.S.S.R. are fairly prominent considering their political characteristics. Africa and Asia hardly figure at all except for Japan. The evidence gives support to the view that there is little mutual awareness among different parts of the developing world, though Mexicans seem in fact to be very conscious of what is going on in Cuba, Chile (1972) and Brazil (World Cup success 1970?).

References

1. Padilla Aragón, E., *México: desarrollo con pobreza,* 1970, Mexico City; Siglo XXI Editores, S.A.
2. Instituto de Investigaciones Sociales de la Universidad Nacional Autónoma de México, *El perfil de México en 1980,* 1971, Mexico City, Siglo XXI Editores, S.A.
3. 'The Little Strike That Grew to La Causa', *Time,* July 4, 1969, pp. 10–13.
4. *Nuevo Atlas Porrúa de la República Mexicana,* 1972, Mexico City, Editorial Perrua S.A., p. 115.
5. As for 4, pp. 118–20.

Sources of material in the figures

12.1, 12.4, 12.5, as for 4 above, pp. 112, 115, 127, 131, 142, 149.

Further sources consulted

Secretaría de Industria y Comercio, Dirección General de Estadística,
   a) *Anuario estadístico compendiado de los Estados Unidos Mexicanos 1970,* Mexico 1971, and earlier years.
   b) *IX Censo general de población, 1970,* Noviembre de 1970, Resumen de las principales características por entidad federativa.
   c) As for b), various volumes for individual states.
Universidad Nacional Autónoma de México,
   a) *Anuario de Geografía* (periodical)
   b) *Boletín del Instituto de Geografía* (periodical)
Centro de Estudios Económicos y Demográficos, *Dinámica de la Población de México,* 1970, Mexico City; El Colegio de México.
Facultad de Ciencias Políticas y Sociales, *Los problemas nacionales,* 1971, Mexico City; UNAM.
Lopez Rosado, D. G., *Problemas económicos de México,* 1970, Mexico City; UNAM.

Further reading

Barkin, D. and King, T., *Regional Economic Development. The River Basin Approach to Mexico,* 1970, Cambridge; University Press.
Bromley, R. J., 'Sierra of Puebla; by-passed zone of Mexico', *Geogr. Mag.,* July 1970, Vol. XLII, No. 10, pp. 752–61.
de la Haba, L., 'Mexico, the City That Founded a Nation', *Nat. Geogr.,* May 1973, Vol. 143, No. 5, pp. 638–69.
Ellis, P. B., 'Changes in Agriculture and Settlement in Coastal Chiapas, South Mexico', *Occasional Papers,* University of Glasgow, No. 2, 1971.
Foster, G. M., *A Primitive Mexican Economy,* 1966, Seattle; University of Washington Press.
Fox, D. J., 'Mexico, The Transport System', *Bolsa Review,* Vol. 6, No. 62, Feb. 1972, pp. ii–xi.
Fox, D. J., 'Patterns of Morbidity and Mortality in Mexico City', *The Geogr. Rev.,* Apr. 1972, Vol. LXII, No. 2, pp. 151–85.

ates, G. R. and Gates, G. M., 'Uncertainty and Developmental Risk in *Paqueña Irrigación* Decision for Peasants in Campeche, Mexico'. *Econ. Geogr.*, Apr. 1972, Vol. 48, No. 2, pp. 135–52.

ill, A. D., 'The Changing Landscape of a Mexican Municipio, Villa las Rosas, Chiapas, *Research Paper No. 91*, Department of Geography, The University of Chicago, 1964.

ewis, O., *The Children of Sanchez,* 1961, New York, Vintage Books.

egee, M. C., 'Monterrey Mexico', *Research Paper No. 59,* Department of Geography, The University of Chicago, 1958.

CHAPTER 15

ARGENTINA

13.1. INTRODUCTION

With a 1970 population of about 23½ million and an area of nearly 2,800,000 sq km., Argentina is the third country in Latin America in population and the se cond in area. From north to south it is about 3,600 km and spans more than 30 of latitude, extending from just within the tropics to within a few hundre kilometres of the fringes of Antarctica. It has a common boundary with fiv other countries and although there have been no serious disputes over frontier in the last few decades there remain questions of the joint use of water resource in these areas.

When Argentina is included in a classification of the countries of the worl (see Chapter 2) on the basis of development criteria, it has many similarities t European countries. In some other respects it resembles Australia anc Canada. Among Latin American countries it comes with Uruguay and Puertc Rico at the top end of the development scale.

Argentina is a highly urbanised country. In 1870, about 30 per cent of it population lived in towns, in 1910 about 50 per cent and in 1970 about 70 pe cent. Though less affluent than Australia or most West European countries i has high educational and health standards and a high level of food consump tion. Its birthrate is much lower than that of any of the other large Lati American countries. Argentina is increasingly becoming part of the Lati American trading community, and its main exports, cereals and meat, are suc that they complement those of other members rather than competing wit them.

There are several broad reasons why Argentina differs from the rest of Lati American. It lies mainly in temperate latitudes and although 'sub-tropical' crop such as cotton and sugar cane are grown to supply national needs, temperate crops form the basis of agricultural production. Argentina has a large area o fertile agricultural land with good soil and climatic conditions, the pampa. I has roughly 15 hectares of cultivated land per person employed in agriculture compared with about 2.5 hectares in Brazil and only 0.2 in Haiti. The popula tion of Argentina is almost entirely of European origin. The country was littl developed during the period of Spanish colonial rule and most immigratior has taken place in the last hundred years. Argentina differs from the other large Latin American countries in the high degree of concentration of population ir the national capital. In 1915, Greater Buenos Aires already had about 25 pe cent of the total population of the country and in 1970 about 35 per cent. A bel of country from Santa Fe to La Plata, including the capital, had about 50 pe cent of the total population.

In a recent economic history of Argentina, the Argentinian economist Aldc Ferrer[1] identifies a number of stages in the development of the country. A period of regional subsistence economies lasted until about 1800. This was followed by a period of transition from 1800–60, during which the dominance of Buenos Aires was established as it became the main outlet for the country, and livestock farming expanded; the interior stagnated. 1860 to 1930 was the great period of development based on the export of primary products; during this period the Indians were cleared from the lands south of Buenos Aires, land was enclosed with the introduction of barbed wire and arable farming spread over the pampa. Most of the railways were built, most of the immigration took place, reinforcing the dominance of the coast, and refrigeration made the export of fresh meat to Europe possible. According to Ferrer, Argentina entered a period of non-integrated industrial economy around 1930, industrial because manufacturing had become by then the key to the economic life of Argentina, but non-integrated because manufacturing depended on the importation of most of its equipment and of fuel and many raw materials. It was developed *at the expense* of agriculture, which was therefore unable to maintain a level of exports sufficient to keep manufacturing expanding. At the end of 1962 it was stated that 'while the industrial and State sectors of the economy had been capitalised by 17 and 42 per cent, respectively, between 1940 and 1955, agriculture and livestock had been decapitalised by 20 per cent and public services by 30 per cent.'

During the colonial period, which ended with the gaining of independence from Spain early in the 19th Century, Argentina was for most of the time in the Viceroyalty of Peru and was controlled from Lima. Direct contact between Buenos Aires and Spain was not usually permitted. Only a small part of modern Argentina was effectively occupied and colonised before 1800. It is shown in *Figure 13.3b*, map *c* as roughly a triangle with Buenos Aires, Mendoza and Jujuy at the corners. This area supplied meat, hides and other agricultural products to the mining areas of the Andes, but itself had virtually no minerals of interest to Spain and did not grow tropical agricultural products for Europe.

The growth of the railway network illustrates the overall development of modern Argentina. The first railways were built before 1860, but not until the 1870s did rapid construction begin. 1900–10 was the decade in which the largest amount was built. Table 13.1 shows the amounts added in successive decades (kilometres).

Table 13.1.

	Additional	Total		Additional	Total
Pre 1880	2,500	2,500	1910-20	5,900	33,900
1880-90	6,900	9,400	1920-30	5,300	38,100
1890-1900	7,100	16,600	1930-40	3,100	41,300
1900-1910	11,400	28,000	1940-50	2,400	43,700

The railways were nationalised in 1948 since which time the route distance has been cut. In 1970 there were only about 41,000 km in use and only 7,000 km were considered to be in good condition. The system is made up mainly of six original companies with three different gauges, so the integrated layout of the system as illustrated in *Figure 13.5* is more apparent than real.

13.2. DEMOGRAPHIC FEATURES

Table 13.2 contains basic demographic data for Argentina on the basis of the 24 major civil divisions. The location of the 22 provinces, the Federal capital and the territory of Tierra del Fuego is shown in *Figure 13.1a*; the numbering of units corresponds to that in the table. From the data in column 2 it can be seen that about half of the population of Argentina is in the Federal capital and the province of Buenos Aires. Great differences in density of population are revealed in column 3, while *Figure 13.1b* shows that the pampa in the east has the highest density, the southern half of the country the lowest. In the topological map the south, Chubut, Santa Cruz and Tierra del Fuego, shrinks dramatically. A large part of the population of Argentina is concentrated in a few large towns. Those with over 100,000 in 1970 are listed in Table 13.3 and located on map *d* in *Figure 13.1*. Several other towns are not far short of 100,000. Almost all the large towns of 1970 were in fact founded in the 16th Century, Buenos Aires itself in 1580.

Two further features of the population of Argentina are shown in Table 13.2. Column 6 shows that in spite of a general decline in net immigration since the 1920s, nearly 10 per cent of the population of Argentina was 'non-native born' in 1970. This included Europeans, particularly prominent in the Capital Federal, and other Latin Americans in 'frontier' provinces, such as Chileans in Santa Cruz. One estimate puts the number of persons in Argentina born in Chile at about 250,000. The proportion of non-native population was much higher in 1914 (see column 5) being nearly 30 per cent in the country as a whole and nearly half in the Capital Federal. New European settlers have nearly all arrived in Buenos Aires and have spread out from the national capital. 'Old' Argentinians have dominated the provinces of the west and north. Since 1870, the inflow of immigrants from Europe has caused a shift in the distribution of population. In 1870 the population was roughly equally divided between the pampa area (units 1, 2, 4, 8, 11 and 21 in Table 13.2) and the north and west. By 1970 about $\frac{3}{4}$ of the population was in the pampa area and 2.5 per cent in the previously uninhabited south.

More recent, shorter term population change is given in column 4 of Table 13.2. With the support of data in columns 7–10 in Table 13.2 the following broad demographic trends may be identified in Argentina.

1. The average rate of growth of 1.5 per cent per year during the 1960s in Argentina is little more than that in many European countries. As in the U.S.S.R., however, it is the combined result of very different elements, a very low birthrate and rate of natural increase in Greater Buenos Aires, other big towns and rural parts of the pampa, and a very high birthrate and a rate of natural increase in many parts of the west and north of Argentina.

2. Internal migration appears to be in two main directions, firstly from the west and north of the country and from the rural pampa to Greater Buenos Aires and to other large towns, and secondly from various parts of the country to areas of new developments, such as agricultural settlement in Chaco and Misiones and mining areas in the south. The result is that the low rate of natural increase in Buenos Aires and other towns due to small families and an ageing population is turned into a high rate of growth through immigration, particularly, presumably, of people of child-bearing age.

3. Internal migration causes a considerable imbalance in the sex structure of

Sources: 1–7 *Censo Nacional de población, familias y viviendas 1970,*
Resultados preliminares.
Instituto Nacional de Estadística y Censos
Presidencia de la Nación Argentina, pp. 16, 34–5, 47
8–10 Arnolds, p. 30 (data for remaining provinces not given)

Legend

1 Area in thousands of sq.km.
2 Estimate of population in 1970 in thousands
3 Density of population in persons per sq.km. to nearest unit
4 Population change 1960–1970, percentage change
5,6 Non-native population as a percentage of total population in 1914 and 1970
7 Males per hundred females in 1970
8 Birthrate per thousand population
9 Deathrate per thousand population
10 Natural increase

	1	2	3	4	5	6	7	8	9	10
	Area	Popn.	Dens	Change 60-70	Pct non-native 1914	1970	Males	Birth rate	Death rate	Nat: incr.
1 Capital Federal		2,972		2.0	49	18	86	22.2	11.1	11.1
2 Buenos Aires	308*	8,733	38*	25.8†	34	12	101	16.5	7.5	9.0
3 Catamarca	100	172	2	2.4	2	0.5	96	30.3	8.5	21.8
4 Córdoba	169	2,060	12	16.1	20	4	98	24.0	7.6	16.4
5 Corrientes	88	564	6	5.6	7	1	98	31.3	9.6	21.7
6 Chaco	100	567	6	4.2	22	4	104	39.8	10.0	29.8
7 Chubut	225	190	1	28.6	48	14	113	34.5	11.7	22.8
8 Entre Rios	76	812	11	0.8	17	2	99			
9 Formosa	72	234	3	26.9	48	15	105			
10 Jujuy	53	302	6	22.4	22	13	103	41.7	16.3	25.4
11 La Pampa	143	172	1	8.0	37	5	109			
12 La Rioja	92	136	1	6.1	3	1	100			
13 Mendoza	151	973	6	16.6	32	6	98	26.3	8.2	18.1
14 Misiones	30	443	15	20.3	37	16	104	34.7	6.9	27.8
15 Neuquén	94	155	2	33.8	45	10	114			
16 Rio Negro	203	263	1	30.4	36	15	110	33.3	11.7	21.6
17 Salta	155	510	3	21.0	8	5	101	27.4	9.1	18.3
18 San Juan	86	384	4	8.7	13	4	96			
19 San Luis	77	183	2	5.1	9	2	101			
20 Santa Cruz	244	84	0.3	45.9	70	29	139			
21 Santa Fe	133	2,136	16	12.5	35	5	99	35.4	8.1	27.3
22 Santiago del Estero	135	495	4	3.9	3	1	99	31.4	9.8	21.6
23 Tucumán	23	766	33	-1.0	10	2	99			
24 Tierra del Fuego	20	16	1	33.1	67	31	173			
ARGENTINA TOTAL	2,777	23,346	8	15.4	29	9	99			

* Including Capital Federal
† 35·1 for area in Greater Buenos Aires, only 12·6 for rest.

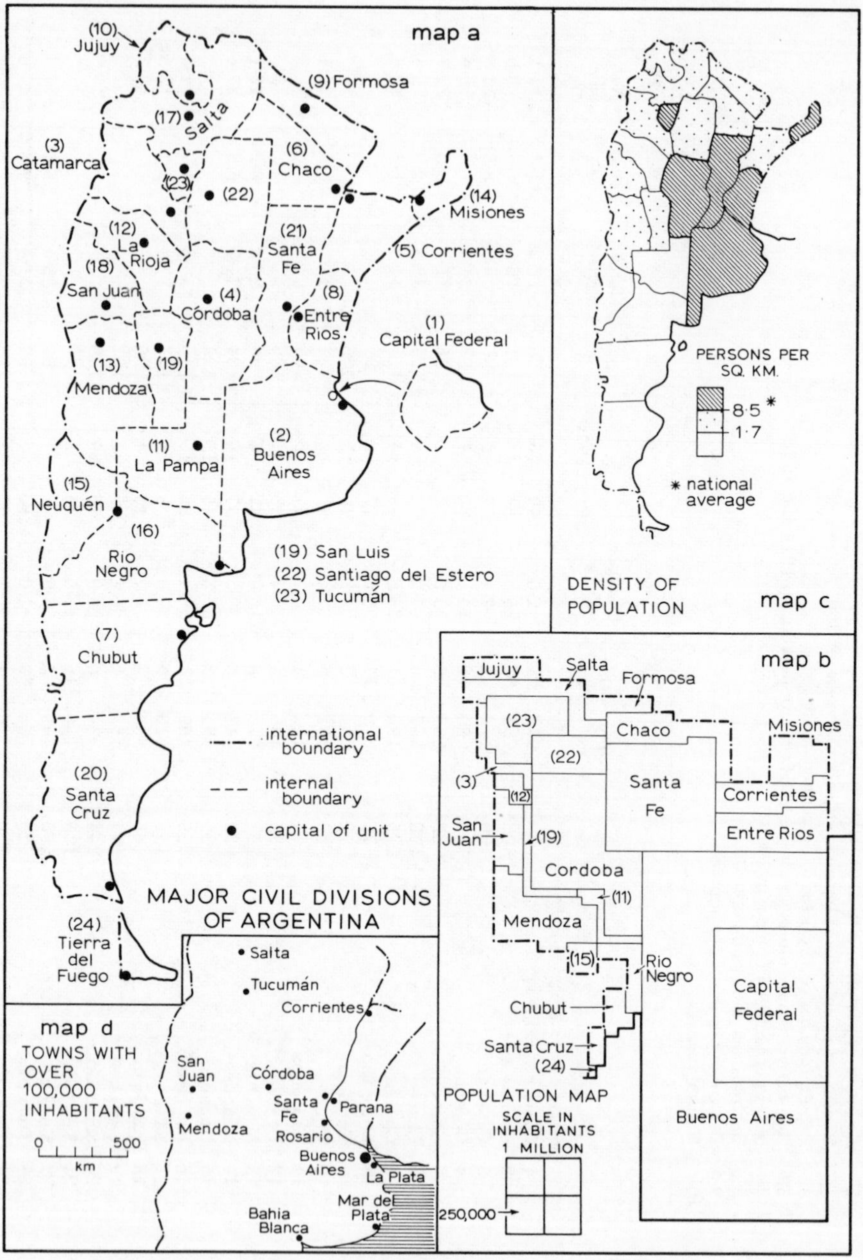
map a
(10) Jujuy
(17) Salta
(9) Formosa
(3) Catamarca
(6) Chaco
(23)
(22)
(14) Misiones
(12) La Rioja
(21) Santa Fe
(5) Corrientes
(18) San Juan
(4) Córdoba
(8) Entre Rios
(1) Capital Federal
(13) Mendoza
(19)
(11) La Pampa
(2) Buenos Aires
(15) Neuquén
(16) Rio Negro
(19) San Luis
(22) Santiago del Estero
(23) Tucumán
(7) Chubut
international boundary
internal boundary
capital of unit
(20) Santa Cruz
MAJOR CIVIL DIVISIONS OF ARGENTINA
(24) Tierra del Fuego
PERSONS PER SQ. KM.
8·5 *
1·7
* national average
DENSITY OF POPULATION
map c
map b
Jujuy
Salta
Formosa
(23)
Chaco
Misiones
(22)
(3)
Santa Fe
(12)
Corrientes
San Juan
(19)
Entre Rios
Cordoba
(11)
Mendoza
(15)
Rio Negro
Capital Federal
Chubut
Santa Cruz
(24)
POPULATION MAP
SCALE IN INHABITANTS
1 MILLION
250,000
Buenos Aires
map d
TOWNS WITH OVER 100,000 INHABITANTS
0 500
km
Salta
Tucumán
Corrientes
San Juan
Córdoba
Santa Fe
Parana
Mendoza
Rosario
Buenos Aires
La Plata
Mar del Plata
Bahia Blanca

Figure 13.1. Argentina: (a) Major civil divisions, (b) Topological map, (c) Density of Population, (d) Towns with over 100,000 inhabitants

opulation in Argentina. More females than males tend to move into the big owns, while more males than females tend to go to remoter areas of new levelopment. There also probably tend to be more male than female immigrants from foreign countries.

Table 13.3.
TOWNS WITH OVER 100,000 INHABITANTS IN 1970

opulation in thousands

Greater Buenos Aires	8,352	Salta	240
Córdoba	846	Paraná	184
Rosario	751	Bahía Blanca	150
Mendoza	500	San Juan	142
La Plata	406	Mar del Plata	140
Tucumán	290	Corrientes	104
Santa Fe	260		

4. If the rate of growth of 1·4 per cent per year around 1970 were to continue anchanged between 1970 and 2000 the population of Argentina would only grow from about 24 million to 40 million. Table 13.4 shows a tendency in reent decades for the gap between birthrate and deathrate to narrow. The influx of young immigrants at certain periods has modified the general trend. With increasing urbanisation, growing awareness of birth control methods, little urther immigration and a slow rate of economic growth, it seems probable that he rate of growth will continue to decline.

Table 13.4.
DEMOGRAPHIC TRENDS 1915–70

Year	Birthrate	Deathrate	Migration	Annual increase
1915	35	16	4	16
1920	32	15	5	21
1925	31	13	7	25
1930	29	12	6	23
1935	25	13	2	14
1940	24	11	1	14
1945	25	10	0	15
1950	26	9	9	26
1955	24	9	3	18
1960	23	9	3	17
1965	21	9	1	14
1970	21	8	1	14

Source: *Censo Nacional de población, familias y viviendas 1970*, Resultados preliminares, pp. 10–11.

The demographic structure of Argentina has been discussed at some length n order to distinguish it from that of the other large countries of Latin America. It is a matter of speculation as to whether Argentina is now at a 'stage' hat other Latin American countries may expect to reach in the future. It is certain that in some quarters in Argentina there is concern about the slow rate of growth of population in a country apparently with large natural resources in a part of the world experiencing a population explosion.

13.3. PHYSICAL FEATURES

Although Argentina is fortunate in having the only large, fertile, relatively
densely populated lowland area in Latin America, much of the country is high
and rugged. *Figure 13.2a* shows the main relief features of the country. The
roughly north-south Argentina–Chile boundary follows the Andes almost the
whole of its length, keeping along or close to the main watershed except in the
southern third. The Andes are higher and wider north of Mendoza, and a small
part of the Altiplano of Bolivia extends into the northwest; much of the way the

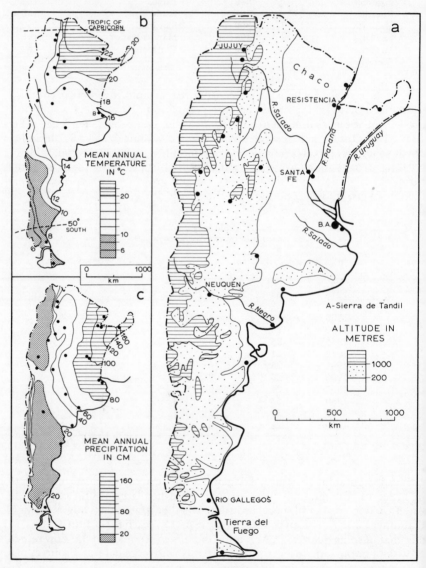

Figure 13.2. Physical conditions in Argentina, (a) Relief, (b) Temperature, (c) Precipitation

crest exceeds 5,000 metres and passes are high and difficult. South of Mendoza the crest is lower and there are many easy passes across the range. The northern part of the Andes is flanked by lower, parallel, ranges, while the mountains of Cordoba stand some 500 km to the east. This is an area with basin and range features, and with extensive salinas. The eastern part of Argentina consists of lowlands rarely exceeding 500 metres, mostly gently undulating, but in places flat and ill-drained, especially between the rivers Paraná and Uruguay. Roughly to the south of the Rio Negro is the plateau of Patagonia, with only limited coastal lowlands, but wide deep valleys.

Mean annual temperature is shown in *Figure 13.2b.* The presence of the Andes in the west greatly modifies temperature here. *Figure 13.2c* shows that mean annual precipitation in Argentina diminishes westwards from over 100 cm in the extreme east (Misiones) to under 20 cm in many valleys in the west and over most of Patagonia. The northern Andes are on the whole dry, and, as in Chile, serve only as a modest source of water for the irrigated areas to the east, but precipitation is higher on the Andes in the south. Many of the rivers flowing east from the northern Andes drain into interior basins, and almost all the water entering the Plate estuary comes from the Paraná and Uruguay rivers.

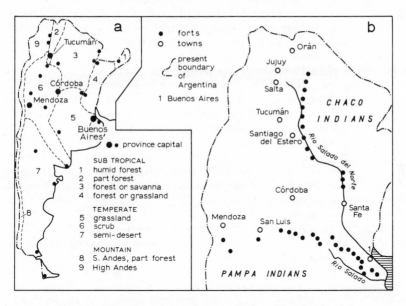

Figure 13.3. Argentina: (a) Vegetation types, (b) Forts of the Colonial Period

The principal types of vegetation according to Rampa[2] are mapped in *Figure 13.3a.* They are divided into sub-tropical and temperate. There are two limited areas (1 and 2) of dense sub-tropical forest, an area in Misiones being the extremity of the forests of South Brazil, and a belt of forest extending along the eastern foot of the Andes to Tucuman. Between these, the Chaco area (3) consists of a mixture of forest and savanna, while the Mesopotamian area lying between the Rivers Paraná and Uruguay, is partly forested, partly open grassland.

The temperate zone consists of the pampa (5) a grassland with virtually no trees originally, and a dry summer period. The northern limit of the pampa is considered to be its junction with the forest and savanna lands, but on the west and southwest, diminishing precipitation is the usual criterion, and an annual rainfall of 50–60 cm is considered to mark the margin. Beyond lies the semi-arid *monte* (6) with a xerophytic vegetation of small trees and shrubs. Patagonia (7) is also semi-arid, but vegetation varies considerably with relief conditions. The valleys have grassland suitable for pasture, but much of the intervening mass is dry and windswept, with a thin cover of shrubs. Only in the Andes in the west (8) is there a forest cover. The northern Andes (9) is distinguished as a separate vegetation region on account of its low temperatures, arid conditions and shrub vegetation.

13.4. AGRICULTURE

It seems both ironical and an indication of development that by the early 1970s agricultural production accounted for only about 10 per cent of the value of goods and services produced in Argentina. Manufacturing and mining accounted for about 30 per cent. In fact the structure of the economy of Argentina in this respect resembles very closely that of Australia. On the other hand, agriculture still accounts for about 15 per cent of the economically active population of the country. In 1970 it employed some 1,350,000 people out of 8,900,000 employed altogether. The productivity of an Australian farm worker is however about 3 times as high as that of one in Argentina.

If agriculture only accounts for 10 per cent of the gross domestic product of Argentina it provides over 90 per cent of the exports and, apart from a few tropical items such as coffee, satisfies the needs of some 25 million Argentinians. Over $\frac{1}{2}$ of the exports of Argentina are normally accounted for by fresh, chilled, frozen, canned or 'extract' meat products, about $\frac{1}{10}$ by hides and wool, about $\frac{1}{4}$ by cereals over $\frac{1}{10}$ by fruit and vegetable oils. The pampa region provides almost all the agricultural exports of Argentina as well as many of the needs of the internal market, whereas the other regions produce almost entirely for local or national needs.

Around 1970, out of a total area of nearly 280 million hectares, about 33 million or nearly 12 per cent of the area of Argentina was classified as being either under cultivation, non-permanent pasture or fallow, though only 24 million was under field crops. About 1·6 million hectares, mostly in the west and northwest, is irrigated. The main areas of irrigation are shown in *Figure 13.4*. About 145 million hectares, or over half of the area of Argentina, is classified as pasture, most of it poor quality land in Patagonia and the north. About 60 million hectares is classified as forest, though most of it is of little commercial value.

Since the Second World War Argentinian agriculture has not experienced the improvements in standards of productivity per unit of area or per worker typical of many developed western countries. The disappointing performance, illustrated by yields around 1950, 1960 and 1970 in Table 13.5, appears to be due to a number of influences, including the following.

1. Land reform in recent decades has led to a more satisfactory position for

tenant farmers and small owners but many very large units still exist and are not being farmed as effectively as they might be.

The high level of natural fertility of the pampa has resulted in a lack of interest in improvements through the use of fertilisers, though the quality of livestock and plant types in Argentina is probably the highest in Latin America. Around 1970, for example, Australia consumed about 5 times as much nitrate fertiliser as Argentina and more than 20 times as much phosphate fertiliser. Argentina hardly produces any fertiliser and imports very little.

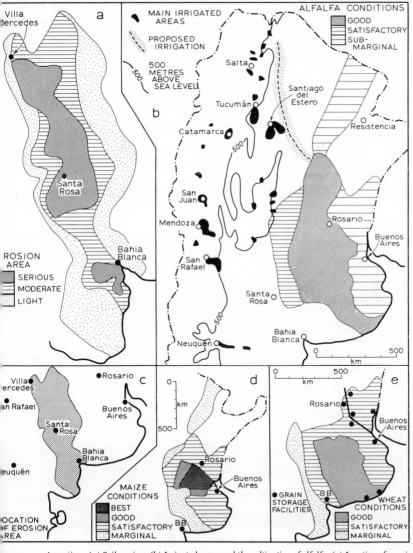

gure 13.4. Argentina: (a) Soil erosion, (b) Irrigated areas and the cultivation of alfalfo, (c) Location of area in (a), (d) and (e) areas of maize and wheat cultivation

Table 13.5.

AGRICULTURAL YIELDS AND PRODUCTION IN ARGENTINA

1-3   Yields in hundreds of kg per hectare
4   Area in thousands of hectares
5   Production in thousands of metric tons

	1 1948-52	2 Yields 1961-65	3 1970	4 1970 Area	5 1970 Production
Maize Argentina	16	18	23	4,020	9,360
Maize U.S.A.	25	42	45	23,210	104,390
Wheat Argentina	12	15	13	3,380	4,320
Wheat France	18	29	34	3,760	12,920
Rye Argentina	7	8	7	530	370
Rye W. Germany	22	27	31	860	2,660
Barley	12	12	11	550	580
Oats	12	13	13	480	600
Millet	8	12	10	130	130
Sorghum	10	16	20	2,080	4,070
Rice	30	35	40	100	410
Groundnuts	10	12	11	210	240
Cotton seed	5	4	7	440	310
Linseed	6	7	9	810	700
Sunflower seed	7	7	9	1,350	1,140
Cotton lint	2·4	2·3	3·2	440	140
Sugar cane	340	500	550	200	10,680
Vines				300	2,130

Source: *FAOPY 1970*, various tables.

3. Although Argentinian agriculture is more highly mechanised than that o other Latin American countries, having more than twice as many tracto as Brazil, it only has half as many as Australia. The number of tractors i use in Argentina rose from about 50,000 in 1950 to about 150,000 in tl early 1960s. There is now about 1 tractor per 8 farm workers in Argenti compared with almost 1 tractor per farm worker in Australia.

4. However excellent the quality of soil in the pampa area, precipitation c the western and southwestern fringes is both low and unreliable. Yiel vary greatly from year to year and excessive use of the land has led to tl destruction by erosion of about 500,000 hectares of farm land. Sever million more hectares are threatened. *Figure 13.4c* shows the main area i which erosion is a potential danger and *Figure 13.4a* the most serious affected area.

In spite of the drawbacks of an organisational, technical and physical natu noted above, Argentinian agriculture is impressively well run and producti by Latin American standards. It is characterised by the very wide range of plan cultivated; a 1970 statistical bulletin lists over 70 different crops grown com mercially, many of them fruits and vegetables. It is predominantly commerci rather than subsistence, with a high degree of regional specialisation and a lar amount of interregional exchange of products, possible thanks to the good ra and road systems. It is dominated by the pampa region, the extent and possib limits of which are shown in *Figure 13.5*, with Britain shown on the same scal

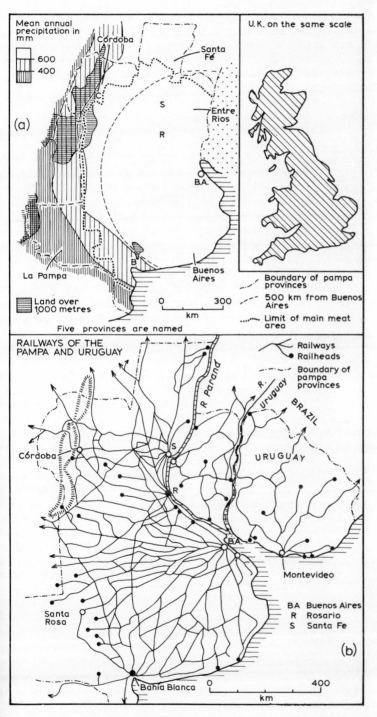

Figure 13.5. (a) The pampa and its limits, (b) Railways of the pampa of Argentina and of Uruguay

Space does not allow a description of the production and distribution of different types of crop and livestock in Argentina. Table 13.5 shows some of the main crops grown in Argentina in 1970 and a comparison of yields in around 1950, 1960 and 1970. Three other countries have been included to contrast their respective performances in maize, wheat and rye yields with those of Argentina.

Table 13.6 shows concisely the regional distribution of different crops in Argentina on the basis of 16 of the 24 major civil divisions; the 5 pampa provinces are indicated. In *Figure 13.4,* maps *b, d* and *e* show the main areas of cultivation of three of the principal crops, alfalfa, maize and wheat. The contrast between the pampa and the rest of the country is brought out in the table. Agriculture in the pampa is based on the cultivation of cereals, both for human consumption and for livestock, of other crops for livestock and of oilseeds, and on permanent pastures that could be improved. These crops are only grown in limited quantities elsewhere in Argentina, but cattle raising is spreading northwards into Chaco and Corrientes-Misiones. Commercial agriculture outside the pampa is based on cotton in the north, sugar in the northwest, vine and deciduous fruits in the west and sheep raising in the south.

Within the pampa there are regional differences in emphasis, with maize, for example, especially important in the area of highest rainfall and wheat in the drier parts. Local differences, on the other hand, depend not so much on physical features, which change only gradually over great distances, but on the choice of particular farmers. Platt[3] illustrates convincingly how two adjacent large units of land tenure, once similar in function, now have very different use of land in virtually identical physical conditions.

In livestock farming there is again a contrast between the pampa region which has most of the cattle, and the rest of the country, especially the south which has most of the sheep, although these are numerous also in the southern part of Buenos Aires province. Pigs and poultry are more widely distributed while the northeast is the area in which most progress has been made in extending cattle raising recently. Cattle numbered about 60 million in 1973 and some 15 million are slaughtered each year.

Forestry and fishing make only a modest contribution to the economy of Argentina. The forests are mostly remote from the main concentrations of population and are of limited commercial quality. Quebracho is the only semi-wild tree comparable in importance to the various species exploited in Brazil. The eucalyptus, introduced from Australia, contributes to the fuel supply locally and also provides shelter belts in grassland areas; timber and timber products are imported. Argentina had a fishing catch of about 230,000 tons in 1971 but since a drive to expand the industry in the late 1950s little growth has taken place.

13.5. ENERGY, MINING AND INDUSTRY

In 1970 mining and manufacturing accounted for about 30 per cent of the gross domestic product of Argentina and employed about 1,500,000 people. Argentina has had a considerable labour force in industry since the last part of the 19th century, about 170,000 in 1895 and 400,000 at the beginning of the First World War. Much of the employment in industry was initially in the processing

Table 13.6.

REGIONAL DISTRIBUTION OF SELECTED CROPS IN ARGENTINA DURING 1969/1970 BY AREA (THOUSANDS OF HECTARES)

	Maize	Wheat	Barley forage	Barley beer	Oats	Rye	Millets	Rice	Ground nuts	Linseed	Sunseed	Cotton	Sugar cane	Vines	Alfalfa	Sorghum
Buenos Aires *	1,340	3,449	161	324	811	733				464	860				1,707	468
Córdoba *	893	848	127	100	57	756	111		216	81	215				1,976	740
Corrientes	93							37				17				240
Chaco	60										62	274	7			164
Entre Rios *	567	361			124			44		275	29				65	
Formosa												60				
Jujuy													27			
La Pampa *		818		81	49	734									557	166
Mendoza														210	46	
Rio Negro														18	20	
Salta	41							3					17			
San Juan														53	13	
San Luis	255		58			45									48	
Sante Fe *	990	629		12	51	210	91	9		124	214	59	10		1,251	485
Santiago del Estero *	86			4								48	136		103	
Tucumán	42												136			
Other provinces	333	134	77		32	13	33	7	3	7	34	9	5	17	71	97
ARGENTINA TOTAL	4,700	6,239	423	521	1,123	2,489	235	100	219	951	1,414	468	201	298	5,585	2,360

* Pampa provinces

Source: *Boletín de Estadística*, Enero/Marzo 1970, Buenos Aires.

of agricultural products, and after the First World War in light industry producing consumer goods such as textiles, clothing and footwear.

During the decade following the Second World War, the policy of the regime of President Perón was to expand and to broaden the base of industry in Argentina at the expense, it is widely agreed, of crop farming and grazing. Even now, however, the average size of industrial establishment in Argentina is small, about 10 persons per unit, and the list of firms includes many self-employed persons and small workshops concerned with small scale manufacturing and the maintenance and repair of machines. There are also a number of very large processing and manufacturing plants such as those concerned with meat processing, oil refining, the manufacture of iron and steel and the production of motor vehicles.

The development of heavy industry in Argentina has been hampered by the lack of energy resources and by the location of the main oilfields in peripheral areas far from Buenos Aires. In 1973 about 70 per cent of the energy in Argentina was supplied by oil, 18 per cent by natural gas, 6 per cent by charcoal, 3 per cent by coal and a small amount from hydro-electric power. Oil and gas have formed the basis of the Argentinian energy supply, and policy has wavered between keeping control of the industry in national hands and enlisting foreign help to boost exploration and production. The national company Yacimientos Petroliferos has virtually controlled the industry since 1935 though the 1967 Hydrocarbons Act allowed the introduction of foreign capital. Oil and gas production rose fast in the 1960s and around 1970–71 the country reached self-sufficiency, while the ratio of reserves to yearly output stood at 17 : 1.

Figure 13.6 shows the position of the five main areas of oil and gas extraction or potential in Argentina. About 21,600,000 tons of oil were produced in 1971 compared with 12,000,000 in 1961. About half of the reserves are in the area of Comodoro Rivadavia and 17 per cent around Mendoza but new finds have been made both in the extreme northwest (Caimancito, 1969) and in Tierra del Fuego, where there are also offshore concessions. Most of the refining capacity in Argentina is in four refineries along the Plate – lower Paraná (San Lorenzo near Rosario, Campana, Dock Sud in Greater Buenos Aires, and La Plata). These receive crude oil from the south by sea and also, when necessary, imported oil. Smaller refineries in or near the oilfields supply regional needs. Argentina has several long natural gas pipelines (see *Figure 13.6*) the main function of which is to convey gas to Buenos Aires and other pampa towns. The latest gas pipeline to be built has a 30 inch diameter and extends some 700 km from Condor/Cerro Redondo to near Comodoro Rivadavia, while gas is also to be supplied to the Argentinian system by pipeline from Santa Cruz in the Bolivian lowlands.

According to one estimate, even assuming that unlocated oil deposits still exist in Argentina, it would require some $6,000 million to have a chance of keeping reserves up to the present level of 17 years of production. It is doubtful if Argentina itself could provide the capital though exploration is in fact continuing on a large scale. Interest is therefore turning to other sources of energy.

1. Argentina, like Brazil and Mexico, may be faced with the prospect of increasing imports of oil in order to keep the desired expansion of its energy base. The 1973 Arab oil strategy and the sharp rise in world oil prices could prove a serious threat to the industrialisation and mechanisation of Latin American countries.

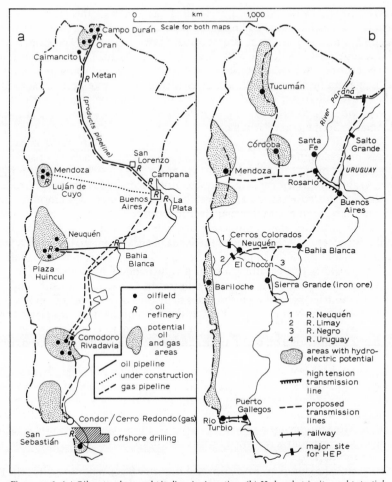

Figure 13.6. (a) Oil, natural gas and pipelines in Argentina. (b) Hydro-electric sites and potential

2. Argentina has considerable moderate quality coal reserves, the biggest deposit being at Rio Turbio in the extreme south (see *Figure 13.6b*). This field had an annual production of only about 600,000 tons in the early 1960s. It is hoped to raise this to 2–3 million tons.

3. In the early 1970s Argentina already had two nuclear power stations under construction, one for completion in 1974 at Atucha northwest of Buenos Aires and one in Córdoba for 1977.

4. Almost all the electricity generated in Argentina comes from thermal electric stations running on oil. There are many small hydro-electric stations in the country but until the early 1970s, no large ones. The first power from the El Chocón-Cerros Colorado scheme in Neuquén province (see *Figure 13.6b*) was generated in 1973. The final capacity is to be 1,200,000 kW, ¾ from El Chocón. The southern Andes of Argentina have many sites suitable for large hydro-electric stations but they are so far from the main centres of population that transmission losses would be large if not excessive. Interest appears to be

directed to the hydro-electric potential of the rivers of the Paraná system, stretches of which form the international boundary with neighbouring countries and would require joint efforts for their development. One scheme is to build a large power station at Salto Grande on the Uruguay river, but a study in 1973 put the cost at $ U.S. 525 million. Other proposals involving flood control and irrigation facilities as well as power include the Santa Fe-Paraná dam (2 million kW potential), the $ U.S. 770 million Piedra del Aguila project and various other projects on the northern rivers, the Paraná, Paraguay, Pilcomayo, Bermejo and Uruguay.

One of the main energy problems of Argentina is the need to satisfy the rapidly increasing demand for electricity. Generating capacity has risen from 1,900,000 kW in 1953 to 4,700,000 in 1963 and 7,100,000 in 1971; even in 1971, however, hydro-electric capacity only accounted for about 10 per cent, and unless the large hydro-electric stations can be financed, increasing amounts of oil will have to be used to fire thermal electric stations.

In addition to its energy minerals Argentina has deposits of a very large number of other minerals. None of these has been large enough to attract large amounts of foreign capital and unlike the other large Latin American countries, Argentina neither exports minerals nor produces enough of most even to support metallurgical industries. Recently, however, Canada, Japan and other industrial countries have shown an interest in the exploration of minerals in Argentina. A large copper deposit at Campana Mahuida in Neuquén province is to be exploited by a joint Argentinian and Canadian enterprise. Argentina also has a number of iron ore deposits and these contribute to the needs of its iron and steel industry.

Argentina has been able to cater for many of its industrial needs thanks to the establishment of textile, footwear, clothing, paper, rubber and cement industries. Since the 1950s engineering has grown and in 1960 the country already produced some 90,000 motor vehicles, a figure that increased to about 250,000 in 1971. The country now produces virtually all its needs of motor vehicles, though in factories largely owned by foreign companies. It even exports motor vehicles and parts.

The establishment of an iron and steel industry has been more difficult. Pig iron and steel are produced in small quantities in several places in Argentina. The Zapla works in the extreme northwest actually uses charcoal for smelting. Only at San Nicolás to the northwest of Buenos Aires is there a large modern integrated iron and steel works; the cost of construction during 1952–62 was some $ U.S. 300 million. This works depends on imported coking coal to be mixed with Argentinian coal, and on imported iron ore, pig iron and scrap. There is a big discrepancy between pig iron production (860,000 tons in 1971) and steel production (1,950,000 tons). In the early 1970s Argentina only produced about 50 per cent of its steel requirements but it is planned to expand the capacity of the San Nicolás works to 4 million tons of steel by 1976.

In recent years several petrochemicals works have been opened or planned. As well as several in the Buenos Aires area there are plants at Comodoro Rivadavia on the oilfield, at Bahia Blanca, a port receiving oil and gas from interior fields, and at Rio Tercero near Córdoba.

Certain industries such as petrochemicals and cement are dispersed among various regional centres but there is concern about the excessive concentration of many others in the Buenos Aires area. In October 1972 a law was passed to encourage the decentralisation of industry in Argentina. No new industries could be established in the Capital Federal itself, while until 1982 those in Buenos Aires province within a 40 km radius of the capital would have to pay a once only tax of 50 per cent of the value of fixed investment and those within 40–60 km a 30 per cent tax.

13.6. REGIONS, REGIONAL PROBLEMS AND FUTURE PROSPECTS

Table 13.7 contains four variables that have been used, for want of better data at the time of writing, to give an approximate idea of regional differences in living standards and levels of development in Argentina. Three of the distributions are mapped in *Figure 13.7*. Column 1a shows per capita electricity production.

Table 13.7.
VARIABLES EXPRESSING DEVELOPMENT IN ARGENTINA

1	Production of electricity in millions of kWh
1a	Production of electricity in kWh per inhabitant
2	Houses in thousands
2a	Houses per 100 inhabitants
3	Bank deposits in millions of pesos
3a	Bank deposits in pesos per inhabitant
4	Infant mortality per 1000 live births, 1963, in selected units

Major Civil Divisions 2-23 *Provincias* (T) *Territorio*	1 Electricity	1a	2 Houses	2a	3 Bank deposits	3a	4 Infant mortality
1 Capital Federal	7,485	640	3,549	30	18,487	1,580	38
2 Buenos Aires							51
3 Catamarca	17	100	41	24	45	260	105
4 Córdoba	740	360	549	27	1,467	710	58
5 Corrientes	99	180	117	21	177	310	72
6 Chaco	39	70	135	24	158	280	71
7 Chubut	17	90	52	27	173	910	
8 Entre Rios	115	140	198	24	295	360	53
9 Formosa	13	60	51	22	64	270	
10 Jujuy	27	90	75	25	127	420	129
11 La Pampa	31	180	52	30	139	810	66
12 La Rioja	14	100	31	23	47	350	
13 Mendoza	577	590	225	23	631	650	57
14 Misiones	24	50	103	23	152	340	
15 Neuquén	12	80	34	22	95	610	118
16 Rio Negro	110	420	68	26	180	680	103
17 Salta	57	110	111	22	186	360	
18 San Juan	70	180	81	21	188	280	
19 San Luis	25	140	46	25	89	490	77
20 Santa Cruz	10	120	23	27	79	940	
21 Santa Fe	486	440	605	28	1,738	810	53
22 Santiago del Estero	42	80	112	23	103	210	
23 Tucumán	153	200	166	22	301	390	
24 Tierra del Fuego(T)	1	60	4	25	12	750	71
ARGENTINA TOTAL	10,167	440	6,429	28	25,268	1,080	

Sources: 1, 4 Arnolds, A., *Geografía* . . ., p. 255, p. 31.
    2   *Censo nacional de población* . . . . . ., p. 53.
    3 *Boletín de Estadística*, July/Sept 1972, Trimestre III, Buenos Aires.

Even when allowance is made for the transmission of some electricity between provinces, big differences are evident. The north and northwest have a level of production and consumption far below the national average. The use of housing data to express differences in living standards is somewhat suspect since family size should also be taken into account. Per capita bank deposits must again be regarded with some reservations since some deposits may be kept in Buenos Aires by people in other provinces. Infant mortality, available only for some provinces, serves as a rough guide to the availability of health services. The general verdict of the four variables is that Buenos Aires has higher standards than the rest of the country and that the northwest and north are the least developed parts. At department level, even more marked differences in living standards occur.

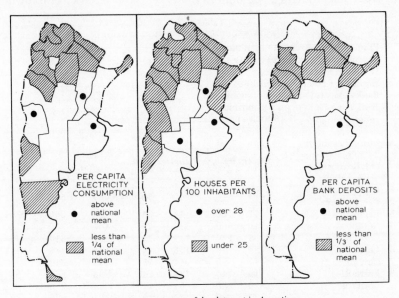

Figure 13.7. Aspects of development in Argentina

Argentina has been subdivided on the basis of its provinces into 7 areas in *Figure 13.8a.* Area 1, the lower Paraná-Plate, contains the Capital Federal and a belt of country from Santa Fe in the northwest to La Plata in the southeast. The places along this belt are linked by a good railway and by a main road on which improvements are continually being made. The individual centres are in fact separated by large stretches of open country and it is not suggested that the 12 million inhabitants of the belt form a conurbation. The distance from Santa Fe to La Plata is roughly equal to that from London to Newcastle or from Boston to Baltimore. The administrative divisions of Greater Buenos Aires are shown in *Figure 13.8c* and their population in Table 13.8.

The Paraná-Plate area has grown in population on account of the strong sea contacts of Argentina with the industrial countries of the world as a result of trade and migration. It is a kind of 'interface' between Argentina and the rest of the world. Routes from the interior focus particularly on Buenos Aires and

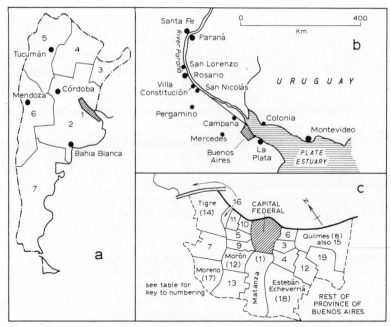

Figure 13.8. (a) Regions of Argentina, (b) Santa Fe – La Plata axis, (c) Districts of Greater Buenos Aires

Table 13.8.
POPULATION OF GREATER BUENOS AIRES

		1970 Population in thousands	Percentage increase 1960-70
	Capital Federal	3,160	7
	Grande Buenos Aires	5,249	39
1	Matanza	659	64
2	Morón	473	38
3	Lanús	450	20
4	Lomas de Zamora	404	49
5	General San Martín	401	44
6	Avellaneda	336	3
7	General Sarmiento	315	87
8	Quilmes	311	38
9	Tres de Febrero	310	18
10	Vicente López	258	4
11	San Isidro	225	9
12	Almirante Brown	208	52
13	Merlo	189	89
14	Tigre	149	62
15	Berazategui	128	38
16	San Fernando	113	23
17	Moreno	111	87
18	Esteban Echeverría	109	56
19	Florencio Varela	98	136
	Total Grande Buenos Aires	8,409	25

Source: *Banas*, 19 October 1970, p. 14.

Rosario. The four ports, Rosario, San Nicolás, Buenos Aires and La Plata handle about $\frac{2}{3}$ of the weight of Argentinian exports and 80–85 per cent of the imports. The fact that fuel and raw materials arrive by sea from southern Argentina and from abroad has made the area attractive to industries. A factory selling its products over the whole national market enjoys the advantage of having nearly 50 per cent of the population, perhaps 60 per cent of the purchasing power, and currently some 70 per cent of industrial production of Argentina, all within relatively easy reach.

The Paraná-Plate area also has disadvantages and problems. Among many are the excessive growth of Buenos Aires itself, the complete absence of energy resources in the area and in its immediate pampa hinterland, and problems of navigation on the Plate estuary and lower Paraná.

The five provinces that contain the pampa area (area 2), as well as fringes of other areas, are predominantly agricultural and have virtually no commercial mineral production. They provide about 80 per cent of the value of Argentinian exports and therefore have a key role in the economy of Argentina. They also contain regional centres such as Córdoba, the main industrial centre of Argentina outside Buenos Aires, and the port of Bahia Blanca. Industry is also spreading from area 1 into adjoining parts of the pampa.

The five areas, 3–7 in *Figure 13.8a,* differ from areas 1 and 2 in their unfavourable peripheral positions in relation to the country as a whole, generally poorer conditions for agriculture, and lack of manufacturing industry. On the other hand they have conditions suitable for specialisation in certain agricultural products and virtually all the known coal, oil, gas and hydroelectric reserves of the country. Each makes a particular contribution to the Argentinian economy. Area 3 is still an area of new settlement, with the need for land reclamation, conditions suitable both for cattle raising and the cultivation of citrus fruits, and a very large hydro-electric potential. Area 4 is also thinly populated and awaits improvements in farming that would enable it to increase its cotton and meat production. Area 5 is the oldest area of settlement in Argentina, has some of the poorest places in the country and a dense rural population. Its future development is tied to its oil and gas deposits and those of the adjoining lowlands of Bolivia and to irrigation schemes. Area 6 specialises in the cultivation of vines and temperate fruits, has only limited scope for the extension of cultivated land, but contains oil and gas deposits and a considerable hydro-electric potential. It is hoped to find metallic ores in the area and to build up heavy industry in Neuquén province. Area 7, Patagonia, is seen by Argentinians as a land of the future. At the moment it contains about 2·5 per cent of the population of the country. It is linked to the rest of the country by coastal shipping and air services, a road, still not completely paved in the early 1970s, and gas pipelines. Since the area is generally very dry, offers little scope for an extension of cultivation, and supports only a limited grazing industry based on sheep-raising, it can hope to create new jobs only in mining, hydroelectric production, forestry and tourism.

Since the late 1960s it has increasingly became both fashionable and highly relevant to study the future. An Argentinian author, Basilio M. Raymundo,[4] published in 1969 a book entitled *Argentina 2000, a semi-deserted nation?* Unconcerned, apparently, about the undeniable successes of Australia and Canada in managing the resources of vast areas with small populations and in achieving very high material standards, Raymundo argues that Argentina,

urrently with 25 million inhabitants, should aim for a 3 per cent annual rate of
opulation growth instead of the current 1·5 per cent. He calculates that the
ountry could produce enough food to feed 100–120 million people by the year
ooo. He seems less concerned about the future of energy and raw materials.
he following lines from the conclusion of the book are a reminder not to
ssume that everyone in Latin America favours zero population growth:

> 'The Neo Malthusian movement, supported by the government
> and institutions of North America and destined for the peoples of
> Latin America, is based on the the erroneous theory that the prin-
> cipal cause of underdevelopment lies in the excessive fertility of
> Latin American women and the best remedy is in contraceptives.
> Such action would aggravate even more the problems of countries,
> like most of those in Latin America, that are underpopulated, and is
> totally contrary to the national interest. It tries to avoid the fun-
> damental solutions: a modification of the socio-economic struc-
> tures that act as a brake on development, and the liberation of the
> country from all monopolistic influence. The determination of
> family size should be left to the decision of parents . . . The State
> should not support, instigate or accept any kind of birth control
> propaganda because this is against the needs of our Republic.'

References

Ferrer, A., *La economía Argentina*, Buenos Aires, 1963, p. 239.
Rampa, A. C., *Geografía física de la República Argentina*, Buenos Aires, 1961, pp. 190–203 and Platt,
    R., *Latin America, Countrysides and United Regions*, 1942, New York; McGraw Hill, pp. 355–361.
Platt, R., *Latin America, Countrysides and United Regions*, 1942, New York; McGraw-Hill, pp.
    355–361.
Raymundo, B., *Argentina 2000, Una nación semideserta?*, 1969, Buenos Aires, Editorial Orbelus.

ources of material in the figures

3.2 Based on maps in A. C. Rampa, *Geografía de la República Argentina*, 1967, Buenos Aires;
    Kapelusz, pp. 114, 127.
3.3 Based on maps in A.C. Rampa (as 2 above), p. 192.
3.4 Based on maps in A. Armolds, *Geografía política y económica de la República Argentina*, 1967,
    Buenos Aires; Kapelusz, pp. 82, 118, 120, 125.

urther sources consulted

nstituto Nacional de Estadística y Censos, *Boletín de Estadística*, Buenos Aires, Enero/Marzo 1970
    and earlier numbers.
rnolds, A., as referred to above in 13.4.
i Tella, T. S. and others, *Argentina, sociedad de masas*, 1965, Buenos Aires; Eudeba.
insberg, M. D., 'Una regionalización estadística de la agricultura en la Pampa Argentina', *Revista
    Geográfica*, No. 72, Junho de 1970, Rio de Janeiro.

Further reading

'Argentina, Political and Economic Hopes', *Bolsa Review,* Jan. 1973, Vol. 7, No. 73.

Eidt, R. C., 'Japanese Agricultural Colonization: a New Attempt at Land Opening in Argentina *Econ. Geogr.,* Jan. 1968, Vol. 44, No. 1, pp. 1–20.

Sargent, C. S., 'Elements of Urban Plot Development: Greater Buenos Aires, *Revista Geográfic* Junho de 1971, No. 74, Rio de Janeiro.

Wilkie, R. W., 'Towards a Behavioural Model of Peasant Migration: An Argentine Case of Spati: Behaviour by Social Class Level,' *Population Dynamics of Latin America,* R. N. Thomas, Ed Conference of Latin Americanist Geographers, Boston, Mass., Apr. 17, 1971.

CHAPTER 14

VENEZUELA

14.1. INTRODUCTION

Venezuela covers about six times the area of England and Wales and is nearly twice the size of Spain. It is situated on the northern side of South America between a point just north of the Equator and 12° North. Before the rapid growth of its oil industry in the 1920s Venezuela was one of the poorer and less modernised Latin American countries. During the colonial period it had few minerals to attract the Spaniards and had a secondary role in the Empire as a supplier of food and livestock products to places in the Caribbean. Before the 1920s it exported small quantities of cocoa beans and coffee. During the last five decades Venezuela has changed enormously and it now belongs to a group of countries that lie between the clearly underdeveloped and clearly developed countries.

In 1921 Venezuela had a population of about 2,700,000. This was mostly concentrated in the Andean region of the northwest and north. In 1971 the population of Venezuela was nearly four times as large, as Table 14.1 shows.

Table 14.1.

Year	Population		Per cent Increase
1941	3,851,000		
1950	5,035,000	1941-50	29
1961	7,524,000	1950-61	50
1971	10,722,000	1961-71	43

The population of Venezuela is made up predominantly of a mestizo population with negro influence and pure Indian elements in some areas. During the 1950s as many as 40–50,000 immigrants were entering the country each year from Italy, Spain and neighbouring Colombia, but since about 1960 there has been little immigration. In 1971 about 45 per cent of the population was under 15 years of age and only 5 per cent was over 60.

In the early 1970s it was calculated that the population of Venezuela was growing at the rate of about 3·4 per cent per year. If this rate were to continue, Venezuela would have about 26 million inhabitants by the year 2000. The figures shown in Table 14.1 suggest that in fact the rate of growth in the 1960s was somewhat lower than that in the 1950s, but the 50 per cent increase during 1950–1961 spans 11 years, not ten, and covers the main period of immigration after the Second World War.

The changing spatial distribution of population in Venezuela is characterised by two trends, a dispersal of population from the Andean region to other parts of the country, particularly the oilfield areas, and a concentration of population in the larger urban centres, all of which are growing fast. The Federal District (Caracas) and the adjoining state of Miranda had about 2,700,000 inhabitants in 1971 compared with little over 1,000,000 in 1950, or 25 per cent of the national population compared with 20 per cent.

Table 14.2 contains area and population data for the major civil divisions of Venezuela. The location of these units is shown in *Figure 14.1*, map *a*. The low density of population and the small number of people in the southern two thirds of the country is shown in different ways in *Figure 14.1*, maps *b* and *c*. The application of the Lorenz curve to the concentration of population in Venezuela gives a gini coefficient of 0·757 in 1950 and 0·758 in 1971. This indicates a high degree of concentration in both years and virtually no change in the basic structure of the distribution during 1950–71. Table 14.3 lists the towns of Venezuela with over 50,000 inhabitants in 1971. Their location is shown in *Figure 14.1*, map *d*, and in *Figure 14.2*.

In 1970 the average per capita gross national product in Venezuela was $ U.S. 1000, almost twice the average of $ U.S. 550 for Latin America as a whole, 2½ times the average for Brazil, roughly equal to the average for Argentina, but less

Table 14.2.
VENEZUELA: AREA AND 1971 POPULATION

1   Area in thousands of sq. km.
2   Population in thousands 1971
3   Density of population in persons per sq. km.

		1 Area	2 1971 Popn.	3 Density
1	Distrito Federal	2	1,861	967
2	Anzoategui	43	506	12
3	Apuré	77	165	2
4	Aragua	7	543	77
5	Barinas	35	231	7
6	Bolívar	238	392	2
7	Carabobo	5	659	142
8	Cojedes	15	94	6
9	Falcón	25	408	16
10	Guárico	65	319	5
11	Lara	20	671	34
12	Mérida	11	347	31
13	Miranda	8	856	108
14	Mónagas	29	298	10
15	Nueva Esparta	1	119	103
16	Portuguesa	15	297	20
17	Sucre	12	469	40
18	Tachira	11	511	46
19	Trujillo	7	381	52
20	Yaracuy	7	224	32
21	Zulia	63	1,299	21
T1	Amazonas	176	22	1
T2	Delta Amacuro	40	48	1
	VENEZUELA TOTAL	912	10,722	12

Source: *Anuario Estadístico 1971*, Ministerio de Fomento.

than half the Puerto Rico figure. In 1971, agriculture accounted for only about
8 per cent of total gross domestic product (but for only 6 per cent in 1960), while
mining and manufacturing each accounted for about 20 per cent. Agriculture
in the early 1970s still employed some 870,000 people, about 26 per cent of the
total economically active population of 3,300,000.

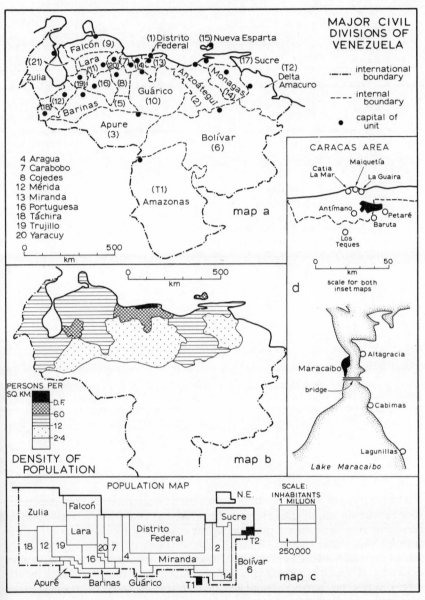

Figure 14.1. Major civil divisions and population of Venezuela. (a) The states and territories of Venezuela
(numbering as in Table 14.2), (b) Density of population, (c) Topological map of population, (d) Caracas and
Maracaibo areas

Table 14.3.

TOWNS WITH OVER 50,000 INHABITANTS IN 1971

Population in thousands, change 1950 = 100

		1971	1950	1950 -71			1971	1950	1950 -71
1	Caracas[1]	2,184			13	Barcelona	76	25	304
2	Maracaibo	650	236	275	14	Valera	74	22	336
3	Valencia	366	89	411	15	Mérida	74	25	296
4	Barquisimeto	334	105	318	16	Puerto Cabello	73	34	215
5	Maracay	255	65	392	17	Coro	69	29	238
6	San Cristóbal	152	54	281	18	Puerto la Cruz	63	28	225
7	San Felix[2]	143	1		19	Los Teques	63	17	371
8	Maturín	122	25	488	20	Maiquetía[4]	59	(40)	
9	Cumaná	120	46	261	21	Acarigua	57	17	335
10	Cabimas	118	42	281	22	Barinas	56	9	622
11	Ciudad Bolívar	104	32	325	23	Punto Fijo	55	15	367
12	Ciudad Ojeda[3]	83	24	346	24	Carúpano	51	30	170

[1] In 1971 Caracas itself had 1,035,000 inhabitants compared with 495,000 in 1950. The larger Area Metropolitana de Caracas includes Petaré, El Valle, Antimano, Baruta, El Recreo, La Vega, Chacao and Leoncio Martínez, each of which had over 50,000 inhabitants in 1971.
[2] San Felix de Guayana, also Ciudad Guayana.
[3] Formerly Lagunillas
[4] In 1971 Catia la Mar, formerly in the Maiquetía total, had 52,000 inhabitants.

Source: X Censo General de Población (2 de Noviembre 1971),
  Venezuela, Resultados Comparativos, Caracas 1972.

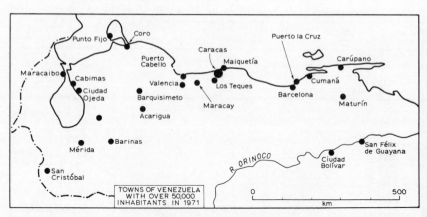

Figure 14.2. Towns of Venezuela with over 50,000 inhabitants in 1971

The great material development of Venezuela since the 1920s has depended very heavily on oil, as the following facts show. The oil industry gives direct employment to less than 1 per cent of the total employed population of the country (one source in the early 1970s gives an estimate of only 24,000). It accounts for nearly all the 20 per cent of the gross domestic product of the country derived from extractive industries, but provides over 60 per cent of the government revenue, takes 70 per cent of foreign investments, and provides 90 per cent of the value of all exports. Venezuela has one of the most favourable balances of trade in the world. The impact of the oil industry on Venezuela will be assessed in Section 14.3, after a brief account of the physical features of the country in the next section. One feature of the economy of Venezuela may already be noted here. If the 1 per cent of the population employed in mining accounts for 20 per cent of gross domestic product and 26 per cent of the population employed in agriculture accounts for only 8 per cent of gross national product, it can be seen that the value of production of an oil worker is over 60 times that of an agricultural worker. Even when the high level of capitalisation of the oil industry is taken into account there still remains a great discrepancy.

14.2. PHYSICAL BACKGROUND

Figure 14.3 shows the main relief features of Venezuela on the main map and precipitation on map *b*. A vegetation map of Venezuela is shown in Chapter 4, *Figure 4.13* on page 92.

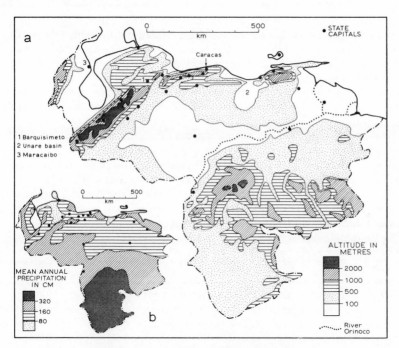

Figure 14.3. Venezuela (a) Relief, (b) Precipitation

Physically, Venezuela may be divided into several fairly distinctive regions, though climate and relief features are only roughly related. A fourfold division of the country distinguishes the cordilleras of the Andes, the lowlands and uplands of the northwest, the lowlands of the llanos, reaching south to the Orinoco, and the uplands and highlands of the Venezuelan Guiana to the south. Within these, subdivisions such as the Orinoco delta may be distinguished.

The Cordillera de los Andes and their continuation eastwards in the Cordillera de la Costa are broken into three parts by the two depressions, one near

Barquisimeto and the other the Unare basin. The Andes are high, exceeding, 5,000 metres in one place, but narrow. For much of the length there are two or more ranges enclosing high valleys and basins (e.g. Mérida, Lake Valencia). There is a considerable area with temperate (*templado*) conditions between about 1,000 and 2,000 metres but the cold (*frío*) and *páramo* zones are much smaller than in other Andean countries. Permanent snow occurs above about 4,600 metres. Mean annual precipitation varies greatly from one part of the cordillera to another, with semi-arid conditions prevailing in places; usually it is steepness of slope and poor quality of soil that limit agricultural possibilities.

On its northwest side, the high Cordillera of the Andes overlooks the lowlands of Maracaibo, partly filled by shallow sea, but almost encircled by mountains or uplands. This lowland is covered by dense tropical rain forest in the south but is dry in the north. There is little agriculture at present but with drainage and control of the rivers in the south and irrigation further north cultivation could be extended.

Roughly between the Andes and the Orinoco lie the llanos. This is a lowland area with a gradual slope east or southeast, filled mainly with relatively new deposits from the cordilleras, with a heavy rainfall in the west and crossed by many large rivers here, but rather more broken, and generally drier in the east. A savanna vegetation is associated with the region, but much of the surface in the west, especially close to the Andes, and in the delta as well, is heavily forested, while the Unare basin has thorn forest rather than savanna. Little of the region is cultivated, though much is used for grazing. Improvements for agriculture depend both on regulating the flow of rivers to prevent flooding and to improve drainage, and on arranging irrigation systems.

Beyond the Orinoco the land rises irregularly towards the southeast of the country, where much of the land is above 1,000 metres, but there are also lowlands, as in the extreme south. Though most of the region receives more than 250 cm of rain per year, patches of savanna occur in places within the tropical rain forest that covers most of the region.

As Venezuela lies well within the tropics, the regional contrasts in its relief, amount of rain, and vegetation, are not matched by contrasts in temperature or seasonal occurrence of rain over most of the country. Over 90 per cent of Venezuela has a mean annual temperature of over 24°C. Even moderate differences in altitude make appreciable differences locally.

Until the 1930s most of the cultivated land in Venezuela was in or on the flanks of the Andean region. The two main oilfield areas, however, are in the Maracaibo lowlands to the northwest of the Andes, and in the eastern part of the llanos. The growth of population in these two areas has led to an extension of cultivation in areas away from the Andes and to improvements in livestock raising, especially in the Maracaibo area.

14.3. THE OIL INDUSTRY OF VENEZUELA

Little oil was produced in Venezuela until the mid-1920s, when several leading oil companies of the time became interested in the exploration of the Maracaibo lowlands. The figures in Table 14.4 show the production of oil in Venezuela in millions of metric tons in selected years since then:

Table 14.4.

Year	Production	Year	Production
1930	19	1961	153
		1962	167
1940	27	1963	170
		1964	178
1950	80	1965	182
		1966	176
1953	92	1967	185
		1968	189
1958	136	1969	188
1959	145	1970	194
1960	149	1971	186
		1972	170

Two features may be noted, firstly the great importance to the U.S.A. of Venezuela during the Second World War, when production expanded greatly, and secondly the levelling out of production in the early 1960s. In 1971 the proved reserves of Venezuela were 1,966 million tons, enough to last only until the early 1980s at production levels of the 1960s. In fact exploration continues and new reserves may be found.

In 1961, the U.S.S.R. replaced Venezuela as the second largest oil producer in the world (the U.S.A. was first) and in the early 1970s Iran and Saudi Arabia both overtook it. In 1961 Venezuela accounted for 14 per cent of the world's oil production, in 1971 for only 8 per cent.

Until the establishment in 1961 of the still small CVP (Corporación Venezolana de Petróleo), the Venezuelan oil industry was exclusively run by foreign companies. Table 14.5a shows the seven leading oil producers in Venezuela in the early 1970s. Creole, with 42–43 per cent of output and Shell with about 25 per cent of output have for several decades dominated the industry. Table 14.5b shows that Creole (Standard Oil), Shell, Mobil and Texaco are among the largest companies in the world according to sales. The giant U.S.

Table 14.5a.
SEVEN LEADING OIL PRODUCERS IN VENEZUELA

Daily average in thousands of barrels

	1972	1973	Per cent 1972
Creole	1,311	1,477	43
Shell	762	781	25
Menegrande	384	405	12
Venezuela Sun	197	179	6
Mobil	102	85	3
Texaco	53	55	1·6
C.V.P.	48	72	1·6
All companies	3,080	3,297	100

Source: *Venezuela Up-to-date*, Summer 1973, Vol. XIV, No. 3, p. 7.

Table 14.5b.
LEADING U.S. AND WEST EUROPEAN COMPANIES

		Sales in millions of £
	U.S. Companies	
1	General Motors	11,330
2	Standard Oil (N.J.)	8,430
3	Ford Motor	6,570
4	Sears, Roebuck	4,000
5	General Electric	3,770
6	Mobil Oil	3,760
7	I B M	3,310
8	Texaco	3,230
9	Chrysler	3,200
10	Gulf Oil	2,950
	European Companies	
1	British Petroleum	3,150
2	Royal Dutch Petroleum	3,020
3	"Shell" Transport and Trading	2,920

Source: *The Times 1000 1972–73*, pp. 10, 55, 67.

motor vehicle companies also have a secondary interest in Venezuela on account of the fact that their products consume petroleum products and in view of their subsidiary plants in Venezuela. The sales of Standard Oil, only a small part of which are actually connected with Venezuelan oil, are alone equal in value to roughly twice the total national income of Venezuela.

For various reasons the oil industry of Venezuela has become less attractive than it was to foreign investors since about 1960 and the value of investments of the main foreign investors, the U.S. oil companies, has changed little in the 1960s. In 1968, U.S. investments in mining in Venezuela were worth about $ U.S. 1,800 million out of about $ U.S. 2,600 million altogether. Receipts from the oil industry were, however, $ U.S. 380 million out of $ U.S. 430 million altogether, still a favourable ratio.

The relationship between foreign oil companies operating in Venezuela and the Venezuelan government has been changed several times since the 1920s, each time in favour of the host country. As a result of the Hydrocarbons Law of 1943, it was established that oil concessions should revert to Venezuela after 40 years, that is by 1983. It was proposed then that as much oil as possible should be refined in Venezuela before export. In the early stages, most Venezuelan oil was shipped out of the country crude, to be refined either in Aruba or Curaçao, or in the consuming countries. The arrangement in the mid-1950s was that approximately half of the profits of the oil companies went to the Venezuelan government through taxes on concessions, exploration rights, production and export.

In 1959 a tougher line was taken towards foreign companies. This led to the establishment of a Venezuelan Oil Company, a new form of association with foreign companies still wishing to extend their operations in Venezuela, and an increase in the share of profits to about 60 per cent for the Venezuelan government. Since 1959, foreign companies have been compelled to work in new areas in association with the Venezuelan government or under contract for it. In 1971 an even more drastic Oil Revision Law stipulated that after 1983 there should be no compensation for foreign companies when their concessions, complete with equipment, are taken over. The world oil crisis following the Arab-Israeli war of October 1973 had considerable implications for Venezuela because it gave Venezuela a chance to raise its oil prices.[1]

The political and organisational background to Venezuelan oil has been discussed at some length because it is vital to an understanding of geographical aspects. In the last two decades production costs of Venezuelan oil have been much higher than those of Middle East oil. Moreover Venezuelan oil tends to be of poorer quality, having a high sulphur content. Higher costs have been offset by the proximity of Venezuela to the U.S.A., its main customer. With the growth in size of oil tankers and a relative decline in transport costs compared with production costs, however, Middle East oil has become more competitive in the U.S.A.

With the prospect of rapidly dwindling reserves in the 1970s and 1980s, Venezuela is interested in conserving these, reducing output and obtaining a very high price for its oil. So long as the industrial countries do not come up with an infallible alternative to oil, the oil producing countries are safe in not expanding production and in keeping prices high.

Brazil, Argentina and other Latin American countries are increasingly interested in the Venezuelan oil industry from which they import already and which they supply with equipment. They could to some extent replace the U.S.A. and West Europe as major importers and also as investors in joint ventures with Venezuela. It was reported[2] that Petrobras of Brazil was seeking the right to prospect for oil in Venezuela on equal terms with CVP.

The relationship of the oil industry to Venezuela as a whole is complex and its influence on the country is profound. The flowchart in *Figure 14.4* includes some of the elements in the relationship. The whole 'system' has depended on the availability firstly of foreign capital, because Venezuela itself could not have financed such an industry, and secondly on the presence of commercial oil reserves for exploration. From the exploitation and exportation of oil the Venezuelan government has received a very large amount of revenue towards its budget. Venezuela has also been able to achieve a high level of energy consumption.

Figure 14.5 shows some of the direct spatial effects of the Venezuelan oil industry. Oil concessions only cover about 6 per cent of the area of Venezuela. Production is highly concentrated, and in the early 1970s about 70 per cent of the total came from the Maracaibo area, where Creole and Shell have their main fields. In 1972 there were about 4,000 active wells in this area but in the early 1970s output was actually falling. Most of the remaining production came from the various more widely scattered eastern oil fields. Two other areas have proved reserves and a small output, Cumarebo in the northwest and Barinas-Apure in the llanos area south of the Andes. Exploration continues in various places including several off-shore areas indicated in *Figure 14.5*.

Although crude oil can be shipped to importing countries more cheaply and conveniently than refined products, the policy of Creole and Shell has been to refine much of the Venezuelan production in the Netherlands Antilles (Aruba

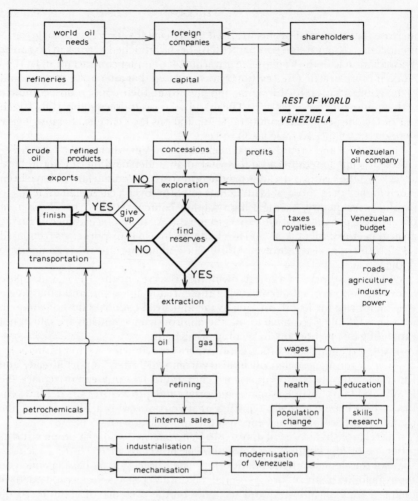

Figure 14.4. Flow diagram of selected aspects of the oil industry of Venezuela and its impact on the economy of the country

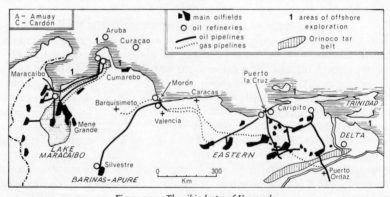

Figure 14.5. The oil industry of Venezuela

and Curaçao). The policy of Venezuela, on the other hand, has been to have oil refineries in Venezuela itself. Among the largest are those at Maracaibo, Amuay, Cardón, Morón and Puerto la Cruz. In 1970 Venezuelan refineries turned out about 66 million tons of refined products, much of this for sale in Venezuela itself, while the Netherlands Antilles produced 47 million tons of refined products.

The transportation of crude oil from the oilfields to Venezuelan refineries or to terminals for direct export is mainly by pipelines, the main routes of which are shown in *Figure 14.5*. Extensive regional road networks have also been built by the oil companies and these have formed the basis of the national system of roads which now covers adequately the northern third of the country from the Maracaibo lowlands in the west to the Orinoco delta in the east.

Since the Second World War the oil industry of Venezuela has given direct employment to 30–50,000 people at different times. For each oil worker, however, several other jobs have been created for people in construction, retail services, transport, food growing and other activities. The benefits of the educational and health facilities provided by the oil companies for their own personnel have also been felt in the oilfield areas. Increasingly even the technical side of the industry has come to be run by Venezuelans. The population of towns in the oilfields and of ports handling oil has grown rapidly.

The deeply traditional and economically dormant Venezuela of the early 20th century has been stirred up and transformed beyond recognition in a few decades as a result of the growth of the oil industry, the direct effects of which have been noted. The use of the great wealth of Venezuela has been a matter of some controversy. Some of it has ended up in the hands of a small very wealthy class whose Caracas flats and villas form some of the most pleasant residential districts in Latin America. The old centre of Caracas has also been modernised at great expense and lavish new express roads ease the heavy road traffic of the capital. At the same time, about ½ million people live in wooden huts in the shanty towns on the hillsides around. Some of the oil wealth has been spent on improving the 'infrastructure' of Venezuela. Improvements in education are illustrated by the growth of literacy (see Chapter 8, Figure 8.4 on page 170). Land reform has been financed and agricultural improvements supported. A new heavy industrial area has been established near the mouth of the Orinoco. Venezuela is increasingly acquiring control of the oil industry itself and is gaining greater benefit from production by adding value to its crude oil not only in refineries but in petrochemicals plants.

14.4. OTHER ACTIVITIES AND FUTURE PROSPECTS

Lack of space prevents the inclusion of more than brief notes on agriculture, other mining activities and manufacturing in Venezuela. Agriculture in the early 1960s is discussed at some length in the first edition of the present book and more recent developments are described in Focus.[3]

The extent of cultivated land has not increased much in Venezuela since the early 1950s. Improvements such as the introduction of irrigation in some areas and an increase in the application of fertilisers have however increased yields of some crops. Land reform measures between 1958 and 1970 have changed the previous situation whereby about 2 per cent of the owners had 80 per cent of the land. About $\frac{1}{5}$ of the agricultural population has been allocated family farms.

Improvements are difficult in the traditional areas of farming where potatoes, maize, wheat and coffee are grown. Maize yields in Venezuela have hardly changed in the last two decades and coffee production increased only slightly in the 1960s. On the other hand the production of rice and sugar in the lowland areas has risen. Increasing attention to fencing, water supply, fodder and breeding should allow an increase in meat, dairy products and hides from the steadily growing number of cattle in the Maracaibo and Orinoco lowlands (5,770,000 around 1950, 8,360,000 in 1969/70). The rugged forest and savanna area of the south of the country seems likely to be shared for some time to come by the shifting Indian cultivators and various mining and timber concerns.

Food production in Venezuela increased faster between the period 1952–56 and 1970 than that in any other Latin American country. In the 1950s considerable quantities of food were imported, but if present trends continue, and in spite of the rapid growth of population and rising standards at home, Venezuela should be able to be a net exporter of agricultural produce.

In addition to its oil reserves Venezuela has reserves of several other minerals and also a large hydro-electric potential in the southern highlands. With capital from the U.S. Steel Corporation and Bethlehem Steel Corporation, Venezuela has become one of the leading exporters of high grade iron ore in the world. The deposit in the El Pao area was discovered in 1941 and since the early 1950s iron ore has been moved by rail from El Pao and Cerro Bolívar to Puerto Ordaz on the Orinoco for export. About 20 million tons of high grade ore (12$\frac{1}{2}$ million tons of iron content in 1971) were being produced annually around 1970. Cerro Bolívar could produce for at least a hundred years at this rate. Another deposit of 650 million tons at San Isidro is to be mined by a Venezuelan Corporation. It is hoped that bauxite deposits will be found in the same area. Two other minerals of interest in Venezuela are nickel, to be mined by a joint Venezuelan and French enterprise at Loma de Hierro 80 km southwest of Caracas, and a coalfield at Guasare in Zulia state to the west of Maracaibo, planned to produce 6 million tons of coal a year by 1976. Of the total electricity generating capacity of Venezuela, about 3 million kW in the late 1960s, only about $\frac{1}{4}$ was in hydro-electric stations, most in the first stage of the Guri plant on the Caroni river in the area of new development around Ciudad Guayana.

Considerable industrial development has taken place in Venezuela in recent decades. Much of the light industry producing such items as cotton yarn and cloth, clothing, footwear, paper and pharmaceutical goods is in Greater Caracas or in the three fast growing urban centres to the west, Maracay, Valencia and Barquisimeto. One use of Venezuelan oil royalties has been the establishment of an integrated iron and steel mill on the lower Orinoco. The first pig iron and steel were produced here in 1963 and in 1971 Venezuela produced about $\frac{1}{2}$ million tons of pig iron and 1 million tons of steel. Ingredients include local iron ore and electric power, and coking coal imported from the U.S.A. Much of the capacity of the rapidly growing petrochemicals industry of Venezuela has been established at Maracaibo and at Morón, both seaports. As yet the engineering industry is not well developed in Venezuela but it is hoped that the needs of the oil industry in metal working and engineering products will be increasingly catered for in the future.

In a country like Venezuela in which plans and projects are turned out and fulfilled or abandoned with alarming frequency, it is difficult to separate the past from the future and difficult to make assessments of the future for more than a few years ahead. The following is no more than a summary of some of the developments that are likely in the 1970s and 1980s. Some of the items are included in the Economic Plan of Venezuela for 1970–74.

1. THE OIL INDUSTRY

(i) Future exploration is needed to locate about 1,000 million tons of new reserves (if these actually exist) by the early 1980s. Since exploration costs are high in offshore areas where reserves are thought to exist, it seems unlikely that Venezuela could itself provide the capital. Disputes over exploration rights on the continental shelf with Colombia, the Netherlands Antilles and Trinidad seem inevitable.

(ii) Venezuela has enormous reserves of oil in its Orinoco tar sands belt (see *Figure 14.5*), an area about 600 km from east to west and 80 km wide.[4] The oil here is estimated to be about 700×10^9 barrels or about 100×10^9 tons. If 10 per cent of this could be recovered, Venezuela could count on reserves about *five times as large* as its 1971 oil reserves. With the increasing price of conventional oil and further research in the extraction of oil from more difficult sources (the oil has a high density, from 8° to 13° and also a large sulphur and metals content), the tar sands of Venezuela could greatly extend the life of the Venezuelan oil industry.

(iii) Much of the natural gas hitherto produced in Venezuela as a by-product of the oil industry has either been fired or pumped back into the ground to facilitate oil production. The gas industry was nationalised in 1971 and Venezuela is now building gas pipelines (see *Figure 14.5*) to deliver gas to the main towns and also to liquefication plants on the coast for export to the U.S.A. by 1976.

(iv) Venezuela is buying a fleet of oil tankers and liquefied gas carriers. CVP has ordered a 35,000 ton tanker.

2. OTHER SECTORS OF THE ECONOMY

The 1970–74 plan[5] allows for the investment of oil revenues in the infrastructure of the country, and in industry, agriculture and social welfare. It is proposed to increase GNP at 6·3 per cent annually, but to emphasise manufacturing, energy and construction (9·6 per cent per year). Dependence on oil among exports should diminish and Venezuela should switch investment from import substitution industries to new export activities, producing a surplus of fruit and vegetables, steel, aluminium, petrochemicals products and natural gas. Investment during 1970–74 includes $ U.S. 316 million to the iron and steel industry (Sidor), $ U.S. 225 million to petrochemicals plants at El Tablazo (Maracaibo) and Morón, and $ U.S. 30 million in an aluminium plant. The El Tablazo plant would eventually have an investment of $ U.S. 1,200 million. Roads ($ U.S. 733 million), the Caracas underground system ($ U.S. 110 million) and Maiquetia Airport ($ U.S. 70 million) are priorities in the transport sector. There has long been talk of building an extensive railway network in

Venezuela, but so far the only railway of more than local or special use is the 175 km line from Puerto Cabello to Barquisimeto.

3. POPULATION

Venezuela in the early 1970s had one of the fastest growing populations in the world. If the present trend were to continue, its population of $10\frac{1}{2}$ million in 1971 would reach 21 million in 1994 and 42 million in 2016. Even if a yearly reduction of 3 per cent on the rate of increase had taken effect from 1971, a drastic slowing down of the rate of growth, Venezuela would still have over 19 million people by the year 2000. If the population of Caracas and Miranda districts continues to grow at recent rates the Greater Caracas area could have about half of the population of Venezuela by the year 2000. Levy and Wadycki[6] have detected a tendency, even in the 1950s, for migration in Venezuela to be less towards the national capital than it was in earlier decades of this century. The establishment of new towns and the provision of new jobs in mining, industry and agriculture away from the national capital and the major oilfield centres, as at Ciudad Guayana, in the Tuy valley south of Caracas and in llanos irrigation projects, provides secondary magnets to migrants.

14.5. REGIONAL DIFFERENCES

One of the obvious questions about the geography of Venezuela, though one not easily answered, concerns the distribution of wealth in the country on a spatial rather than a class basis. Enough data are available on a state basis from sources dating from the 1960s and from the 1971 census to allow a tentative multi-variate study of the recent situation in Venezuela. Tables of numerical data have been included in this section for the reader to study and use.

Table 14.6 contains data for the 1960s used by the author for the application of factor analysis before 1971 census material became available. It should be noted that in the arrangement of values, high to low means 'good' to 'bad' except for variables 1, 5 and 6, where the opposite is true; variable 3 is indifferent. As a result there are high negative correlations between some of the variables. Table 14.7 shows the matrix of correlation coefficients between the 11 variables. There are remarkably high negative correlations (-0.96) between percentage of population in agriculture on the one hand and percentage of population literate and having electricity supply on the other.

The application of oblique factor analysis to the data in Table 14.7 produces two closely correlated factors ($+0.76$), I and II. Factor I highlights the employment variables (1 and 2), literacy and electricity, while factor II places more emphasis on birthrate and car ownership. Factor III does not correlate with the other two, but brings out the independent dimension of deathrate and infant mortality. The factor loadings are shown in Table 14.8.

Each state has a score on each of the three factors. The matrix of state scores is shown in Table 14.9. In *Figure 14.6* the seven states with the highest level of literacy (column 7 in Table 14.6) and the seven with the lowest are shown in map *a*. This variable reflects so closely factor I that an identical distribution is given in map *b*, showing the upper and lower 7 states on this factor (column I in Table

1 Persons employed in agriculture as a percentage of total employed population
2 Professional and white collar workers as a percentage of all employed population
3 Population change 1950-70 (1950 = 100)
4,5 Birthrate, deathrate, 1960
6 Infant mortality, deaths under 1 year per 1000 live births
7 Literate population as a percentage of total population over 10 years of age, 1961
8 Percentage of dwellings having electricity in 1961
9 Percentage of dwellings having running water in 1961
10 Cars (automóviles) registered in 1968 per 1000 inhabitants
11 Municipal income in sucres per inhabitant in 1969

		1 Agr.	2 Prof.	3 Popn.	4 Brate	5 Brate	6 Inf.	7 Lit.	8 Elec.	9 Water	10 Cars	11 Inco.
1	Distrito Federal	2	22	262	45	6	38	88	95	71	28	215
2	Anzoátegui	31	9	209	51	6	40	64	54	32	11	38
3	Apuré	60	6	185	44	6	28	47	26	20	8	25
4	Aragua	22	11	286	41	7	39	71	74	62	48	47
5	Barinas	63	5	289	52	9	54	46	32	23	15	21
6	Bolívar	29	11	309	45	6	37	69	52	29	28	28
7	Carabobo	20	13	271	43	8	50	70	72	53	34	60
8	Cojedes	59	9	181	46	10	47	43	31	28	45	32
9	Falcón	37	10	158	48	7	37	59	45	27	13	14
10	Guárico	51	7	193	46	7	40	52	40	32	33	29
11	Lara	37	8	182	48	9	51	54	49	40	15	37
12	Mérida	58	7	164	47	11	55	48	33	42	20	42
13	Miranda	21	17	310	27	6	40	73	74	55	96	112
14	Monagas	50	7	169	54	6	28	59	41	32	14	42
15	Nueva Esparta	26	9	157	42	7	29	62	62	18	18	35
16	Portuguesa	61	4	243	54	12	67	42	30	34	22	31
17	Sucre	51	7	140	52	7	30	53	37	25	10	22
18	Táchira	48	8	168	53	11	40	60	48	69	25	55
19	Trujillo	57	6	139	47	11	60	46	35	32	14	24
20	Yaracuy	57	6	169	52	10	61	49	43	40	28	29
21	Zulia	22	12	232	45	6	41	70	77	52	24	45
	VENEZUELA TOTAL	41	9	210	47	8	43	58	50	39	26	49

Sources: *Anuario estadístico de Venezuela 1969*, Ministerio de Fomento, Dirección General de Estadística y Censos Nacionales, Caracas 1972.
Columns: 4, 5, pp. 26–7; 6, pp. 101–88: 10, p. 243; 11, p. 312.

Noveno Censo General de Población, 26 de Feb. de 1961.
Resumen General de la República, Parte A, Caracas 1966, Parte B, Caracas 1967.
Columns: 1, pp. 162–3; 2, pp. 162–3; 7, p. 89; 8, pp. 84–9; 9, pp. 29–39.

Table 14.7.

MATRIX OF CORRELATION COEFFICIENTS (PEARSON r) FROM TABLE 14.6

	1	2	3	4	5	6	7	8	9	10	11
1 Agr.	1·00										
2 Prof.	−0·88	1·00									
3 Popn	−0·49	0·51	1·00								
4 Brate	0·55	−0·62	−0·45	1·00							
5 Drate	0·61	−0·52	−0·31	0·41	1·00						
6 Inf.	0·37	−0·30	0·07	0·23	0·80	1·00					
7 Lit.	−0·96	0·90	0·52	−0·48	−0·65	−0·44	1·00				
8 Elec.	−0·96	0·88	0·51	−0·53	−0·51	0·26	0·95	1·00			
9 Water	−0·56	0·64	0·37	−0·26	0·03	0·09	0·64	0·70	1·00		
10 Cars	−0·36	0·53	0·56	−0·78	−0·12	0·03	0·37	0·44	0·46	1·00	
11 Income	−0·66	0·87	0·40	−0·38	−0·27	−0·13	0·72	0·73	0·69	0·40	1·00

Table 14.8.

FACTOR LOADINGS

Variables	I	II	III
1 Agr.	0·97	0·72	0·16
2 Prof.	−0·92	−0·86	−0·01
3 Popn	−0·52	−0·61	0·06
4 Brate	0·53	0·81	0·15
5 Drate	0·61	0·41	0·74
6 Inf.	0·38	0·18	0·77
7 Lit.	−0·98	−0·72	−0·16
8 Elec.	−0·97	−0·75	0·00
9 Water	−0·65	−0·58	0·49
10 Cars	−0·40	−0·79	0·18
11 Income	−0·74	−0·71	0·23

14.9). A somewhat different view of the least sophisticated 7 states on factor II is given in map *c*. Cluster analysis has been applied to the data in Table 14.9 to give the linkage tree in *Figure 14.7*. On the basis of this multi-variate classification, the Distrito Federal (Caracas) and the adjoining state of Miranda each form single-member 'groups'. There is less differentiation among the group of 8 states (group 6 in *Figure 14.7,* map *a*) that make up the least sophisticated part of Venezuela. The main oilfield area of Venezuela, the state of Zulia (with Maracaibo) joins Carabobo and Aragua in group 5.

In conclusion, it appears from data in Table 14.6 and from more recent data in Table 14.10 that there were very marked differences in the level of development between different states of Venezuela with the oldest areas of settlement, the densely populated, deeply rural western Andes remaining the least changed part of the country, with only half its population literate, generally poor housing conditions and few motor vehicles.

Table 14.9.

SCORES OF STATES ON FACTORS I–III

		I	II	III			I	II	III
1	Distrito Federal	24	31	58	12	Mérida	59	54	62
2	Anzoategui	46	55	41	13	Miranda	37	18	50
3	Apuré	60	55	34	14	Monagas	53	59	38
4	Aragua	39	41	51	15	Nueva Esparta	45	51	36
5	Barinas	61	58	53	16	Portuguesa	67	59	67
6	Bolívar	44	47	38	17	Sucre	55	59	39
7	Carabobo	39	42	56	18	Tachira	51	55	64
8	Cojedes	61	47	55	19	Trujillo	60	57	60
9	Falcón	50	54	40	20	Yaracuy	58	56	62
10	Guárico	55	51	44	21	Zulia	39	46	48
11	Lara	51	54	54					

Note that as the negative signs in Table 14.8 are against the variables indicating a high level of development on factors I and II, scores on factors I and II in Table 14.9 may be switched about the mean of 50 (e.g. Distrito Federal 24 on 1 to 76).

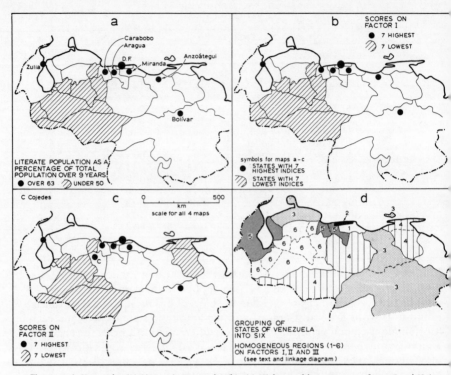

Figure 14.6. Venezuela: (a) Literacy in Venezuela, (b), (c) Highest and lowest states on factors I and II (see Tables 14.8 and 14.9), (d) Grouping of the states of Venezuela on the basis of three factors

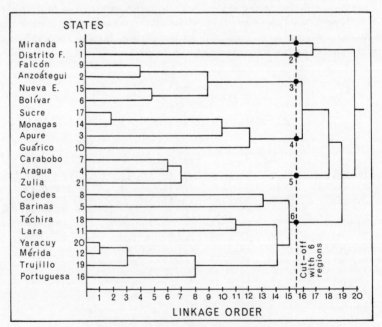

Figure 14.7. Linkage diagram for the states of Venezuela

1 Population growth 1950-1971 (1950 = 100)
2 Illegitimate births as a percentage of total births
3 Immigrant population as a percentage of population born in the unit
4 Housing *without* running water as a percentage of all housing
5 Housing *without* any system of sewage disposal as a percentage of all housing
6 Doctors per 10,000 inhabitants
8 Bolívars spent on public works (*obras públicas*) per inhabitant
9 Urban population as a percentage of total population

		1 Popn	2 Illeg.	3 Immig.	4 Water	5 Sewage	6 Doctors	7 Lit.	8 Public Works	9 Urban
1	Distrito Federal	262	29	47	10	10	24	86	353	99
2	Anzoategui	209	89	20	41	24	6	74	271	71
3	Apuré	185	200	7	63	56	4	58	236	33
4	Aragua	286	44	48	15	8	5	83	153	90
5	Barinas	289	75	34	53	45	4	60	251	41
6	Bolivar	309	71	32	39	19	7	80	431	76
7	Carabobo	271	50	41	24	10	9	82	398	92
8	Cojedes	181	89	13	44	38	6	61	298	49
9	Falcón	158	44	4	46	36	6	71	245	57
10	Guárico	195	120	11	49	35	4	64	307	60
11	Lara	182	69	9	34	29	6	69	161	68
12	Mérida	164	33	10	26	41	11	65	274	42
13	Miranda	310	57	77	15	11	2	85	162	86
14	Monagas	170	120	16	42	33	6	71	121	70
15	Nueva Esparta	157	52	50	36	10	9	74	286	85
16	Portuguesa	243	120	32	41	36	4	62	222	63
17	Sucre	140	111	3	50	43	5	65	190	60
18	Tachira	168	42	4	14	32	6	73	155	58
19	Trujillo	139	63	4	38	42	6	61	168	46
20	Yaracuy	169	67	13	36	23	4	65	336	65
21	Zulia	232	61	16	24	32	11	81	521	85
T1	Amazonas	200	117	15	45	50	8	59	364	45
T2	Delta Amacuro	141	145	12	56	43	4	64	333	44
	VENEZUELA TOTAL	207	81	23	37	31	7	68	271	65

Sources: *Anuario estadístico 1971*, pp. 41, 56, 58, 98-9.
Venezuela Resultados Comparativos, p. 6.

References

1. *The Times,* 2 Jan., 1974, p. 15, reported a rise in the posted price of crude oil in Venezuela from $ U.S. 7·74 a barrel to $ U.S. 14·08.
2. *Bolsa Review,* Oct. 1972, Vol. 6, No. 70.
3. Crist, R. E. and Leahy, E. P., 'Venezuela', *Focus,* Sept. 1973, Vol. XXIV, No. 1.
4. *Venezuela Up-to-date,* Summer 1973, Vol. XIV, No. 3, p. 4 and *Bolsa Review,* Feb. 1973, Vol. 7, No. 74.
5. *Peruvian Times,* Oct. 29, 1971 and Feb. 4, 1972.
6. Levy, M. R. and W. J. Wadycki, 'Lifetime versus one-year migration in Venezuela', *J. Reg. Sci.,* 1972, Vol. 12, No. 3, pp. 407–17.

Sources of material in the figures

14.3 Based on maps in *Atlas Agrícola de Venezuela,* Ministerio de Agricultura y Cría, 1960, Caracas.
14.5 Based on a map in *Petroleum Press Service,* Dec. 1972, p. 450.

Further sources consulted

Dirección General de Estadística y Censos Nacionales (Ministerio de Fomento)
    a) X Censo General de Población, *Venezuela Resultados Comparativos,* Caracas 1972 and regional volumes, Caracas 1973.
    b) *Anuario estadístico,* 1971.
Revista Geográfica, Universidad de Los Andes, Mérida (periodical).
Echevarría Salavat, O. A. and others, *Venezuela 1950–1967, Variables, Parameters and Methodology of the National Accounts,* 1968, Washington D.C.; IADB.
Chavez, L. F., *Sobre la base económica y la estructura funcional de las ciudades venezolanas,* 1971, Mérida, Universidad de los Andes.
Gormsen, E., *Barquisimeto, una ciudad mercantil en Venezuela,* 1963, Caracas; Editorial Arte.

Further reading

Best, R., 'Caracas develops upward', *Geogr. Mag.,* Apr. 1973, Vol. XLV, No. 7, pp. 501–5.
Harris, D. R., 'The Ecology of Swidden Cultivation in the Upper Orinoco Rain Forest, Venezuela', *Geogrl Rev.,* Oct. 1971, Vol. LXI, No. 4, pp. 475–95.
Rodwin, L., 'Ciudad Guayana: A New City', *Sci. Am.,* Sept. 1965, Vol. 213, No. 3, pp. 122–32.
'Venezuela' in *Focus* (see 3 above).

CHAPTER 15

COLOMBIA

15.1. POPULATION

Colombia covers roughly twice the area of France. It is situated between 4° S at Leticia on the Amazon and 12° N in the Guajira Peninsula and is therefore crossed by the Equator. According to the census of 1964 it had $17\frac{1}{2}$ million inhabitants in that year. The total had risen to an estimated $21\frac{3}{4}$ million in 1971 and the country currently has an annual rate of population growth of about 3·2 per cent. Population is very unevenly distributed over the national area, most of it being in a number of clusters in the north western half of the country.

In 1970 about 45 per cent of the employed population of Colombia was in agriculture (2,750,000 out of 6,085,000) and this branch of the economy accounts for about 27 per cent of gross domestic product, compared with industry which provides only 22 per cent. Per capita gross domestic product in Colombia around 1970 was only about $\frac{2}{3}$ as high as that of Venezuela but fairly close to the levels in Brazil and Peru.

There is less of a concentration of population in the national capital of Colombia, Bogotá, than in the capitals of other Latin American countries of comparable size. The Distrito Especial of Bogotá, formerly part of the Department of Cundinamarca, has 11 per cent of the total population of the country, while Greater Medellín and Cali each have about 5 per cent. All three towns are growing fast, as are most of the other larger towns of the country. There is also a shift of population into some parts of the thinly populated northern and eastern lowlands.

The latest census of Colombia at the time of writing was that of 1964 and any data published since then are only estimates. Table 15.1 shows the major civil divisions of Colombia as they were in 1967 after various changes in the mid-1960s. They are numbered as they were before 1964, and the location of the units in the older system is shown in map *a* of *Figure 15.1*. As a result of recent changes, four new Departments have been created and the former Intendencia of La Guajira has become a Department. Table 15.1, column 1, shows the small number of people in the Intendencias and Comisarias and column 5 shows their very low density of population. Table 15.2 shows towns with over 50,000 inhabitants in 1964.

The density of population in Colombia is mapped in map *c* of *Figure 15.1* on a major civil division basis and the distribution of population is shown on a topological basis in map *b*. Although Bogotá is well to the west of the centre of area of Colombia, map *b* shows that it is on the eastern side of the centre of population. The marked differences in rates of growth of population shown in column 2 of Table 15.1 are due to migration between units rather than differences in natural increase, which appears to be fairly uniform over the country. In fact, data for birthrate, deathrate and other demographic features are deficient in many parts of Colombia due to inadequate records.

Table 15.1.

COLOMBIA: AREA AND POPULATION DATA FOR MAJOR CIVIL DIVISIONS, 1967

1   Population in thousands according to the census of July 15, 1964
2   Annual rate of increase of population in persons per thousand
3   Estimate of population in 1967 in thousands
4   Area in thousands of sq.km.
5   Density of population in persons per sq.km.

	Major civil division		1 Popn. 1964	2 Growth rate	3 Popn. 1967	4 Area	5 Density
DEPARTMENTS							
1	Antioquía		2,477	35	2,737	63	44
2	Atlántico		717	40	803	3	246
(8)	Bogotá D.E.		1,697	68	2,028	2	1,278
3	Bolívar		694	35	766	26	29
4	Boyacá		1,058	21	1,122	68	17
5	Caldas		713	23	759	7	104
6	Cauca		617	24	649	30	21
(11)	César	(1967)	261	66	315	24	13
7	Córdoba		586	45	666	25	26
8	Cundinamarca		1,122	16	1,155	22	52
9	Chocó		182	25	195	47	4
10	Huila		416	27	449	20	22
I 3	La Guajira	(1964)	147	28	186	20	9
11	Magdalena		528	45	601	23	26
12	Meta		166	70	202	86	24
13	Nariño		706	19	744	31	24
(5)	Quindío	(1966)	306	22	325	2	178
(5)	Risaralda	(1966)	437	27	472	4	119
14	Norte de Santander		534	25	573	21	28
15	Santander		1,001	22	1,065	31	34
(3)	Sucre	(1966)	313	25	335	11	32
16	Tolima		841	13	870	23	37
17	Valle del Cauca		1,733	35	1,911	21	90
INTENDENCIAS							
I 1	Arauca		24	47	28	23	1
I 2	Caquetá		104	73	128	90	1
I 4	San Andrés		17	85	21	–	–
COMISARIAS							
C 1	Amazonas		13	41	14	121	0·1
C 2	Putumayo		56	54	65	26	2·5
C 3	Vaupés		13	48	15	91	0·2
C 4	Vichada		10	9	10	99	0·1
C 5	Guainía		4	48	4	78	0·1
	COLOMBIA TOTAL		17,485	32	19,215	1,139	17

Source: *Anuario General de Estadística 1966–67*
    Tomo I, p. 15

15.2. PHYSICAL FEATURES

Figure 15.2a shows the main relief features of north western Colombia.
Although Colombia lies within the tropics, much of the population lives in a
sub-tropical or temperate environment in the mountain areas of the country.
From the extreme southwest of the country the Andes, which are under 150 km

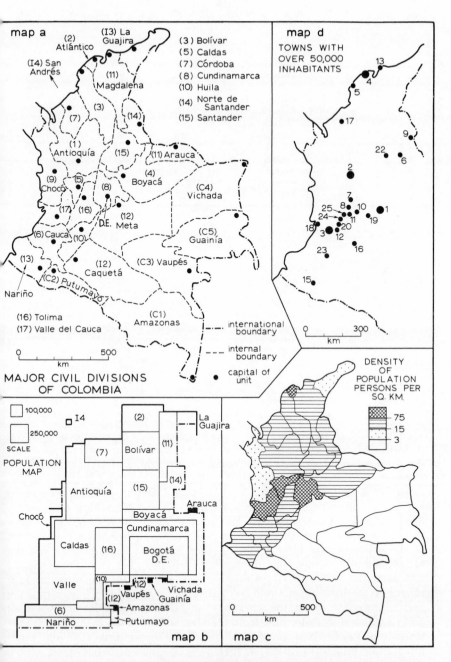

map a

(2)
Atlántico

(I3) La
Guajira

(I4) San
Andrés

(11)
Magdalena

(3) Bolívar
(5) Caldas
(7) Córdoba
(8) Cundinamarca
(10) Huila
(14) Norte de
Santander
(15) Santander

(7)

(3)

(14)

(1)
Antioquía

(15)

(11) Arauca

(9)
Chocó

(5)

(4)
Boyacá

(C4)
Vichada

(8)

(17)

(16)

(12)
D.E. Meta

(6) Cauca

(10)

(C5)
Guainía

(13)

(12)
Caquetá

(C3) Vaupés

Nariño

(C2) Putumayo

(16) Tolima
(17) Valle del Cauca

(C1)
Amazonas

international
boundary

internal
boundary

capital of
unit

0   500
km

MAJOR CIVIL DIVISIONS
OF COLOMBIA

map d

TOWNS WITH
OVER 50,000
INHABITANTS

13

4

5

17

9

22

6

2

7

8
25
24
18
3

10
11
20
12

1

19

16

23

15

0   300
km

100,000

I4

250,000

SCALE

POPULATION
MAP

(2)

La
Guajira

(7)

Bolívar

(11)

(15)

(14)

Antioquía

Chocó

Boyacá

Arauca

Cundinamarca

Caldas

(16)

Bogotá
D.E.

Valle

(10)

(12)

Vaupés

Vichada
Guainía

(6)

(12)

Amazonas

Nariño

Putumayo

map b

DENSITY
OF
POPULATION
PERSONS PER
SQ. KM.

75

15

3

0   500
km

map c

Figure 15.1. Colombia: (a) Major civil divisions, (b) Topological map, (c) Density of population, (d) Towns
with over 50,000 inhabitants (see Table 15.2)

Table 15.2.

COLOMBIA: TOWNS, WITH OVER 50,000 INHABITANTS, IN THE *CABECERA* OF THE MUNICIPIO IN 1964

		1964	*1969**
1	Bogotá D.E.	1,662	2,294
2	Medellín	718	1,196
3	Cali	618	821
4	Barranquilla	493	817
5	Cartagena	218	299
6	Bucaramanga	217	280
7	Manizales	190	268
8	Pereira	147	224
9	Cucutá	147	207
10	Ibagué	125	179
11	Armenia	125	163
12	Palmira	107	164
13	Santa Marta	89	137
14	Bello	88	(127)†
15	Pasto	83	123
16	Neiva	76	112
17	Montería	71	167
18	Buenaventura	70	113
19	Girardot	67	n.a.
20	Buga	66	n.a.
21	Itagüí	60	(101)†
22	Barrancabermija	60	n.a.
23	Popayán	59	n.a.
24	Tuluá	57	n.a.
25	Cartago	56	n.a.

* This source also lists Ciénaga (143) and Valledupar (120)
† Included with Medellín in 1969 data and on map
Sources: 1964 data: XIII Censo Nacional de Población (Julio 15 de 1964), *Resumen General*, p. 32.
1969 data: *United Nations Demographic Yearbook 1970*.

wide, but high, with two parallel ranges separated by a high plateau, open out to form for much of the length of Colombia three main ranges, called very simply the Cordillera Occidental (western), Central, and Oriental (eastern). These are separated by two depressions, the Cauca and Magdalena valleys. The crests of the western and central Cordilleras run roughly parallel, only 70–80 km apart, with summits well over 3,000 metres along most of the central one. They close at the northern extremity, only allowing the River Cauca to pass through a narrow valley to the wide lowlands to the north. Northwards the crest of the eastern range increases in distance from the central range and the Magdalena valley widens into the northern lowlands. The Cordillera Oriental widens north of Bogotá to form a high plateau with parallel but discontinuous ranges. At the Venezuelan boundary it divides, the main branch becoming the high Andes of Venezuela, the other separating the Maracaibo lowlands, a small part of which is in Colombia, from the Magdalena lowlands. A fourth range close to the Pacific coast runs roughly parallel to the western Cordillera, but is much more limited in scale. The high Sierra Nevada de Santa Marta, with a 5,800 metres high snow clad peak, stands apart from the rest of the Andes and exceeds even the highest points in the main ranges. East of the Andes almost all the land is below 500 metres but it contains upland areas as well as an isolated range south of Bogotá.

The crest of the eastern range forms the main watershed between rivers draining to the Caribbean or Pacific and those draining to the Orinoco or Amazon. Only short rivers drain to the Pacific, except in the extreme southwest, where the western range is broken and the southern continuation of the Cauca valley drains westwards. Large areas in the Magdalena and Atrato lowlands are ill-drained.

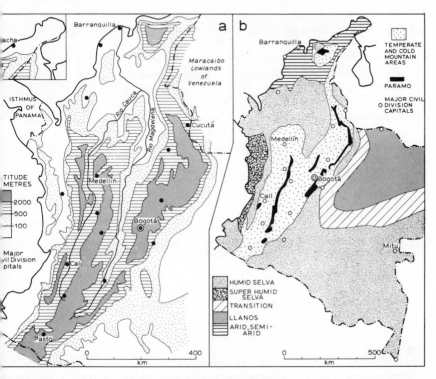

Figure 15.2. Colombia, (a) Relief, (b) Vegetation

Figures 15.2b and *15.3a* show the main vegetation types of Colombia and mean annual rainfall. The extremely complex and varied relief conditions already described produce very diverse climatic, vegetation and soil conditions. Marked changes in conditions due to altitude and to the barrier effect of the mountain ranges occur in a matter of 10–20 km in places.

Rainfall is heavy over most of Colombia and semi-arid conditions only occur locally in the north of the country and in some of the Andean valleys and basins. Elsewhere the lowlands are either covered with tropical rain forest or, in the Orinoco lowlands, llanos, with gallery forest. The Pacific coast is one of the wettest places in the world, receiving 600–700 cm of rain per year in places. The Amazon lowlands of the southeast receive less rain but are still heavily forested. The remaining variations in climate and vegetation are caused by altitude, with many of the lower slopes of the Andes clothed in mountain forest but the higher parts predominantly grassland. Lowland Colombia is hot throughout the year with a mean annual temperature around 25°C and a small annual range, but

many areas of settlement lie either in the so-called temperate zone (1,000–2,000
metres) or the cold zone (over 2,000 metres), and above about 2,000 metres
frosts may occur.

Physical conditions restricting agriculture include low temperatures, but
only in the very limited areas above about 3,000 metres, and inadequate rainfall
along the northeast coast and in some valley floors. The main obstacles have

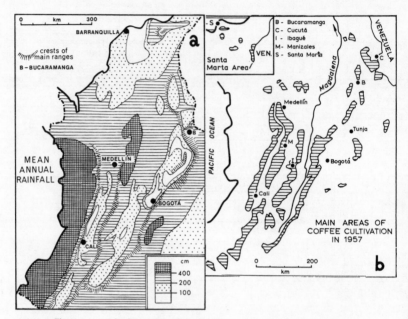

Figure 15.3. Colombia: (a) Rainfall, (b) Main areas of coffee cultivation in 1957

been steep slopes in the Andes, dense forest, poor drainage and poor soils in the
forested lowlands. In fact the agricultural possibilities of most of the surface of
Colombia have not been fully assessed yet, and the lowland areas of the country, whether grassland or forest, have so far mostly been used only to support
large herds of cattle or shifting cultivators. There is little need for irrigation
except in certain localities, but some is practised to supplement rainfall.
Physical conditions also profoundly affect the economic life in Colombia by
making movement in certain directions extremely difficult.

15.3. ECONOMIC ACTIVITIES

In spite of a decline in the relative importance of agriculture as an employer of
labour from about 70 per cent in the 1930s to 45 per cent in 1970 the absolute
number of persons working on the land has not changed much. Nearly 3
million agricultural workers use a mere 3 per cent of the total area of Colombia
for the production of field crops and another 1·5 per cent for tree crops.
Another 15 per cent of the area is classed as pasture and is used mainly for cattle
raising. Over 60 per cent of the total area of the country is forested.

During the 1960s it was hoped to extend the cultivated area in Colombia, to achieve higher yields, and to reduce dependence on coffee, the main export crop, which in the late 1960s still accounted for 60–65 per cent of the value of exports. In fact total agricultural production and food production both increased by about 40 per cent between 1960 and 1970. Mechanisation made little progress in the 1960s but the consumption of nitrate and phosphate fertilisers has been rising. Population increased by about the same percentage as agricultural production and average per capita food consumption, at the low level of 2,260 calories per day in 1960, actually dropped to 2,140 per day in 1970.

The coffee tree is grown in Colombia between a few hundred and about 2,000 metres above sea level in long narrow zones along the sides of the main ranges. The main producing Departments are Caldas, Valle del Cauca, Antioquía and Cundinamarca. The main areas of cultivation are shown in *Figure 15.3b*. Coffee is exported from the northern areas of cultivation via the Caribbean ports and from the southern area through Buenaventura. There has been a steady increase in both the area under coffee plantations (650,000 hectares in 1950 to 820,000 in 1968) and in the weight of coffee produced (350,000 tons in 1950, 510,000 tons in 1970). Colombian coffee is a mild variety, obtaining a high price abroad, and its quality is carefully preserved. The land tenure situation is satisfactory, most of the coffee being grown in family farms with a few thousand trees each. The crop is gathered throughout the year, and this places a minimum strain on the difficult transport facilities of the country.

The varied physical conditions of Colombia allow the cultivation of almost any field or tree crop and the list of crops grown commercially is very large. Conditions for cultivation are often difficult and yields are generally low even by Latin American standards. Maize, occupying about $\frac{1}{3}$ of the area under crops (700–800,000 hectares a year in the last two decades) is the principal cereal. Yields, however, increased little, though 1971 yields of 1,280 kg per hectare (cf. U.S.A. 5,450) were above the yearly average of 1,030 kg around 1950. The cultivation of rice, the second cereal of Colombia, increased in extent in the 1950s and in yields in the 1960s, and prospects for a further extension of its cultivation in the northern and eastern lowlands seem good. The areas suitable for wheat cultivation are very restricted, wheat yields are low, and most of the wheat consumed in Colombia has to be imported.

Many other food crops are grown in Colombia, including barley and potatoes in the Andes, bananas, sweet potatoes and oilseeds in the lowlands. In the last two decades there has been a steady increase in the area under sugar cane cultivation, especially in the Cauca valley, but between 1950 and 1970 average yields only increased by 10 per cent. The expansion of cotton cultivation has been even more marked, the area increasing 5 times since 1950 and production more than 10 times. Even so, most of the sugar and cotton produced in Colombia are consumed internally and in the late 1960s only cotton fibre (5 per cent of exports), bananas (4 per cent) and sugar (3 per cent) could be said to supplement coffee among agricultural exports. The large number of cattle in Colombia (14 million around 1950, 21 million in 1971), raised mainly in the northern lowlands, might with improvements in quality and management contribute to exports in the future.

Colombia has not been distinguished among the countries of Latin America for its mineral resources or production. It produces small quantities of metallic minerals and non-metals for its own use. Coal, oil and natural gas account for nearly all the value of Colombian mineral production and together with a large hydro-electric potential, give the country a solid energy base. In 1971 Colombia had about 230 million tons of proved oil reserves, enough to allow current rates of production (11 million tons in 1971) to continue for about two decades. Natural gas reserves (80 × 10⁹ cubic metres in 1971) are also considerable. Colombia also has the biggest coal reserves in Latin America and was producing about 3 million tons a year in the early 1970s. A surplus of crude oil and oil products allows Colombia to export these items, which account for about 10 per cent of the value of exports.

The oil reserves of Colombia (see *Figure 15.4b*) occur in several different parts of the country. One of the areas of production, the Barco fields, is in a continuation of the Maracaibo lowlands of Venezuela, northwest of the town of Cucutá. There are several groups of fields along the Magdalena valley, the principal one being the De Mares fields centred on Barrancabermeja. Finally, in the extreme southwest of Colombia, adjacent to the very promising area of oil reserves in Ecuador, there appear to be considerable potential reserves, as yet only partly explored. There are several oil refineries in Colombia and crude oil is piped from the oilfields to these or direct to the ports for export. Refined oil is distributed to the main urban and industrial centres by products pipelines, the three largest centres, Bogotá, Medellín and Cali being away from the oilfields.

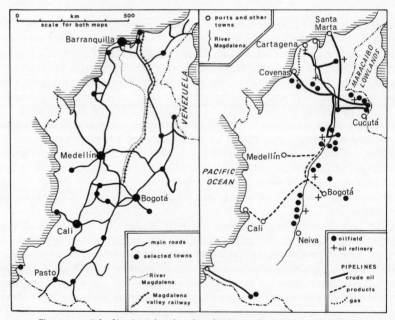

Figure 15.4. Colombia: (a) Selected roads and railways, (b) Oil fields and pipelines

In 1970 Colombia had an installed electricity generating capacity of 2,700,000 kW. Hydro-electric stations account for about 60 per cent of the capacity and 75 per cent of output. Hydro-electricity is regarded as a major source of energy for the future and it was announced in 1972[1] that five projects with a total capacity of 10 million kW and a capital cost estimated to be $ U.S. 2000 million are under study.

The process of industrialisation has continued gradually in Colombia since the end of the 19th century. Even so, Colombia in 1970 was less highly in-dustrialised than the U.S.A. in 1870.[2] The main clusters of population in the country have tended to be isolated from the outside world, the unreliable Magdalena navigation being the main link via the Caribbean ports until the Panama Canal came into use in 1918 and the port of Buenaventura could be used. Isolation to some extent protected Colombian industrialists who, ob-taining capital within the country, were able to set up light industries in Medellín and Bogotá to use primary products of the country such as cotton, wool and hides, and more recently iron ore and oil. Much of the industry of Colombia is at present concentrated in four main areas.

1. The Caribbean ports of Covenas, Cartagena, Barranquilla and Santa Marta have plants processing agricultural products, oil refineries and petrochemicals plants. The completion of the Magdalena valley railway in 1961 greatly improved access to the rest of the country and the continuing construc-tion of new roads and the paving of existing ones has given the northwestern part of the country a satisfactory system (see *Figure 15.4a*).

2. The national capital, Bogotá, is an attractive area for new industries as it has more than 10 per cent of the national population and probably over 15 per cent of the national market as well as good road and air links to other parts of Colombia. The establishment of an integrated iron and steel works at Paz del Rio, north of Bogotá, to use nearby iron ore, coal and limestone, was intended to provide a heavy industrial base for Colombia. Stagnation in production, amounting only to about 200,000 tons of pig iron and of steel per year throughout the 1960s, suggests the project is in some way unsatisfactory. Steel consumption in Colombia has been growing fast and imports have been increasing.

3 and 4. Medellín and Cali are the centres of the two other main industrial areas of Colombia. Medellín is the older centre and still specialises in the manufacture of textiles while Cali has a wide range of industries including the manufacture of paper, tyres, cement and food products.

15.4. PRESENT PROBLEMS AND FUTURE PROSPECTS

A number of studies have been made of recent trends in Colombia and future prospects. Space allows only a brief reference to some of these. For convenience specific topics have been chosen for discussion separately below.

During the 1960s much of the fairly steady economic growth in Colombia was absorbed by increasing population. In real terms the per capita income of the average Colombian was about 15 per cent higher in 1970 than in 1960. Table 15.3 shows the growth rate of gross internal product (Producto Interno Bruto) in real terms, firstly in absolute terms and then in per capita terms.[3] Between 1960 and 1968, the contribution to gross national product of agriculture and mining diminished, but that of industry hardly changed.

Population is increasing at about 3.2 per cent per year in Colombia. While there are no clear signs that the rate of population increase is slowing down ap-preciably, estimates of births and deaths[4] suggest that in the 1960s the gap

Table 15.3.

Year	Absolute	Per capita	Year	Absolute	Per capita
1960	4·3	1·1	1965	3·6	0·4
1961	5·1	1·9	1966	5·4	2·2
1962	5·4	2·2	1967	4·2	1·0
1963	3·3	0·1	1968	5·8	2·6
1964	6·2	3·0			

between birthrate and deathrate did begin to narrow. *Figure 15.5* shows that the total population of Colombia grew from under 9 million in 1938 to over 19 million in 1967. At the beginning of the period the number of extra people gained each year was about 200,000, by the end, about 600,000. Birthrate and deathrate (births and deaths per 1000 inhabitants) were fairly stable and not very far apart until 1945 when birthrate began a period of 15 years of growth while deathrate steadily declined. The most recent stage, from about 1960 to the present, is characterised by a drop in birthrate, possibly caused by the increasing urbanisation of the country and the pressure to have smaller families in urban environments.

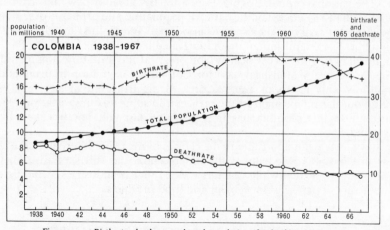

Figure 15.5. Birthrate, deathrate and total population of Colombia, 1938–1967

There is considerable local and interregional movement in Colombia.[5] In Table 15.4, the percentage of population of a given Department born in other Departments (column 6) is an indication of the attraction of certain regions compared with others. Cundinamarca (area 8) includes Bogotá (D.E.), and the capital itself has been the focus of migration rather than the predominantly rural areas of the Department surrounding it. Valle de Cauca, with the town of Cali, is a secondary focus while Barranquilla attracts population from several northern Departments. Medellín draws population mainly from its own Department of Antioquía. A. Gilbert[2] has identified two main directions of flow in Colombia, one directly from rural areas to the larger urban centres and one from various parts of the country to empty areas in Meta and some of the Intendencias and Comisarias. He considers the migration to be mainly economic in motive.

1,2   Employment in agriculture (1) and in manufacturing (2) as a percentage of total economically active population
3   Literate males over the age of 7 years as a percentage of all males over 7
4   Persons with secondary education as a percentage of all persons with education
5   Urban population as a percentage of total population
6   Population born in other Departments as a percentage of total population
7   Population change 1951–64, percentage increase
8   Deaths with a medical certificate as a percentage of all deaths
9   New bank loans in pesos per capita in 1962

		1 Agr.	2 Mf.	3 Lit.	4 Edn.	5 Urb.	6 Migr.	7 Change	8 Cert.	9 Banks
1	Antioquiá	45	15	74	12	55	7	35	76	360
2	Atlántico	16	24	79	14	94	23	40	83	456
3	Bolívar	54	7	55	10	60	8	32	63	156
4	Boyacá	68	7	67	6	18	7	21	34	57
5	Caldas	53	10	76	11	56	18	24	61	227
6	Cauca	72	5	63	5	22	11	24	27	77
7	Córdoba	68	6	45	7	32	9	45	39	125
8	Cundinamarca[1]	25	17	83	17	70	35	43	85	884
9	Chocó	64	3	45	6	22	8	25	23	8
10	Huila	61	8	63	8	41	15	27	38	178
11	Magdalena	61	8	57	9	54	18	51	48	217
12	Meta	64	6	71	7	45	53	70	61	388
13	Nariño	59	16	65	6	27	2	19	28	61
14	Norte de Santander	52	10	65	10	49	9	25	50	195
15	Santander	52	12	67	9	42	10	22	43	207
16	Tolima	61	7	66	7	43	14	13	40	155
17	Valle del Cauca	32	15	79	11	71	33	35	80	400
I1	Arauca	69	5	63	5	30	29	47	n.a.	n.a.
I2	Caquetá	75	4	57	5	25	56	73	n.a.	n.a.
I3	La Guajira	59	8	42	9	39	7	28	66	n.a.
C1	Amazonas	53	7	69	9	31	18	41	n.a.	n.a.
C2	Putumayo	68	3	72	4	19	47	54	n.a.	n.a.
C3	Vaupés	87	2	40	3	12	10	48	n.a.	n.a.
C4	Vichada	79	1	32	7	0	27	n.a.	n.a.	n.a.
	COLOMBIA	47	13	70	11	53	18	32	60	327

• Includes Bogotá D.E.

Sources: XIII Censo Nacional de Población (Julio 15 de 1964), *Resumen General*, Bogotá 1967
Columns: 1, 2, pp. 124–5; 3. pp. 74–7; 4. pp. 80–3; 5. p. 41; 6, pp. 52–6.
Anuario General de Estadística 1966–67, Tomo I Column: 8, p. 44.
Anuario General de Estadística 1962, Bogotá 1964, p. 496.
Column 9.

As in other Latin American countries big differences in per capita income exist both between classes and between regions. Various data suggest, however, that disparities are not so marked as in Brazil, Mexico, Venezuela or Peru. This feature seems to be due to the lack of one dominant urban centre or leading region in the country. The data in Table 15.4 show nevertheless that regional disparities do exist and that there appear to be strong correlations between backwardness (e.g. in education in columns 3 and 4) and dependence on agriculture (column 1). The three distributions in *Figure 15.6* show that variables 3 (literacy), 8 (medical services as represented by issue of death certificates) and 9 (bank deposits) tell roughly the same story about the regional distribution of wealth in Colombia. They suggest two broad influences, the advantages of a central position in the country and the influence of urban population.

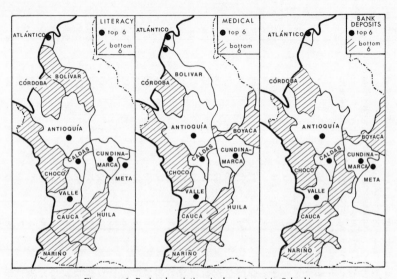

Figure 15.6. Regional variations in development in Colombia

In a more detailed study of municipios in the Department of Antioquía, A. Gilbert[6] identified two similar associations, firstly a reduction in the level of development with distance from Medellín and secondly a relationship between level of development and presence of urban population. The maldistribution of services in Colombia is further illustrated by data for the availability of dentists and doctors in Colombia.[7] Table 15.5 shows the number of persons per doctor and per dentist according to the population size of the municipio capital. In the largest cities there are more doctors than required. Many work only part time as doctors. In small towns and rural areas doctors are far too few.

There has been increasing concern over two aspects of Colombian foreign trade, firstly the heavy dependence on coffee exports and secondly the small per capita value of trade. Colombia started a Four Year Plan (1971–74)[8] to increase export diversification by expanding trade in 'non-traditional exports'. For example it is proposed to raise textile and clothing exports ($ U.S. 20 million in

1971 to $ U.S. 50 million in 1974). Meat and cattle worth $ U.S. 70 million should be exported in 1974. Such export products as chemicals and petrochemicals, metal products, wood and furniture, leather and shoes would also figure in the plan. In the longer term, Colombia hopes to reach an agreement with Brazil to develop its resources of coking coal and to produce 10 million tons a year by 1980. It has a copper deposit (625 million tons of ore) at Pantanos 120 km northwest of Medellín that could also contribute to exports.

Table 15.5.

Size	Persons per	
	Doctor	Dentist
Over 500,000	700	2,500
100–500	1,300	4,300
50–100	1,700	8,500
30–50	3,100	8,100
20–30	3,300	12,300
15–20	3,300	10,500
10–15	4,100	14,700

The trend towards exporting processed and manufactured goods is likely to bring further prosperity to urban areas at the expense of many rural areas, such as those in the south of Colombia, unable to diversify agriculture or attract industry.

References

1. *Bolsa Review*, Oct. 1972, Vol. 6, 'Urban Growth and Industrial Development: The Colombian Case', No. 70, p. 573.
2. Gilbert, A., IGU Commission on Regional Aspects of Economic Development, Rio de Janeiro, 1971.
3. *Planes y programas de desarrollo 1969/72*. República de Colombia, Departamento Nacional de Planeación, Doc. DNP 417, 1 Diciembre, 1969, p. 1.1.
4. Departamento Administrativo Nacional de Estadística, *Anuario General de Estadística, Población, Asistencia Social e Higiene*, Tomo I, p. 16.
5. See 2.
6. Gilbert, A., 'The Spatial Distribution of Social Variables in Antioquía, Colombia', *Discussion Paper* No. 38, Graduate School of Geography, London School of Economics.
7. Gilbert, A., in talk at seminar in the Centre for Latin American Studies, Liverpool University, 2 Mar. 1973.
8. *Peruvian Times*, Oct. 8, 1971 and Aug. 25, 1972.

Sources of material in the figures

15.2 Based on maps in *Atlas de economía colombiana* (see full details below).
15.3 (a) as for 15.2.
15.5 as for reference 4 above.

Further sources consulted

Departamento Administrativo Nacional de Estadística,
   a) XIII Censo Nacional de Población (Julio 15 de 1964), *Resumen General*, Bogota, 1967

b) *Anuario General de Estadística,* 1962, Bogota, 1964
c) *Informe al Congreso 1971.*

Further reading

'Colombia, The Development of Tourism', *Bolsa Review,* July 1973, Vol. 7, No. 79.

Gilbert, A., 'Stagnant Schooling in Rural Colombia', *Geogr. Mag.,* Oct. 1972, Vol. XLV, No. 1, pp. 8–12.

Sandilands, R. J., 'The Modernisation of the Agricultural Sector, and Rural-Urban Migration in Colombia', *Occasional Papers,* University of Glasgow, No. 1, 1971.

Shlemon, R. J. and Phelps, L. B., 'Dredge-Tailing Agriculture on the Rio Nechí, Colombia, *Geogrl Rev.,* July 1971, Vol. LXI, No. 3, pp. 396–414.

CHAPTER 16

PERU

16.1. INTRODUCTION

Peru is situated on the western side of South America between the Equator and 18°S. Although it lies well within the tropics, about half of its population lives in temperate conditions at altitudes of more than 2000 metres above sea level. Most of the remainder lives in the coastal region which for several months in the year has temperatures that are anomalously cool for the latitude. Peru is about 2½ times as large in area as France and over 5 times as large as the United Kingdom. The 1972 census figure for the population of the country was 13,570,000. About 60 per cent of the population is urban according to the census definition, compared with only 35 per cent in 1940. In the early 1970s pop-. ulation was growing at about 3·1 per cent per year (birthrate 42 per 1000, deathrate 11 per 1000).

The main map in *Figure 16.1* shows the major civil divisions of Peru, the Departments (Callao has the special status of Provincia Constitucional). The area, the 1972 population and the density of population of the 24 units are given in Table 16.1. The uneven distribution of population over the national area can be seen from the contrasts in density of population in column 3. The interior Department of Loreto has only about 1 person per sq. km. compared with the Department of Lima, containing the capital, with over 100 persons per sq. km. The topological diagram, map *b* in *Figure 16.1,* shows clearly the concentration of population in the area of Lima, which, with its port Callao, had about ⅕ of the population of Peru in 1972. Table 16.2 contains all towns in Peru with over 40,000 inhabitants in 1972. Greater Lima had in that year about twice as many inhabitants as the next 15 towns combined.

In 1970 the total gross domestic product of Peru was $ U.S. 5,440 million, or 400 dollars per capita. In that year the corresponding U.K. figures were $ U.S. 119,200 million and 2,140 dollars per capita. In *Figure 16.2*, England and Wales is drawn on the same scale as Peru. To appreciate the meaning of the values in dollars given above it helps to realise that the two English counties of Derbyshire and Nottinghamshire, the small shaded area on the inset map of the U.K. in *Figure 16.2,* produce roughly the same value of goods and services as the whole of Peru, though the composition of these is very different. If the two counties were 'inflated' to the size of Peru, everything would be extremely thinly spread on the ground.

The total number of persons employed in Peru in 1970 was about 4,050,000, less than ⅓ of the total population in that year. The labour force of about 1,850,000 in agriculture was 46 per cent of the total, a proportion very similar to that found in Mexico, Brazil and Colombia but far above the comparable figures for Venezuela and Chile (about 25 per cent) or Argentina (about 15 per cent). Although agriculture employs such a large part of total population in

Peru, it only accounted in 1971 for about 18 per cent of total gross domestic product, compared with 30 per cent from industry and 52 per cent from all kinds of tertiary activities including construction. Although the per capita gross domestic product of Peru is some way below the average for Latin America of 550 dollars in 1970 it has become less dependent on agriculture than most

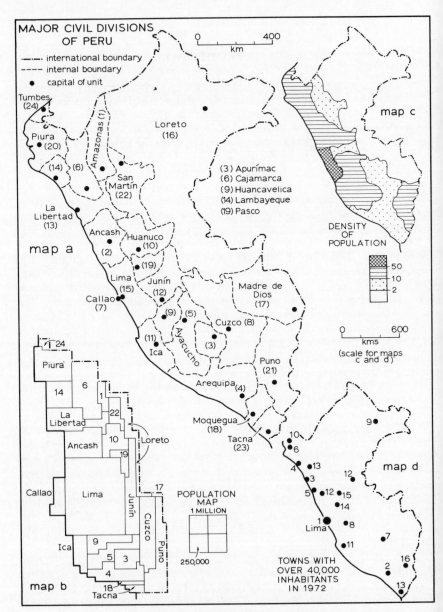

Figure 16.1. Peru: (a) Major civil divisions, (b) Topological map, (c) Density of population, (d) Towns with over 40,000 inhabitants (see Table 16.2)

Table 16.1.

PERU: AREA AND POPULATION DATA

1   Area in thousands of sq. km.
2   Population in thousands, 4 June 1972
3   Density of population, persons per sq. km.

		1 Area	2 Popn.	3 Dens.			1 Area	2 Popn.	3 Dens.
1	Amazonas	41	197	5	14	Lambayeque	17	515	30
2	Ancash	36	727	20	15	Lima	34	3,485	103
3	Apurímac	21	308	15	16	Loreto	478	495	1
4	Arequipa	64	531	8	17	Madre de Dios	78	22	0·3
5	Ayacucho	44	460	10	18	Moquegua	16	75	5
6	Cajamarca	35	916	26	19	Pasco	22	177	8
7	Callao	*	316	†	20	Piura	33	855	26
8	Cuzco	76	713	9	21	Puno	74	780	11
9	Huancavelica	21	331	16	22	San Martín	53	224	4
10	Huánuco	35	421	12	23	Tacna	15	96	6
11	Ica	21	358	17	24	Tumbes	5	75	15
12	Junín	43	691	16					
13	La Libertad	23	806	35		PERU TOTAL	1,285	13,572	10·6

* Only 76 sq. km in area
** Very high

Source: Población del Perú, Censo del 4 de Junio, 1972, *Resultados Provisionales*

Table 16.2.

PERU: POPULATION IN THOUSANDS OF TOWNS WITH OVER 40,000 INHABITANTS IN 1972

1	Lima-Callao	3,318	10	Sullana	88
2	Arequipa	305	11	Ica	74
3	Trujillo	242	12	Callaría*	58
4	Chiclayo	190	13	Tacna	56
5	Chimbote	159	14	Cerro de Pasco	47
6	Piura	140	15	Huánuco	41
7	Cuzco	121	16	Puno	41
8	Huancayo	116			
9	Iquitos	111			

* Formerly Pucallpa
Source as for Table 16.1.

developing countries in Africa and Asia. Its problems are more acute in some respects than those of most Latin American countries but basically it can be taken to exemplify all underdeveloped countries.

16.2. THE THREE REGIONS OF PERU

It is no criticism of air services in Peru to draw attention to three air crashes that occurred there in a matter of a few months in 1955 to illustrate three different physical environments. One aircraft crashed in the tropical forest of the interior of Peru and was never found. Another aircraft crashed into a snowfield on the side of a mountain in the Cordillera Blanca, the scene in 1970 of a disastrous avalanche; the plane has never been reached but can still be seen. A third aircraft crashed in the coastal desert region and was located by rescuers, but they found difficulty reaching it due to the absence of roads in the area.

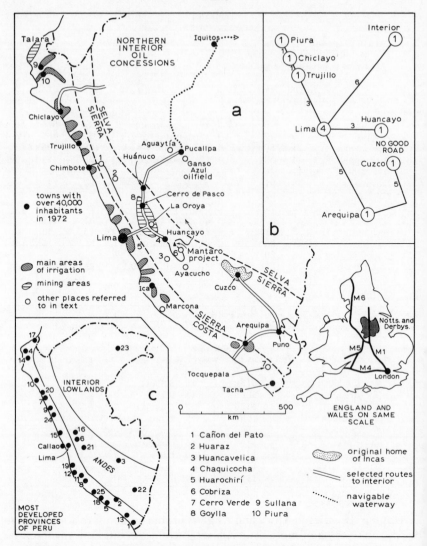

Figure 16.2. Peru: (a) General location map showing places referred to in the text. (Note that England and Wales are on the scale of the main map (a)), (b) See Table 16.3, (c) Provinces in Table 16.11

To many Peruvians it is self-evident that their country is divided into three distinct regions, the coast (*costa*), Andes (*sierra*) and Amazon lowlands (*selva*). Such a threefold division is convenient but oversimplified. It will be used as a basis for a geographical description of Peru in this section but with reservations. Firstly, on the physical side there are considerable transition zones between the coastal desert region, the mountain environment of the Andes and the forest or savanna covered lowlands of the interior. Secondly, cultural and economic conditions vary greatly within each of the three regions. Recently, in view of the great economic importance of fishing, there has been reference to a fourth major region, the coastal waters of Peru, and it would not be difficult to justify a fifth one, the Greater Lima area.

In *Figure 16.3* the main relief features of Peru are shown in map *a* and vegetation types in map *b*. The great altitude of the Andes in Peru can be appreciated from the fact that except in the extreme north, all roads and railways from the coastal region to places beyond the Western Cordillera of the Andes, the Pacific-Atlantic watershed, cross passes in excess of 4,000 metres. Many towns in the Andes are over 3,000 metres above sea level. Although there are some areas of plateau, as around Lake Titicaca in the south and Huancayo in the centre, intervening areas are very rugged and on the eastern flanks, rivers run in deep valleys and gorges parallel to the Andes. There are many peaks above 5,000 metres.

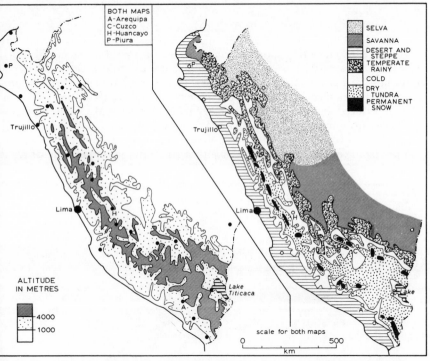

Figure 16.3. Relief and vegetation in Peru. Department capitals are shown on both maps, but as open circles on the vegetation map

The coastal region of Peru is one of the driest regions in the world. Lima itself averages only about 4 cm of rain a year. Cultivation is possible only with the help of water from the many rivers flowing from the Andes into the Pacific. Rainfall in the Andes is highest in the north and on the interior side and low in the south where desert conditions extend to a high altitude on the Pacific side. It is seasonal, but where relief, soil and temperature conditions are suitable, usually adequate for agriculture and grazing.

On the interior side of the Andes, rainfall is very heavy on the flanks of the mountains and the area called the *ceja de la montaña* (eyebrow of the montaña) is heavily forested, unlike the rest of the Andes which has a grassland or tundra vegetation. The Amazon lowland is often referred to, confusingly, as the *montaña* (mountain in Spanish). To Peruvians the term suggests forest, also described as selva. Most of the interior lowland of Peru is covered with dense tropical rain forest but in the extreme southeast the vegetation is more open. Some idea of the complexity of the distribution of different types of climatic and vegetation conditions can be gained from map *b* in *Figure 16.3*.

The relative importance of the regions of Peru has changed through time (see *Figure 1.4* on page 11). In pre-Columbian times, civilisations have flourished for thousands of years in both coastal and Andean regions, though apparently not in the Amazon region. Towards the end of pre-Columbian times, the Incas dominated Peru from Cuzco in the southern Andes and arable farming, grazing, mining and domestic industries were found wherever people could settle in either region.

During the colonial period the Andean region was the part of the Viceroyalty of Peru that most interested the Spaniards on account of its many mineral deposits. Although the capital of Peru was at Lima on the coast and other colonial towns existed in various coastal oases, much effort was spent in establishing towns and mines in the Andes. In the 19th and 20th centuries the Andes have declined in relative importance, as a whole range of new products greatly reduced the relative importance of the precious metals of Peru. Among the newer products are guano, fish and more recently fishmeal from the Pacific *(Figure 16.4)*, cotton and sugar from the coastal oases, and oil, iron ore and copper from coastal mining areas. Even the Amazon region came to life for a

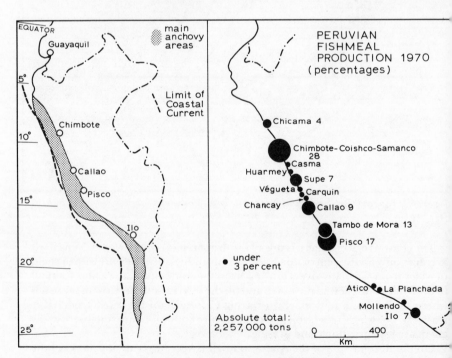

Figure 16.4. Peru: Fisheries and fishmeal processing

time during the period of gathering of wild rubber around 1900. In the Second
World War the U.S.A. became interested in tropical forest products, after the
Japanese occupation of Southeast Asia, and interest in the selva region revived.
The Andean region has declined relatively throughout the modern period,
maintaining for export only a production of non-ferrous metals from the Cen-
tral Andes and a surplus of some pastoral and arable products.

In the early 1970s the coastal region provided about 80 per cent of the value
of Peruvian exports and had most of the industries while the Andes had become
one of the poorest regions of Latin America, its predominantly agricultural
population making a living from the land in difficult physical conditions with
primitive methods and limited opportunities for improvement. The selva
region remains one of considerable potential not only for its timber but also
because it apparently has considerable oil reserves.

1. AGRICULTURE

In 1970 about 2,400,000 hectares of land or 2 per cent of the total area of Peru
was arable and about 200,000 hectares were under tree crops. About 1 million
hectares are irrigated, including virtually all the land in the coastal region.
There is very little cultivated land in the Amazon region. About 27 million hectares of land in Peru are classified as pastures, mostly in the Andes, while 87
million hectares, over $\frac{2}{3}$ of the total area of Peru, is forested.

Where water is available for irrigation, conditions are excellent for
agriculture in the coastal region of Peru. Water supply is reasonably reliable,
land flat or gently sloping, soil fertile and temperatures, which rarely drop
below 10°C, are hot enough for the cultivation of sub-tropical or temperate
crops. Until recently much of the land in the coastal oases was in big holdings,
some foreign owned. Sugar and cotton are grown for export as well as home
consumption and thanks to the generous use of both nitrate and phosphate fertilisers, yields are very high. Peruvian yields of sugar cane are three times the
world average, which is also the Latin American average, and cotton yields
twice the world average. Sugar cane, occupying about 50,000 hectares, is grown
especially in the oases around Trujillo. Cotton, occupying about 150,000 hectares, is grown throughout the coastal region. Rice, mainly around Chiclayo,
maize, alfalfa, and, to the south of Lima, the vine, are also grown. Cattle are
raised in the coastal region primarily for meat or dairy produce rather than as
work animals, and agriculture is fairly highly mechanised.

The main drawback of agriculture in the coastal region is the high cost of
extending cultivation. Many rivers still have water that might be used for irrigation before it reaches the sea, but dams and canals have to be constructed to
make it available. Already at least three tunnels bring water from the
headwaters of the Amazon under the main watershed of the Andes to feed rivers
on the Pacific side.

Cultivation in the Andes is practised in a large number of small, relatively
favourable regions separated by vast areas of poor pasture or waste land.
Reasonably flat areas are found on the shores of Lake Titicaca and in the Mantaro valley around Huancayo. In other places, valley side river terraces, narrow
valley floors and even steep mountain sides, partially terraced, are cultivated to
the limit. Rainfall in the Andes tends to be unreliable, frosts are a hazard at

higher altitudes and soil on steep slopes is easily washed away. Access to many villages is still only on foot or by pack animal. In many parts of the Andes land is very unevenly divided among the farm population.

Altogether, then, conditions for agriculture tend to be very difficult in the Andean region and yields of the main crops, maize at lower altitudes, barley, wheat and potatoes in higher areas are generally low. Cattle, sheep, goats and llamas are kept not only for meat and dairy produce to be sold outside the region but also for hides and wool and as transport and ploughing animals.

On the interior slopes of the Andes, coffee, the coca shrub and tea can be cultivated. Where conditions permit, the interior lowlands of Peru can be used to grow the rubber tree and the oil palm, bananas and various other tropical plants as well as manioc, and fodder for livestock. It is appreciated, however, that the scope for growing field crops is limited.

During the 1960s, the agricultural production of Peru increased by about 30 per cent, while the number of persons employed in agriculture changed little. Food production increased by 40 per cent, but consumption at the low level of an average of 2,200 calories per inhabitant per day remained steady. While it is accepted that further improvements are needed in agriculture in Peru it is difficult to know where to invest limited capital. As long as there is scope for extending irrigation in coastal areas this seems the best way of increasing production. Land tenure conditions and educational levels in the Andes are unsatisfactory in many places, roads poor and physical conditions marginal. It is costly to transport fertilisers into the region, not feasible to manufacture them there, and risky to use them when they might be wasted or misused. Indiscriminate mechanisation could increase the problems in the Andes by reducing the number of jobs. The Amazon region remains difficult to develop for agriculture both on account of physical conditions and through its remoteness. Plans in the 1950s to use the selva region more fully by resettling Andean farmers there and by building a marginal highway to open up the region had apparently been abandoned in the early 1970s.

2. ENERGY, MINING AND MANUFACTURING

Until the late 1960s Peru had a surplus of oil for export but by 1971 energy consumption exceeded production. Oil remains the main source of energy in Peru but the old oilfields of the extreme north coastal area, owned by International Petroleum Co. before being taken over by the Peruvian government in 1969, were already well on the way to becoming exhausted. In fact new finds both in the northern coastal area and in the interior (see *Figure 16.5*) seem likely to extend Peruvian reserves far beyond the 70 million tons of proved reserves quoted for 1971 against an annual production of about 3 million tons. As in Colombia and Ecuador it will be necessary to build a pipeline to take the oil over the Andes to the coast. Peru also has reserves of natural gas, put at 85×10^9 cubic metres in 1971 against a small production of 0.5×10^9 in that year. There appear to be large reserves in the area of Aguaytía in the Amazon region (see *Figure 16.2*).

Peru only has a small output of coal, mainly from a coalfield at Goylla associated with the Cerro de Pasco mines. Its proved reserves are 200 million tons but there are thought to be much bigger reserves of both coal and lignite.

About ⅔ of the output of electricity comes from hydro-electric stations and their annual output of about 3 × 10⁹ kWh is equivalent to the amount of electricity that would be generated by 2 million tons of coal. The largest hydro-electric power stations in use in Peru in the early 1970s are at Huallanca (Cañon del

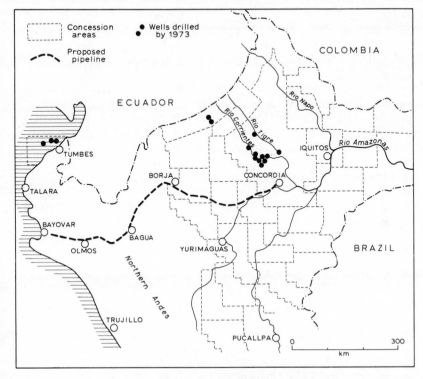

Figure 16.5. Oil concessions and oilfields in northern Peru

Pato in the Northern Andes) and in the Andes behind Lima. Delays have prevented the completion of the ambitious Mantaro project (see *Figure 16.2*), which eventually should supply both the adjoining Andean region and Lima. The Andean region has altogether a very large hydro-electric potential but the best sites are remote from existing communications and centres of consumption.

3. OTHER MINERALS

There is a large number of mining areas and mines in Peru but much of the production comes from a few localities. One of the principal mining towns is Cerro de Pasco, which produces non-ferrous metal ores, smelted at La Oroya before export. Cobriza is another place in the Andes with non-ferrous metals. Tocquepala in southern Peru has one of the largest copper mines in the world. In the same area, the Cerro Verde copper deposit is also to be exploited. On the coast at Marcona Peru has large desposits of high grade iron ore. Peru produces about $\frac{1}{8}$ of the world's silver, 6 per cent of the world's zinc (300,000 tons), 5 per cent of the world's lead (150,000 tons) and 3 per cent of the world's copper (200,000 tons) as well as about 10 million tons of iron ore. Typically it exports to the industrial countries virtually all these minerals either as pure ore, pelletelised or refined. It in no way benefits from adding value to the raw materials except in the manufacture of silver and the production of small quantities of pig iron and steel. The value of gold production is now very small.

4. MANUFACTURING

Peru has made less progress in industrialisation than the other large Latin American countries. Much of its industrial capacity is in fact concerned with processing food and raw materials either for export or for home use. The coastal region has virtually all the capacity of the country for oil refining, fishmeal production, cotton ginning and sugar refining and has the only iron and steel works in the country at Chimbote. Most light manufacturing and the relatively recent engineering industry are in Lima and Callao, though there have been plans to put new industries in other big towns of the coastal region.

5. LOCATION

From what has been said it is evident that the coastal region has better conditions for agriculture than the Andean region, one of the world's richest fishing areas, and many of the mineral resources of Peru. It also has most of the modern industrial capacity and in Lima, many of the administrative, educational, military and other non-goods sectors of the economy. The coastal region has at least one other major advantage over the other two regions of Peru, that of favourable position or location, an attribute that is difficult to assess numerically. Table 16.3 and diagram *b* in *Figure 16.2* are intended to

Table 16.3.
HYPOTHETICAL TRANSPORT COSTS IN PERU

Every journey to Lima is made four times

	P	C	T	L	I	H	A	C	TOTAL
Piura	0	1	2	20	11	8	10	15	67
Chiclayo	1	0	1	16	10	7	9	14	58
Trujillo	2	1	0	12	9	6	8	13	51
Lima	5	4	3	0	6	3	5	10	36
Interior	11	10	9	24	0	9	11	16	90
Huancayo	8	7	6	12	9	0	8	13	63
Arequipa	10	9	8	20	11	8	0	5	71
Cuzco	15	14	13	40	16	13	5	0	106

show in a very simple way what favourable position means in Peru and how an index can be worked out. It should be remembered, however, that to a self-supporting community such as an isolated agricultural valley, spatial position in the national context matters little. The greater the interdependence between regions, the greater the movement of goods, people and information between them, the more critical to the development and success of a region its position becomes.

In the example illustrated in *Figure 16.2b* and Table 16.3 a hypothetical factory, producing for the national market, has to deliver products to eight areas, represented by the circles. The amount to be delivered to Lima–Callao is four times as great as the amount to any of the other places. Transport costs are shown along each link between the nodes. Table 16.3 shows the total cost of delivering 11 loads of goods from a hypothetical factory at each of the 8 places shown. Lima-Callao is the most favourable or accessible location, Cuzco the least favourable. Places in coastal Peru have an additional advantage over the rest of the country in being close to seaports and links with other countries.

Some features of the communications network of Peru are shown in *Figure 16.6*. The rail network is of limited extent and importance, serving mainly to provide links between the coast and parts of the Central and Southern Andes. Most of the movement of goods and passengers in Peru is on the road system, shown in the main map. Although Lima is located on one side of the area of Peru, it is 'central' in the road system being on the Pan-American highway along the coast. In view of the lack of an all-weather road along the Andes many journeys between places in different parts of the Andes follow routes down to the coast, along the coastal highway and into the Andes again. However inadequate the highway system of Peru in linking centres in the Andes and interior by direct good quality roads it has been a remarkable achievement (with resources equal to those of a couple of English counties) to provide so many motor roads; there are many additional local roads not actually shown on the map.

The 'central' position of Lima in the communications network of Peru is especially noticeable in the system of internal airlines. Only the services of one company, Faucett, are shown. Other services follow a similar pattern. Any journey between southern and northern Peru has to be broken in Lima, which is the centre of a radial system of services. Only in the north are certain secondary centres linked by regular services.

From what has been said about the three regions of Peru in this section it is evident that some places are more favoured than others. Relative advantage is a combination of various features. Four sets of influences may be identified, firstly the nature of the population/resource balance, secondly the educational level of the population, thirdly the kind of job available and fourthly position in the national context. It will be shown in the next section that these influences contribute to explain differences in levels of development in Peru at Department level and at Province level.

16.3. REGIONAL DIFFERENCES IN PERU

With the help of P. M. Mather,[1] the author has applied factor analysis to the study of regional problems in Peru. Several sets of data, both at Department and at Province level, have been studied. In this section some of the data and some of the findings are discussed. Unfortunately treatment has to be brief and superficial but it is hoped that the possibilities of such studies will be appreciated by the reader. The following studies are referred to:

1. 1972 demographic data for the Departments
2. Various Department data from the 1961 census and more recent years
3. Province data from the 1961 census
4. Province data from the 1961 census with additional data and oblique factor analysis.

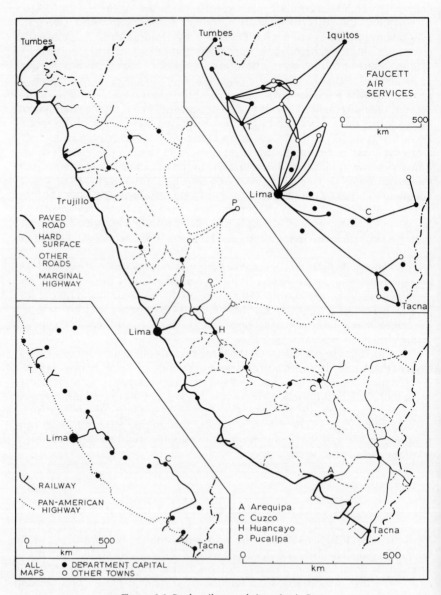

Figure 16.6. Roads, railways and air services in Peru

STUDY 1

Table 16.4 contains 1972 population data for the Departments of Peru. The Departments have been placed in five groups, A–E, shown below the main table.

Columns 1–3 show population in thousands at the time of the three most recent censuses. The Department of Lima contains a considerable area in the Andes as well as along the coast.

Columns 4–5 show relative and absolute population change in the Departments during 1940–72. In column 4, 1940 population equals 100. In column 5, absolute growth is in thousands. The two fastest growing areas during 1940–72 were Lima-Callao and the interior Department of Madre de Dios. About 40 per cent of the absolute growth of population took place in Lima-Callao, due to increasing flows of migrants from other regions during the period in question.

Columns 6–7 show relative and absolute population changes during 1961–72, data being represented as in columns 4 and 5. Over 40 per cent of the absolute gain took place in Lima–Callao.

Columns 8–9 show the percentage of the total population of Peru in each Department in 1940 and in 1972. A comparison of the two columns shows which Departments have gained and which have lost relatively. Since the rate of natural increase probably does not vary greatly from one region to another the changes in relative share of population in columns 8 and 9 are due largely to migration between Departments. The main flow has been from the Andean area to Lima–Callao. The share of the population of Peru in the former dropped from about 50 per cent to 35 per cent in three decades while the share of the latter grew from 15 per cent to 28 per cent. There have been secondary relative gains in the rest of the coast and in the interior. In spite of the net flows of migrants from the Andes the overall population figure for the region in 1972 was 4¾ million compared with 3 million in 1940. Actual decreases of population in the Andes have only been of a local nature.

Columns 10–11 show the total population and the percentage living in towns with more than 10,000 inhabitants.

STUDY 2

Table 16.5 contains data for 22 variables summarising physical, economic, demographic, social and financial aspects of the 24 Departments of Peru. Two drawbacks in the nature of the data in this study must be noted. Firstly, most data are for 1961 but some variables are for later years. It seems reasonable to assume that the *relative* positions of the Departments on the later data are not very different from what they were in 1961. Secondly, on the 'coarse' scale of the network of Departments, the same Department may contain very different kinds of physical and social conditions. For example Ancash (2) includes provinces in the coastal zone, in the Callejón de Huaylas and in the interior of the Andes. An average value for the whole Department is not characteristic of any of the areas. This second drawback is partly removed in studies based on data for the 144 provinces in 1961.

CHACAYAN, CENTRAL ANDES

SMELTER AND HOUSING, LA OROYA, CENTRAL ANDES

• *Chacayán and La Oroya Central Andes*

Rural housing in Huallay and Chaquicocha, Central Andes

Table 16.4.

PERU: 1972 POPULATION DATA

		1	2	3	4	5	6	7	8	9	10 Towns gt. 10,000	11 Towns gt. 10,000
		1940	1961	1972	1940-72 Rel.	1940-72 Abs.	1961-72 Rel.	1961-72 Abs.	Pct. 1940	Popn 1972	Popn	Pct.
1	E Amazonas	65	118	197	301	131	166	78	1·1	1·4	10	5
2	C Ancash	425	583	727	171	302	125	144	6·8	5·4	201	28
3	D Apurímac	258	288	308	119	50	107	196	4·2	2·3	12	4
4	C Arequipa	263	389	531	202	267	136	142	4·2	3·9	331	62
5	D Ayacucho	359	411	460	128	101	112	49	5·8	3·4	43	9
6	D Cajamarca	494	747	916	185	422	123	169	8·0	6·8	52	6
7	A Callao	82	214	316	383	233	148	102	1·3	2·3	316	100
8	D Cuzco	487	612	713	146	226	146	101	7·8	5·2	145	20
9	D Huancavelica	245	303	331	135	87	109	28	3·9	2·4	16	5
10	D Huánuco	234	329	421	180	187	128	92	3·8	3·1	61	14
11	B Ica	141	256	358	254	217	140	102	2·3	2·6	136	38
12	D Junín*	316	521	691	219	375	133	170	5·1	5·1	184	27
13	C La Libertad	383	582	806	211	423	139	224	6·2	5·9	364	45
14	B Lambayeque	193	342	515	267	323	151	173	3·1	3·8	287	56
15	A Lima	828	2,031	3,485	421	2,657	172	1,454	13·3	25·7	3,137	90
16	E Loreto	169	337	495	293	326	147	158	2·7	3·6	186	38
17	E Madre de Dios	5	15	22	440	17	148	7	0·1	0·2	0	0
18	C Moquegua	34	52	75	218	40	145	23	0·6	0·6	39	52
19	D Pasco	113	138	177	156	64	128	38	1·8	1·3	47	27
20	B Piura	409	669	855	209	446	128	186	6·6	6·3	321	38
21	D Puno	548	686	780	144	231	114	93	8·8	5·7	79	11
22	E San Martín	95	162	224	237	130	139	63	1·5	1·7	31	14
23	C Tacna	36	66	96	263	59	145	30	0·6	0·7	56	58
24	A Tumbes	26	56	75	293	50	135	20	0·4	0·6	33	44
	PERU TOTAL	6,208	9,907	13,572	219	7,364	137	3,665	100·0	100·0	6,178	46
A	Lima-Callao	911	2,247	3,801	418	2,890	169	1,554	14·7	28·0	3,453	93
B	Rest of coast	742	1,267	1,728	233	986	136	461	11·9	12·7	744	43
C	Intermediate	1,142	1,671	2,334	205	1,192	140	663	18·4	17·2	991	42
D	Andean	3,054	4,036	4,796	157	1,742	119	760	49·2	35·3	639	13
E	Interior	334	632	938	281	604	148	306	5·4	6·9	227	24

* In 1940 Pasco was part of Junín, 1940 population is estimated.

No attempt is made here to justify the inclusion of each of the 22 variables in Table 16.5. Some reflect social conditions and problems characteristic of developing countries (15, literacy, 11, lack of hospital facilities) while others are peculiar to the Andes (17, chewing of coca).

The 22 variables in Table 16.5 were correlated, but the correlation matrix is not included here. Most of the variables correlated highly with one of the first three factors that were produced from the application of rotated factor analysis. The percentage of the variation of each variable on the first three factors is shown in Table 16.7. Associated with factor I are the variables reflecting income levels, medical facilities and employment. In Table 16.8 the scores on factor I show the positions of the Departments on this development scale. Lima, Callao, Ica, Arequipa and Tacna turn out to be the most developed on the criteria used while various Andean Departments are the least developed. Factor II distinguishes altitude and with it some of the features of the *'mancha india'* the 'Indian patch', that part of the Andes extending from Huancavelica to Puno in which only a small part of the population is Spanish speaking, deathrate is high, and the socially undesirable habit of coca chewing is widespread.

Four other factors (III–VI) were also used in the study to group the Departments according to the linkage tree shown in *Figure 16.7*. Each of the factors III–VI had associated strongly with it variables that were largely independent of the two main groups, namely birthrate (see Table 16.7, col. III), precipitation, marriage status and industry. From the present study and those made with the more detailed province level data it became evident that development in Peru could not be completely summarised on one factor or dimension. At least three associated dimensions could be identified, one that seemed to stress technological modernisation, one cultural modernisation (from indigenous to European) and one demographic features.

In the linkage tree in *Figure 16.7* it is characteristic that most of the more similar pairs or groups of units are the less developed ones. Thus Puno, Apurímac and Huánuco in the Andes are very similar, as a comparison of their indices on the original 22 variables in Table 16.5 will show (compare rows 3, 10 and 21). Lima and Callao join one another but remain separate from the rest of Peru until the last stage of linkage. Tacna, a 'special' coastal Department adjoining Chile, and the almost empty Madre de Dios, are also late joiners, which means that they are very different from the rest of Peru. The six groups that emerge from the tree if it is 'cut' where indicated in *Figure 16.7d* are mapped in *c*.

STUDY 3

Two studies were made of data with a regional breakdown at province level. At the time of the 1961 census there were 144 provinces, though the number was increased to 150 in the 1960s. 28 variables were used in the first study. In the second study, certain variables were removed, some new variables added, and the number of provinces reduced to 139 with the removal of Lima, Callao and the three provinces of Madre de Dios. Many of the 33 variables used in the second study were the same as those used at Department level, described in Table 16.6. From the study, three main oblique, partially correlated, factors emerged.

Table 16.5.

PERU: SELECTED DATA FOR THE DEPARTMENTS

Departments	1 Alti.	2 Rain	3 Non agr.	4 Min Mf.	5 Serv. Com.	6 Urb.	7 Sex	8 Age	9 Migr.	10 Doct.	11 Hosp. Beds	12 Brate	13 Drate	14 Span.	15 Lit.	16 Matr.	17 Not Coca	18 Shoe	19 Elec.	20 Bnk.	21 Budg.	22 Inco.
1 Amazonas	20	100	26	5	14	39	104	472	18	9	10	35	13	88	58	30	79	52	4	168	13	3,008
2 Ancash	25	30	37	14	14	33	93	468	9	8	11	39	12	33	48	29	80	86	291	520	55	3,808
3 Apurímac	30	60	23	8	11	20	91	480	3	3	5	38	17	4	23	34	68	71	9	151	11	2,675
4 Arequipa	20	20	65	18	31	65	105	482	22	48	28	36	10	66	74	70	93	95	139	1,770	134	5,697
5 Ayacucho	30	70	23	7	12	25	89	472	4	5	6	31	14	5	27	107	54	89	6	164	16	2,566
6 Cajamarca	23	70	22	11	8	15	95	486	4	3	4	35	9	97	45	15	89	61	5	98	17	2,873
7 Callao	0	0	92	25	42	96	110	506	51	61	45	39	8	90	94	46	100	100	548	3,260	187	9,689
8 Cuzco	32	80	34	13	20	32	100	500	7	5	10	35	17	10	33	26	56	74	135	425	33	3,721
9 Huancavelica	34	50	22	9	9	19	91	430	4	2	4	33	15	6	29	87	27	79	7	54	5	2,848
10 Huánuco	23	80	24	6	10	21	98	446	7	8	8	32	16	29	43	20	56	65	13	224	24	2,589
11 Ica	3	5	50	16	23	54	109	446	22	29	38	35	8	83	84	37	99	98	73	1,580	129	6,258
12 Junín	31	80	47	19	19	49	98	468	14	12	15	39	14	39	61	63	68	92	25	640	36	4,547
13 La Libertad	23	70	43	15	19	42	98	454	12	21	22	38	9	99	63	16	84	95	10	748	85	4,196
14 Lambayeque	0	10	52	17	22	62	104	466	17	15	14	46	9	96	70	15	99	91	62	994	122	4,532
15 Lima	19	20	85	22	45	86	101	500	40	60	40	36	8	81	90	46	98	99	548	6,180	222	9,869
16 Loreto	1	300	42	8	26	39	106	400	8	4	9	28	5	81	67	11	100	57	25	496	104	2,966
17 Madre de Dios	5	320	47	20	25	25	157	462	40	7	8	46	7	68	72	14	95	83	8	154	113	4,308
18 Moquegua	18	20	42	13	20	48	108	486	25	20	39	42	15	59	64	42	89	90	30	1,690	29	7,205
19 Pasco	32	80	52	30	14	35	106	454	18	15	21	38	16	35	52	29	65	91	9	290	36	5,491
20 Piura	7	15	44	15	20	45	101	432	4	9	10	43	9	99	55	40	100	78	36	600	51	4,259
21 Puno	36	60	28	11	13	18	93	482	2	3	3	30	14	51	34	44	54	64	7	173	16	3,223
22 San Martín	6	150	24	7	13	59	99	394	6	3	9	42	9	88	68	59	97	47	3	212	17	2,364
23 Tacna	18	15	61	19	31	70	119	492	39	47	53	42	14	60	74	45	90	96	69	2,790	75	9,543
24 Tumbes	0	40	57	10	40	61	116	436	22	17	17	45	9	99	77	36	100	94	57	336	51	4,861

Table 16.6.

DEFINITIONS OF VARIABLES IN TABLE 16.5

1 Mean *altitude* of Department above sea level in hundreds of metres
2 Mean annual *precipitation* in centimetres
3 Persons employed in activities other than *agriculture* as a percentage of total employed population
4 Persons employed in *mining* and *manufacturing* as a percentage of total employed population
5 Persons employed in *commerce* and *services* as a percentage of total employed population
6 *Urban* population as a percentage of total population
7 *Sex* ratio: males per 100 females
8 *Age*: persons over 19 years of age per 1,000 total population
9 *Migration*: persons born in other Departments as a percentage of total population
10 *Doctors* per 100,000 inhabitants
11 *Hospital beds* per 10,000 inhabitants
12 *Birthrate*: live births per thousand total population
13 *Deathrate*: deaths registered per thousand total population
14 *Spanish*: persons over 5 with Spanish as their 'mother language' as a percentage of all persons over 5
15 *Literacy*: persons over 17 able to read as a percentage of all persons over 17
16 *Marriage*: men classified as 'married' (casados) per 10 men classified as 'living with' (convivientes)
17 *Coca chewing*: adults not chewing coca as a percentage of total adult population
18 Persons using *footwear* as a percentage of total population
19 *Electricity* consumption in kWh per inhabitant
20 *Bank deposits* in soles per inhabitant
21 Department *expenditure* in soles per inhabitant
22 Department *income* in soles per inhabitant

Sources:
Variables 1, 2: various sources
Variables 3–9 and 14–18: Tomos I–V del *Censo Nacional de Población* (1961) Dirección Nacional de Estadística y Censos
  Variables 6, 7, 8, 9, Tomo I, Cuadros 14, 10, 16, 24
  Variable 16, Tomo II, Cuadro 33
  Variables 14, 15, Tomo III, Cuadros 49, 60
  Variables 3, 4, 5, Tomo IV, Cuadro 92
  Variable 17, 18, Tomo V, Cuadros 147, 141
Variables 10, 11: Ministerio de salud pública y asistencia social, *Censo de recursos humanos de salud* (informe preliminar) Peru 1964 (Nov. 1965), Cuadro 3: pp. 11–15 y Cuadro 1, p. 3–6
Variables 12, 13, 19–21: *Anuario Estadístico Peruano* 1966
  Variables 12, 13, pp. 529, 591
  Variable 19, p. 1108
  Variable 20, p. 1454
  Variable 21, p. 1516
Variable 22: Banco Central de Reserva del Perú, 1968, *Cuentas Nacionales del Perú 1950–1967*, Cuadro 10.

Table 16.7.

VARIABLE LOADINGS ON EACH OF FIRST THREE ROTATED FACTORS*

		Rotated factors		
		I	II	III
1	Altitude	5	61	7
2	Precipitation	10	2	2
3	Not agriculture	67	9	1
4	Mining and manufacturing	29	0	4
5	Commerce and services	60	14	1
6	Urban	65	16	5
7	Males/females	7	7	16
8	Age	15	8	0
9	Migration	66	4	6
10	Doctors	84	4	0
11	Hospital beds	85	1	1
12	Birthrate	2	6	90
13	Deathrate	2	84	0
14	Spanish speaking	4	82	2
15	Literacy	48	39	3
16	Marriage	1	7	1
17	Coca chewing	13	66	7
18	Using footwear	32	0	5
19	Electricity	44	1	0
20	Bank deposits	80	2	0
21	Department budget	48	20	1
22	Department income	86	1	2

* The indices show the percentage of the variation of each variable accounted for by each factor. This is the correlation coefficient squared and multiplied by 100.

Table 16.8.

SCORES OF DEPARTMENTS ON FIRST THREE ROTATED FACTORS

		I	II	III
1	Amazonas	− 6·5	−1·2	1·4
2	Ancash	− 3·0	−2·7	0·8
3	Apurímac	−10·5	−8·0	2·3
4	Arequipa	9·2	3·0	−0·8
5	Ayacucho	− 9·5	−8·6	3·9
6	Cajamarca	− 8·8	−1·3	1·9
7	Callao	23·7	9·8	−3·9
8	Cuzco	− 5·8	−7·0	2·1
9	Huancavelica	−11·5	−9·8	3·9
10	Húanuco	− 9·8	−5·9	3·1
11	Ica	7·4	5·4	−1·3
12	Junín	− 1·1	−3·2	0·1
13	La Libertad	0·2	1·9	−0·2
14	Lambayeque	3·7	5·4	−3·1
15	Lima	23·3	8·1	−1·9
16	Loreto	− 4·6	5·2	2·3
17	Madre de Dios	1·4	5·6	−3·9
18	Moquegua	3·9	−0·3	−1·9
19	Pasco	− 0·7	−3·9	−0·3
20	Piura	− 1·9	3·0	−1·4
21	Puno	− 9·7	−6·9	3·9
22	San Martín	− 7·1	2·6	−0·1
23	Tacna	13·4	2·8	−3·4
24	Tumbes	4·2	6·2	−3·5

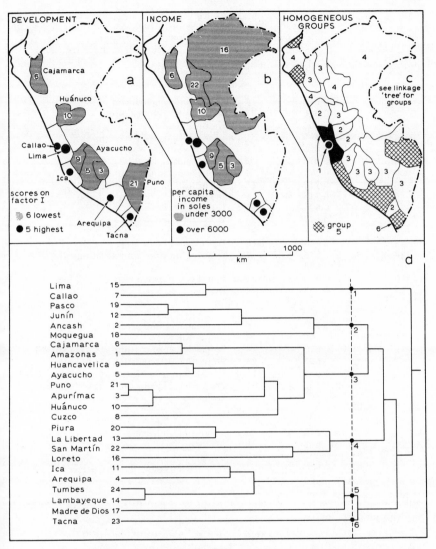

Figure 16.7. Peru: (a) and (b) development by Department according to factor I in Table 16.8 and variable 22 in Table 16.6, (c) and (d) six homhomogeneous groups on six factors, map and linkage diagram

Table 16.9 shows the variables with a correlation of more than ± 0·5 on each of the three factors.

Each factor tells a somewhat different story of the complex ingredients that make up the reality of regional differentiation in Peru. Factor I highlights the contrast between agricultural employment and white collar employment, carrying with it a whole range of health, financial and educational features that are of low standard in predominantly rural, agricultural areas and high in urban ones. Factor II brings to light a second axis of development, one related to the superimposition of European on pre-Columbian ways of life. Factor III

Table 16.9.

VARIABLES MOST CLOSELY ASSOCIATED WITH FACTORS, I, II AND III RANKED IN
ORDER OF DEGREE OF ASSOCIATION

Rank	Pattern coefficient	Variable
Factor I		
1	+0·986	14 : Agricultural employment
2	−0·876	27 : Office workers (empleados)
3	−0·850	13 : Hospital beds
4	−0·845	31 : Bank deposits, type 1
5	−0·823	16 : Employment in commerce/services
6	−0·812	32 : Bank deposits, type 2
7	−0·775	4 : Urban population
8	−0·723	15 : Mining and manufacturing
9	−0·718	8 : In-migration from Lima
10	−0·691	19 : Use of footwear
11	−0·671	26 : Workers (obreros)
12	−0·636	33 : Province budgets
13	−0·614	18 : Domestic workers
14	−0·543	7 : In-migration from other departments
15	+0·538	2 : Precipitation
16	−0·508	21 : Franchised population
17	−0·507	12 : Doctors
Factor II		
1	−0·799	6 : Proportion of population aged over 19 years
2	−0·706	17 : Proportion of population economically active
3	+0·677	24 : Proportion of population speaking Spanish
4	−0·668	23 : Proportion of population chewing coca
5	+0·588	11 : Rate of natural increase of population
6	+0·552	21 : Proportion of population eligible to vote
7	+0·508	25 : Proportion of state employees
Factor III		
1	−0·814	5 : Males per 100 females
2	+0·641	1 : Altitude
3	+0·589	10 : Deathrate
4	−0·516	7 : In-migration from other departments

combines altitude and demographic features. Each gives a different view of development in Peru.

The three factors combined represent a scale of modernisation in Peru. Two of many possible interpretations of the results are given below.

1. Factor I represents development in Peru particularly as it is reflected in the shift of emphasis from employment in agriculture to employment in other branches of the economy. The area scores of the 139 provinces in the study are dispersed about a mean of 0 (zero). Table 16.10 lists all provinces more than 1 standard deviation from the mean on this factor. The negative signs indicate high level of development and positive ones low level of development (note the positive correlation of + 0·986 of the agricultural employment variable with the factor). Thus the highest and lowest levels of development are identified in the table. All the 20 least developed are situated in the Andes or interior of the country. They are all deeply rural and depend very heavily on agriculture. None has a town of appreciable size. The 25 most developed according to factor I, on the other hand, are 'developed' for many different reasons. Most but not all are

Table 16.10a.
PROVINCES WITH HIGHEST SCORES ON OBLIQUE FACTOR I

(Location reference number in brackets : see *Figure 16.8* for location)

	(LIMA		13	Mariscal Nieto (108)	−1·64
	(CALLAO)		14	Piura (113)	−1·37
1	Tacna (135)	−2·69	15	Chancay (99)	−1·34
2	Arequipa (27)	−2·57	16	Pasco (110)	−1·34
3	Cuzco (51)	−2·51	17	Tumbes (137)	−1·23
4	Talara (119)	−2·20	18	Camaná (28)	−1·23
5	Islay (33)	−2·18	19	Chincha (77)	−1·23
6	Yauli (85)	−2·17	20	Pacasmayo (90)	−1·20
7	Trujillo (86)	−2·03	21	Huancayo (80)	−1·14
8	Nazca (78)	−1·98	22	San Román (128)	−1·12
9	Santa (18)	−1·92	23	Maynas (102)	−1·10
10	Chiclayo (9)	−1·82	24	Casma (10)	−1·05
11	Ica (76)	−1·81	25	Caravelí (29)	−1·03
12	Pisco (79)	−1·80			

Table 16.10b.
PROVINCES WITH LOWEST SCORES ON OBLIQUE FACTOR

(Location reference number in brackets : see *Figure 16.8* for location

139	Cangallo (36)	1·57	129	Santa Cruz (50)	1·22
138	Cotabambas (25)	1·49	128	Chumbivilcas (57)	1·15
137	Cutervo (46)	1·46	127	Loreto (105)	1·15
136	Ayabaca (114)	1·35	126	Chota (47)	1·14
135	Hualgayoc (48)	1·31	125	La Mar (38)	1·13
134	Acobamba (65)	1·28	124	Huari (12)	1·11
133	M.Luzuriaga (14)	1·27	123	Pachitea (74)	1·10
132	Chucuito (123)	1·25	122	Dos de Mayo (71)	1·08
131	Huancané (124)	1·23	121	Maranon (73)	1·07
130	V. Fajardo (41)	1·22	120	Huancabamba (115)	1·01

on the coast and all 10 of the towns with over 100,000 inhabitants in 1972 (see Table 16.2) are represented.

Table 16.11 is an attempt to account for the relative success of the top 25 provinces in Table 16.10a and located in map *Figure 16.2c*. The essence of development in Peru is that with modernisation in the last hundred years or so a relatively small number of places have pulled ahead of a large number of others. Each of the modernised provinces has 'succeeded' through a combination of a number of favourable attributes. For example province 3, Cuzco, is small in area and therefore consists almost exclusively of the town of Cuzco itself. This town has been developed as the tourist capital of Peru and has attracted or deliberately been given a number of industries. Talara, province 4, owes its development to the presence of the main oilfields of Peru. Province 9, containing Chimbote, has changed rapidly thanks to the availability of hydro-electric power, the presence of an iron and steel works, and a huge fishmeal processing capacity. Province 6, Yauli, contains the Cerro de Pasco Corporation's main smelter in La Oroya, a plant that provides several thousand jobs outside agriculture. So the high position of most of the 25 provinces can easily be accounted for once local conditions are examined in sufficient detail. Perhaps $\frac{1}{4}$ or $\frac{1}{3}$ of the 144 provinces of Peru have something positive and dynamic about them. It may be asked what the prospects of the remainder are. Should future development be directed to them or should it be concentrated in the already more modernised provinces?

Table 16.11.
ATTRIBUTES OF THE TOP 25 PROVINCES OF PERU

1 represents the presence of the attribute

		Department capital	Town over 100,000	Town over 20,000	Mining	Export agriculture	Industry	Commercial	Tourism	Seaport, fishing
	Lima*	1	1	1		1	1	1	1	
	Callao*		1	1			1	1		1
1	Tacna	1		1				1		
2	Arequipa	1	1	1			1	1	1	
3	Cuzco	1	1	1			1	1	1	
4	Talara			1	1		1			1
5	Islay							1		1
6	Yauli			1			1			
7	Trujillo	1	1	1		1	1	1	1	1
8	Nazca				1	1				1
9	Santa		1	1		1	1			1
10	Chiclayo		1	1		1	1	1		1
11	Ica	1		1		1	1	1		
12	Pisco			1		1				1
13	M. Nieto				1		1			1
14	Piura	1	1	1		1	1	1		
15	Chancay			1		1			1	1
16	Pasco	1		1	1					
17	Tumbes	1		1				1		
18	Camaná									
19	Chincha			1		1				1
20	Pacasmayo					1				1
21	Huancayo	1	1	1			1	1	1	
22	San Román			1				1		
23	Maynas	1	1	1			1	1	1	(1)†
24	Casma					1				
25	Caravelí									1

* Not included in the 139 provinces studied.
† Amazon port.

2. The second and final study in this section is summarised in *Figure 16.8*. Each of the 144 provinces has been given a score between +3 and −3 according to its performance on each of the three factors identified in the study and already referred to. Since all three factors are to some extent correlated, in most cases if a province has a high score on one factor it should have a fairly high one on the others and if it has a low score on one it should have a low score on the others. The result of the combination of the three factor scores for each province is to produce a consensus that gives a picture of backwardness and of modernisation in Peru.

The prize in backwardness goes to province 65, Acobamba, in the Department of Huancavelica, scoring more than 1 standard deviation on all three factors. Reference to the original data matrix shows that this province, located

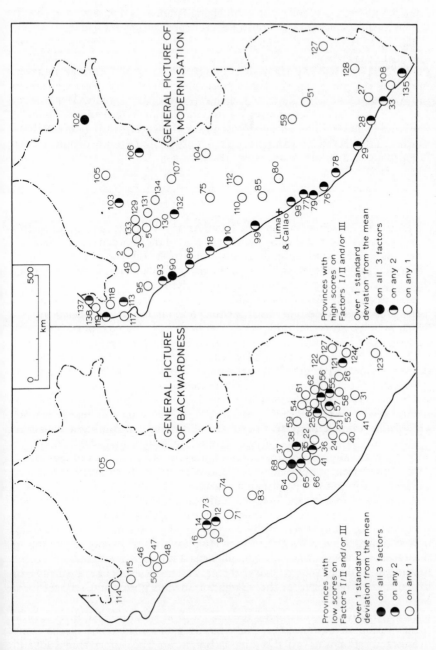

Figure 16.8. Provinces of Peru with scores indicating backwardness and modernisation on three factors (see Tables 16.9 and 16.10)

about 3,400 metres above sea level, has 88 per cent of its employed population in agriculture, only 2 per cent in mining and manufacturing, 78 per cent of the populate illiterate and only 3 per cent giving Spanish as their first language. It has no hospitals or banks and only 3 doctors per 100,000 inhabitants.

The three remaining sections of this chapter contain descriptions of three places of Peru known to the author first hand. Chaquicocha is a village in one of the poorer parts of the Andes, in the province of Concepción, rated about 110th out of the 144 provinces. The Huarochirí valley contains a group of villages in the province of the same name. Huarochirí is in the Andes of Lima Department and is rated about half way among the provinces. Lima is the national capital of Peru and comes out highest on almost all variables representing development in spite of the fact that it contains not only most of the wealthy people of Peru but also about a million shanty town dwellers.

16.4. CHAQUICOCHA, AN ANDEAN VILLAGE

Chaquicocha is a settlement on the Central Andes of Peru at about 3,500 metres above sea level, located about 50 km to the west of the regional centre of Huancayo. The present study is an impression of a brief visit to the village in 1970. The aim is to illustrate the general problems of a small rural settlement rather than to give exact detail about Chaquicocha itself.

Chaquicocha had about 600 inhabitants in 1970. Administratively it is part of a Distrito, San José de Queros. It is situated in an undulating treeless area in which browns, greys and dull greens are the predominant colours. The snow clad peaks of the Cordillera Occidental can be seen in the far distance. The village receives a moderate rainfall with a maximum around January and a long dry season around August. Diurnal temperature variations are more marked than seasonal ones. Frosts occur fairly frequently.

The area of the community of Chaquicocha is about 650 hectares. The natural resources consist of the soil and a supply of water coming partly from the seasonal rainfall, partly from a stream descending from the higher village of Quero, and shared with that village. Temperatures are usually high enough to allow the cultivation of potatoes, barley and some other cereals and vegetables. At any given time about half of the land is used for the cultivation of crops, some is fallow and some is permanent pasture.

An unpaved motor road between Huancayo and the coast of Peru passing through Chaquicocha was completed in 1965 giving the village a modern transport link with the rest of the country for the first time. Previously communication had depended on a track to Huancayo, difficult if not impassable in the wet season. Before the road, Chaquicocha was largely a self-contained community, but since 1965 it has become easier to exchange a surplus of agricultural products from the village for various goods and services from outside.

In a virtually self-contained settlement such as Chaquicocha, there is little specialisation in occupations. Every family grows field crops, keeps some livestock and builds its own dwellings as best it can. The women spin wool and weave it for clothing. There is some communal effort, as in the maintenance of the water supply.

As the community depends exclusively on agriculture it is inevitably faced with a set of basic problems. Firstly, yields of crops and the carrying capacity of the pasture vary greatly from year to year. Production of food from crops and of various items from livestock may therefore be adequate to provide a surplus for sale outside the village in some years but inadequate to feed the population of the village in others. Secondly, facilities for storing food are limited and stored food is vulnerable to moulds and vermin. If there is a sequence of two or three bad years, then either food has to be obtained from outside the village or people starve. But the purchase of food outside depends on a surplus of agricultural products. It may be noted that on a larger scale, such sequences of bad years for agriculture have afflicted Northeast Brazil on various occasions, and affected about 2 million people in Ethiopia during 1971–73.

What happens in Chaquicocha if the potato crop is ruined by heavy frosts, the barley yields are low and pasture poor? It was reported that in 1969 about $\frac{1}{4}$ of all the children of 'school age' died through various diseases, about 50 out of 200. Since women have a large number of children there is always a supply to replenish population after a demographic setback and a kind of equilibrium seems to exist in which the population stays around several hundred, the maximum number that can be supported at a subsistence level. It is worth noting, however, that one could find in Australia a single farm of 650 hectares, the area of Chaquicocha, run by a single family, perhaps with some further labour. With machines for ploughing and harvesting, and fencing to control livestock, 6 people on the Australian farm could produce as much as 600 people in Chaquicocha. In Chaquicocha agricultural equipment is limited to such tools as spades and mattocks. Virtually no chemical fertilisers are used.

What do people get for their efforts in Chaquicocha? Most of the families live in a single room dwellings with walls built of adobe (mud brick) and a roof with thatch, corrugated iron or tiles. The use of timber and glass is very limited. The village was laid out in a grid iron plan and each dwelling set in a small, walled field, with four fields to a block. The streets of the village are mostly grass tracks. The water supply runs in a ditch along one of the streets. There are no sewage facilities.

There is no doctor in Chaquicocha or in any nearby village. An unqualified person visits the village from time to time to sell pharmaceutical goods but the services of a doctor and the facilities of a hospital have to be obtained in Huancayo. As it is, the children of the village are more susceptible to diseases than their elders. Inadequate food and an unbalanced diet no doubt contribute to the widespread occurrence of intestinal diseases such as worms, and pulmonary diseases such as pneumonia and bronchitis. Most children have sores on exposed parts of their body.

Education is provided in the village by a single school which in 1970 had three teachers for about 150 children. The materials for the present school buildings were provided by the government and a new building with three classrooms was constructed by the villagers. The salaries of the three teachers are paid by the government. The present building replaces one that was no better than a barn with an earth floor and no proper lighting or ventilation. The present building has three classrooms with wooden floors, proper windows and rough desks. The school has virtually no other equipment.

Among subjects being taught, the author noticed the following. Children are taught to tell the time, yet there are no clocks in the village. They are taught about different kinds of vitamin yet none of the sources mentioned are available in the village. They are taught Inca history yet this is of no relevance to the present problems of the village. The teachers reported that while primary education is theoretically compulsory, some families did not allow their children to go to school at all. In fact many children spend a great deal of time looking after small herds of livestock. The teachers found on the other hand that some parents themselves were glad to attend 'evening' classes. More aspiring parents paid for their older children to stay in Huancayo to obtain secondary education there.

At a distance the school children of Chaquicocha make a colourful picture as they leave their school in the afternoon sunshine. The girls wear blue and the boys have wine colour jersies. Close up, the children smell and they probably never wash themselves or change their clothes.

The money available to the population for the purchase of all outside goods and services is very limited. Equipment, seeds and building materials have high priority, but a large number of other items can be obtained in the one shop in the village, run by an outsider. The items for sale in the shop in 1970 included:

kerosene	bread	sardines
petrol	biscuits	tuna
candles	spaghetti	lard
matches	condensed milk	cooking oil
batteries	beer	fresh fruit
salt	soft drinks	cigarettes
soap	sweets	writing equipment
detergents	sugar	aspirins

There are poorer places than Chaquicocha in the Andes of Peru. Many villages are not served by a motor road. Some are culturally handicapped through the presence of a quechua speaking population. Nevertheless, if the aspirations of the Peruvian government and the expectations of the people of Chaquicocha are to be satisfied, the standard of living must be raised in some way. It may be helpful if initially confusing to see the working of the village as a rough kind of system. A change in the values in the existing system and/or the addition of new elements to the system or the removal of existing ones from it potentially have repercussions throughout. The system of Chaquicocha is represented in *Figure 9.6* on page 184.

Three possible futures for Chaquicocha may be noted. Firstly it could continue very much on present lines. Secondly, gradual improvements might be introduced. These will be described below. Thirdly, a drastic remedy, quite out of the question in practice, might be applied. For example, $\frac{9}{10}$ of the population might be resettled elsewhere and the remaining $\frac{1}{10}$ left in the village with a greatly superior population resource balance. Such a remedy for all the villages of the Andes of Peru is impossible.

The following gradual improvements are of the kind widely being tried out in places in the world like Chaquicocha.

1. More artificial fertilisers should be used, but these have to be bought outside the village. The practice of using dung as a fuel should somehow be abandoned in order to return manure to the land.
2. The livestock population should be reduced and its quality improved.

Pastures should be fenced off to prevent the terrible over-grazing found at the moment.

3. Water supply should be improved by the construction of reservoirs. Domestic water should be separated from the stream running through the village which collects rubbish and animal manure while also providing drinking water.

4. An electricity supply should be provided, and various services such as a post office and library provided. Health and educational facilities should be improved.

The annual per capita income in Chaquicocha is somewhere between $ U.S. 50–100 per year. This is the figure for much of the Andes, for the poorest parts of Northeast Brazil and for Haiti in Latin America. It is the level widely found in India and in the poorer parts of Africa such as Ethiopia. The inescapable fact about such places is that the present level cannot be replaced by a per capita income several times as high (but still very low by the standards of developed countries) unless either a given area loses 80–90 per cent of its population, or unless it gets massive aid from elsewhere to make a profound change in technology, education and health. As it is, unless cultural and social attitudes change, any improvements in a place like Chaquicocha, and particularly any improvement in health services, would have the effect of lowering mortality, thereby keeping more children alive and building up an even greater population.

Such places as Chaquicocha are losing population through migration. It is widely held now that the better educated and/or more enterprising people are the ones who tend to leave. The number of people that can be absorbed elsewhere, either in new farming areas, or in towns, does not offer a solution to the demographic pressures that can build up in rural areas. A comparison of 1961 and 1972 census data for Peru shows that in fact many rural areas of the Andes do have 5–10 per cent fewer people in the latter year than in the former. This kind of loss of population in certain places is nothing like the reduction that would be needed to bring about a population size to match the resources available and to give conditions for commercial agriculture.

16.5. HUAROCHIRÍ, A VALLEY IN THE ANDES BEHIND LIMA

The valley of Huarochirí is located in the western Andes of Peru on the Pacific side of the main watershed in the headwaters of the River Mala. These streams have cut a great hollow in the high plateau with its surface at about 4,000 metres above sea level. The Mala leaves this valley through an impassable gorge starting about 2,000 metres above sea level. The Huarochirí area has according to the 1972 census about 8,000 inhabitants in a cluster of villages in an area about 25 × 10 km set in a virtually uninhabited area of poor pasture. Population is mainly found at a number of nucleated settlements between about 2,000 and 4,000 metres above sea level. The only resource of this small region is its cultivated and pasture land, for there is very little timber, no economic minerals are produced other than building materials, and no hydro-electricity is generated. Until 1946 the region could only be reached from the outside world along tracks suitable for pack animals. Integration into the national economy has been very gradual and has still not proceeded far.

The valley was absorbed in the Inca empire during its expansion in the 15th century and a main road passed through it at this time, but it must have been almost entirely self-sufficient. Tubers, maize and beans were grown and the land was tilled by hand. The llama was the only form of livestock. Metals were virtually unknown and the wheel was not used for transportation. In the 16th century the area began to feel the influence of Spanish conquest. For military and administrative purposes population was grouped into nucleated settlements. The population was theoretically converted to Christianity, but many old beliefs and customs last to this day. Spanish began to be used and gradually came to replace quechua, but many quechua words are still used and the two languages occur side by side, as for example in the place name Santiago de Anchucaya. New plants and livestock were introduced, and Old World cereals, cattle and sheep have come to supplement the range of New World items, but new methods of cultivation made little impact. Some new techniques were adopted, such as weaving with a more complicated form of loom.

For almost four centuries the valley of Huarochirí remained very much on the fringe of Peruvian economic life, with a mestizo culture superimposed on a predominantly Indian people. By 1900, wool and food products, such as potatoes and dried meat, could be taken to the growing market in Lima by pack animal, but early in the 20th century a railway was completed in the neighbouring Rimac valley and this could be reached in 1½ days, thus making Lima more accessible. In 1920 a road was started to Huarochirí, but the whole length of the road was not completed until 1946. The road climbs altogether more than 4,000 metres from the coast before it descends about 1,000 metres into the Huarochirí valley. There are some 40 hair-pin bends in this last stretch alone. The direct distance from Lima to Huarochirí is about 80 km but the road distance is about twice this length. As the road has no paved surface it is out of use throughout the rainy season, about half the year. For much of its length it is too narrow for vehicles to pass and traffic has to go in different directions on alternate days. The journey up takes from 10–20 hours and the return journey from about 8–16. Obviously transport costs are still very high, but this link is vital to the valley because only by selling surplus agricultural products to the outside world can anything be brought in.

The Huarochirí valley is a deep hollow with very steep sides, cut by the Mala and its tributaries in the plateau. The only level or gently sloping land is provided by terraces left on either side of the Mala as a result of rejuvenation. Slumping and landslides occur frequently, soil is generally thin and poor, and much of the cultivated land has been terraced. Annual rainfall in the higher part of the valley is about 50 cm but at the lower end much less.

All but the highest part of the valley depends on an intricate pattern of irrigation channels taking water from the Mala itself and from the tributaries coming in on the eastern side from the snow-clad Cordillera Occidental of the Andes. Temperatures vary enormously with altitude over a very short distance and the range of crops grown varies from village to village, from potatoes in the highest to sub-tropical crops in the lowest. Cultivation is largely by hand or occasionally by ploughs drawn by livestock, but the possibility of mechanising agriculture on conventional lines is out of the question, when there are in places as many as 50 'fields' per hectare. The arable land grows fodder crops for livestock as well as food crops for human consumption, but fodder crops supplement the pastures on higher land around, which vary in productivity with the seasons.

Movement of goods between the various settlements in the area is difficult and inconvenient, for the motor road only reaches Huarochirí and Santiago. Virtually all the possible land that could be cultivated is already in use, slopes are too steep to extend cultivation, and no more water is available for irrigation. Yields could be increased by bringing in fertilisers and improving the quality of seeds and livestock; hence the need for closer contact with other parts of Peru.

The population of about 8,000 gives a very high density per unit of cultivated land but this cannot be worked out precisely on account of lack of data. About half the population is in the two largest villages which, like most of the others, are laid out on a grid-iron pattern with a central square. Almost all the buildings have adobe walls and thatched roofs. Eucalyptus timber and corrugated iron are used by the more affluent members of the community. Furniture is usually very poor, the kitchens outside the main building are traditionally too low to stand up in, and cooking is done on open fires. Water supply is provided in the villages from a few communal taps. Fuel is too scarce for heating and there is no gas and no electricity. Again, sanitation is almost unknown. Considering the size of the villages, they all have a surprisingly large number of shops, but the turnover is small and most shopkeepers have other occupations as well. Each village has a church, but difficulty is experienced in keeping a permanent priest. The valley has no doctor and no hospital facilities. There are primary schools in most of the villages and education is available for most of the children up to the age of about eleven, but facilities for secondary education had to be found outside the region until a small start was made in the 1950s to provide this locally.

Not surprisingly the inhabitants of the valley, many of whom have travelled to the capital, or have relatives who have settled there, are conscious of the need to improve conditions in their own area. To do this they have to bring in an enormous number of ingredients: fertilisers, better implements, seed and stock for agriculture, fuel (mainly kerosene), building materials such as corrugated iron and glass, and all the machinery and consumer goods beyond the limited range of clothing produced locally, as well as the services of teachers and doctors. These can be obtained only through the sales of agricultural products which, in fact, are marketed now in a reasonably well-organised way in the wholesale markets of Lima. If variety in diet is desired then items such as sugar, rice and tinned foods also have to be brought into the valley.

The valley of Huarochirí is isolated and is relatively though not desperately poor. Many other areas in the Andes of Peru are both more isolated and poorer. There appears to be considerable out-migration from the valley and the population itself did not change much between 1961 and 1972. The census figures for the two largest villages are as follows:

	1961	1972
Huarochirí	2125	2066
San Lorenzo de Quinti	1580	1717

It is difficult to increase agricultural production on account of the many reasons already suggested but it is unthinkable at the moment to try to diversify the economy by introducing non-agricultural activities. There seem to be three possible lines of approach. Firstly, the region could be left to itself, in which case nothing very much would change. Secondly, a massive attempt could be made to improve it; in the case of Huarochirí for example a first class road could be built right into the valley, eliminating its isolation. The cost of building such a road could not possibly be offset by the limited advantages to the economy of the country as a whole of integrating such a region. Thirdly, the region could be deliberately abandoned, retaining only a caretaker population to keep agriculture going and having the rest of its population resettled in some more promising agricultural area or in an urban centre. As already noted in the last section, such a solution could be possible only for a small part of the Andean population. In conclusion, it may be noted that basically the situation in Huarochirí and its prospects and problems are very similar to those in Chaquicocha.

16.6. LIMA AND CALLAO

The following brief account of Greater Lima provides both a contrast with the rural areas described in the two previous sections and a case study of a large urban centre in Latin America typical basically, though not in detail, of most of the other large towns of the continent. For the purposes of this section, Greater Lima is defined as the Province of Lima and the Provincia Constitucional of Callao. Some features of Greater Lima are mapped in *Figure 16.9*.

Greater Lima occupies only a tiny fraction of the total area of Peru but in 1972 it had about 3,320,000 inhabitants, nearly 25 per cent of the total population of the country. Its population grew from about 650,000 in 1940 to nearly 2 million in 1960. According to the 1961 census, about half of the population was born elsewhere in Peru. A high proportion of women of child bearing age, a high birthrate plus large-scale in-migration have resulted in a five-fold increase of the population of Greater Lima in three decades.

Ever since the 16th century Lima has been a key centre in Peru but the growth in the last few decades has caused numerous problems of two main kinds. In the first place, a large part of the industry, services and wealth of Peru have become concentrated in one place. Secondly, such a rapid growth of population has outpaced the capacity of the city to provide housing, roads, water, electricity, educational and health facilities and other needs. Lima is in a desert region, but the area in which it is situated is supplied with water by three rivers, the central one being the Rimac, on which Lima is located. These three rivers irrigate the rich alluvial soils of the area, but the local farms have long ceased to satisfy the food requirements of the capital. The built-up area of the town has itself taken up considerable areas of former farm land.

Lima was founded in 1535 by the Spaniards who, after some indecision, chose a site for the future capital of their new empire in South America near the coast and not in the Andes. They chose an area in which there was already an agricultural population and therefore a local food supply, as well as water. An almost level site was used so that the town could spread indefinitely, and the streets were laid out in the usual grid-iron fashion. It was not long before Lima began to have at least six clearly defined functions. It was a military base for the continuation of the Conquest, an administrative centre, becoming the capital of a viceroyalty soon after its foundation, a religious centre, an educational centre (with a University from about 1550), the main commercial centre handling the trade with Spain, and in a limited way a manufacturing centre.

Between 1550 and 1850 the population of Lima grew only gradually, rising from about 40,000 in 1700 to about 100,000 in 1850, by which time it was the capital of Peru, its original sphere of administration, which for a time around 1600 spread over the whole of South America, having been progressively reduced through the Colonial period. The building of walls in the 17th century and a very serious earthquake in 1743, which attracted attention in Europe at that time, were outstanding events in an otherwise undistinguished history.

Technological changes spreading to Latin America from Europe and North America began to transform the economy of Peru from about 1840. Shipping services along the coast grew more efficient and frequent and first guano and then cotton, metals and sugar were exported to Europe. From this time on Lima began to grow both in population and in area, at first slowly and then more rapidly. Its links with the rest of the country were strengthened, first along the coast by shipping services, then with the central Andes by rail, and especially since the Second World War with the rest of the country by road. Population grew from about 100,000 in 1850 to about 250,000 in 1910 and 650,000 in 1940.

The improvement of roads and air services since the 1930s has changed travel times in Peru drastically. A journey to Lima that took several weeks by land from the southern Andes can now be accomplished in a day or two by bus, and the hazardous journey from Iquitos, which lasted about a month, now takes only 2 hours by air.

The built-up area of Lima has spread in three successive phases. Until the latter part of the 19th century most of the population was still within the limits of the walls, which were demolished late in the 19th century. Railways were built in the 1860s and tramways around 1900 in three directions towards the nearby coast to Callao, Magdalena and Miraflores and the built up area began to spread along these transport axes. By the 1930s these had been supplemented by good roads, and by the early 1950s a Greater Lima region was recognised by planners to fill the triangle Lima–Callao–Chorrillos, though some agricultural land remained within this triangle. By the early 1950s it was also possible to recognise several distinct land-use zones, including a central business district, the remains of the old town around this, by now largely consisting of slum dwellings, areas of better-class suburbs, especially in Miraflores, an industrial zone extending most of the length of one of the avenues between Lima and its port, the port area itself, and finally the shanty towns. The latter already housed about 100,000 people by 1955 and occupied land of no use for agriculture or other developments including hillsides close to or even within the built-up area, the gravel covered bed of the River Rimac, places in the desert outside the town, and even blocks awaiting development within Lima.

In the 1960s, planners recognised an extended Greater Lima, stretching in a discontinuous urban area some 80 km along the coast and some 40 km from San Lorenzo island, inland up the Rimac valley. This includes a considerable number of new shanty towns, the total population of which was estimated to be around 350,000 in the early 1960s and had probably reached 1 million by 1972, and at least three new satellite towns, one of which, Ventanilla, was completed in the early 1960s to house 100,000 people. Many new resorts serving as outer suburbs of Greater Lima have also grown up along the coast, thanks to the excellent conditions for motor transport. The construction of new fishmeal factories, a large new airport and oil refineries outside the established triangle of Greater Lima, and the plan to link the island of San Lorenzo to Callao by a causeway, all add to the reality of the concept of a Greater Greater Lima.

Lima retains the six functions it already had in the 16th century but its commercial and industrial functions have grown relatively. The disproportionate share of the amenities and wealth of Peru found in the provinces of Lima and Callao as a result of 20th century expansion can be gauged from a selection of figures from the 1961 census. The proportions have probably only changed slightly in the 1960s. In 1961 Lima and Callao had about 20 per cent of the total population of Peru but the following percentages of other ingredients of the country:

professional workers	40
gross national product	45
managerial personnel	55
office workers (*empleados*)	60
motor vehicles	60
doctors	65
industry	70
bank deposits	80
value of imports	80
international air services	90

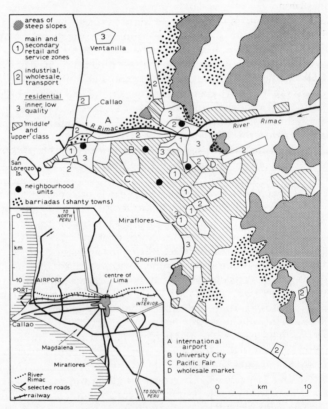

Figure 16.9. The Greater Lima area. The main map shows functional zones and units while the inset map shows the principal roads and other transport features. Source: Jean Paul Deler, Lima 1940–1970 *(Centro de Investigaciones Geograficas, Lima, Enero 1975)*

The standard of living in Greater Lima is about twice the national average and about five times the average for the Andes. Lima is both the commercial and financial capital of the country and the place where most of the key decision makers reside and work. The banks, ministries, airline offices and hotels which form both the control centre of the internal affairs of Peru and the interface through which transactions with the rest of the world are organised, occupy a few streets in the old central area, once the place from which Spain controlled a large part of South America through its viceroy.

References

1. Mather, P. M. and Cole, J. P. *Peru Province Level Factor Analysis,* 1971, duplicated discussion paper, Geography Department, Nottingham University.

Sources of material in the figures

16.3 Based on maps in *Atlas histórico, geográfico y de paisajes peruanos* (see full details below).
16.4 (a) Based on map in *Sci. Am.*, June 1973, p. 24, (b) Data from *Peruvian Times*, Mar. 3, 1972, p. 63.
16.5 Based on map in *Peruvian Times*, Mar. 9, 1973.
16.6 As for 16.2.

Further sources consulted

Oficina Nacional de Estadística y Censos
  a) VI Censo Nacional de Población, various volumes
  b) *Anuario estadístico del Perú*
  c) *Población del Perú*, Resultados Provisionales, Lima, Agosto de 1972.
Instituto Nacional de Planificación, *Plan Nacional de Desarrollo para 1971–1975, Volumen I: Plan General,* 1971, Lima.
Matos Mar, J. and others, *Dominación y cambios en el Peru rural,* 1969, Lima, Instituto de Estudios Peruanos.
Oficina Nacional de Planeamiento y Urbanismo, *Plan de desarrollo metropolitano Lima-Callao, Esquema director 1967–1980* (undated).
Peñaherrera del Aguila, C., *Geografía General del Perú, Tomo I, Aspectos físicos,* 1969, Lima; 'Ausonia Talleres Gráficos' S.A.
Instituto Nacional de Planificación, Asesoria Geográfica, *Atlas histórico geográfico y de paisajes peruanos,* 1963–1969, Lima.
Peruvian Times (periodical), from Oct. 1973, *Andean Times*.

Further reading

Adams, R. N., *A Community in the Andes, Problems and Progress in Muquiyauyo,* 1959, Seattle; University of Washington Press.
Clapperton C. M. and Hamilton, P., 'Peru Beneath its Eternal Threat', *Geogr. Mag.,* June 1971 Vol. XLIII, No. 9, pp. 632–39.
Mangin, W., 'Squatter Settlements', *Sci. Am.,* Vol. 217, No. 4, pp. 21–29.
Smith, C. T., 'Problems of Regional Development in Peru', *Geography,* Vol. liii, Part 3, July 1968, pp. 260–81.

CHAPTER 17

CHILE

17.1. POPULATION, PHYSICAL FEATURES AND RESOURCES

Chile is distinguished from other Latin American countries by its long, narrow shape. Although it covers about the same area as Venezuela or Bolivia it extends more than 4000 km from north to south while rarely exceeding 200 km from east to west. If population were distributed evenly over the area of Chile, average distances between places in the country would be great. In fact in 1970 about 45 per cent of the total population of Chile lived in the two provinces of Santiago and Valparaíso, on less than 3 per cent of the national area. With nearly 2,600,000 inhabitants in that year, Greater Santiago alone had nearly 30 per cent of the population of the country. The provinces at the northern and southern extremities have only a few per cent of total population. In practice the long, narrow form of Chile has not been altogether a disadvantage. The resources of the country are all located within a short distance of the coast and with good shipping services they can easily be exported or moved relatively cheaply from one region of Chile to another.

Area and demographic data for Chile are given in Table 17.1 on the basis of the 25 provinces, the location of which are shown in *Figure 17.1,* map *a.* The data in columns 1 and 2 show that while the four most northerly and two most southerly provinces are large in area they are not among the largest in population. The arid northern and the mountainous southern areas of Chile shrink to a very small size on the topological map, *Figure 17.1c.* The data for birthrate, deathrate, migration and urbanisation are unfortunately for 1960, not 1970, but the *relative* positions of the provinces on these variables are unlikely to have changed much during the 1960s. The data in column 8 show population change between 1960 and 1970. The varying rates of growth are due more to inter-province migration within Chile than to differing birthrates. Increases were in the provinces with the three largest towns, Santiago, Valparaíso and Concepción, and in the thinly populated northern and southern provinces.

Chile is a highly urbanised country, with 76 per cent of its population classified as urban (see column 7 in Table 17.1), and migrants continue to move out of the predominantly agricultural and rural areas of Central Chile. Table 17.2 lists the towns with over 50,000 inhabitants in 1970 and their location is shown in *Figure 17.2.* The rate of growth of population in Chile has diminished considerably since the 1950s and during 1963–71 the average annual rate of growth was only 1·4 per cent, a figure much closer to European rates than to most Latin American ones. There has been little immigration into Chile in recent decades but some movement of Chileans into Argentina.

In 1970, 26 per cent of the employed population of Chile was in agriculture, about 700,000 persons out of 2,700,000. Mining and manufacturing accounted for about 400,000 people. The familiar efficiency gap between agriculture

Table 17.1.

CHILE: DEMOGRAPHIC DATA

1   Area in thousands of sq.km.
2   Population in thousands, 1970
3   Density of population, persons per sq.km.
4,5   Births, deaths per 1000 inhabitants in 1960
6   Persons born in other provinces as a percentage of total population in 1960
7   Urban population as a percentage of total population in 1960
8   Percentage increase of population 1960-70

		1 Area	2 Popn	3 Dens.	4 Brate	5 Drate	6 Migr.	7 Urb.	8 Change
1	Aconcagua	10	161	16	32	10	18	56	14
2	Antofagasta	123	252	2	27	9	33	95	16
3	Arauco	6	99	17	35	12	14	36	10
4	Atacama	80	152	2	32	9	30	74	31
5	Aysén	89	48	1	9	9	47	53	35
6	Bio-Bio	11	193	17	36	14	15	37	14
7	Cautín	17	421	24	26	12	13	39	7
8	Colchagua	8	169	20	33	10	13	33	6
9	Concepción	6	638	112	34	12	26	82	18
10	Coquimbo	40	339	8	32	10	10	52	9
11	Curicó	6	114	20	33	12	24	41	7
12	Chiloe	23	111	5	29	12	7	22	12
13	Linares	10	189	19	34	12	17	36	10
14	Llanquihuo	18	199	11	31	10	18	42	18
15	Magallanes	135	89	1	25	9	46	83	21
16	Malleco	14	177	12	30	12	17	45	1
17	Maule	6	83	15	26	10	11	40	3
18	Nuble	14	315	22	33	12	12	40	10
19	O'Higgins	7	306	43	33	11	22	53	18
20	Osorno	9	160	18	28	11	17	46	10
21	Santiago	17	3,218	186	55	17	31	90	32
22	Talca	10	231	24	32	12	22	44	12
23	Tarapacá	55	175	3	28	8	24	87	42
24	Valdivia	21	275	13	31	12	21	44	6
25	Valparaíso	5	727	152	40	15	27	89	18
	CHILE TOTAL	742	8,841	12					

Sources: 1. *Síntesis Estadística*, Julio 1971, p. 15
4, 5. *Demografía*, Año 1966, pp. 6–32
6, 7. XIII Censo de Población, Serie A, *Resumen del país*, p. 60, p. 124
8. XIV Censo Nacional de Población, *Resultados provisorios*, 1970

and industry can be observed in Chile. Agriculture only accounts for about 7 per cent of gross domestic product, industry for about 40 per cent (28 per cent from manufacturing, the rest from mining).

For simplicity Chile can be divided into three very narrow regions extending from north to south, the Andes in the east, a central depression, and a western coast range. All three features diminish progressively in altitude southwards, and in the south the Andes range is not only lower but discontinuous, the central depression largely submerged, and the coast range a number of islands. The southern part of Chile has been heavily glaciated. In the north the continuity of the central depression is in reality interrupted in several areas by ridges linking the Andes and the coastal range. There is a paved motor road all the way from Arica in the north to Puerto Montt in the south. This follows the central depression nearly all the way but touches the coast in a few places. In Central Chile access from the coast to the central valley is generally difficult.

Northern Chile is one of the driest regions in the world. There are places where it has hardly rained at all for hundreds of years. Precipitation increases from north to south and the annual amount is 200–300 cm in south central Chile and even higher in the south. It occurs mainly in the winter in central Chile but throughout the year in the south. As far south as Santiago rainfall is inadequate for most kinds of agriculture unless supplemented by irrigation,

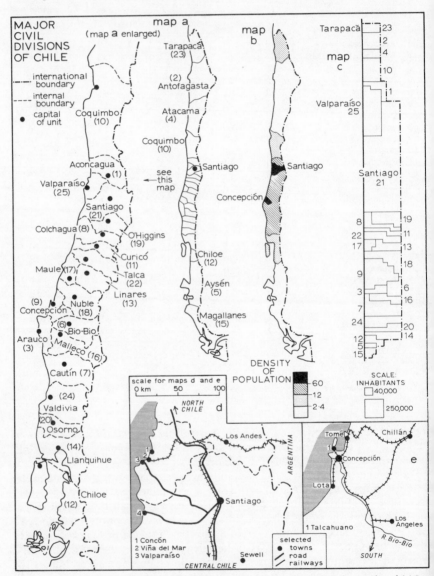

Figure 17.1. Chile: (a) Major civil divisions, (b) Density of population, (c) Topological map, (d) and (e) Santiago and Concepción areas

but since the rivers draining northern Chile are short and originate in the near-by Andes, which themselves are dry, little is available north of Coquimbo, and desert conditions prevail. There is only thin vegetation as far south as Santiago, south of which first in the Andes, and then in the valleys and along the coast south of the Bio Bio river, there are extensive forests.

Table 17.2.
TOWNS IN CHILE WITH OVER 50,000 INHABITANTS IN 1970

1	Santiago[1]	2,587	13	Los Angeles	90
2	Valparaíso[2]	436	14	Puerto Montt	87
3	Concepción[3]	340	15	La Serena	72
4	Temuco	146	16	Calama	72
5	Antofagasta	126	17	Iquique	65
6	Coronel[4]	125	18	Magallanes	65
7	Osorno	106	19	Linares	61
8	Talca	103	20	Curicó	60
9	Chillán	102	21	Quilpué	56
10	Rancagua	95	22	Coquimbo	55
11	Arica	92	23	Ovalle	53
12	Valdivia	91	24	Copiapó	52

[1] Greater Santiago figure
[2] With Viña del Mar
[3] With Talcahuano
[4] With Lota
Source: *Muestra adelantada*

Thanks to its shape, Chile can be divided into five reasonably clear-cut regions from north to south, each containing part of the three elements, the coastal range, the central depression and the Andes. The first area colonised by the Spaniards lies roughly in the centre between Santiago and the Bio Bio valley. This now contains nearly ⅔ of the population of the country and includes much of Chile's agricultural land. To the north, between Santiago and Copiapó, agriculture depends almost entirely on irrigation, and the cultivated area is very limited. Here, on the other hand, are most of the iron ore deposits worked at present. To the north again there is virtually no agriculture, but the presence of both nitrates and copper has brought considerable activity to the region, and the development of fishing is reviving stagnating ports in the extreme north. To the south of the Bio Bio, settlement has mainly taken place since 1870 and agriculture, forestry and a considerable hydro-electric potential have formed the basis for the opening up of this region in the last hundred years. To the south again, the rugged mountains and inaccessible forests of most of southern Chile at present make virtually no contribution to the economic life of the country, but the extreme south has Chile's only oilfield and some grazing land.

17.2. ECONOMIC ACTIVITIES

According to the agricultural census of Chile in 1964–65,[1] in 1965 the sown area (*superficie sembrada*) was 1,583,000 hectares, just over 2 per cent of the total national area. There had been no increase between 1955 and 1965 and even in 1936 the area was 1,340,000 hectares. The truth is that unfavourable rainfall, altitude, slope and soil conditions confine cultivation almost entirely to certain areas in Central Chile and to limited irrigated areas to the north of Santiago. The prospects for extending cultivation are very limited and significant increases in agricultural production can only be expected from an increase in yields. About 10 million hectares in Chile is classed as pasture land, most of it only of moderate quality. There are over 10 million hectares of forest, more

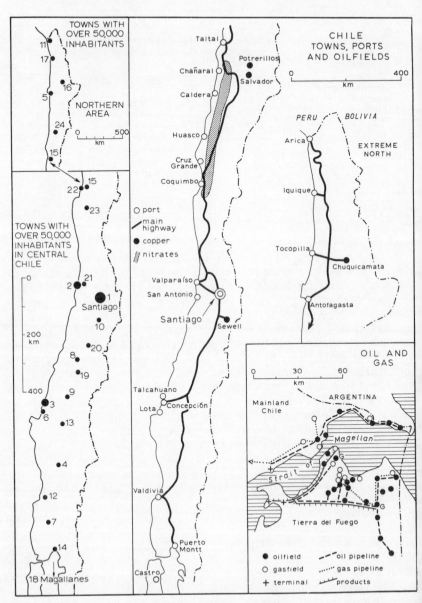

Figure 17.2. Chile: (a) Towns with over 50,000 inhabitants, (b) Location map of places mentioned in text, (c Oil and gas fields of Southern Chile

than ¼ of the national area. Table 17.3 shows the distribution in 1965 by provinces of total cultivated land, of land under wheat, which occupied nearly half, and of cattle.

Table 17.3.
CHILE: ECONOMIC ACTIVITIES BY PROVINCES

1 Cultivated area (*tierras de cultivo o de labranza*) in thousands of hectares
2 Area under wheat in thousands of hectares in 1965
3 Cattle in thousands in 1965
4 Timber produced in millions of *pulgadas*, 1965
5 Production of copper in thousands of tons
6 Persons employed in manufacturing in thousands

		1 Crops	2 Wheat	3 Cattle	4 Timber	5 Copper	6 Manu-facturing
1	Aconcagua	34	13	54		10	4
2	Antofagasta	3		1		327	7
3	Arauco	25	13	90	2		1
4	Atacama	7	3	10		118	2
5	Aysén	5		102	1		1
6	Bio-Bio	99	49	138	5		4
7	Cautín	243	127	370	4		5
8	Colchagua	88	39	95			2
9	Concepción	34	18	52	10		35
10	Coquimbo	53	21	86		16	4
11	Curicó	52	16	48			1
12	Chiloe	17	6	99	1		1
13	Linares	101	42	102	1		3
14	Llanquihué	31	12	213	1		4
15	Magallanes	1		46			2
16	Malleco	130	79	166	1		3
17	Maule	29	20	37	2		1
18	Nuble	156	92	149	3		4
19	O'Higgins	88	21	94		154	5
20	Osorno	48	22	270	1		3
21	Santiago	132	53	176		27	206
22	Talca	88	32	77			5
23	Tarapacá	4		4		1	9
24	Valdivia	83	41	337	10		9
25	Valparaíso	30	14	54		13	32
	CHILE TOTAL	1,583	734	2,870	43		

Sources: Cols. 1–4 *Agricultura e Industrias Agropecuarias*
   Año agrícola 1964–1965, pp. 30, 9, 36, 84
   Col. 5   *Minerla*, Año 1968
   Col 6 See Table 17.6; col. 1

The growth of agricultural production in Chile has been hindered both for organisational reasons and on account of physical limitations. Land in the oldest area of agricultural settlement in Chile was very unevenly distributed among the farming population and in the 1960s various measures were taken to redistribute the land. In view of the drastic political changes it is difficult in 1973 to assess the present land tenure position and future policy. On the production side, recent trends reveal only limited progress. Between the early 1950s and 1970, food production in Chile rose only by about 30 per cent. The area under wheat hardly changed, but average wheat yields rose from about 1200 kg per hectare around 1950 to 1700 kg per hectare in 1970. The number of cattle was 2,400,000 in 1930 and only 2,900,000 in 1970, while the number of sheep, about 6,000,000, has hardly changed in recent decades. The warm temperate climatic conditions of Central Chile allow the cultivation of many crops. The cultivation of barley and oats has declined in recent decades but that of maize, yields of which have roughly doubled between 1950 and 1970, and of rice, has increased. Beans, potatoes, sugar beet and the vine as well as alfalfa and other fodder crops are also cultivated. Agricultural production is insufficient, however, to satisfy the needs of Chile, and cereals, sugar and coffee are among agricultural products imported, mainly from other South American countries.

Like Venezuela, Chile depends heavily on one mineral for its exports. Around 1970, copper accounted for about 75 per cent of the value of exports. Table 17.4 shows the position of Chile in world copper production (thousands

Table 17.4.

| | Production | | Percentage from |
	Chile	World	Chile
1953	361	2,790	13
1963	602	4,630	13
1970	711	6,320	11
1971	716	6,390	11
1972	593	n.a.	9 ?

of tons of copper content). In 1970 most of the copper in Chile came from three places (see *Figure 17.2*, map *b*), the Chuquicamata (290,000 tons) and El Salvador (103,000 tons) mines of the Anaconda Company and the El Teniente mine (194,000 tons) of Kennecott. Large mining companies accounted for about 600,000 out of the 700,000 tons produced. Almost all the copper produced in Chile is exported, about one third of it in blister or unrefined form, about two thirds already refined. During the period when Allende was President of Chile (1970–73) a complete takeover of the U.S. owned Chilean copper mines was staged. The companies had been working closely with the Chilean government since the late 1960s. In 1971 however it was argued, very much along the lines used by the Peruvian government to take over the Esso oil operations in Peru in 1969, that the copper companies owed Chile $ U.S. 774 million in excess copper profits. Since their investments were calculated to be worth only $ U.S. 710 million they could be taken over without any compensation. It should be noted that all the main industrial countries of the world, including the U.S.A. and the U.S.S.R., have to import copper, and that the struggle for Chilean copper in the early 1970s had strong political undercurrents. Unfortunately for Chile it seems likely to have to continue to depend on copper as its principal export commodity, as the 10 million tons of iron ore exported annually account for only a few per cent and the scope for achieving surpluses of such items as nitrates, timber and its products, fish and fishmeal is very limited. Fortunately, new reserves of copper ore are being found in Chile. Recently, for example a deposit was located at Las Pelambres in north Chile, with 300 million tons and a 1 per cent copper content.[2]

Chile has a varied and considerable energy base. Its coal and lignite reserves would last many decades at the present rate of extraction. The annual production of coal is about 1½ million tons, almost all from the provinces of Concepción and Arauco. Some of the coal is used for coking in the iron and steel works near Concepción. In 1971 Chile also produced about 1½ million tons of oil, but in that year reserves were only 15 million tons. Chilean oil comes entirely from the many small fields in Tierra del Fuego and the nearby mainland (province of Magallanes, see *Figure 17.2*). It is shipped to refineries at Concepción and Concón (near Valparaíso). Exploration for oil continues offshore in the Strait of Magellan. The natural gas of Chile also comes from the extreme south of the country. In 1971, $3.6 + 10^9$ cubic metres (about 5 million tons of coal equivalent) were produced. Liquefied gas is shipped to various Chilean ports from the terminals shown in *Figure 17.2*. Reserves in 1971 were estimated to be 66×10^9 cubic metres. Chile also has a number of moderate sized hydro-electric stations (capacity about 1,100,000 kW out of a total of 2,100,000 including thermal) and these produced electricity that in a thermal station would have required about 2½ million tons of coal (only 600,000 at official equivalent). In spite of having considerable mineral resources, Chile in 1971 consumed 15 million tons·coal equivalent of energy while producing only about 9 million. Copper processing takes a considerable part of the total consumption. Chile is therefore depending increasingly on imported oil, and in 1971 nearly ⅔ of the oil refined in Chilean refineries came from abroad.

Modern mining and industrial techniques have been used in Chile for at least a century in the extraction and processing of nitrates and copper. For several decades now the economy of the country has depended more on mining and manufacturing than on agriculture. Most of the light manufacturing is in Greater Santiago which in 1967 had about 60 per cent of all employment in industry. Much of the remaining manufacturing capacity is located at Valparaíso, the main port for Santiago, and at Concepción and the adjoining town of Talcahuano. The establishment of an iron and steel industry at Huachipato in Talcahuano dates back to 1950. The industry is based on local coal and on iron ore from northern Chile. Output has not been expanded as quickly as was hoped in the early 1960s (see Table 17.5). Since the early 1960s, steel consumption

Table 17.5.

	Pig iron	Steel	Steel consumed
1953	286	313	261
1963	418	489	628
1970	481	547	795
1971	500	607	692

has considerably exceeded steel production. Other branches of heavy industry that have been developed in recent years are petrochemicals and the processing of timber to produce pulp and newsprint.

17.3. REGIONAL DIFFERENCES AND FUTURE PROSPECTS

In the 1960s Chile was widely regarded as one of the most developed and politically stable countries of Latin America. Events between 1970 and 1973 drew attention to the persisting poverty and underprivileged status of the rural population and the poor and unstable conditions of many urban dwellers. The supposed political 'maturity' of Chile, strained by drastic changes under the Allende government, vanished with the military coup in 1973. It seems unlikely that underlying economic and social conditions and problems have changed much since 1970 and data for the 1960s and 1970 (census) illustrating spatial aspects of these are therefore still broadly valid and relevant.

Table 17.6 contains data for 10 variables that in various ways reflect levels of economic development and material standards in the 25 provinces. Some are for 1960, others for the late 1960s or 1970. A brief comment follows on each variable.

Column 1. *Manufacturing*. The absolute number of persons employed in manufacturing in 1967 (353,000 in total) is broken down on a province basis in Table 17.3 (column 6). In Table 17.6, manufacturing population has been expressed, for want of figures for total employed population, in terms of per 1000 total population. The provinces of Santiago, Concepción and Tarapacá (with the free trade area of Arica) are well above the national average. Chiloe, Arauco and some other provinces are hardly industrialised at all. In *Figure 17.3*, the third diagram shows the distribution of manufacturing in Chile and brings out the heavy concentration in the national capital.

Column 2. *Electricity*. The interpretation of this variable must be made with reservations because it measures electricity consumption in manufacturing against total population. The provinces with the processing of minerals and with heavy industry have very high indices.

Columns 3, 4. *Literacy and secondary education* measure different levels of education available. In contrast to most other Latin American countries the highest standards of education in Chile are not in the capital, which in fact contains a large number of relatively poor migrants, but in certain other urbanised provinces with a background of modernisation such as Tarapacá and Antofagasta in the north and Magallanes in the south.

Columns 5, 6. *Infant mortality* and *births with medical certificate* are rather devious ways of measuring the availability and/or efficiency of medical services. They are only approximate, as records are incomplete and are for 1960 only.

Columns 7, 8. *Savings and bank deposits* per inhabitant reflect broadly purchasing power and living standards, though the indices for Santiago may be affected by the presence of money kept there by people living in other provinces.

Column 9. *Taxes* are raised in Chile from various sources including income and imports. However approximate the figures are, they reveal enormous differences in the taxability of different provinces.

Column 10. *Private cars* per 1000 inhabitants also show greatly varying degrees of motorisation in Chile.

The general picture of the regional distribution of wealth (and poverty) in Chile, provided by the data in Table 17.6 and represented visually in *Figure 17.3* alongside agriculture, mining and manufacturing, brings out the following features.

1. The Santiago-Valparaíso area, depending on manufacturing and various services, is the most prosperous part of Chile, though within it there are big discrepancies.

Table 17.6.
CHILE: DEVELOPMENT DATA

1   Persons in manufacturing per 1000 total population in 1967
2   Consumption of electricity in industry in kWh per inhabitant in 1967
3   Literate population over the age of 14 as a percentage of total population over the age of 14 in 1960
4   Children receiving secondary education as a percentage of total population, 1970
5   Deaths of children under 1 year of age per 1000 live births in 1960
6   Births with medical assistance per 100 live births in 1960
7   Savings (*Depósitos de ahorro*) in escudos per inhabitant in 1970
8   Deposits (*Depósitos en moneda corriente*) in escudos per inhabitant in 1970
9   All tax collected in escudos per inhabitant in 1968
10   Private cars in circulation per thousand inhabitants in 1970

		1 Manu.	2 Elec.	3 Lit.	4 Sdy Educ.	5 Inf. Mort.	6 Assist.	7 Savs	8 Deps	9 Tax	10 Cars
1	Aconcagua	23	57	80	15	95	85	361	750	230	17
2	Antofagasta	27	182	93	24	104	94	345	1,500	270	13
3	Arauco	8	7	69	11	172	49	131	290	70	4
4	Atacama	12	80	87	17	111	75	288	990	290	9
5	Aysén	11	4	82	20	397	64	223	1,080	280	10
6	Bio-Bio	22	294	71	10	167	56	144	490	170	8
7	Cautín	13	22	73	18	145	51	111	460	170	6
8	Colchagua	14	30	68	13	92	57	208	510	500	8
9	Concepción	54	747	84	25	145	69	270	1,160	430	12
10	Coquimbo	13	22	77	16	111	58	232	750	230	9
11	Curicó	13	36	71	20	137	58	223	790	240	11
12	Chiloe	5	3	79	7	131	40	176	470	90	4
13	Linares	15	89	72	14	121	66	188	510	170	7
14	Llanquihué	18	66	80	12	120	53	123	610	210	7
15	Magallanes	23	172	94	21	69	98	826	2,610	830	29
16	Malleco	14	24	70	14	163	54	144	390	150	6
17	Maule	15	20	71	19	91	50	216	540	100	5
18	Nuble	13	55	70	13	140	49	150	450	190	6
19	O'Higgins	17	201	77	15	119	84	302	970	270	13
20	Osorno	21	79	79	16	158	57	133	810	350	11
21	Santiago	64	198	91	23	76	91	404	2,320	1,740	27
22	Talca	23	46	73	16	129	64	187	740	330	10
23	Tarapacá	53	130	92	24	73	91	385	1,910	760	19
24	Valdivia	34	84	78	14	157	58	143	550	230	8
25	Valparaíso	44	252	92	26	80	90	462	1,880	1,110	24
	CHILE TOTAL	40			20			310	1,460	890	17

Sources: 1, 2, IV Censo Nacional Manufacturas, *Tomo Tercero*, pp. 237–56 (1971).
3, XIII Censo de Población, Serie A, *Resumen del país*, p. 71.
4, 7, 10, *Síntesis Estadística*, Junio 1970, pp. 23–4; Mayo 1971, p. 16; Diciembre 1971, p. 18.
5, 6, *Demografía*, Año 1966, pp. 6–32, pp. 57–60.
8, Banco Central de Chile, *Boletín Mensual*, No. 536, Oct. 1972, p. 1265.
9, *Finanzas, Bancos y Cajas Sociales*, Año 1969, p. 26.

2. The extreme north and south of Chile, depending on mining, fishing and grazing, and the Concepción area, with heavy industry, are above the Chilean average.
3. To the south of Santiago, and extending to the province of Aysén, most areas depend heavily on agriculture and tend to be poorer than the

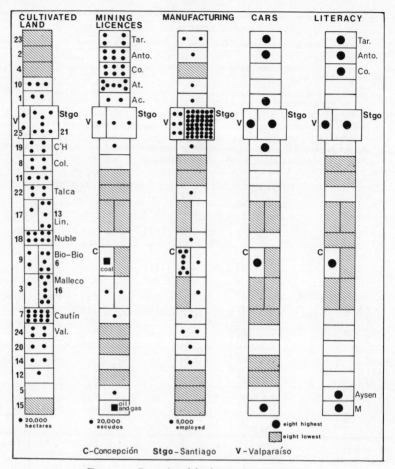

Figure 17.3. Economic and development features of Chile

Chilean average. Some provinces, such as Arauco and Chiloe are however considerably worse off than others.

A further study was carried out by the author on data for the 1970 census grouped into 12 areas. Table 17.7 breaks the population of each areal unit into two types, urban and rural. Six variables, the first three expressing the quality of housing, the second three reflecting mobility, awareness and educational levels, were selected to show contrasts of two kinds. Firstly, differences between the twelve areas can be seen by comparing percentages down any column. For example in column 6 (URB) the extremes of radio ownership among the *urban* population ranges from 76 per cent of families in area C (Atacama) to only 50 per cent in area E (Santiago). Secondly, differences between the urban and rural population can be seen by comparing any pair of indices in a given column. For example, in column 3, for area D (Valparaiso), 74 per cent of urban dwellings have a water supply in the house while only 22 per cent of rural dwellings in the same province do. A comparison of urban and rural percentages for Chile as a

Table 17-7.

INDICATION OF URBAN AND RURAL LIVING STANDARDS IN 12 REGIONS OF CHILE

1 Urban population as a percentage of total population
2 Permanent dwellings (*viviendas*) as a percentage of all dwellings
3 Percentage of dwellings with running water available in the dwelling
4 Percentage of dwellings with more than two rooms
5 Percentage of households (*hogares*) having a motor vehicle
6 Percentage of households having a radio
7 Literate population over the age of 10 as a percentage of all population over the age of 10

Grouping of provinces

C Atacama, Coquimbo   H Nuble, Concepción, Arauco, Bio-Bio, Malleco
D Aconcagua, Valparaíso J Valdivia, Osorno
F O'Higgins, Colchagua   K Llanquihué, Chiloé, Aysén
G Curicó, Talca, Linares, Maule

		1 Urban	2 Permanent dwelling		3 Water in dwelling		4 More than two rooms		5 Motor vehicle		6 Radio		7 Literate over 10	
			Urb.	Rur.	Urb.	Rur.	Urb.	Rur.	Urb.	Rur.	Urb.	Rur.	Urb.	Rur.
A	Tarapacá	81	82	67	84	30	74	49	13	7	56	48	96	78
B	Antofagasta	96	94	82	84	52	71	67	10	10	60	54	96	88
C	Atacama	67	92	71	66	11	68	46	11	3	76	58	92	76
D	Valparaíso	86	90	77	74	22	71	64	10	6	56	65	95	82
E	Santiago	94	86	81	79	27	71	64	14	8	50	63	95	81
F	O'Higgins	47	92	90	68	12	69	62	11	5	52	62	90	75
G	Curicó	48	93	88	70	11	71	56	11	3	63	55	90	73
H	Concepción	66	92	84	61	10	72	57	8	3	63	41	90	72
I	Cautín	50	94	77	52	5	72	52	9	2	61	35	91	74
J	Valdivia	56	92	89	61	12	76	65	9	3	71	49	89	77
K	Llanquihué	45	92	94	53	9	71	64	9	3	73	61	91	82
L	Magallanes	89	98	91	79	41	76	62	23	15	51	68	96	92
	CHILE	76	89	84	73	12	72	59	12	4	55	52	93	76

Source: XIV Censo Nacional de Población y III de Vivienda, abril 1970, *Muestra de adelanto de cifras censales*, in 13 volumes, tables 1, 2, 4, 7, 12.

whole shows very marked differences for domestic water supply, motor vehicle ownership and literacy, not such marked contrasts in the quality of dwellings or their size, and little difference in ownership of a radio. The advantage of transistor radios in rural areas without electricity supply must be taken into account here.

Chile is one of the few Latin American countries in which measures to distribute the wealth of the country more equably have not only been discussed but actually carried out. Even so the 'cake' is still very unevenly shared out. Comparisons are odious, but if Chile is compared with Sweden, which has roughly as many inhabitants, it emerges that the total national income of Chile in 1970, $ U.S. 6,000 million was only about $\frac{1}{5}$ that of Sweden, $ U.S. 30,000 million. Corresponding per capita figures were $ U.S. 680 and $ U.S. 3,700. The truth is that if income were shared out evenly in Chile, everyone would be poor. The socially well intended measures of the Allende government in 1970–73 to raise the standard of living of the poorer section of the Chilean community would probably have increased consumption in Chile, reduced savings, and slowed down further expansion of the means of production. It could be argued that what Chile needs is a larger 'cake' before the shareout of the cake is altered.

Future prospects for Chile seem favourable in two respects, firstly population is increasing relatively slowly and secondly educational levels are high by Latin American standards. On the other hand, natural resources are limited, with few prospects of extending cultivation, a danger of over exploitation of forest and fish resources, and an ominous increase in dependence on imported oil, the price of which increased enormously in 1973–74.

References

1. Dirección de Estadística y Censos, IV Censo Nacional Agropecuario, Año Agrícola 1964–1965, Tomo 1, *Resumen General del País,* Dic. de 1969.
2. *Peruvian Times,* 27 Aug. 1971.

Further sources consulted

Dirección de Estadística y Censos, XIV Censo Nacional de Población y III de Vivienda, *Muestra de adelanto de cifras censales,* by groups of provinces.
Instituto Nacional de Estadísticas
  a) *Síntesis Estadística* (Periodical)
  b) XIV Censo Nacional de Población, *Resultados Provisorios,* 1970.
Revista Geográfica de Valparaíso (periodical)
Flores, E., *et al., Estudios Geográficos* (Homenaje de la Facultad de Filosofia y Educación a Don Humberto Fuenzalida Villegas), 1966, Santiago; Universidad de Chile.
Corporación de Fomento de la Producción, *Geografía económica de Chile, Primer Apéndice,* 1966, Santiago; CORFO.

Further reading

Blakemore, H., 'Chile elects for a wind of change', *Geogr. Mag.,* Nov. 1970, Vol. XLIII, No. 2, pp. 137–43.

Glassner, M. I., 'Feeding a Desert City: Antofagasta, Chile', *Econ. Geogr.*, Oct. 1969, Vol. 45, No. 4, pp. 339–48.

Herrick, B. H., *Urban Migration and Economic Development in Chile,* 1965, Cambridge, Mass.; The M.I.T. Press.

Porteous, J. D., 'Urban Transplantation in Chile', *Geogrl Rev.*, Oct. 1972, Vol. LXII, No. 4, pp. 455–78.

Smole, W. J., 'Owner-cultivatorship in Middle Chile', *Research Paper* No. 89, 1963, Geography Dept., The University of Chicago.

Wadhams, P., 'Ocean surveyors in the Chilean fjords', *Geogr. Mag.*, May 1972, Vol. XLIV, No. 8, pp. 563–7.

CHAPTER 18

FUTURES FOR LATIN AMERICA

18.1. INTRODUCTION

Although the study of the future remains a controversial and emotional matter it grew in respectability in the 1960s and has now become widely accepted and practised. It may be stating the obvious to point out that nothing can be done to change the past (except by rewriting history books) whereas apparently something can be done to shape the course of events in the future by planning and controlling them. Indeed, one justification for studying history is that it throws light on the present and presumably the future.

The study of the future has been marked in recent years by the use of more flexible approaches than previously. The aim often used to be to predict *the* future as accurately as possible. Currently the aim is to produce alternative futures, each depending on a particular set of assumptions. Much credit for this new approach is due to H. Kahn and his colleagues, who in *The Year 2000*[1] discuss methods of studying the future and also sketch out various possible future situations or scenarios. The new approach to the study of the future, then, is to work out what could happen, given a certain set of circumstances, rather than what will happen. The contribution of the electronic computer in allowing the handling of much information and in performing many calculations should also be appreciated.

One of the themes of the present book has been to review the present economic, social and political geography of Latin America and to offer some views about future development prospects. The present chapter takes a comprehensive view of some recent trends in Latin America. These help to establish the limits within which future trends *could* continue. Projections of population and production are then made for selected countries, and possible different futures are considered. The optimism found among many Latin Americans towards the possibility of greatly rising living standards in the next few decades has been referred to in various chapters. The prospect is accepted by the author only with severe reservations.

In a given country or in a region within a country, goods and services are produced over a given period, a year for example, and are distributed in some way among a given population. In many Latin American countries, the total 'cake' is shared out very unevenly both by type of employment and by region. The size of production of goods and services in a country (gross domestic product indices will be used in this chapter) depends ultimately on the size of the natural resources available. The countries of Western Europe and also Japan depend very heavily on the natural resources of other parts of the world, whereas those of Latin America tend to export primary products. More immediately, the level of production of goods and services depends on the rate at which resouces are used and on the use made of them. The 'production' of services or 'non-goods' activities depends heavily on the production of material goods, a basic fact of economic development recognised more explicitly in communist countries than in western industrial ones.

A change in the population size of a country depends on births and deaths and on migration into and out of the country. It seems unlikely that international migration will play much part in demographic changes in the larger Latin American countries in the next few decades. It will therefore be assumed that population change in Latin America will depend mainly on the difference between the number of births and deaths within each country.

There is a very broad relationship between the population size of a country, the ability to use natural resources, and the amount of goods and services produced in a given period. This relationship tends to lead to the argument that population growth is needed to produce economic growth. In the opinion of the author this argument is spurious and circular, because, as has been shown in various situations in the present book, unemployment and underemployment are very high in Latin America and productivity per worker generally very low due to the lack of mechanisation. The result of this situation is illustrated by the following example. It has been shown that 14 million Australians produce roughly the same value of goods and services as 90 million Brazilians. It would seem more reasonable to expect higher per capita levels of production and therefore consumption in Brazil from an increase towards the Australian level in the productivity of the 90 million Brazilians there already, than to argue that Brazil is still 'empty' and needs far more people.

In the rest of this chapter, the future of population and of production in Latin America are first considered separately and then together. The possibility of political changes in Latin America are considered with reference to the Latin American Free Trade Association and to other regional groups. Latin America is then set in a world context.

18.2. POPULATION TRENDS AND PROJECTIONS

From time to time, historical and future population data are published in United Nations and other sources. Table 18.1a contains United Nations population data for five major Latin American countries. The two main sources are indicated below the table. Some of the data have been modified by the author on the evidence of recent census data for 1970–72 from the five countries concerned. The following features may be noted:

1. During the 50 years from 1920 to 1970 the population of all five countries increased greatly, but there was a marked difference between the fastest and slowest growing.
2. In almost every instance the *absolute* gain in population grew with each successive five year period. Minor anomalies in the general trends may be accounted for to some extent by inaccuracies of estimates during intercensal periods and, in the cases of Argentina and Venezuela, by immigration at certain periods.
3. Table 18.1b shows the percentage increase of each population on the population five years previously. Thus for example between 1920 and 1925 the population of Brazil grew from 27·4 million to 30·3 million, an

Table 18.1a.

POPULATION IN MILLIONS OF 5 LATIN AMERICAN COUNTRIES, 1920–85

	1920	1925	1930	1935	1940	1945	1950	1955	1960	1965	1970	1975	1980	1985
Brazil	27·4	30·3	33·6	37·2	41·1	46·2	51·9	60·0	71·0	82·0	94·5	107·3	123·7	142·5
Mexico	14·0	15·2	16·6	18·1	19·8	22·6	25·8	29·7	35·0	41·4	49·1	60·2	71·4	84·4
Argentina	8·9	10·4	11·9	13·0	14·2	15·4	17·2	19·1	21·0	22·5	24·3	25·7	27·8	29·5
Venezuela	2·4	2·8	3·1	3·3	3·7	4·3	5·3	6·4	7·7	9·1	10·7	12·7	15·0	17·4
Peru	5·2	5·6	6·0	6·5	7·0	7·7	8·5	9·4	10·9	12·0	13·6	15·9	18·5	21·6

Table 18.1b

PERCENTAGE INCREASE OF POPULATION DURING FIVE YEAR INTERVALS IN ABOVE COUNTRIES, 1920–70

	20-25	25-30	30-35	35-40	40-45	45-50	50-55	55-60	60-65	65-70
Brazil	11	11	11	10	12	12	16	18	15	15
Mexico	9	9	9	9	14	14	15	18	18	19
Argentina	17	11	9	9	8	12	11	10	7	8
Venezuela	17	8	6	12	16	23	21	20	18	18
Peru	8	8	8	8	10	10	11	12	11	13

Sources: *UNDYB 1960*, Table 4, *UNSYB 1972*, Table 20, and various yearbooks of countries.

absolute gain of 2·9 million and a percentage increase of 11 per cent. An increase of 15 per cent in five years is slightly less than a 3 per cent annual increase (the latter takes into account 'compound interest'). In all the countries in the table except Argentina, the five-yearly rate of increase itself tended to grow, at least until 1960. The slight downward trend in Brazil and Venezuela after 1960 may mark the beginning of a long term reduction in the rate of growth of population. Nevertheless the effect of such a trend would not be felt much for some decades since the absolute population continues to grow. Thus, for example, a 20 per cent increase on 25 million people and a 10 per cent increase on 50 million people both produce an absolute increase of 5 million.

4. The last three columns of Table 18.1a show United Nations estimates until 1985. They assume roughly a continuation of the rate of growth experienced during a period before 1970.

5. Tables 18.1a and b illustrate the difficulty of forecasting population trends. There are two extreme possibilities for each country. Firstly, through some disaster the population in a given country could be wiped out altogether. Secondly, as discussed in Chapter 6, every woman could have as many children as is biologically possible, which could theoretically produce a doubling of population in a decade or an even shorter time. Neither of these extremes would be considered probable. A more conservative approach would be to assume a continuation of recent trends, whatever they are considered to be from the evidence available, and to experiment with variations on such a basis. In the projections that follow, one projection assumes that recent trends will continue, while others assume that the rate of increase will itself *diminish* at varying rates in the future. A more detailed study of population projections for Mexico is given in Appendix 3. Some of the drawbacks and possibilities of making computerised projections are noted there.

Figure 18.1 shows with the help of three topological maps how the population of South America* changed from about 26 million in 1870 to about 180 million in 1970. If the trend of the last hundred years were to continue for the next hundred, South America would have about 1,250 million people in the year 2070. In fact, a considerable part of the increase up to 1960 was due to the arrival of permanent migrants from Europe. On the other hand the rate of natural increase (birthrate minus deathrate) was much greater in most parts of South America around 1970 than around 1870.

For the purposes of this chapter a series of projections was made to the year 2070 of the population of the seven largest Latin American countries and of the population of the remaining countries in three groups. The starting point was the 1970 population of each area. It was assumed that initially the rate of population change would be the *average* observed during 1937–1970. This rate was calculated from various intercensal change rates and is given in Table 18.2, in the column 1970, under change rates. A yearly increase of 2·8 per cent on a given population may be calculated by adding to the original population (95 million for 1970 in this case) 0·028 of itself to give the new population. Thus 95 million becomes 95 million + 2,660,000 or 97,660,000 in 1971.

---

* The trend in the rest of Latin America has been similar to that in South America.

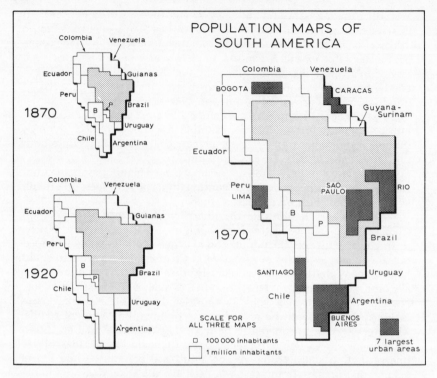

Figure 18.1. The growth of population in South America, 1870 to 1970, represented by topological maps. The area of each unit on the maps is proportional to the population of the unit

Four projections were made on a year to year basis, *A, B, C* and *D*. In these projections it was assumed that in *A* the *rate of population change* for 1970 in Table 18.2 would continue indefinitely, while in *B, C* and *D* it would decrease year by year by 1 per cent, 2 per cent and 3 per cent respectively. The effect of the reducer on the original rates of increase after 30 years is shown in the last four columns of Table 18.2. Thus by the year 2,000 there has been no change in the rate of increase in projection *A*, whereas the effect of multiplying each rate of change by 0·97 every year for 30 years in projection *D* is to reduce all the 1970 change rates drastically by the year 2000. No assumptions are made as to what exactly might cause the changes in rate of growth. None of the four projections assumes an *increasing* rate of growth in the future, in spite of the fact that this has been the trend in many areas in the last two or three decades.

In Table 18.2, the 2nd to 5th columns show the expected population of the ten regions of Latin America in the year 2000 according to the four projections described. The data in the table show clearly that even if the drastic reduction of 3 per cent per year in the rate of increase in projection *D* had started in 1970 (there is no obvious evidence to suggest it did), the population of Latin America would still increase enormously between 1970 and 2000.

Some implications of the results in Table 18.2 give concern. Even the *B* projection gives a doubling of the total population of Latin America by the year 2000. If Latin America hoped or expected to obtain the *present* per capita

Table 18.2.

POPULATION PROJECTIONS FOR LATIN AMERICAN COUNTRIES 1970–2000

	Population in millions					Yearly change rates				
	1970	A 2000	B 2000	C 2000	D 2000	1970	A 2000	B 2000	C 2000	D 2000
Reducer used						1·0	0·99	0·98	0·97
Brazil	95	218	196	179	166	·028	·028	·021	·015	·011
Mexico	51	119	107	97	90	·029	·029	·021	·016	·012
Argentina	24	40	38	36	34	·017	·017	·013	·009	·007
Venezuela	10	27	24	21	20	·032	·032	·024	·017	·013
Colombia	21	47	42	39	36	·027	·027	·020	·015	·011
Peru	14	29	27	24	23	·026	·026	·019	·014	·010
Chile	10	18	17	16	15	·021	·021	·016	·011	·008
Central America	17	40	36	32	30	·030	·030	·022	·016	·012
Islands	25	44	41	38	36	·020	·020	·015	·011	·008
Smaller S. America	17	34	31	29	27	·022	·022	·016	·012	·009
Latin America	284	617	557	512	476					

national income of West Europe, which is about five times as high as the present Latin American level, the production of goods and services in Latin America would have to be increased *ten times* in three decades.

Table 18.3 shows longer term projections continuing those already described. The A projection for Latin America, continuing the 1937–70 trend, begins to reach astronomical proportions by 2030, and by 2070 is greater than the 1970 total population of the world. The D projection, with a constant reduction of the initial rate of growth by 3 per cent per year, gives a reasonably stable population in Latin America after about 2010 at little more than double the present level. The A and D long term projections are shown in *Figure 18.2*. In *Figure 18.3*, individual projections of A type and C type are shown for the three largest countries of Latin America.

Table 18.3.

POPULATION PROJECTIONS FOR LATIN AMERICAN COUNTRIES 1970–2070

Population in millions

	1970	In the year 2030				In the year 2070			
		A	B	C	D	A	B	C	D
Brazil	95	500	334	253	207	1,508	553	318	230
Mexico	51	282	186	139	113	884	313	176	126
Argentina	24	67	52	44	39	131	71	51	42
Venezuela	10	69	44	32	25	243	77	41	28
Colombia	21	104	71	54	45	303	115	67	49
Peru	14	63	44	34	28	177	70	42	31
Chile	10	34	25	20	18	78	37	24	19
Central America	17	97	63	47	38	318	109	60	43
Islands	25	80	60	49	43	178	86	58	46
Smaller S. America	17	64	47	38	32	154	70	45	35
Latin America	284	1,361	926	709	588	3,973	1,500	883	650

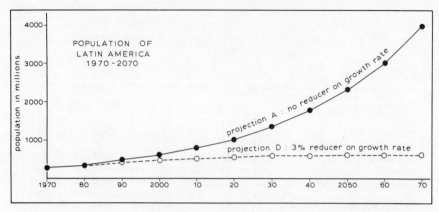

Figure 18.2. Two projections of the total population of Latin America, 1970 to 2070. Projection A assumes no change in the average rate of growth observed in the decades up to 1970 while projection D assumes the initial rate of growth will diminish by 3 per cent per year from 1970 on

In a general survey of world population trends,[2] 'The Prospects for a Stationary World Population', T. Frejka reaches the conclusion that a levelling off in the population of the developing countries is not likely or even feasible for many decades to come. Even if Latin American governments wanted to control population growth, little could be done at once to change trends. Some of

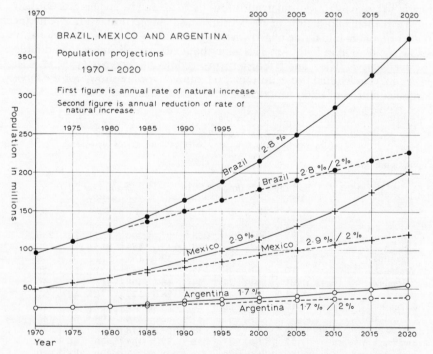

Figure 18.3. Projections of the population of Brazil, Mexico and Argentina from 1970 to 2020

the difficulties were noted in Section 6.7. During the 1960s the average growth rate in Latin America was 2·9 per cent per year and the fertility was 5·5. As it is, little has been done so far and several countries with large expanses of empty territory seem intent on filling these with the help of large increases. While the Mexican government is reported[3] to have accepted the need to reduce the rate of population growth, many Brazilians want a much bigger population and the President of Peru is reported in 1971 to have rejected the introduction of birth control on the grounds that the country is big enough to hold far more people. The view of one Argentinian economist on the need to increase the population of Argentina enormously was quoted in Chapter 13.

In Section 18.4, it will be assumed that the population growth of Latin American countries in the next few decades will follow the *B* or *C* projections. This allows a moderate diminution of the rate of natural increase, for which there is limited evidence in the 1970 and 1971 censuses of certain countries.

18.3. PRODUCTION AND CONSUMPTION TRENDS

In order to estimate possible future living standards for Latin American countries it is necessary to know both future population size and the future value of production of goods and services. It is difficult to compare the gross domestic product of a country at different times on account of the almost constant tendency for currency units to drop in value over time, and therefore difficult to measure real rather than apparent changes in production over time if these are assessed in money terms rather than specific items such as food, steel or energy. In this section, therefore, trends and future prospects for the production and consumption of energy, agricultural items and mineral raw materials are considered, as well as gross domestic product (at constant prices). The three sectors of the economy to be considered together make up a large proportion of the more basic side of the production of goods and services, though the present and presumably the future importance of manufacturing and services in Latin America should not be overlooked.

1. ENERGY

Table 18.4 shows the production of oil, natural gas and electricity in Brazil, Mexico, Argentina, Venezuela and Peru in recent decades. In Table 5.13 in Chapter 5, energy consumption and surplus are shown. Electricity includes both thermal and hydro-electricity. If the rates of increase in production observed during the last 3–4 decades were to continue, some very large production totals could be expected by 1990 or 2000. When an economic activity is small in absolute terms however it is more easy to achieve high rates of increase than when it is large. A feature of Soviet growth, widely publicised in the U.S.S.R. as evidence of a superior economic system, were the high increase rates in the 1930s and 1950s in many industrial sectors.

With regard to the future of energy production in Latin America, the following problems face the industry to varying degrees in every country. Since oil and natural gas are non-renewable resources and many of the oilfields in

Latin America have been producing for several decades, many of the more easily accessible reserves, particularly in Mexico and Venezuela, have already been used. Exploration costs tend to be high in such new areas as the forests of Amazonia and offshore concessions. The large reserves of tar sands in Venezuela can be used commercially only with new technology. Many Latin American countries are in fact faced with the need to import increasing quantities of oil, presumably from areas such as the Middle East and Nigeria, which will still have surpluses in the 1970s and 1980s. During the world oil 'crisis' of late 1973 more publicity was given in Britain to the impact of higher oil prices on the economies of the developed countries than on the economies of developing countries importing oil.

Table 18.4.

PRODUCTION OF OIL, NATURAL GAS AND ELECTRICITY IN FIVE COUNTRIES 1937–1970

The following energy equivalents are used in *United Nations Statistical Yearbook* (e.g. 1972, p. 846).

> 1 ton of crude oil is equivalent to 1·3 tons of coal
> 1000 cubic metres of natural gas are equivalent to 1·332 tons of coal
> 1000 kWh are equivalent to 0·125 tons of coal

For comparison, in 1970 the U.K., produced 145 million tons of coal.

	1930	1940	1950	1960	1970
OIL (millions of tons)					
Brazil	—	—	—	3·9	8·2
Mexico	5·7	6·3	10·3	14·2	21·5
Argentina	1·3	2·9	3·4	9·1	20·0
Venezuela	20·1	27·5	78·2	149·4	193·9
Peru	1·7	1·6	2·0	2·5	3·6
NATURAL GAS (cubic metres $\times 10^9$)					
Brazil	—	—	—	0·5	1·3
Mexico	0·3	1·1	1·7	9·7	18·8
Argentina	0·3	0·5	0·6	1·4	6·0
Venezuela	—	—	1·5	4·6	9·0
Peru	—	—	—	—	0·5
ELECTRICITY (kWh $\times 10^9$)					
Brazil	0·5	1·3	8·4	22·9	45·5
Mexico	1·2	2·5	4·4	10·7	28·6
Argentina	1·2	2·6	4·4	10·4	21·7
Venezuela	—	0·1	0·5	3·0	12·6
Peru	—	0·1	0·8	2·7	5·3

– Negligible or none.

The exploitation of hydro-electricity is a slow process and involves hydrological and transmission problems. Several examples have been given in earlier chapters of the slow progress in the construction of hydro-electric stations in Latin America. In the Soviet Union in the 1950s and 1960s delays occured in the completion of several large hydro-electric stations. Coal reserves are generally limited in extent and quality; Latin American countries might increase their imports of coal. They are certainly beginning to import nuclear power station. In view, however, of the slow rate of development of nuclear power for the generation of electricity in the pioneer countries in this field, the U.K., U.S.A. and U.S.S.R., Latin America can hope to obtain little energy from this source for at least two or three decades.

Altogether, then, energy supplies in Latin America could fall short of the amount required to maintain an increase in consumption of the kind shown in Table 18.5. It will be shown in Section 18.4 that when population increase is taken into account, the arithmetic of the prospective energy gap in some Latin American countries is most depressing. Likely achievements in the next three decades appear to fall far short of present hopes, expectations and long term plans.

Table 18.5.
ENERGY CONSUMPTION IN FIVE COUNTRIES, 1937–70

	1937	*1950*	*1960*	*1970*
ENERGY CONSUMPTION (millions of tons of coal equivalent)				
Brazil	5·0	11·5	24·5	44·6
Mexico	8·2	15·4	31·9	59·3
Argentina	9·2	13·1	22·3	39·2
Venezuela	1·0	3·9	19·3	26·8
Peru	0·8	1·6	3·8	8·6
Ethiopia	—	—	0·2	0·8
Belgium*	34·7	37·4	37·6	59·7
ENERGY CONSUMPTION (Kilograms per capita)				
Brazil	130	220	330	470
Mexico	440	660	900	1,200
Argentina	650	760	1,100	1,690
Venezuela	300	770	2,700	2,500
Peru	130	190	330	610
Ethiopia	0	2	8	30
Belgium*	4,020	4,160	3,970	6,120

– Negligible
* Includes Luxembourg.

2. AGRICULTURAL PRODUCTS

Table 18.6 gives a brief picture of the kinds of increases achieved in the production of important agricultural items in selected countries. During the same period, the population of the five countries in question more than doubled. Yields fluctuate from year to year, and a considerable amount of the variations in Table 18.6 are accounted for by this random element. The per capita consumption of food has increased in all the five countries in the last 2–3 decades but except in Argentina it is still low by the standards of most developed countries.

From what has been said about agriculture in previous chapters of this book it will be appreciated that there is scope in many Latin American countries for increasing agricultural production, usually through a combination of various improvements rather than through a single line of attack. In summary, the

Table 18.6.

PRODUCTION OF SELECTED AGRICULTURAL ITEMS 1940–70 IN SELECTED COUNTRIES

	Crops in thousands of tons, cattle in millions			
	1940	*1950*	*1960*	*1970*
Wheat				
Mexico	350	550	1,190	2,440
Argentina	8,150	5,800	3,960	4,920
Maize				
Brazil	5,440	6,000	9,040	14,220
Mexico	1,665*	3,120	5,390	9,000
Argentina	10,238	2,670	4,850	9,360
Venezuela	360	360	440	710
Peru	450	290	340	620
Sugar				
Brazil	1,190	1,900	3,320	5,020
Mexico	320	670	1,520	2,400
Argentina	520	610	820	980
Peru	430	460	810	770
Cotton				
Brazil	540	390	540	670
Mexico	70*	260	460	310
Peru	80*	80	130	90
Coffee				
Brazil	1,000	1,070	1,800	760
Mexico	50	70	70	180
Cattle				
Brazil	41	51	74	97
Mexico	18	15	21	25
Argentina	33	45	43	50

* Mid or late 1930s.

following directions, listed for convenience, could lead perhaps to a doubling of agricultural production between 1970 and 2000.

1. Land reform
2. The greater use of potential land in existing farming areas by transference from grazing to crop farming and by the application of fertilisers
3. The cultivation of new areas
4. Experimentation with new crops in areas with a few traditional crops
5. A reduction of the number of animals used for ploughing and transport, releasing fodder for the raising of stock to provide meat, milk and other items.

From the many examples for specific countries in previous chapters it must be added that all five approaches above must be considered with serious reservations. For example the clearance of hitherto uncultivated land for cultivation requires careful assessment of the potential there. The indiscriminate settlement of new areas with unknown conditions can lead to economic waste and ecological disaster.

Though agricultural production could perhaps be doubled between 1970 and 2000, it must be remembered, as shown in Section 18.2, that population is also expected to double during 1970 and 2000. The longer term prospect is more gloomy. It is doubtful if a further doubling of population between 2000 and 2030 could be matched by an equivalent doubling of agricultural production again. The doubling between 2000 and 2030 would involve absolute values twice as great as the doubling between 1970 and 2000.

3. OTHER SELECTED PRIMARY PRODUCTS

Mineral reserves do not last for ever and there are many now abandoned mines in Latin America where at one time precious metals and precious stones were mined. It is less widely realised that Peru, which in 1948 produced ⅓ of the world's vanadium, ceased production in 1956. This trivial example is a reminder of the way in which minerals run out. So much of Latin America remains to be explored for its minerals that it is impossible to estimate reserves of most minerals. A shortage of easily extracted minerals in the world as a whole could intensify the search for minerals in Latin America. Nevertheless the pattern of mineral discoveries and production over time is less predictable than that of agricultural production or industrial production.

Table 18.7 shows the production of non-ferrous metals in Peru and Mexico in recent decades. Two features of the trends may be noted. The fairly steady

Table 18.7.
COPPER, LEAD AND ZINC PRODUCTION IN PERU AND MEXICO, 1930–70

	Thousands of tons of metal content				
	1930	1940	1950	1960	1970
Copper					
Mexico	70	40	60	60	60
Peru	50	40	30	210	210
Zinc					
Mexico	120	120	220	260	270
Peru	10	20	90	280	320
Lead					
Mexico	230	200	240	190	180
Peru	20	50	60	170	160

upward trends observed in the production of most energy and agricultural items in Tables 18.4 and 18.6 do not occur. In the case of copper and lead in Mexico there has been an absolute decline in production. In the case of the Peruvian production of all three metals, between 1950 and 1960, sharp increases in production occurred in a matter of a few years due to the opening of large new mining capacity.

There is a big element of uncertainty in some other branches of production, particularly fishing. Table 18.8 shows the weight of the Peruvian fishing catch between 1957 and 1972. In 1964 a projection of past trends into the future would have given a continuing yearly increase to perhaps 20 million tons in 1970. In spite of a setback in 1965 and a levelling off in production after 1967, a projection of past trends into the future made in 1970 would have given perhaps a continuing production level of about 10 million tons a year in the

Table 18.8
PERUVIAN FISH CATCH, 1957–72
(millions of tons)

1957	0·5	1961	5·2	1965	7·6	1969	9·2
1958	0·9	1962	6·8	1966	8·8	1970	12·6
1959	2·2	1963	7·1	1967	10·2	1971	10·6
1960	3·5	1964	9·3	1968	10·6	1972	4·5

forseeable future. In 1972 the catch dropped drastically on account, it is thought, of a combination of the negative effects of a warm current from the north reducing fish food in the sea, and over-fishing, reducing breeding fish. In 1974 the fish catch was about 4 million tons.

4. GROSS DOMESTIC PRODUCT

Even from the limited evidence in this section it can be seen that some branches of the economy change more smoothly and predictably than others. Since overall economic growth includes all elements of the economy the tendency is for drastic ups and downs in different sectors to cancel one another out to some extent. Even so, data for the growth of gross domestic product in various Latin American countries in the last two decades show rates varying in the same country over a short period from no change in one year to as much as 10 per cent in another. Continuous periods of more than a few years of a high rate of growth have been unusual, though Puerto Rico, Venezuela and Mexico have achieved rates of growth at times since the Second World War comparable with those in some communist countries, and in Japan and certain West European countries. Table 18.9 shows the achievements in selected countries in Latin America and

Table 18.9.
AVERAGE ANNUAL RATES OF GROWTH OF GROSS DOMESTIC PRODUCT* AT CONSTANT PRICES

	Period	Gross domestic produce	
		Total	Per capita
Brazil	1960-70	5·5	2·3
Mexico	1960-70	7·3	3·6
Argentina	1960-70	4·2	2·6
Venezuela	1960-71	5·4	1·8
Peru	1968-71	5·5	2·3
Haiti	1960-69	0·6	−1·4
Puerto Rico	1960-70	7·4	5·5
Uruguay	1960-70	1·0	−0·3
U.S.A.	1960-71	4·3	3·0
U.S.S.R.	1960-70	7·2	5·9
U.K.	1960-71	2·8	2·2
Japan	1960-71	10·7	9·6
Spain	1960-71	7·0	5·9
Romania	1960-69	8·8	7·9

* For the U.S.S.R. and Romania the definition is 'net material product'.

Source: *UNSYB 72*, Tables 184–6.

among developed countries elsewhere in the world. The table shows that rates of growth (at constant prices) varied from one country to another in both groups. Since population was growing at about 3 per cent per year in Latin America and at about 1 per cent per year in the developed group of countries, a Latin American country needs a 'start' of 2 per cent growth of gross domestic product to offset its fast population growth and achieve a per capita growth similar to that in a developed country.

18.4. POPULATION AND PRODUCTION

In this section two types of projection have been made to illustrate ways of studying the prospects of Latin American countries in the future and of answering questions such as: 'What would Mexico have to do to reach the 1970 per capita gross domestic product of France (or the U.S.A., or Spain) in the year 2000 (or 1990 or 2010)'?

Various studies of development have shown that there is a broad correlation between the per capita consumption of energy in a country, and its per capita gross domestic product. Energy therefore 'stands in' for total gross domestic product and has constant values over time whereas money has to be converted to constant prices. The first type of projection in this section combines population and energy consumption in Brazil, Mexico and Argentina. On *Figure 18.4,* the position of a country on the graph in a given year depends on the two coordinates, its total population size on the horizontal axis and its total energy consumption in millions of tons of coal equivalent on the vertical scale. The reader should note that it is more convenient to express per capita energy consumption in kilograms and that there are 1000 kilograms in a metric ton.

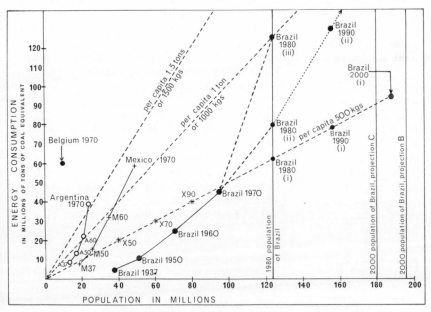

Figure 18.4. Population and energy consumption trends in Argentina, Mexico and Brazil

Over a period of time, presumably both the population size and the energy consumption of a country change. The position of a country on the graph therefore also changes. As its total population grows, it moves from left to right while as its total energy consumption grows it moves from bottom to top. The values for population and energy consumption for Brazil, Mexico and Argentina in 1937, 1950, 1960 and 1970 have been taken (or estimated) from Tables 18.1a and 18.5. A feature of the graph is the fact that whatever the size of a country, a given level of per capita energy consumption falls on a line originating at the bottom left hand corner of the graph and running in a direction towards the upper right. If total population and total energy consumption both grow at the same rate, *per capita* consumption stays the same. On the graph in *Figure 18.4,* a hypothetical country (X) is represented by an asterisk. In 1950 it had 40 million people and consumed 20 million tons of energy; in 1970, 60 million people and consumed 30 million tons; and in 1990, 80 million people and consumed 40 million tons. Per capita consumption was 0.5 tons (500 kilograms) in all three years. On the graph, the fact that *per capita* consumption in Argentina, Mexico and Brazil increased in every period (see Table 18.5) is shown by the way the points representing the countries fall on a slight curve (joined on the graph by continuous lines) between 1937 and 1970. The 1970 position of Belgium is shown for comparison. It should be noted that per capita values increase from lower right to upper left on the graph. Once the layout of the graph has been appreciated, it brings home strikingly the interdependence of population size, production and level of development. Such graphs have been used by H. Kahn in *The Year 2000.*[1]

A graph of the kind used in *Figure 18.4* also helps to appreciate possible future situations. The future of energy consumption in Brazil to the year 2000 will be considered. It is not known what the population of Brazil will be during the next three decades. Various futures could be tried. It will be assumed here that a rate of growth somewhere between the *B* and *C* projections in Section 18.2 will occur. This anticipates 124 million in 1980 (see vertical line on graph), 156 million in 1990 and 188 million in 2000. It is not known how much energy will be consumed each year in Brazil over the next thirty years. It *is* known, however, that there are difficulties in expanding energy consumption in Brazil because increasing amounts will have to be imported unless dramatic new discoveries of oil and natural gas occur.

Three projections of energy consumption in Brazil will be made. In Table 18.10a the trend from 1937 to 1970 is shown. In Table 18.10b the figures arrived at in three projections, (i), (ii), and (iii) are given. They are represented graphically in the right hand part of *Figure 18.4.*

Projection (i). It is assumed that in 1980 a per capita consumption of 500 kilograms tons of coal equivalent is reached and after that, consumption grows with population. In the year 2000 Brazil would need to consume about twice as much energy as now, but would be at a level of development far below that hoped for.

Projection (ii). It is assumed that the trend observed during 1937 to 1970 is approximately continued to the year 2000. In 2000, Brazil reaches a per capita level of consumption of 1000 kilograms of coal equivalent, but needs to consume 188 million tons of energy, four times as much as in 1970, to do this.

Projection (iii). This projection takes Brazil to a per capita level of energy consumption in the year 2000 of 2000 kilograms per capita, *half* the 1970 French

Table 18.10.

POPULATION AND ENERGY PROJECTIONS FOR BRAZIL

(a)

	Population millions	Energy consumption in millions of tons of coal equivalent	Per capita energy consumption in tons of coal equivalent
1937	39	5	120
1950	52	12	220
1960	71	25	330
1970	95	45	470

(b)

	Population estimate	Projection (i) Energy		Projection (ii) Energy		Projection (iii) Energy	
		cons.	capita	cons.	capita	cons.	capita
1980	124	62	500	80	645	124	1,000
1990	156	78	500	130	830	234	1,500
2000	188	94	500	188	1,000	376	2,000

level. But Brazil has to consume 376 million tons of energy to achieve this level, eight times as much as at present.

The reader is left to decide which projection seems feasible, realistic or possible. To be sure, the performance of Argentina and Mexico is greatly superior to that of Brazil and there is at least a prospect that by the year 2000 they might each come somewhere near the 1970 level of France of 4000 kilograms per capita. Brazil, on the other hand, is similar to Colombia, Peru, and many smaller Latin American countries.

A similar exercise follows with gross domestic product data. Four countries are considered, Venezuela, Chile and Peru, and the Netherlands for comparative purposes. The population of the four countries is given in Table 18.11a, that for 1980, 1990 and 2000 assuming for the three Latin American countries a diminution of the annual rate of natural increase of 2 per cent each year observed in the period before 1970. This is a fairly 'generous' assumption based on the C projection in Section 18.2. A continuation of the 1950–70 population growth rate would give considerably bigger populations with correspondingly lower per capita gross domestic product estimates for 1980–2000. The rate of increase of the population of the Netherlands (1·2 per cent per year around 1970) is also assumed to diminish during 1970–2000.

Gross domestic product is measured in terms of 1970 values in U.S. dollars to allow comparability among the countries. Other years are measured in dollars of the same value. This means that the 'projection' of gross domestic product back to 1960 has the effect of expressing values for that year in 1970 dollars, not 1960 dollars, which were worth considerably more. Future estimates of gross domestic product are also in 1970 dollars.

It is assumed that the rates of growth of gross domestic product (at constant prices) observed during the decade 1960–70 are maintained in each of the four countries for the thirty years 1970–2000. The percentage rates of increase each decade are shown in Table 18.11b. These are calculated from annual rates of 5·3 per cent for the Netherlands, 5·4 per cent for Venezuela, 4·4 for Chile and

Table 18.11.

PROJECTIONS OF POPULATION AND GROSS DOMESTIC PRODUCT FOR 4 COUNTRIES

(a) Population estimates
population in millions

	1960	1970	1980	1990	2000
Netherlands	11·5	13·0	14·7	16·3	17·8
Venezuela	7·7	10·4	13·9	17·6	21·3
Chile	7·3	8·8	10·7	12·6	14·4
Peru	10·9	13·6	17·2	20·8	24·4

(b) Gross domestic product growth rates assumed, 1970-2000.

Percentage increase per decade

Netherlands	67	Chile	54
Venezuela	69	Peru	59

(c) Gross domestic product in millions of 1970 dollars
U.S. dollars at 1970 prices (T) and per capita (C)

	1960		1970		1980		1990		2000	
	T	C	T	C	T	C	T	C	T	C
Netherlands	18,800	1,630	31,400	2,410	52,400	3,560	87,500	5,370	146,000	8,200
Venezuela	6,150	800	10,400	1,000	17,600	1,270	29,700	1,690	50,200	2,360
Chile	4,350	600	6,700	760	10,300	960	15,900	1,260	24,500	1,700
Peru (i)	3,400	310	5,400	400	8,600	500	13,700	660	21,800	890
Peru (ii)	3,400	310	5,400	400	10,800	630	21,600	1,040	43,200	1,770

Source of 1960 and 1970 figures: *UNSYB 72*, Tables 184, 188.

4·8 for Peru. The resulting absolute values of gross domestic product and resulting per capita values (total GDP in Table 18.11c divided by total population in Table 18.11a) are given.

It could be argued that the rates of growth of gross domestic product in the 1960s will not continue in the next three decades. The point of view might be put that faster rates of growth have been observed both in Latin America (e.g. 7 per cent per year for Mexico) and elsewhere (e.g. 10 per cent per year in Japan) and that a faster rate of growth could be maintained under certain circumstances. A second projection is given for Peru (referred to as Peru (ii)), assuming a doubling of gross domestic product each decade from 1970–2000, an almost inconceivable achievement. The results of the projection are shown graphically in *Figure 18.5* and the two projections for Peru are compared.

Many points could be made in connection with the study described above. A much more elaborate set of projections could be made, including more countries and giving various alternative futures. Certain conclusions may however be stated with some conviction from the case considered.

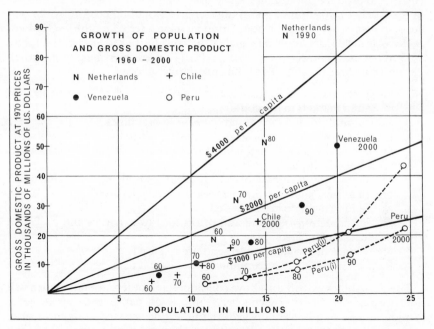

Figure 18.5. Population and gross domestic product trends and projections 1960 to 2020 for the Netherlands, Venezuela, Chile and Peru

Of the three Latin American countries selected for study, only Venezuela, on a continuation of performance during the 1960s, has a chance of reaching in the year *2000* the *1970* level of the Netherlands. Unless population growth slowed down greatly in Venezuela, the attainment of the 1970 Netherlands level would however require approximately a five-fold increase in the production of goods and services in 30 years. The argument that because in the 30 years 1940–1970 Venezuela already achieved roughly a five-fold increase in the production of goods and services and therefore could do the same again in the next three decades is utterly spurious. The *absolute* increase would have to be five times greater in the second period, as may be illustrated by the following numbers: 1 unit in 1940 to 5 units in 1970, absolute increase 4 units; 5 units in 1970 to 25 units in 2000, absolute increase 20 units.

With regard to the possible aspirations of the poorest of the three countries, Peru, a number of points may be made. Projection Peru (i) gives a fairly generous future for Peru, assuming less than a two-fold increase of population from 13½ million in 1970 to 24½ million in 2000 (one 'official' Peruvian estimate[4] of population in the year 2000, made in 1972 was 30 million). To reach a per capita level of about 900 dollars in the year 2000 (below the 1970 Venezuela level), an average yearly growth rate of 4·8 per cent per year would have to be maintained every year for 30 years, and GDP would have to grow absolutely four times. In a country in which man has been active for several thousand years it is hard to see how in a mere three decades such an increase could take place.

Projection Peru (ii) assumes an average annual rate of increase of 7–8 per cent per year every year between 1970 and 2000 (the effect of this *annual* rate of increase is to produce a doubling each decade). In this way an eight-fold increase in the yearly production of goods and services would be needed by the year 2000. *Even then,* assuming the population increase referred to, the level in Peru in the year 2000 would only be equal to the West European level of the 1950s.

Even the more conservative projection Peru (i) needs everything to go well in Peru for the three decades. The following should all occur:

1. Large reserves of oil and/or natural gas must be found, extracted *and* moved to markets in the country.
2. Agricultural production should increase several times.
3. Large new reserves of non-ferrous metals must be found and exploited.
4. Fishing must at least be maintained at 1970 levels and the forest resources used extensively.
5. The heavy industrial base of Peru needs improvements. A steel production of at least 5 million tons per year would be an asset.
6. An engineering industry is needed.
7. Foreign trade must expand and prices for raw materials and processed products remain favourable.
8. Many kinds of social improvements are required.
9. Political stability and a continuity of policy and plans is desirable.

The probability that all the above conditions and others not mentioned will hold throughout 30 years seems very unlikely on past experience in Peru. Without question, however, any growth of the kind referred to requires large amounts of capital and their effective use. This could mean that most of the expansion would have to be in the coastal region and Amazon rather than in the Andes. Regional differences would therefore increase in the next 30 years. Most of the employed population has a very low productivity, many people are underemployed, and many of employable age are unemployed, so the idea that a bigger population is needed is ridiculous in the view of the author. On the contrary, any reduction in the rate of population growth would either lessen the need to achieve such a high rate of economic growth or for the same rate of economic growth would allow higher living standards.

What has been said specifically about Peru applies broadly to most Latin American countries. The final point made in this section with reference to Peru is therefore also valid in a much broader context. Table 18.12 sets out in the simplest terms possible the apparent paradox of a country like Peru. Suppose an arbitrary level of $500 per capita GDP (in 1970 U.S. dollars) is taken as a threshold between poor and not poor. Then it is suggested that while the *proportion* of poor people in Peru diminished between 1940 and 1970, the *absolute*

Table 18.12.
POVERTY IN PERU

	Total population (millions)	Percentage poor	Absolute number poor (millions)
1940	7	90	6·3
1970	14	80	11·2
2000	25	60	15·0

number increased. Even if great improvements take place in Peru between 1970 and 2000, the process is likely to be repeated. What should not be overlooked is that *higher standards* may be expected in the year 2000 than in 1970 and the perceived poverty threshold could therefore itself actually be higher too.

18.5. GROUPINGS OF LATIN AMERICAN COUNTRIES

The political fragmentation of Latin America reached its greatest extent with the creation after the Second World War of several independent countries from British colonies. Since the 1950s, however, there has been a trend towards the establishment of trading groups and free trade associations. The earliest groups, the Organisation of Central American States and the Federation of the British West Indies, formed in the 1950s, preceded the much larger Latin American Free Trade Association (LAFTA).

LAFTA was established in 1960 to bring about a reduction in and eventually the elimination of tariffs on trade between member countries. The countries in Table 18.13 apart from the U.S.A. were members by the late 1960s but Venezuela and Bolivia joined late. One of the aims of LAFTA was to encourage and increase trade between Latin American countries and to increase economic interdependence. Some of the countries were not satisfied with the slow progress towards economic integration and the Andean Group was formed. The three largest Latin American countries, Brazil, Mexico and Argentina appear to have been reluctant to commit themselves far in the move towards economic integration.

A measure of the success of LAFTA in achieving its aims is a comparison of trade between member countries before LAFTA (1959) and after nearly a decade of LAFTA (1969). Table 18.13 shows along each row the percentage of the value of exports of each LAFTA country going to every other one and also to the U.S.A. and the other main destination apart from the U.S.A. Percentages for 1959 and 1969 may be compared. They show that most of the eleven countries were sending a bigger proportion of their exports to other LAFTA countries in 1969 than in 1959, indicating a general growth of trade within the group. Peru and Venezuela were two notable exceptions. On the other hand, even in 1969

Table 18.13.

INTER LATIN AMERICAN TRADE 1959 AND 1969

Each number is the percentage of the value of exports of the country of origin to the particular destination to nearest one per cent

Country of origin (Exports from)	Year	1 ARG.	2 BOL.	3 BRZ.	4 CHI.	5 COL.	6 ECU.	7 MEX.	8 PAR.	9 PER.	10 URU.	11 VEN.	1-11	U.S.A.	OTHER	
1 Argentina	1959	—	1	9	3	0	0	1	1	1	1	1	16	11	23	U.K.
	1969	—	1	8	6	1	—	1	1	3	1	1	23	9	14	Italy
2 Bolivia	1959	6	—	2	—	0	0	1	—	1	—	0	10	35	46	U.K.
	1969	5	—	1	1	0	0	1	0	2	0	0	10	31	46	U.K.
3 Brazil	1959	3	0	—	1	0	0	—	0	0	2	—	6	46	7	W.G.
	1969	7	—	—	1	—	0	1	—	—	2	—	11	26	10	W.G.
4 Chile	1959	5	—	2	—	—	—	1	0	1	0	—	8	39	16	W.G.
	1969	6	—	3	—	—	—	—	0	—	0	—	10	17	14	U.K.
5 Colombia	1959	0	0	0	0	—	1	0	0	0	0	—	1	68	10	W.G.
	1969	1	0	—	1	—	1	—	0	1	0	1	5	42	13	W.G.
6 Ecuador	1959	—	0	—	2	5	—	1	0	0	0	2	10	59	11	W.G.
	1969	2	0	0	3	4	—	—	0	0	0	0	10	41	12	W.G.
7 Mexico	1959	—	0	—	0	0	0	—	0	0	0	1	1	70	9	Japan
	1969	1	0	1	1	1	0	—	0	0	0	1	5	57	7	Japan
8 Paraguay	1959	21	1	—	0	0	0	0	—	0	3	0	25	33	(21)	Arg.
	1969	29	0	—	3	0	0	1	—	0	4	0	37	21	(29)	Arg.
9 Peru	1959	3	1	1	9	1	1	—	—	—	—	—	16	31	10	U.K.
	1969	2	—	1	1	1	—	1	0	—	—	1	7	35	16	Japan
10 Uruguay	1959	—	0	1	0	—	—	—	—	1	—	—	3	12	10	Neth.
	1969	2	0	5	2	3	—	—	1	2	—	—	15	7	14	U.K.
11 Venezuela	1959	4	0	4	0	1	0	—	0	—	1	—	8	42	24	Neth.A.
	1969	1	0	2	1	1	—	—	0	—	—	—	5	34	20	Neth.A.
U.S.A.	1959	1	—	2	1	1	—	4	0	1	—	4	15		21	Canada
	1969	1	—	2	1	1	—	4	—	—	—	2	11		24	Canada

Sources: *United Nations Yearbook of International Trade Statistics, 1959* and *1969.*
W. G. – West Germany.
Neth. A. – Netherlands Antilles

the U.S.A. alone still took several times as many of the exports of each country as the rest of LAFTA. Perhaps the most notable aspects of the development of LAFTA in the 1960s have been the growth of trade between Argentina and Uruguay, exporting temperate agricultural products, and various South American countries, and the greatly increased, though still small participation of Mexico and Colombia. The fact remains that food and raw materials still form the bulk of Latin American exports and manufactured goods the principal type of imports.

Brazil, Mexico and Argentina are increasingly exporting manufactured goods and they are interested in markets in less industrialised Latin American countries. The latter, however, are also trying to establish their own industries and, as was stated in Bolivia as a reason for not joining LAFTA, they tend to prefer to buy good quality manufactured goods from established industrial countries rather than less known manufactures of Latin American partners. The great distances between many pairs of Latin American countries and the lack of regular efficient shipping services have also discouraged trade. It seems reasonable to predict that in the next decade or two the presence of LAFTA will not make much difference to the development of Latin American countries.

The Andean Group, a sub-group of LAFTA, had in the early 1970s ambitious plans for integration. Bolivia, Chile, Colombia, Ecuador, Peru and Venezuela form the Andean Group. In the short term their mutual trade has increased somewhat in the early 1970s but of the total imports of the six members, only about 5 per cent came from partners in the Andean Group in 1972.[5] Trade includes the export of Venezuelan oil and Colombian meat to the other countries, but by 1973 there was still little exchange of manufactured goods.

18.6. LATIN AMERICA AND THE REST OF THE WORLD

It was pointed out at the beginning of this book that on average Latin America is the most developed of the developing regions of the world. Table 18.14 has been included both to emphasise this point and to show how dubious the projection of recent trends into the future can be.[6] For the purposes of this study the countries of the world have been placed in ten groups, the main components of which are noted.

A study was made of recent trends in the growth of population, food and energy consumption, the availability of doctors, and gross domestic product or some equivalent measure of total economic size during the 1950s and 1960s. Projections were then made for five-year periods from 1970 to 2000. Rates of change based partly on recent trends, partly on a subjective assessment of prospects, were then made. The per capita values of each of the four indices of living standards and development were then calculated. On the basis of the particular changes used in this projection, Latin America maintains its position at the top of the six developing regions though it is challenged by South West Asia and North Africa. It remains far below the level of the four developed regions. The share of the total world population in the four developed regions drops from about 30 per cent in 1970 to 20 per cent in the year 2000.

It is with regret that the author feels forced to conclude this book by saying that the weight of evidence presented at various stages shows convincingly that unless a complete change of trends occurs in the world very soon, the

Table 18.14.

1 North America plus Australia and New Zealand
2 Non-communist Europe
3 U.S.S.R. plus communist East Europe
4 Japan
5 Latin America
6 Africa except the five northern countries
7 Asia from Turkey to Afghanistan plus North Africa
8 Indian 'sub-continent'
9 Asia from Burma to Indonesia and South Korea
10 China plus small communist neighbours

AT Population in millions
AP Percentage of world total population
B Food in thousands of calories per inhabitant per year. e.g. 3000 calories per day would be about 1,100.
C Energy consumption per capita in kilograms of coal equivalent
D Doctors per million people
E Gross national product in 1970 U.S. dollars

	Year	1 NAM	2 WEU	3 USR	4 JAP	5 LAM	6 AFR	7 SWA	8 SAS	9 SEA	10 CHI
AT Total population	1970	242	354	350	104	283	270	176	704	351	760
	2000	320	429	412	133	583	557	363	1,211	736	1,114
AP Per cent population	1970	7	10	10	3	8	7	5	19	10	21
	2000	6	7	7	2	10	9	6	21	13	19
B Food per capita	1970	1,165	1,130	1,131	913	912	804	909	730	803	730
	2000	1,180	1,240	1,410	1,050	1,110	980	860	750	1,010	920
C Energy per capita	1970	10,330	3,760	4,340	3,130	870	320	510	180	240	550
	2000	23,270	9,230	11,440	17,610	2,540	580	2,460	630	1,000	1,440
D Doctors per million	1970	1,450	1,360	1,740	1,060	560	70	340	90	110	100
	2000	1,940	1,980	2,830	1,460	1,820	100	490	120	160	200
E GNP per capita	1970	4,460	2,370	1,360	2,260	420	190	370	90	110	100
	2000	7,790	5,830	4,390	8,660	790	320	770	150	210	200

development gap will be wider in absolute terms in the year 2000 than in 1970. Within the developing world, South Asia seems destined to deteriorate while some countries of Latin America, Africa and Southwest Asia could move into the developed group.

Even if a dramatic rethinking of population and economic growth were to take place and a political climate favourable to a reshaping of the human community came into existence, it seems doubtful if the organisational and institutional means are available to make very big changes over two or three decades. Demographic processes cannot be changed quickly and the transfer of wealth from the developed countries to the developing ones may be easy to advocate and work out in theory but difficult to put into practice.

References

1. Kahn, H. and A. J. Wiener, *The Year 2000*, 1967, New York; Macmillan.
2. Frejka, T., 'The Prospects for a Stationary World Population', *Sci. Am.*, Mar. 1973, Vol. 228, No. 3, pp. 15–23.
3. 'Population Year in Review – 1972', *Population Bulletin* (Population Reference Bureau), Dec. 1972, Vol. 28, No. 6, p. 6: 'Perhaps stimulated by the results of the 1971 census, which showed a population increase of almost 40 per cent in 10 years, Mexican President Luis Echeverria in 1972 reversed long-standing official opposition to family planning and announced that a government program to encourage lower fertility would be set up'. (President Echeverría himself has eight children.)
4. *Peruvian Times*, 29 Sept. 1972, p. 2.
5. *Andean Times*, 19 Oct. 1973, p. 6.
6. The table shows a small part of the results of one of several runs made by the author in collaboration with Mr. D. S. Ebdon, using programs in Focal and Fortran languages.

Further reading

Cole, H. S. D. (Ed.), *Thinking about the Future, A Critique of the Limits to Growth,* 1973, London; Chatto and Windus.
Ehrlich, P. R., *Population, Resources, Environment,* 1970, San Francisco; W. H. Freeman & Company.
Kearns, K. C., 'International Co-operation for Development: The Andean Common Market', *Focus,* Nov. 1973, Vol. XXIV, No. 3.
Russett, B. M., 'Delineating International Regions', in *Quantitative International Politics: Insights and Evidence* (J. D. Singer, Ed.), 1967, New York; The Free Press.

NOTES ON QUANTITATIVE METHODS

Several quantitative methods have been used for various purposes in this book. They will be discussed briefly. All calculations have been made by computer.

1a Multivariate analysis
1b Linkage analysis
2   Lorenz curve
3   Spearman rank correlation coefficient
4   Population projections are discussed in Appendix 3.

1. MULTI-VARIATE ANALYSIS

Multi-variate analysis, particularly factor analysis, has now been used in a large number of geographical publications and its various procedures, advantages and disadvantages have received considerable publicity in geography as well as in other subjects. References are given at the end of this Appendix. Linkage analysis can be carried out from factors derived from factor analysis. The basic ideas behind factor analysis and linkage analysis will be illustrated with a very simple example.

Table A1.1.

1	Area size	1	Large	0	Small
2	Population size	1	Large	0	Small
3	GDP per capita	1	High	0	Low
4	Literacy level	1	High	0	Low
5	Spanish colonial	1	Yes	0	No

| | Cases | *Attributes or variables* | | | | |
		1 *Area*	*2* *Popn.*	*3* *GDP*	*4* *Lit.*	*5* *Spanish*
A	Argentina	1	0	1	1	1
B	Brazil	1	1	0	0	0
C	Chile	0	0	1	1	1
D	Colombia	0	0	0	0	1
E	Mexico	1	1	1	1	1
F	Peru	0	0	0	0	1
G	Venezuela	0	0	1	1	1

Table A1.1 is a case by variable data matrix similar basically to many given in the book. It differs from most in that its variables are expressed only in a yes/no form, 1 and 0 being used to represent nominal data.

Table A1.2 is similar to the various matrices of correlation used in the book but an index of similarity is given for the relationship between each pair of variables rather than a Pearson or Spearman Correlation coefficient. A similarity point is scored each time a pair of variables has 1 and 1 or 0 and 0 against a particular case (country). Thus variables 1 and 2 in Table A1.1 agree on all countries except Argentina where they have 1 and 0 rather than 1 and 1 or 0 and 0. Variables 1 and 2 therefore agree on 6 out of 7 countries, a high degree of similarity. Variables 3 and 4 agree completely, on 7 out of 7 countries.

Table A1.2.

ATTRIBUTE SIMILARITY MATRIX

	1	2	3	4	5
1	7	6	4	4	2
2	6	7	3	3	1
3	4	3	7	7	5
4	4	3	7	7	5
5	2	1	5	5	7

Table A1.3.

CASE SIMILARITY MATRIX

		A	B	C	D	E	F	G
Argentina	A	5	1	4	2	4	2	4
Brazil	B	1	5	0	2	2	2	0
Chile	C	4	0	5	3	3	3	5
Colombia	D	2	2	3	5	1	5	3
Mexico	E	4	2	3	1	5	1	3
Peru	F	2	2	3	5	1	5	3
Venezuela	G	4	0	5	3	3	3	5

Table A1.2 contains the similarity indices between all pairs of variables. Basically, factor analysis identifies pairs or larger groups of variables that are similar and reduces these to single new variables or factors. In this example the five original variables might be reduced to three factors by selecting the most closely correlated variables:

Factor I   Area size and population size
Factor II   GDP and literacy
Factor III   Spanish speaking.

The position of each country in relation to the new factors would then be calculated and given an area scores matrix.

Table A1.3 shows that basically the idea of linking most similar cases comes from a calculation of the degree of similarity of pairs of cases (countries) according to their values on each variable, or, if factors are used for the classification, on each factor. Colombia and Peru agree on all five of the variables in Table A1.1 and achieve a maximum similarity score of 5, which is recorded in Table A1.3 (see the crossing of row D and column F). Venezuela and Chile also turn out to be identical. Brazil is the least similar to any of the other countries, differing on all five variables from Chile and Venezuela. A linkage tree might be constructed joining countries in the following sequence.

Stage 1	Stage 2	Stage 3
Brazil	Brazil	
		⎧Brazil ⎨Peru ⎩Colombia
⎧Peru ⎩Colombia	⎧Peru ⎩Colombia	
⎧Venezuela ⎩Chile	⎧Venezuela ⎪Chile ⎨Mexico ⎩Argentina	⎧Venezuela ⎪Chile ⎨Mexico ⎩Argentina
Mexico Argentina		

2. THE LORENZ CURVE

The Lorenz curve is widely used in social science subjects as a concise way of representing graphically, and in the gini coefficient also numerically, the degree of concentration or dispersion of a distribution. The basis of the distribution may or may not be spatial. The following simple example illustrates the Lorenz curve by using the area and population size of the five major regions of Brazil (see *Figure 11.4c* on page 223). Area is in thousands of sq. km., population in thousands.

Table A1.4.

		Area	Population	Density
1	North	3,554	3,650	1·03
2	Northeast	1,542	28,680	18·54
3	Southeast	919	40,330	43·90
4	South	562	16,680	29·68
5	Centre-West	1,897	5,170	2·75

Two sets of data, area and population in this case, are given. The aim of the Lorenz curve is to show how evenly or unevenly population is distributed over area.

Step 1. Calculate the density of population (persons per sq. km.)

Step 2. Reorder the cases under consideration in descending order of density, as shown in Table A1.5, and record area and population again:

Table A1.5.

		Area	Population
1	Southeast	919	40,330
2	South	562	16,680
3	Northeast	1,542	28,680
4	Centre-West	1,897	5,170
5	North	3,554	3,650
	Total	8,457	94,509

Step 3. Calculate the percentage of total area and of total population in each unit and add these cumulatively (Table A1.6).

Table A1.6.

		Area		Population	
		Percentage	*Cumulative*	*Percentage*	*Cumulative*
1	Southeast	10·9	10·9	42·7	42·7
2	South	6·8	17·7	17·7	60·4
3	Northeast	18·2	35·9	30·3	90·7
4	Centre-West	22·1	58·0	5·5	96·2
5	North	42·0	100·0	3·8	100·0
	Total	100·0		100·0	

Step 4 on a piece of graph paper with 100 units on the horizontal and on the vertical axes, plot the five areas in the order they appear in Table A1.6 according to the population value of the horizontal axis and the area value on the vertical axis in the columns of cumulative values.

This has been done in *Figure A1.1*.

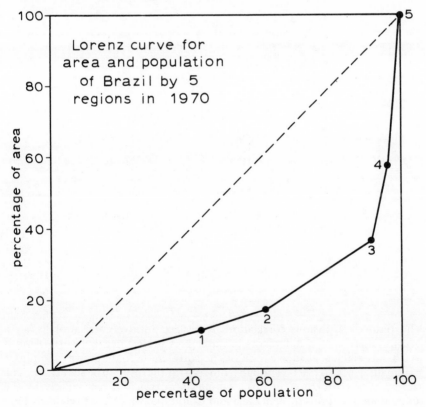

Figure A1.1

Step 5 the gini coefficient of concentration may be calculated as follows:

    a) calculate the area between the diagonal (dashed line on the graph) and the line joining the areas of Brazil

    b) calculate the area of half the square occupied by the graph (5000 units)

    c) express (a) as a proportion of (b).

Note that the nearer the gini coefficient is to 0 (zero) the more even is the distribution, and the nearer it approaches 1, the more concentrated it is.

3. THE SPEARMAN RANK CORRELATION COEFFICIENT

This is easy to calculate and to appreciate. The following simple worked example used Latin American data from Table 9.1 (page 174). The first seven countries in the table are ranked according to their scores on two variables, level of literacy (variable 8) and national income per capita (variable 18). The formula is

$$r = 1 - \frac{6\Sigma d^2}{n^3 - n}$$

where n is the number of cases (7 countries in this example) and d is the difference of rank of each country on the two variables

Table A1.7.

	Original data		Ranked data			
	Literacy	*Income*	*Literacy*	*Income*	*d*	d^2
Brazil	61	341	6·5	7	−0·5	0·25
Mexico	76	632	4	3	+1	1
Argentina	93	914	1	1	0	0
Venezuela	63	837	5	2	+3	9
Colombia	73	358	3	6	−3	9
Peru	61	363	6·5	5	1·5	2·25
Chile	84	613	2	4	−2	4

$$\Sigma d^2 = 25·5$$

$$r = 1 - \frac{6 \times 25·5}{7^3 - 7}$$

$$r = 1 - \frac{153}{336} = 1 - 0·45$$

$$r = + 0·55$$

The result is a positive correlation. A perfect positive correlation is $+1·0$ because there are no differences in ranking. A perfect negative correlation is $-1·0$. A coefficient around 0 indicates no correlation. In the above example, as n is small, $+0·55$ is not far enough from zero for the result to be significant. The closeness of correlation in this example is thrown out particularly by the anomalous situations in Venezuela and Colombia, which have relatively high income and low literacy and the opposite respectively.

Further reading

Baggaley, A. R., *Intermediate Correlational Methods,* 1964, Wiley; New York.
Davis, J. C., *Statistics and Data Analysis in Geology,* 1973, Wiley; New York.
King, L. J., *Statistical Analysis in Geography,* 1969, Prentice Hall; Englewood Cliffs.

TOWNS WITH OVER 100,000 INHABITANTS IN 1970, A CONTINUATION OF TABLE 6.3 (POPULATION IN THOUSANDS)

			Population				Population
51	ARG	Tucmán	290	94	COL	Palmira	164
52	BRZ	Manaus	286	95	COL	Armenia	163
53	COL	Bucaramanga	280	96	MEX	Saltillo	161
54	BRZ	Brasília	277	97	MEX	Morelia	161
55	MEX	Támpico	271	98	ARG	Salta	160
56	COL	Manizales	268	99	BRZ	Londrina	160
57	MEX	Mexicali	267	100	SAM	Cochabamba	157
58	CAM	Managua	262	101	ISL	Ponce	156
59	ARG	Santa Fe	260	102	BRZ	Campos	155
60	MEX	Chihuahua	257	103	BRZ	Pelotas	155
61	BRZ	Natal	256	104	VEN	San Cristóbal	152
62	VEN	Maracay	255	105	MEX	Durango	151
63	ARG	Mar del Plata	250	106	ARG	Bahía Blanca	150
64	ISL	Santiago de Cuba	250	107	MEX	Nuevo Laredo	149
65	BRZ	Maceió	249	108	PER	Trujillo	149
66	CAM	Tegucigalpa	232	109	BRZ	Jundiaí	147
67	MEX	San Luis Potosí	230	110	CHI	Témuco	146
68	COL	Pereira	224	111	COL	Ciénaga	143
69	BRZ	Juiz de Fora	224	112	VEN	San Félix	143
70	MEX	Torreón	223	113	ARG	San Juan	142
71	MEX	Veracruz	214	114	MEX	Matamoros	138
72	MEX	Mérida	212	115	COL	Santa Marta	137
73	COL	Cucutá	207	116	MEX	Reynosa	137
74	BRZ	João Pessoa	204	117	MEX	Cuernavaca	134
75	CAM	San José	203	118	BRZ	Campo Grande	134
76	BRZ	Riberão Preto	197	119	PER	Chiclayo	134
77	BRZ	Teresina	190	120	ISL	Santa Clara	133
78	SAM	Georgetown	190	121	ISL	Guantánamo	131
79	PER	Arequipa	187	122	BRZ	Feira de Santana	129
80	ARG	Paraná	184	123	BRZ	Piracicaba	128
81	SAM	Paramaribo	182	124	BRZ	Gov. Valadares	127
82	BRZ	Aracajú	182	125	CHI	Antofagasta	126
83	MEX	Aguascalientes	181	126	CHI	Lota	125
84	COL	Ibagué	179	127	BRZ	Vitória	125
85	MEX	Hermosillo	177	128	BRZ	Santa Maria	125
86	MEX	Acapulco	174	129	COL	Pasto	123
87	BRZ	São Luis	171	130	BRZ	Baurú	123
88	ISL	Camagüey	171	131	BRZ	Volta Redonda	122
89	BRZ	Sorocaba	168	132	MEX	Jalapa	122
90	MEX	Culiacán	168	133	VEN	Maturín	122
91	CAM	Santa Ana	168	134	VEN	Cumaná	120
92	COL	Montería	167	135	PER	Chimbote	120
93	BRZ	Campina Grande	165	136	MEX	Poza Rica	120

			Population				Population
137	MEX	Mazatlán	120	153	CAM	San Miguel	108
138	COL	Valledupar	120	154	PER	Piura	106
139	BRZ	Florianópolis	120	155	CHI	Osorno	106
140	BRZ	Petrópolis	119	156	PER	Cuzco	105
141	VEN	Cabimas	118	157	ARG	Corrientes	104
142	MEX	Irapuato	117	158	VEN	Ciudad Bolívar	104
143	MEX	Ciudad Obregón	114	159	CAM	San Pedro Sula	103
144	MEX	Toluca	114	160	ISL	Port of Spain	103
145	MEX	Querétaro	113	161	CHI	Talca	103
146	COL	Buenaventura	113	162	CHI	Chillán	102
147	BRZ	Uberlândia	112	163	BRZ	Caruarú	102
148	COL	Neiva	112	164	BRZ	Taubaté	101
149	BRZ	Uberaba	110	165	BRZ	Rio Grande do Sul	100
150	BRZ	São José do Rio Preto	110	166	PER	Iquitos	100
				167	MEX	Villahermosa	100
151	BRZ	Caxias do Sul	109	168	MEX	Oaxaca	100
152	SAM	Santa Cruz	109				

POPULATION PROJECTIONS IN MEXICO

The application of computers to the study of population makes it possible to carry out a very large number of calculations. Hitherto, projections have tended to be 'best estimates' of the future, given previous trends. With the help of computers it is possible to create various futures, based on different assumptions, and to compare them.

This section contains five projections of the population of Mexico, using two basically different methods, A and B. Method A takes the population of each member of a given set of divisions (the 32 major civil divisions of Mexico) and modifies this on a year to year basis, firstly according to natural change and secondly according to net migration between selected pairs of divisions. Method B, referred to sometimes as cohorts, takes the total population of Mexico, subdivided into 17 5-year age groups and into male and female. Every five years population moves from one group to the next. Births are determined by female fertility and deaths by male and female mortality.

PROGRAM A

Refer to Table A3.1.

Column 1 contains the 1970 population of each of the 32 states of Mexico.

Column 2 contains the index used to change the existing population year by year. Projection A1 uses for *example* 1·040 to increase population by 4 per cent. Projections AII and AIII are programmed somewhat differently, not using the whole number part (i.e. using ·040 not 1·040) and adding ·040 of the initial population to that population to increase it by 4 per cent.

Column 3 data as used in projection AI modify Column 2. For example multiplying 1·04 by ·9996 has the effect of reducing it very gradually towards 1·00 in about 100 years. In projections AII and AIII only the fractional part of Column 2 is used and this is reduced throughout in projection AII by 1 per cent a year and in projection AIII by 2 per cent a year, the Column 3 indices being ·99 and ·98 respectively for all 32 states.

Column 4 values have the effect of delaying or retarding the use of the reducer index in Column 3. In all three projections the values given for Column 4 in Table A3.1 were used to delay the application of Column 3 indices to Column 2, the assumption being that natural increase would begin to slow down only after a delay of 10 or 20 years in the less developed and less urbanised states.

In projections AI–AIII it was also assumed that 68 migration flows would take place between specified pairs of states. Migration was calculated from that observed during the decades up to 1970 and was assumed to continue throughout the projection at rates indicated in Table A3.2. For example 1–9,

Table A3.1.

		1	2	3	4
1	Aguascalentics	338	1·040	·99960	10
2	Baja California	870	1·037	·99963	0
3	Baja California (T)	128	1·037	·99963	0
4	Campeche	252	1·038	·99962	20
5	Coahuila	1,115	1·041	·99959	0
6	Colima	241	1·037	·99963	10
7	Chiapas	1,561	1·028	·99972	20
8	Chihuahua	1,613	1·033	·99967	0
9	D.F.	6,864	1·032	·99968	0
10	Durango	939	1·040	·99960	10
11	Guanajuato	2,270	1·034	·99964	10
12	Guerrero	1,597	1·040	·99960	20
13	Hidalgo	1,194	1·035	·99965	20
14	Jalisco	3,297	1·036	·99964	0
15	México	3,833	1·026	·99974	10
16	Michoacán	2,320	1·039	·99961	10
17	Morelos	616	1·034	·99966	20
18	Nayarit	544	1·038	·99962	10
19	Neuvo León	1,695	1·036	·99964	0
20	Oaxaca	2,172	1·027	·99973	20
21	Puebla	2,508	1·031	·99969	10
22	Querétaro	486	1·040	·99960	10
23	Quintana Roo (T)	88	1·036	·99964	20
24	San Luis Potosí	1,282	1·037	·99963	10
25	Sinaloa	1,267	1·043	·99957	0
26	Sonora	1,099	1·038	·99962	0
27	Tabasco	768	1·037	·99963	20
28	Tamaulipas	1,457	1·032	·99968	0
29	Tlaxcala	421	1·040	·99960	20
30	Veracruz	3,815	1·026	·99974	20
31	Yucatán	758	1·034	·99966	20
32	Zacatecas	951	1·040	·99960	20

·0025, means that ·0025 (i.e. 0·25 per cent) of the population of Aguascalientes (1) migrates to the Distrito Federal (9) every year.

Projection AI has two basic assumptions, a gradual reduction of the 1970 rate of natural increase (as in Column 2, Table A3.1) and a continuation of the considerable inter-state migration observed up to 1970 (Table A3.2). Table A3.3 shows the results of projection AI for each state at ten yearly intervals between 1970 and 2069. Table A3.4 shows the percentage of the population expected in each unit. Note that by the year 2000, the D.F. and the State of Mexico are together expected to have nearly 30 million inhabitants, or over 25 per cent of the total population of Mexico and by 2070 nearly 100 million or about 30 per cent of the total population of the country. In the year 2000, Guadalajara would probably have 4–5 million and Monterrey 3–4 million inhabitants.

Projection AII assumes a yearly reduction of 1 per cent in the natural increase subject to an initial delay in some units (see Table A3.1, Column 4). Migration is as in AI. The national totals according to projection AII are shown in Table A3.5, but space does not allow the inclusion of data for individual states according to projection AII.

Table A3.2.
MIGRATION

States From To	Proportion	States From To	Proportion
1- 9	·0025	16-15	·0015
5- 8	·0005	17- 9	·0015
5- 9	·001	18- 2	·001
5-19	·003	19- 9	·0005
5-28	·001	20- 9	·003
7- 9	·001	20-15	·001
8- 2	·0005	20-30	·001
8- 9	·001	21- 9	·0025
8-25	·0005	21-15	·001
8-26	·0005	21-30	·001
9-15	·002	22- 9	·004
10- 2	·0005	22-15	·001
10- 5	·0005	24- 9	·002
10- 8	·002	24-19	·004
10- 9	·001	24-28	·002
10-19	·0005	25- 2	·001
10-25	·001	25-26	·001
11- 2	·0005	26- 2	·001
11- 9	·0004	27- 9	·001
11-15	·0015	27-30	·001
11-28	·0005	28- 9	·001
12- 9	·002	29- 9	·005
12-15	·0005	29-21	·002
12-17	·0015	30- 9	·002
13- 9	·006	30-15	·0005
13-15	·0015	31- 9	·001
13-30	·0005	31-23	·002
14- 2	·001	32- 1	·001
14- 6	·0005	32- 2	·001
14- 9	·001	32- 5	·001
14-18	·0005	32- 8	·001
16- 2	·0005	32- 9	·002
16- 9	·004	32-14	·003
16-14	·001	32-20	·004

Projection AIII assumes a yearly reduction of 2 per cent in the natural increase subject to an initial delay in some units (as for AII). Migration is as in AI and AII. Results are given in Table A3.6. As the falling off in the rate of natural increase is very marked in this projection totals after the first decades drop well below those in projections AI and AII (see Table A3.5). *Figure A3.1* compares the results of the three projections graphically.

METHOD B

Uses the data in Table A3.7. Note that this method calculates changes on a *basis of 5 years* so that fertility and mortality rates have to be five times as large as they would be for yearly groups and changes. The first two columns contain the male and female population of Mexico in 1970. Column 3 contains the fertility index expressing the average number of children from each woman from appropriate

Table A8-8.
PROJECTION AI

Population in thousands

	1970	1980	1990	2000	2010	2020	2030	2040	2050	2060	2069
TOTAL	48,062	66,458	90,113	118,639	151,043	185,927	221,273	254,593	283,217	304,639	316,120
1 Aguascalientes	338	501	724	1,004	1,335	1,703	2,084	2,447	2,757	2,981	3,088
2 Baja Calif.	870	1,381	2,085	3,001	4,129	5,436	6,856	8,290	9,617	10,708	11,396
3 Baja Calif.T.	128	181	247	324	410	500	588	666	727	765	776
4 Campeche	252	366	531	756	1,034	1,363	1,729	2,112	2,484	2,812	3,043
5 Coahuila	1,115	1,568	2,115	2,738	3,402	4,057	4,644	5,102	5,380	5,445	5,315
6 Colima	241	370	552	790	1,083	1,425	1,780	2,183	2,545	2,852	3,055
7 Chiapas	1,561	2,037	2,658	3,416	4,268	5,185	6,126	7,038	7,862	8,540	8,982
8 Chihuahua	1,613	2,190	2,879	3,664	4,513	5,380	6,205	6,924	7,474	7,803	7,883
9 D.F.	6,864	10,334	14,099	19,084	24,904	31,346	38,066	44,616	50,482	55,154	57,973
10 Durango	939	1,316	1,803	2,374	3,003	3,650	4,263	4,783	5,156	5,341	5,327
11 Guanajuato	2,270	2,971	3,813	4,721	5,637	6,493	7,215	7,734	7,997	7,976	7,716
12 Guerrero	1,597	2,271	3,230	4,494	6,006	7,713	9,517	11,282	12,850	14,062	14,738
13 Hidalgo	1,194	1,554	2,024	2,584	3,187	3,795	4,363	4,844	5,193	5,375	5,381
14 Jalisco	3,297	4,553	6,064	7,790	9,652	11,534	13,294	14,776	15,839	16,372	16,351
15 México	3,833	5,558	7,872	10,784	14,302	18,374	22,876	27,610	32,312	36,678	40,057
16 Michoacán	2,320	3,171	4,242	5,458	6,754	8,038	9,200	10,126	10,720	10,915	10,729
17 Morelos	616	881	1,261	1,769	2,399	3,142	3,975	4,855	5,725	6,517	7,106
18 Nayarit	544	805	1,168	1,638	2,220	2,909	3,684	4,510	5,339	6,113	6,711
19 NuevoLeón	1,695	2,489	3,521	4,799	6,304	7,981	9,740	11,459	13,000	14,221	14,947
20 Oaxaca	2,172	2,745	3,472	4,327	5,252	6,203	7,130	7,974	8,673	9,175	9,423
21 Puebla	2,508	3,265	4,179	5,188	6,246	7,292	8,256	9,064	9,649	9,961	9,983
22 Querétaro	486	684	942	1,247	1,586	1,937	2,273	2,563	2,777	2,890	2,895
23 Quintana Roo	88	146	237	369	546	770	1,038	1,339	1,656	1,966	2,216
24 San Luis P.	1,282	1,702	2,213	2,774	3,351	3,900	4,374	4,728	4,925	4,944	4,806
25 Sinaloa	1,267	1,880	2,671	3,633	4,730	5,897	7,040	8,084	8,813	9,243	9,298
26 Sonora	1,099	1,583	2,194	2,928	3,761	4,651	5,536	6,342	6,994	7,424	7,581
27 Tabasco	768	1,083	1,526	2,108	2,805	3,598	4,448	5,298	6,082	6,727	7,138
28 Tamaulipas	1,457	2,013	2,691	3,481	4,358	5,279	6,186	7,013	7,690	8,156	8,358
29 Tlaxcala	421	581	802	1,082	1,404	1,750	2,094	2,409	2,662	2,827	2,884
30 Veracruz	3,518	4,315	5,298	6,418	7,582	8,735	9,812	10,745	11,471	11,937	12,104
31 Yucatán	758	1,028	1,393	1,854	2,384	2,964	3,561	4,136	4,642	5,037	5,265
32 Zacatecas	951	1,236	1,606	2,042	2,494	2,927	3,300	3,575	3,721	3,721	3,596

Table A3.4.
PERCENTAGE OF POPULATION EXPECTED IN EACH UNIT, 1970–2069

		1970	1990	2010	2030	2050	2069
1	Aguascalientes	0·7	0·8	0·9	0·9	1·0	1·0
2	Baja California	1·8	2·3	2·7	3·1	3·4	3·6
3	Baja California T.	0·3	0·3	0·3	0·3	0·3	0·2
4	Campeche	0·5	0·6	0·7	0·8	0·9	1·0
5	Coahuila	2·3	2·3	2·3	2·1	1·9	1·7
6	Colima	0·5	0·6	0·7	0·8	0·9	1·0
7	Chiapas	3·2	3·0	2·8	2·8	2·8	2·8
8	Chihuahua	3·4	3·2	3·0	2·8	2·6	2·4
9	D.F.	14·3	15·6	16·5	17·2	17·8	18·3
10	Durango	2·0	2·0	2·0	1·9	1·8	1·7
11	Guanajuato	4·7	4·2	3·7	3·3	2·8	2·4
12	Guerrero	3·3	3·6	4·0	4·3	4·5	4·7
13	Hidalgo	2·5	2·2	2·1	2·0	1·8	1·7
14	Jalisco	6·9	6·7	6·4	6·0	5·6	5·2
15	México	8·0	8·7	9·4	10·3	11·4	12·7
16	Michoacán	4·8	4·7	4·5	4·2	3·8	3·4
17	Morelos	1·3	1·4	1·6	1·8	2·0	2·2
18	Nayarit	1·1	1·3	1·5	1·7	1·9	2·1
19	Nuevo León	3·5	3·9	4·2	4·4	4·6	4·7
20	Oaxaca	4·5	3·9	3·5	3·2	3·1	3·0
21	Puebla	5·2	4·6	4·1	3·7	3·4	3·2
22	Querétaro	1·0	1·0	1·1	1·0	1·0	0·9
23	Quintana Roo	0·2	0·3	0·4	0·5	0·6	0·7
24	San Luis P.	2·7	2·5	2·2	2·0	1·7	1·5
25	Sinaloa	2·6	3·0	3·1	3·2	3·1	2·9
26	Sonora	2·3	2·4	2·5	2·5	2·5	2·4
27	Tabasco	1·6	1·7	1·9	2·0	2·1	2·3
28	Tamaulipas	3·0	3·0	2·9	2·8	2·7	2·6
29	Tlaxcala	0·9	0·9	0·9	0·9	0·9	0·9
30	Veracruz	7·3	5·9	5·0	4·4	4·1	3·8
31	Yucatán	1·6	1·5	1·6	1·6	1·6	1·7
32	Zacatecas	2·0	1·8	1·7	1·5	1·3	1·1

Table A3.5.
FIVE PROJECTIONS FOR THE TOTAL POPULATION OF MEXICO TO THE YEAR 2070 IN MIL-
LIONS (1970 POPULATION IS 48 MILLION)

	1980	1990	2000	2010	2020	2030	2040	2050	2060	2070
AI	66	90	119	151	186	221	255	283	305	317
AII	66	90	120	155	195	240	290	345	402	463
AIII	66	88	112	136	160	183	204	222	239	253
BI	65	87	112	140	171	203	234	262	285	300
BII	65	83	101	118	132	140	141	136	125	110

*Decennial change in millions according to data in above
projections*

	1970–1980	1980–1990	1990–2000	2000–2010	2010–2020	2020–2030	2030–2040	2040–2050	2050–2060	2060–2070
AI	18	24	29	32	35	35	33	29	20	12
AII	18	24	30	34	40	45	50	54	58	61
AIII	18	22	24	24	24	23	21	18	17	14
BI	17	22	25	28	31	32	31	28	23	16
BII	17	18	18	17	14	12	1	−5	−11	−15

Table A8.6.

PROJECTION AIII

		Population in thousands				Percentage of population				
	1970	1980	2000	2030	2070	1970	1980	2000	2030	2070
1 Aguascalientes	338	501	947	1,676	2,377	·7	·8	·8	·9	·9
2 Baja California	870	1,362	2,723	5,419	9,271	1·8	2·1	2·4	3·0	3·7
3 Baja Calif. T	128	179	293	462	623	·3	·3	·3	·3	·2
4 Campeche	252	366	743	1,471	2,324	·5	·6	·7	·8	·9
5 Coahuila	1,115	1,544	2,456	3,582	4,222	2·3	2·3	2·2	2·0	1·7
6 Colima	241	370	745	1,454	2,375	·5	·6	·7	·8	·9
7 Chiapas	1,561	2,037	3,372	5,423	7,301	3·2	3·1	3·0	3·0	2·9
8 Chihuahua	1,613	2,164	3,353	5,007	6,477	3·4	3·3	3·0	2·7	2·6
9 D.F.	6,848	9,917	17,583	31,257	48,595	14·3	15·0	15·7	17·1	19·2
10 Durango	939	1,316	2,237	3,417	4,064	2·0	2·0	2·0	1·9	1·6
11 Guanajuato	2,270	2,971	4,504	6,116	6,589	4·7	4·5	4·0	3·3	2·6
12 Guerrero	1,597	2,271	4,414	8,033	11,074	3·3	3·4	3·9	4·4	4·4
13 Hidalgo	1,194	1,554	2,544	3,755	4,152	2·5	2·4	2·3	2·1	1·6
14 Jalisco	3,297	4,493	7,075	10,551	13,286	6·9	6·8	6·3	5·8	5·3
15 México	3,833	5,557	10,351	19,639	33,283	8·0	8·4	9·3	10·7	13·2
16 Michoacán	2,320	3,171	5,150	7,411	8,218	4·8	4·8	4·6	4·1	3·2
17 Morelos	616	881	1,742	3,430	5,541	1·3	1·3	1·6	1·9	2·2
18 Nayarit	544	805	1,527	2,760	4,132	1·1	1·2	1·4	1·5	1·6
19 Nuevo León	1,695	2,454	4,324	7,476	11,148	3·5	3·7	3·9	4·1	4·4
20 Oaxaca	2,172	2,745	4,274	6,327	7,643	4·5	4·2	3·8	3·5	3·0
21 Puebla	2,508	3,265	4,951	6,931	8,025	5·2	4·9	4·4	3·8	3·2
22 Querétaro	486	684	1,175	1,822	2,210	1·0	1·0	1·1	1·0	0·9
23 Quintana Roo T.	88	146	363	890	1,726	0·2	0·2	0·3	0·5	0·7
24 San Luis Potosí	1,282	1,702	2,625	3,560	3,719	2·7	2·6	2·3	1·9	1·5
25 Sinaloa	1,267	1,851	3,241	5,359	7,341	2·6	2·8	2·9	2·9	2·9
26 Sonora	1,099	1,560	2,642	4,324	6,094	2·3	2·4	2·4	2·4	2·4
27 Tabasco	768	1,083	2,073	3,798	5,473	1·6	1·6	1·9	2·1	2·2
28 Tamaulipas	1,457	1,989	3,194	5,019	6,918	3·0	3·0	2·9	2·7	2·7
29 Tlaxcala	421	581	1,063	1,768	2,160	0·9	0·9	1·0	1·0	0·9
30 Veracruz	3,518	4,315	6,340	8,739	9,883	7·3	6·5	5·7	4·8	3·9
31 Yucatán	758	1,028	1,825	3,077	4,109	1·6	1·6	1·6	1·7	1·6
32 Zacatecas	951	1,236	2,006	2,785	2,677	2·0	1·9	1·8	1·5	1·1

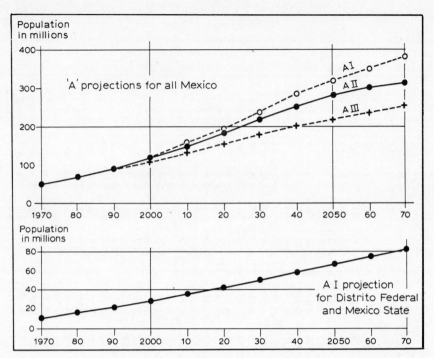

Figure A3.1

Table A3.7.
DATA FOR PROJECTION BI

| | Population in thousands | | Fertility | | Mortality | |
	Males	Females	Index	Modifier	Females	Males
	1	2	3	4	5	6
0–4	4,164	4,029	0·00	1·000	0·100	0·100
5–9	3,947	3,802	0·00	1·000	0·010	0·010
10–14	3,281	3,135	0·00	1·000	0·005	0·005
15–19	2,498	2,570	0·40	0·950	0·007	0·010
20–24	1,935	2,107	1·50	0·950	0·010	0·015
25–29	1,580	1,691	1·50	0·950	0·016	0·020
30–34	1,290	1,315	1·20	0·950	0·017	0·023
35–39	1,239	1,281	1·00	0·950	0·020	0·030
40–44	963	977	0·40	0·950	0·025	0·035
45–49	832	810	0·00	1·000	0·035	0·045
50–54	592	604	0·00	1·000	0·045	0·060
55–59	503	512	0·00	1·000	0·060	0·090
60–64	453	468	0·00	1·000	0·080	0·120
65–69	346	358	0·00	1·000	0·130	0·170
70–74	243	247	0·00	1·000	0·180	0·220
75–79	120	133	0·00	1·000	0·350	0·450
80+	153	197	0·00	1·000	1·000	1·000

Source 1 : IX Censo General de Población 1970
Source 2, 3 : Centro de Estudios Económicos y Demográficos, *Dinámica de la Población de México*, Mexico 1970, p. 53 fertilidad, p. 43
y 33 mortalidad.

age groups. The 4th column is an index that modifies the fertility index, ·95 having the effect of reducing it by 5 per cent over each 5 year period or by about 1 per cent a year. The last two columns give the mortality indices for each female and male age group.

Projection BI assumes a reduction of fertility of 5 per cent every 5 years. No changes occur in mortality rates. The results of the projection, shown in Table A3.5 and again in more detail in Table A3.8, compare closely with those for projection AI. Note how the shares of the youngest age groups diminish throughout the projection.

Projection BII changes only one assumption in BI, the fertility reduction rate. This is ·90 for each of the six 'fertile' age groups instead of ·95 in BI. The effect is to reduce fertility below even the level at which population would stabilise itself and after about the year 2040 to reduce the total population of Mexico sharply.

CONCLUDING POINTS

1. Table A3.5 shows that all five projections give at least a doubling of the population of Mexico during the last 3 decades of the 20th century. Results diverge more and more noticeably after the year 2000. The three A type projections are shown graphically in *Figure A3.2*.

2. Note that in Mexico during the period 1940–1970 the rate of natural increase itself *tended to increase*. That is, the gap between birthrate and deathrate tended to widen. The relevant data are given below. *All five projections* given in this section therefore *assume* after 1970 a marked change in the 1940–70 trend by making natural increase (AI–AIII) or fertility (BI and BII) diminish in the future. The increase in the population of Mexico *could be* much greater than any of the five projections given in Table A3.5. The current rate of over 3 per cent per year, if it continued, would give a doubling of population about every 23 years, and therefore at least a population of 100 million by 1995, 200 million by 2020, 400 million by 2045 and 800 million by 2070.

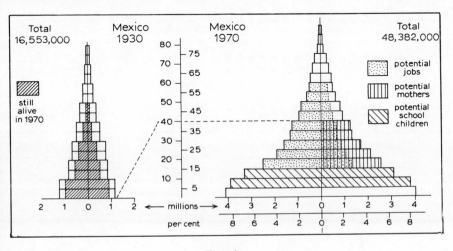

Figure A3.2

Table A3.8b.
RESULTS OF PROJECTION BI

Population in thousands

	1970	1980	1990	2000	2010	2020	2030	2040	2050	2065
0-4	8,193	11,396	14,789	17,136	20,015	21,927	24,777	26,076	26,780	25,897
5-9	7,749	8,977	11,810	14,271	16,699	19,437	21,550	22,914	23,899	23,776
10-14	6,416	7,300	10,154	13,177	15,268	17,833	20,428	22,077	23,234	23,816
15-19	5,068	7,633	8,843	11,633	14,057	16,450	19,146	21,228	22,571	23,742
20-24	4,042	6,329	7,202	10,018	13,000	15,062	17,593	20,153	21,780	23,341
25-29	3,271	4,962	7,473	8,658	11,390	13,764	16,106	18,746	20,785	22,635
30-34	2,605	3,920	6,137	6,983	9,714	12,606	14,606	17,061	19,543	21,702
35-39	2,520	3,184	4,776	7,191	8,333	10,962	13,246	15,500	18,041	20,698
40-44	1,940	2,489	3,747	5,863	6,672	9,283	12,046	13,957	16,302	19,504
45-49	1,642	2,384	2,979	4,518	6,801	7,882	10,368	12,529	14,662	18,116
50-54	1,196	1,807	2,319	3,492	5,460	6,213	8,646	11,219	12,999	16,383
55-59	1,015	1,493	2,169	2,711	4,112	6,186	7,171	9,434	11,400	14,389
60-64	921	1,048	1,584	2,034	3,066	4,786	5,447	7,583	9,840	12,346
65-69	704	846	1,244	1,809	2,264	3,430	5,155	5,980	7,866	10,272
70-74	490	705	804	1,215	1,560	2,356	3,667	4,175	5,817	8,093
75-79	253	479	577	848	1,236	1,548	2,344	3,516	4,083	6,053
80+	350	236	342	390	590	758	1,150	1,778	2,025	3,254
TOTAL	48,375	65,156	86,948	111,947	140,235	171,482	203,447	233,926	261,626	294,019
Shows*	46	42	42	40	37	35	33	30	28	25

* Per cent under age of 15.

Table 3A.8b.
THE STATE OF FERTILITY DURING THE COURSE OF PROJECTION BII

	1970	1980	1990	2000	2010	2020	2030	2040	2050	2065
15-19	0·380	0·343	0·310	0·279	0·252	0·228	0·205	0·185	0·167	0·14
20-24	1·425	1·286	1·161	1·048	0·945	0·853	0·770	0·695	0·627	0·53
25-29	1·425	1·286	1·161	1·048	0·945	0·853	0·770	0·695	0·627	0·53
30-34	1·140	1·029	0·929	0·838	0·756	0·683	0·616	0·556	0·502	0·43
35-39	0·950	0·857	0·774	0·698	0·630	0·569	0·513	0·463	0·418	0·35
40-45	0·380	0·343	0·310	0·279	0·252	0·228	0·205	0·185	0·167	0·14

FURTHER READING ON CENTRAL AMERICA, THE ISLANDS AND THE SMALLER SOUTH AMERICAN COUNTRIES

CENTRAL AMERICA

Billard, J. B., 'Panama, Link Between Oceans and Continents', *National Geographic,* Vol. 137, No. 3, March 1970, pp. 402–40.

Browning, D., *El Salvador, Landscape and Society,* 1971, Oxford; Clarendon Press.

Furley, P., 'A capital waits for its country' (Belize), *Geographical Magazine,* July 1971, Vol. XLIII, No. 10, pp. 713–6.

Hanbury-Tenison, R., 'Darien Indians in the shadow of progress' (Panama), *Geographical Magazine,* Sept. 1972, Vol. XLIV, No. 12, pp. 831–7.

Nott, D., 'Central America: Common Market reconstruction proposals', *Bolsa Review,* Vol. 7, Aug. 1973, No. 80, pp. 373–8.

Severin, T., 'Pressure in El Salvador', *Geographical Magazine,* Jan. 1969, Vol. XLI, No. 4, pp. 278–86.

Whetten, N. L., *Guatemala, The Land and the People,* 1961, New Haven: Yale University Press.

THE ISLANDS

Bryden, J. M., *Tourism and Development, A Case Study of the Commonwealth Caribbean,* 1973, Cambridge University Press.

Cerruti, J., 'The Netherland Antilles, Holland in the Caribbean', *National Geographic,* Vol. 137, No. 1, Jan 1970, pp. 115–46.

Cracknell, B. E., 'Caribbean island with a problem' (Dominica), *Geographical Magazine,* April 1971, Vol. XLIII, No. 7, pp. 463–70.

Crozier, B., 'Soviet Pressures in the Caribbean, The Satellization of Cuba', *Conflict Studies,* No. 35, May 1973.

Eyre, L. A., 'The Shantytowns of Montego Bay, Jamaica', *The Geographical Review,* Vol. LXII, July 1972, No. 3, pp. 394–413.

Lewis, O., 'The Culture of Poverty' (Puerto Rico), *Scientific American,* Oct. 1966, Vol. 215, No. 4, pp. 19–25.

Lowenthal, D., 'Black Power in the Caribbean Context', *Economic Geography,* Vol. 48, 1972, pp. 116–34.

Moss, R., *The Stability of the Caribbean,* 1973, London; Institute for the Study of Conflict.

Soviet Geography: Review and Translation, January 1967 (American Geographical Society) contains several papers on Cuba.

Wood, H. A., *Northern Haiti: Land Use and Settlement,* 1963, University of Toronto Press.

SMALLER SOUTH AMERICAN COUNTRIES

Baitx, A., 'Uruguay, the Problems of the New Government', *Bolsa Review,* Vol. 6, No. 71, Nov. 1972, pp. 613–9.

'Ecuador, Petroleum and the Future', *Bolsa Review,* Vol. 7, No. 75, March 1973, pp. 94–100.

Momsen, R. P., 'Priorities for the Guayas Basin' (Ecuador), *Geographical Magazine,* Dec. 1970, Vol. XLIII, No. 3, pp. 167–76.

Preston, D. A., 'Negro, Mestizo and Indian in an Andean Environment', *Geographical Journal,* Vol. 131, Part 2, June 1965, pp. 220–34.

Preston, D. A., 'Changes in the Economic Geography of Banana Cultivation in Ecuador', *IBG Transactions and Papers,* 1965, No. 37, pp. 77–90.

Preston, D. A., 'Pimampiro, Equateur, Géographie d'une ville andine', (Ecuador), *Les Cahiers d'Outre-Mer,* tome XIX (1966), pp. 57–72.

Preston, D. A. 'Life without landlords on the Altiplano' (Bolivia), *Geographical Magazine,* Aug. 1969, Vol. XLI, No. 11, pp. 819–27.

Tata, R. J., 'Bolivia', *Focus,* Vol. XXIV, No. 2, Oct. 1973.

INDEX

Numbers in italics refer to information in the form of tables or maps. Bold type numbers refer to important sections.